PAUL
THE
APOSTLE

PAUL
THE
APOSTLE

The Triumph of God in Life and Thought

J. Christiaan Beker

T. & T. CLARK LTD.
36 GEORGE STREET, EDINBURGH

COPYRIGHT © FORTRESS PRESS 1980

Printed in the United States

for

T. & T. CLARK LTD., EDINBURGH

0 567 09309 3

First Printed. . . . 1980

To Wilfred
in commemoration of fifty years
of friendship

and to Ada
a constant support in all seasons

Contents

Indexes

Preface

Paul has been a controversial figure throughout history and has provoked extreme reactions of admiration and dislike. The complexity of his thought is in no small way responsible for this.

However, when we turn to the world of scholarship for a more balanced judgment, we encounter similar extremes. The history of interpretation presents us with a bewildering variety of evaluations: portraits of Paul the rationalist and systematic theologian, and of Paul the mystic or religious genius, have claimed equal validity. Champions of a pervasive Hellenistic influence on Paul have vied with those who claim his purely Jewish provenance.

Although in recent years the sharp alternatives have been reduced to a broader consensus, the nature of Paul's thought and its relevance for the variety of human circumstance in his mission field have not been sufficiently clarified. Too often analyses of various segments of Paul's thought have been made to appear as if they comprehend the whole of Paul; and too often the "original" of Paul's thought has been distorted for the sake of modern relevance and instant edification.

This study attempts to move toward an understanding of "the whole Paul" by focusing on two fundamental questions. What is the coherent theme of Paul's thought and what is the texture of his hermeneutic?

I posit the triumph of God as the coherent theme of Paul's gospel; that is, the hope in the dawning victory of God and in the imminent redemption of the created order, which he has inaugurated in Christ. Moreover, I claim that Paul's hermeneutic translates the apocalyptic theme of the gospel into the contingent particularities of the human situation. Paul's ability to correlate the consistent theme of the gospel and its contingent relevance constitutes his unique achievement in the history of early Christian thought.

Paul neither imposes a doctrinal system on his hearers nor compromises the truth of the gospel for the sake of strategic victories nor celebrates spiritual immediacy at the price of consistency.

The book attempts throughout to make the historical understanding of Paul hermeneutically relevant for our own theological situation. For not only Paul's method of doing theology but also his apocalyptic-cosmic theme should be able to stimulate a fresh interpretation of the gospel in our day—all the more so when we recall the efforts of Third World theologians to conceive of theology as praxis and when we reflect on the need for a gospel and ethic that encompass God's redemptive plan for the whole created order and thus give Christian world-responsibility a new urgency.

Part One (Chapters 1 and 2) introduces Paul the apostle and the character of his thought. It sets the stage for Parts Two and Three, which delineate the twofold theme of the study, the coherence and contingency of Paul's gospel. To be sure, my outline is more rigid than the actual content of the chapters themselves. I have attempted to correlate the theme of contingency and coherence throughout the book but considered it necessary to accentuate these two themes separately in Parts Two and Three.

Moreover, a thesis always exaggerates. It would be an error to suppose that Paul consistently integrates the coherent theme of the gospel and its contingent interpretation. There are clearly instances where the situational demands suppress the apocalyptic theme of the gospel (e.g., Galatians), or where the theme seems to impose itself on the situation (e.g., 1 Corinthians 15). However, notwithstanding Paul's occasional inconsistencies, his hermeneutical intent is clear.

Because Paul's letters are substitutes for his personal presence in the churches, they testify to the concrete appeal of the gospel for particular occasions (Chapter 3).

The letters to the Galatians and Romans—often considered to be timeless construals of Paul's dogmatic thought—demonstrate his interpretive ability to proclaim the one truth of the gospel according to the argumentative needs of the hour (Chapters 4–6). And Paul's interpretation of the tradition shows this from another angle: amid the variety of theological traditions in the early church, he is able to grasp the basic truth of the gospel without minimizing its situational relevance (Chapter 7).

Part Three turns to the question of the coherent theme of Paul's gospel and locates it in his apocalyptic world view, which is both affirmed and modified by the resurrection of Christ (Chapter 8). The apocalyptic world view determines as well Paul's view of the death of Christ (Chapter 9). At first glance, Chapters 10 and 11 seem to disrupt the flow of the argument. However, the defeat of the apocalyptic powers in the death and resurrection of Christ (Chapters 8 and 9) necessitates a critical look at the complex function of two power structures: the powers of death and the law. For how can death still be operative as a power if its ally, sin, has been defeated (Chapter 10)? And how can the law be both the instrument of God and also the obedient servant of sin (Chapter 11)?

Paul's thought on redemption and the Christian life (Chapters 12 and 13) focuses on the consequences of Paul's apocalyptic gospel for ethics. Here I attempt to put the indicative-imperative scheme in its correct setting and to emphasize Christian responsibility in the world. A similar apocalyptic perspective pervades Paul's treatment of the church (Chapter 14) and of Israel (Chapter 15). Part Four (Chapter 16) summarizes the argument of the book and concludes that all elements of Paul's thought are distorted unless they are viewed from the perspective of the dawning triumph of God, which constitutes the coherent theme of Paul's gospel.

A study that owes so much to previous New Testament scholarship is not complete without thanking all those who have taught me to appreciate Paul, especially W. C. van Unnik, A. N. Wilder, R. M. Grant, and John Knox. I also thank Mr. C. D. Myers for his invaluable help in preparing the notes and bibliography; Martha Onusconich and Theodore McConnell of Fortress Press for their counsel and encouragement; Ms. Teri Betros for her patience in typing an often illegible script; Ms. Eve Hanle for her editorial work; and my colleagues, G. W. Stroup, T. W. Mann, and D. L. Migliore, who—notwithstanding their suspicion of all things apocalyptic—offered constructive criticisms.

J. C. BEKER
Princeton, New Jersey

PART ONE

INTRODUCTION

1

Paul: Apostle to
the Gentiles

CONVERSION EXPERIENCE AND APOSTOLIC CALLING

One of the most remarkable things about the life of Paul is how little we really know about him and how little he tells us about his life. How is it possible for a man so little given to self-confession to emerge as such a distinct and clear person from his letters and to convey such an intense personal identity to us?* This is a curious phenomenon, especially when we recall the passionate soliloquies of a Jeremiah—in many ways Paul's prophetic model—or Marcus Aurelius's *Meditations*, or even the *Confessions* of Augustine, for whom psychological autobiography is the point of departure for speculative thought. We tend to forget that Paul gives only hints about his external career and internal religious reflections. And so we ignore not only the occasional character of his letters but also the incidental nature of his self-preoccupation.

How different in this respect is Paul from Ignatius of Antioch, the bishop who desires to be martyred in Rome as Paul had been. How self-reflective and introspective—if not masochistic—is Ignatius about his way to discipleship and his imitation of Christ. Both Ignatius and Paul have a sense of authority and humility, but how flowery and sensuous is Ignatius's sytle compared to the concise staccato style of Paul; and how differently they conceive of their role. Ignatius writes:

> Suffer me to be eaten by the beasts, through whom I can attain to God. I am God's wheat and I am ground by the teeth of wild beasts that I may be found pure bread of Christ. Rather entice the wild beasts that they may become my tomb and leave no trace of my body, that when I fall asleep I be not burdensome to any. Then shall I be truly a disciple of Jesus Christ, when the world shall not even see my body. . . . Now I am learning in my bonds to give up all desires.[1]

When Paul is in prison and on trial, his conviction expresses itself in sober and extroverted language:

---

*This study bases its interpretation of Paul on the seven authentic letters: Romans, 1 Corinthians, 2 Corinthians, Galatians, Philippians, 1 Thessalonians, and Philemon. Second Thessalonians, Colossians, Ephesians, and the pastoral Epistles are viewed as pseudepigraphical documents that transmit Pauline traditions.

3

For to me to live is Christ, and to die is gain. If it is to be life in the flesh, that means fruitful labor for me. Yet which I shall choose I cannot tell. I am hard pressed between the two. My desire is to depart and be with Christ, for that is far better. But to remain in the flesh is more necessary on your account. [Phil. 1:21-24]

Although Ignatius has often been characterized as theologically close to Paul,[2] his mystic striving for perfect discipleship is quite different from Paul's apostolic self-understanding.

Were it not for the Book of Acts, we would not be able to sketch a coherent life of Paul or his itinerary, or even know the circumstances of his conversion. Paul himself mentions his call only when forced to do so in polemical contexts (Gal. 1:15-16; 1 Cor. 15:9-10; Phil. 3:4-11) and never as an example of personal piety. Acts is more interested in a psychological description of its hero Paul and in relating his conversion on appropriate occasions (Acts 9, 22, 26). In a similar vein, the author of the pastoral Epistles highlights Paul's inner life:

[Christ] judged me faithful by appointing me to his service, though I formerly blasphemed and persecuted and insulted him; but I received mercy because I had acted ignorantly in unbelief. . . . And I am the foremost of sinners; but I received mercy for this reason, that in me, as the foremost, Jesus Christ might display his perfect patience for an example [pros hypotypōsin] to those who were to believe in him. [1 Tim. 1:12-16]

Paul's own lack of narcissistic self-concern and introspection is not due to any personal sense of timidity or humility. More than any other apostle in the New Testament, Paul is extremely self-conscious about his apostolate. He has an acute sense of authority and of territorial rights over his mission field. Günter Klein surmises that Romans was written by Paul in order to give the church there its apostolic credentials—credentials it had lacked heretofore.[3] Although this assumption is wrong, Klein's emphasis on Paul's apostolic authority is correct. Texts like 1 Cor. 4:15 and 2 Cor. 10:13-18 demonstrate that Paul exercised his "father right" over his churches as a claim to absolute authority. Moreover, he identifies his own message with the truth of the gospel in Gal. 1:7-10 and utters an eschatological curse on those who disagree with his gospel. He writes in 1 Cor. 14:37 in a similar vein: "If any one thinks that he is a prophet, or spiritual, he should acknowledge that what I am writing to you is a command of the Lord. If any one does not recognize this, he is not recognized."

It is not correct to cast Paul as a humble man, but neither should we view him as a passionate fanatic who identifies his ego with the truth. It is amazing that the man who writes Gal. 1:7–10 can also write Phil. 1:15–18:

> Some indeed preach Christ from envy and rivalry, but others from good will. The latter do it out of love, knowing that I am put here for the defense of the gospel; the former proclaim Christ out of partisanship, not sincerely but thinking to afflict me in my imprisonment. What then? Only that in every way, whether in pretense or in truth, Christ is proclaimed; and in that I rejoice.

What is intriguing about Paul is the concurrence of his sense of authority and his lack of pious self-concern. Paul is extremely reticent about his conversion experience and yet extremely outspoken about his apostleship.

This emphasis is reversed in Acts. Here Paul's conversion experience is central, and despite Acts 14:4, 14, he is refused the title of apostle because he does not have the proper historical "apostolic" credentials (Acts 1:21–22; cf. Acts 13:31).

Therefore, Paul's claim to be an apostle is so important to him because it authorizes him to be an authentic, Christ-appointed interpreter of the gospel. Becoming a Christian does not primarily mean discipleship to Paul, or even the call to be a "witness" in dependence on Jerusalem (Acts); rather, for him the call is to the apostolate. Therefore, he is engaged not in an introspective analysis of his conversion but in the extraverted character of his apostolic call: "Paul, a servant of Jesus Christ, called to be an apostle, set apart for the gospel . . . concerning his Son . . . through whom we have received grace and apostleship to bring about the obedience of faith . . . among all the Gentiles" (Rom. 1:1–5).[4]

Discipleship and Apostolate

For Paul, discipleship and the apostolate are not successive stages on life's way; such was the case for Jesus' disciples, who were first disciples and later appointed as apostles after Jesus' resurrection. Paul is not "a disciple" in this sense, because his apostleship does not build upon a prior discipleship. Jesus' instruction of the disciples was probably not based on the rabbinic model of teacher/disciple, of learning and memorization, and of transmitting the halakah of the teacher.[5] Nonetheless, we may suppose a period of learning, if not of a slowly maturing insight (however much all broke down at the moment of the crucifixion). The resurrection appearance of Jesus to his disciples, and their subsequent apostolic mission (Matt. 28:16–20; Luke 24:36–49), certainly meant an integration of their memory of Jesus with their new confession of him as the risen Christ. Their former discipleship was not ignored but illumined by new insights.

Paul does not fit this model, not only because his apostolic call was not based on a prior discipleship but also because the quality of his illumination was different. No disciple of Jesus could claim the radical reversal which he experienced from zealous persecutor to zealous witness for Christ, that is, from Pharisaic missionary to anti-Pharisaic apostle.

Paul's call, then, is unique: he is not only "the least of the apostles," the "stillborn child," but also "the last" of the apostles (1 Cor. 15:8-9). Although every Christian is "called"[6] (*klētos*; cf. "called saints," *klētois hagiois* [Rom. 1:7]), Paul is a "called apostle" (Rom. 1:1) and thus the direct mediator of the gospel and its authoritative interpreter. His call is unique in that he is not "sent out" (*apostellein*) to the "circumcised"—like Peter—but to the "uncircumcised" (Gal. 2:7-8). He is indeed *the* apostle to the Gentiles (Gal. 1:15-16; Rom. 11:13: *eimi ego ethnōn apostolos*), commissioned to proclaim God's grace in Jesus Christ to *all* the nations— Jew and Gentile alike—which means that the gospel is "apart from law" (Rom. 3:21).

Paul's conversion experience is absorbed by the greater reality of his apostolic calling. He does not celebrate his "conversion experience" to mark his own spiritual grandeur, because he understands it as the commission to proclaim the gospel, that is, to serve Christ among the Gentiles.

THE CONTENT OF THE GOSPEL

Paul's conversion experience then is not the theme of his theology. Such a view distorts Paul's gospel pietistically. It is a methodological error to dig behind the text of the Pauline letters in order to find an underlying psychological "pretext" that is hidden from us. In fact, "conversion" terminology is absent in Paul: verbs like "repent" (*metanoein*) and "turn to" (*epistrephein*) rarely occur (2 Cor. 3:16; 1 Thess. 1:9; but cf. Acts 3:19; 9:35; 11:21; 14:15; 15:19; 26:18, 20; 28:27). Moreover, Paul does not use the vocabulary of "religion" and "piety" (cf. *eusebeia, thrēskeia*). Scholarship at the turn of the century, with its strong psychological and romantic interests,[7] was preoccupied with Paul's "conversion experience." Friedrich Nietzsche provided a classical model for such a psychological interpretation of Paul. He was "the dysangelist" who, "hungry for power," saw at last in Jesus the solution to the problem of his soul.[8] Paul himself hardly fosters psychological speculation, for the thrust of his gospel runs the opposite way—away from introspective self-concern and mystic self-analysis to an objective, almost sober, assessment of his apostolic task. As we noted before, the "conversion story" (Phil. 3:4-11; Gal. 1:12-17; 1 Cor. 15:8-9) is introduced only to illustrate the nonhuman origin of his gospel; its purpose is to emphasize God's justifying grace, a grace that cannot be explained by human-psychological criteria. The "conversion story" then documents the Christ-event as the reversal of the ages: "once a Pharisaic persecutor, now an apostle" (Gal. 1:23). It is a commentary on the gospel of radical grace for all people and not an occasion for private, self-serving "boasting."

The correlation between apostolate and gospel indicates the extraverted character of Paul's call and the objective content of his theological thought. The universality of the gospel is matched by the universality of the apostle's task, that is, to herald God's saving victory over His creation. The conversion experience and the accompanying mystical phenomena are simply absorbed by the content of the gospel and its universal claim. "For though I am free from all men, I have made myself a slave to all, that I might win the more. . . . I have become all things to all men, that I might by all means save some" (1 Cor. 9:19, 22b). The center of the gospel is not constituted by mystical introspection or private individualism. Paul is not preoccupied with his own religious experience, because the righteousness of God that has dawned with the death and resurrection of Christ must be conveyed to all people as God's liberating act for his creation. Therefore, Paul confesses: "a 'fateful' necessity [ananke] is laid upon me" (1 Cor. 9:16; trans. mine).

Experience and Thought

The emphatic correlation in Paul between apostleship and gospel calls for further clarification. Does it really make sense to distinguish Paul's conversion experience from his apostolic call and thus to downgrade the experiential-personal element of Paul's gospel in favor of the more extraverted and objective character of his apostolic call and gospel? Is not, after all, Paul's conversion experience the secret center behind his theological thinking, thus making his thought rooted in his conversion experience and inexplicable apart from it? Is not religious language to a great extent a product of personal experience,[9] and does not the passionate character of Paul's theological language point to its origin and source in his dramatic conversion experience?

Gustav Adolf Deissmann's *Paul* provided a new perception of the mystic religiosity of Paul, one that showed the error of the prevalent interpretation of Paul as dogmatic theologian.[10] Moreover, can it not be argued that Paul's theological thinking is the projection on a universal screen of a very existential and personal truth? Does not the conflict between experience and theological construct account for the antinomies and inconsistencies of Paul's thought?[11] And if we divorce the extraverted character of his apostleship and gospel from the inward nature of the conversion experience, are we not in danger of reintroducing a scholastic rationalism into Paul's theology, so that doctrinal constructions collide with religious experience? The "Jesus versus Paul" debate of an earlier decade urged us to return from Paul, "the first theologian of Christianity," to the "religious posture of Jesus."[12] And was not this return to the "simple gospel" of Jesus to a great extent motivated by the fact that in the history of dogma Paul the theologian had drowned Paul the man of piety? Is it simply theological bias to downgrade Paul's religion in favor of his theology because we want to ignore the fact that religious experience is after all the source of all theology?

It would be an error to oppose experience and thought, as if we have to choose between them. Champions of these contradictory positions (cf., respectively, Deissmann[13] and Wrede[14]) obscure the nature of Paul's apostolate and gospel, because in his apostolic call both experience and thought cohere. What is at issue is not experience itself but its quality, function, and direction as these come to expression in Paul's theological language.

The gospel for Paul is not contracted to a personal subjectivism that would reduce his preaching of the gospel to a pious retelling of his conversion experience. Moreover, the gospel is not primarily an intra-psychic phenomenon that limits itself to the conversion of individual souls climbing out of a lost world into the safety of the church, like drowning people climb aboard a safe vessel.[15] Rather, the gospel proclaims the new state of affairs that God has initiated in Christ, one that concerns the nations and the creation. Individual souls and their experience are only important within that worldwide context and for the sake of the world. Christ as the object and content of the gospel is not simply the means for individual holiness and private experiences; rather, he remains the transcendent Lord and Judge over all people's experiences: "we shall all stand before the judgment seat of God" (Rom. 14:10). Thus, Paul's conversion experience is taken up and absorbed by God's redemptive purpose for his whole creation.

In accordance with its worldwide claim, Paul's gospel has both a theocentric dimension and a Christocentric dimension. The "gospel of God" (Rom. 1:1; 1 Thess. 2:2, 8, 9; 2 Cor. 11:7; Rom. 15:16) is identical with the "gospel of Christ" (Rom. 15:19; 1 Cor. 9:12; 2 Cor. 2:12; 4:4; 9:13; 10:14); and both dimensions fuse into the one cosmic-redemptive purpose of God for which Christ died and was raised. The experiential-subjective dimension of Paul's apostolic life must serve this worldwide purpose of God, and thus he proclaims God's act in Christ as the imminent manifestation of his cosmic, world-encompassing glory.

Experience, then, is not opposed to thought but brought into thought as its dynamic power. Therefore, Rudolf Bultmann is quite correct when he defines Paul's theology in this way:

> Paul's basic position is not a structure of theological thought. It does not take the phenomena which encounter man and man himself whom they encounter and build them into a system, a distantly perceived cosmos (system), as Greek science does. Rather, Paul's theological thinking only lifts the knowledge inherent in faith itself into the clarity of conscious knowing—the act of faith is simultaneously an act of knowing and correspondingly theological knowledge cannot be separated from faith.[16]

The correlation of apostle and gospel means that "the clarity of conscious knowing" is an integral part of Paul's apostolate. Indeed, experience and thought are defined by the content of the gospel. Faith and the Spirit, for example, are never extolled as saving virtues in and by themselves, as if their opposites, "works" and "the body," are by definition inferior religious categories; they are saving virtues only in terms of Christ as their object and content. The objective content and universal claim of the gospel compels Paul to give an orderly intelligible account of God's act in Christ to *each specific need and situation*, in order that everyone may *know* what God has done—so that, for instance, the relationship of Israel to the Gentiles may be *understood*, or the concrete need of the neighbor may be intelligibly observed and served in the context of the church. Faith in Christ, then, is never divorced from knowledge and intelligible coherence (cf. 1 Cor. 14:19). Paul's apostolic task does not exhaust itself in charismatic enthusiasm or miraculous sensationalism (cf. 2 Corinthians 10–13), because he must convince and convict the nations with a timely and intelligible kerygma.

Thus, we cannot excuse or celebrate the alleged inconsistencies, unclarities, and non sequiturs in Paul by pointing to his mystic feelings or passionate incoherence, as if thought does not matter to him and as if he is instead a man of action and religious feeling. Adolf von Schlatter observed correctly that *Denkakt* and *Lebensakt* cannot be divorced in Paul:[17] practice and thought interact and determine each other. Therefore, the thought of the apostle remains focused on the specificity of his apostolic-missionary service: "I am under obligation both to Greeks and to barbarians, both to the educated and to the uneducated" (Rom. 1:14; trans. mine).

In short, Paul's conversion experience is not the entrance to his thought. Paul is preoccupied by his call to the apostolate and gospel as service to the world, not by his conversion experience. Therefore, he patterns his call after that of Jeremiah, who like Paul was "appointed . . . a prophet to the nations" (Jer. 1:5; cf. Gal. 1:15–16); and he uses not the language of conversion but the language of the prophetic call. Paul's interpretation of his conversion experience concentrates on its function and absorption into God's plan for his world rather than on a mere retelling of the experience itself.

2

The Character of Paul's Thought

At this point it would be helpful to discuss in a preliminary way the character of Paul's thought. I propose that its specificity is marked by two of its components—contingency and coherence—and their interaction.

CONTINGENCY

Paul's hermeneutic cannot be divorced from the content of his thought, because he relates the universal truth claim of the gospel directly to the particular situation to which it is addressed. His hermeneutic consists in the constant interaction between the coherent center of the gospel and its contingent interpretation.

Paul's hermeneutical ability stands out when we consider the nature of this interaction. We could argue, for instance, that Paul simply imposes the objective content of the gospel on his various audiences and that his apostolic preaching is actually a monstrous repetition of "Pauline doctrine" to which intellectual assent must be given. Or we could argue the opposite and claim that he accommodates the gospel to "what the market will buy," so that scoring points over opponents or intuitive feelings are more important than the integrity of the gospel. His interpretation of the gospel may simply be a dogmatic pronouncement that is valid for all situations, or it may be an incoherent display of incidental, opportunistic, and compromising thoughts that vary from situation to situation.

In a remarkable piece of writing, Søren Kierkegaard seems truly to grasp the nature of Paul's apostolic call and gospel.

If a man can be said to be situated absolutely teleologically, then he is an apostle. *The doctrine communicated to him is not a task which he is given to ponder over*, it is not given him for his own sake; he is, on the contrary, on a mission and has to proclaim the doctrine and use authority. Just as a man, sent into the town with a letter, *has nothing to do with its contents, but has only to deliver it*; just as a minister who is sent to a foreign court is *not responsible for the content of the message*, but has only to *convey it correctly*; so, too, an apostle has really only to be faithful in his service, and to carry out his task. Therein lies the essence of an apostle's life of self-sacrifice, even if he were never persecuted, in the fact that he is "poor, yet making many rich," that he never dares take the time or the quiet or carefreeness in order to grow

11

rich. Intellectually speaking he is like a tireless housewife who herself hardly has time to eat, so busy is she preparing food for others, and even though at first he might have hoped for a long life, his life to the very end will remain unchanged, for there will always be new people to whom to proclaim the doctrine. Although a revelation is a paradoxical factor which surpasses man's understanding, one can nevertheless understand this much, which has, moreover, proved to be the case everywhere: that a man is called by a revelation to go out in the world, to proclaim the word, to act and to suffer, to a life of uninterrupted activity as the Lord's messenger. But that a man should be called by a revelation to sit back and enjoy his possessions undisturbed, in active literary farniente, momentarily clever and afterwards publisher and editor of the uncertainties of his cleverness: that is something approaching blasphemy. The lyrical author is only concerned with his production, enjoys the pleasure of producing, often only perhaps after pain and effort; but he has nothing to do with others, *he does not write "in order that"*: in order to enlighten men or *in order to* help them along the right road, *in order to* bring about something; in short, he does not write *in order that*. The same is true of every genius. No genius has an *in order that*; the apostle has absolutely and paradoxically an *"in order that."*[1] [Italics mine.]

Kierkegaard's insistence on the objective content of the gospel and his teleological description of the apostle's task are persuasive. However, the interaction between coherent content and situational contingency is here misconstrued. For "the doctrine" is indeed "a task which the apostle is given to ponder over," and apostolic authority is not that of the man who "has nothing to do with its contents, but has only to deliver it."

The apostolic "in order that" is exactly the reason for both the contingency and the coherence of the gospel. Just because the apostle writes "in order to bring about something," his gospel is necessarily contingent; and just because the gospel itself has as its content the "in order that" of God's coming triumph, it has a coherent core.

Views similar to Kierkegaard's noncontingent characterization of the gospel appear frequently in the landscape of Pauline scholarship, that is, whenever scholars suppress or play down the contingency of historical situations and arguments in favor of Paul's systematic doctrine or *Lehrbegriff* (see below). Yet Paul is neither a rationalistic dogmatist nor a Mishnaic traditionalist; nor is he an opportunistic compromiser or a thoughtless charismatic. Rather, he is able to make the gospel a word on target for the particular needs of his churches without either compromising its basic content or reducing it to a petrified conceptuality.

COHERENCE

The second component of Paul's thought lies in its coherent center. Because we cannot celebrate the contingency of Paul's hermeneutic at the expense of the specific content of his gospel, it is imperative to explicate what we mean by Paul's "coherent center." If Paul's gospel is neither a doctrinal system nor a selective "essence" nor an unspecifiable kerygma, how shall we characterize the content of his thought?

The Search for a Doctrinal Center

The character of Paul's thought has preoccupied scholars ever since Ferdinand Christian Baur's work on the historical investigation of the Pauline Epistles.[2] Until that time, the view of the Reformation largely prevailed. It had characterized Paul's thought as "doctrine" and had focused its center in his anti-Judaistic debate, that is, in justification by faith. Whereas Baur still cast Paul's thought in terms of a doctrinal core, the history-of-religions school temporarily effected a profound change. For a time "the religious Paul" supplanted "the doctrinal Paul." Richard Reitzenstein characterized Paul as "the greatest Gnostic of them all";[3] William Heitmüller and Wilhelm Bousset introduced the "cultic Paul,"[4] and in their footsteps Heinrich Weinel, Gustav Adolf Deissmann,[5] and others centered on the "mystic Paul." Yet the doctrinal core surfaced in a new manner: Paul's thought was assigned to either "mystic" or "doctrinal" centers or to a combination of them.

Preceded by Heinrich Julius Holtzmann, Otto Pfleiderer, and William Wrede,[6] Albert Schweitzer formulated the issue in a classic way that preoccupies scholarship even today.[7] Schweitzer located the center of Paul's thought in his eschatological mysticism; he rejected Paul's doctrine of justification as the central core, which had been the prevalent option since the Reformation, and instead advocated a two-crater scheme, in which a main crater of eschatological mysticism was posited against a secondary crater of rabbinic-juridical thought forms that Paul only used as a polemical weapon against Judaism.

Thus, righteousness of faith was downgraded as a "survival" in favor of eschatological mysticism. Along these lines the quest for the doctrinal center continued. However, the "whole" gospel of Paul could not be accounted for with this selective method. Paul had to be truncated—as Marcion had already done in the second century (see Chapter 3, below)—or at least some sections of his letters had to be assigned to a "secondary" crater. Schweitzer believed Romans 1–5 and chunks of Galatians to be peripheral to Paul's real substance. And so the debate continued between "rabbinic" and "Hellenistic" selections of Paul's "core."

New Perspectives

Bultmann opened up a new perspective that seemed to provide a solution to the impasse between the various "cores" of Paul's thought. Bultmann pointed to the contingency of Paul's thought by correlating Paul's theology and his anthropology. His distinction between the kerygma and its theological expression allowed him to deny that the kerygma had a specific content. Because "Paul's theological thinking only lifts the knowledge inherent in faith itself into the clarity of conscious knowing," Paul's "basic position is not a structure of theoretical thought."[8] Indeed, "theological understanding has its origin in faith."[9] Although Bultmann was able to move away from a doctrinal-propositional core, to which intellectual assent must be given, his emphasis on the kerygma as the act of preaching to which faith responds in terms of a new self-understanding neglects the content of the kerygma and so introduces a split in the kerygma between the act and content of preaching, a split that Paul never intended.

Today it is widely recognized that Paul's thought cannot be grasped in terms of a systematic doctrinal core. Modern scholarship has reacted against a narrow "conceptual" definition of Paul's thought and has defined it in terms of a broader, more encompassing framework in which false dichotomies are overcome. However, this recognition often produces ambivalence and obfuscation and has rarely led to new creative insights. A glance at the confusing variety of terms that are employed to characterize and clarify Paul's thought clearly manifests this. Paul's thought is described as "kerygma," "core," "essence," "Paulinism," "mysticism," "eschatological participation," "*Glaubenslehre*," "*Lehrplan*," "motifs and perspective" (Keck), "pattern of religion" (Sanders), "co-inherent" patterns and "fundamental doctrines" (Whiteley), and "coherent thought" (Sanders).[10] The *Mitte* (center) of Paul's thought is located either in justification by faith (Wendland, Kümmel, Käsemann)[11] or sacramental participation (Schweitzer, Davies)[12]* or both (Sanders);[13] others locate its "quintessence" in Ephesians (Bruce)[14] or in "the identity of the risen Lord with the crucified Messiah, Jesus" (Dahl).[15] Others reject the idea of Paul as a

---

*Davies is arranged under this view, although he does not use this terminology. He emphasizes the idea of corporate solidarity, allocates a secondary role to justification by faith, and names the notion of "being in Christ" Paul's central soteriological concept (William David Davies, *Paul and Rabbinic Judaism*, pp. 177, 86–110).

thinker: "more a man of prayer—than a learned exegete and close thinking scholastic" (Deissmann).[16]

Ernst Käsemann correctly complains about the frequent unclear characterizations of Paul's thought:

> The inclination of earlier times to view Paul as the first Christian dogmatist has swung to the other extreme. He is conceded the honour of being the most important reflective theologian in the New Testament; but it would be generally denied today that he developed a system [Bornkamm] or possesses a firm methodology [Luz; Vielhauer]. Both these opinions may be correct. But that does not mean that the dominating centre of Paul's theology must be denied as well. Although he composed no *Summa Theologica*, it would probably be going too far to set in its place a collection of interrelated ideas about the encounter between God and man, with at most a general thesis about "judgment and grace" [cf. Bornkamm]. Such statements are so general that they no longer allow the specific character of Pauline theology to emerge, a character which simply cannot be overlooked and which distinguishes him from all other New Testament writers.[17]

Indeed, the reasons for a particular terminology that purports to characterize the center of Paul's thought are often not explicated or set in the context of a discussion of the nature of Paul's language and thought. However, there are notable exceptions to this verdict.[18]

A NEW METHOD

The presence of a coherent center in Paul's thought cannot be denied. However, we need a method that will enable us to describe and understand this center more clearly. Our habit of systematic denotative thinking in terms of finished structures of thought and restrictive conceptual units has too often suggested false alternatives, as when scholars oppose "doctrine" and propose "mysticism" because of their abhorrence of a "rationalistic" Paul.

Paul's center is not a theoretical proposition that is subsequently applied to sociological contingencies; it is not a frozen tradition that needs casuistic explication for concrete cases. Indeed, the gospel is not a legal structure or a finished product of thought that permits a pyramid of propositional deductions.

Rather, Paul's coherent center must be viewed as a symbolic structure in which a primordial experience (Paul's call) is brought into language in a particular way. The symbolic structure comprises the language in which Paul expresses the Christ-event. That language is, for Paul, the apocalyptic language of Judaism, in which he lived and thought. The symbolic structure then is the result of the translation of Paul's primordial experience into his basal language and constitutes for him the necessary interpretation of the Christ-event. The primordial experience of the Christ-event then nourishes, intensifies, and modifies Paul's traditional apocalyptic language. It is in this sense that I speak about the coherent center of Paul's gospel as a symbolic structure: it is a Christian apocalyptic structure of thought—derived from a constitutive primordial experience and delineating the Christ-event in its meaning for the apocalyptic consummation of history, that is, in its meaning for the triumph of God.

It is necessary, however, to make certain distinctions within the symbolic structure, for unless we distinguish between a primary and secondary level of language, we too easily identify a particular symbol with the whole of the symbolic structure. I refer to the range of symbols like righteousness, justification, reconciliation, freedom, adoption, being in Christ, being with Christ, glory, and so on, that in their totality constitute Paul's symbolic structure but in their particularity interpret the gospel according to the contingent needs of a particular situation.

Therefore, the primary language of the symbolic structure or its "deep structure" signifies the Christ-event in its meaning for the apocalyptic consummation of history, whereas the secondary language of the symbolic structure, or its "surface structure," signifies the contingent interpretation of Paul's Christian apocalyptic into a particular situation.*

In this way, the often arbitrary selective bifurcation of Paul's thought (i.e., "justification" vs. "participation in Christ"), which imports a rigid conceptuality into it, can be overcome and the unity of his thought be honored within its diversity. The search for one dominant symbol, "concept," or "essence" betrays the error of both misplaced concretion and conceptual fallacy.

THE APOCALYPTIC TEXTURE OF PAUL'S THOUGHT

The quest for a more comprehensive understanding of Paul's "core" characterizes modern scholarship (see above). Moreover, many scholars

---

*The language of structuralism may be helpful to clarify the delineation of Paul's coherent core. The symbolic structure can be called a paradigmatic structure that contains the totality of the syntagmatic symbols. In other words, the traditional symbols that are juxtaposed to each other in Paul's letters (syntagmatic) constitute in their totality the paradigmatic structure of Paul's thought, just as all the elements of language are contained in its basic grammar. In this sense, the "coherent center" is the synchronic-paradigmatic structure of Paul's thought, which should not be splintered into its diachronic and syntagmatic elements if we intend to understand the coherence of Paul's thought.

locate the "core" in the apocalyptic texture of Paul's thought.[19] Yet by and large, Paul's christological reinterpretation of apocalyptic is usually considered to be such a radical modification of it that apocalyptic no longer functions as the crucial carrier or abiding center of his thought. Rudolf Bultmann, Hans Georg Conzelmann, and Charles Harold Dodd are typical in this respect: Paul's apocalyptic is either demythologized into existential self-understanding (Bultmann)[20] or deemed to be peripheral to his interpretation of the creed (Conzelmann)[21] or dismantled in terms of a psychological development of his thought (Dodd).[22]

Ernst Käsemann and his pupil Peter Stuhlmacher clearly steer a different course. Käsemann has impressively demonstrated that apocalyptic is "the mother of Christian theology" and has made Paul his key witness for this assertion.[23] However, it is necessary to press Käsemann's thesis, especially his distinction between the *regnum Christi* and the *regnum Dei*. Apocalyptic is not merely a Pauline *Kampfeslehre* against Hellenistic Christian enthusiasm (as Käsemann's repeated use of "eschatological reservation" seems to suggest); rather, it constitutes the heart of Paul's gospel, inasmuch as all that is said about Christ refers to that process of salvation which will imminently climax in the *regnum Dei*.

Moreover, Käsemann so fuses the theme of righteousness by faith with apocalyptic that he characterizes the symbol "righteousness" as *the* theme of Paul's thought: "Paul has not developed a fixed exegetical method or a closed dogmatic system. He has, however, a theme which dominates his whole theology, i.e., the doctrine of justification."[24]

Thus Käsemann identifies *one* theme as *the* theme and does not distinguish the primary language of the symbolic structure (the Christ-event in its apocalyptic meaning) from the *variety* of symbols that interpret it. Thus, righteousness must be viewed as *one* symbol *among* others and not as *the* center of Paul's thought.

The most striking aspect of Paul's thought is his hermeneutic, that is, the interface between contingency and coherence. I called Paul's coherent center a symbolic structure that contains a "deep" structure of Christian apocalyptic and a "surface" structure of a variety of symbols. The "surface" structure now operates as an interpretive field that mediates between the coherent center and its relevance to contingent situations, that is, the authentic truth of the coherent center aims at relevance according to the demands of the dialogical situation.

Thus, the gospel is for Paul both "truth" and "effective word": it is verified not only by its content but also by its "fruit," or effectiveness. Moreover, just as the coherent center participates in a primordial experience (Paul's call), so it gives rise again to a new primordial experience in that the gospel's symbolic power is able to evoke the response of faith in its hearers.

The interface between coherence and contingency then resembles a military command center that dispatches the necessary material according to the needs of the various field units. The symbol of "righteousness," for example, is proper for the situation in Galatia and Rome, but it does not meet the needs in Corinth, where "wisdom" is employed.

This analogy lacks, however, the reciprocal and dialogical element of Paul's hermeneutic. It is this remarkable interaction between coherent core and contingent diversity that I will attempt to demonstrate subsequently.

THE OBJECTION TO APOCALYPTIC

A final observation: My coherent theme runs contrary to the heart of Bultmann's position.[25] Bultmann argues that the core of the kerygma must be freed from its obsolete husk, the mythological-apocalyptic world view of Paul, for unless the kerygma is demythologized, the core of the gospel cannot speak authentically to the modern person. Moreover, Paul himself—according to Bultmann—already initiated this hermeneutical task that subsequently was accomplished more adequately by John. However, what is husk to Bultmann belongs in our construal to the core of Paul's gospel, because the removal or existential interpretation of apocalyptic distorts the truth of the gospel. It is my contention that Paul locates the coherent center of the gospel in the apocalyptic interpretation of the Christ-event. Paul's thought is misinterpreted when this central affirmation of his is distorted, ignored, or collapsed into the Christ-event itself.

The objection to apocalyptic runs deep in our theological veins. Indicative of this is that the term *eschatology* has widely displaced the pejorative term *apocalyptic*. There are at least two reasons for this. In the first place, apocalyptic suggests armchair speculation, sectarian rigidity, egocentric particularity, ethical passivity, and an adherence to an obsolete world view and to misleading language that cannot and should not be resuscitated. In the second place, there is a profound theological objection to the apocalyptic theme. If the saving grace of the gospel is conditioned by the intellectual acceptance of a particular world view, a sacrifice of the intellect and an intellectual "works"-righteousness jeopardizes the liberating power of our stance in faith. Although this is not the place to discuss these issues, three observations should be made. First, Paul does not divorce the centrality of the death and resurrection of Christ from its apocalyptic coordinates, and he does not simply equate the apocalyptic world view with any other world view. Second, we cannot simply dismantle apocalyptic in Paul and hope to retain the meaning of the Christ-event. Third, it is a gross misunderstanding to equate apocalyptic in Paul with a philosophy of history, idle speculation, ethical passivity, and escape from the created world.

For Paul, then, apocalyptic is the indispensable means for his interpretation of the Christ-event. And the interaction between coherent center and contingent interpretation accords with the theme of hope that is inherent in his Christian apocalyptic. For unlike a Greek dualistic apprehension of divine reality, in which time will eventually be swallowed up by eternity, Paul views God as the coming one who has already come to his creation in Christ. In other words, God is the contingent-historical intervener in a process that—in hidden and contrary ways—already manifests the imminence of his final glory. Only at the time of his final glory and triumph will his living presence in Christ and in the Spirit—now only visible to the eyes of faith—climax in his public presence to "sight" (2 Cor. 5:7).

Thus, there seems to be a basic relationship between the two components of Paul's thought, for the nature of the coherent core is such that it searches for contingent historical concreteness. To be sure, the interface between coherence and contingency characterizes the gospel as such and does not seem to depend on a *specific* definition of coherence, that is, on the apocalyptic delineation of Paul's gospel. It applies, for instance, as well—if not better—to a definition of Paul's coherent core as the present but hidden lordship of Christ, for that lordship searches necessarily for its contingent expression in history.

My claim, however, is that the *character* of Paul's contingent hermeneutic is shaped by his apocalyptic core in that in nearly all cases the contingent interpretation of the gospel points—whether implicitly or explicitly—to the imminent cosmic triumph of God.

Indeed, after the Christ-event, the imminent apocalyptic triumph of God already discloses its proleptic presence in history to the eyes of faith in the power of the Spirit and so foreshadows its public manifestation in glory, when "God will be everything to all things" (1 Cor. 15:28; trans. mine).

PART TWO

THE CONTINGENCY OF
THE GOSPEL

3

Contingency and Coherence in Paul's Letters

THE LETTERS: OCCASIONAL AND AUTHORITATIVE

Robert Funk has shown that Paul's letters are a substitute for his personal presence.[1] It is therefore no accident that most of the letters include an itinerary, information about Paul's plans, and his desire to visit the church personally and/or reasons for his inability to do so. This demonstrates the eminently practical and occasional nature of Paul's letters. Since Deissmann's *Light from the Ancient East*, it has been customary to distinguish between official-public epistles and private letters and to arrange the Pauline correspondence under the latter nonliterary category. Although the distinction serves to underline the occasional personal character of Paul's letters (according to Deissmann they are documents of personal piety), it should not mislead us. Paul did not—as many scholars would have it—dash off casual and incidental observations to his various churches. His letters are occasional, but not casual; they are not private, but personal; they are authoritative and not simply products of the moment. Hans Dieter Betz has performed a valuable service in comparing the official style of Roman letter-writing and rhetoric to the structure of Galatians. He concludes that even a polemic "fly sheet" like Galatians reflects careful composition.[2] Because Colossians transmits Pauline tradition, it demonstrates the semiofficial character of Paul's letters: "When this letter has been read among you, have it read also in the church of the Laodiceans; and see that you read also the letter from Laodicea" (Col. 4:16). Even a letter as personal as Philemon is directed to Philemon's house church (Philem. 2). Furthermore, from the beginning, Pauline letters were read in the context of the public worship service of the church (1 Thess. 5:27; cf. Eph. 3:4).

The letters are not only personal, occasional documents aimed at particular situations in particular times and places, but they are also authoritative documents. This is indicated by the official form of the letter, especially by the opening and closing formulas that make the letters a unique phenomenon among the Hellenistic-Roman letters. The formula "Grace to you and peace" (*charis hymin kai eirēnē*) is not simply an addition to a Jewish letter or a substitution for the usual "greeting" (*chairein*).

Moreover, the phrase "From God our Father and the Lord Jesus Christ" (*apo tou theou patros kai kyriou Iēsou Christou*) is a unique feature, because in Hellenistic-Roman letters the preposition "from" (*apo*) always indicates the human sender (Berger).[3] The letter form thus points to the apostolic self-estimate and authoritative claim of the letters. Their official structure, liturgical clues, and personal address to house churches indicate that Paul meant them to be read in the churches as messages that substituted for his apostolic presence and that conveyed the living word of the gospel to those present. Ernst Fuchs[4] reminds us that Paul writes reluctantly because the letter is a substitute for the living word (*viva vox*) of the gospel. This means that the letter is a curious phenomenon. It does not pretend to be "literature," which has a universal claim for all situations and subsequent generations.

Thus, Paul's letters, with their particularity and occasionality, are quite different from the literary genre of the "gospel," which intends to be a lasting literary testament. Because the letter is eminently particular and occasional, it wants to be a substitute for the dialogical directness of the apostolic word *hic et nunc* and yet claims divine authority and binding revelation, just like the prophetic word and letter in the Old Testament and apocalyptic literature (cf. the Jeremiah-Baruch cycle and the letters in Revelation). In other words, the occasional character of the letters does not imply their incidental character. The letter form, then, with its combination of particularity and authoritative claim, suggests something about Paul's way of doing theology. It suggests the historical concreteness of the gospel as a word on target in the midst of human, contingent specificity. Therefore, the letter must be bent toward the oral, dialogical nature of the gospel. The coherent center of the gospel is never an abstraction removed from its "address" and audience; it cannot be a *depositum fidei* or doctrinal abstraction that as a universal, timeless substance is to be poured into every conceivable situation regardless of historical circumstance. In other words, the truth of the gospel is bound up with its contingency and historical concreteness. Particularity and occasionality do not constitute a contamination of Paul's "pure thought"; rather, they serve to make the truth of the gospel the effective word of God.

Therefore, the interpreter of the Pauline letters cannot focus on the "substance" of the letter apart from its contingent setting. Too often, interpreters act as if the situational particularity of the letter is merely peripheral; sometimes they can even turn the obscurity of the contingent occasion to their advantage, for example, when the obscure occasion for the letter to Rome allows them to turn the letter into a timeless treatise (cf.

Nygren[5]). Thus theologies of Paul often tend to forget that Paul's thought is geared to a specific situation and that his arguments cannot be divorced from the need of the moment.

The Hermeneutical Obstacles of the Letters

The particularist and yet authoritative revelational claim of the letters proved to be a hermeneutical obstacle from the beginning. Where amid the variety of concerns and multiformity of occasions was the unity and core of the Pauline message to be found? What does constitute the universality, uniqueness, and center of Paul's message? Within the New Testament itself, the deutero-Pauline Epistles already struggle with this issue: How is the particularity and apostolic authority of Paul's gospel to be conveyed to a new generation and a new climate of thought after the death of the apostle? The pastoral Epistles solve the problem in a practical way by making Paul's "sound doctrine" (hygiainousa didaskalia, 1 Tim. 1:10; 2 Tim. 4:3) and "the deposit of truth" (paratheke, 1 Tim. 6:20) the authoritative criterion for ecclesiological problems of heresy and church organization. Ephesians tries to solve it in a speculative way: The author does not mention concrete ecclesiological problems but portrays Paul as the foundation stone of the church and as the mystagogue of God's revelation about the ontological being of the church.

There is a movement under way to diffuse the particularity of the Pauline letters in order to save Paul's authority for the church universal. In this light, the "encyclical"-letter theory—as proposed by recent scholarship—reveals a basic misunderstanding about the nature of Paul's letters. The theory, which has been argued especially for Romans and Ephesians, suggests that Paul at times writes a theological treatise that is meant not for any particular situation but for *all* his churches or for *all* his churches in certain Roman provinces. Thomas Walter Manson and John Knox, for instance, posit that the body of Romans consists of Romans 1:1—14:23, with 15:15-33 added for the church at Rome and 16:1-24 added when the letter was sent to Ephesus.[6] Thus, they argue, Paul composes a universal encyclical (Rom. 1:1—14:23) that is used for a variety of purposes. Other scholars propose a similar theory for Ephesians, because of its lack of address, among other reasons. Edgar Johnson Goodspeed and Knox even suggest that Ephesians was originally a cover letter for the first collection of the Pauline letters, a type of summary of Pauline theology, written by Onesimus, the first collector, who was the runaway slave from Philemon's house and who later became Bishop of Ephesus (Knox).[7] Such theories diffuse the particularity of the Pauline letters and suggest that a fixed body of Pauline thought was transmitted either by Paul or by his disciples to various churches as a sort of theological compendium.

The specificity and occasional character of the letters was felt to be a hindrance to their catholicity once the letters were collected and later canonized. Therefore, steps were taken to minimize their particularity and heighten their catholicity and doctrinal uniformity.

There is evidence that when 1 Corinthians headed the list of the Pauline collection, the superscription was enlarged in a catholic sense (cf. 1 Cor. 1:2, "together with all those who in every place call on the name of our Lord Jesus Christ, both their Lord and ours"). Because in all probability (cf. Tertullian and the Muratorian Canon) Corinthians opened the original list of the Pauline letters and Romans closed it, Rom. 16:25–27 functioned as the ending of the total collection. Its peculiar style, terminology, and general tone point to a non-Pauline hand; it most certainly displaced Rom. 16:24 when the letters were collected.[8] On the basis of evidence of the early use of Romans, 1 Corinthians, and Ephesians, Nils Alstrup Dahl correctly surmises that even before the "official" collection of the Pauline letters, individual letters circulated in the churches.[9] In all these cases, geographical particularity was omitted for catholic reasons. This would explain, according to Dahl, the omission of Rome in Rom. 1:7 and 15, the omission of a geographic reference in Eph. 1:1–2 (which Dahl considers to be a Pauline letter), and the catholic address of 1 Cor. 1:1. Moreover, 2 Thessalonians may have circulated as well without geographic address. (Polycarp points to a Philippian address [Pol. *Phil.* 11.3; cf. 3.2].)

The Diffusion of Particularity and Specificity

The particularity of the Pauline letters was diffused more decisively by the formation of the New Testament canon. The "ecumenical" Paul of Acts—who preaches the same message to a variety of churches and who, as a supreme witness for Christ, faithfully adheres to the one Christian kerygma as authorized by the Jerusalem church—was placed before the historical Paul and his collected letters. This placement actually functions as a hermeneutical key to the understanding of the Pauline letters, because the one ecumenical Paul speaks supposedly in them all with the same message. Second Peter 3:14–16, although acknowledging the difficulty of interpreting the Pauline letters, testifies that Paul proclaims the same catholic message, "speaking of this [the forbearance of our Lord] as he does in all his letters." When the "Catholic Epistles" were placed in the canon after the Pauline letters, they suggested not only the "catholicity" of the Pauline letters but also the idea that the apostle Paul was one harmonious catholic voice among the unanimous voices of all the apostles. At the time of the canonization of the Pauline letters then, both their particularity and the specificity of Paul's gospel were felt to be a problem. Because the "apostolic" witness of the canon claimed universal relevance, Paul must have addressed himself to "all Christian churches," just as such a universal address was ascribed to the so-called Catholic Epistles. After all, canonicity meant catholicity. The problem with "the apostolos" of the canon was not the plurality of the gospels but the particularity of the letters. Indeed, the plurality of the gospels in the canon was acutely felt, as the superscriptions reveal (e.g., *the* Gospel *according to* Matthew) and to which the longevity of the Diatessaron in the Syrian church testifies. How could the gospel be one and yet be present in four different forms? How could the "apostolic" witness be applicable to the universal church if Paul had simply written to specific churches about specific problems? Plurality and particularity are part of the same problem: How can the universality and the unity of the gospel be maintained in the face of them? Irenaeus argued for the universality of the gospel by speculating on the number four as a universal number. Just as the number four functioned as the universal number for Irenaeus, so did the number seven for the Pauline Epistles, as the Muratorian Canon discloses: *in catholica habentur* (1.69). And so Hebrews was finally conjoined to the Pauline letters to create a Pauline canon of 2 × 7. The catholic church then solved the issue of particularity by diffusing the occasional character of the letters, that is, by positing their universal "catholic" relevance. This in effect negated the problem of the particularity of the letters and allowed a general consensus of apostolic doctrine to overshadow not only the contingent character of the gospel within the Pauline letters but also the specificity of the Pauline gospel among the other books of the New Testament. Dahl correctly blames the Muratorian Canon for its false assumption that catholicity depends on the removal of particularity, and he points over against a docetic theology to the historicalness of all theology.[10]

THE SEARCH FOR DOCTRINAL UNITY

However, we must go further and notice the enormous hermeneutical consequences of this docetic move by the agents of the collection and canon. Not only was Paul harmonized with other canonical witnesses, but the "catholic" Paul now was viewed in terms of the doctrinal unity that he had supposedly preached to all the churches in harmony with the other apostolic witnesses. The creation of a "catholic" Paul by the makers of the canon has had dire consequences for the estimate of the "historical" Paul in the church. The "catholic" Paul is a "synthesized" Paul, built from the Acts of the Apostles, the Pauline letters, and the deutero-Pauline letters (Colossians, Ephesians, and the pastoral Epistles). *This* Paul won acceptance in the canon. Even so, he was silenced in the church until the time of Augustine and the Reformation. It was not until the time of the Reformation that the historical Paul could exert his basic influence on the church, which is all the more remarkable when we realize that the Reformers' critical grasp of the issue raised by the long-standing acceptance in the church of a "catholic" Paul was more intuitive than historical. Furthermore, because the "catholic" Paul of the canon was transmitted as doctrinal authority for orthodoxy, the *specificity* of both Paul's gospel and his interpretive contingent method were soon forgotten. The center of Paul's theology was now stated in terms of a doctrinal criterion that was abstracted from the particularity of its expression in the letters. In this way, Paul's theology was bequeathed to subsequent generations as revealed doctrine. The coherent center of Paul's gospel was bought at the expense of its contingency. The search for the center of Paul's thought became henceforth a search for dogmatic timeless truth, a search that continued essentially until the nineteenth century (Baur).[11]

Those who reacted negatively to Paul the "dogmatic theologian" and the search for a doctrinal center proposed a questionable alternative: The center now was not doctrine but religious intensity or religious feeling (cf. Deissmann,[12] among others). In both cases, the originality of Paul's theological thought and the versatility of his hermeneutic were overlooked, that is, the peculiar interrelation of "catholicity" and "particularity," of thematic coherence and situational contingency, or of "authoritativeness" and particularity. The "doctrinal" center aimed at an abstract definition and a conceptual consistency and so froze Paul's language. When this method was rejected in favor of an "experiential" center, a new error was introduced. The "experiential" center searched for an entity behind the language of the text and so abstracted itself away from the text of the letters to a coherent unity that was now located in Paul's religious experience.

The Three Solutions

This discussion can be summed up by outlining three solutions in the history of doctrine that were offered to solve the problem. I will call them (1) the catholic solution; (2) the Marcionite solution; and (3) the psychological solution.

1. I select Luke-Acts as an example of the catholic solution. Although Colossians-Ephesians and the pastoral Epistles also belong to this category, these deutero-Pauline letters portray the catholic solution on a different level (see above). The principal contribution of Luke-Acts to the Pauline problem of singularity and multiformity is to minimize the question of the center of Paul's thought. It focuses on Paul, the convert who became the chosen witness of God and the worldwide missionary. What distinguishes the apostle is not his thought and the question of its distinctiveness but rather his remarkable career and missionary success. Because the outstanding eminence of the apostolic person legitimizes the authority of Paul, the relation between kerygma and apostle is here decided in favor of apostolic greatness; it is not the message that evokes admiration, at least not its distinctiveness, but rather the person of the apostle. We must not forget that, according to Luke, Paul is not a writer of letters at all, and Luke-Acts is strangely silent about them. As Knox puts it, the Paul of the letters is a great letter writer and a poor speaker (2 Cor. 10:10), whereas the Paul of Acts is a great speaker and no letter writer at all.[13] Because Paul is underplayed theologically in Acts, Luke is unable to give Paul's thought any distinctiveness. All his speeches are similar, if not parallel, to those of "the apostolic kerygma" (Dodd[14]), especially similar to those of Peter, and do not point to any particularity or originality on Paul's part. Paul's thought in Acts is in no way distinctive but rather part and parcel of the unified kerygma of the early church. Subsequently, the catholic solution simply diffuses the specificity and contingency of Paul's thought and even silences his thought when it needed to combat gnosticism, which considered Paul its ally. In fact, Paul's thought did not achieve any prominence in the early church until (perhaps) the time of Augustine. Until that time and even up to the Reformation, the catholic solution largely prevailed. Although Paul's letters were collected early and subsequently canonized, and although they were read in the churches, alluded to in the apostolic fathers (Clement, Ignatius), and even quoted (Polycarp), it cannot be said that they had any theological impact. Second Peter 3:15–16 and Polycarp are evidence that, although Paul was accepted and even admired, the early church was more interested in his ethical apostolic admonitions than in his theological thought. In view of early heretical antinomianism (which already surfaces in the Epistle to James) and Marcion's Pauline canon, it was imperative that the church not surrender Paul to the heretics but claim him, although not in any preponderant way. Thus, the thought of the apostle was minimized and domesticated, so as to integrate the witness of

Paul with the other witnesses of the apostolic college. Paul's theological influence on the patristic period was minimal. The complete silence of the apologists indicates that Paul was felt to be an alien, if not a danger to the interests of the apologists. The teachings of Jesus—the *Nomos*—and the stoic conception of the *Logos* with its possibilities of bridging the logos in every man with Christ as the true preexistent Logos were more germane to the apologists' attempt of bridging culture and Christ. Eva Aleith sums it up this way:

> The institution of the ancient church does not want to be Petrine or Pauline, but apostolic. Because of this, it cannot use any extreme genius and outsider. The diligent way in which Paul as representative of the harmonious company of the apostolic college and as a faithful member of a uniform tradition is represented, is therefore not so strange, because the understanding of the particularity of Pauline theology is actually absent. . . . We cannot discover any trace of the Pauline teaching of sin and redemption in the early Christian apologists. The doctrine of the seminal Logos and the freedom of will favor a consistent moralism. None of the old theologians was able to penetrate into the essence of Paul's teaching of faith. The apologists learned nothing else from the post-apostolic writings, but that faith was a free assent to doctrine, and subsequent times would add little to this. . . . Paul experienced as hardly any other writer the fate to be read diligently and with admiration, but to be rarely understood.[15][Trans. mine.]

2. Whereas the catholic solution removes the problem of thematic coherence and contingency and tends to concentrate on Paul's personal apostolic greatness or on his harmony with the other canonical witnesses, the Marcionite solution focuses on the center and unity of Paul's thought. Here, a hermeneutical method selects a center and pushes the rest to the periphery. In Marcion, this hermeneutical method operates with selectivity, emendation, and a falsification theory (earlier employed by the Ebionites). Marcion limits his canon to ten Pauline Epistles and the Gospel of Luke and subsequently undertakes to emend the Pauline corpus, that is, to cleanse "the true Pauline doctrine" from its falsifications by Judaizers. Marcion then achieves a center by removing the "peripheral"; thus, Galatians comes first in his canon, and an emended version of both Galatians and Romans acts as the canon within the canon. It was Marcion's genius to search for a Pauline center of thought within the variety of the letters. We must recall here, however, the words of Franz Overbeck: "In the second century nobody understood Paul except Marcion, who misunderstood him."[16] Marcion's intent comes very close to Paul's own, to

present the true gospel of Christ amid the theological diversity of the early church. And Marcion's intent became in different ways the model for most subsequent scholarship when it searched for the unity and core of Paul's thought. This is evident in Baur's method of positing a Pauline antithesis to the Petrine thesis[17] and his way of deciding for—or against—Paul's authorship of particular letters; in Wrede's characterization of Paul's theology as a *Kampfeslehre*;[18] and in Schweitzer's "primary crater" of eschatological mysticism over against a survival-like secondary crater of rabbinic thought.[19] All these attempts carry on Marcion's search for the core of Paul's thought. The question, however, is whether Marcion's valid intent was correctly executed and whether subsequent scholarship repeated his mistake in its own way. Marcion found a canon within a canon, that is, a "cleansed" Paul. But hermeneutically, he imposed a unity of thought on Paul and thus destroyed the variety of thought in the Pauline letters. In other words, a center was imposed on Paul, and Paul's contextual way of doing theology was ignored. Marcion's error was not his search for a Pauline center but his inability—due to his own theological convictions— to discover how Paul himself interpreted the coherent center of the gospel. For Marcion and those who impose a unity of thought on Paul, the core of Paul's gospel was a systematic, doctrinal unity that, as Paul's abiding center, could be abstracted from the particularity and occasionality of the letters. In this way, Paul's "system" was focused on a set of primary concepts, in terms of which other concepts were downgraded (see Chapter 2, above). Linguistic concepts and dictionary meanings became increas- ingly a hermeneutical criterion for Paul's theology, and his thought was divided into either rabbinic or Hellenistic elements in order to arrive at a coherent conceptuality of Pauline theology. So it appeared that Paul simply imposed a unified center on the historical contingencies of every church, as if he emptied out a ready-made system into the diversity of historical situations and imposed unity and universality of doctrine upon particularity of circumstance. The Pauline letters, however, demand a hermeneutical clarification of the relation between contextualism and thematic construal, of contingency and coherent center. We must resist on the one hand the attempt to reduce occasionality and specificity to accidental, ad hoc, casual composition, or to the category of the haphazard, and so turn the letters into "fly sheets" that have no abiding center or authority. On the other hand, we must resist the attempt to equate the coherent core of Paul's gospel with a systematic set of propositions or a doctrinal set of categories, a "compendium of doctrine" (Melanchthon). Even in the pastoral Epistles this movement is under way (see above).

Paul's pneumatic, flexible interpretation of the *paradosis* has now become a *parathēkē,* a juridical *depositum fidei,* which is on the way to becoming a "frozen language." However, the Pauline letters demonstrate a hermeneutical versatility that explicates the center of the gospel in such a way that contextual situation is not suffocated by imposition from without but rather illumined in the light of the gospel. In other words, the gospel becomes *viva vox* only there, where it inserts itself with linguistic variety into the contingency of the human situation and so achieves its intended incarnational depth.

In summary, the Marcionite solution teaches us that however legitimate the search for the center of Paul's thought is, that center cannot be bought at the price of emendation, selective concepts, and a priori decisions about what is central and peripheral. Imposing a doctrinal unity on the variety of the letters needs to be avoided (see Chapter 2, above).

3. A third and final attempt to come to terms with the problem of the coherence and contingency of the letters—and thus, with their singularity and multiformity and occasional character—is the psychological approach. This approach is heavily indebted to the psychology of religion and the history-of-religions school. Over against a catholic, "apostolic" stance, and in opposition to a search for a doctrinal core, the psychological approach is basically developmental. Originally, it was a reaction to the doctrinal treatment of Paul. Scholars like Heinrich Weinel, Gustav Adolf Deissmann, and Johannes Schneider[20] intended to free the religious person of Paul from sterile, dogmatic thought categories. However, the psychological approach had a fatal flaw. Although this method was able to do justice to the variety of the Pauline letters, it could only achieve a Pauline "core" by locating it in his pretextual psyche. Paul's center becomes located in his religious personality rather than in his thought. And the variety of theological responses in the letters is attributed to Paul's psychoreligious development, a development that is reflected in the change between his early and his late correspondence. The developmental scheme has found its classical expression in discussions about Paul's eschatology and Christology. Dodd and other scholars[21] trace a line from Paul's earlier futurist apocalyptic eschatology to its mature ecclesiological expression in Colossians-Ephesians, where the "divine commonwealth" (Dodd) displaces the early Jewish apocalyptic expectations. In this way, the variety of Paul's thought is given expression, and the imposition of the doctrinal system is avoided. However, it is problematic whether a developmental process can be demonstrated in Paul's career in such linear fashion, especially when we realize that the total Pauline correspondence took

place within the span of no more than six years (A.D. 50–56) and that the letter period was preceded by almost fifteen years of nonliterary, apostolic activity (Gal. 2:1). Thus, there is no clear evidence for a maturing in Paul during his letter-writing period.

There are merits and dangers in all three approaches. The apostolic-catholic approach minimizes the quest for Paul's thought and its variety and celebrates his apostolic activity and the apostolic unity of the canon. It stresses that all Paul's apostolic utterances cohere within the one person of the apostle, who, moreover, is in harmony with all the other apostolic voices. The Marcionite approach correctly searches for the specificity of Paul's thought and its core, yet it forces an arbitrary mold on that thought by emendation, selectivity, and doctrinal imposition. The psychological approach intends to do justice to the variety of Paul's thought; in doing so, however, it assumes an evolutionary process that is difficult, if not impossible, to demonstrate. Furthermore, it often locates "the center" of Paul in his prelinguistic religious experience.

PAUL'S HERMENEUTIC

All three approaches fail in one decisive way: they do not honor the singularity and specificity of the Pauline letters in their hermeneutical interaction with the coherent center of Paul's gospel. This is obvious in the first and second approach: here unity and coherence are bought at the expense of variety and diversity and are located either in the "apostolic" person of Paul or in a selective, doctrinal core. The third approach comes close to respecting the situational variety of the letters. Yet, it exhibits a crucial failure in that it employs the situational variety to construct a developmental scheme, Paul's evolutionary growth as a thinker. The relation between "situation" and "thought" is not explored in its integrity, because the situation is viewed in terms of Paul's greater or less mature development, as the case may be.

The nature of Paul's hermeneutic needs more careful attention. Authority and particularity, coherent core and contingent contextualism constitute a dialectical movement in Paul's thought in which those elements continually interact.

Paul's hermeneutical skill exhibits a creative freedom that allows the gospel tradition to become living speech within the exigencies of the daily life of his churches. The "core" is for Paul not simply a fixed, frozen message that must either be accommodated to more or less adaptable occasions or simply imposed upon them as immutable doctrine. For Paul, tradition is always interpreted tradition that is executed in the freedom of

the Spirit. I intend to show that the interaction between the constant
elements of the gospel and the variable elements of the situation characterizes Paul's special—if not unique—hermeneutic. He was able to bring the
gospel to speech in each new situation without compromising either the
wholeness of the gospel or the specificity of the occasion to which it was
addressed. The interaction comes to speech in Paul's reflections on the
truth of the gospel and its concrete effectiveness. The power (*dynamis*) of
the gospel is for Paul the verification of its truth (*alētheia*; cf. Gal. 2:5, 14).
But the reverse is true as well: because the gospel is true, it manifests itself
as power, that is, it is effective (Rom. 1:16; 1 Cor. 1:18–25). The effective
power and the truth of the gospel are thus held in a dialectical tension:
They are inseparable, because for Paul the gospel contains both a coherent
truth and an inherent power. On the one hand, the power of the gospel is
evident in the existence of the churches, Paul's "fruit" (Rom. 1:13; 15:28;
trans. mine); "glory and joy" (1 Thess. 2:20); "joy and crown" (Phil.
4:1); the "seal of my apostleship" (1 Cor. 9:2) and the reason for his pride
"in the day of Christ . . . that I did not run in vain or labor in vain" (Phil.
2:16). Thus the emphasis on the concrete effectiveness of the gospel comes
to clear expression in 1 Thess. 1:5: "For our gospel came to you not only
in word, but also in power and in the Holy Spirit and with full
conviction." On the other hand, the power of the gospel depends on the
truth of the gospel, that is, on its specific identity as the one gospel of
"Jesus Christ and him crucified" (1 Cor. 2:2), besides which there is no
gospel (Gal. 1:6, 7; 2 Cor. 11:4). The correlation between the truth and
the power of the gospel indicates the amazing interaction between the
content of the gospel and its effective-contingent interpretation. "Core"
and particularity are not related in terms of a body of law and its casuistic
interpretation, or in terms of doctrinal propositions that now need to find
application. Rather, they are related as the mode in which the crucified
and risen Lord (1 Cor. 2:2; Rom. 8:34) in his significance for God's final
triumph is present in the historical particularity of the church's life. As I
mentioned before, the letter form is an emergency measure for Paul and
his theological method because it is the substitute for his personal presence
and for the oral living communication of the gospel in a dialogical
situation.[22] The letter, then, is not a dogmatic text or a fixed tradition that
from now on can be subjected to a rational delineation of Christian faith
as if it contained a series of propositions. Nor is the letter an accidental
feature in Paul's theology, so that its occasionality must be grudgingly
acknowledged before we can treat the essence of Paul's thought.[23]

Can we, in dealing with the Pauline letters, interpret them as they should be interpreted, or do we universalize them and abstract them away from their immediacy into a set of propositions or doctrinal centers? They should be interpreted as gospel for particular situations, "enfleshing" the gospel into human particularity. And the question is whether we allow the hermeneutical particularity of Paul's method to function in our own theological situation. For the way in which Paul allowed the gospel to incarnate itself can never be divorced from the doctrinal core of his gospel.

We can say then that the hermeneutical interaction between the coherent center of the gospel and its contingency—that is, the manner in which the one gospel of "Christ crucified and risen" in its apocalyptic setting achieves incarnational depth and relevance in every particularity and variety of the human situation—constitutes Paul's particular contribution to theology. His way of doing theology and the versatility of his language in interpretation are the marks of his genius, a genius that the letters richly document. His ability to focus in the midst of the early churches' variety of theological expressions on the one central core of "Christ crucified and risen," together with his ability to allow that focus to light up and interact with every conceivable variety and particularity of human life, is a feat that—with perhaps the exception of Luther—no other apostle or theologian has achieved. In that sense the letter form with its directness and its multiform response to contingent situations is not merely an accidental feature or a regrettable obstacle that prevents us from getting to the core of Paul's thought. Rather, it conforms most appropriately to Paul's way of doing theology. Leander Keck expresses it well:

> If the interpreter first finds the particularity of the original occasions to be an obstacle to appropriating Paul, it is probably because one expects the letters to be articulate timeless truths and principles to be applied, rather than timely words to concrete situations which are prototypes of our own. In other words, in the long run it is precisely the particularity of the occasions that make Paul's letters perennially significant.[24]

A FINAL OBSERVATION

Bultmann's hermeneutic deserves special mention because he broke with the nineteenth-century hermeneutical tradition of Pauline research.[25] To be sure, the Marcionite danger surfaces here again: Bultmann imposes his own hermeneutical conviction on the Pauline letters and therefore undercuts Paul's reflections on Israel's destiny, his apocalyptic eschatology, social solidarity, and cosmic theological horizon. He interprets Paul via Johannine categories. However, Bultmann's demythologizing breaks away from an interpretation of Paul in terms of doctrinal blocks and rabbinic or Hellenistic "craters." His interpretation intends to discover the existential self-understanding of Paul in his gospel and the challenge to human existence that Paul calls for in his various letters. Nevertheless, Bultmann's synchronic-topical treatment of Paul's thought cannot do justice to the particularity of the letter situations. Although in his interpretation of Paul a doctrinal "core" is not imposed on the hearers of the gospel in terms of intellectual assent, his existential hermeneutic blurs the historical distinction between Paul's kerygma and our twentieth-century situation, and the split between Historie and Geschichte does not permit the hermeneutical question its historical distance and depth.

The relation between "core" and "particularity" is here not actually resolved. The "core" for Bultmann is not any "objective doctrine" or "body of truth" but the word or kerygma of cross and resurrection that challenges man's self-understanding and quest for authenticity. Thus, the "core" is not an objective content and the "particularity" is that not of a particular situation but of every human situation everywhere as addressed by the gospel throughout the ages as an invitation to an existential decision. The "core" is not a specific identifiable content, and the "particularity" is not the historical particularity of the Pauline letters. In this way, Bultmann bypasses the nature of Paul's theological language in its historical versatility and specificity, that is, the way in which it functions within the particularity of the letter situation.

Bultmann's demythologizing passes too quickly from an investigation of the historical function of Paul's language ("mythology") to its demy-thologized, universal-existentialist function, and so Paul's historical her-meneutic becomes here a philosophical hermeneutic. Although Bult-mann's hermeneutical move achieves a remarkable unity and coherence of Paul's thought, which marks the thus far unsurpassed greatness of his essay on Paul in his New Testament Theology, the kerygma of Paul becomes abstracted from the letters and bypasses the hermeneutical interaction between coherence and letter situation in Paul's own theological language and world view.

4

Contextual Interpretation I: Galatians

CONTEXTUAL METHOD

The next three chapters will explore the contextual nature of Paul's theological thinking. The choice of Galatians and Romans for this purpose may seem surprising because these letters are often used together to exhibit Paul's systematic doctrinal thought. Romans seems the least occasional of all the Pauline letters, and although this does not apply to Galatians, it has always provided a rich quarry for the doctrinal essence of Paul's thought. In descriptions of Paul's thought, Galatians frequently functions as the hermeneutical supplement to Romans, because—although both letters betray a similarity of vocabulary and themes—Romans is much more explicit and extensive than Galatians. Both letters seem to set forth a unified theme that exhibits Paul's doctrinal center: justification by faith. According to a long-standing hermeneutical method, what is obscure in one text in Scripture is clarified with the help of another text, so that Scripture may be harmonized. In this way, theological thought is abstracted from its specific function and occasion in each particular situation, and one receives the impression that Galatians might just as well have been sent to Rome or Romans to Galatia. To be sure, there is good reason to conflate Galatians with Romans in a systematic treatment of Paul's thought. The similarity of themes and vocabulary, and the analogous movement from justification by faith in the first chapters to sacramental participation in Christ and to ethical exhortation in the later chapters, suggests a unitary treatment that can ignore incidental historical circumstances and context. This method becomes all the more attractive because Romans is the least occasional and most systematic letter of Paul. Romans seems capable of drawing Galatians, its "helpmate," into its own timeless current so as to minimize or at least neutralize the occasional nature of both letters, especially the explicit situational character of Galatians.

Therefore, it might seem an exercise in futility to select Galatians and Romans for an investigation of Paul's contextual way of doing theology. If—as I contend—Paul's theological method is a method of embodying the coherent center of the gospel into the particularity of a given situation, it would seem that the Corinthian correspondence should be our test case, and certainly not Romans. First Corinthians especially invites contextual interpretation because of Paul's question-and-answer method. However, if it can be shown that Paul uses a similar method in the "doctrinal" letters of Galatians and Romans, it would demonstrate that all Paul's theological thought is contextual-particularist. It would open our eyes to the fact that Paul's theological method is essentially a method of "ortho-praxis," a method of doing theology in the empirical mode, and that Paul's contextual method cannot satisfy our desire for "pure cognitive thought," as if a "timeless doctrinal system" can be abstracted from it. It is not by chance that the contextual particularity of Paul's thought has often been resisted by systematic theologians, because it constitutes a hermeneutical problem of the first order. Abstract timeless products of thought allow a facile transfer to new situations and world views and overcome more easily the problem of distance and historicity, which the emphasis on contingency poses. Therefore, the "doctrinal" letters of Galatians and Romans are an important test case for exploring the contingent nature of Paul's theological thought.

DIALOGICAL AND DIALECTIC THINKING

A situational approach to Paul's thought requires a contextual-dialogical method. "Dialogical thinking" is a more suitable term for Paul's thought than dialectical thinking. Dialogical thinking occurs within the "covenantal" context of persons and involves all the human elements that make up a conversation or confrontation. It is appropriate to oral discourse and is directly audience centered (see Chapter 7, below) because it posits that the intent and thrust of Paul's thought is inseparable from the specific situation that evokes it. In other words, it does not permit us to abstract Paul from the historical nexus of his thinking that addresses the partner(s) in the dialogue. The diatribe style of the Pauline letter confirms this dialogical thinking when, for instance, Paul introduces opponents into the discourse, repeats their key words, dismantles their objections, and interrupts his own arguments with emotional exclamations and non sequiturs.

Since the rise of Neoorthodoxy, it has become customary to refer to Paul's thought as dialectical. The term, however, often lacks precision, because it functions frequently as an umbrella for thought forms like paradox, antinomy, and even contradiction. "Dialectical" is a process of thinking that in Hegel, for example, advances a thought by moving it via thesis and antithesis to a new synthesis. Sometimes, as in Kierkegaard's paradox of the incarnation, the outcome of dialectical thought is the paradox or antinomy. Paul's thought, notwithstanding its occasional dialectical moments, cannot properly be called dialectical in its whole range, because Paul is not a philosopher who allows us an insight into the cognitive processes of his thought. To characterize Paul as a dialectical thinker makes of him a person who is engaged in a project of thought for the sake of thought and who allows his various thoughts to fall into their systematic place. Whereas dialogue subjects thought to the dialogical situation of speaker and audience, dialectic subjects the audience to the refinement of thought itself, which subsequently is either appropriated or rejected on the basis of the strength of the arguments and their logical sequence, as in the Platonic dialogues. Paul certainly exhibits dialectical insights, especially when the antitheses between life in the world and life in Christ begin to overlap. Such statements as "When I am weak, then I am strong" (2 Cor. 12:10), or passages where the foolishness of the cross is contrasted with the power of God (1 Corinthians 1), certainly suggest paradox. But these paradoxes occur at quite specific moments in Paul's thought; they do not allow us to characterize his overall thought as dialectical. "Dialectical" is unfitting to Paul's thought not only in a formal sense but also in a material sense. Neoorthodoxy derives "dialectical" largely from Kierkegaard's "infinite qualitative difference between eternity and time": The supreme paradox is the incarnation as the moment where eternity touches time. Dialectics aim at this paradox. The consequence of such dialectical thought as applied to Paul is the evaporation of the historical concreteness of his thought. The Word of God, to be sure, touches time in dialectical theology but does not enter a particular time or incarnate itself into human language and history in its contingent specificity.[1] Therefore, the "incarnational" concreteness and specificity of Paul's theological method is not recognized in a "dialectical" theology, where God's Word threatens to become a timeless Word. The Word means here the permanent crisis of "history" rather than signifying its timely relevance for a specific historical occasion.*

---

*This is not to deny that an interpretive *analysis* of Paul's thought must employ a dialectical method. How else can we describe the interaction between coherence and contingency or between the authenticity and the relevance of the gospel? In other words, a dialectical method grasps the interface between the unity of the gospel and its diverse expressions more appropriately than a developmental scheme. A developmental scheme uses the contingency of the letters to trace a theological process in Paul's mind from, for example, Galatians via the Corinthian correspondence to Romans (cf., e.g., the recent attempts of Hans Hübner, *Das Gesetz bei Paulus*, and John William Drane, *Paul, Libertine or Legalist?*; see Chapter 6, below, p. 94).

DIALOGICAL THINKING AND
THE TOPICAL-DOGMATIC METHOD

A contextual-dialogical method must resist as well the topical-dogmatic method that is employed in most Pauline theologies. Here Paul's reflections on such things as sin, the law, the flesh, Christology, eschatology, and ethics become building stones for an abstract system that constitutes the essence of his thought. Even the New Testament theologies of Bultmann and Conzelmann or Oscar Cullmann's Christology[2] or the essays on Paul's thought by Günther Bornkamm and Herman Nicolaas Ridderbos[3] follow a topical-dogmatic method that—notwithstanding its often anthropological focus—moves away from the contextual meaning of Paul's themes and language. Thus these scholars subject themselves to James Barr's indictment of New Testament word studies: "Theological thought of the type found in the New Testament has its characteristic linguistic expression not in the word individually, but in the word-combination or sentence."[4] Bornkamm, for example, separates Paul's "Life and Work" (Part One) from his "Gospel and Theology" (Part Two).[5] Part One treats the outline of Acts and the occasions for the letters, whereas Part Two is set aside for Paul's systematic thought. To be sure, Bornkamm sees the danger of his method:

> First, however, let us refer to an important characteristic of Paul's theology which is generally too little attended to. Paul's theology resists all efforts to reproduce it as a rounded-off system carefully arranged under headings, as it were, a *Summa Theologica*. Much erudite exposition proceeds as if there were no such difficulty and diligently *arranges into groups* the apostle's various statements about God, Christ, man, redemption, the sacraments, the church, last things, and so on. Indeed, the more it succeeds in turning the scattered data into *an aggregate classified under heads*, the more respect it is accorded. But that is quite wrong, even if the requisite reference is given for each proposition. The *plain fact* is that Paul's statements are just not found thus arranged *as fundamental doctrines of dogmatics*; practically always they are in *fragmentation and invariably woven in with others*. Admittedly, no exposition, the present one included, can avoid ordering Paul's trains of thought under leading topics and problems. Yet *this is make-shift; in actual fact, everything is intertwined.*[6] [Italics mine.]

Bornkamm's *schlichte Beobachtung* ("plain fact") does not cause him to reconsider his own thematic-topical method, and his valid criticism of other theologies does not seem to affect his own procedure. He may be correct when he rejects the "fortuitous" circumstance of "the changing situation from letter to letter" as ground for the absence of systematic "stock themes" in Paul,[7] but he does not contemplate the implications these fortuitous situations carry for Paul's theological thought. Bornkamm's solution to the problem is identical with Bultmann's definition of Paul's theology: "Every statement about God, Christ, Spirit, Law, judgment and salvation is at the same time one about man in his world."[8] Bornkamm reveals the difficulty of appreciating Paul's contextual way of doing theology. A thematic-topical approach achieves coherence of systematic content at the price of specificity of circumstance and context. The possibility of a different method is evident in Johannes Munck's *Paul and the Salvation of Mankind*.[9] Munck's method moves toward a dialogical approach that—in treating the four main letters in terms of their particular problems and settings—is superior to the topical-thematic approach. Indeed, contextual interpretation allows Paul's way of doing theology to surface more properly.

The criticism of the method of New Testament theologies does not intend to reject the need for a synchronic treatment of Paul's thought. There is indeed a paradigmatic structure to Paul's thought that forms its basic coherence and must be derived from the contingent variety of his arguments in his letters. However, the need for a comprehensive structure of Paul's thought too often disregards the particularity of that thought and therefore endangers the character of Paul's way of doing theology, that is, his hermeneutic. Moreover, it often forces Paul's thought into a systematic-logical coherence, where actually fortuitous or incidental juxtapositions may occur (vs. Bornkamm). And these may well be evoked by particular contingent argumentative situations rather than being constituent parts of Paul's logical structure of thought.

THE LETTER TO THE GALATIANS

I will explore Paul's contextual method by comparing his interpretation of the Abraham story and of the Torah in Galatians and Romans.[10] The result of this investigation will not become clear until Chapter 6, where the interpretation of these themes in Galatians (Chapter 4) and Romans (Chapter 5) will be compared. However, only when the total context of each letter is understood are we able to avoid atomistic comparisons, harmonizations, and construals of a timeless essence. I propose to investigate first of all the Galatian situation and Paul's apostolic self-defense in Gal. 1:11—2:21, because the function of the Abraham story and of the Law (Galatians 3) must be viewed within the total context of the letter.

Galatians was written for a specific purpose. The Galatian churches (Gal. 1:2) were located in the northern part of Asia Minor, that is, in the territory around Ancyra and Pessinus (and not in the Roman province "Galatia"). "The first time" of Paul's visit (Gal. 4:13)[11] confirms the sequence of Acts 16:6 and 18:23, where a second visit of Paul to the area is mentioned. The address, "Galatians" (Gal. 3:1), normally applies to the inhabitants of the territory rather than to those of the Roman province. Moreover, Galatia cannot refer to Iconium, Lystra, and Derbe (Lycaonia) with their strong Jewish populations (Acts 13, 14) because the letter is addressed to Gentiles. The Galatian churches, then, are composed of Gentiles who after their initial conversion are now in a quick process (tacheōs) of turning to a "different gospel" (Gal. 1:6). Paul's inability to come personally to Galatia (Gal. 4:20) suggests that he is somewhere in Europe, probably in Corinth, where he composes Romans shortly afterward. Thus, Galatians is probably one of Paul's latest letters.

The polemical, emotional, official, and almost nonpersonal character of the letter is evident both in the extensive and aggressive self-introduction and in the omission of laudatory attributes in the preface. Paul's customary thanksgiving is omitted, and the letter ends abruptly (Gal. 6:17) without greetings from co-workers or news about them. The variety in literary style shows the passionate character of the letter: apologetic self-defense (Gal. 1:10—2:10), accusation (2:11–21), attack (3:1–5), scriptural midrash (3:6–14), and allegorical interpretation (4:21–31) mix with tender appeal, sorrow (4:12–20), and bitter sarcasm (5:12). If anywhere, the whole range of Paul's personality and hermeneutical ability comes to light here.

The Theology of the Galatians

The Galatians were converted by Paul to the gospel. After his last visit to them (Acts 18:23), itinerant Jewish-Christian missionaries had arrived (cf. Gal. 1:7; 4:17; 5:10; 6:12). The scene resembles that of 2 Corinthians, where traveling Jewish-Christian missionaries had invaded the Corinthian church with a "different Jesus" and a "different gospel" (2 Cor. 11:4). In Galatia the Jewish-Christian missionaries were able—to Paul's astonishment—to convince the Galatians of the truth of their cause.

What, then, were their convictions, and how did they manage to make such a convincing appeal? To be sure, the opponents do not intend to apostatize from the gospel; they only want to perfect what Paul has commenced (epiteleisthe, Gal. 3:3). In order to accomplish their primary objective—to discredit Paul's gospel—they devise a strategy that combines personal attack and theological subject matter: If they can undermine Paul's apostolate, they can undermine his gospel as well. The issue is sensitive and explosive, because Paul also posits apostolate and gospel as interlocking realities. Paul, however, intends to subordinate his apostolate to the gospel (cf. Rom. 1:1–17), whereas the opponents concentrate their attack primarily on Paul's apostolate. They are convinced that once this has been accomplished Paul's gospel will be discredited as well. Thus, they force Paul into a personal defense of his person. Indeed, the hermeneutic of the apostolate is Paul's primary concern in Galatians, just as it is in 2 Corinthians 10–13, for if that fails, the truth of the gospel is likewise surrendered. Paul must defend both his apostolic status and the truth of the gospel together (Gal. 1:1, 11–12).

The argument of the opponents runs along the following lines: You Galatians were Gentiles when, through the gospel which Paul preached, you turned to Christ. This turning away from idols and the "elemental spirits of the universe" (Gal. 4:3, 9) is an important first step. It is like the step Gentiles take when they turn from idols to the God of Israel and attach themselves as semiproselytes or God-fearers to the synagogue. However, do not mistake the first step for the end of the road (Gal. 3:3). Paul misled you when he told you that your new status as sons of God in Christ depends on faith alone. That is an opportunistic misconstruction of the gospel and short-circuits its full implications. You realize—of course— that our Christ was the Messiah promised to the people of Israel, the true sons of Abraham. Jesus Christ is indeed the messianic fulfillment of the promise to Abraham, and therefore the promise pertains to those who belong to the people of Israel. It does not mean that Gentiles are excluded from the promise: They can participate in the full blessings promised to Abraham if they join the people of the promise. When Paul opposes the Torah and Christ, he is not only wrong but also opportunistic, because he wants to make it religiously and sociologically easy for Gentiles to become Christians, in order to enhance his apostolic grandeur. It is simply false that Gentiles can remain participants in pagan society without the "yoke of the Torah." The Torah and Christ cohere, because it is only within the realm of the Torah that the promise is fulfilled in Christ. To be sure, the observance of the Torah does not mean the observance of *all* its statutes and ordinances (cf. "the whole law": Gal. 5:3, 14; 6:13). Although Jesus Christ, the Messiah, acknowledged their validity, they have been fulfilled by him in his death for us. Nevertheless, "Torah-keeping" means the obligation to become a member of the Jewish people and therefore circumcision marks your entrance into the line of salvation-history that started with Abraham and finds its fulfillment in Christ. The Torah, then, has primarily salvation-historical significance; it assures your participation in Christ by placing you in the correct salvation-historical scheme. What counts is its cosmic-cultic meaning as law of the universe. Therefore circumcision and Jewish calendar-observances (Gal. 4:10) complete your status as full Christians and guarantee God's divine blessing upon you as true sons of Abraham. Paul should have taught you the gospel in this way. His claim to apostolic independence is actually a combination of opportunism and disobedience. His opportunism is directed at painless mass conversions, which must enhance his ego, whereas his disobedience is apparent when he—contrary to directions from Jewish-Christian headquarters in Jerusalem—preaches *an abbreviated gospel*. He should have behaved in accordance with his real status and have told you that he was an apostle in dependence on Jerusalem and have preached to you the proper and authentic gospel, as he was taught it. Instead, this latecomer to the apostolic circle acts illegitimately and disobediently when he preaches a gospel that rests on *sola fide*, ignores the law and the Jewish antecedents of the Messiah, destroys the continuity of Israel with the church, and lacks a proper ethic. The Jerusalem apostles are the true authority in the church because they are the disciples of the historical Jesus (cf. Gal. 2:6) and provide the continuity between Israel and the church. Therefore they are the pillars (*styloi*)[12] of the new temple and the true source of Paul's apostolate, as his relation to Jerusalem in the past clearly indicates.*

Paul's Response

Paul intends to dismantle the opposition by arguing for the integrity of his apostolate and his gospel. Therefore, the relation of the apostle to the gospel constitutes the theme that dominates the literary structure of the letter. The theme, which is subsequently unfolded chiastically, is stated in Gal. 1:11–12: "The gospel which was preached by me is not man's gospel [*kata anthrōpon*]. For I did not receive it from man [*para anthrōpou*], nor

---

*The preceding reconstruction can only claim reasonable accuracy. Specifically, two items are open to discussion: (1) The opponents may have presented a "softer" picture of Paul than we suggest. The harsh picture, presented above, may well be due to Paul's sensitive reaction to the opponents' argument. In other words, the opponents may not have attacked Paul outright but simply have tried to put Paul in his place. He was—to be sure—an apostle, but he was dependent on Jerusalem. His gospel was—to be sure—not a false gospel, but it was incomplete. Paul, in other words, may argue with opponents who do not simply deny all he has done but who discredit him in a subtle way. If this is the case, the opposition in 2 Corinthians is quite different, because it is acutely hostile to Paul. (2) The status of the Torah in the opponents' scheme is unclear and ambivalent (Gal. 3:3; 4:9, 21; 5:13–15; 6:12). Do they adhere only to the cultic salvation-historical meaning of the Torah or to its strict "covenant-keeping" sense as well, that is, to the Torah as an indivisible totality? The observance of the moral Torah is implied in Gal. 2:16—3:5 and 5:14, 23b, whereas Paul, to the contrary, argues in Gal. 4:9–10, 6:13, and 5:3 that circumcision and cultic observances as practiced by the Galatians are inconsistent with the Jewish understanding of Torah as an indivisible unit (cf. "the whole law" in Gal. 5:3, 14).

was I taught it, but it came through a revelation about [of?] Jesus Christ."

1. *"The apostle": Gal. 1:13—2:21.* Paul's gospel does not derive "from a human source" (*para anthrōpou*); to the contrary, it is directly from God, and this constitutes his apostleship.

2. *"The gospel": Gal. 3:1—5:25.* Paul's gospel is not "according to human standards" (*kata anthrōpon*); to the contrary, it is according to Scripture (*kata graphēn*, Gal. 3:1—4:31) and verified by the Spirit (Gal. 5:1-25).

The appeal of the "different gospel" of the Judaizers is the promise of becoming a "whole" Christian. It requires a Gentile's incorporation in the domain of Israel through circumcision, that is, incorporation in the people of the covenant and the promise. The opponents claim to represent the Ur-gospel of the Jerusalem church, and they charge Paul with preaching a "mini-gospel" that distorts the Jerusalem gospel. As a Jerusalem delegate, he should have been obedient to Jerusalem and consequently concur with the gospel that the Judaizers preach to the Galatians.

Paul's response betrays his precarious situation and the finesse of the opposition. Because he is aware of the crisis of the situation and the impending defection of the church (Gal. 4:11, 19), he cannot simply appeal to his apostolic "right" or "fatherhood" over his churches (cf. 1 Cor. 4:15; 9:1-2). The crisis situation dictates the form and substance of the argument with its sharp antitheses and invective dialogue. Paul aims at an either/or decision and argues on the basis of principle, because all is either won or lost. Not until Gal. 4:12, 19 does he allude to the Galatians as his "brothers" and "my little children." It is part of his strategy (but cf. 2 Corinthians 10-13) to leave the identity of the opponents in the shadow in order to diffuse their stature and "legal" right over the Galatians (cf. "some" [Gal. 1:7]; "any one" [1:9; cf. 1:7; 5:12]; the clearest reference: "the circumcision party" [6:13]). Moreover, he carefully steers a course between an image of himself as a defector from Jerusalem and as a dependent servant of Jerusalem, because he intends to demonstrate both the independence of his apostleship and gospel and the basic agreement between Jerusalem and himself. But how can he maintain his independence and yet refute the charge of being a runaway, rebellious apostle? And how can he argue his agreement with Jerusalem without forfeiting his freedom and admitting his dependence? In other words, how can he argue agreement and not dependence, and how can he argue freedom and not rebellion?

Paul defends the independence and truth of both his gospel and his apostolate in Gal. 1:13—2:21. Their source is not explicable on human grounds (1:11–17), because Paul's pre-Christian career demonstrates that his Christian apostolate was impossible in terms of his own volition (1:13–14). Moreover, there was no need for human authorities to teach him the gospel (1:16–25; cf. 1:12b) after his call (1:15); in fact, apart from a fourteen-day visit with Peter three years later, he had no contact with Jerusalem but preached the gospel in Syria and Cilicia.

The Galatian opponents distort the truth when they charge Paul with perverting his apostolic dependence on Jerusalem and the Jerusalem gospel (Gal. 2:1–4). To the contrary, Paul's law-free gospel was acknowledged by the so-called "pillars" in Jerusalem. Although Paul did go up to Jerusalem, he went on his own initiative (2:1), and the apostolic decree and the collection agreement show the substantial unity of the church in the truth of the gospel. Paul now reinforces his "independence-in-agreement" claim by acknowledging the pillars without giving them superior status in the cause of the gospel (2:6). And even when a super-pillar like Peter defects from the truth of the gospel, Paul is anything but subservient, because he publicly called Peter to account (2:11–14). Although Paul does not mention Peter's possibly angry reaction to this heavy-handed action at Antioch, Paul implies that his argument settled the matter once and for all for the sake of the "truth of the gospel" (cf. Gal. 2:5, 14; 2:11–21).

What, we may ask, is the force of this argument, and what did Paul hope to accomplish? Paul's personal, apostolic defense occupies center stage in Gal. 1:11—2:21 (cf. also 2 Corinthians 10–13; Phil. 3:4–11). In 1 Corinthians the situation is different. Here Paul still trusts the weight of his apostolic authority and does not debate it (except for 1 Cor. 9:1–27; cf. 1 Cor. 15:8–10). Rather, he points away from himself to the one foundation, Jesus Christ (1 Cor. 3:11), in relation to whom all others are subordinate agents. Elsewhere he can rejoice when others preach the gospel, even when they slander him (Phil. 1:15–16). However, in Galatians and 2 Corinthians he is engaged in an extensive personal defense and self-legitimation. But why does he argue that way? Why did Paul not negate himself and concentrate instead on the substance of the gospel? Why did he not follow his own dictate, "We put no obstacle in any one's way" (2 Cor. 6:3), by putting himself out of the way for the sake of Christ. It is the nature of the attack on Paul in Galatians and 2 Corinthians that compels this particular response. Although he knows himself to be a "slave of Christ" (Gal. 1:10; trans. mine) and subject to the gospel (1 Cor. 9:24–27), and although he does not want to elevate himself by means of the gospel (2 Cor. 12:10), he is forced to authenticate himself in this situation, because the truth of the gospel in Galatia (and Corinth) stands or falls with the truth of his apostolate. Paul cannot say, "Forget about me—only the gospel counts." The gospel and its bearer are interlocked, because if Paul is discredited in Galatia—as he is—the only gospel that remains is the "different gospel," which in fact is "no gospel" (Gal. 1:6). The bearer of the gospel becomes all-important in Galatians and 2 Corinthians because the issue is the true gospel as opposed to the pseudo-gospel and because the apostle is responsible for the truth of the gospel against the lie. Wherever Paul perceives that the situation has not reached a crisis (cf. 1 Corinthians, Romans), he does not feel compelled to conflate the apostle and the gospel into an undivided whole (cf. Rom. 1:1-16; 15:15-19). A relativizing of his apostolic self-awareness in Galatia would have meant a surrender of the truth of the gospel. That is how Paul perceives it. He is not just a preacher of the gospel but the apostle who interprets the gospel with the authoritative, unique claim of a resurrection witness and as the founder of the church. Paul's self-defense, then, shifts into a demonstration of his exemplary apostolic life. Because he lives the truth of the gospel (Gal. 4:12; cf. 2:14 and 5:1-12), he becomes the apostolic paradigm for the Galatians. In that sense the gospel and the apostolate cohere as well. The correlation of apostle and gospel, which dominates Gal. 1:12—2:21, continues to be a prominent theme in Gal. 3:1—5:25, when Paul moves from personal to material considerations.[13]

THE MIDRASH ON ABRAHAM

The argument in Gal. 3:1—5:25 centers on the interpretation of Scripture (cf. Gal. 3:6-18 and 4:21-31). Paul extends his first exegesis (3:6-18) into an explication of the function of the law (3:19—4:11); the second exegesis (4:21-31) issues into a call for Christian freedom (5:1-12) with its ethical consequences (5:13-26).

A contextual study of Paul's thought points to the variety of ways in which Paul uses Scripture to his advantage in a particular situation. Because Abraham played a central role in the theology of the opponents, Paul's midrash on Gen. 15:6 (Gal. 3:6; cf. Rom. 4:3) constitutes his polemic against their position. Although it is probable that a Christian interpretation of Gen. 15:6 existed before Paul (cf. James 2:11-24), he develops it in his own way whenever "the Jewish question" arises, in order to ground his conception of justification by faith in Scripture. Notwithstanding their similarity, the Abraham chapters in Galatians 3 and Romans 4 have a different hermeneutical function, because Paul does not intend to score identical points or to "dump" a fixed exegetical product on two different situations (see Chapter 6, below).

The issue in Galatians is: Who are the true sons of Abraham? (Gal. 3:7) The Judaizers argue that because both Abraham and Christ—as the heir to Abraham's blessing—were circumcised, only sons of Abraham through circumcision belong to the domain of blessing. Gentiles cannot be full Christians without living within the domain of salvation, that is, without adopting circumcision and the Torah. Instead of emphasizing, as he does in Romans 4, Abraham and his personal stance in faith, Paul discusses in Galatians 3 the principle that the Abraham story reveals. In Galatians 3, the references to Gen. 15:6 and 18:18 (Gal. 3:6–9) center on the scriptural principle that justification is by faith for the Gentiles. The fact that Paul argues on the basis of principle is clear in his opening question: "Did you receive the Spirit by works of the law or by the message of faith?" (Gal. 3:2; trans. mine). Over against the Judaizers, who coalesce Christ and the Torah, Paul posits the antithesis of the Torah and Christ, which the Abraham story must undergird. It is interesting in this context that— whereas circumcision is Paul's real target in Galatians (2:3; 5:2, 3, 6, 11; 6:12, 13, 15)—he argues in Galatians 3 the principle of the Torah and its function and omits references to circumcision (cf. the theme of 3:1–5; however, "ending with the flesh" in 3:3 no doubt refers to circumcision).

Galatians 3:6–9. Paul places the Abraham story in this either/or context in order to counter the "surplus" argument of his Judaizing opponents. While they insist on the privilege of Abraham and his seed (the Jews) over the Gentiles, Paul interprets Gen. 15:6 in conjunction with Gen. 18:18[14] and Hab. 2:4. The observance of the Torah (and circumcision) did not make Abraham pleasing to God, only his faith. Furthermore, Gentiles are the recipients of God's promise to Abraham (Gal. 3:8). "Faith" (vv. 7 and 9) and "Gentiles" (v. 8, twice) are the key words of this section. Galatians 3:9 now seems to conclude the necessary argument: "Therefore those who are *of faith* are blessed with the believing Abraham" (trans. mine). If faith is the only condition for being a son of Abraham, and if Gentiles are the object of the blessing, the Judaizing argument is uprooted.

Galatians 3:10–18. At this point the status of the Torah in its relation to the promise to Abraham needs to be clarified in the light of the basic theme of Gal. 3:1–5. Instead of integrating Abraham-Torah-circumcision and Christ, Paul drives a radical wedge between Abraham and the Torah on the one hand and between Torah and Christ on the other hand, by arguing that the blessing (= promise) and faith belong together, just as do the curse and the works of the law (Gal. 3:10–13). Paul now connects the promise (blessing) and Christ with a double argument: (1) Christ by lifting the curse of the law enables "the blessing to Abraham" to flow to the Gentiles (v. 14), and (2) because Christ is the exclusive "seed" of

Abraham according to Gen. 17:7 (v. 16), Christ is discontinuous with the era of the Torah and directly related to the promise. The Torah came upon the scene 430 years after the promise and had nothing to do with God's promise to Abraham (vv. 17–18). Christ is the one who fulfills the promise to Abraham, for with him the Spirit (v. 14) and faith have come (v. 25).

We can summarize the argument as follows:

1. An argument of principle dominates the discussion. The principle of faith for the Gentiles is antithetical to the principle of the Torah and its works (Gal. 3:2–5).

2. The argument of antithetical principles takes a salvation-historical form through the use of the Abraham story (Gal. 3:6–18). It has in Galatians an outspoken discontinuous thrust, because the blessing and promise to Abraham are antithetical to the curse and the Torah.

3. The relation between Abraham and Christ is that between promise and exclusive seed (Gal. 3:16). Both are opposed to the Torah, and Abraham seems to have had no "seed" before Christ, because the actualization of faith has come only since Christ (vv. 19, 23).

4. Christ actually came to undo the law and its curse, and thus the promise to the *Gentiles*—in accordance with God's promise to Abraham (Gal. 3:7)—cannot be blocked by the Torah (v. 14). In arguing this way, Paul demonstrates to the Gentile Galatians the incongruity and impossibility of "returning" to the law (Gal. 4:7).*

The Logic of the Argument

Because the Abraham midrash has an inherently salvation-historical thrust, but is interpreted by Paul in a discontinuous manner, the question

---

*What remains unclear in the argument is the status of the Gentiles before Christ. One could argue that the section is primarily directed to *Jewish* Christians (cf. Gal. 2:15: "*We* ourselves, who are Jews by birth . . ."; cf. the first person plural: Gal. 2:16, 17; 3:13, 14; 3:23–25; 4:3, 5) over against the Galatian Gentile Christians (cf. the second person plural and "Gentiles": Gal. 3:2–5, 8, 14; 3:26, 27, 29; 4:6, 7, 8–11). In other words, the argument turns so sharply to a denial of the Jewish privileges claimed by Judaizers that all those "privileges" are shown to be obstacles to salvation and thus things that Gentiles should not be concerned with—least of all Gentiles who, ironically enough, now desire to "return" to the law (Gal. 4:7). This interpretation seems strained, however, because Paul strongly implies that the curse of the law would also have made Abraham's blessing void for Gentiles (Gal. 3:13–14). Galatians 3:22 ("all things"; cf. "all men" in Rom. 11:32) particularly suggests the universal curse of the law and the "no exit" status for all "before faith came" (Gal. 3:23). Again in Gal. 4:3, 9, the "renewed" (*palin*) return of Gentiles to the "elemental spirits of the universe" is equated with a return to the domain of the Torah, from which Christ has redeemed us (4:5). The anti-Jewish argument, however, so pervades Galatians 3 that the relation of Gentiles to the Torah before Christ is unclear. The accent falls on the Christocentric confession of Gal. 3:26–29, which for Gentiles is the only reality that matters, for to be in Christ is to live in the reality of the new creation (Gal. 3:28), and that reality excludes the Torah but confirms the promise to Abraham.

arises how this discontinuous hermeneutic affects the logic and consistency of the argument.

In Gal. 3:6–9 we are led to believe that sons of Abraham are all those who belong to his seed (v. 8, "in you"). Abraham is their father because they believe (v. 9: "those who are men of faith"). We are not prepared for the sudden introduction of verse 16 (Gen. 17:7), where Christ alone—and not "those who are men of faith"—constitutes Abraham's seed.

Thus, Gal. 3:6–9 suggests that "the seed of Abraham" refers to "those who believe" rather than to Christ exclusively (v. 16), just as Rom. 4:14–16 interprets "seed" in terms of a plurality of believers. Even Gal. 3:10–14 does not clearly prepare the way for Christ as "the seed of Abraham," that is, for Christ as the sole content of God's promise to Abraham, because Paul argues here that apart from Christ the blessing to Abraham would have been forfeited. The principle of faith as such does not save Gentiles— as verses 6–9 have it—nor is Christ the sole content of the promise (v. 16). Rather, in verses 10–14, Christ is the object of faith because he is the "enabler" of the promise. He has lifted the curse of the law in his death on the tree, so that the blessing of Abraham—interrupted by the curse of the Torah—can now flow freely to the Gentiles: "That in Christ Jesus the blessing of Abraham might come upon the Gentiles" (v. 14). Christ then is here the enabler of the blessing, not its sole content or representative, because he enables the prior promise to Abraham to flow. In other words, he is "the emergency measure" of God that allows the blessing to flow, after its interruption by the period of the law with its curse.

The christological argument shifts again in Gal. 3:16–29. Paul now underscores the uniqueness of Christ as the sole recipient and content of the promise. The Gentiles are no longer directly the "sons of Abraham" and recipients of the promise because of their faith (vv. 8, 9), for now Christ is the sole recipient in his status as the exclusive seed. Furthermore, Christ is here no longer the enabler of the promise to Abraham (Gal. 3:14), that is, God's emergency measure that permits the blessing of Abraham to flow to the Gentiles. To the contrary, in verses 16–29 Christ is the blessing and the fulfillment of God's promise. Paul now states that faith did not become a reality until Christ came (vv. 23–25), and he seemingly ignores both the case of Abraham (vv. 6–9) and the function of Christ as the enabler of the promise (vv. 10–14).

The introduction of Christ as Abraham's exclusive seed gives the Abraham midrash a Christocentric focus that climaxes in the sacramental-baptismal confession: "For in Christ Jesus you are all sons of God, through faith" (Gal. 3:26). Christians are not primarily sons of Abraham because of their "faith" (vv. 6–9) or because of Christ's lifting of the curse (vv. 10–14); they are primarily sons of God (v. 26) because they have been incorporated in Christ, and as such they are "Abraham's seed" as well (v. 29), because Christ is "the seed of Abraham" (v. 16).

We have come full circle. The argument started with the faith of Abraham and his believing "sons" (seed); subsequently, it moved to Christ as the one who removed the curse of the law and enabled the blessing (= promise) to Abraham to flow to the Gentiles, and finally we end with Christ as Abraham's exclusive seed, who alone actualizes faith and makes faith our possibility (Gal. 3:23–29). The emphasis now falls on "belonging to Christ" (v. 29) and on being "sons of God" in Christ (v. 26). Whereas we expect to hear, "You are the true sons of Abraham because Christ has confirmed Abraham's faith which the law threatened to undo," we hear instead, "Because you are sons of God through baptism in Christ, you are seed of Abraham as well" (vv. 26–29).

In Galatians 3 the element of discontinuity dominates the Abraham story. The peculiar shifts in the argument indicate that Paul bends the Abraham story—which the opposition used for its benefit—to his own purpose. He carries out a Christocentric argument that confirms faith for the Gentiles and annuls the Torah. Therefore, Abraham can only be maintained in salvation-history as a figure of the promise, one who "contains" Christ as "his one seed" (Gal. 3:16). The "Jewish" dispensation of circumcision and the Torah has only been a curse and an obstacle: a curse that threatened to undo the blessing promised to the principle of faith (vv. 9–10) and an interloper that inserted itself illegitimately between the promise to Abraham and its exclusive fulfillment in Christ.

The peculiar logic of the argument shows that the salvation-historical thrust of the Abraham story can be used by Paul against the Judaizers only if he centers the story Christocentrically (Christ as the exclusive seed) and therefore discontinuously. Before Christ came, faith was a promise—even to Abraham—and not a reality, because only those incorporated in Christ actualize faith.

Paul uses the Abraham story in a polemical setting, because in the hands of the opponents Abraham has become "Judaized" and Christ has been subordinated to their Judaizing interpretation. Because the Judaizers stress the continuity in salvation-history between Abraham, Torah, circumcision, and Christ, Paul can use the Abraham story only in terms of discontinuity. Before Christ came in the "fullness of time" (Gal. 4:4; trans. mine), there was only the promise of God and bondage to the law. The keys to the Abraham midrash in Galatians 3 are the "promise" (*epangelia*) and Christ, because faith has become an actuality in history only *since* and *in* Christ. And because the Galatian Gentiles are the intended objects of the promise, they are in Christ "sons of God"[15] and the "seed of Abraham." Christians believe not in the promise (but cf. Rom. 4:20 and 24a) but in Christ who has fulfilled the promise. Therefore, a return to the Torah (Gal. 4:9, 21) means a regression to the period of the curse and a rejection of God's salvation-historical plan, that is, a fall from grace (Gal. 5:4), thus making the Judaizers in Galatia enemies of the gospel who stand under its curse (Gal. 1:6–9).

THE TORAH

Paul uses the Abraham story to dismantle his opposition, but in the midst of the process he opens himself up to such a radical antithesis between faith and the law that an urgent defense on behalf of the law becomes inevitable: "Why then the law?" (Gal. 3:19). Whereas the "chain" argument of the Judaizers connects Abraham, circumcision, the Torah, and Christ, Paul drives a wedge between Abraham and the Torah. We must not overlook the fact that the Judaizing interpretation of the Abraham story has a compelling logic. Abraham's circumcision defines the domain of the messianic blessing in Christ and marks the proper line of salvation-history. According to the Judaizers, the Torah confirms primarily the line of salvation-history rather than its halakic dimensions. Therefore, Paul condemns the Galatians and their new leaders repeatedly for not obeying the whole law:[16] "Cursed be every one who does not abide by all things written in the book of the law, and do them" (Gal. 3:10; cf. Deut. 27:26, LXX);[17] "I testify again to every man who receives circumcision that he is bound to keep the whole law [*holon ton nomon*]" (Gal. 5:3); "For the whole law [*ho gar pas nomos*] is fulfilled in one word . . ." (5:14); "Even those who belong to the circumcision party do not themselves keep the law" (6:13; trans. mine).

The Galatians do not seek to reintroduce the strict observance of the Torah or to undo the act of God in Christ but intend to give it its completed meaning. Therefore, circumcision does not mean a return to Judaism, or an apostasy from Christ, but a full appropriation of the Christ-event, that is, without the antinomian consequences of Paul's gospel (Gal. 5:14, 23). Paul now attacks this position by radicalizing it: Circumcision means a reintroduction of the Torah in its totality and does not permit a neglect of any of its demands.

Because it is probable that Paul was formerly a Shammaite radical and not a liberal Hillelite,[18] he insists that a reintroduction of the Torah means strict Torah observance for Gentiles. What the Galatians perceive as a necessary supplement to their faith Paul views as a radical break with faith. In order to score that point decisively, Paul discusses the law in such a radical fashion that it threatens to become a demonic, antidivine principle. The Galatian situation dictates an interpretation of the law that is quite different from the one in Romans, because—as I will argue—Romans is addressed not to a critical situation or to Judaizers but to recent converts from the synagogue, both God-fearers and former Jews (see Chapter 5, below).

In Galatia, to the contrary, Paul faces Gentile Christians who want to incorporate the *best* of Judaism. Far from apostatizing to Judaism and the Jewish law, they recognize that Christ has changed the observance of Torah so that it is no longer the sole criterion of salvation. They simply insist on the correlation of certain abiding Torah principles and observances with faith in Christ, because Christ did not so much abrogate the law as fulfill its legal demands in his life, death, and resurrection (cf. Gal. 2:18-21). Paul, then, cannot risk a positive posture toward the law in this context. Therefore, he radicalizes the issue by declaring that even a minimum of law observance implies an obedience to "the whole law." In the very different situation of Romans—where, for instance, the phrase "the whole law" does not occur—the apology of the law is much more positive. Paul speaks there about the law as "holy, righteous, and good" and "spiritual" (Rom. 7:12, 14) and claims that "we uphold the law" (Rom. 3:31). He makes appropriate distinctions between the inherent goodness of the law and its abuse in the human situation and speaks directly about such things as the fulfillment of "the just requirement of the law" (Rom. 8:4).[19] However, the crisis situation in Galatians, where the law is co-opted into the gospel, forces Paul to such a radical hermeneutic of the law that it becomes almost a totally negative power in history; moreover, it endangers Paul's own view of it, because it seems to drive him into the hands of Gnostics and antinomians (cf. Gal. 5:13-24). It is therefore no wonder that many interpreters detect a gnosticizing treatment of the law in Gal. 3:19-20.[20]

Galatians 3:10-29 carries out a twofold attack on the law and climaxes in a discussion of the function of the law in salvation-history. The first line of attack is presented under the categories of blessing and curse (Gal. 3:10-14), the second line under those of the promise and the law (vv. 15-29).

Galatians 3:10-14. Paul almost slides into a dualism between two antithetical powers, because he opposes radically the blessing of faith to

Abraham and "his sons" to the curse of the law and its works. The law curses Christ, and Christ simply annuls the law, in order that faith and the blessing can flow to the Gentiles.[21] The dualism between the law and faith is here heightened by the opposition of Hab. 2:4 (Gal. 3:11) to Lev. 18:5 (Gal. 3:12). "Faith" is opposed to "doing," because God has ordained faith as the principle of salvation-history (Gal. 3:11, 12). In a daring move, Paul opposes Scripture to Scripture (cf. Rom. 10:5–9) and thus splits Scripture apart, because Lev. 18:5 is antithetical to God's will in Christ. The law then seems indeed an antidivine agency.

Galatians 3:15–29. This "gnosticizing" interpretation is reinforced by Paul's second line of attack: the promise as opposed to the law. Although in Gal. 3:10–14, faith and the law collide, Christ's sacrifice "for us" resolves the conflict between the law and the promise of faith, because his death is an acknowledgment of the validity of the law. In verses 15–29, however, the law does not seem to have *any* role at all in the sequence from the promise to Christ[22] because it is simply an interloper (v. 17). Paul here radicalizes his salvation-historical argument. He does not discuss the principle of the law as in verses 10–14 ("faith" vs. "doing") but stresses instead the temporality of the law in salvation-history between the period of the promise and that of Christ. The law is inferior to the promise on three counts: (1) because of its temporary nature (430 years after the promise, and only until Christ—v. 17); (2) because of its inferior origin (it was ordained through the mediation of angels and it made a mediator necessary—vv. 19–20); and (3) because it was unable to give life and was never intended to do so (vv. 21b). In Gal. 3:10–14, the law and faith are on a collision course because they are in principle incompatible (vv. 11, 12), whereas in verses 15–25 the law and the promise are successive, independent, and inversely related entities. Paul uses this "gnosticizing" opposition of gospel and law in order to make his opponents realize that their gospel of circumcision and Torah destroys the very purpose of God's work of salvation in Christ, because the synthesis of law, circumcision, and gospel perverts the essence of the gospel.

Nevertheless, the opposition between the law and the gospel does not lead to a demonizing of the law. Paul does not simply eliminate the Torah from his Bible. Although Paul comes close to invalidating the Torah by opposing it to faith and to the promise (Gal. 3:11–12, 15–18), he wants to demonstrate as well the indispensable place of the Torah in salvation-history. The question, however, is whether Paul's intent is matched by his logic. He seems so carried away by his thematic point of radically opposing gospel and law, faith and works, that his "defense" of the law (Gal. 3:19–

20) is only sketched in cryptic strokes. To be sure, the contradiction in Scripture between Hab. 2:4 and Lev. 18:5 (Gal. 3:11–12) is clarified in Gal. 3:19–22. The "doing" of the law (Gal. 3:12)—although opposed to the rule of faith (v. 11)—is nevertheless a divine necessity in salvation-history, for it represents the dark but necessary foil for the coming of faith with Jesus Christ. And yet the relation between the divine origin of the law (cf. Rom. 7:12, 14) and its disastrous anthropological function does not come into focus, because Paul stresses the negative ontology of the law so heavily in Gal. 3:19–20. The law seems simply a hostile power that, contrary to God's will, imprisons mankind. Nevertheless, this impression is mistaken: (1) The law becomes a curse, rather than is itself a curse, because it curses those who do not obey God's commands (Gal. 3:10); (2) Christ is indeed cursed by the law (Deut. 21:23), but his curse is a curse for us, that is, Christ is not simply victimized by the demonic agency of the law but expiates our transgressions and thus submits to the divine requirement of the law (Gal. 3:13). (3) In Christian hindsight, the law was given by God to increase the trespasses, so that it might be the prison and taskmaster that highlights the coming of faith in Christ (Gal. 3:19, 21–25).

Despite the dualistic opposition between the law and the promise (Gal. 3:11–18), the Torah has an essential function in salvation-history. However, we must be aware that its function is not that of a tutor who sharpens our consciousness of sin and need for forgiveness and so leads us to Christ: "Now before faith came, we were confined under the law, kept under restraint until faith should be revealed. So that the law was our custodian until Christ came [*paidagōgos hēmōn—eis Christon*], that we might be justified by faith" (Gal. 3:23–24). Because the words "until Christ" (*eis Christon*) have the same meaning as the temporal phrases of verses 23–29, Paul does not speculate here about the law as the agent that evokes our consciousness of sin (cf. Luther: "it drives us to Christ"[23]) but rather describes our objective status before God "until Christ came," that is, our no-exit situation before God. Indeed, the pivotal text of Romans 11— "God has consigned all men to disobedience, that he may have mercy upon all" (Rom. 11:32)—is adumbrated in Gal. 3:22: "But the scripture consigned all things to sin, that what was promised to faith in Jesus Christ might be given to those who believe." The term "scripture" (*graphē*) suddenly appears in the argument about "the law" (*nomos*, Gal. 3:22; cf. v. 8), in order to show that the law is an inalienable part of salvation-history. The discontinuity between the law and gospel is corrected by verse 22: God's plan of salvation in Scripture embraces both the condemning effect of the law and the promise of faith. Thus, the necessary relation between the promise and law in salvation-history prevents a Marcionite disjunction between the law and the gospel. It was the law's necessary function to "increase the trespasses" (Gal. 3:19), so that in the midst of man's hopeless situation, faith in Christ might become a new reality. Moreover, verse 22 demonstrates that the law is applicable not only to Jews but also to the Gentiles. Indeed, without the death of Christ (v. 13), the blessing to the Gentiles (v. 8) would also have been nullified. Within the course of the argument, then, Paul extends the influence of the Torah over the Gentile world, for he includes the Gentiles under the "all things" (*ta panta*) of verse 22 and climaxes the section with the "all" (*pantes*) of verse 26: "for in Christ you are *all* sons of God, through faith." When we review the argument as a whole, we can only conclude that it is disruptive because the apology of the law is cryptically inserted into an argument that logically seems to negate the law.

CONCLUSION

Galatians shows that Paul's theology is a contextual theology; it is shaped by the interaction between situational contingency and the material coherence of the gospel. Paul's interpretation of the Abraham story is dictated by the Judaizing scheme of synthesizing Abraham, Torah, circumcision, and Christ. Thus, Paul divorces Abraham from the law and its works and joins him to the "pro-evangelion" of faith for the Gentiles (Gal. 3:8). The Christocentric thrust of the Abraham story is apparent, because the promise of the blessing to Abraham is actualized only in Christ, who as Abraham's exclusive seed (v. 16) fulfills the promise and breaks the curse of the law (vv. 13–14). His death on the tree allows the promise to flow to the Gentiles, and his exclusive status as "seed of Abraham" (and "son of God," cf. Gal. 4:4) actualizes faith (Gal. 3:23–26). Salvation-history is not constituted by an empirical continuity that moves from Abraham via the Torah and circumcision to Christ but is located solely in God's promise to Abraham and the response to Christ in faith, which is antithetical to the law and its works.

The Torah cannot be integrated into the gospel, as the Judaizers claim. The combination of promise, Torah, circumcision, and Christ must be broken apart for the sake of "the truth of the gospel" (cf. Gal. 2:5, 14), because Christ and the Torah are contradictory principles, as Hab. 2:4 and Lev. 18:5 testify (Gal. 3:11–12). The death of Christ has wiped out the curse of the law and enables the promise to flow to the Gentiles (Gal. 3:14). Furthermore, Christ as Abraham's exclusive "seed" has brought the temporary and inferior dominion of the law to an end. In Christ, saving faith has become a reality, and the law's condemnation and imprisonment is overcome. In retrospect, God's negative intent with the law in salvation-history is clear; it was the necessary foil for our new freedom in Christ (Gal. 3:22), so that a return to the law can only mean severance from Christ (Gal. 5:4; cf. 4:8–11).

In tracing Paul's argument, we have become aware of the fact that Galatians does not render a consistent picture of the relation between law and gospel. Thus, we are tempted to interpret Galatians with the help of Romans, in order to clarify the "hidden layers" beneath Paul's argument. However, a letter written with a specific polemical purpose is not a systematic treatise. If we treat it as such, we are unable to grasp the *mode* of Paul's theological thinking. Paul's aim in Galatians 3 is to oppose the Judaizers, and in the process of radicalizing their position, he radicalizes his own. Because Galatians is a first-level polemical response and not a second-level dogmatic proposition, a fundamentally consistent picture of the argument does not emerge. Its flow is complex and cryptic, as the relation between law and gospel discloses. Paul opposes law and gospel in such a way that the triumph of the gospel of faith for the Gentiles necessitates the utter negation of the law, with the result that its positive function and divine origin hardly surface.[24] Although the argument is complex, the basic theme is clear: slavery or freedom, Torah or Christ (Gal. 2:4; 3:2–5; 4:9, 22–26; 5:1–4). We conclude, then, that situational discourse cannot sacrifice the "language-event" of the gospel to systematic balance and timeless truth.

Paul intends to turn the gospel of the Judaizers into an antigospel and to indict his churches for (re)turning to that domain of slavery, from which Christ has set them free. The Abraham story was God's promise of faith for the (Galatian) Gentiles, which is realized by Christ. Because the law has always been the enemy of faith, it is impossible to combine it with the promise and faith.

Therefore, the crisis situation in Galatia compels Paul to an argument of principle: faith versus works of the law, freedom versus slavery. Abraham is not cast as a believing person (but cf. Romans 4) but instead illustrates a principle, God's promise of faith that Christ actualizes. Likewise, the law illustrates the principle of the curse and bondage and is thus radically opposed to the new age of Christ. Galatians is definitely marked by the particularity of the situation to which it is addressed. The contingent nature of the argument is clear. Paul responds to a crisis of apostasy. Although the antithetical power of Paul's argument is apparent, its logic is cryptic, intuitive, and often inconsistent, because it is dictated by the crisis at hand. Both the Abraham story and the apology of the law show that Paul bends theological tradition radically to his own purpose and comes close to a Marcionite split between law and gospel. All this makes Galatians one of Paul's most difficult letters, as the history of interpretation shows. The situation also dictates the virtual absence of an otherwise central feature in Paul's letters—the future apocalyptic dimension of the gospel. Apart from Gal. 5:1, 5, 21b, and 6:7-8, this topic is completely ignored.

Galatians threatens to undo what I have posited as the coherent core of Pauline thought, the apocalyptic coordinates of the Christ-event that focus on the imminent, cosmic triumph of God. Indeed, the eschatological present dominates the letter, for the crisis situation demands the either/or of bondage under the law or freedom in Christ. And this either/or is so centrally grounded in the death of Christ as the annulment of slavery under the Torah (Gal. 2:19-21; 3:1, 13-14; 4:5; 6:14) that the apocalyptic future with its basis in the resurrection of Christ does not receive its proper emphasis. (Note also the virtual absence of the resurrection of Christ in Galatians.)

This contrasts sharply with Romans 5-8, where the key word, "life," points both to the *presence* of the apocalyptic future and to the apocalyptic *future* of our present life in the Spirit. The crisis in Galatia shows the remarkable contingency of Paul's theology. Because the Christocentric focus of Galatians pushes Paul's theocentric apocalyptic theme to the periphery, Galatians cannot serve as the central and normative guide for all Paul's letters and theology. Indeed, if we ignore the future apocalyptic hints in Galatians, the letter can easily be interpreted as a document of realized eschatology by a Paul who is "the greatest of all the Gnostics."[25]

Galatians demonstrates that the interaction between theological coherence and situational particularity can lead to emphases and construals that are clearly one-sided because they are dictated by the contingency of the situation. If we lose sight of this utterly contingent character of Galatians and use it without qualification as the "core" of Paul's thought, we misconstrue both the coherence of Paul's gospel and his theological method (see Chapter 6, below). In this sense, the Christocentrism of the Reformation's interpretation of Paul depends more on an exclusive doctrinal use of Galatians than on the totality of Paul's thought (see, e.g., Luther: "The Epistle to the Galatians is my epistle, to which I have wedded myself. It is my Catherine von Bora").

5

Contextual Interpretation II: The Structure and Argument of Romans

THE PROBLEM OF ROMANS

It has been customary to treat Romans as Paul's most systematic letter, the one that summarizes the totality of his thought. Since Philipp Melanchthon characterized Romans as a *"compendium doctrinae Christianae,"*[1] the comprehensive and systematic nature of Romans has been taken for granted until recently and still finds adherents. Scholars have spent much energy on the architectonic structure of Romans, while largely ignoring its character as a letter.[2] Ferdinand Christian Baur's insistence on a historical explanation of the letter[3] opened up a new approach in the nineteenth century. However, this approach seemed to lead to a dead end theologically, and the rise of Neoorthodoxy stimulated anew the view of Romans as a "dogmatics in outline" or as a literary treatise that summarizes the essence of Paul's thought.

There is certainly justification for this latter interpretation. Not only does Paul write to a church which is unknown to him and with which he has had no apostolic relations, but he also composes a letter that is not (or hardly at all) interrupted by problems and questions of a local-contingent character. In fact, the letter reads like a carefully composed treatise on the permanent and universal elements in Paul's thought. The structural argument (Rom. 1:16—8:39; 9:1—11:32; 12:1—15:13) is, to be sure, framed by introductory questions (1:1-15) and the announcement of Paul's plans (15:14-33), but these elements seem at first glance to have little relation to the "heart" of the letter. Even when the "frame" is taken seriously, it seems to yield no direct assistance in clarifying the "occasional" character of the letter.

First, there is the textual problem of chapter 16 and the place of the doxology, Rom. 16:25-27. In some manuscripts the doxology occurs after Rom. 14:23; in P46, after 15:33; in most manuscripts, after 16:23. Does this indicate that Romans existed in several versions and that it was originally composed as an encyclical letter to various Pauline churches as a general compendium of Paul's thought (cf. Chapter 3, above)?

Second, the character of chapter 16 seems to speak against Rome as a destination, for it is hard to imagine that Paul would have so many friends in a church unknown to him. Besides, the list seems more appropriate for Ephesus than for Rome.[4]

Third, the discrepancies between Rom. 1:1–15 and Rom. 15:14–33 enhance the theory of an encyclical letter. The "catholic" tone of 1:1–15 seems to have been concretized and supplemented when the letter was sent to Rome (15:14–33). The discrepancies appear to be weighty, especially with respect to two problems: the problem of Spain and the problem of apostolic fruit (karpos). As to the first problem, it is curious indeed that in chapter 1 Paul expresses his deep longing to come to Rome in order to instruct and share fellowship with the Roman church, without even mentioning his trip to Spain, whereas in chapter 15 Spain is announced as Paul's real goal, with Rome serving only as a transit point (diaporeuomenos, 15:24). Moreover, it is also curious that Paul, who in chapter 15 exults in his pride to preach the gospel "not where Christ has already been named, lest I build on another man's foundation" (v. 20) and thus intends to come to Rome only "in passing" (v. 24), mentions in chapter 1 explicitly that his longing to come to Rome is related to his desire to have "fruit" (karpos) "among you as well as among the rest of the Gentiles" (1:13). In chapter 1, then, he plans missionary activity in Rome; in chapter 15 he makes it a point of pride not to missionize where others have founded a church before him (cf. 2 Cor. 10:13–18). All these elements make it difficult to view Romans as an occasional letter that was written not only at a specific hour of need but also for the specific purpose of addressing particular problems in the church at Rome.

In addition to the difficulties of the frame, there is insufficient external information about the Roman church to clarify the letter's "occasional" character. Although Judaism was strong in Rome and there were a considerable number of synagogues in the several districts of the city,[5] the precise origin of the church and its constitution in Paul's time are uncertain. Was there, for example, a plurality of house churches, or one assembly? Because the church(es) lacked an apostolic foundation, it (they) probably grew out of the synagogue(s) and attracted many "God-fearers." Suetonius's remark in his Life of Claudius, "Since the Jews constantly made disturbances at the instigation of Chrestus, he expelled them from Rome" (Judaeos impulsore Chresto assidue tumultuantes Roma expulit), refers in all likelihood to messianic revolutionary troubles that caused Claudius (A.D.

39–54) to expel the Jews in A.D. 49 (there had been a prior veto of assembly under Tiberius, A.D. 14–37). Jewish Christians were no doubt among them. However, under Nero (A.D. 54–68) the edict was retracted, and presumably many Jews (Jewish Christians) returned to Rome.[6] It is possible that Romans 14 and 15 reflect a church in which returning Jewish Christians found a preponderance of Gentile Christians, a situation that led to friction among them. The earliest available history of the church points to a (Jewish-) Hellenistic Christian, non-Pauline institution (cf. 1 Clement, A.D. 95; Hermas, A.D. 150). Even those scholars who stress the occasional character of Romans and locate its main purpose in chapters 14 and 15 cannot sufficiently explain the exceedingly lengthy prolegomena of chapters 1–12, if all Paul intended was to address the problem expressed in chapters 14 and 15.[7]

THE RELATION OF STRUCTURE AND OCCASION

In the face of these difficulties, most scholars—even those who, unlike Manson[8] and Knox,[9] reject an encyclical theory and characterize the letter as specifically addressed to Rome—adopt a position that minimizes its occasional character and locates its motivation in Paul's own situation. The contingent character of Romans is here connected with Paul's own situation and not with the needs of the Roman church. Romans is either an apology or self-introduction of Paul's theology to a church unknown to him and suspicious of him, and/or an appeal for help for his Spanish mission in the West, in the way Ephesus had served as his base of support in the East. Such explanations at least recognize some importance of Rome itself for Paul.[10]

Less acceptable are theories that locate the purpose of Romans almost exclusively in the mind of Paul. After the completion of his mission in the East (Rom. 15:23), Paul enjoys a period of relative rest in Corinth; the conflicts in Galatia and Corinth now prompt Paul to reflect on his basic theological convictions before he commences a new period in his life. To this end he combines the basic elements of Galatians and Corinthians in a new synthesis.[11] According to this view—very similar to the encyclical theory—Romans could just as well have been written to some other church, because its Roman destination is purely accidental. The abstract theological structure of Romans is thus enhanced and its occasional character bypassed. Romans would indeed be unlike any other Pauline letter because of its universal-systematic or purely "confessional" character. It is therefore curious that although modern scholarship almost universally objects to Melanchthon's description of Romans as "a compendium of doctrine," it is itself engaged in dissipating the contingency of the argument of the letter.[12]

The presupposition that Romans is a "theological confession" or a "dogmatics in outline" is the real reason for the immense interest in the letter's architectonic structure and the neglect of its "frame." Indeed, Romans is in many ways unlike any other Pauline letter. It is composed neither in the question-and-answer style of 1 Corinthians (*peri*, 1 Cor. 7:1, etc.) nor as a direct response to heretical teachings (as, e.g., Galatians). Romans has the appearance of a tractate, for it is carefully composed and reflects a basic theological argument. The combination of structural coherence and temporal contingency is a challenge to the interpreter of Romans, because the relation between structure and occasion has profound consequences for Paul's "epistolary" theology. William G. Doty expresses it well:

> Epistles seem to have presented a unique genre for expression of the early growth of the churches; they were transformed into what was probably the most important literary genre of the early church. . . . Why was it that someone such as Paul wrote epistles rather than gospels? Why did the epistolary genre continue into the ecclesial letter genre, while the gospel genre effectively came to an end with the canonical gospels? Can we conclude that there were ontological features of the epistolary genre that corresponded to the existential needs of the primitive Christians—needs not satisfied by the gospel or the history?[13]

Letters are words on target because of their contingency. Because they are much closer to oral dialogue and living word than to either gospel or history, they pose a hermeneutical difficulty (cf. Chapter 3, above). Their temporal historical relevance and relation to a past closed to us resists timeless relevance or doctrinal universality. Thus the Pauline letters may indeed be an eye-opener to the nature of Christian theology as a theology in living process rather than "as a religion characterized by recourse to solidified and frozen traditions of the past."[14]

The balance in Romans between structure and occasion thus poses a profound theological question. And we avoid this question when we strip the letter of its epistolary form and transform it into a piece of "timeless Christian doctrine" or into "the essence" of abstract Pauline thought. The traditional focus on the structure of Romans, with its double quest for the literary architecture of the letter and for the abiding dogmatic "essence" of Paul's thought, needs to be radically questioned. Too often, uncritical prejudice can determine our hermeneutic. Paul is assumed to be not only a literary genius who, in the style of classic authors, composes well-balanced literary units but also a thinker engaged in the construal of carefully consistent thought sequences that have the quality of eternal verities. One forgets that Paul did not write a gospel story or a history such as Acts but a variety of contingent letters. Thus we must acknowledge their epistolary integrity and avoid treating them as merely the accidental pretext for a systematic statement of a "timeless" Pauline thought.

The exclusive focus on the structure of Romans and on Paul's unity of thought creates havoc with the interpretation of Romans. First, the main part of Romans is separated from its frame, that is, from 1:1–15 and 15:14– 16:25. Subsequently, chapters 14 and 15 (if not chapters 12 and 13 as well) are detached from the main body because of their parenetic content and their sometimes disjointed character.[15] In the search for the architecture of Paul's thought, then, an increasingly abstract core is often postulated.

The Debate about Romans 9–11

How do chapters 9–11 fit into the structure of Romans? This section is frequently viewed as an appendix or an afterthought.[16] Bultmann attributes Romans 9–11 to "the speculative fantasy" of Paul.[17] Francis Wright Beare is typical of many when he writes:

> We have left out of consideration three chapters (9–11) of this letter, chiefly because they do not form an integral part of the main argument. They are a kind of supplement in which Paul struggles with the problem of the failure of his own nation. . . . We cannot feel that the apostle is at his best here and we are inclined to ask if he has not got himself into inextricable (and needless) difficulties by attempting to salvage some remnant of racial privilege for the historic Israel—Israel "according to the flesh"—in spite of his own fundamental position that all men are in the same position before God.[18]

Charles Harold Dodd posits likewise that Rom. 12:1 is the immediate sequel to 8:31–39, because Paul begins there the treatment of Christian ethics: "But once again the sequel is postponed, while *certain theological difficulties* left over from the foregoing discussion are dealt with [i.e., in chapters 9–11]."[19] Romans 9–11 originally formed a separate treatise, according to Dodd—"the kind of sermon that Paul must often have had occasion to deliver."[20] William Sanday and Arthur Cayley Headlam concur with this view of chapters 9–11 as an appendix.[21]

It seems, then, that the quest for the structural logic of Romans 1–8 requires a hermeneutical procedure that amputates a part of Paul, truncating the historical Paul in favor of a so-called "theological" Paul. And even when more constructive approaches appear,[22] chapters 9–11 are often not explored for the sake of a concrete view of the actual purpose of Romans. The search for a "doctrinal core" or a "dogmatics in outline" naturally has a general hermeneutical appeal, because it eases the way toward minimizing the historical particularity of Paul's situational theology. Interpreters have been offended by the issue of the particularity and theological specificity of first-century Judaism (reflected throughout Romans but especially in chapters 9–11 and in 2:1—3:20) and have ascribed it either to Paul's sentimental (ethnic) bias or to the utterance of an apostate (cf. Karl Barth's equation of Israel with "the church, the world of religion").[23]

Even when Romans 9–11 was taken seriously,[24] the Jewish question could at times be transposed into the issue of the universal *homo religiosus* (Barth[25]) without regard for Paul's historical view of Israel and salvation-history. The distaste for the particularity of Romans 9–11 and the preference for Romans 1–8 as a dogmatic monologue by Paul, that is, as the systematic-universal "core" of Romans, not only prevented a correct assessment of the purpose of Romans but also contributed to an inaccurate historical picture of Paul. Baur's Hegelian view of early Christian history was built on the opposition of Paul to Peter. It led subsequently to a romantic conception of Paul as "the lone revolutionary" who after the Antioch incident (Gal. 2:11–14) turned his back on Jerusalem and Jewish Christianity, went it alone, and stuck to a gospel of absolute liberty, free from tradition and inherited positions and inspired by the Spirit alone. This "emancipated Paul" became the founder of a new divine common-wealth and of a new view of humanity, led by the Spirit and fed by universal love. Even as great a commentator and historian as Hans Lietzmann states:

> From that time forward [after Antioch], Paul took his own path separately from that of Peter and Barnabas. . . . His relationship with the original apostles at last broke down completely. Paul stood alone among the Christians whom he had converted, and very dangerous opponents [the great figures in Jerusalem] worked behind his back.[26]

This picture of an emancipated Paul, relying on the Spirit alone to work out his universal calling, was supposed to fit neatly into the view of Romans as the basic manifesto and self-confession of the emancipated, universal apostle.

THE QUEST FOR THE "CORE" OF PAUL'S THOUGHT

The basic quest for the "core" of Paul's thought focused in the major commentaries on the theological structure of Romans 1–8. The exclusive attention to Romans 1–8 enhanced a view of the letter as a systematic thought structure and increasingly abstracted it from its historical grounding and specificity.[27]

Both Barth[28] and Nygren[29] exemplify this tendency. Barth paved the way for a new generation of commentators and in his commentary paid no attention to Rom. 1:1-15 and 15:14—16:25. This is not surprising in view of his basic hermeneutical rule:

> Paul, as a child of his age, addressed his contemporaries. It is, however, far more important that, as Prophet and Apostle of the Kingdom of God, he veritably speaks to all men of every age. The differences between then and now, there and here, no doubt require careful investigation and consideration. But the purpose of such investigation can only be to demonstrate that these differences are, in fact [*im Wesen der Dinge*] purely trivial.[30]

Thus Barth bypasses the historical issues and consequently the possibility of a hermeneutic different from that which sovereignly disregards the hermeneutical "ditch" between the times.

Nygren[31] likewise considers it an advantage that the letter resists explanation, either in the situation of the Roman church or in the circumstances of Paul himself, and so it becomes for him a pure theological exposition of the Pauline gospel. Nygren plays off theological content against "accidental circumstances." "It is only a disservice if, instead of looking deeply into them [i.e., into purely theological problems], one concerns himself with the external and incidental circumstances which gave Paul the occasion for dealing with the problems."[32] Nygren structures the course of Paul's thought remarkably consistently and aesthetically;[33] I reproduce it here in an abbreviated way.

The Theme: (a) "He who is righteous by faith
              (b) shall live." (1:17)
  (a) He who through faith is righteous (1:18—4:25)
      1. The old aeon (1:18—3:20)
      2. The new aeon (3:21—4:25)
  (b) He who through faith is righteous—*shall live* (5:1—8:39)
      1. Free from wrath (5:1-11)
         The two aeons: Adam and Christ (5:12-21)
      2. Free from sin (6:1-23)
      3. Free from the law (7:1-25)
      4. Free from death (8:1-39)

The aesthetic beauty and clarity of this outline should not deceive us, for it attributes to Paul an architectonic rigor that cannot stand close scrutiny. It is a methodological error to view Romans as a theological structure developed in a vacuum—a view that portrays Paul as engaged with himself in thought, wrestling with the perennial truth of the gospel. The hermeneutical advantage of "timelessness" cannot silence the historical illegitimacy and impossibility of this procedure. It is illegitimate to turn a lack of historical evidence to theological-hermeneutical advantage and to conceive of any Pauline letter as an exercise in thought without concrete historical mooring.

Close inspection of Nygren's outline establishes its untenability. The freedom series is quite arbitrary. "Freedom from death" is only one theme among others in Romans 8; freedom from the law occupies only Rom. 7:1-6, especially because, on Nygren's own showing, 7:7-25 applies to the Christian conscience under the law; 6:1-23 is as much concerned with newness of life (6:4) and with death (6:23) as with sin; and 5:1-11 focuses more on the Christian's new joy and hope than on freedom from wrath. Furthermore, Rom. 5:12-21 is a curious interloper in the structural scheme. These verses form; according to Nygren, the hidden "two-aeon center" for all of Romans. But why, then, do they occur here and not at Rom. 1:17?[34] Nygren's commentary is typical of many in its concentration on the thematically compact thought sequence of Romans 1-8.[35] André Feuillet, for instance, stresses the literary aesthetic of Romans and detects a threefold scheme, indicative of a Trinitarian principle of composition.[36] Even the balanced essay by Ulrich Luz states as methodological principle: "Its [Romans'] composition must be understood from the material center and cannot be gained from the concrete occasion of the letter."[37]

We must be aware that Rom. 5:1-11 and 5:12-21 have been and continue to be "a stone of stumbling" for the architectonic structure of the "main section" of the letter (Romans 1-8). Melanchthon[38] had divided Romans into three main parts; he associated Rom. 5:1-11 with the first section (Rom. 1:16—4:25) but did not link the sections organically:

1. *Praecipua disputatio* (1:16—5:11).
2. *Quasi novus liber* (5:12—8:29) (*peccatum, lex,* and *gratia* treated as theological concepts).
3. *Nova disputatio* (chaps. 9-11).

Reformation orthodoxy and pietism alike favored the dogmatic scheme, "justification" and "sanctification," as the explanation for the sequence of Romans 1-4 and Romans 5-8. This scheme proved to be influential in subsequent scholarship. It suggested that Paul had planned a structural composition of, essentially, two main parts. What remained unsolved was the question of the divisional break between the parts (Rom. 5:1; 5:12; or 6:1?) and their organic relation. Luther downplayed the significance of Rom. 5:12-21 and called it an appendix.[39]

The rise of the history-of-religions school instigated a new perspective on Paul. Due to the influence of Wernle and Wrede, Romans became the key witness for the so-called "two-crater theory."[40] Over against the Reformation's insistence on the centrality of the righteousness of God (Rom. 1:16-17) and of justification by faith (Rom. 3:21-30), righteousness by faith now becomes a secondary, juridical-rabbinic crater, a *Kampfeslehre* (Wrede) that serves Paul's polemical purpose against Judaism. Paul's "main crater," and his mature thought, is located in his eschatological mysticism that—according to this scholarship—expresses itself so clearly in Romans 6-8. The "crater" theory could appeal to a shift in terminology within the letter: "righteousness" and "faith" (*dikaiosunē, pistis*), so prominent in Romans 1-5, retreat almost completely in Romans 6-8, where they are displaced by the "Spirit" (*pneuma*) and a sacramental-ontological terminology (*syn/en Christō*). Hermann Lüdemann's work was important for the "two-crater theory," because he uncovered not only a distinct Jewish and Hellenistic use of "flesh" and "Spirit" but also two distinct schemes of redemption.[41] Subsequently, the Jewish and Hellenistic elements of Paul's thought were played off against each other, so that a "two-crater theory" became inevitable, especially because it seemed to correspond to the two main parts of Romans 1-8. The search for architectonic structure and consistency of thought patterns thus prevailed, and a structural division within Romans 1-8 between chapters 1-4 (and 5) and 6-8 was the logical outcome.[42] The essence of Pauline thought—although confined to a "main crater"—had been uncovered for all time!

However, the exact location of the division remained a problem that concerned chiefly the place of Romans 5:1-11 and 5:12-21. Does the "new" or "mature" thought structure begin with 5:1, 5:12, or 6:1? What is the place of chapter 5 within the structure of the letter? Do 5:1-11 belong with 1:16—4:25 (as its climax), or do they—together with 5:12-21—belong to 6:1—8:39 (as its introduction)? Furthermore, how are 5:1-11 and 5:12-21 related? How does one explain specifically the "therefore" (*dia touto*) of 5:12?[43] Although agreement on this issue has never been reached, the quest for a systematic thought structure remains for most scholars the unquestioned presupposition.[44] The influence of Schweitzer's crater theory continues, however modified, in the perennial debate about the main structure of Romans 1-8. Does 5:1-11 (12-21) still belong to the "justification language" of 1:16—4:25, or does it belong to the "participation language" (Sanders's term) of chapters 6–8? How craterlike is Paul's thought? Does he integrate his two thought structures or not? And if he does, how and where? Wilhelm Lütgert[45] and James Hardy Ropes[46] supported the crater theory with their view of a multiple audience for both Galatians and Romans in order to explain the sequence of Paul's thought and his linguistic shift from rabbinic to "Hellenistic" categories. According to this view, Romans 1–4(5) is addressed to the Jewish nomistic audience of the Roman church, while chapters 6–8 are addressed to the Gentile antinomian section of the church. Franz J. Leenhardt suggests as an alternative a parallel structure of 1:18—5:11 and 5:12—8:33.[47] Both sections deal with sin (1:18; 5:12); the death of Christ (3:21; 6:1); the law (3:27; 7:1–25); the promise (4:1–25; 8:1–4); and the hope (5:1–10; 8:18–25). In a similar vein, one could devise a speculative structure that—with Rom. 5:12–21 as summary and transition, and 6:1–23 as refutation of antinomianism—shows a parallel argument with a "double" audience and a "double" language:[48]

Theme	Rabbinic	Hellenistic
The Old Adam	1:18—3:20	7:7–25
The New Adam	3:21—4:25	8:1–17
The Hope of the New Adam	5:1–11	8:10–39

Rom. 5:12–21 (Summary and transition)

[6:1–23; 7:1–6] (Response to objections)

The attractiveness of such schemes is the hermeneutical harvest they carry, because it can now be argued that Paul employs a variety of linguistic schemes in order to preach the one gospel to a variety of situations and world views (i.e., Paul is "a Jew to the Jews / a Gentile to the Gentiles").[49] Furthermore, such "crater" structures overcome the traditional "justification/sanctification" scheme that turns the complex relation of Romans 1–4/5–8 into a simple linear progression from forgiveness to the moral life.

The attractiveness of these structural schemes should not tempt us. Where is the evidence for such a distinct Pauline usage of language and for such a divorce between language games? What is the place of Romans 9–11 in these schemes? Are chapters 9–11 a return to "Jewish" language and a surrender of the "universalistic" language to the Gentiles? How do chapters 12–15 function in this scheme, and how can the "framework" (Rom. 1:1–15; 15:14—16:24) be so completely neglected? The diligent search for the architectonic structure of Romans—whether in its totality or in "craters"—suffers from an unexamined presupposition, for it imposes a dogmatic premise on the exegetical task. Dogmatic language requires systematic coherence and architectonic logic (cf. *loci*-dogmatics), and far too often New Testament scholarship has not resisted this dogmatic prejudice in its investigation of Romans.

THE OCCASIONAL CHARACTER OF ROMANS

Its Specific Address

The preceding review of the history of research has indicated the persistence of the "epistolary" problem of Romans. The relation of its artistic-literary and dogmatic structure to its epistolary particularity demands to be clarified, so that new insights into Paul's way of doing theology may emerge.[50]

If Romans is indeed a situational and particular letter, it can no longer be treated as the compendium or essence or confessional monologue of Paul's thought to which the other letters are purely fragmentary contributors. Whether Romans is viewed as a theological treatise apart from any specific historical motivation (Nygren[51]), or as a compendium of Paul's thought, a "last testament" (Bornkamm[52]), in both cases its situational particularity is denied. To be sure, recent scholarship has increasingly recognized the untenable character of this position. Many scholars point in various ways to the historical occasion and purpose for the letter and to its contingent character.[53]

However, old views rarely die. Even in studies as recent as those by Frederick Bruce[54] and Leander Keck,[55] Romans is said to be an exception to the contingent character of the Pauline letters. Bruce quotes Joseph Lightfoot with approval: "The manner, which in the one epistle [Galatians] is personal and fragmentary, elicited by the special needs of an individual church, is in the other [Romans] generalized and arranged so as to form a comprehensive and systematic treatise."[56] Keck correctly argues that the letters were written for particular congregations that had particular problems,[57] but then he states that "to some extent Romans is an exception because Paul had not yet been to Rome" (cf. "behind Romans, the most mature statement of Paul's theology, lie *the controversies worked through in previous letter-writing*"[58] [italics mine]).

I dwell on this issue because the recognition of the particularity of Romans—notwithstanding its coherent character—remains clouded by ambivalent gestures. What needs to be acknowledged is that the occasion for Romans primarily lies not in external factors or within Paul himself but in Paul's argument with the Roman Christians. The ambivalence on this point is highlighted by Kümmel:

> It is quite appropriate that he presents himself to them and tells them what is the essence of Christianity and what is the content of the gospel that he preaches as apostle to the Gentiles. The desire to introduce himself to the Christians in Rome and to tell them who he is and what he preaches gives Paul the occasion to express himself at some length about the basic truths of Christianity as he sees and teaches it. Though it arose out of concrete necessity for his missionary work, Romans is the theological confession of Paul, which has been appropriately characterized as "the testament of Paul."[59]

In opposition to such statements, it is encouraging to hear the conclusion of Harry Gamble: "But at the least, it is clear that no interpretation of Romans will be adequate, if it fails to make sense of the fact that in Romans we have a letter addressed to a specific community and, as it appears, *only to that community*"[60] (italics mine). Moreover, Gamble correctly sees as the basic issue in interpreting Romans "how to correlate satisfactorily the *content* of the letter with its *ostensible occasion*"[61] (italics mine). The letter is not only written from a specific situation but also addressed to a specific situation; therefore, its arguments and structural form are dictated by specific needs and circumstances, so that Romans is not simply a summary or dogmatic substance of Pauline thought. Such a view discards the problem that the letter form raises for canonical-"catholic" universality, because in that case Romans ceases to be a letter and becomes instead a dogmatic essay, a *summa theologica* that summarizes the occasional content of the other Pauline letters.

Paul intends to score very specific points in Romans. His argumentation and purpose are quite different from, for instance, his procedure in Galatians, so frequently viewed as a supplement and companion letter to Romans (see Chapter 4, above). In Rome, he is dealing with a mixed church, not a purely Gentile church as in Galatia; moreover, he is not dealing with a Judaizing heresy, that is, with Gentile Christians who desire circumcision, or with an anti-Pauline opposition in an organized form, as there is in Galatia. In Romans, Paul uses polemics for the sake of apologetic persuasion; in Galatians he is primarily engaged in heated and sarcastic polemics. The Galatian Gentiles seek to complete and perfect their Christian status by submitting to circumcision, whereas in Rome the reverse may be the case, because Paul must warn Gentiles against showing any religious superiority over the Jews (Rom. 11:13–25a). Galatians deals with antithetical theological principles (i.e., law and circumcision over against Christ and faith), whereas Romans places its polemics in a wider context: it focuses on the church as the one people of God, constituted by Jewish and Gentile Christians (3:21–30; 5:18–21; 10:12; 11:32; 15:8–12). In other words, in Romans the relation of peoples (Jews and Gentiles) in God's salvation-historical plan is central, whereas in Galatians the focus is on the inferiority and obsolescence of the law.

Because of the different occasions and motivations for the letters, it is a fallacy of misplaced concretion to claim that the Roman and Galatian letters have a single thematic unity. Topics like the promise, faith and the law, and terms like "righteousness," "boasting," and "to reckon" are used differently or far less prominently in Galatians when compared with Romans. Particularity of theological concern, then, cannot be sidestepped in favor of a perennial structure of Paul's thought, because Paul's way of doing theology is ignored in that case (see Chapter 6, below).

A CONVERGENCE OF MOTIVATIONS

What, then, is the occasion that motivates Romans? It is impossible to pinpoint one decisive cause. The motivation of the letter lies both in Paul's concrete situation and in that of the Roman church. In other words, there is a convergence of several factors behind the occasion for the letter, which explains its occasional yet "systematic" form.[62]

1. When Paul writes Romans, he finds himself in a new situation. The mission work in the east has been accomplished: "From Jerusalem and as far round as Illyricum I have fully preached the gospel . . . but now, since I no longer have any room for work [*mēketi topon echōn*] in these regions . . . I hope to see you . . ." (Rom. 15:19, 23–24). "From Jerusalem and *in a circle [kuklō]* as far as Illyricum I have fully preached the gospel of Christ" (Rom. 15:19) suggests, as John Knox[63] has shown, that Paul is a world apostle with a specific strategy: "their voice has gone out to all the earth, and their words to the ends of the world" (Ps. 19:4; *eis ta perata tēs oikoumenēs*, Rom. 10:18; cf. 15:11). He does not haphazardly missionize the Roman Empire but conceives of his mission in terms of a "circle." Thus far it has reached only Dalmatia (Illyria), but it will stretch from Jerusalem, via Europe and Spain, to Africa and back to Jerusalem. Romans, then, has a specific connection with Paul's mission to Spain. Although it does not occupy center stage in chapter 15 and is not even mentioned in chapter 1, Paul wants to use Rome as a point of transit and possibly as headquarters for his mission in the west. "To be sped on my journey there by you" (Rom. 15:24) suggests the support Paul expects from Rome for his Spanish

mission (cf. also 15:28). Paul's central purpose seems clear: he does not go to Rome primarily to missionize (15:20) but wants to use Rome in some way for his world-apostolic task (15:16–24). Paul's mission to Spain is thus a reason for writing the letter, because Paul would not have visited Rome without his plans for Spain.

2. Paul's forthcoming visit to Jerusalem seems even more important than his Spanish mission. The collection visit, which is in preparation (Rom. 15:25), occupies center stage in chapter 15. Paul's apostolic appeal in 15:30–32 is for Rome's active intercession on his behalf, so that the collection from Macedonia and Achaia may be augmented and supported by the famous Christian church of the west ("your faith is proclaimed in all the world," Rom. 1:8).[64] The collection visit is the fulfillment of Paul's pledge to the apostolic council (Gal. 2:10), but its meaning transcends the issue of economic support for the "poor among the saints" (Rom. 15:26) in Jerusalem. It expresses symbolically the eschatological unity of the church of "Jews" and "Gentiles" in the purpose of God as the fulfillment of Paul's apostolic mission.[65]

The collection is a decisive step on the way to the eschatological hour and the beginning of what soon will come to pass. What deserves our attention is that it not only symbolizes the unity and equality of Jew and Gentile in the one church of God but also expresses the salvation-historical priority of Israel and Jewish Christianity over the Gentiles (Rom. 15:27; cf. 15:8). The "material blessings" (*ta sarkika*) of the Gentiles in the collection are a grateful response to the "spiritual blessings" (*ta pneumatika*) given to the Gentiles by Jerusalem (15:27). Thus, the theme of Romans (1:16–17) is confirmed by the urgency about the collection (15:25–28). For it is indeed the integration of particularism and universalism that marks the theme of the letter; the gospel "is the power of God for salvation to *every one* who has faith, to the Jew *first* and also to the Greek" (Rom. 1:16).

Paul's anxiety about the collection is evident: he has doubts about its reception by the pillars in Jerusalem (*hoi hagioi*), and he fears the Jews in Judea (Rom. 15:30). In that connection, Paul appeals for Rome's intercession: "to strive together with me in your prayers to God on my behalf" (15:30). From this, we see that the letter is also an appeal to win the Romans to Paul's side, and its theological structure is no doubt related to this appeal. Paul challenges the Romans to stand in the gospel as he preaches it[66] and in this way to support his effort in Jerusalem. Romans is in that sense a "hidden letter to Jerusalem"[67] in that Paul rehearses before the Roman church his impending dialogue with Jerusalem.

3. But why is Paul so anxious about the collection visit? It is interesting

that Galatia—prominently mentioned in 1 Cor. 16:1 as a contributor to the collection—is absent from the list in Romans 15, where only Macedonia and Achaia are named (15:26). What has happened? The apostolic council is far in the past. If Paul was already suspect then, there was nevertheless a fraternal agreement: "We to the Gentiles, they to the circumcised" (Gal. 2:9). However, that agreement left a gray area for disagreement, as the Antioch case subsequently showed (Gal. 2:11–14). Although Jerusalem agreed to Gentile missions without circumcision, did they view Gentile Christians as the equals of Jewish Christians, or as (semi-) proselytes? Jerusalem probably did not believe that Jews should forsake "to live like Jews" (ioudaizein, Gal. 2:14) and should surrender the laws of purity, and so on. Under the agreement, a disagreement could easily brew regarding the social and/or religious status of Jewish life. When was life according to the Torah a religious issue (a principle of salvation), and when was it purely ethnic-cultural conformity? There is no doubt historical truth to the words with which James and the elders greeted Paul in Jerusalem in Acts 21:20–21:

> And they said to him, "You see, brother, how many thousands there are among the Jews of those who have believed; they are all zealous for the law, and they have been told about you that you teach all the Jews who are among the Gentiles to forsake Moses, telling them not to circumcise their children or observe the customs [ta ethē].

The omission of Galatia in the collection list could point to the fact that just prior to the writing of Romans, Paul had not only written Galatians but had lost his case with the Galatian churches as well.[68] Although it is highly improbable that Jerusalem emissaries were directly responsible for the Galatian apostasy, the conflict with Galatia and Paul's radical response to it could not have but worsened his relations with Jerusalem. In this light, Paul's fear about Jerusalem and his appeal to Rome can be rightly interpreted, because the Galatian situation, and Paul's response to that crisis, had created the impression that the place of the Jew in salvation-history was a purely negative one and had in fact become obsolete with the coming of Christ. Romans attempts to discuss the "Jewish question" within the context of Paul's thought. Not only is it an urgent question for the largely Gentile church in Rome, but it also serves to defuse the hostile reaction to the Galatian letter—probably not only in Jerusalem but also in Rome.

4. At this point the importance of chapters 14 and 15 can be correctly assessed. The tension between the weak and the strong concerns Jewish

Christians and Gentile Christians, as Rom. 15:8–9 indicates ("circumcised" vs. "Gentiles"). (Cf. also 15:10: "Rejoice, O Gentiles [*ethnē*], with his people [*ho laos autou*]," Deut. 32:43, LXX.) Paul was not as ignorant about Rome as many commentators suggest, since there is no compelling reason to cut chapter 16 from the letter.[69] This chapter shows that Paul had many friends and associates in Rome who could have informed him about the situation there. Prisca and Aquila (Rom. 16:3) belong to the group that was banned under Claudius (Acts 18:1–2) but returned to Rome under Nero. It is significant—in the light of the Jewish-Christian presence in Rome—that two Jewish-Christian apostolic figures, Andronicus and Junias, are mentioned in Rom. 16:7 ("my kinsmen"; cf. also Herodion, "my kinsman," v. 11; "Lucius and Jason and Sosipater, my kinsmen" [*syngeneis mou*], v. 21). Paul's basic apostolic effort—to establish the one church of Jews and Gentiles—is jeopardized in Rome, where disunity threatens in the factions of "the weak" and "the strong." To Paul this disunity reflects a disobedience to the gospel, arising out of a fundamental misunderstanding of it both in Rome (Romans 14 and 15) and in Jerusalem (Rom. 15:30–32), because the gospel means the basic equality of Jew and Gentile. And because the church is neither a pure Gentile church nor an antithesis to Jewish Christians, its oneness of Jew and Gentile marks it as the people of God within a unity that nevertheless preserves the salvation-historical priority of Israel. For the righteousness of God (Rom. 1:17) signifies both "the end of the law" (Rom. 10:4) and the ratification of God's promises to Israel (Rom. 1:1–2; 4:1–12; 15:8). Inasmuch as *all* have sinned (Rom. 3:9, 23), Christ alone can bring forgiveness of sins and new life to those who believe in him. Both Israel and the Gentiles can live only when they stand *sola fide* in the *sola gratia* of God's righteousness in Christ.

ROMANS AS A DIALOGUE WITH JEWS

The Mixed Character of the Church in Rome

The hermeneutical key to Romans is primarily situational. Paul's apostolic calling was to the Gentiles (Gal. 1:15; Rom. 1:5, 13–14; 11:13; 15:16). His early struggle focused on a Torah-free gospel for the Gentiles. In the course of that struggle he had created the suspicion that he wanted to overthrow Judaism, the law, and the scriptural roots of the gospel—a suspicion that the Galatian crisis had increased. Paul's response to that crisis no doubt had aggravated the situation. The Corinthian letters show that Gentile Christianity increasingly moved from a defensive posture into an offensive one, and from a minority to a majority position. Paul's apostolic calling had succeeded only too well. Of course—before A.D. 70 and the destruction of land, temple, and city—the mother church in Jerusalem still exercised a position of dominance, a fact that Paul himself affirmed. Only after the Jewish-Christian crisis, after the war and the evacuation to Pella, did Gentile Christianity become the dominant form of Christianity. Once the church became practically synonymous with Gentile Christianity, its understanding of Paul became problematic. The situation before A.D. 70, in which a Gentile law-free mission was a daring revolutionary break with everything Judaism stood for, was no longer a problem. Later generations of Christians, now completely Gentile and out of sociological-cultural touch with Jewish-Christian life and thought, could only view Jewish Christianity as a (heretical) minority, and the struggle over the Torah as a debate around ethnicity and cultic particularities that did not touch the consonance of the Old Testament moral law with the "law of nature" (*lex naturae*). This alienation from Judaism—especially after the mission to the Jews had failed and Christians had turned their backs on the Jews—meant an alienation from Paul (see Chapter 15, below). Although he was now revered as the great missionary and martyr, his theological thought was misunderstood, redirected, or neglected.

In first-century Rome the Gentile majority felt that it was in a superior position over the Jewish-Christian section of the church. Therefore, the apostle to the Gentiles (Rom. 1:5) must warn Gentile Christians against pride:

> We who are strong ought to bear with the failings of the weak, and not to please ourselves. . . . [Rom. 15:1]

> If your brother is being injured by what you eat, you are no longer walking in love. [Rom. 14:15]

> Now I am speaking to you Gentiles. . . . So do not become proud, but stand in awe. For if God did not spare the natural branches, neither will he spare you. [Rom. 11:13, 20–21; cf. 11:25: "Lest you be wise in your own conceits. . . ."]

Is Paul in Romans assisting Jewish Christians who are being oppressed by Gentile Christians?[70] This cannot explain the whole letter, because Gentiles are not warned in the other sections of the letter but only in Rom. 11:13–25 and in chapters 14 and 15. To the contrary, the main body of the letter confronts Judaism (cf. Rom. 2:1–11, 17–29; 3:1–8, 9–20; 4:1: "Abraham, our natural forefather" [trans. mine]; 6:1–15; 7:1: "For I am speaking to those who know the law"; 7:4–6; chaps. 9–11). This aspect of

Romans has often been neglected because the letter seems so clearly directed to a Gentile church:

> . . . among all the Gentiles, *including* yourselves. . . . [Rom. 1:5–6; trans. mine]

> . . . among you as well as among the rest of the Gentiles. [Rom. 1:13]

> I am under obligation both to Greeks and to barbarians. . . . [Rom. 1:14; Jews are omitted!]

> . . . to be a minister of Christ Jesus to the Gentiles. . . . [Rom. 15:16]

And yet the focus and scope of Paul's argument contradict the exclusively Gentile character of the Roman church. Adolf von Schlatter (1952), preceded by Wilhelm Julius Mangold (1884), translated Rom. 1:5b–6a (*en pasin tois ethnesin . . . en hois este kai hymeis*)[71] as follows: "among all the Gentiles, *in the midst of* whom you live" (warrant: the text reads *en hois* rather than *ex hōn*). This translation facilitates a view of the Roman church as a mixed congregation.[72]

A more decisive argument for a mixed congregation is the character of the "Gentile" audience. The *ethnē* in the Pauline letters and Acts are on the whole not pure Gentiles but those "God-fearers" among the Gentiles who had been attracted to the synagogue as semiconverts or sympathizers (Schmithals[73]). They have now been converted to the gospel. Indeed, Paul's Gentile mission found its converts largely among those groups, and their "apostasy" from the Jewish synagogue must have made the former "missionary" Pharisee a special object of hatred among the Jews. Thus, the frequent allusions to the Old Testament and Jewish terminology in Romans, and a statement like Rom. 7:1 ("I am speaking to those who know the law"), are intelligible even when Paul addresses the "Gentile" majority of the Roman church.

Even so, the "Jewish"-Gentile character of the church does not exclude its mixed character. It is probable that former Jews also belonged to the congregation. Not only Romans 14 and 15, and 7:1–6, but also the basic Jewish form of the argument confirm this. Kümmel states the problem as follows:

> Romans manifests a double character: it is essentially a debate between the Pauline gospel and Judaism, so that the conclusion seems obvious that the readers were Jewish Christians. Yet the letter contains statements which indicate specifically that the community was Gentile-Christian.[74]

THE FUNCTION OF ISRAEL IN THE GOSPEL

The relation now between the Jewish argument and the "Jewish"-Gentile Christian audience needs urgent clarification, because, on the basis of internal evidence, Romans seems mainly a dialogue with Jews. The convergence of causes that motivate the letter indicates Paul's need, at this particular point of his career, to develop and clarify the fundamental issue behind his apostolate, the question of Israel's function in the gospel. This is the issue behind the collection, and it will be a central topic of conversation in Paul's forthcoming visit to Jerusalem; but it is also the issue that troubles the most illustrious church in the West, Rome.

The occasional character of Romans should not detract from its fundamental-theological importance for Paul's thought. A well-ordered theological composition allows a type of response different from ad hoc solutions to contingent problems (cf. 1 Corinthians 5-11). When a letter assumes the features of a treatise, a problem of major proportions is under discussion. And yet a treatise-type letter does not necessarily negate its particularity. The situational motivations behind Romans, then, must be distinguished from the distinctly different situations of the other letters. Although Romans seems to be in some sense a "dogmatics in outline," it is not a timeless theological product but a "treatise" that is evoked by—and addressed to—specific problems.

Romans is a Christian response to Jewish questions such as "What is Israel's role in salvation-history?" and "What is the function of the Torah and circumcision?" Romans is a dialogue with Judaism, because Paul does not attack a Judaizing heresy (as in Galatians) but is forced by the exigencies of the time and the problem in Rome to contemplate the proper role of Judaism in salvation-history.

Behind the Jewish-Christian and Gentile-Christian conflict in Rome, and behind the "God-fearing" Gentiles—only recently withdrawn from the Roman synagogue—stands the profound issue of the role of Israel in salvation-history. Is the gospel the abolition of or the fulfillment of Israel's election and salvation-history? Are the Scriptures still Scripture for Israel? Above all, what is the unity and continuity of salvation-history? Is the God of Christ a faithful God or an arbitrary God (*pistis theou*, Rom. 3:3)? If he has ceased to be faithful to *Israel's* promises, how can he be trusted by the Gentiles? In Romans, Paul does not attack Christians for adopting Jewish ways or circumcision[75] but demonstrates instead the way in which Judaism is accounted for in the gospel. The dialogue with the Jews is at the same time an apology for the gospel. Indeed, the hidden and open addressee of Romans 1–4 is the Jew, who is addressed directly in 2:1–29, 3:1–20, and 4:1–25. Paul has the Jew in mind when he calls Abraham "our natural forefather" (Rom. 4:1; trans. mine). To be sure, the direct dialogue with the Jew ceases with Rom. 5:1 and moves into the eschatological confession of the Christian community celebrating its new life in Christ (cf. the beginning of the first person plural in 5:1; 6:1). The confessional character of Romans 5:1—8:39, framed by the eschatological sections of 5:2b, 9–11, and 8:18–30, and concluded by the victory hymn of 8:31–39, transcends "the Jewish question," although it still has the Jewish question as its continuous backdrop (Rom. 5:20–21; 6:1–15; 7:1–25; 8:1–4 ["the just requirement of the law"]; 8:7, 15 ["to fall back into fear," *palin*]; 8:33).

The Jewish Character of the Argument in Romans 1:16—4:25

The Old Testament Jewish nature of the argument should be noted: Paul selects "righteousness" as the theme of the gospel (not "the wisdom of God" or "the word of the cross"; cf. 1 Corinthians 1); scriptural citations abound in Romans 1–5; Romans 4 constitutes a midrash on Scripture (Gen. 15:6); the Christology of Rom. 3:24–25 is heavily indebted to Jewish-Christian tradition, with its emphasis on expiation, forgiveness, blood, and covenant. Nestle's text has twenty-two Old Testament passages in boldface between Rom. 2:1 and 5:11.[76] Despite Paul's focus on the universal (cf. the frequency of "everyone," "all" [*pas, pantes*]), the presence of the particularist argument is quite evident: it is posited in Rom. 1:16b, repeated in 2:9–10, and picked up again in 3:1–8, after its apparent demise in 2:26–29. The theme "to the Jew first and also to the Greek" (Rom. 1:16b) must not, however, be understood in terms of a neatly divided structure, as if chapters 1–5 are addressed only to Jews and chapters 6–8 only to Gentiles. Instead, Paul weaves the universalist theme (*panti tō pisteuonti*, 1:16) into his argument with the Jew (*ioudaiō te prōton*, 1:16b; cf., esp., 3:9–20) and likewise does not forget "the Jewish question" in chapters 5–8. But it is the Jew whom Paul wants to convince about the universalistic claim of the gospel in chapters 1–4. Paul's argument for the particularism of Jewish priority in the scheme of the gospel is alluded to within chapters 1–4 (cf. 3:1–20) but firmly established only in chapters 9–11 (esp. chap. 11). It is interesting to note Paul's versatility in arguing contingently; when Gentile universalism is the focus, the Jew is addressed (cf. Rom. 3:9–20), but when Jewish particularism is underscored, the auditor is specifically the Gentile (cf. Rom. 11:13–14, 17–25a).

The characterization of Romans 1–4 as a "dialogue with Jews" is contradicted by the prominent place of Rom. 1:18–32, which (sometimes with 2:1-16) is usually named "the indictment of the Gentiles" or "the Gentiles under sin." According to most scholars, the two sections 1:18-32 and 2:1-29, as addressed to, respectively, Gentiles and Jews, climax in 3:9, which accuse both alike: "We have already charged that all men, both Jews and Greeks, are under the power of sin" (*pantas hyph hamartīan*). This climax concludes with a Scripture catena (Rom. 3:10-20) and forms the negative foil for 3:21-30, with its positive proclamation of "the righteousness of God through faith in Jesus Christ for all who believe" (Rom. 3:22, *pantas tous pisteuontas*). According to this view, Rom. 1:18–4:25 is addressed to both Jew and Gentile, and no overall argument with Jews is to be seen in the section as a whole. The polemic with the Jews in 3:1-9 is thus viewed as an intrusion into the argument—a Pauline "aside"[77]— necessitated by the radical, polemical nature of 2:26-29, which seems to undermine all Jewish privileges. This systematic, doctrinal characterization of Rom. 1:18—3:20 as "the indictment of all humankind" overlooks the fact that 1:18-32 (and 2:1-16?) is not simply a Gentile counterpart to the Jewish argument of 2:17-29. Although the gospel is to the Jew first, the Gentile is indicted first and the Jew last.[78] The weight of the indictment falls on the Jew (last in sequence, first in importance). The style of Rom. 1:18-32 is different from that of 2:1-29; compare, for example, the direct address and the diatribal character of 2:1-29 with the descriptive, nondialogical character of 1:18-32. Moreover, the "therefore" (*dio*) of Rom. 2:1 indicates that 1:18-32 is integrally connected with 2:1-29, the indictment of the Jew. However, Rom. 1:18-32 and 2:1-29 are not simply juxtaposed indictments of Gentiles and Jews but are interwoven. Although Paul employs a traditional Jewish/Hellenistic scheme in Rom. 1:18-32—used by the synagogue in its indictment of the idolatry, adultery, and social vices (1:20-31) of the Gentile world—it seems that he generalizes the scheme so that it is applicable to the whole world ("men," 1:18: *anthrōpōn*, not *ethnōn*), that is, to both Jews and Greeks; in Rom. 1:23, he may even be alluding to the Genesis story of the fall of humankind.[79]

But even if—as seems likely—the Gentile world alone is Paul's focus here, he invites Jewish agreement with his description of that world and its vices because he intends to set a trap for the Jewish auditor: he is in the same condemnable condition before God as is the Gentile world in Jewish eyes (Rom. 2:1-11). In other words, Paul elaborates in Rom. 1:18—3:20 the succinct statement in Galatians, "We ourselves who are Jews by birth and not Gentile sinners" (Gal. 2:15). The argumentative point of Rom. 1:18—3:20 is not an equal and separate indictment of Gentile and Jew. Although Paul does not spare the religious and moral bankruptcy of the

Gentile world, his specific aim is directed against Jewish superiority and pride. After all, both Paul and the Jew already know from their heritage the self-evident sinful condition of the Gentile; it is a point that does not need to be argued. What is argued is the equal status of Jew and Gentile under sin; what is presupposed is the self-evident character of the Gentile under sin.

This line of argument is confirmed by the peculiar reasoning of Rom. 3:19: "Now we know that whatever the law says it speaks to those who are under the law, so that every mouth [*pan stoma*] may be stopped, and the whole world [*pas ho kosmos*] may be held accountable to God." If the law speaks only to "those under the law," why does it apply to "the whole world"? Paul does not suddenly introduce "the (universal) law of the heart" (cf. Rom. 2:15) into the picture, for that law has no direct relation to the Old Testament scripture of Rom. 3:11–18. Rather, Paul addresses his Jewish target. For if it can be shown that the catena of scripture of 3:11–18 applies to the Jews, then it is self-evident that the whole world (i.e., the Gentiles) is accountable to God as well, for Gentiles are by nature sinners (cf. The Wisdom of Solomon). They are "without God in the world" (Eph. 2:12; cf. Gal. 4:8) and "alienated from the life of God" (Eph. 4:18), because of "the old nature [*palaios anthrōpos*] which . . . is corrupt through deceitful lusts" (Eph. 4:22).

The Jewish target of Rom. 1:18—3:20 is evident not only in 2:1-11 ("for God shows no partiality," 2:11) but equally in 2:12-16. Bornkamm's analysis is not convincing here, as if 2:12a and 2:12b are the theme, respectively, for verses 13-16 (indictment of the Gentile) on the one hand and for verses 17-18 (indictment of the Jew) on the other hand.[80] Instead, Paul is again engaged in an indictment of the Jew. The emphasis is on verse 12b: "And all who have sinned under the law will be judged by the law," because the statement of verse 12a is self-evident: "All who have sinned without the law will also perish without the law." In this context Paul treats the Gentiles and "the work of the law written on their hearts" (Rom. 2:15; trans. mine) so mildly because he uses the law-abiding impulses of the so-called despised Gentiles to scathe the ethnic superiority and election pride of the Jews. And although Paul wants to uphold "the advantage of the Jew" (Rom. 3:1), he again levels against the Jews the seemingly contradictory sentence: "We do *not* have an advantage" (3:9a). Paul's aim, then, is the demolition of Jewish pride in the Torah and the destruction of Jewish narcissistic self-elevation over the Gentiles.

Romans 3:21-31 once more reveals the Jewish, dialogical character of Paul's argument. It tears apart the Jewish conviction that righteousness and

the law form an integral unity, that works of the law are the sole condition
for God's forensic judgment and thus for eternal life. Because the true
function of the law is the knowledge and conviction of sin (3:20),
righteousness can be obtained only "apart from the law," that is, apart
from its sentence of death. This possibility lies in the free grace of God as
manifested in the death of Christ, who is our expiation and "place" of
forgiveness (hilastērion, 3:25). Thus, faith in the redemptive death of Christ
constitutes our justification, and not the law of condemnation. Are faith
and the law, then, antithetical realities? If this were true, the Torah, as
constitutive of Israel's election and existence, would simply be an antidivine power. "The righteousness of God apart from the law" (3:21) seems
to negate the law. Paul rejects this assertion succinctly, almost cryptically,
in Rom. 3:21–31: "Do we then overthrow the law by this faith? By no
means! On the contrary, we uphold the law" (3:31). However, how can
this square with the claim "apart from the law" (3:21)? The answer lies in
verse 21b: "the righteousness of God has been manifested apart from the
law, although the law and the prophets bear witness to it."* Yet this
positive claim about the law (3:21b, 31) remains cryptic until Rom. 4:1–
12, where the midrash on Gen. 15:6 must demonstrate its truth. In Rom.
3:21–31, then, there is a double thrust—indicated by the phrases "apart
from the law/testified to by the law" (v. 21): (1) the exclusion of the
works of the law (v. 27) and (2) the affirmation of the law (v. 31). The
Jewishness of this argument is especially clear when we notice the
conclusion in 3:27–30. We expect Paul to say, after Rom. 3:21–26, "Where
then is sin?" That, after all, is the theme of 3:23. "All have sinned and fall
short of the glory of God." The burden of sin is indeed lifted by God's
forgiveness and justification (3:23–26). But now we hear suddenly the
climactic question: "Where then is boasting?" Paul demolishes the Jewish
claim to God's righteousness based on the law, that is, the works of the law
(3:20–21), and wants to destroy the preeminently Jewish sin of boasting.

Romans 3:21–31 is not primarily a discourse within a theological
vacuum concerning the doctrine of justification by faith applicable to all

---

*Paul uses "the law" (nomos) in 3:31; we would have expected in 3:21b ("the law and the
prophets") "scripture" (graphē), as in Gal. 3:22 (cf. "scripture" [graphē] in Rom. 4:3). The
argument "apart from the law/testified to by the law" creates at first glance confusion, because
Paul operates with two concepts of "law" (nomos): "law" (nomos) as "scripture" (graphē) and
"law" (nomos) as moral, cultic law (cf. "the works of the law," Rom. 3:20), that is, nomos as gramma
("letter," 2 Cor. 3:6; Rom. 2:29). Nomos as "Scripture" (graphē, 4:3; cf. 1:2: en graphais hagiais)
confirms justification by faith, whereas nomos as inciting to erga ("works") is gramma ("the letter
that kills," 2 Cor. 3:6) and effects the opposite of justification, that is, condemnation (cf. 2 Cor. 3:6;
see Chapter 11, below).

humankind. That may be true as well, but it is not Paul's primary intent. Justification by faith applies to both Jew and Greek ("man," 3:28; "the circumcised and the uncircumcised," 3:30). But it is argued here against a Jewish position of boasting and superiority. Thus, verses 27–31 are directed specifically to Jews (cf. Rom. 3:29: "Or is God the God of Jews only? Is he not the God of Gentiles also?"). The Jews refuse to submit to God's equal judgment over Jew and Gentile and to his radical grace that equalizes and unites both peoples before God. Paul turns the Shema confession of Israel, "Hear, O Israel, the Lord our God is one Lord" (Deut. 6:4), radically against Israel (Rom. 3:30) to emphasize the oneness of both Jew and Gentile in judgment and grace by faith alone. Romans 3:21–31 overthrows any Jewish claim to superiority over the Gentiles, because *sola fide* (3:28) is incompatible with distinctions of race and privilege. Thus, *sola fide* is the ground of the oneness of "all" (cf. vv. 22, 23), of both Jew and Gentile, in the Pauline gospel. The Jewish pitch of the argument continues in 4:1–12, where the Jewish theme of boasting is again taken up and refuted in the case of Abraham (4:2).

The Jewish thrust of Rom. 3:21–31 unveils something significant about Paul's conception of sin and his (later) discussion of the law. Although at this point Paul does not unfold his reflections on sin, flesh, death, and the law (Romans 5–8), he profoundly conjoins law and boasting (3:27). The real sin of the Jew is not the indulgence of the flesh (cf. 1 Pet. 4:3; Eph. 2:3; Col. 3:5–7) or the sin of hypocrisy (Rom. 2:17–29[81]). Instead, the Jew highlights sin in its most demonic aspect, because he believes that in observing the Torah he exhibits a true zeal for God (Rom. 10:2). Paul calls this phenomenon "boasting" (Rom. 3:27), which is akin to a state of illusion or blindness. The Jews are sinful precisely because the power of sin blinds them to their transgression. And thus the law, which should have led them to a recognition of sin (3:20), binds them "under the power of sin" (3:9). The effect of that power is pride, the proud self-awareness of their moral stature and achievement. Indeed, the Jews' failure to recognize and acknowledge their transgression leads them to boasting and blindness. In Rom. 3:21–31 the interpretation of sin as pride and as self-deception foreshadows 7:7–25, where Paul analyzes man's plight under the law. However, in Romans 2 the Jew is indicted in traditional Jewish (Christian) terms, that is, in terms of the hypocritical contradiction between oral confession and moral acts; his boasting in God (2:17) and in the law (2:23) is empirically contradicted by his immoral behavior and the public transgression of the law (2:23–24). The "boasting" of Rom. 2:23 is deepened in 3:27, for here the Jew transgresses the law of God not by immoral behavior but by his very attempt to be moral. Sin is here not the contradiction between confession and act but that between moral intent (to obey God's will) and moral result (self-righteousness).

Romans 3:27 awaits the full elaboration of sin and law in 7:7–25. Why this comes so much later in the letter is difficult to say, although the letter clearly shows a progression of the argument, because chapter 7 cannot occur before 5:12–21 has laid its foundation and presuppositions. Although Paul in 3:27 moves beyond the hypocrisy argument of 2:1–29, in 1:18— 4:25 he emphasizes responsible guilt and moral failure, whereas in 5:12–21 the issue of culpable illusion and tragic failure surfaces in a manner not presented before.*

Romans 1:18—4:25, then, is essentially a dialogue with the Jews. The gospel for Jew and Gentile confines them both under sin and liberates and unites them both through faith in Christ, but it is primarily the Jewish auditor who is the target of Paul's exposition. Indeed, God's salvation-history reaches its eschatological stage in the creation of the one people of God, the one church of Jew and Gentile.[82]

THE ARGUMENT OF ROMANS 5-8

It would be an exaggeration, however, to claim that all of Romans is simply a dialogue with Jews or a situational address. The confessional character of Rom. 5:1—8:39 transcends "the Jewish question," for it explores the meaning of life in Christ. The doxological tone at the end of every chapter highlights this:

---

*Likewise, moral accusation based on moral responsibility dominates Rom. 1:10–32 and 2:1–29, whereas Rom. 5:12–21 describes the tragic situation of humankind "in Adam." It is as if Paul deliberately moves the discussion in Romans to a level where a prior argument is transcended by new elements introduced into the discussion (cf., e.g., "therefore" in Rom. 5:12, which both summarizes the preceding argument and moves it to a new level). This is especially clear with the issue of Torah; it is only at Rom. 7:1 that the references to law in 2:13, 3:19–21, 31, 4:15, 5:13, 20, and 6:14–15, which thus far had not been clarified, compel Paul to a fuller discussion. And yet that discussion cannot occur until 5:12–21 and 6:1–15 have laid the foundations. Thus Rom. 7:1–25 functions as a necessary excursus. It clarifies the earlier, cryptic reference to the law, but it does so at the point in the argument where it fits best, after the human condition in Adam (5:12–21) under sin (6:1–23) has been discussed. Romans 7:1–25 functions as a necessary excursus—not as an arbitrary appendix. Apart from different levels of argumentation, there are also differences in tone. The polemical tone of Rom. 1:18—4:25 differs from the more apologetic, didactic tone of 7:7–25—a tone that, in the midst of its penetrating analysis of sin, makes concessions that were almost unthinkable in Romans 1-4. Again, the polemical tone of 1:18—4:25 shifts into the joyful tone of Christian confession in 5:1-2: "Therefore, since *we* are justified by faith, we have peace with God through our Lord Jesus Christ. . . . We have obtained access to this grace in which we stand, and we rejoice in our hope of sharing the glory of God"! The existence of the Christian community with its blessings through and in Christ both highlights the fall of Judaism and transcends it. When we reach Romans 11, the anti-Jewish polemic of chapters 9 and 10 is displaced by a didactic discourse concerning "the Jewish question," now specifically directed not to the Jews but to Gentiles (11:13–25).

through our Lord Jesus Christ (5:11, 21)

in Christ Jesus our Lord (6:23)

(Thanks be to God) through Jesus Christ our Lord (7:25a)

in Christ Jesus our Lord (8:39)

Structurally the section is quite complex. The coherent clarity of Rom. 1:18—4:25 should not deceive us into thinking that 5:1—8:39 is equally coherent, as if, for instance, "sanctification" follows "justification" in a process from "forgiveness of sins" (1:18—4:25) to "moral holiness" (5:1—8:39). Unlike Nygren, who has imposed an artificial structural composition on Rom. 5:1—8:39,[83] Dahl has clarified the problem of Romans 5–8 by pointing out that 5:1-11 introduces the themes of "glory," "Spirit," "hope," "love," and "salvation," which are not explicated until Romans 8.[84] Dahl surmises that the intervening chapters are ad hoc answers to previous objections and are without a clear, logical structure. Paul's epistolary method militates against the systematic, dogmatic structure that is usually sought after in these chapters.

At least two questions about Rom. 5:1—8:39 need clarification: (1) What constitutes the coherence of Romans 5–8? (2) Is there any continuation here of the Jewish dialogue that we discovered in Rom. 1:18—4:25? As to the first question, if—as Dahl suggests—5:1-11 is the thematic preface to 8:1-39, do the other sections constitute a coherent structure that moves from 5:1-11 to 8:39? In other words, when chapter 8 picks up 5:1-11, what is the function of the intervening sections, especially 5:12-21? The exegetical difficulty around "therefore" (dia touto, 5:12) pinpoints the issue, as we have seen. Luther called Rom. 5:12-21 a lustigen Spaziergang[85] (i.e., an appendix); others describe it as both transition and core[86] or as the beginning of a new section.[87] Does 5:12-21 summarize 1:18—5:11 and mark as well the transition to chapters 6–8? Does this mean, then, that 5:1-11 belongs to the previous section 1:18—4:25? But if that is true, how is the new beginning at 5:1 to be explained, with its first person plural, confessional character (cf. already 4:24-25)? Ad hoc epistolary transitions may provide a better answer than the search for a dogmatic structure because they point to the flowing contextual movement of the argument. For example, Rom. 5:1-11 picks up 4:24-25 and moves the argument to the new level of eschatological life and hope; 5:20-21, with its radical claims, compels the discussion of 6:1-23; and 7:5-6 sets the theme for both 7:7-25 and 8:1-17. Within the flow of the argument, Romans 7 comes naturally, because the discussion of the law (3:20; 4:15; 5:14, 20-21; 6:14,

15) is "overdue."[88] In my opinion Rom. 5:12–21 is both a summary of 1:18—5:11 and a transition to 6:1—8:39: it sums up in apocalyptic, typological language the plight of humankind *before* Christ and its new life *in* Christ. But it is also a transition, because Paul shifts in 5:12–21 to the universal, ontological, and eschatological dimensions of Christian life that dominate 6:1—8:39 ("death," "life," "the flesh," "the power of 'sin,'" the "Spirit"). Jew and Gentile are now subsumed under the one figure of Adam, who by his transgression sealed "all men" (*pantas anthrōpous*, 5:18) under sin and death. The subject is no longer Jew or Gentile but "the many" (*hoi polloi*, 5:19). The scheme of "the one and the many" with its incorporation motif introduces a universalistic argument that concludes with the confidence and hope of eternal life (5:21). The Jewish argument of Rom. 1:18—4:25 has been transcended, and we find ourselves on a new ontological level, the level of existence in Adam and in Christ, which 5:1–11 introduced. Because of "the new age" of "life" that has come in Christ, the difference between Jew and Gentile is neutralized, for both belong equally to "the old age" that Christ has undone.

As to the second question, can the contingent character of Romans still be maintained in view of the very different character of Romans 5–8? What has happened here to "the Jewish question"—which seems absent both in 5:1-11 and in 5:12-21? There can be no question about the different character of chapters 5–8. However, we should not dismiss too rapidly the persistence of "the Jewish question." The joyful confession of 5:1-11, celebrating the Christians' new access to God through Christ and their "boasting" in the hope of the glory of God, cannot but evoke the contrast to Judaism with its boasting (3:27; 4:2), its loss of glory (3:23), and its condemnation before God (3:19-22; cf. 5:9: "much more shall we be saved by him from the wrath of God"). Although the drama of history has been decided by the actions of the two Adams, and although the law has "slipped in" (*paraeisēlthen*) on a scene already decided by the other protagonists, the law has a crucial function.[89] It prevents the Adam typology from sliding into a mythological, Gnostic scheme and so guarantees its historical character and humankind's moral responsibility before God. Although the law is impotent in verses 13, 14, and 20, it has a positive salvation-historical function. Paul claims that Adam and his fall are prior to Moses and the law, and that consequently the law arrives on a scene already characterized by sin and death. However, although the law is impotent (8:3) and cannot change the human condition, its impotence does not mean it is useless: "Law came in, to increase the trespass" (5:20). The law, then, not only has the legal function of holding persons accountable for their sin (5:13; cf. 4:15) but also causes them to sin more. Indeed, because a person's being determines one's actions, the imperative of the law can only confirm a person's plight; it cannot change the human condition. Therefore, when persons confront the law, the law concretizes their sinful being by evoking their sinful actions. As Luther put it, "Good works do not make a good man, but a good man does good works" (see Chapter 11, below). However, the evocation of sin is the purpose of the law in God's plan of grace (5:20–21).

Thus Rom. 5:12–21, 6:1–23, and 7:1–25 occur against the background of a renewed argument with Jews about the consequences of Paul's gospel of justification by faith and its salvation-historical and ethical implications. Just as 5:12–21 unveils the true function of the law, so 6:1–23 and 7:1–25 are elaborate replies to Jewish synagogal protests that are aroused by 5:20–21. For the Jew claims that if grace is fully given only where sin abounds, sin must be the necessary condition for the reception of grace, and Christian life becomes radically immoral. Moreover, if the law functions "to increase sin," then the law becomes a demonic agency. Thus, Paul's position is absurd and bypasses the "covenant-keeping" conviction of Judaism on sin, law, and atonement. Furthermore, Paul's position demonstrates that the law is a necessary ingredient for the moral life because it is the opponent rather than the ally of sin. The hidden but central place of the Torah in the discussion is clearly evident in Rom. 6:14, because Paul claims that not grace and sin but the law and sin are allies in the Christian view of life. The cryptic statements of 6:14, 15 are evoked by 5:20–21 and will be elaborated in 7:7–25 ("the law is sin?" [7:7]), where again the Jewish nature of the discussion is apparent, as the midrash on Genesis 3 in Rom. 7:7–10 and the stress on the divine character of the law in Rom. 7:12, 14, 22–23 (cf. Rom. 8:4) demonstrate. (Cf. also the explicit reference to people familiar with the Torah and Judaism in Rom. 7:1, 4–6: "Likewise, my brethren, you have died to the law through the body of Christ. . . . But now we are discharged from the law.")[90]

Conclusion

Romans must be characterized primarily as a dialogue with Jews. Even when Paul does not speak as directly to Jews as he does in Rom. 1:18—4:25, the Jewish debate about the law and salvation-history is always in the background. To be sure, Rom. 5:1—8:39 cannot be characterized as a direct debate with Jews. Here Paul transcends the Jewish-Gentile question and focuses on the new reality of the lordship of Christ in the church as the proleptic manifestation of God's imminent eschatological triumph. Although the Jewish question is not forgotten and provides the background against which Paul posits the new reality of life in Christ, that reality collapses the Jewish-Gentile issue into an apocalyptic either/or; one belongs either to the old Adam or to the new Adam: "Then as one man's trespass led to condemnation for all men, so one man's act of righteousness leads to acquittal and life for all men" (Rom. 5:18). Where Christ becomes the dividing point between life and death, flesh and the Spirit, sin and grace, the law and freedom, there the ontology of the new eschatological life transcends the historical "advantage" of the Jew, although it does not negate it. Indeed, the dialogical focus of Romans 1–4 shifts here to a confessional Christian celebration.

However, the combined factors of the forthcoming debate in Jerusalem, the Galatian crisis, the mixed and troubled character of the Roman church, and Paul's appeal for Rome's intercession compel him to reflect on "the Jewish question" as a constitutive element of his gospel. Is the gospel a betrayal of Jewish salvation-history and the law? Must Christianity be characterized as a heretical offshoot of its parent, Judaism, or simply as another *nova religio* of the Roman Empire? Did Paul's response to the Galatians amount to a demonizing of Jewish religion? The question of God's faithfulness to his promises to Israel, and their proleptic fulfillment in Christ, is more than ever evoked by the convergence of circumstances that prompted Paul to write Romans. Those promises of God concern the creation of the eschatological people of God, the church of Jews and Gentiles: "Praise the Lord, all Gentiles [*ethnē*], and let all the peoples [*pantes hoi laoi*] praise him" (Rom. 15:11). Paul's gospel is a gospel for the Gentiles, just because it is not a betrayal of Israel but the fulfillment of God's promise to Israel: "The root of Jesse shall come, he who rises to rule the Gentiles; in him shall the Gentiles hope" (Rom. 15:12 [Isa. 11:1; Gen. 49:10]; cf. also Rom. 11:26), and "That is why it depends on faith, in order that the promise may rest on grace and be guaranteed to all his descendants—not only to the adherents of the law but also to those who share the faith of Abraham, for he is the father of us all" (Rom. 4:16). The gospel is "to the Jew first, but also to the Gentile," because Israel's priority is not to be dismissed. It will disclose itself in the eschaton, when all Israel will be saved through the intervention of the Gentile mission (Rom. 11:25–26). At the end, Israel's beginning, that is, its election by God, will be confirmed.

Romans exhibits a basic apology for Israel. Therefore, chapters 9–11 are not an appendix but a climactic point in the letter. And yet the apology takes a curious form, for throughout Rom. 1:18—8:39 and until 11:11 (except for the interruption at 3:1–4) the apology has the character of a radical polemic. The reason for this is the Jewish doctrine of election. For the Jew, God's faithfulness and election mean the segregation of the Jew from the Gentile, because the covenant, the Torah, and circumcision constitute the essential privileges of Israel. Although the Jews are, to be sure, aware of their sins, they know themselves not to be sinners in the manner of the Gentiles because they live in the domain of the Torah and circumcision, where forgiveness is available to them as it is not to the Gentiles. A full integration of Jew and Gentile in terms of their status before God simply contradicts everything Judaism stands for in its "covenantal nomism." The Jew's attitude to proselytes and God-fearers—often sympathetic, sometimes ambivalent—reflects this self-awareness. Paul conducts his polemic against this position. Indeed, he blames Gentiles for their idol worship (Rom. 1:18–32; cf. Gal. 4:3–11), but his focus is on equalizing Gentile and Jew, for both are under the power of sin. Therefore, he "paganizes" the Jews in Rom. 2:21–29 by indicting them for those cardinal Gentile sins (1:18–32) that the Jews have always abhorred about Gentile life: idolatry ("robbing temples," v. 21), adultery (v. 22), and social vices ("stealing," v. 21). Paul concentrates primarily on the Jewish sins of hypocrisy (2:26–29) and boasting (3:27), whereas typical Gentile sins do not fill the pages of Romans (except for 1:18–32; but cf. Colossians; Ephesians; 1 Peter).[91]

Paul strongly advocates the "advantage of the Jew" (Rom. 3:1), but it lies exclusively in the "faithfulness of God" that persists amidst the "faithlessness" and "unbelief" of the Jews (3:3, *pistis/apistia*; cf. 4:20; 11:20, 23). Israel's tragedy is that it blindly claims what it has lost. It rejects the gospel, because its claim to privilege has made it immune to God's new gift of grace (10:18, 21). Unless Israel acknowledges that "*all* are under sin" (3:9), it faces a possibly ultimate rejection (11:23–24). However, Paul's polemic against Israel's election self-consciousness does not invalidate his apologetic. Marcion and many Jewish interpreters[92] fail to see that the sharpness of the polemic is for the sake of the apologetic. Israel's betrayal does not thwart Israel's destiny in the plan of God. Thus, Paul's polemic is a polemic of sorrow (Rom. 9:1–2), induced by Israel's high calling in history: "Of their race, according to the flesh, is the Christ" (9:5). And because Israel—notwithstanding its own disobedience—has been and remains the vessel of God's promises, the Gentiles cannot look down on Israel (11:13–32). For the boasting of the Jew (3:27), or the Gentile (11:18), destroys the unity of both in the one eschatological body of Christ (12:4–5). Whereas in Galatians Paul fights for the universality of the gospel and argues mainly against a Jewish understanding of salvation-history, in Romans he integrates the universality of the gospel and the particularity of Israel. Thus, Romans gives a much more balanced picture of the place of Israel in salvation-history than Galatians does. As we have seen, the particularity of the situation dictates this. The occasion in Romans is "right" for stimulating Paul's most important theological reflection. Situational contingency becomes the occasion for food for thought.

JEWS, JEWISH CHRISTIANS, AND GOD-FEARERS IN ROMANS

If Romans is a tractate evoked by historical circumstances, why does the letter address itself to a Jewish issue and present itself as a dialogue with Jews rather than with Jewish Christians—because they, and not Jews, are members of the Roman church? In fact, Paul's plea for Rome's intercession concerns not only fear for the Jews in Judea but especially fear about the attitude of the Jewish-Christian community in Jerusalem toward the collection (Rom. 15:30–32), which symbolizes the relation of Jewish Christians to their Gentile brothers and sisters. If Paul's concern is the unity of Jewish and Gentile Christians in the church, why does he carry on a dialogue with synagogue Jews in Romans?

Paul acknowledges the salvation-historical priority of Jewish Christianity and the Jerusalem church because he views Judaism as the major heritage and source of Jewish Christianity. Or rather, he regards Jewish Christianity as the proleptic salvation-historical fulfillment of the divine promises to Israel. Jewish Christianity would have no special status for Paul except for God's promises to Israel. Jewish Christianity is special because Israel is special. Although Paul is regarded by the Jews as the great apostate, he does not reject Isreal. He remains an Israelite ("I myself am an Israelite," 11:1) and calls Israelites "my brethren, my kinsmen by race" (Rom. 9:3). Paul's conversion is in no way a rejection of Israel and of "ethnic" religion in favor of a new cosmic universal religion of the Spirit (Baur). The gospel does not come to the Gentiles because of the permanent eclipse of Israel or because Paul denies Israel's particularity. Rather, it comes to the Gentiles as God's ratification of his promises to Israel in Christ. The issue is not particularism versus universalism but universalism within the context of particularism. Thus Paul speaks about the dependence of the Gentiles on the "spiritual blessings" of Jerusalem, to which they should respond with their "material blessings" (Rom. 15:27), and he stresses that "Christ became a servant to the circumcised to show God's truthfulness, in order to confirm the promises given to the patriarchs" (15:8). Before A.D. 70 the priority of Jerusalem was generally acknowledged in the Gentile churches, just as all the apostles were Jewish

Christians. Moreover, Paul's fight for his independent apostolic status had to be argued in the face of his necessary relation to Jerusalem, and—however illegitimately—the opposition in Galatians and 2 Corinthians certainly claimed in some sense the support of the authority of the Jerusalem church and its pillars.

The status of Cephas as the "rock" of the church emerged rapidly (Matthew 16)—at least after James's and John's martyrdoms had dissolved the triumvirate of "the pillars" in Jerusalem (cf. Gal. 2:1–10). In any case, Peter's role must have been considerable from the start (Gal. 2:7, 11–14; 1 Corinthians 1–4, Cephas party). Moreover, the "pillars" (*styloi*) in Jerusalem underscore the eschatological importance of the city for the expectation of the Parousia (cf. Rom. 11:26: "The Deliverer will come from Zion . . ."; cf. also 15:12). Indeed, Acts vividly describes Jerusalem's supervisory role over the mission field. Because an eschatological pilgrimage of the Gentiles to Jerusalem (Isaiah 2; Micah 2; Isa. 66:23) had long been fostered in the traditions of Israel, the locus of the Parousia in Jerusalem probably constituted the mission theology of the apostolate to the circumcised (Gal. 2:7).

Paul's own relation to Jerusalem was a sensitive matter. His mission would have been in vain (Gal. 2:2) unless Jerusalem agreed with his law-free gospel, because a divided apostolate was unthinkable to Paul (1 Cor. 15:11).

And so, the forthcoming visit to Jerusalem produced in Paul a renewed anxiety about the reaction of Jewish Christianity in Jerusalem to the collection gathered from the Gentiles, and thus to Paul's gospel of the one eschatological church of Jews and Gentiles. Indeed, Paul's anxiety was not without cause. According to Acts 21:20–24, he is greeted with concern over his apostasy from the Torah, and seemingly few Jewish-Christian friends were willing to help him during his time of trial in Jerusalem.

Jerusalem's importance, then, is linked to the importance of Israel for the gospel. Jewish Christianity signified "the first fruits" of the ingathering of all Israel (Rom. 11:16), and thus the beginning of the fulfillment of God's promises to the patriarchs (11:15–16, 28–29). Because the priority of Jewish Christianity is insolubly connected with the priority of Israel in salvation-history, the nature of the priority had to be delineated, lest Jewish Christianity become either sectarian and divorced from Gentile Christianity or a negligible item in an increasingly Gentile church, which in this manner would lose its salvation-historical base in Israel.

A dialogue with Jews, then, was necessary to determine not only the legitimate role of Jewish Christianity but especially that of the law-free

Gentile mission. The key to the dialogue is the abiding faithfulness of God in the light of the faithlessness and unbelief of Israel, manifested in its rejection of Christ. And if God's act in Christ confirms his faithfulness to Israel, God becomes as well the ground of trust for the Gentiles.

The faithlessness of Israel is due to its inability to understand and keep the law in terms of God's promise. And that inability is confirmed by their rejection of Christ (Rom. 10:3, 18–21). Thus the law condemns Israel and provides no "life." Israel can be "Israel" only when it lives by God's promise as confirmed by Christ. "Christ is the end of the law" (10:4) both in terms of its goal and its termination, for the law constitutes Israel's self-aggrandizement and boasting in its rebellion against God. Jewish Christianity owes its priority to God's promise alone and not to any ethnic pride or boasting in the Torah. A Jewish Christianity that does not live by grace alone has in fact returned to Judaism in its rebellion against God: "But of Israel he says, 'All day long I have held out my hands to a disobedient and contrary people' " (10:21).

The primary audience of Romans is, as Schmithals has shown, those "Gentiles" who recently abandoned the synagogue as "God-fearers" (and/or proselytes) and who now—along with their Jewish-Christian brethren—must understand that the gospel both confirms and abolishes Israel's privilege.[93] They are thus admonished to "stand" in the gospel (Rom. 11:20; and also warned against a possible backsliding to the synagogue?) For although the gospel equalizes "all" before God's grace in Christ and gathers them into the one church of Jews and Gentiles, this equality confirms as well Israel's priority in the gospel, as located solely in God's promises and in his faithfulness to Israel in Christ.

Paul's dialogue with the Jews is the necessary background for his gospel to former Gentile "God-fearers" and to former Jews in Rome. He claims that their stance in the gospel does not mean a betrayal of Judaism but constitutes God's faithfulness to his promise to Israel in Christ. Therefore, Roman "Gentile" Christians and Jewish Christians alike must understand that Israel's priority in salvation-history signifies in Christ the equality of both in the one body of the church.

CONTINGENCY AND COHERENCE IN ROMANS

I have devoted considerable attention to the contingent character of Romans. It was my intent to show that Romans is not a systematic treatise or compendium of Christian doctrine but rather a theology in process, one that was evoked by the concrete demands of the Roman church. I agree with Dahl's judgment:

Like Paul's other letters, Romans has the characteristics of a genuine letter. It is a written communication between two parties who are spatially separated and is a substitute for personal presence. . . . The relationship between theology and missionary activity is as intimate in Romans as in any of Paul's letters, but the perspective is different. . . . Paul's letter to the Romans gives us the most comprehensive representation of Paul's theology because it was written for a very particular purpose. The theology of Romans is closely tied to the Pauline mission with its historical and eschatological perspectives.[94]

Although I have stressed the relevance of Romans to the internal problems of the church more than Dahl does, Dahl opens up a perspective on the letter which permits us to see the characteristically Pauline interaction between coherence and contingency. It is foolish to deny that Romans has a more systematic form and structure than the other letters of Paul. What must be denied, however, is the choice between either contingency or coherence, because it is the interaction between these components that characterizes the letter.

Specifically, the convergence of motivations for the letter indicates that the situations of the Roman church and Paul at the time of writing Romans evoke fundamental themes of Paul's theology. Romans functions as the catalyst for integrating contingency and coherence. The overarching theme of Romans is the righteousness of God (Rom. 1:17), a righteousness that has appeared in Christ as the prelude to God's apocalyptic triumph.

God's righteousness in Christ now vindicates his unswerving faithfulness (Rom. 3:1) to his promises to Israel (Romans 11), and it promises the imminent salvation of God to his created world (Rom. 5:1–11; 8:17–39). And the guarantee of the imminent triumph of God is the eschatological community of the one church of Jews and Gentiles, which already celebrates the dawn of God's victory and groans for its full actualization (Romans 5, 8). The Roman church is an integral part of the eschatological perspective of Paul's missionary theology. However, its mixed character has produced problems. A conflict between Jewish and Gentile Christians threatens to dissolve its unity. This particular problem gives Paul the opportunity to address the church about the fundamental role of Israel in salvation-history in the framework of the universality of God's grace in Christ for all people.

There is no room in the church as the beachhead of God's coming triumph of grace for Jewish superiority or Gentile pride, because "God has consigned all men to disobedience, that he may have mercy upon all" (Rom. 11:32). And this mercy of God will be fully realized shortly, because "the night is far gone, the day is at hand" (13:12). And so Paul concludes the body of the letter: "May the God of hope fill you with joy and peace in believing, so that by the power of the Holy Spirit you may abound in hope" (Rom. 15:13).

6

Contextual Theology in Romans and Galatians

PAUL'S INTERPRETIVE METHOD

I have attempted to demonstrate the occasional and contextual character of both Galatians and Romans. Despite the thematic similarity of the two letters, they must be understood in their particularity.* Even Rom. 5:1—8:39 (one of Paul's most systematic reflections) is permeated by "the Jewish question," which constitutes the occasion for Romans. We cannot construct from these letters an abiding, timeless theological structure comprising the "essence" of Paul's thought without destroying his theological method. In his letter to the Romans, Paul is not setting forth a *summa theologica*, nor is he engaged in an exposition of the "eternal verities" of the gospel or in a dogmatic monologue. His aim is kerygmatic, not dogmatic, that is, the gospel has the power to illumine a particular situation in the light of God's redemptive purpose in Christ.

Paul is not a dogmatic theologian but an interpreter of the gospel who is engaged in a hermeneutic that fits the occasion. I will discuss the issue of particularity and universality, that is, the relation between the contingency and the coherent "core" of Paul's gospel, by comparing two parallel themes in Galatians and Romans: faith (Galatians 3; Romans 4) and the law (Galatians 3; Romans 7).† These themes invite doctrinal integration: Galatians and Romans are usually treated in Pauline theologies as complementary building stones for Paul's "doctrine" of faith and the law. Although there is a need for a coherent view of Paul's thought, this procedure becomes especially dangerous when "coherence" is displaced with "timeless doctrine" or with the search for a narrowly defined *Mitte* (center) of Paulinism that will absorb all facets of Paul's thought.[1] In that case, Paul's theological method is neglected, and our insight into the historical nature of his theology is blocked. I intend to show that the particularity of an occasion compels Paul to differentiation and discrimi-

---

*After completing the manuscript, I discovered that John William Drane (*Paul, Libertine or Legalist?*) and Hans Hübner (*Das Gesetz bei Paulus*) argue a similar thesis. However, both scholars press contextual arguments into a developmental scheme of Paul's thought, which seems to me quite speculative (see Chapter 4, above, p. 39).

†The different eschatology of the two letters has been discussed in Chapters 4 and 5, above.

nation in argumentation and kerygmatic pitch, because different occasions necessitate different theological emphases and construals. Instead of blaming Paul for inconsistency of thought or lack of intellectual power, as a long-standing tradition of scholarship has maintained[2] (cf. Schoeps: "Das grundlegende paulinische Miszverständnis"[3]), we should question instead our own doctrinal premises and prejudices. Paul's theological method has a very different intent. Theology in the empirical mode has a particularist focus that a systematic construal of Paul's thought has always deplored because of its own universalist-abstract tendencies.[4] Paul's particularity of argument and kerygmatic focus suggest the singularity of his hermeneutical method. Although the quest for the coherent "core" of Paul's gospel is important in any construal of the specificity of "Pauline thought," it must embrace Paul's hermeneutical method as possibly his greatest achievement (see Chapters 2 and 3, above). Paul's interpretive method is not a hindrance to extrapolating his "core" but rather the necessary entrance into the uniqueness of his thought.

"FAITH" IN GALATIANS 3 AND ROMANS 4

The theme of faith is particularly prominent in the Abraham story of Galatians 3 and Romans 4. In both chapters the key text is Gen. 15:6: "Abraham believed God, and it was reckoned to him as righteousness" (Gal. 3:6; Rom. 4:3). The difference in the movement of the argument between Galatians 3 and Romans 4 does not strike us at first, because in both chapters Abraham is cast as the prototype of faith, a man who is justified by God because of his faith and whose faith has been fulfilled by Christ. He is the key figure in Scripture: the man of faith and the promise, realities that are prior to the coming of the law and incongruent with it. Whereas the law is opposed to faith, faith is saving faith, because it is radical trust in the God of the promise and does not rely on the works of the law. As saving faith it breaks down the barrier between Jew and Gentile, because the Scripture foretold and demonstrated in Abraham its inclusive character (Gal. 3:8; Rom. 4:11). However, this general interpretation is inadequate because it abstracts from Paul's particular focus in each of the parallel chapters.

Galatians 3 is dominated by the key word "promise" (*epangelia*: noun and verb: 9 times), Romans 4 by the verb "to reckon" (*logizomai*: 10 times). "Promise" is also an important term in Romans 4 (5 times), but not until verse 13; however, apart from the quotation of Gen. 15:6 in Gal. 3:6, the verb "to reckon" is absent from the Galatian discussion. Paul's interpretation of Gen. 15:6 focuses here not on "to reckon" (*logizomai*) as in Romans but on "faith" (*episteusen/pistis*, vv. 6–14) and on "promise" (vv. 14–22). Moreover, there is a different pitch in the argument; in Romans 4 Abraham is introduced in the context of boasting (4:2; cf. 3:27), and his own status is that of the "godless one" (4:5). The focus is on God's act of "reckoning" in the context of sin and boasting.

In Galatians 3, however, the terms "boasting," "godless," and "reckoning" do not occur. Here the emphasis is not on that triangle, but on "faith," "Gentiles," and "works." This does not constitute a contrast with Romans 4, but it nevertheless makes for a different nuance. In this context we should note the absence of Hab. 2:4 from the discussion in Romans 4 and its very different position and importance in both letters (Rom. 1:17; Gal. 3:11). It constitutes the theme of Romans (1:17), but in Galatians 3 it is only a running commentary on Gen. 15:6. It seems likely that the faith argument of Galatians 3 drew Hab. 2:4, with its emphasis on faith, into the picture, whereas the stress on God's act of reckoning in Romans 4 (cf. Psalm 32 in Rom. 4:7–8) did not necessitate the use of Hab. 2:4. It is also interesting that Hab. 2:4 is used differently in Rom. 1:17 and Gal. 3:11; the emphasis in Galatians 3 is primarily on "faith" as opposed to "doing"; that in Rom. 1:17 on the unilateral gift of righteousness (Rom. 1:16) which is apprehended by faith. In fact, in Galatians 3 faith is strictly defined in terms of its object, Christ, and so means "obedience" or "belief" in Christ (vv. 5, 7, 9, 11, 12, 14, 22, 23, 24, 25, 26); in Romans 4 the picture is more ambiguous; faith can mean belief in the God of Christ (v. 24) or acceptance of God's gratuitous gift (vv. 13, 14, 16), but more often it refers to "trust" (vv. 5, 17, 18, 19, 20), especially because Abraham's "trust" is opposed to "distrust" (*apistia*) in verse 20.

"Seed" (*sperma*) in Galatians (3:16 [3 times], 19, 29) does not mean Abraham's descendants as in Romans, but exclusively Christ (Gal. 3:16); it designates Christians only insofar as they are "in Christ" (Gal. 3:18–29). However, in Romans (4:13, 16, 18) "seed" refers to a twofold "seed": the people of the Jews and the people of the Gentiles (vv. 16, 18; cf. v. 12). In Romans 4 the emphasis is on Abraham as "the father of many peoples" (vv. 17, 18), that is, on the unity of Jew and Gentile in the one church (cf. "father": vv. 1, 11 [2 times], 12, 16, 17, 18). This focus is absent from Galatians. In Romans 4, Paul interprets Gen. 15:6 in the light of Gen. 15:5 (v. 18) and draws Gen. 17:5 into the discussion, where God names Abram Ab-raham (*patēr pollōn ethnōn*). Abraham is the figure who unifies the peoples of Jew and Gentile and whose seed is a plurality of peoples (cf. also Rom. 9:4), whereas in Galatians, Christ as the singular seed is the one in whom all are one (3:16, 20).

In Galatians 3 the actual content of the promise is Christ (v. 19b), who is Abraham's exclusive seed (v. 16). The movement in Galatians 3 is from Abraham to Christ, the fulfillment of the promise (v. 19b). Galatians 3 is Christocentric, because Christ is the object of faith (vv. 22, 23, 25) and because faith was not a real possibility before Christ came. Abraham represents here the "pro-evangelion" (v. 8); he is the figure of the promise that is only now realized in Christ (v. 25: "but now that faith has come").

Moreover, the discontinuity in salvation-history is much more apparent in Galatians than in Romans: (1) the promise and the Torah are antithetical principles, for the Torah is a later interloper into salvation-history (Gal. 3:17); (2) the curse of the Torah makes Christ's sacrifice necessary (3:13). Only because of Christ's death on the cross is "the curse" on humankind lifted, thus making it possible for "the blessing" to Abraham once again to flow to the Gentiles (Gal. 3:10–14). Thus, the reality of faith, which was promised to Abraham, is only possible because Christ has broken the curse (v. 13) and has liberated us from the "custodian" of the law (v. 25). Genesis 15:6 is interpreted more in terms of the promise than of the actuality of faith, because the reality of faith is possible only in Christ and was not really available prior to his coming. The salvation-historical discontinuity of Galatians 3, with its Christocentric scope and its antithesis to the Torah, is much less apparent in Romans 4. Here the focus is more on the continuity of salvation-history and on the abiding nature of faith in pre-Christian and Christian reality, that is, on the inherent quality of faith as trust and obedience rather than on Christ as the sole object and possibility of faith.

The object of faith in Galatians 3 is strictly Christ, for whom Abraham figures only as promise; in Romans 4 the object of faith is the God of Abraham, who is the same as the God of the Christians, that is, the one who justifies the ungodly (Rom. 4:5) just as he justified Abraham, the one who raises the dead (4:17) just as he raised up new seed for Abraham. In other words, God is the one who reckons righteousness to faith alone (Rom. 4:3, 23). Abraham's faith and Christian faith are so integrated that the christological focus of faith appears explicitly only at the very end of the chapter (Rom. 4:24–25). Therefore, the structural analogy between Abraham's faith and Christian faith is much more apparent in Romans 4 than in the promise-fulfillment scheme of Galatians 3. The shift from the Christocentric emphasis in Galatians 3 to the theocentric argument in Romans 4 serves the continuous thrust of the salvation-historical argument in Romans 4.

The person of Abraham is much more central in Romans than in

Galatians. He is the believer whom God "reckons" just because he incorporates the abiding trust of faith and is, as such, the exemplar for both Jews and Gentiles. Romans 4:17–21 gives, as it were, a psychological sketch of Abraham's faith and describes the empirical attitude that faith dictates. No such attitudinal description can be found in Galatians 3 or anywhere else in Paul (but cf. Hebrews 11). We can say, then, that the inherent quality of faith is described in Romans 4, but not its direct Christocentric focus, as in Galatians and elsewhere in Paul.

Moreover, the character of the promise differs. In Galatians 3 the promise of Abraham is fulfilled in Christ (3:22: "that what was promised to faith in Jesus Christ might be given to those who believe") or in the gift of the Spirit (3:14). Usually the "promise" is, for Paul, no longer the object of hope for Christian believers because it has been confirmed and fulfilled in Christ (cf. Gal. 3:22; also Rom. 15:8; 2 Cor. 1:20). The Christian hopes no longer in "the promise" but in the "glory of God" (cf. the transition from "promise" in Rom. 4:16–21 to "hope" in Rom. 5:1–2). In this way, Paul distinguishes between the Old Testament believer ("promise") and the Christian ("hope"). However, in Romans 4 the promise seems to be the abiding object of faith (4:20), for it characterizes Abraham's faith as an example for Christians. Faith in the promise characterizes here both the Old Testament believer and the Christian,[5] and faith-righteousness is indeed the means for "Abraham and his descendants" to secure the promise (4:13). Galatians 3, to the contrary, does not dwell on Abraham and his personal stance of faith or on the abiding reality of faith in the promise. Faith, in fact, is only possible now that the promise has been fulfilled (v. 22). Salvation-history here portrays in Abraham the principle of faith, which includes the Gentiles and excludes the Torah. Genesis 15:6 is interpreted in the light of both Gen. 18:18 ("In you [Abraham] shall all the Gentiles be blessed" [Gal. 3:8; trans. mine]) and Hab. 2:4 ("He who through faith is righteous shall live" [Gal. 3:11]). This principle of faith collides with the curse of the law (Gal. 3:10, 12), which Christ has removed (v. 13). Abraham is illustrative of a basic salvation-historical principle: the gospel is for the Gentiles by faith alone and stands over against the curse and condemnation of the Torah. Thus, we can say that although both chapters interpret salvation-history, Galatians 3 focuses on the principles that constitute that history, whereas Romans 4 centers on the existential stance of Abraham's personal faith as example for all believers.

Galatians 3, with its emphasis on a fulfilled promise and its omission of hope (*elpizō* is absent from Galatians; *elpis* occurs only in Gal. 5:5), suggests a structure of realized eschatology in which the fullness of eschatological reality coincides with the Christ-event. In Romans, however, the future-eschatological thrust is much more prominent (cf. Romans 5–8). Faith in the promise characterizes both Abraham and Christians (Rom. 4:20–25), and promise and hope (5:1–2) seem to fuse into each other.

CONTINUITY AND DISCONTINUITY

Romans 4 allows for the continuity of salvation-history, whereas Galatians 3 focuses on its discontinuity. To be sure, Rom. 4:13–16 also opposes the Torah to the promise and states that faith is "emptied" when it is based on the law (v. 14). On this point Paul never wavers. However, the movement of the argument in Galatians 3 is different from that in Romans 4.

Because Galatians 3 combats Judaizers who argue for the salvation-historical combination of Torah and Christ, Paul's response is polemical and antithetical. He insists that the scope of the promise is blessing for the Gentiles by faith alone. Because Christ has destroyed the curse of the law, those who compromise the antithesis between faith and the law are severed from Christ (Gal. 3:25; cf. 5:4). Christ then fulfills the promise to Abraham but inserts himself as a discontinuous reality in a salvation-history that after Abraham was dominated by the prison of the law (v. 17).

Romans 4, to the contrary, is engaged in a dialogue with Jews. Its scope is suggested by Rom. 3:29: "Or is God the God of Jews only? Is he not the God of Gentiles also?" The key of the argument extends beyond "faith in Christ" versus "the works of the law" (cf. Gal. 3:2, 5) to the theme "I have made you the father of many nations" (Rom. 4:17; cf. Gen. 17:5). In other words, Abraham's seed (*sperma*) is constituted by two peoples: the "uncircumcised" (*akrobystia*) and the "circumcised" (*peritomē*; cf. Rom. 4:16: ". . . not only to the adherents of the law but also to those who share the faith of Abraham, for he is the father of us all"; cf. also v. 12). The unity and coequality of these peoples in the one church of Jews and Gentiles in the gospel is the focus of the argument.[6] Abraham is the origin and living exemplar of justifying faith in salvation-history: those who "walk in his footsteps" (v. 12: *tois stoichousin tois ichnesin*, i.e., both Jews and Gentiles) constitute the one church of Christ.

The dialogue with Jews in Romans 4 has a more conciliatory tone than the polemic against the Judaizers in Galatians 3. Notwithstanding Rom. 4:13–16, Paul attempts to demonstrate from Scripture—which is the common bond between Jew and Christian—the salvation-historical reality of faith in God's justifying act. Faith as trust is the basic principle for the interpretation of Scripture, and its christological "confirmation" is added at the end as a capstone (Rom. 4:24–25). Christology does not serve (as in Galatians 3) to pinpoint the curse of the law and its inferior origin and status. Rather, it acts as a final confirmation of the interpretation of Scripture (Rom. 4:23–25), so that indeed "the law is upheld" (Rom. 3:21, 31). The reader of Romans 4 is not confronted as is the Judaizer in Galatians 3 with a sharp Christocentric discontinuity in salvation-history. Instead, Paul underlines the facticity of Abraham's faith as example for both Jews and Gentiles (Rom. 4:12); and it is this continuous reality of faith, beginning with Abraham and confirmed by Christ, that constitutes, notwithstanding verses 14–16, the major emphasis of the passage. The polemic in the dialogue is, to be sure, present: the blindness of the Jew who rejects his forefather Abraham as the one who lives by faith and not by Torah and circumcision (vv. 13–15). The Jew is here admonished to become a "true" Jew like Abraham, but Judaism is not "demonized," as threatens to occur in Galatians 3. It is apparent that Romans 4 and Galatians 3 explicate different "situational" interests: Romans 4 unfolds the thesis of Rom. 3:29–31 (God justifies both Jew and Gentile by faith; "we uphold the law"), whereas Galatians 3 explicates the antithesis of verses 2–5 (faith vs. law).

The Abraham Story and the Adam Story

We should be aware of the fact that Romans introduces both Abraham and Adam, whereas the Adam story is absent from Galatians. Abraham and Adam complement each other in Romans (chapters 4 and 5:12–21). Abraham typifies salvation-history, and Adam typifies the dualistic apocalyptic theology of the two ages. The focus of the Abraham story is the relation of Jew and Gentile within the basic continuity of God's faithfulness to his plan of salvation. Christ functions here to confirm the stance of faith that Abraham has already exhibited and that applies to all "who walk in his footsteps," both the circumcised and the uncircumcised (Rom. 4:12; cf. vv. 24–25).

The Adam typology, to the contrary, operates not in terms of continuity but in terms of discontinuity. Here, the last (eschatological) Adam reverses radically what the first Adam has initiated in world history (Rom. 5:12–21; cf. 1 Cor. 15:20–22), so that the dualistic, apocalyptic thrust of the Adam typology underscores the radical newness of God's act in Christ. Thus, the Adam typology centers on the ontological antithesis of death and life, whereas the Abraham story focuses on the continuity of faith within salvation-history. In the Adam typology the death of Christ functions as the negation of the old world's values and as the transformation of the believer into a resurrection mode of existence. Christ is here the initiator of the new eschatological world of "life" (Rom. 5:17, 18, 21) and the "new creation" (cf. Gal. 6:15; 2 Cor. 5:17). Within this apocalyptic Adam typology, there is no room for a figure like Abraham who already constitutes within the old the seed or reality of the new to come. Adam and Abraham cannot be integrated easily into a "systematic" view of history, because both figures operate on different tracks and levels in Paul's thought. The Adam story, indeed, transcends "the Jewish question" of the relation between Jew and Greek, for the ultimate division in humankind is not between Jew and Greek but between being "in Adam" or "in Christ." The religious-cultural dualism of Jew and Greek is transcended by an ontological dualism that provides the ground for the celebration by the church of its new being in Christ. In the light of his redemptive reversal of the human condition "in Adam," all other distinctions fall away. According to Paul, Christ is not a new Abraham* or a new Moses but the new eschatological Adam.

We can say, then, that Christ confirms and fulfills Abraham's faith (Romans 4) but that he, as the new Adam, reverses the ontological, cosmic consequences of Adam's deed, because in his obedience the "new man" and the "new creation" are realized. Along these lines Paul can confirm both the continuity with the old dispensation (Romans 4) and the discontinuity of the new dispensation (Romans 5; cf. also 2 Corinthians 3, where both the continuity and discontinuity with the old dispensation are stressed).

The Abraham story in Galatians 3 has a different focus. Here the interpretative key is discontinuity. The new age of faith is only actualized in Christ (Gal. 3:22, 23, 25), whereas the old age is characterized by bondage to sin (v. 22), which is evoked by the law (v. 19). Although Abraham constitutes an enclave of faith in the old age (vv. 6–9), he is cast not so much as the actualizer of faith but as the recipient of God's promise, and thus represents the pro-evangelion (v. 8; cf. vv. 15–18). It strikes us that the Abraham story of Galatians incorporates features of both the Abraham story and the Adam story of Romans. But because Paul does not employ the Adam story in Galatians, he cryptically inserts the dualistic

---

*We expect Abraham rather than Adam to be "the type of the coming one" (Rom. 5:14). In that case, Christ fulfills the obedience of Abraham and so undoes the disobedience of Adam. It seems that Hebrews connects the obedience of Abraham with the superior obedience of Christ (Heb. 11:8–10; 12:2; 13:13, esp. 2:10; 4:15; 5:8–10). However, in Rom. 5:14 the context dictates the translation of *typos* not as type but as antitype (cf. Käsemann: "*Gegenbild*").

Adamic motif of the two ages into the Abraham story for the sake of his argument and thus disrupts the logical sequence of his thought (see Chapter 4, below). The new age of faith and our being in Christ annuls the old age of our service under the "custodian" of the law (Gal. 3:24–28). This apocalyptic motif of discontinuity dominates Paul's interpretation of the Abraham story in Galatians, because the promise to Abraham— actualized by Christ as his exclusive seed—is sharply contrasted with the law and its curse.

In Romans 4 and 5:12–21, Paul demonstrates the continuity and the discontinuity with the old age. God confirms Abraham's faith as the prototype of our faith in Christ (Romans 4), but the possibility of such a faith is ultimately dependent on the ontological renewal of our being in Christ, who abolishes our old being in Adam (Rom. 5:12–21).

In Galatians 3 Paul attacks Judaizers, who fuse Abraham, the Torah, and Christ. Because he is not interested in showing the continuity of the new and the old, he therefore interprets the Abraham story in an utterly discontinuous way. It seems as if the Abraham story of Galatians has more features in common with the Adam story of Rom. 5:12–21 than with its parallel story in Romans, notwithstanding the common emphasis on the promise. The reason for this lies in Paul's need to interpret the Abraham story in Galatians dualistically, because he must safeguard the *solus Christus* and the *sola fide* of his gospel against the Judaizing synthesis of law and gospel (cf. the incorporation motif of Rom. 5:12–21 which occurs in Gal. 3:27–29). The extremely different situations in Galatia and Rome dictate the different emphases of the argument.

The Jewish-Dialogical Thrust of Romans 4

The Jewish-dialogical thrust of the argument is indeed prominent in Romans 4 in at least three separate areas:

(1) Circumcision—explicitly avoided in Galatians 3, and condemned throughout the letter (Gal. 5:2, 3, 11; 6:12, 13, 15)—emerges in Rom. 4:11 in a positive light. This occurs nowhere else in the Pauline letters (cf. its metaphorical interpretation in Phil. 3:3; cf. Col. 2:11). Paul accepts circumcision here as a physical seal of faith-righteousness and appeals to Genesis 17, the "circumcision chapter" of Scripture—something he avoids in Galatians 3 (cf. Gen. 17:10 in Rom. 4:11). Moreover, the attack on circumcision in Galatians is practically absent in Romans.

(2) The Jewish Abraham ("our natural forefather," Rom. 4:1 [trans. mine]) appears in a Christianized form in Rom. 4:1–12. He is the "godless one" (*asebēs*), who in terms of Ps. 32:1 (Rom. 4:7–8) receives justification

(v. 13). Paul emphasizes "to reckon" (*logizomai*) seven times in verses 1–11 in order to characterize Abraham as the example of the *justificatio impii* (cf. v. 5). The "promise" (Rom. 4:13–21) is subsumed under God's gracious "reckoning" in Romans 4, whereas Galatians 3 highlights the "promise" in its salvation-historical character and in its fulfillment in Christ. Because faith is, in Romans 4, not just a promise to Abraham, which is only actualized in Christ (cf. Galatians 3), promise and faith are permanent realities for both Old Testament believers and Christians. But how can Abraham be both a Jew and a "Christian"? Paul's hermeneutical skill is apparent here, for he weaves past and present together and contemporizes Abraham as a Christian type. In Abraham's case the Old Testament is consonant with the Christian gospel and proclaims the same "gospel." Because Abraham is committed to justification by faith (Rom. 4:5, 13), he is the father of two peoples—Jews and Gentiles—in one church. The ecclesiological focus of unity is present in both chapters but executed in a very different way. The christological focus of Galatians 3 serves the antithesis between law and gospel, whereas the theocentric thrust of Romans 4 brings Scripture and gospel together in Abraham.

(3) The Old Testament characterization of faith as unconditional trust marks Romans 4, especially in its description of the attitude of faith (Rom. 4:17–21). In contrast to the Christocentric content of faith in Galatians 3, where faith can only be "belief in Christ," faith is, in Romans 4, essentially "trust" and is theocentric (Abraham trusts in the God who raises the dead, in the God who justifies the ungodly); it is defined as obedient trust, and hope in God. Faith is trust in the promise of God and thus stubborn hope as opposed to empirical "hopelessness" (4:19) and "distrust" (4:20). The christological object of faith comes only at the end (4:24–25), and then in a theocentric-credal formulation: "[we] who believe in him that raised from the dead Jesus our Lord" (v. 24). The function of the theocentric focus is to stress the analogy between our faith and Abraham's justification. This "soft" christological emphasis on faith in Romans 4 has often misled interpreters into thinking that Paul simply celebrates the phenomenon of "faith" rather than its object, Christ. "When Paul speaks of faith, he is referring to something which did not begin with Christianity, but is an original and permanent element of all genuinely religious life, even though in some forms of religion, as in the extreme legalist form of Judaism, faith is empty of meaning."[7] Romans 4 inclines toward a celebration of faith for the sake of faith, although Paul clearly "Christianizes" Abraham, because the object of Abraham's faith, "the God who raises the dead," is the same God as he "who raised Jesus our Lord from

the dead" (vv. 17, 24–25). Paul's focus on faith in Romans 4 is not exclusively Christocentric but has a more comprehensive character, for he invites Jews to the saving reality of justifying faith as the clue to their own scriptures, a clue that the Christ-event has disclosed.

THE LAW IN GALATIANS 3 AND ROMANS 7[8]

Galatians is a polemical letter and addresses itself to a crisis situation in which clear-cut decisions are demanded. The Judaizing synthesis of Abraham-promise-Torah and Christ demands a response that opposes Torah and Christ as antithetical principles, so that confessing Christ negates Torah and circumcision.

In Romans, Paul does not face an apostasy of Judaizers but is engaged in a dialogue with Jews and Jewish Christians about his stance toward the Torah as consistent with the faithfulness of God toward Israel in the gospel. In Galatians, Paul is on the attack against Christians who have reintroduced the Torah into the gospel, whereas in Romans he argues with Jews, who fail to see that only God's act in Christ can save them from the condemnation of the law. Romans exhibits a polemic of persuasion, Galatians a polemic of confrontation; Romans offers a balanced, well-ordered discussion, whereas Galatians is a "combat" letter. It is written in a sarcastic and aggressive mood; the argument is disruptive, fragmentary, and at times ambiguous, and its polemical debate does not yield a systematic order.

Although Romans 7 makes statements about the law that are even more shocking and radical than their counterparts in Galatians 3, the context is different, as a comparison of the "apologies of the law" in Rom. 7:7–13 and Gal. 3:19–20 reveals. The argument in Gal. 3:19–20 is fragmentary and has a distinctively negative flavor, so that even the divine origin of the Torah is called into question (3:20). The "apology" is cryptic and surfaces only after the law has been characterized as a curse that is opposed to the promise and its blessing. The Torah not only curses Christ on the tree, but it is also an illegitimate interloper that splits salvation-history apart and inserts itself between the promise and Christ. It is denounced by Scripture (Hab. 2:4 vs. Lev. 18:5 [Gal. 3:11, 12]) and is an illegitimate codicil to the "testament" of the promise (Gal. 3:15). The law has a negative ontological dimension (3:19b, 20), whereas its positive function is restricted to the retrospect of salvation-history. The prison and custodian status of the law is a divine necessity only in hindsight; the law functions to increase the trespasses as the necessary and negative counterpart of the new reality of Christ and faith. Bondage under the law is the dark foil for our freedom in

Christ. The divine nature of the law, however, is hardly alluded to in Galatians 3 (v. 19a) and the cryptic "apology of the law" (3:19-22) does not fully succeed.

In Romans, to the contrary, there is a full apology of the law (Rom. 7:7-13) that spills over into verses 14-25 and serves to put Paul's radical statement of 7:5 in its proper light: "While we were living in the flesh, our sinful passions, aroused by the law, were at work in our members to bear fruit for death." The apology in Romans succeeds because here Paul not only gives a positive ontology of the Torah but also makes important distinctions between the law's ontological and ontic functions—something Galatians does not do. Where in Galatians 3 can we find statements like "The law is holy, and the commandment is holy and just and good" (Rom. 7:12) or "the law is spiritual" (Rom. 7:14)? Where in Galatians do we hear, "For I delight in the law of God, in my inmost self" (Rom. 7:22)? Galatians 3 does not posit, "Do we then overthrow the law by this faith? By no means! On the contrary, we uphold the law" (Rom. 3:31). It offers only a negative counterpart, "Is the law then against the promises of God? Certainly not!" (Gal. 3:21). Paul's claim that for believers "the just requirement of the law is fulfilled" (Rom. 8:4: *plērōthē*) is only cryptically and negatively stated in Gal. 5:23 (but cf. Gal. 5:14). It would be strange indeed for Paul in Galatians to extol the "giving of the law" as one of Israel's privileges (Rom. 9:4-5) or to discuss the "advantage of the Jew" (Rom. 3:1). A "third use" of the law for Christians must rely almost completely on Romans, because it has no solid support in Galatians. It is interesting that Galatians speaks about "fulfilling the law of Christ" (*ton nomon tou Christou*, 6:2)—an expression not used in Romans—but not about "upholding the law" (Rom. 3:31).[9] The "law of Christ" refers no doubt to Gal. 5:14, where Paul claims that the "one word" of the Old Testament love commandment (Lev. 19:18) fulfills "the whole law" (cf. Rom. 13:9). However, the precise relation of the Torah to "the law of Christ" remains unclear.

The "Jewish question" in Romans gives the law a profile that we do not expect after reading Galatians. The distinction between the ontology of the law and its anthropological function in Romans 7 permits Paul to differentiate between the law's divine origin and its abuse in the human situation by the power of sin. Thus, he is able to stress its positive function both in God's salvation-history (i.e., its ability to unmask the power of sin for what it really is [v. 13]; cf. Gal. 3:19) and as the expression of God's will for Christians (Rom. 8:4, 7). The relation of law to gospel is therefore different in Galatians and Romans. In Galatians the antithesis between law and gospel dominates the discussion, because the law and Christ collide at the tree (Gal. 3:13), where the law curses Christ. Furthermore, the law inserts itself illegitimately between the promise and Christ and blocks the line of salvation-history (Gal. 3:17–18).

Although there is in Romans a similar collision between the promise, Christ, and the law (Rom. 4:13–14; 7:5–6; 8:1–3), the scope of the argument is different. The law's inability is stressed (Rom. 8:3) rather than its curse. Christ does not "abolish" the law (Rom. 3:31) but rather fulfills the law's intent (Rom. 8:4; cf. 9:31). To be sure, in Romans, Christ is also "the end of the law" (Rom. 10:4)—in a context where this can only mean "the law is finished"—and the salvation-historical dualism of Galatians is likewise present in Rom. 4:13–14 and Rom. 7:4–6. Yet the law-gospel issue is here much less antithetical, because the positive ontology of the law allows its divine intent to be taken up into the gospel. Therefore, although Christ is the end of the law, he also fulfills its intent (Rom. 10:4; cf. 3:31; 8:3, 4, 7; 9:31).

The apology of the law in Rom. 7:7–13 actually extends itself into a discussion of the human plight under the law in Rom. 7:14–25. In the course of the argument, Paul unfolds an anthropology that in autobiographical manner depicts the schizoid status of the old Adam under the law. Just because the law expresses the divine will, and because "my inmost self" (v. 22) and "the law of my mind" (v. 23) consent to the law, the experience of the power of sin as constitutive of my being (v. 14) is all the more desperate. Sin executes its power in me not only by paralyzing my will but also by deceiving me through the law (Rom. 7:11). However, the demonic use of the law by sin does not mean that the law itself is satanic. Although the law, like Satan, incites me, condemns me, and kills me, the law uncovers the power of sin within me as my principal enemy. Thus the law becomes my enemy not because of its ontological status and its illegitimate incursion into salvation-history (as in Galatians 3) but because it confronts me with who I am: a person who "covets" (Rom. 7:7).

In Romans, Paul develops in the context of the law a specific anthropology (Rom. 7:7–25); Galatians has a cryptic parallel to this in Gal. 5:13–24 but not in chapter 3. The anthropological, subjective dimension of the law is much more apparent in Romans than in Paul's salvation-historical and ontological language about the law in Galatians. Whereas in Galatians the law functions in the retrospect of salvation-history to seal our sin before God, whether we are aware of it or not, in Romans the subjective, existential element surfaces. Here the issue of my "own righteousness" (*idia dikaiosunē*, Rom. 10:3) appears; it is absent in Galatians. It follows, then, that the theme of "boasting" is focal in Romans (2:17, 23; 3:27; 4:2), whereas it is much less central, if not peripheral, in Galatians (6:13; cf. also 6:4, 14). The experience of sin, evoked by the law (Rom. 3:20; 7:7–13), is not simply a confession of Christian hindsight, as if it is unknown to the pre-Christian Jew (cf. esp. Paul's appeal to Jewish experience in Rom. 2:1–29). Romans at least suggests that faith in Christ answers on some level the Jew's awareness of sin, which the confrontation with the law brings about (cf. Luther's "second use" of the law that convicts the person of sin). Faith in Christ is, to be sure, a transfer from the blindness and ignorance of sin to a radical new level of perception of my plight before God in Christ. However, the hindsight of faith is accompanied in Romans by a sense of relief from previous awareness of sin and from the condemning effect of the law. In other words, Romans—but not Galatians—leaves some room for the "pedagogy" of the law (see Chapter 11, below).

Romans is a "dialogue with Jews" and addresses former God-fearers, proselytes, and Jews. Therefore, "the Jewish question" in Rome necessitates a posture which differs from that toward the Judaizing problem in Galatia.

Paul argues in Romans the function of the law within the compass of God's faithfulness and salvation-historical plan. Although Christ is "the end of the law" (Rom. 10:4), he is also the one who fulfills the intent of the law (Rom. 8:3–4). The antithesis between Christ and the law is not due so much to the ontological status of the law (Galatians 3) as to its anthropological failure (Romans 7). Although Christ brings the era of the Torah to an end (Rom. 10:4), the law was necessary because it functioned as the negative counterpart (Rom. 4:13; 5:13, 20; 7:13) to the positive righteousness of God in Christ (3:21). On this point Romans and Galatians agree (Gal. 3:19–25). However, in Romans, Paul also leaves room for the suggestion that the law brings knowledge of sin (Rom. 3:20; 7:7–25), not only when we in Christ look back on our former life under the law (Gal. 3:22–26) but also while we were still under the law (Rom. 2:1–29).

Since the dialogue with the Jew in the context of God's faithfulness (Rom. 3:3; 9:6, 14) stresses the priority of the Jew in the gospel, the apology of the law becomes necessary in a more vital sense than in Galatians, where the antithesis between promise, faith, and the law leaves room for only a questionable, or at least cryptic, apology of the law that hardly relieves the law's inferior status. In Romans, to the contrary, the law and Christ are not—as it were—ontological counterparts; they have become so only because of the depth of the human fall. In this way the

Marcionite tendencies of Galatians are overcome in Romans, not in the least because of the different contingency and argumentation of both letters.

The different emphases of Paul's interpretation of the law in Galatians and Romans may well have affected the discussion of the law in the history of doctrine. Edward A. Dowey states, "For Luther the chief connotation of law is self-salvation and condemnation, whereas for Calvin it is the structure of love."[10] Paul's contextual interpretation of the law in Romans and Galatians is not far removed from these various connotations of law, although—just as in Luther and Calvin—the coherent core of his teaching about the law remains constant.

I conclude, then, that—in spite of the basic coherence of Paul's interpretation of faith and the law in Galatians and Romans—the different contextual situations necessitate a contingent argument that reveals both the versatility of Paul's hermeneutic and the richness of his thought. The gospel indeed allows a wide diversity of interpretation without sacrificing its coherent center.

7

Tradition and Gospel

PAUL AS INTERPRETER

Paul's originality and creativity are to be found not in his doctrinal architecture but in his hermeneutic. Understanding Paul, then, means understanding the relationship between tradition and interpretation in his thought.

The perennial Jesus-Paul debate, which arose around the turn of the century, has blinded many interpreters to the texture of Paul's thought. Paul has been indicted as the doctrinal theologian who perverted the Galilean gospel of Jesus and turned it into theological doctrines about the Son of God, original sin, the atonement, and so on. Paul was considered to be the "first theologian of the church," the "true founder of Christianity," the "Hellenizer" of the gospel, or the hairsplitting scholarly rabbi who perverted the simple gospel of Jesus.[1]* "Before Paul came," William Wrede argued, Christianity was only "an inner Jewish sect," but after Paul there was a "Christian Church."[2] He characterizes Paul as "the second founder of Christianity," who pushed "the greater one, whom he meant to serve completely into the background."[3]

The tide turned when Wilhelm Heitmüller pointed to Hellenistic Christianity as the necessary intermediary between Jesus and Paul;[4] and more recently, Jewish-Hellenistic Christianity was described as a separate entity alongside Hellenistic Christianity. Some scholars even disclaimed Paul's originality almost completely and turned him into a traditionalist.[5] He became someone who stood on the shoulders of Christian theologians and missionaries who are unknown to us and whose writings have not survived. However, with the form-critical investigation of the Pauline letters,[6] a more fruitful approach has dawned. Paul was discovered to be an interpreter of the tradition rather than a systematic theologian or mere traditionalist. Attention now focused on the character of Paul's interpretation of the tradition.

What, then, is the specific character of Paul's interpretation of the tradition? Is he a traditionalist who adopts the Antiochene gospel and

---

*The Jesus versus Paul debate still continues in the dialogue between Judaism and Christianity (cf. Martin Buber, Leo Baeck, Hans Joachim Schoeps, Schalom Ben-Chorin); cf. also Ethelbert Stauffer (*Jesus, Paulus und wir*); John Knox (*The Ethic of Jesus in the Teaching of the Church*); and Gerhard Ebeling, "Jesus and Faith," in *Word and Faith*, pp. 201–46.

simply transmits it to the people of his mission field? Does he, in fact, continue his former rabbinic-exegetical training? Is he engaged with the gospel in the same way he was engaged with the halakah and the Torah, that is, with the "traditions of my fathers" (Gal. 1:14)? If this is the case, Paul simply transferred his traditional Jewish hermeneutic to the new content of the gospel.

Or is Paul a revolutionary, who adopts the Antiochene gospel only in order to transform it, so that his interpretation does not conserve the tradition but becomes instead the occasion for new structures of thought and heterodoxy (cf. Marcion and the Gnostics). In fact, has Paul not often been viewed as friend of heretics and Gnostics and as an enemy of the traditional catholic orthodox consensus (cf. Reitzenstein, "Paul the greatest Gnostic of them all")?[7] His influence in church history has indeed been that of a revolutionary; we have only to remember Marcion, Valentinian Gnostics, Augustine, Luther and the Reformation, John Wesley, and Neo-orthodoxy with its inception in Barth's *Commentary on Romans*. But we must also recall the suspicion, suppression, and misinterpretation of Paul's fate in the church (2 Pet. 3:15–16; Acts; the Pastorals; the Apologists).

The Nature of Interpretation

The discovery of Paul the interpreter strengthens the case for the particularity and linguistic versatility of his thought. An interpreter concentrates on the function of language in a specific historical context because his hermeneutic loses its motivational power and focus without the specificity of the context.

We must remember here the complexity of the term "interpretation." After all, every translator is an interpreter unless he chooses to be simply a transliterator like, for instance, Origen in the second column of his *Hexapla* or Aquila in his Greek translation of the Old Testament. Translation is always a form of transposition. The burden of every interpretation is "that sayings which originally meant one thing later on were interpreted to mean something else, something which was felt to be more relevant to human conditions of later times."[8] An interpreter, then, is involved in the business of being faithful to the old text for a new situation, and the implicit or explicit "transformation" of the original that this procedure involves.

An interpreter may well have a revolutionary effect, but he does not think of himself as a creative genius or a revolutionary in the usual sense— someone who breaks with the old and who creates *de novo*. Although his interpretation may break new ground, he does not purposely negate the tradition in order to found a new movement in the history of thought. Although every revolution in the history of thought owes more to the tradition than it wants to acknowledge, the intent and attitude of the interpreter toward the tradition is decisive.

Paul is not a self-styled revolutionary, nor is he a schismatic who breaks the continuity with the past and founds a "new church"—like, for instance, a Simon Magus or a Valentinus. Jesus and Paul differ decisively in this respect; Jesus indeed breaks with the Jewish tradition, which is confirmed by the creation of the Gospel genre after his death and resurrection, whereas Paul consciously adopts the tradition of the Antioch church after his conversion and interprets it in his gospel.

Interpretation both preserves and transforms, because continuity and discontinuity, stability and adaptability, are inherent in every process of interpretation. Every interpreter insists that he is not an innovator but a faithful translator of the tradition, and Paul is no exception: "This is how one should regard us, as servants of Christ and stewards of the mysteries of God. Moreover it is required of stewards that they be found trustworthy [*pistos*]" (1 Cor. 4:1-2). However, Paul's self-estimate occurs in the face of an opposition that accuses him of innovation (Galatians), apostasy (Romans 9–11), or distortion (2 Corinthians 10–13). And our reflections on interpretation should not import into Paul the modern historical distinction in interpretation between the "original" and the "translation."[9]

Faithfulness (cf. 1 Cor. 4:2) to the tradition is difficult to measure. Novelty of language cannot be a criterion because it may signify either distortion or faithful rendering of tradition. In fact, an interpreter becomes faithless if he rigidly uses language that was meant for a different time and place in the present. In that case, tradition becomes a frozen, dogmatic language that is supposedly valid for all occasions. In other words, the tradition becomes "traditionalist" and—however sacrosanct—unintelligible. Language manifests our historicity; unless "new" language is found, the "old" tradition cannot come to speech again for new occasions. Language is faithful when the *Sachverhalt* (the material content) of the tradition is preserved in a new *Sprachgestalt* (linguistic expression). Because stability and adaptability dominate the hermeneutical process, the interaction between preservation and transformation is crucial in interpretation. A new hermeneutical situation and a new hearing of a text may uncover deeper meanings that the "old" text did not seem to contain in its own historical context. Because every text enters history and begins its own history of interpretation, interpretations of a text allow both surface and deeper meanings to emerge.

PAUL AND THE TRADITION

Paul's apostolic authority complicates his relation to the tradition, for he claims to be not just *an* interpreter but *the* interpreter of the tradition (or at least one of *the* interpreters). Because he is not a slave of the tradition but a "slave" of Christ and called to be an apostle (Rom. 1:1; Gal. 1:10), he is its free interpreter. "Am I not free? Am I not an apostle? Have I not seen Jesus our Lord? Are not you my workmanship in the Lord?" (1 Cor. 9:1); "Where the Spirit of the Lord is, there is freedom" (2 Cor. 3:17); "The letter kills, but the Spirit gives life" (2 Cor. 3:6; trans. mine). This is especially true for an apostle who in sovereign freedom shifts or expands the tradition in his interpretation, in order to bring its true meaning to life for the particular concerns of his churches (1 Cor. 15:3–5; cf. vv. 6–8). 1 Corinthians 15:1–11 illustrates it vividly: Paul's preparation for his debate with the Corinthians on the resurrection of the dead (vv. 12–50) has a twofold function. It establishes not only the apostolic consensus about the resurrection of Christ (vv. 1–7, 11) but also the unique authority of Paul's apostolic interpretation of this tradition (vv. 1, 8–10). Paul is not only a transmitter of the apostolic tradition (vv. 1–7) but also an independent apostle, because he is the "last" apostle to receive a resurrection appearance and mandate from Christ. Because his *logos* (account, interpretation; v. 1) of the tradition is faithful, it has a fundamental authority and thus makes his interpretation of the resurrection in verses 12–50 authoritative and binding on the Corinthians.

In considering Paul's free interpretation of the tradition, we should notice the disagreements among scholars when they try to isolate pre-Pauline tradition. Those disagreements testify to the interpretive freedom with which Paul handles tradition in his gospel. In Rom. 3:24–26, for example, it has proven difficult to delineate precisely where Pauline additions occur and even where the tradition begins (in v. 24 or v. 25?). However, at the time of the Pastorals the tradition is much more clearly delineated because it is now on the way to becoming a sacrosanct text (e.g., 1 Tim. 3:16, with its introductory formula; cf. also 2 Tim. 2:11).

A similar phenomenon occurs with Paul's interpretation of Old Testament texts. Citation formulas are interspersed with running commentaries, allusions, and free citations. In this context the comments of Thomas Walder Manson are relevant:

> We are long accustomed to distinguish carefully between the text which—
> in more senses than one—is sacred, and the commentary upon it and
> exposition of it. We tend to think of the text as objective fact and
> interpretation as subjective opinion. It may be doubted whether the early

Jewish and Christian translators and expositors of Scripture made any such sharp distinction. For them the meaning of the text was of primary importance; and they seem to have had greater confidence than we moderns in their ability to find it. Once found it became a clear duty to express it; and accurate reproduction of the traditional wording of the Divine oracles took second place to publication of what was held to be their essential meaning and immediate application. Odd as it may seem to us, the freedom with which they handled the Biblical text is a direct result of the supreme importance which they attached to it."[10]

And Edward Earle Ellis comments:

In selecting a particular version or in creating an *ad hoc* rendering Paul views his citation as thereby more accurately expressing the true meaning of Scripture. For Paul, as for the rabbis, the "letter" was sacred; but unlike some rabbis, Paul valued the "letter" not for itself alone but for the meaning which it conveyed. His idea of a quotation was not a worshipping of the letter or "parroting" of the text; neither was it an eisegesis, which arbitrarily imposed a foreign meaning upon the text. It was rather, in his eyes, a quotation-exposition, a midrashpesher, which drew from the text the meaning originally implanted there by the Holy Spirit and expressed that meaning in the most appropriate words and phrases known to him.[11]

THE IMMEDIACY OF REVELATION

Non verba sed tonitrua, Jerome says about the Pauline letters;[12] he hears "the thunder" when he reads "the words." The relation between tradition and gospel in Paul is marked by the *prophetic-pneumatic* character of his apostolate and hermeneutic. Although Paul does not employ the prophetic "Thus says the Lord," he is as aware as the Old Testament prophets of the immediacy of the divine word in his preaching and word (1 Thess. 1:8; 2:13; Rom. 1:16; 2 Cor. 2:14–16, etc.).

However, because he is an apostle, Paul is not simply a successor to the Old Testament prophets but the prophet-apostle who bridges the time between the resurrection of Christ and the general resurrection of the dead, when God's promises to Israel and the Gentiles will find their cosmic fulfillment. Although Paul does not describe his authority in the imagery of the prophets who claim to have been privy to the "council of God," Paul knows himself to be entrusted with the "mysteries of God" (1 Cor. 2:7–16; 4:2), which only a *pneumatikos* can grasp and which gives him an authority beyond human criticism: "The spiritual man judges all things, but is himself to be judged by no one" (1 Cor. 2:15); "and I think that I have the Spirit of God" (1 Cor. 7:40).

Paul almost arrogantly identifies himself with the gospel, as if the apostle *himself* is the incarnation of the truth of the gospel. But how can Paul identify obedience to the gospel with obedience to himself? Where is Paul's sense of humility in all this, especially as he declares, "I am . . . unfit to be called an apostle" (1 Cor. 15:9)? Moreover, how can he be so flexible in one situation (Phil. 1:15), so careful in another (1 Cor. 4:1–4), and yet claim his interpretation of the gospel to be the only true version in still other situations (Gal. 1:6–9; 2 Corinthians 10–13)? How can he demand that Christians imitate *him* (1 Cor. 4:16; 1 Cor. 11:1; 1 Thess. 1:6) and yet refuse "fan club" recognition (1 Cor. 1:14–17)? When the interpreter becomes himself the criterion of the truth, objective norms and warrants are ignored. What then does legitimize and authenticate Paul's interpretation as divine, authoritative word, and what are the limits of an interpretation inspired by the Spirit or given by direct revelation (Gal. 1:12; cf. 1 Cor. 14:6)? Is the Spirit here the sole criterion? And if not, how can a confession as brief as "Jesus is Lord" exercise any meaningful control (1 Cor. 12:3)? The wrestling of the Old Testament with false prophecy emerges here in ·a new way. Thus, before long, the church—like the Old Testament (Deut. 13:1–3; 18:20–22; Jer. 28:9)—established objective criteria for the utterances of the Spirit by means of explicit christological confessions or the *regula fidei* (cf. already John 4:1–6).

What shall be the criterion for interpretation at a time when credal confessions have not yet been established or are too succinct and fragmentary to act as controls over the Spirit? Does the effectiveness of an interpretation denote its truth in that case? When Paul locates the authenticity of the gospel in its power (*dynamis*, Rom. 1:16) and in its empirical effectiveness (1 Thess. 1:5; 2:13; 1 Cor. 4:14) or in his apostolic fruit (*karpos*; cf. "work," *ergon*; 1 Cor. 9:1), how shall the content and identity of the gospel be checked, when no explicit "rule of faith" or normative "sayings of Jesus" or "authoritative confessions" exist that can arbitrate the truth-claim of this "power"?

Paul's apostolic calling now gives him an immediate access to the truth (1 Cor. 9:1; Gal. 1:12), that is, pneumatic immediacy (1 Cor. 2:7–16), because it disallows human mediation (Gal. 1:12), human criteria, or human criticism (1 Cor. 2:15; 4:3–4): "For I did not receive it [the gospel] from man, nor was I taught it, but it came through a revelation of Jesus Christ" (Gal. 1:12). This claim makes the hermeneutical relation between pneumatic immediacy and human mediation an urgent problem, for how does Paul understand his function as an interpreter of the transmitted tradition when he, as an apostle, claims immediacy of access to the gospel without human mediation (Gal. 1:11–12)? And how is Paul's claim of absolute authority, based on the immediate reception of the gospel (Gal. 1:11–12), balanced by his own admission of its human mediation (1 Cor. 11:23; 15:3)?

The problem is even more complex, for Paul cannot simply be cast as a fanatic or mystagogue whose authority is in all cases inviolable and absolute. He is no *theios aner* like Apollonius of Tyana or an epiphany of the deity. It is therefore important to understand the various levels of his claims to authority. For example, when the truth of the gospel is at stake Paul appeals rarely to himself but regularly to the gospel. Furthermore, there are at least three restraints on his authoritative immediacy: (1) the words of the Lord (1 Cor. 7:10, 25; 9:14); (2) a "judgment" (*gnōme*) on ethical matters (1 Cor. 7:25, 40) that is open to discussion; (3) an eschatological reservation that leaves the final judgment to God (1 Cor. 4:4; cf. esp. Paul's own subjection to it in 1 Cor. 9:24–26).

Therefore, even when Paul claims pneumatic immediacy in his apostolic mission, it transgresses neither the freedom of his churches, for which the truth of the gospel has set them free, nor the final eschatological judgment on Paul's own faithfulness (1 Cor. 4:1–5). The delicate balance between apostolic authority and the freedom of the churches explains Paul's almost contradictory speech in Rom. 1:11–12 (cf. Rom. 15:14–16). "For I long to see you, that I may *impart* to you some spiritual gift to strengthen you, that is, that we may be *mutually encouraged* by each other's faith, both yours and mine" (italics mine).

TRADITION AND GOSPEL

Paul and the Old Testament Prophets

The apostle stands on the shoulders of the prophets. Paul proclaims to the Gentiles *the gospel* which the prophets proclaimed before him as *promise* (Rom. 1:1–15). Moreover, he calls himself "a servant of Christ Jesus, called to be an apostle, set apart for the gospel of God" (Rom. 1:1). The term "servant" or "slave" (*doulos*) is not a term of humility but a prophetic title[13] and is nowhere used for church members in the Pauline letters. Paul then adopts the Old Testament prophetic function of the *ebed* (servant; cf. also Gal. 1:10) and describes his call in terms that are analogous to the call of the prophet Jeremiah and the *Ebed* in Second Isaiah (cf. "set aside from the womb" [Gal. 1:15, trans. mine; cf. Rom 1:1]). Acts 13:47 correctly understands the apostle Paul as the successor of "the servant": "I have set you to be a light for the Gentiles, that you may bring salvation to the uttermost parts of the earth" (Isa. 49:6, trans. mine).

The apostle then is the eschatological successor of the prophets, just as "the gospel of God" (Rom. 1:1) is the eschatological confirmation of God's promises to the prophets (Rom. 1:2). Paul derives the term "gospel" in all likelihood from Second Isaiah: "How beautiful upon the mountains are the feet of him who brings *tidings of good* [LXX: *podes euangelizomenou*], who publishes salvation, who says to Zion 'Your God reigns' " (Isa. 52:7); "The Spirit of the Lord God is upon me, because the Lord has anointed me to bring good tidings [LXX: *euangelisasthai*] to the afflicted" (Isa. 61:1).

Like Second Isaiah, Paul interprets Israel's traditions in the light of new divine eschatological acts in history. As the apostle of Jesus Christ, Paul is the herald of the gospel of God, which announces the impending fulfillment of Second Isaiah's eschatological promise of liberation, because he knows himself to be standing at the dawn of that promise: "And the glory of the Lord shall be revealed, and all flesh shall see it together" (Isa. 40:5).

According to Walther Zimmerli,[14] there is a twofold literary genre of the prophetic call in the Old Testament. One genre describes its visionary motifs: the throne of God, the divine council, the act of grace to the chosen, his purification, and the sending of the word into the mouth of the prophet (cf. Isa. 6:2–13; 1 Kings 22:19–22). Zimmerli calls this genre a *Sendungserzählung* ("sending narrative"). The other genre—the *Berufungserzählung* ("call narrative")—describes the call as a word event. Here there is dialogue, protest, commission, and exhortation (cf. Jer. 1:4–19 and Exod. 3:1—4:17).

In contrast to the visionary "sending narrative" of Acts 9, Paul himself describes his call after the "call narrative" of Jeremiah (Gal. 1:15–16) with its emphasis on a nonvisionary word event. This suggests that—although Paul is an apocalyptic theologian—he shares the prophetic heritage of the Old Testament and not the visionary characteristics of the apocalyptic "seers" (cf., e.g., his reluctant reporting of visions in 2 Cor. 12:1–6). Paul's proclamation of the gospel is not based on visionary constructions or apocalyptic revelations, and he does not ground his apostolic authority on an exaltation to the heavenly regions (cf. The Apocalypse of Paul).

Like his call, Paul's hermeneutic is in the prophetic manner. The time is past when the Old Testament prophets were considered as the great innovators and founders of Israel's ethical religion in contrast to its "legalistic" traditions.[15] Because the prophets are not innovators but stand within the basic covenant traditions of Israel, they interpret Israel's tradition to its new historical situation. Although according to Gerhard von Rad[16] their message is radically eschatological so that "the former things" are no longer to be remembered (Isa. 43:18) and old traditions are nullified because of God's new historical acts, the tension between the old and the new, or between the continuous and the discontinuous, is never surrendered. Isaiah exhorts Israel not only to forget "the former things" but also to remember them (Isa. 42:9; 43:9). Indeed, the characteristic of the prophetic interpretation of the tradition is typology (the "new" Exodus; the "new" or "eternal" covenant, etc.). To be sure, the interpretive tension may reach a breaking point when crucial Israelite traditions are ignored or so transformed that innovation collides with tradition (e.g., the omission of covenant terminology in the preexilic prophets; the transformation of the Davidic covenant into a "covenant of the people"; and the absence of the Mosaic covenant tradition in Second Isaiah). Nevertheless, the prophets view themselves as interpreters of Israel's traditions rather than as revolutionaries who negate them.

The interpretation of the tradition naturally differs from prophet to prophet. For some, the future of Israel depends on its response to the prophetic kerygma as it actualizes the tradition for the present (preexilic prophets). For others, a new eschatological act of God overshadows the "conditional" character of Israel's salvation, which is now viewed as an act of pure grace (e.g., Isaiah 40–45; Jer. 31:31–34; Ezek. 36:26–32).

Different interpretations of the tradition are evident when we compare, for instance, Deuteronomy and Second Isaiah. The Deuteronomist is a retrospective interpreter and Second Isaiah a prospective one. However, both are engaged in actualizing Israel's traditions for the present—Deuteronomy probably in the time of Josiah before the crisis of the exile, and Second Isaiah shortly after Cyrus's edict that permitted the exiles to return to Palestine.

Second Isaiah interprets the tradition in the light of God's new historical acts, that is, the homecoming of the exiles, whereas the Deuteronomist has no such new divine action to report. He calls upon Israel to remember and live out of the "openness of the past." The continuity with the past is therefore much stronger in Deuteronomy than in Second Isaiah, who balances the openness of the past with God's impending eschatological victory in his new creation of Israel.

In some sense the interpretative postures of Deuteronomy and Second Isaiah resemble respectively those of the Jewish tradition and Paul. For whereas Judaism is, like Deuteronomy, committed to the "openness" of the past in its halakic midrashim, Paul—like Second Isaiah—lives out of the eschatological future of God's promises. And again like Second Isaiah,

Paul interprets in however discontinuous ways God's new act also in a typological-eschatological manner, that is, in the context of Israel's covenant traditions and promises (cf. "the *new* covenant"; "the law of Christ"; "the Jerusalem above," etc.).[17] However, Paul as apostle of the Christ-event announces that the promises to Isaiah have entered their time of fulfillment because Christ has brought about "the end of the ages" (1 Cor. 10:11) and the eschatological ratification of the promises. Because typology intersects with an apocalyptic understanding of the "fullness of time," the prophets—as indeed all Scripture—have now become promise.

The prophets were no innovators but took their stance within Israel's covenant traditions and claimed to be interpreters of those traditions for the sake of Israel's response to her God in new historical situations. In a like manner, Paul takes his stance within the apostolic tradition and interprets it as God's living word for his churches.

He claims that his "immediate" revelation of the gospel from God (Gal. 1:12) is continuous with the gospel he received from Antioch (1 Cor. 15:3–5; cf. 11:23). However contradictory this may seem, the claim to immediacy is, for Paul, never divorced from his acknowledgment of the apostolic tradition. He is not "the only true" apostle, because all the apostles are one in the gospel (1 Cor. 15:11). The Antioch gospel tradition does not collide with Paul's gospel but is fused with it so as to constitute the one gospel of Christ. The relation of gospel and tradition needs urgent clarification, because related to it is not only the issue of immediacy and mediacy but also the problem of the continuity and discontinuity of Paul's gospel with that of Jerusalem and Antioch.

PAUL AND THE WRITTEN TRADITION

The debate about gospel and tradition in the history of Christian thought should not be transferred to the thought of Paul. The issue of tradition and gospel in Paul does not concern tradition as an additional source of revelation that is coequal with the written gospel (cf. the Tridentine question). In fact, in the Pauline context, the problem is the reverse, because "the tradition" is prior to "Paul's gospel."

Tradition as a written body of doctrine that is transmitted to new generations via tradents, or the distinction between the content of a written tradition (*tradendum* or *traditum*) and the act of its transmission (*actus tradendi*; cf. the issue of *traditio activa* and *passiva*) can be applied to Paul only in a cautious way. The Christian *tradendum* in Paul is neither a written corpus nor a body of dogmatic material; it contains not a holy written text but a variety of holy words—not *the* tradition but a *variety* of traditions; it contains elements for a gospel story (cf. 1 Cor. 15:3-5) and not official documents or normative, universally valid liturgical formulas and creeds.

The "scripture/tradition" problem applies to Paul's hermeneutic of the Old Testament scripture rather than to his interpretation of the gospel tradition. In the one case, we deal with a normal hermeneutical situation that is, in principle, applicable to every written-authoritative text; in the other case, we are concerned with oral transmission, flexible units of tradition, and oral proclamation.

A written text of the past poses hermeneutical problems that do not apply in the same way to oral tradition: (1) there is *distance* of place and time, that is, discourse remote from the directness of an oral dialogical situation; (2) moreover, we deal here with literary artistry and composition, which stimulates analysis, reflection, and an exploration of hidden meanings and demands exegetical methods and/or translation into a different tongue or into different thought structures. Furthermore, (3) a written text goes "public"; it possesses catholicity of meaning, because it transcends the particularity of its first occasion and can now be transmitted to other places and times; (4) in the case of the Old Testament, it now claims canonical status and becomes an inspired and infallible text; (5) written texts are fully appropriated only through a prior act of understanding: however subconscious the process may be, empathy precedes sympathy or antipathy.

Understanding and Appropriation

Written texts must be brought to speech again after their distance from the present time has been overcome. In Judaism, for instance, the Torah can remain intelligible only through halakic or midrashic interpretation. The scribe is a student of hermeneutics and the *beth hammidrash* a school for hermeneutical training (cf. the seven exegetical rules of Hillel [Tos. Sanhedrin 7:11]). Jewish tradition recognizes that hermeneutical adaptation is necessary for the Torah to be "appropriated." In fact, oral tradition itself (*masorah = paradosis*; cf. the *Torah shebe ᶜal peh*) receives canonical status along with the written Torah. Because the Torah is the inspired Holy Scripture, the hermeneutically distinct moments of "understanding" and "appropriation" fuse, as it were, into the one indivisible movement of obedience to the text. And because the inspired status of this text assumes its divine relevance and authority, the possibility of unintelligibility and obsolescence—inherent in a secular text of the past—in principle cannot arise. Indeed, obedience to the whole Torah in all its "inspired" parts and details marks the faithful Jew, and the obscurity of particular passages is removed by a hermeneutical process that moves from "understanding" to "appropriation."

Paul's interpretation of Holy Scripture is similar to Judaism's hermeneutic in that it aims at understanding for the sake of appropriation. Indeed, Paul needs to demonstrate with exegetical arguments his claim that Christ has become the key to Scripture (cf., e.g., Gen. 15:6 in Galatians 3 and Romans 4).

Because the hermeneutical method interprets Scripture "prophetically" and "messianically" in order to make Scripture "understandable" in the new Christian situation, it becomes the bridge between the inspired authority of the Old Testament text and its appropriation by Christians. The method thus removes obstacles to the appropriation of the text by providing a new understanding of it.

The *midrashic pesher*-method of Qumran and the early church demonstrates how the "understanding" of the text is fused with its "appropriation." The apocalyptic self-understanding of the communities applies Scripture immediately to their own situation "at the end of time." Scripture then is understood as predictive prophecy that enables people to appropriate its living authority: "Now these things happened to them as a warning, but they were written down *for our instruction*, upon whom the end of the ages has come" (1 Cor. 10:11); "Does not the law say the same? For it is written in the law of Moses, 'You shall not muzzle an ox when it is treading out the grain.' Is it for oxen that God is concerned? Does he not speak *entirely for our sake*? It was written *for our sake* . . ." (1 Cor. 9:8–10); "For whatever was written in former days was written *for our instruction*, that by steadfastness and by the encouragement of the scriptures we might have hope" (Rom. 15:4).

Like Judaism, Paul never argues the authority and relevance of Scripture, for in most cases an appeal to Scripture ends all theological debate (cf. "as it is written"; "the scripture says"). And yet Scripture itself is, of course, not the gospel. Because it does not have the immediate impact of the oral gospel or provide the same immediate access to God's eschatological act in Christ, Paul often characterizes it by the preposition "before" (*pro-*, Gal. 3:8–25; Rom. 1:1; 15:4), that is, it is promise, not gospel.

CHRIST, THE KEY TO SCRIPTURE

Paul's hermeneutic of Scripture (= *graphē*) has Christ as its key. And this means for Paul a hermeneutic of "pneumatic" freedom: "Where the Spirit of the Lord is, there is freedom" (2 Cor. 3:17). The life-giving freedom of the Spirit displaces the killing "letter" (*gramma*) of Scripture (2 Cor. 3:6) because it uncovers the "veil" on the Jewish reading of Moses (2 Cor. 3:15) that is "taken away only through Christ" (2 Cor. 3:14). As opposed to the Jewish misunderstanding of the Scripture—"because their minds were hardened" (2 Cor. 3:14)—Paul posits its understanding by the Spirit. Because he knows Scripture to be a closed book unless it is read in the light of Christ, he establishes "a canon within the canon" and can even quote Scripture against itself (Rom. 10:4–8; Gal. 3:11). Contrary to the Jewish hermeneutical method that introduces a third passage as mediator between two contradictory passages in Scripture,[18] Paul simply allows the contradiction to stand for the sake of his Christocentric argument. He cites Hab. 2:4 against Lev. 18:5, because Hab. 2:4 agrees with the gospel (Gal. 3:11); likewise, he opposes Lev. 18:5 to Deut. 30:14 (Rom. 10:4). Moreover, he does not hesitate to distort the meaning of Deut. 30:14 (LXX) in the process by omitting its final and crucial phrase: "to *do* them" (Rom. 10:8). A literal reading of Deut. 30:14 would have destroyed Paul's antithesis between doing and faith: "the man who does the righteousness which is based on the law" (Lev. 18:5) versus "the word is near you, on your lips and in your heart" (that is, the word of faith that we preach; Deut. 30:14; Rom. 10:8).

Luther understood Paul's sure grasp of Christ as the hermeneutical key to Scripture when he formulated as the key to all of Scripture: *was Christum treibet*. Therefore, Scripture (*graphē*) remains a dead letter (*gramma*) unless the Spirit of Christ intervenes (2 Cor. 3:14–17; see Chapter 11, below).

THE IDENTITY OF THE GOSPEL

Paul's hermeneutic of the gospel tradition differs from his interpretation of the Scriptures. The gospel is not a written text about the life, death, and resurrection of Christ; rather, it is oral proclamation that dictates its own hermeneutical method. The interpretive content (the *interpretandum*) and the interpretive act (the *interpretatio*) fuse here more directly than in the interpretation of a written text of the past. Because oral interpretation involves a live audience, it is dialogically centered and decisively situational. The proclamation of the gospel is directed to a specific group in a specific time and place. The content of the gospel, its understanding, and its appropriation fuse in the interpretive act, inasmuch as the gospel aims directly at the "Amen" of the obedience of faith. The oral gospel does not require the elaborate exegetical methods of a written text, because it encounters fewer hermeneutical obstacles. Paul can verify the truth of the gospel simply by an appeal to its "power" (Rom. 1:16), or its empirical effectiveness (1 Thess. 1:15; 2:13), and often legitimizes the authority of his gospel by its success in eliciting faith and in establishing churches (1 Cor. 9:12; 4:15; cf. 2 Cor. 10:12–18). There is a directness to it all—an appeal to an immediate commitment of faith—"an authority not as the scribes" (Mark 1:22)—that does not apply in the same way to a written text.

Lest these distinctions between interpretations of written texts and of oral tradition become too analytical, it must be remembered that Paul's freedom with the written Old Testament text signifies an apocalyptic-pneumatic claim of immediate access to its meaning. The "original" of the text and its "translation" for the present fuse for Paul as directly as in his interpretation of the oral apostolic tradition. Nevertheless, the distinction seems valid, not in the least because of Paul's conscious use of a variety of exegetical methods.

The "gospel" (*euangelion*; cf. also *kērygma*) refers both to the content of preaching and the act of preaching. However important situational immediacy is, it cannot be divorced from the doctrinal content of the gospel, because content, direct address, and obedience coincide. The interrelated terms *pistis, akoē,* and *hypakoē* illustrate this: *pistis* means both faith as obedience and the "message" or "the faith"; *akoē* refers both to "the message" and "the hearing" of the gospel and is closely related to *hypakoē* (*hypakouein* [obedience—to obey]; cf. Gal. 3:1–5; Rom. 1:5; Rom. 10:14–15). The gospel then has an identifiable coherence. Because it is not only power (*dynamis*, Rom. 1:16) but also "tradition" (*paradosis*, 1 Cor. 11:23; 15:3–5; cf. 11:2), it is characterized by both its contingency and its coherence.

Paul's emphatic denial that the gospel he received is "from man," and his claim that it came "through a revelation about Jesus Christ" (Gal. 1:12), seem to collide with his admission that he "received" (*parelabon*) the gospel from the Antioch church via traditional channels: "For I delivered to you as of first importance[19] what I also received" (1 Cor. 15:3). Because the verbs "to receive" and "to deliver" (*paralambanein; paradidonai,* 1 Cor. 11:23; 15:3) are technical terms for the transmission of tradition (cf. *kibbel; masar = paralambanein; paradidonai*), this terminology makes Paul a link in the chain of tradition; just as the rabbis claimed to transmit the oral tradition that Moses handed down to Ezra and to the "men of the great synagogue" who in turn handed it down to the rabbis, their successors, so Paul *transmits* the gospel.

However, we must be aware of the fact that the verb "to receive" has a multivalent meaning. It denotes both the reception or transmission of tradition and its saving significance. Paul indeed "received" the tradition from the Antioch church on a human level. In fact, as a Pharisee he could not have persecuted the church without knowledge of its tradition. Although the "reception" of tradition can mean the reception of a body of information (cf. 1 Cor. 11:2; Rom. 6:17: *paradosis* = *didachē*), usually it means more than that, because it has both a horizontal and a vertical dimension. Therefore, it refers regularly to the *believing* acceptance of the gospel tradition (cf. 1 Cor. 11:23; 15:1, 3; Gal. 1:9, 12; cf. Phil. 4:9; 1 Thess. 2:13; 4:1). The horizontal and vertical aspects of "receiving" *coincide* when the reception of "the tradition" (*paradosis*), or of "the teaching" (*didache*), is equated with the saving power of the gospel, that is, when "receiving" is synonymous with "acceptance" (*dechesthai*). The horizontal and vertical aspects can also be contrasted when the "reception from man" is opposed to "the revelation about Jesus Christ" (Gal. 1:12; cf. Col. 2:8) or to "receiving the word of God" (1 Thess. 2:13). The two moments within the one process of coming to faith, that is, *reception* and *acceptance* (= appropriation), are clearly distinguished in 1 Thess. 2:13. "When you *received* the word of God which you heard from us, you *accepted* it not as the word of men but as what it really is, the word of God." Likewise, in 1 Cor. 15:1–5 the elements of tradition and gospel can not only be distinguished but can be fused as well: "The gospel which you *received*," is the gospel "in which you *also stand*." "Receiving" is indeed the guarantee of salvation, although it can turn into a "believing in vain," if the Corinthians do not accept Paul's "account" (*logos*) of the gospel, which explicates the tradition (1 Cor. 15:2).

Paul never admits that "receiving tradition" marks him as a "dependent" apostle, because the vertical dimension of "receiving" is uppermost in his mind. Therefore, he equates the "receiving" of the tradition with the immediate "revelation" of Gal. 1:12, when he significantly adds the clause "from the Lord" to the tradition terminology (1 Cor. 11:23; cf. also 1 Thess. 4:15). In other words, the risen Lord himself stands behind the tradition as Paul's direct source of the gospel.[20]

Human mediation and divine immediacy are related in a complex way. Pneumatic freedom of interpretation, apostolic immediacy, and the effective power of the gospel cannot hide the fact that the gospel has a specific identity and content that Paul received, both from his apostolic predecessors (1 Cor. 15:3) and from the Lord (Gal. 1:12). Paul's apostolic freedom in the Spirit is bound not only by the contours of the tradition but also by the content of the direct revelation from God.

The Apostolic College

Paul's assessment of his apostolate bears directly on his hermeneutic of the gospel. He himself probably created the idea of a *numerus clausus* of the apostolate. Although the apostolate was not restricted to a certain number (cf. Didache 11) and referred to missionaries who founded churches or to delegates from local churches (2 Cor. 8:23; Phil. 2:25; Acts 14:4, 14; cf. 1 Cor. 15:7: "all the apostles"), Paul argues that he is "the last of the apostles" and thus of equal authority with the other apostles (1 Cor. 15:8).

Although the Book of Acts restricts the apostles to a *numerus clausus* as well, it denies to Paul what he so ardently claims. Acts limits the apostleship to *the twelve disciples*, that is, to those who were not only witnesses to Christ's resurrection but also his historical disciples (Acts 1:21–22; 13:31). The "dogmatic"-orthodox formula of Acts necessarily excludes Paul, together with "all the apostles" of 1 Cor. 15:7. Paul does not subscribe to the specific apostolic criteria of Acts, but he—like Acts— views the apostolate as a unique institution, an institution that is restricted to a limited time and number. It is limited to those who witnessed the resurrection and who were the first to receive a missionary mandate from the risen Lord during the short period in which resurrection appearances took place.

Apostolate constitutes the source of the tradition, so that in theory no conflict can arise between the apostolate and the tradition. A divided apostolate is simply unthinkable for Paul (1 Cor. 15:11) because the apostolic tradition and "his" gospel have an identical source. In fact, the expression "my gospel" is quite rare in Paul (Gal. 1:10; Rom. 2:16), for according to his conviction, "his gospel" does not in any way deviate from "the gospel" or the apostolic tradition.

It is interesting that Paul's exclusion from the apostolate by Acts goes hand in hand with the remarkable consensus in Acts about the content of the gospel that Paul and the apostles share. Acts posits a regular, uniform outline of the apostolic kerygma,[21] which constitutes the source of Paul's gospel, because Paul is dependent on the apostolic kerygma of the twelve disciples/apostles.

Although the Paul of the letters also finds himself in agreement with the other apostles about the content of the gospel (1 Cor. 15:11; Gal. 2:6–9), his apostolic self-awareness permits him to interpret the gospel in such a way that it produces tensions, if not conflicts, with the interpretation of the other apostles (cf. the Antioch case of Gal. 2:11–14). Such conflicts are in principle impossible for the Paul of Acts, who is dependent on others for the fixed content of the gospel and is in total harmony with the other apostles. Thus, Paul's conflicts with other missionaries are reduced in Acts to personal squabbles (cf. Acts 15:37–40).

PAUL'S HERMENEUTIC

Paul fuses the gospel tradition and his hermeneutic so smoothly that it is noticeably difficult for form critics to isolate the tradition from its Pauline interpretation (Rom. 3:24–26; 4:24–25; 8:3–11, 32–34; 1 Cor. 15:3–8). But how can he fuse the tradition into his interpretation when he knows that his opponents also interpret and appeal to the tradition (cf. "the different gospel" of Gal. 1:7; 2 Cor. 11:4) and when Jewish Christianity interprets it in a manner that so compromises law and gospel that Paul even accuses "the pillar" Cephas and his co-worker Barnabas of betraying "the truth" of the gospel (Gal. 2:12–14)? Paul does not attack the tradition or isolate himself from it when conflicts arise. Instead, he appeals to it and attacks its false interpretations (as in Antioch or Corinth [Gal. 2:11–21; 1 Cor. 15:12–19; 2 Cor. 11:4]). In other words, when he fuses his interpretation with the tradition, he claims that both are the one true gospel that he (and the apostles) preach (1 Cor. 15:1–11). Paul dismantles "false" interpretations of the gospel tradition by claiming that his own interpretation is not just an "alternative" option but represents "the truth" of the gospel.

To be sure, Paul can be tolerant at times by allowing diversity of interpretations for the sake of the unity of the church (Phil. 1:15; cf. also the issue of "the weak" and "the strong" in Romans 14 and 15 and in 1 Corinthians 8–10). Moreover, Jewish Christians no doubt differed from Paul on such things as the validity of Jewish kosher laws, and the apostolate "to the circumcised" (Gal. 2:7) certainly articulated the gospel in a way different from Paul. However, although Paul allows variety, toleration stops when the "truth" of the gospel is at stake (Gal. 2:5–14; cf. Gal. 1:6–9 and Paul's *anathema*). His gospel represents the "truth" of the gospel and determines what is false or what is a tolerable variant in its interpretation (cf. Paul's adamant defense of the integrity and coherence of the gospel in Galatians 1–5; 1 Corinthians 15; 2 Corinthians 10–13; Phil. 3:1–11; Rom. 3:1–8; 6:1–23).

The Antioch "gospel tradition" proclaims the death and resurrection of Christ as a sacrifice "for us" (1 Cor. 15:3; cf. 8:11),[22] and Paul adopts this tradition as his own (1 Cor. 15:1–11). Although Paul claims that the distinct and prior Antioch tradition coincides with his gospel, he interprets the tradition specifically and radically as the law-free gospel for the Gentiles, because this was the content of God's revelation to him (Gal. 1:15–17).

However, Paul never concedes that *the* common gospel tradition diverges in any way from his gospel (Gal. 2:1–21; 1 Cor. 15:11). *His* gospel simply explicates "the truth" of the apostolic tradition about God's act in Christ's death and resurrection, and its "coherent core" does not permit any compromise. If other apostles would have disagreed with his gospel—something that is inconceivable to him (Gal. 2:1–10, 11–21)—he would certainly have branded them as "false apostles disguising themselves as apostles of Christ" (2 Cor. 11:13). However, because Paul is convinced that the apostolic college is in agreement on the core of the gospel, the authority of the other apostles is as weighty in the churches as Paul's own.

Church members, to be sure, do not share this authority. Although they also have the freedom of the Spirit in Christ (2 Cor. 3:17) and exercise the ability "to distinguish between the spirits" (*diakrisis pneumatōn*, 1 Cor. 12:10), they are dependent on the "traditions" of the apostles (1 Cor. 11:2, 23; 15:2–11; Rom. 6:17), that is, on the apostolic hermeneutic of the gospel. The apostle, as resurrection witness and "father" of his churches, has a relation to the gospel tradition that differs from his "children" in Christ, for he himself is the source of the tradition. Consequently, the apostles are not grouped along with teachers, prophets, and miracle workers or under the charismatic gifts of the Spirit (cf. 1 Cor. 12:4–11). The apostolate is a unique phenomenon in the church, because of its unique witness to the resurrection of Christ and his mandate. Therefore, the idea of successors to the apostles is, in principle, impossible, even though the construct of the "apostolic succession" (since 1 Clement and Irenaeus) attempts to continue the authority of the apostolic office in the church. In Paul's time the apostles are unique, because they exist *prior* to the church and are its founders. The "grace" (*charis*) of the apostolate is therefore qualitatively different from the "grace gifts" (*charismata*) of the members of the church, because apostolicity constitutes a truth claim about the essence of the gospel. The uniqueness of the apostolate coincides with the uniqueness of the apostolic hermeneutic. Its authority is not open to debate, at least not when the center of the gospel is under debate (cf. 1 Cor. 15:12–19; 2 Cor. 10:4–6).

It is erroneous to equate "tradition" and "gospel" in Paul with respectively the "objective content" and the "subjective inspiration" of revelation ("the revelatory moment"),[23] just as it is erroneous to oppose the letter and the Spirit in terms of "outward" and "inward." The "revelation" of Gal. 1:12 does not exclusively refer to divine "inspiration" that lights up the content of the tradition. Rather, it refers to an *apocalyptic* experience, one in which content and inspiration coincide, just as the "seeing" of the risen Lord (1 Cor. 9:1; 15:1–8) refers not to an inspirational experience but to a commission to a specific gospel: "in order that I might preach him among the Gentiles" (Gal. 1:16).

What then constitutes the specificity and particularity of Paul's gospel? Although Paul has "received" the gospel tradition from the Antioch church, he fuses this tradition with his interpretation of it: "If you hold it *in the way* [*tini logō*] I preached the gospel to you" (1 Cor. 15:2, 3; trans. mine). He is able to see a depth in the tradition which others did not perceive previously in its radicality: the gospel he received through the direct revelation about Christ (Gal. 1:12) is *for the Gentiles, apart from the law* (Gal. 1:15–16). Paul's apostolic hermeneutic thus breaks open the deep meaning and universal-cosmic scope of the gospel tradition.

Paul's own stance, however, is rarely polemical toward the other apostles (but cf. Gal. 2:11–14). He never indicts them with lack of perception or with distortion of the heart of the gospel (cf. 1 Cor. 15:11; Gal. 2:6–10). We have noticed before that Paul rarely speaks of "my gospel." However, although the radicality of his own interpretation actually suggests a phrase like "my gospel," Paul's insistence on the unity of the apostolic college in "the gospel" does not really allow him to use it. This phenomenon actually symbolizes the built-in tension of Paul's interpretation of the gospel: his double-edged emphasis on the truth of the gospel *and* on the unity of the church; his knowledge of the particularity of his gospel *and yet* his stress on a common apostolic consensus demonstrate not only Paul's equation of his interpretation with *the* truth of the gospel but also the uneasiness with which other apostles regarded him.

The Multiplicity of Traditions and Paul's Hermeneutic

We must remember in this context the variety and multiplicity of pre-Pauline traditions in the early church. Klaus Wengst[24] and Hans von Campenhausen[25] have shown that no fixed credo or normative baptismal confession existed in the apostolic church. Credal formulas, acclamations, hymns, incipient "passion stories," catechetical materials, and gospel traditions (later incorporated in the four Gospels) circulated in various forms in various regions.[26] The one *kerygma* of Jesus' death and resurrection circulated as a plurality of *kerygmata* (cf. the synoptic Gospels) and interpretations. Although traditional formulations enjoy authoritative status in the churches, they do not possess the authority of written texts and creeds because they are often not clearly defined and because they are, moreover, too succinct to function as controls over interpretation (cf. 1 Cor. 12:3; Rom. 1:3-4; 10:9).

Although 1 Cor. 15:3-5 belongs—at least according to Paul—to the "core" of the tradition, it certainly is not the only, or the only normative, tradition in the early church; moreover, it permits a variety of interpretations and is therefore more a building block for a gospel story than a fixed normative creed.[27]

Paul's hermeneutic is distinct in two respects: First, he is able to focus on a coherent core within the early church's multiple traditions, that is, he selectively grasps what to him is the essence of the gospel in its apocalyptic setting and so achieves a consistency of interpretation amid a contingency of gospel situations and a variety of gospel traditions. Second, he is able to infuse the traditions with a deeper—or a different—meaning that was not evident on the surface. In other words, Paul identifies a specific apocalyptic "core" of the gospel amid a variety of theological traditions in the early church and interprets that specific core—"Jesus Christ and him crucified" (1 Cor. 2:3)—as the prelude to God's triumph within a variety of contingent situations.

Why, for instance, should the Jewish-Hellenistic-Christian tradition of 1 Cor. 15:3-5 involve the end of the law and a law-free gospel to the Gentiles? Moreover, why should the resurrection of Christ or the death of Christ "for us" mean the end of the law rather than the forgiveness of sins *under* the law? And why should not the resurrection of Christ mean the heavenly exaltation of believers—as the Corinthians believed? Do not they already participate with the risen Christ in his heavenly glory? The interpretation of the resurrection of Christ as His spiritual victory over death seems to make a final apocalyptic resurrection of dead bodies superfluous. We will see that in some ways the theology of the Corinthians has a more compelling logic than Paul's insistence on a future resurrection of the dead (see Chapter 8, below). What is more, who can doubt that Jewish Christianity—notwithstanding the harmony of the apostolic council (Gal. 2:1-10; cf. 1 Cor. 15:11)—interpreted the gospel tradition in a way that was different from Paul and must have felt very ambivalent about his law-free gospel to the Gentiles (cf. Acts 21:17-25)?

Paul interprets the tradition in accordance with his apostolic call and immediate revelation from God (Gal. 1:12; 1 Cor. 9:1): Christ crucified means the gospel for the Gentiles without the Torah, which signifies the proleptic realization of God's coming universal reign and triumph over his rebellious creation. This interpretation of the tradition raises questions about the relation of Paul's hermeneutic to (1) that of the Jewish-Hellenistic church in Antioch and (2) to that of the Jerusalem church.

Paul and the Antioch Tradition

The Antioch tradition was probably a "selective" tradition. It may not have been the only one available in the Syrian region, because Matthew's Gospel—which is located in Syria as well—contains a multiplicity of traditions. What strikes us especially is the absence of Jesus traditions in Paul, for after all, he belonged to the Antioch church. Although he adopts "Jesus sayings" as normative for his churches in 1 Cor. 7:12, 25; 9:14 (1 Thess. 4:15?), they are not a constitutive part of the *kerygma* (cf. their wholesale omission in credal formulations). It is even more curious that when Paul introduces Jesus sayings he does not mention the authority of their dominical author (Rom. 12:14-21). How is this silence to be explained? Does the Antioch tradition(s) lack a dominical *logia-* or *vita* tradition? Was this due to the selectivity of the Stephen group and Jewish-Hellenistic Christianity as it consolidated itself in Antioch? Did they simply bypass the Jerusalem tradition of the sayings of Jesus? Is this perhaps the reason for the different focus of the synoptic gospel tradition (the Q-source)? Or was such Jesus tradition in the time of Paul unavailable, at least in the Antioch area? Or do we have to suppose that Paul simply avoided Jesus sayings in controversial situations because they were used by his opponents against his apostolate and gospel? In other words, were they used in a "sarkic" way (2 Cor. 5:16), in order to appropriate Jesus' power as a miracle worker? (See Chapter 13, below.) But if Antioch did not possess Jesus traditions, it is difficult to explain its close relation to Matthew. The building blocks of the later synoptic Gospels (cycles of aretologies, "miracle stories," *logia*, and incipient passion stories) were undoubtedly in the process of being formed and must have circulated in church circles like Antioch.

Although this unresolved issue[28] illustrates how little we know about the character and extent of theological traditions in the pre-Pauline church, their fluid character is clear. They are not a body of law as in Judaism or blocks of Jesus' teachings as in Matthew.

Matthew and Paul, for instance, differ considerably in their interpretation of the gospel tradition. Jesus' *didache* (teaching) is normative for Matthew and becomes the substance for the Gentile mission: "*teaching them to observe* all that I have commanded you" (Matt. 28:20). Although Matthew combines Jesus' "teaching" and the promise of Jesus' divine presence (Matt. 28:20; cf. 18:20), he focuses on Jesus' radical interpretation of the Torah that is confirmed by his death and resurrection.

It is, to the contrary, not the teachings of Jesus but the crucified and risen Christ himself who constitutes the new Torah for Paul (cf. *ennomos Christou*, 1 Cor. 9:21; cf. also Gal. 6:2). The tradition Paul inherits from Antioch is *kerygma* rather than *didache* in Matthew's sense, or the *life* and teaching of the suffering prophet-Messiah in Luke's sense. The story of Jesus is for Paul a "kerygmatic story" and is centered solely in Jesus' death and resurrection. Thus, the kerygma actually is less a story than, as it were, the punch line of a story. Nor is it like the "kerygma stories" in Acts, which incorporate important aspects of Jesus' historical ministry. Paul's hermeneutic of the tradition no doubt allowed him considerable freedom, because the declaratory character of the kerygmatic formula (cf. the *hoti*-clauses in 1 Cor. 15:3-5) is brief and succinct and therefore not under the control of a full-fledged gospel story or of a fixed, normative body of tradition.

Although the postapostolic church subsequently tightened this freedom and controlled the "apostolic" canon with an "apostolic" interpretation (the *regula fidei*) and an "apostolic" interpreter (the episcopate), orthodox interpretations of the tradition had still to wage a continuous battle against heretics and Gnostics, notwithstanding these fixed confessional boundaries.

In the early apostolic church the situation is different because it is characterized by a multiplicity of traditions. The church then was held together less by dogmatic uniformity than by hermeneutical multiformity.[29] The unity of the church was the focus, and theological diversity served that purpose. In this context of multiformity, Paul may indeed have been the first "dogmatic" theologian in the sense that he could not sacrifice the specificity of "the truth of the gospel" to the unity of the church. Indeed, the unity of the church and the truth of the gospel constitute the permanent uneasy dialectical components of Paul's apostolate and thought.

Paul and the Jerusalem Tradition

We do not know Paul's precise relation to the hermeneutic of the Jerusalem church (or the Jewish-Hellenistic church). The thesis of the Tübingen school is no longer viable (i.e., the opposition of Pauline vs. Petrine Christianity), because the relation of Paul to Jerusalem was characterized by tension rather than by schism and separation (vs. Lietzmann) and because Paul is nowhere in open disagreement with Jerusalem (cf., to the contrary, 1 Cor. 15:11 and Gal. 2:7-10. The Antioch case was an incident, not a split (Gal. 2:11-14). Moreover, Paul's final trip to Jerusalem and the gathering of the collection (see Chapter 5, above) demonstrate both his concern for the unity of the church of Jew and Gentile and his anxiety about his reception in Jerusalem. Jerusalem probably considered Paul a difficult "brother" because of his extreme radicalization of the gospel, but a brother nevertheless. No doubt the situation worsened after the Galatian crisis, for help from the Jerusalem church is noticeably absent at the time of Paul's last visit to Jerusalem (Acts 20, 21). However, the Galatian and Corinthian apostasy cannot be ascribed to Jerusalem's intrigue (cf. the Tübingen school). Even though Jerusalem may lurk behind "these superapostles" (2 Cor. 11:5), Paul's opponents probably did appeal illegitimately to their Jerusalem connections.

CONCLUSION

Multiformity within unity seems to be the overriding issue in the early church, and thus we must not impose on it a doctrinal uniformity. However, it was Paul, more than any other early theologian, who opened the way to the doctrinal purity of the gospel. Both his reduction of the gospel traditions to the gospel of "nothing except Jesus Christ and him crucified" (1 Cor. 2:2) and his radical hermeneutic of it as the law-free gospel to the Gentiles, which anticipates God's universal triumph, paved the way not only for the distinctness of his theology (cf. its aftermath in the "Pauline school" of Colossians, Ephesians, the pastoral Epistles, Polycarp, and Marcion) but also for the open confrontation with other interpretations of the gospel. In that sense it was Paul who, notwithstanding his contextual way of doing theology, prepared the way for the later theological battles about the "doctrinal essence" of the gospel and the exclusion of deviant heresies.

PART THREE

THE COHERENCE OF
THE GOSPEL

8

Paul's Apocalyptic Theology: Apocalyptic and the Resurrection of Christ

This chapter will discuss the basic framework of Paul's thought and determine its coherent center (see Chapter 2, above). It argues that Paul's thought is anchored in the apocalyptic world view and that the resurrection of Christ can only be understood in that setting. The interpretation of 1 Corinthians 15 will back that claim. The argument rejects those construals of Paul's thought that suppress, delimit, or compromise its apocalyptic texture. In that context the interpretative bias against apocalyptic in the history of doctrine will be criticized, a bias that until recently has dominated the treatment of apocalyptic.

The coherent center of Paul's gospel is constituted by the apocalyptic interpretation of the Christ-event. "Paul's outlook is at bottom that of Jewish apocalyptic. While conceptions from other sources . . . have to be taken into account, they are superimposed on an apocalyptic groundwork."[1]

First I will discuss what apocalyptic is and how Paul is related to that movement.

THE APOCALYPTIC WORLD VIEW

Philipp Vielhauer[2] and Klaus Koch[3] have outlined the basic components of apocalyptic as a movement of thought. For Vielhauer this includes:

1. The doctrine of the two ages with its radical dualism.

2. Pessimism and otherworldly hope, which expresses the fundamental thought of apocalyptic dualism, that is, the radical discontinuity between this age and the coming age.

3. Universalism and individualism, that is, the cosmic, universal scope of apocalyptic and its view of the person as no longer a member of a collective entity.

4. Determinism and imminent expectation of the kingdom of God, which involves God's prefixed plan of history, calculations about the end of history, and its periodization (four, seven, or twelve periods).[4]

Koch gives a more comprehensive picture which differs in many ways from Vielhauer's:

1. An urgent expectation of the impending overthrow of all earthly conditions in the immediate future.

2. The end appears as a vast cosmic catastrophe.

3. The time of this world is divided into segments.

4. The introduction of an army of angels and demons to explain the course of historical events and the happenings of the end time.

5. Beyond the catastrophe a new salvation arises, paradisal in character and destined for the faithful remnant.

6. The transition from disaster to final redemption takes place by means of an act issuing from the throne of God, which means the visibility on earth of the kingdom of God.

7. The frequent introduction of a mediator with royal functions.

8. "The catchword *glory* is used wherever the final state of affairs is set apart from the present and whenever a final amalgamation of the earthly and heavenly spheres is prophesied."[5]

Koch's interpretation is preferable to Vielhauer's because it is more precise and more critical. He deplores the usual ascription to apocalyptic of radical dualism, otherworldly utopianism, remote transcendence of God, and utter determinism and suggests instead the components of continuity, of the hidden presence of the kingdom, and of history as a meaningful process.

From these descriptions one can deduce that apocalyptic revolves around three basic ideas: (1) historical dualism; (2) universal cosmic expectation; and (3) the imminent end of the world. However, a systematic description of apocalyptic should not deceive us into viewing it as a purely speculative and abstract phenomenon. To the contrary, apocalyptic is born out of a deep existential concern and is in many respects a theology of martyrdom. The apocalyptist has a profound awareness of the discrepancy between what is and what should be, and of the tragic tension between faithfulness to the Torah and its apparent futility. Therefore, he lives a hope that seems contradicted by the realities of his world but that is fed by his faith in the faithfulness of the God of Israel and his ultimate self-vindication. Will God keep his promises to his people and reward their faithfulness to the covenant? Will he, notwithstanding present persecution, establish his people in victory over their enemies and thus vindicate his glory in the glorious destiny of his people? Contrary to a long trend in scholarship that since Julius Wellhausen[6] has viewed apocalyptic as speculative armchair academics and as a degeneration of Israel's prophetic religion, apocalyptic is not to be understood without the existential realities of martyrdom, persecution, moral fiber, and encouragement and the longing for a final theodicy. The discontinuity between this age and the age to come points to a radical transformation of the present world order, because the world is presently ruled by Satan, death, and the forces of evil. This dialectic of negation and affirmation is accompanied by a sense of imminent expectation of God's universal reign. The cry of imminent expectation: "O Sovereign Lord, holy and true, how long before thou wilt judge and avenge our blood on those who dwell upon the earth?" (Rev. 6:10) is conjoined to the universal-cosmic hope of "a new heaven and a new earth" (Rev. 21:1).

In this context we must correct some basic misconceptions about apocalyptic. It is erroneous to play off "Pharisaic" Judaism against "apocalyptic" Judaism, as if both constituted distinct "parties" in Palestinian Judaism with quite different conceptions of the law.[7] This distinction has become popular since the classic works of George Foot Moore[8] and Wilhelm Bousset.[9] Moore depicted first-century Judaism along the lines of "normative" Judaism (i.e., the Tannaite tradition after Jamnia (A.D. 90), when Pharisaism became the norm for Jewish religion. Bousset, to the contrary, stressed the "popular" religion of the times as opposed to "legalistic" Pharisaism and assigned a predominant role to apocalyptic conventicles. This division in scholarship is still operative in the work of Dietrich Rössler,[10] who opposes a rabbinic casuistic observance of the Torah to its apocalyptic salvation-historical conception. He views the Torah in an apocalyptic context as the domain of God's faithful covenantal pledge to Israel. Especially since the discovery of Qumran, the pervasive apocalyptic character of pre-Jamnia Judaism has been increasingly recognized. Apocalyptic fervor no doubt inspired the movement behind the Jewish war of A.D. 66–70, which was supported by the Pharisees. Josephus tells us of a series of messianic movements that attempted to overthrow the Roman occupation[11] (cf. also Theudas and Judas the Galilean in Acts 5:36–37). The Zealots, the Sicarii, and the Qumran community are inexplicable without this apocalyptic fervor, and The War Scroll testifies to the (Essene) preparedness for the final eschatological battle against "the children of darkness." Because it was this apocalyptic stimulant that according to the fathers of Jamnia had been responsible for the war and the destruction of Jerusalem, they purged and/or softened the apocalyptic element from the Mishna (A.D. 180) and became exceedingly cautious about apocalyptic speculation. Louis Ginsburg gives a good example of the new sobriety of the rabbis after the war: "If thou hast a sapling in thy hands and thou art told: Behold, the Messiah has come, plant thy sapling and then go to meet him" (R. Johanan ben Zakkai).[12] In this early article (1922) Ginsburg cautions against a split between "Pharisaic" and "apocalyptic" Judaism: "It would be very difficult to prove the contention that the attitude of the apocalyptic authors toward the Torah was different from that taken by the Rabbis."[13] It is only after the wars of A.D. 70 and A.D. 132 that "normative" Judaism excises its apocalyptic components. However, we will see (Chapter 9, below) that the relative weight of "apocalyptic" as compared to "rabbinic" must be acknowledged in the period before Jamnia, for the multiformity of the Judaism of the Second Commonwealth is obvious and does not allow us simply to fuse rabbinic and apocalyptic traditions and groups[14] or to make Second Commonwealth rabbinic Judaism the norm of pre-Jamnia Judaism.[15]

It is also an error to make a hard-and-fast division between so-called messianism and apocalypticism, as if the former is nationalistic and confined to Israel with a Davidic messiah as warlord and conqueror who will subject the enemies of Israel to his throne in Jerusalem, and the latter is transcendental and universalistic. To be sure, apocalypticism often comprises a universal history that concerns the rise and fall of world empires and expects a cosmic redemption that will be inaugurated by a preexistent redeemer figure.[16] Although there are remarkable differences between, for instance, the eschatological picture of the Psalms of Solomon and 4 Ezra or the Apocalypse of Baruch, the nature of apocalyptic does not allow its stock of images to be classified along nationalistic or cosmic-universal lines. In the vision of Judaism, the eschatological hope is intertwined with miraculous, cosmic happenings, and universal cosmic expectations of God's intervention regularly blend with "national" messianic figures. This has been characteristic of apocalyptic thinking from its early appearance in Isaiah 24–27, Zechariah, and Daniel, and it is apparent in Qumran with its twin messianic figures.

Dualism, the cosmic rule of God, and the hope of its imminent coming form the crux of apocalyptic thought. It is, however, erroneous to press dualism into a blatant unconcern for this world or to interpret the hope in God's imminent rule as an escape from ethical responsibility. Although there is disagreement about these issues in scholarship, we will see that Paul's apocalyptic cannot be thus interpreted.

THE INTERPRETATION OF
APOCALYPTIC ESCHATOLOGY

It must be pointed out that the interpretation of the future eschatological dimension of the hope has been largely a stream of misinterpretation in the history of the church. To be sure, both Albert Schweitzer and Martin Werner have drawn attention to the de-eschatologizing of the early Christian message in the history of the church.[17] However, their basic insights have until recently been neglected by systematic theology and biblical scholarship alike. The history of futurist eschatology in the church has been one long process of spiritualization and/or ecclesiologizing or institutionalizing, especially under the influence of Origen and Augustine. From the condemnation of Montanism in the second century and the exclusion of chiliastic apocalypticism at the Council of Ephesus (A.D. 431) through its condemnation by the reformers (in the Augsburg Confession) and until today, future eschatology was pushed out of the mainstream of church life and thus pushed into heretical aberrations. The impact of this spiritualizing process and the distaste for apocalyptic speculations made by sectarian groups have no doubt contributed to the overwhelmingly negative estimate of apocalyptic by biblical and theological scholarship since the Enlightenment.

It is necessary to gain a more adequate and historical view of apocalyptic in view of a long tradition of antiapocalyptic sentiment. From Julius Wellhausen and Bernhard Duhm[18] until recent times, apocalyptic has been villified as armchair sophistry, degeneration of prophecy, utopian speculation, ethical passivity, and so on. In 1959, Rudolf Schnackenburg can still claim:

> This dwelling on fantastic nightmares, this conscious excitement of anxiety and fear, this deliberate indulgence in an emotional expectation of the end of the world, coupled with the hammering on the theme of apocalyptic's secret knowledge . . . its concealment from the multitude and its delivery to the wise . . . the pride of the elect and the contempt for the *massa damnata*—indeed the positive thirst for revenge and pleasure in the destruction of the wicked: all these things are a heavy shadow on the picture, otherwise so radiant, of universal perfection; and they are a blot on the apocalyptic writers who created them.[19]

Thus it comes as no surprise that Neoorthodoxy collapsed apocalyptic eschatology into Christology. "Eschatological" was no longer an ontic event expected in the future but a noetic-hermeneutical tool, that is, a linguistic concept, defining Christology as God's ultimate revelatory word. In the modern era the world view of the Enlightenment has shaped the hermeneutic of future eschatology in a threefold way: (1) the demything by historical-critical liberalism; (2) the demythologizing by the Bultmann school that has its roots in David Friedrich Strauss's conception of myth;[20] (3) the solution of realized eschatology, popularized by Charles Harold Dodd.[21] I mention this broad movement of the spiritualization and excision of apocalyptic eschatology because it has greatly influenced Pauline scholarship and has caused a misconstrual of the eschatological hope in Paul's thought. It has contributed to a wrong hermeneutic of Pauline thought, as if apocalyptic was a vestige on the periphery of Paul's theology. Liberal interpreters of the past considered the apocalyptic framework an ornamental husk that could be removed without affecting the core of Paul's thought. William Morgan speaks for many when he states:

> In expositions designed for edification it is inevitable that the original framework, foreign as it has to a large extent become, should be for the most part discounted and that the apostle's central ideas should receive a more modern setting. With such procedure no fault can be found; and that it is possible is a proof that these ideas are at bottom of permanent validity.

The dimension of the apocalyptic hope is here a framework that is in any event peripheral to Paul's timeless "central ideas."[22]

Rudolf Bultmann, to the contrary, deserves merit for recognizing the arbitrary method of liberalism in picking and choosing between husk and core. He posits that the whole of Paul's thought occurs within an apocalyptic-mythical world view and that therefore all Paul's thought must be reinterpreted or demythologized.[23] Bultmann subjects Paul to an existential interpretation, that is, an interpretation in terms of the anthropological self-understanding that myth contains. The cosmological-futurist elements of myth constitute obsolete and misleading language when interpreted literally, and they are to be read anthropologically. Thus, the apocalyptic myth intends to speak about the transcendence of God, "who is always the One, who comes to us from outside our known and manageable world."[24]

> The understanding of Christian existence as a life in which God is always one who comes and as a life which is always a future possibility is—of course—not always fully explicit in the New Testament in all its ramifications. In fact, there was at the outset a serious obstacle to its full realization. The obstacle was the eschatology which the early church took over from Judaism, with its expectation of an imminent end of the world and the ushering in of ultimate salvation by a cosmic catastrophe. Only the author of the Fourth Gospel has emancipated himself from this eschatology. But when Paul says that faith, hope and love remain even when "that which is perfect" is come [1 Cor. 13:13], he is bringing an important truth to light. This is, that if real life means being open to the future, it can never be regarded as a definitive state of bliss. Faith and hope are the dispositions of those who are always looking for the grace of God as a future possibility.[25]

Radical openness for the future means "that we are always in via, that we have never reached the end."

> We may—it is true—still find in the New Testament, including the Pauline writings, the Jewish belief in the transcendent glory as the compensation for suffering in this world [e.g., Rom. 8:18-25; 2 Cor. 4:17-18], but for Paul such a belief has lost its motive power.[26]

Although Bultmann criticizes the liberal interpretation of apocalyptic myth, he likewise surrenders the integrity of Paul's thought, although in a more sophisticated way. Both Morgan and Bultmann adopt a stance toward myth that contrasts the scientific world view with the world of myth and seeks to rob apocalyptic myth of its cosmic-historical intent. The real stumbling blocks of Paul's apocalyptic world view for modern mentality are here conveniently removed, that is, the dimensions of imminence and cosmic-universal expectation. In fact, Bultmann can do justice only to the dualistic dimension of Paul's apocalyptic world view. This dimension is easily open to a spiritualism of "the finite over against the infinite" or to a scheme of spiritual transcendence. Thus, in Bultmann's *New Testament Theology* the "not yet" of eschatological hope is interpreted as the permanently valid dialectical opposite of the "already," that is, as man's utter dependence on the transcendent God[27] (see Chapter 12, below). The chronological dimension between the present and the future is to be understood not in temporal but in existential terms, something the post-Pauline writings failed to do.[28] Bultmann's interpretation of Paul, however impressive, is essentially a Johannine interpretation, and it is no surprise that the only commentary Bultmann has written is on the Gospel of John. The demise of apocalyptic categories in John's spiritualistic interpretation of the Christ-event is, as it were, imported into Paul. Hermeneutically, Bultmann arranges apocalyptic under the general category of myth and opposes a literal understanding of myth to its anthropological intent. However, he ignores the historic-cosmic intent of the apocalyptic world view, and the antithesis between literal and figurative speech now becomes a denial of the realistic intent of the language.[29] The language of apocalyptic myth is more than an existentialist projection of man's plight because it concerns the reality of the cosmic victory of the creator over his created world.

John Goodrich Gager[30] detects a similar anthropological function in Paul's apocalyptic language about the end time. He points out that end-time language often functions either to exhort Christians to moral behavior or to console them in their present afflictions (cf., e.g., 1 Cor. 6:9, 10; Gal.

5:21; Rom. 8:18–25; and 2 Cor. 4:1—5:10). There is no question that these hortative conclusions do exist at the end of apocalyptic sections (cf. 1 Thess. 4:18; 5:11; 1 Cor. 15:58). However, there is a question as to whether these exhortations and consolations are the primary function of the apocalyptic sections or whether they must be seen as belonging to a wider cosmological context that is part of Paul's world view. Demything and demythologizing, then, seriously jeopardize the integrity of Paul's thought. Paul's language is here interpreted as in need of correction, and we must either disregard the language (Morgan) or reinterpret its "literal" character (Bultmann). To be sure, a "literal" reading of apocalyptic images (in Evangelical and Pentecostal circles) derives from a modernistic, denotative conception of language and thus signifies a distortion of apocalyptic in the scientific mood. However, the question remains whether the alternative to the "literal" is the "existential" (anthropological), because the category of the "literal" threatens to become a convenient instrument to amputate Paul's intent. The relation between the literal and the real in apocalyptic language is too easily solved in terms of a spiritualistic interpretation.

The solution of "realized eschatology" is subject to a similar verdict, for here a unilinear developmental scheme is introduced into the Pauline letters and is subsequently used to deapocalypticize Paul's thought. A primitive apocalyptic stage (1 Thessalonians) is opposed to the "divine commonwealth" stage of Paul's maturity (Ephesians), so that the apocalyptic-future hope is eliminated in favor of a realized eschatology in the later Paul. This scheme assumes the authenticity of Colossians and Ephesians and neglects the fact that all the Pauline letters were composed in a very short period (A.D. 50–56), which makes any extensive revision of Pauline thought patterns unlikely. Furthermore, future apocalyptic references in late letters like Galatians (5:5), Romans (13:11), and Philippians (3:21) resist any such major revision (see Chapter 3, above).

"Eschatology" in Neoorthodoxy becomes a term that no longer has any precise meaning; it is usually opposed to the "bad" term "apocalyptic" and signifies the transcendent, ultimate character of the Christ-event as God's new self-revelation. When Karl Barth writes that "if Christianity be not altogether thoroughgoing eschatology, there remains in it no relationship whatever with Christ,"[31] the term "thoroughgoing eschatology" refers not to future eschatology but to the Christ-event as God's transcendent revelation, which is and remains God's alone and touches history only tangentially. Resurrection is now defined as *Ewigkeit im Nu*. The early Barth is a Christomonist for whom Christology swallows up future eschatology. Paul Althaus's evaluation of apocalyptic is typical of that held by many theologians:

> The world has in principle its end in the judgment and the kingdom in Christ. In this sense every time in history and likewise history as a whole, is an end-time, because both individually and as a whole it borders upon eternity and has an immediate relation to its judgment and its redemption. *To this extent all the hours of history are the self-same last hour.*[32] [Italics mine.]

To be sure, the post-Bultmannian period has reversed in many ways this low estimate of apocalyptic in theology and biblical scholarship. Theologians like Jürgen Moltmann and Wolfhart Pannenberg,[33] biblical scholars like Ernst Käsemann, Peter Stuhlmacher,[34] and others express a new appreciation for apocalyptic and its positive contribution for understanding early Christianity and Paul in a new way (see Chapter 2, above). Käsemann's thesis—"apocalyptic was the mother of all Christian theology"[35]—opened up a new era of interpretation. As Klaus Koch says:

> Up to then apocalyptic had been for biblical scholarship something on the periphery of the Old and New Testaments—something bordering on heresy. Käsemann had suddenly declared that a tributary was the main stream, from which everything else at the end of the Old Testament and the beginning of the New was allegedly fed.[36]

It is my intent to press this new appreciation of apocalyptic for a fresh understanding of Paul, because only a consistent apocalyptic interpretation of Paul's thought is able to demonstrate its fundamental coherence.

PAUL AND APOCALYPTIC

No doubt Paul was an apocalyptist during his Pharisaic career. As a Pharisee of the Diaspora, he lived his life in hope of the fulfillment of the messianic promises. Pharisaism was a party, "extremely zealous for the traditions of the fathers" (Gal. 1:14); its "zeal for the law" (Phil. 3:5) expressed itself in its separation from the rest of Judaism, a separation that was linked to the idea of the *Kadoshim* and *Zedakim*, the successors to the "faithful remnant" of Old Testament times, as reformulated in the Maccabean struggle. Paul's zeal for Torah and halakah had been the catalyst for his persecution of the church: "As to zeal a persecutor of the church, as to righteousness under the law blameless" (Phil. 3:6). His theological reason for persecuting the church was evoked by the heretical consequences that Hellenistic-Jewish Christians like the Stephen group drew from their confession of the crucified Jesus as the Messiah. We can be sure that Paul, like Judaism in general, did not consistently persecute the

Jerusalem Christians but rather persecuted the Hellenistic-Jewish Christians who gathered, for instance, in Damascus (Acts 9:1), that is, those Christians who had relaxed their observance of the Torah and who, according to Acts 6:11, 13, spoke "against Moses and the temple." These Hellenistic-Jewish Christians had started the Gentile mission (Acts 11:19–26) and had committed a cardinal sin in the eyes of the Pharisees. They had breached the domain of Judaism in allowing Gentiles to participate in the messianic promises without circumcision and without observance of the "whole law" (Gal. 5:3). They regarded Gentiles as Christian proselytes who were admitted to the Christian "way" but without obligation to the whole law.

Paul's apocalyptic conviction was not initiated by his conversion to Christ but formed the background of his Pharisaic world view. The discontinuity between Paul the Pharisee and Paul the Christian lies in a different posture toward the relation between the Torah and the messianic promises and not in a change from "legal casuistic Pharisaism" (Paul the Pharisee) to "universalistic apocalyptic thinking" (Paul the Christian). Because Paul had probably been an apocalyptic Pharisaic "missionary" before his conversion, if we can trust Acts 9:1–2, the apocalyptic structure of his thought remains the constant in his Pharisaic and Christian life.

The truth of this assertion is evident from the Pauline letters, because apocalyptic persists from the earliest letter (1 Thessalonians) to the latest (Philippians). Apocalyptic is not a peripheral curiosity for Paul but the central climate and focus of his thought, as it was for most early Christian thinkers. This has been almost dogmatically denied by New Testament scholarship, notwithstanding the researches of Schweitzer and Bousset.[37] Leonhard Goppelt, for example, argues that typology is the crucial category in Paul and opposes it to apocalyptic;[38] Willi Marxsen claims, "Although we quite often find . . . apocalyptic material in Paul's letters, he himself was not an apocalypticist";[39] and Conzelmann states that Paul's theology is based on nonapocalyptic credal formulations.[40] Even Sanders, who emphasizes the apocalyptic stream in Judaism, can say:

> Since the conventions of apocalypticism had so little influence on him, the hypothesis might be put forward that before his conversion and call Paul was not especially apocalyptically oriented. This is one more reason for not supposing that Paul began with a set apocalyptic view and fitted Christ into it.[41]

Paul's passionate temper and life-style are not the result of a personal idiosyncrasy but are part of his awareness that he is the man of the hour whose mission takes place in the last hours of world history. He knows himself to be the eschatological apostle who spans the times between the resurrection of Christ and the final resurrection of the dead.

Paul's gospel is formulated within the basic components of apocalyptic. To be sure, apocalyptic undergoes a profound modification in Paul, but this does not affect the intensity of its expectation (vs., e.g., Baumgarten[42]). Both modification and intensity are henceforth determined by the Christ-event.

The modification of apocalyptic is evident in the fact that Paul (1) does not employ the traditional apocalyptic terminology of "this age" in conjunction with that of "the age to come"; (2) significantly modifies the traditional apocalyptic view of the escalation of the forces of evil in the end time; and (3) rarely uses the terminology "the kingdom of God" (or "the day of the Lord"), and when he does, it is mainly in traditional contexts.

As to point 1, when we compare Paul's writing to Jewish apocalyptic literature (4 Ezra; Apocalypse of Baruch; Qumran) and to, for example, the apocalyptic section of Ephesians, we notice that he uses little of the traditional apocalyptic terminology. The language of "powers," "rulers," "lordships," "thrones," "world rulers of darkness" (Eph. 6:12; cf. Col. 1:16) is restricted mainly to the apocalyptic sections of 1 Cor. 15:24–28 and Rom. 8:38–39 (cf. 1 Cor. 2:6–9). In fact, Paul does not engage in apocalyptic timetables, descriptions of the architecture of heaven, or accounts of demons and angels. He does not relish the rewards of the blessed or delight in the torture of the wicked (cf. Revelation).

The major apocalyptic forces are, for him, those ontological powers that determine the human situation within the context of God's created order and comprise the "field" of death, sin, the law, and the flesh. Paul does not oppose "this age" to "the coming age" (but cf. Ephesians). The reduction of apocalyptic terminology and the absence of apocalyptic speculation signifies that the Christ-event has strongly modified the dualistic structure of normal apocalyptic thought. Although death is "the last enemy" (1 Cor. 15:26), Paul strongly emphasizes both the openness of the present to the future glory of God and the incursion of the future into the present. No apocalypse ever posits the intimacy of communion in "this age" between God as "Abba" and the believers as his "children" and "sons" (Gal. 4:6; Rom. 8:15). The "age to come" is already present, so that Christians can already rejoice, can already claim "the new creation," and can already live in the power of the Spirit.

As to point 2, the presence of the new age in the old entails a modification of the concept of the escalation of evil in the last times as this is found, for instance, in the Jewish doctrine of the messianic woes.* The apocalyptic terminology of the "present age" and the "coming age"[43] is at times present in a different guise.[44] Although Paul adopts the contrast of "the sufferings of the present time" versus "the coming glory" from Jewish apocalyptic (Rom. 8:18), he modifies the doctrine of the messianic woes (*thlipseis*): Christians do not simply "endure" the tribulations of the end time and do not simply "wait" for the end of suffering in God's glorious new age. Christians can already "glory" in sufferings (Rom. 5:2), because God's power manifests itself in the midst of suffering. Suffering signifies a redemptive possibility because it takes its stance in the redemptive cross of Christ and is a token of the extension of God's love in Christ for the redemption of the world (Rom. 8:17-30).

As to point 3, the proleptic presence of the new in the old is probably the reason for Paul's sparing use of the terminology of the kingdom of God (*basileia tou theou*) as the future reality of salvation. And when he uses it, it is in clearly traditional contexts, borrowed from the Jewish-Hellenistic church: "king" (*basileus*; cf. 1 Tim. 1:17; 6:15) and "kingdom" (*basileia*) are not terms that are integral to Paul's thought, although the verb "to reign" (*basileuein*) occupies an important place (Rom. 5:14, 17, 21; 6:12; 1 Cor. 4:8; 15:25). The phrase "kingdom of God" occurs eight times in the authentic letters: Rom. 14:17; 1 Cor. 4:20; 6:9, 10; 15:24, 50; Gal. 5:21; 1 Thess. 2:12. The inclusive view of the age to come as an already operative reality is especially clear in Rom. 14:17: "For the kingdom of God is not food and drink but righteousness and peace and joy in the Holy Spirit." Paul, however, never refers to the kingdom as "the kingdom of Christ" (but cf. Col. 1:13). We can say, then, that traditional apocalyptic thinking in terms of the two ages and their strict temporal dualism is only peripherally present in Paul because the old age has run its course already: "the end of the ages has come" upon us (1 Cor. 10:11; perfect tense, *katēntēken*) and the "fulness of time" has occurred in Christ (Gal. 4:4).[45]

The intensity of Paul's apocalyptic religion is characterized by hope (*elpis*).

> Through him [Jesus Christ] we have obtained access to this grace in which we stand, and we rejoice in our hope of sharing the glory of God [Rom. 5:2].

---

*However, this concept is not documented in Jewish literature until A.D. 135.

> For in this hope we were saved. Now hope that is seen is not hope. For who hopes for what he sees? But if we hope for what we do not see, we wait for it with patience [Rom. 8:24, 25].

> For they themselves report . . . how you turned to God from idols, to serve a living and true God, and to wait for his Son from heaven, whom he raised from the dead, Jesus who delivers us from the wrath to come [1 Thess. 1:9–10].

> For we must all appear before the judgment seat of Christ, so that each one may receive good or evil according to what he has done in the body [2 Cor. 5:10].

Because hope in Paul is not simply a component of faith, Bultmann's characterization of hope as an inherent quality of faith is to be rejected. Hope is, for Bultmann, no longer hope in a specific object.[46] For Paul, hope is not only a believing posture, but something that has a specific content. Abraham epitomizes the hope of the believer: "In hope he believed against hope" (Rom. 4:18). Here hope is a characteristic of faith and identical with the attitude of the Old Testament believer whose faith is simultaneously a hoping in the Lord (cf. especially the Psalms). Faith, hope, and trust are synonyms in the Old Testament (*batah; kawah; amān*) and this meaning persists in Paul and the New Testament.

However, hope has also a specific content and signifies the hoped-for reality. Thus the "waiting" and "patience" that accompany hope, along with the "sighing" of the Christian, have a specific object. Hope is not simply the possibility of an open future or faith in God "who always comes to us from the future"[47] but also the glory of the age to come (Rom. 5:2; 8:18) or the redemption of the body (Rom. 8:23) or the Parousia of Christ (1 Thess. 1:10) or cosmic peace (Rom. 5:1; cf. also Gal. 5:5), that is, the specific blessings of the kingdom of God. Faith not only is hope but it has a hope; it cannot exist without the specific object of the hope.

Paul posits a distinct difference between the promise and the hope and rarely uses the promise for the hope of the Christian or as the content of the Christian hope (except for the probably non-Pauline interpolation of 2 Cor. 6:14—7:1, Paul alludes in Romans 4 to Abraham's faith in the promise as constitutive of Christian faith; see Chapter 6, above). The promise refers exclusively to the Old Testament promises, which according to Paul are "confirmed" by Christ (2 Cor. 1:19–20; Rom. 4:16). Thus, the Gentiles have received in Christ the "promised Spirit" (Gal. 3:14; cf. also Gal. 3:22 and Eph. 1:14; *epangelian pneumatos*). The promise and the hope refer to different objects, as the terminological shift from promise

(Romans 4) to hope (Romans 5) in Romans shows. Whereas the object of the promise is the Christ-event that is its "confirmation," the object of Christian hope is directed not to the death and resurrection of Christ but rather to those realities of glory that the Christ-event has opened up for the future (Rom. 8:18–30; cf. Col. 1:27, "Christ, the hope of glory"). The hope shares with the promise its specific content, for example, "the redemption of our bodies" (Rom. 8:23) or "an eternal weight of glory" (2 Cor. 4:17; cf. Col. 1:5). Hebrews differs from Paul on this point, because for that author the promise and the hope are fused and both Old and New Testament believers are united in the same "hope" and "promises." Paul's strong christological emphasis makes him differentiate between the promise and the hope: Christ not only "ratifies" the Old Testament "promises" but also opens them up anew as "hope," because in Christ the promises have been given a new basis. In other words, the Old Testament promises are not made obsolete by the Christ-event but are taken up in the hope. Thus, Paul speaks not about the fulfillment of the promises but about their confirmation in Christ (Rom. 4:16, *bebaios*). Indeed, the Christ-event ratifies the Old Testament promises, but it is not a closure event, because it reactivates the hope of his Parousia in glory (1 Cor. 1:7, 8). And it seems that the hope entails the expectation of new revelation and new acts of God. For although the Christ-event as confirmation of the promise and as catalyst of the hope determines the quality of the future hope, the eschatological hope contains the expectation of new acts of God, such as Israel's eschatological conversion or the liberation of creation or the "mystery" of change (1 Cor. 15:50) or the "mystery" of Israel's way of salvation (Rom. 11:25).

In summary, just as "glory" is not only an attribute of the majesty of God but also a dominion and state of glory in the new age (Rom. 8:18), so hope in its relation to glory (Rom. 5:2) is not just the posture of faith but is directed toward a specific object, time, and place: the time and place of the Parousia and the glory to come.

Faith, like hope, has for Paul a specific object. Faith is "saving faith," because Christ is its object and content; it has no inherent virtue in and of itself. The gospel is not distinct from the law because it celebrates "simple trust" or inarticulate "goodwill" instead of "works" and a search for "merits." Judaism, of course, also knows the reality of faith and mercy, so that a faith/works antithesis in this simplistic form would not have served Paul at all in his polemic with Judaism. In Paul as in Luther, *sola fide* is inseparable from *solus Christus*. Faith, to be sure, has a variety of connotations. It can mean assent, obedience, trust, commitment, or the message of faith (cf. *akoē*, Gal. 3:5; Rom. 10:16). It often occurs within a setting of endurance (*hypomonē*), patience (*makrothymia*), and waiting (*apodechomai*), that is, within a context of the practice of hope (cf. Rom. 5:3–5; 8:25; especially 1 Thess. 1:3: "Remembering before our God and Father your work of faith and labor of love and steadfastness of hope in our Lord Jesus Christ"; Gal. 5:5: "For through the Spirit, by faith, we wait for the hope of righteousness"). Just as "the Spirit" is the drawing power of the future "glory" in the present, so "faith" is the power of "salvation" (*sōtēria*) in the present, and makes us eagerly wait for its future realization (Rom. 5:1–11; 4:20–25). Faith motivates our endurance because it is the first installment of that future salvation that we now possess in Christ as righteousness (Rom. 5:9–11). "We walk by faith, not by sight," says Paul (2 Cor. 5:7), but that means that faith itself waits for the consummation of sight. "For now we see in a mirror dimly, but then face to face" (1 Cor. 13:12). Thus, faith relates to hope in the way that righteousness relates to salvation, and "faith-righteousness" (Rom. 4:13) is inseparable from that righteousness or salvation that is our eschatological destiny (Gal. 5:5).

In Paul hope has an apocalyptic specificity. It centers on a happening in time and space that is the object of the yearning and sighing of the Christian, that is, the victory over evil and death in the Parousia of Christ or the kingdom of God (1 Cor. 15:24). Paul's apocalyptic dualism is not a Gnostic dualism of contempt for this world, or otherworldliness. It is determined by the event of Christ, an event that not only negated the old order but also initiated the hope for the transformation of the creation that has gone astray and is in travail because it longs for its redemption from decay (Rom. 8:20). Although the glory of God will break into our fallen world, it will not annihilate the world but only break off its present structure of death, because it aims to transform the cosmos rather than to confirm its ontological nothingness.

The resurrection of Christ marks the beginning of the process of transformation, and its historical reality is therefore crucial to Paul because it marks the appearance of the end in history and not simply the end of history. It is not an intrapsychic event; rather, it appeals to the Christian's solidarity with the stuff of creation that God has destined for "resurrection" glory.

Critical Evaluation

A final observation: Paul's modification of apocalyptic should not be exaggerated or be construed in terms of an abstruse dialectic. Jürgen Becker and Heinz-Wolfgang Kuhn have pointed out that the distinction between primitive Christianity and Judaism does not lie simply in their different conceptions of salvation, with one viewing it as present reality and the other as a purely future hope. Qumran has demonstrated clearly that the new age is already appropriated as a present reality and is not simply a future expectation. The community knows itself to be the new temple and the new covenant and celebrates the Spirit in its midst.[48] This means that the difference between at least a form of apocalyptic Judaism and Pauline Christianity must not be drawn in terms of temporal distinctions. Rather it raises the question about the mode and quality of the new in the present. And as we shall see, the issue of the Torah will turn out to be the decisive difference in the Jewish and Christian understandings of the quality of the new age.

Moreover, the presence of the new in the old is often interpreted in terms of the distinction "presently hidden" versus "publicly revealed in the kingdom of God."[49] This interpretation can certainly draw on Paul inasmuch as he opposes "faith" to "sight" (2 Cor. 5:5), speaks—although rarely—about "revelation" (apokalypsis) as a future phenomenon (1 Cor. 1:7; Rom. 8:19; but Gal. 1:12), and views the Christ-event as a proleptic anticipation of God's final glory. However, the Lutheran emphases on the word of God and faith as revelation of the hidden God (deus absconditus) constitute too narrow an interpretation of Paul's view of the reality of the new age in the present. Because the Catholic interpretation of "the new creation" in Christ as a sacramental reality ex opere operato errs in the opposite direction, and because Paul cannot be drawn into a scheme of "realized eschatology," the precise interpretation of the presence of the new in the old is still a hotly debated issue (see Chapters 11 and 12, below). At this point, two observations are in order.

The interpretation of the new in the old in terms of "hidden" versus "public" imposes upon Paul a dualism between the old and the new that seems unwarranted. The history of Israel is for Paul not simply the old age of darkness;[50] he softens the dualism between the ages by interpreting Israel's history in a typological light. Thus, the past is not just the age of sin and death but also the era of God's salvation-historical imprint. The era of "the old covenant" has its own (temporary) "splendor" (2 Cor. 3:7–11); the Exodus story has eschatological meaning for believers (1 Cor. 10:1–13); the privileges of Israel are real and abiding (Romans 9–11), and although Christ is the end of the law (Rom. 10:4), the law is "holy and righteous and good" and plays a necessary part in salvation-history (see Chapter 11, below). The past contains the footprints of the promises of God, and these promises are taken up into the new rather than cast aside.

Therefore, if the past of the old age already contains the hidden presence of God's promises, then the presence of God's act in Christ is not simply a hidden presence: "Therefore, if any one is in Christ, he is a new creation" (2 Cor. 5:17). This issue is crucial for Paul because God's righteousness and his faithfulness to his promises to Israel are at stake. Romans demonstrates that the question of God's faithfulness to Israel is answered in the gospel, and the affirmation of God's faithfulness demonstrates in turn the reliability of God's act in Christ for the salvation of the Gentiles.

The "hidden"/"public" scheme rests on an interpretation of Paul that views him in combat with Gnostic religious convictions. Thus, Paul stresses the utter dependence of the believer on the word of God, who justifies the ungodly by faith alone, instead of the sacramental realism of proto-gnosticism or Gnostic religion. The believer is the *simul justus et peccator* who lives by faith in the "nude" promise of God, and so Christian visibility in the world tends to be exclusively defined in terms of "weakness" that is made perfect by the grace of God alone (2 Cor. 12:9–10). This construal is promoted by the Lutheran emphasis on faith in the word of God and on the correlation of *sola fide* and *solus Christus* that corresponds to Paul's view.

However, the interpretation of Paul in terms of a Gnostic combat situation has been eroded by the Nag Hammadi evidence, because it has become increasingly difficult to detect a coherent Gnostic system in the pages of the New Testament. Moreover, the resurrection of Christ has a clear historical-ontological referent in Paul; it is attested to by witnesses (1 Cor. 15:6) and is therefore not just a "kerygmatic" event. Indeed, the resurrection of Christ releases the Spirit, which manifests itself concretely in "signs, wonders and mighty works" (2 Cor. 12:12; Rom. 15:18–19) and in glossolalia, prophecy, and healings (1 Corinthians 12–14). Moreover, the believer is "a new creation" in Christ (2 Cor. 5:17; Gal. 6:15) and participates in the life of Christ in such a way that his Christian status is visible in the world; nonbelievers confess to the presence of Christ in the church (1 Cor. 14:25) and believers can resist the "deeds of the body" (Rom. 8:13) and can live like "shining lights in the world" (Phil. 3:15). In this light, unqualified speech about the "incognito life" of Christians or about the "hidden" character of life in Christ is clearly insufficient. The contextual situation determines for Paul his particular theological pitch (see Chapter 12, below), and his response to enthusiasts is quite different from his response to Judaizers and Jews. It is clear, however, that Paul integrates the categories of justification by faith and those of participation in Christ. Therefore, the antithesis "hidden"/"revealed" is too one-sided because it imposes upon Paul's christological modification of apocalyptic a dualistic scheme that characterizes more the old age of darkness and the invisibility of faith than the new age that detects the coming dawn of God's glory on the horizon of the world. The radical difference between the old and the new is no longer the same as in apocalyptic Judaism, and it is not to be interpreted exclusively in terms of the dialectic of the hidden presence of the new within the old. The Christ-event makes it possible for Paul to speak about the proleptic new in the present that is ushering in the full glory of God.

THE RESURRECTION OF CHRIST AND THE
FUTURE RESURRECTION OF THE DEAD

The Resurrection of Christ as Apocalyptic Event

We must remember that the resurrection of Christ heightened rather than relaxed the longing for the Parousia.

> For they themselves report concerning us what a welcome we had among you, and how you turned to God from idols, to serve a living and true God, and to wait for his Son from heaven, whom he raised from the dead, Jesus who delivers us from the wrath to come [1 Thess. 1:9–10].

> But our commonwealth is in heaven, and from it we await a Savior, the Lord Jesus Christ, who will change our lowly body to be like his glorious body, by the power which enables him even to subject all things to himself [Phil. 3:20–21; cf. 1 Cor. 15:20–28].

Resurrection language is end-time language and unintelligible apart from the apocalyptic thought world to which resurrection language belongs. Resurrection language properly belongs to the domain of the new age to come and is an inherent part of the transformation and the recreation of all reality in the apocalyptic age. Thus, the resurrection of Christ, the coming reign of God, and the future resurrection of the dead belong together. The new creation in Christ (*kainē ktisis*, 2 Cor. 5:17; Gal. 6:15) is an anticipation of the final resurrection of the dead and a new act of creation by the God who "raises the dead and who calls into existence the things that do not exist" (Rom. 4:17). "Resurrection," then, has not just ideational significance, as if it marks a new perception of things (resurrection as language, or kerygmatic, event); it also has a clear historical and ontological reference because it addresses itself to the transformation of the created order. Therefore, the resurrection of Jesus is not simply synonymous with a heavenly "translation," "assumption" (Enoch, Elijah), "ascension" or "rebirth" (cf. the mystery religions). Paul does not think of Jesus' ascension in terms of a removal scene, as if a Gnostic savior figure leaves the scene of corrupted matter by shedding his body on the cross and by ascending to his proper heavenly abode, where Spirit conjoins Spirit. Neither is Jesus' resurrection a "historical reunion scene," as if Jesus returns to the flesh and continues in some sense his earlier companionship with his disciples, eating with them, talking with them, and so on (Luke 24). We must not forget that empty-tomb traditions do not play any role in Paul's thought. "He was buried" (*etaphē*, 1 Cor. 15:4) underscores the reality of the death of Christ. The resurrection of Christ means primarily the "bodily" exaltation of Christ by God and his enthronement to his heavenly lordship (Phil. 2:11). It signifies the exaltation of the crucified Christ, that is, it is a proleptic event that foreshadows the apocalyptic general resurrection of the dead and thus the transformation of our created world and the gift of new corporeal life to dead bodies. Resurrection is a historical-ontological category, manifesting in this world the dawning of the new age of transformation. Thus, the God "who gives life to the dead" (Rom. 4:17; 2 Cor. 1:9) is not so much the God of miraculous intervention in general but specifically the God who since the resurrection of Christ has initiated the resurrection world as the creator-redeemer, who "calls into existence the things that do not exist" (Rom. 4:17). Resurrection language expresses the new age in the midst of the old: Paul stresses the resurrection of the body, not the resurrection of the flesh.[51] A resurrection of the flesh signals a loss of Paul's apocalyptic thinking; it underscores the continuity between the old age and the new age to such an extent that the spiritual transformation of the new age is ignored.

The final resurrection is total renewal in an apocalyptic sense: "the new world" (*palingenesia*, Matt. 19:28; 1 Clem. 9:4; cf. Mark 12:23: "In the resurrection [*anastasis*] whose wife will she be?"). And so Paul can call Israel's conversion in the eschatological age "life from the dead" (Rom. 11:15). Because resurrection is an apocalyptic category, the resurrection of Christ can only be understood apocalyptically as the preliminary manifestation of the general resurrection in the age to come. Therefore, Paul characterizes the risen Christ as "the first fruits of those who have fallen asleep" (1 Cor. 15:20) or as "the first-born among many brethren" (Rom. 8:29; cf. Col. 1:16), so that the resurrection of Christ announces the imminent dawn of the general resurrection to come.

The Resurrection of Christ as Isolated Event

We must be aware of the fact that resurrection language cannot function properly when it is divorced from this temporal and cosmological framework, because there is a necessary correlation between the resurrec-

tion of Christ and the age to come. If we divorce the two events by
allocating the age to come to a far-off point, or if we retain one event and
discard the other by eliminating the age to come as myth and by retaining
the resurrection of Christ as in some sense a historical event, resurrection
language is forced to function in a new semantic field, where it loses its
intended meaning. In a Gnostic setting, resurrection of the dead becomes
a heavenly ascent of the pneumatic self, shedding the material body in
order to be absorbed in the unity of the Pleroma. In later Catholic
Christianity, it becomes synonymous with the immortality of the individual soul after death, a development that was foreshadowed in Hellenistic
Judaism, which conceived of the resurrection in an immaterial way, that
is, as the ascension of the soul to heaven (Wisdom of Solomon; 2 and 4
Maccabees). However, when the resurrection of Christ is divorced from
the new age to come (cf. Bultmann), its cosmological aspect is not only
individualized and spiritualized but its temporal aspect is also reduced to a
"postmortem" immortality of the soul. Even when interpreters unmask
the Greek anthropology of a dualism between spirit and body as nonbib-
lical and reject the doctrine of the immortality of the soul, the failure to
acknowledge Paul's apocalyptic eschatology as the carrier of his thought
undermines the significance of the resurrection for Paul and so miscon-
strues Paul's thought as a whole. As I noted earlier, Neoorthodoxy in all
its forms collapses apocalypticism into Christology. Bultmann defines
Paul's eschatology as the "now" of God's salvation in Christ and rejects
his apocalypticism as a survival.[52] Eschatology becomes the possibility for
genuine human authenticity due to the word of Christ in the gospel, and
the resurrection of Christ is reduced to an intrapsychic event or to an
existentialist event, that is, to a new self-understanding in the world. It
becomes the perception of the meaning of the cross and thus loses both its
character as event and its temporal apocalyptic mooring. The resurrection
event is thus isolated from its apocalyptic setting with the assistance of an
interpretation of myth that centers on the historicity of man.[53] If anthropology becomes the sole criterion for Pauline theology, the resurrection
no longer has an ontological-cosmological meaning and instead is conflated exclusively with the realm of human decision and possibility.

    The collapse of apocalypticism into Christology or anthropology causes
a disorientation of Paul's proclamation of the resurrection, which has
grave consequences for Paul's thought. Individualism and spiritualization—if not ecclesiastical self-aggrandizement—are the inevitable results
of such an interpretation. Moreover, the neglect of the cosmic-temporal
elements of Paul's apocalyptic thought leads to a neglect of his "ecologi-

cal" and cosmic themes and so to a misconstrual of both his anthropology and ecclesiology, for the somatic worldly component of that anthropology cannot be spiritualized away—as Käsemann correctly observes.[54] Paul's church is not an aggregate of justified sinners or a sacramental institute or a means for private self-sanctification but the avant-garde of the new creation in a hostile world, creating beachheads in this world of God's dawning new world and yearning for the day of God's visible lordship over his creation, the general resurrection of the dead (see Chapter 14, below).

The relation between apocalyptic cosmology and anthropology is, to be sure, crucial in Paul. Bultmann has underscored Paul's anthropological focus in his *New Testament Theology*. Pauline theology is discussed there under the themes "Man [*der Mensch*] prior to the revelation of faith" and "Man [*der Mensch*] under faith."[55] After a discussion of Paul's anthropological concepts and the forces that imprison man ("flesh, sin, world and the law"), the theme is explicated under the concept "righteousness," which Bultmann understands in Lutheran fashion to be a divine gift to man.[56] Throughout the discussion the cosmological-ontological aspects of Paul's thought are subjected to an existentialist interpretation. The themes of the person in solidarity with the created order; the resurrection as a distinct historical event and as inaugurating the final resurrection of the dead; the world (*kosmos*) as the created order that involves more than "humankind"—all are neglected or demythologized. Notwithstanding the crucial importance of anthropology for Paul and his rejection of apocalyptic speculation, anthropology becomes disoriented if it is not viewed within the coordinates of the "objective" categories of the Christ-event and of the created order. The resurrection of Christ and the final resurrection of the dead are crucial events, not because they are the guarantee of eternal personal survival but because they express the inner connection of the salvation of the created order with the final triumph of God. For the resurrection of the dead signals the liberation of the created order "to the freedom of the glory of the children of God" (Rom. 8:21; trans. mine).

When the resurrection of Christ is isolated from its linguistic apocalyptic environment and from the reality of future apocalyptic renewal, it may well retain its traditional nomenclature in expositions of Paul's thought, but it becomes something radically different. It becomes actually a docetic miracle in the midst of history without affecting the historical process itself, that is, an event in the midst of history rather than at the end of history for the sake of history's transformation. Attention now shifts to the resurrection as the end of the incarnation, as a closure event rather than as an inaugural event. This happens, for instance, in John, where—notwithstanding 16:13 ("the Spirit will declare to you the things that are to come")—future eschatology is absorbed by the resurrection of Christ and the gift of the Spirit. Given John's Christocentric emphasis, the future becomes purely an unfolding of what has happened once for all in the Christ-event. Thus, the resurrection completes the itinerary of the Son of God from pre- to postexistence and simply confirms the truth of the incarnation. The identity between the Jesus of history and the risen Christ is asserted in such a way that the risen Christ is portrayed as "divinity in the flesh" on earth (John 20:20, 24–29; 21:4–8; Matt. 28:9; Luke 24:38–43). Such a portrayal necessitates logically an ascension, separable from the resurrection and the forty days of Jesus' postresurrection stay on earth with his disciples (Acts 1). From now on, empty-tomb traditions are used to stress Christ's divine character on earth after his resurrection or to show the divine continuum between Jesus' pre- and postresurrection life. In John, for instance, Jesus' historical life seems to be a theophany of a deity in "rabbinic clothes," because the distinction between the historical and resurrection life of Jesus becomes blurred.* The resurrection of Christ is interpreted as the exaltation of Christ, that is, as his present lordship in heaven and his present activity in the Spirit, but in such a way that it is no longer connected with the imminent resurrection of the dead and the cosmic renewal of creation. Even in the synoptic Gospels (especially Matt. 28:18) the present "authority" (*exousia*) of the risen Lord seems more important than his Parousia at "the close of the age" (Matt. 28:20, *synteleia tou aiōnos*), and none of the Synoptics makes any reference in its resurrection stories to Christ as the "first born" of the dead or to the final resurrection of the dead (but cf. Matt. 27:52–53). The conception of resurrection as exaltation without an inherent connection with the final resurrection and God's imminent apocalyptic triumph leads to the problem of Hellenistic Christianity (cf. 1 Corinthians 15). For Paul, resurrection as exaltation is the first stage toward the resurrection of the dead, whereas for the Corinthians the exaltation of Christ simply means the completed eschatological glory of Christ. Thus, exaltation Christology is capable of minimizing the final resurrection of the dead. Death is no longer the last enemy to be overcome (1 Cor. 15:26), it has been overcome (cf. 2 Tim.

---

*Cf. also the glorification on the Mount (Mark 9:1–8) and the stories of Jesus walking on the sea as composed of resurrection traditions. Cf. also Luke 5:1–11, originally the resurrection appearance to Peter?

1:10; 2:18); the final resurrection has already occurred in—and with—the resurrection of Christ. In a Gnostic environment, stories and sayings like Luke 16:19–31 and 23:32 (cf. Luke 23:46; Ps. 31:6) are interpreted as "realized eschatology." Chrysostom reports that the Manichaeans interpret Luke 23:43, "Truly, I say to you, today you will be with me in Paradise," as the full presence of salvation in the present, which according to them makes a resurrection of the dead superfluous. The heretics of 2 Tim. 2:18 may have had similar thoughts.[57] Furthermore, an exaltation Christology allows a dualistic interpretation and a denial of a "resurrection body": Hippolytus tells us that Justin, the Gnostic, taught that Jesus' body remained on the cross, whereas his pure Spirit went to the Father.[58]

Along these lines, the resurrection, with its apocalyptic coordinates of the general resurrection and the imminence of the Parousia, was reinterpreted nonapocalyptically in the postapostolic era.

(1) The resurrection interprets Jesus' life as a closure event, that is, as the final confirmation of the divine status of Jesus in his incarnate life. And so the "life of Jesus" becomes a "foundation story" that occupies the position of the "center of history" and loses its firm connection with the coming kingdom of God and the final resurrection of the dead (cf. already Luke).

(2) It stresses in antidocetic fashion the reality of Jesus as the Christ and thus centers more on the identity of Jesus as the eternal Son of God than on Jesus as the inaugurator of the final resurrection and the kingdom of God.

(3) It confirms the divine preexistence of Christ and his incarnation and so construes an analogy between the incarnation and the resurrection: Just as the postresurrection Jesus is divinity in the flesh, so the incarnate Jesus is divinity in the flesh.

(4) The resurrection signifies the exaltation of Christ, whose grace is available through the sacraments of the church, "the kingdom of Christ," and whose reign can now be located in the hierarchical offices of the church.

(5) The resurrection of the dead becomes an individualistic postmortem immortality and an individualistic "last" judgment.

(6) The cosmic resurrection of the dead and the future kingdom of God become a far-off proper "conclusion" to the created order. They function, as it were, as the proper end for systematic doctrinal thought: Just as our transient creation has a beginning, it has an end in the eternal being of God, so that both "beginning" and "end" are embraced by the timelessness and eternity of God.

We conclude that the intrusion of Hellenistic categories in the history of doctrine has pushed aside the apocalyptic coordinates of the resurrection of Christ and the final resurrection of the dead, with the result that the triumph of God through Christ has become solely the triumph of Christ over our personal death, and the kingdom of Christ as present in the church has displaced the expectation of the coming triumph of God over his creation.

Indeed, increasingly in the history of the early church, the resurrection of Christ propels the question of his preexistence. Although Paul himself relates the resurrection to Christ's preexistence, his focus is not on Christ's preexistence but on his resurrection as the open horizon for the apocalyptic future.

However, the delay of the Parousia, the shifting philosophical and cultural climate, and the new apologetic missionary demands of the church contributed to a slackening interest in apocalyptic matters; protological rather than eschatological categories became the central concern (cf. the Greek quest for the *archē*). This movement climaxes—via the logos-doctrine of the apologists—in the Nicene struggles and subsequently at Chalcedon. The interest shifts from the resurrection status and imminent return of the Son of God at the right hand of God to the relation between the Father and the Son in preexistence. The development of the logos-theology furthered this tendency, as can be seen in the prologue of John and subsequently in the logos-theology of the apologists. Reflection on God's action "in the end" is displaced by that on God's action "in the beginning." However, the logos speculation contained a twofold danger: (1) a docetic interpretation of the incarnation; (2) a view of the resurrection as a confirmation of the eternal status of the Son of God rather than as the inaugural event of the Parousia. The movement from the resurrection to the incarnation could borrow from Jewish-Hellenistic ontological wisdom categories that were now applied to the Christ-event (cf. Col. 1:15, 18, where "first-born" [*prōtotokos*] as reference to the resurrection of Christ shifts toward "first-born" [*prōtotokos*] as Christ's mediating function in creation [1:15]). Similarly, the meaning of "Parousia" changes. Whereas it is always applied to the future "coming" of Christ in the New Testament, it now refers not to the "second coming" but to the incarnation as the "first coming" (Ignatius; Justin Martyr).

Moreover, because the resurrection of Christ is conceived as a divine miracle within the ongoing historical process and has no basic meaning for the redemption of the created order, it becomes, with the incarnation, the metaphysical junction of matter and spirit, that is, the place where the heavenly world touches the material sphere. The non-Pauline resurrection of the flesh of Christ (cf. Tertullian), that is, of his divine "materialization" on earth, no longer has a forward-eschatological look that views Christ as "the first in a series to come"; instead, it has a backward look, in order to prove the reality of the incarnation.

THE BIFOCAL CHARACTER OF THE RESURRECTION

For Paul, the historicity of the resurrection of Christ and its "bodily" character are crucial. The historicity of the resurrection signifies its eschatological-temporal significance, that is, it is a proleptic event that inaugurates the new creation. The "bodily" character of the resurrection manifests the resurrection as an event that not only occurs in time but also signals the "bodily" ontological transformation of the created order in the kingdom of God. Therefore, the resurrection of Christ is both crucial and yet provisional. It is crucial because it marks the beginning of the new creation; it is provisional because it looks forward to the consummation of that beginning. The resurrection of Christ thus underscores two interrelated features of Paul's thought: the abiding significance of the apocalyptic framework, and the Christ-event as both crucial and yet provisional.

The resurrection of Christ heightens the tension in the Jewish-apocalyptic scheme of the two ages between the "already" and "not yet." Contrary to widespread opinion (cf., e.g., Cullmann), this tension is not unique to the gospel because Jewish apocalyptic circles like Qumran exhibit a similar tension. The Qumran community knows itself to be alive in the end time and to be "the new covenant" of the saved, in possession of the eschatological Spirit,[59] so that it already claims the gifts of the end time in its midst. Therefore, it is not the tension itself, but the interpretation of its particular quality, that must be explored in Paul. Although the new age has already dawned with the resurrection of Christ, and although faith in Christ means a life of eschatological peace with God (Rom. 5:1), the "already" is not to be fused with the "not yet." The time of the consummation or the Parousia of Christ is "not yet," and "sight" has "not yet" displaced "faith" (2 Cor. 5:5). Cullmann introduces the analogy of D-Day and V-Day of World War II to illustrate this tension.[60] A. M. Hunter describes it as follows:

> But Paul's gospel like that of the whole New Testament was set in a framework of both realized and futurist eschatology. D-Day was but the prelude to V-Day, the Day of Christ, the parousia, the day of the final victory of God in Christ. It is the conviction that though the campaign may drag on and V-Day, the day of final glory may still be out of sight, D-Day is over and the powers of evil have received a blow from which they can never recover.[61]

Paul's thought, then, is bifocal. With the Christ-event, history has become an ellipse with two foci: the Christ-event and the Parousia, or the day of God's final victory. The dynamic tension between the two foci character-izes Paul's thought. He considers the Parousia to be imminent and his apos-tolic mission to be the preparation for its coming. Therefore, its success will be his eschatological reward on the day of the last judgment (1 Thess. 2:20; Phil. 2:16; 4:1) and its possible failure a reason for his exclusion from eternal life (1 Cor. 9:24–27; 1 Thess. 2:19). "We shall not all sleep, but we shall all be changed" (1 Cor. 15:51; cf. 1 Thess. 4:13; 5:23). And even where this confidence is shaken by the perilous events of his life (2 Cor. 1:9; Phil. 1:19–26; 2:17), the hope persists that "not much time is left" (1 Cor. 7:29) and that the true "commonwealth" of the Christian is in heaven, from where Christ will imminently return (Phil. 3:20–21).

THE TRANSPOSITION OF THE APOCALYPTIC FRAMEWORK

However, although this dynamic tension is the lifeblood of Paul's eschatological self-understanding, Christian religious life is unable to maintain its fervent longing for the end time. An atmosphere may prevail in which the Jewish apocalyptic world view—with its passion for the public manifestation of God's final righteousness and victory—ceases to be the focal concern. In such a situation, the apocalyptic framework is being discarded and transposed into something else. The tension of the gospel, inherent in the interaction of the two foci of the Christ-event and the final glory of God, snaps and collapses. In the course of church history the tendency has been to stress one of the foci over the other, so that either the "already" or the "not yet" receives almost exclusive attention. Some-times—as in apocalyptic sectarianism—a purely apocalyptic outlook rees-tablishes itself and minimizes the "already" of God's action in Christ. Yet the prevailing option in the history of Christian thought collapses the "not yet" into the "already," so that the eschatological future becomes purely a "doctrine about the last things" (*doctrina de novissimis*), like purgatory, the interim state of the dead, and the far-off conclusion of God's dealing with the created world.

In the New Testament we notice this movement away from the temporal tension inherent in Paul's apocalyptic theology. Two solutions seem to present themselves: (1) a diffusion of the tension between the foci, or (2) a conflation of the foci. The first solution postpones the apocalyptic hour (cf. esp. 2 Peter, 2 Thessalonians, Luke-Acts); the second solution spiritualizes it (cf. esp. Colossians, Ephesians, John).

Second Peter alters the conception of time from historical chronology into a divine conception of time, in order to come to terms with the delay of the Parousia. The question of the heretics is, "Where is the promise of his coming? For ever since the fathers fell asleep, all things have continued as they were from the beginning of creation" (3:4). And Peter answers, "Do not ignore this one fact, beloved, that with the Lord one day is as a thousand years, and a thousand years as one day" (3:8).

Although we may appreciate Peter's attempt to retain the apocalyptic Parousia (2 Pet. 3:8–14), his attempted solution is a peculiar mixture of the Stoic-philosophical doctrine of the end of the world ("conflagration," *ekpurōsis*; cf. 2 Pet. 3:7, 10) and the traditional Christian teaching of the "day of the Lord" coming "like a thief" (3:10). Peter changes chronological time into a scheme that, although not timeless, is no longer able to address the early Christian urgency of time. He postpones the Parousia for the sake of the repentance of all (3:9). The tone has changed. The imminence of the Parousia does not motivate man's urgent need for repentance (as, e.g., in Heb. 6:4–8; 9:27–28); rather, man's need for repentance makes the delay of the Parousia necessary (cf. the "second chance" to repent in Hermas).

In a similar way, 2 Thessalonians snaps the tension between the two foci when the author inserts a specific apocalyptic program between the present and the Parousia (2 Thess. 2:1–12). He intends to retain the emphasis on the future age, especially because he struggles against an enthusiastic spirtualism that knows itself to be participating already in the kingdom of God. "Now concerning the coming of our Lord Jesus Christ and our assembling to meet him, we beg you, brethren, not to be quickly shaken in mind or excited, either by spirit or by word, or by letter purporting to be from us, to the effect that the day of the Lord has come" (2 Thess. 2:1–2).[62] The author—unlike Paul—defines in his apocalyptic program the impending future as the time of the messianic woes. The future is not the time of the Parousia but the time of the messianic woes that precede the Parousia (cf. "first," *prōton* [2 Thess. 2:3] vs. "then," *tote* [v. 8]). The apocalyptic time of the Antichrist is not yet; it is "held up" (v. 7) by a mysterious "restrainer," probably the apostle Paul himself in his missionary career. Although the author characterizes the present time as a time of affliction (*thlipseis; diōgmoi;* 2 Thess. 1:4), the present "tribulation" (*thlipseis*) will be followed by a time of extreme crisis, "the rebellion" (*apostasia,* 2:3) before the Parousia. In other words, more "tribulations" are to come. The author argues for a delay of the Parousia with the help of an apocalyptic timetable. Unlike Paul, he is unable to stress the imminence of the Parousia and to resist enthusiasm (cf. 1

Corinthians). Paul relates the two foci—Christ and the Parousia—in such a way that he is able to maintain both the presence of salvation and its future consummation. Second Thessalonians, to the contrary, responds to a spiritualistic interpretation of the kingdom with a postponement of the Parousia and a need for endurance. The balance between Christ and the Parousia is here surrendered for the sake of an apocalyptic program, with the result that the tension between the two foci of Christ and the Parousia is no longer maintained in its integrity.

The writer of Luke-Acts is a master theologian who is not, like the authors of 2 Peter and 2 Thessalonians, satisfied with a simple correction of the problem of the delay of the Parousia. Instead, he restructures the relation between the two foci and places the Christ-event at "the center of time" (Conzelmann). His salvation-historical sketch turns attention away from the problem of the delay of the Parousia. What occupies him is the present time as a time of missions. Although he does not deny the Parousia and its expectation (Acts 1:11; 3:20–21), he allows it to fade away to the periphery (cf. his use of *basileia* = preaching the gospel: Acts 8:12; 19:8; 20:25; 28:31). Luke aptly uses the solution of apocalyptic postponement to concentrate on the missionary demands of the church. The temporal end of time is diffused for the sake of the mission of the church. It is displaced, as it were, by the geographical end of the mission to the ends of the earth (Acts 1:1–8), that is, to Rome as the center of the Roman Empire (Acts 28).[63]

At the other end of the spectrum, the apocalyptic future is not postponed but conflated with the Christ-event. Here the "not yet" focus disappears in favor of the "already." Present and future are not stretched apart but collapse into each other. The author of 2 Tim. 2:18–19, for example, indicts the opponents of Paul in the following way: "Among them are Hymenaeus and Philetus, who have swerved from the truth by holding that the resurrection is past already. They are upsetting the faith of some." Indeed, it was easy to misunderstand Paul's preaching of the Christ-event in this manner, given the enthusiastic atmosphere of the early church with its abundance of Spirit-gifts and prophetic inspirations, especially when we remember the psychological impact that the sociological atmosphere of conflict must have had on the early churches. Eschatological and charismatic phenomena readily abound in sectarian groups that are alienated from the society at large and subjected to its hostility.

When Paul writes, "Behold, now is the acceptable time; behold, now is the day of salvation" (2 Cor. 6:2) or, "Therefore, if any one is in Christ, he is a new creation; the old has passed away, behold, the new has come" (2 Cor. 5:17), the focus of "the already" certainly seems to blot out the "not yet." The demand of the moment within the context of a particular argument can easily lead to a noncontextual hearing of Paul's total message. In 2 Cor. 5:17, for instance, the stress on "the already" appears in a setting that combats adversaries who claim to have esoteric, "sarkic" knowledge of the historical Jesus. In that context the new being of the believer in Christ makes a purely historical knowing of Jesus, that is, a knowing "according to the flesh," irrelevant, because it ignores the eschatological shift that Christ has initiated. However, this contextual argument is easily distorted into "realized eschatology" when it is read apart from its total context. The relation of "the parts to the whole" is a major hermeneutical problem, especially in an author who is engaged in contingent argumentation. When people interpret Paul on the basis of isolated proof texts, which are taken out of the "whole" of his message, Paul is open to misinterpretation.

Elaine Hiesey Pagels has shown how the Valentinian Gnostics could claim Paul as their ally with this proof-text method.[64] It is quite probable that the "selective hearing" of the Corinthians tripped up their interpretation of Paul's gospel and so distorted it enthusiastically in a Gnostic sense. When in a Hellenistic atmosphere the apocalyptic world view is no longer operative, Paul's so-called "eschatological reservation" can be discarded. When in Colossians and Ephesians baptism signifies that Christians have not only been buried with Christ but have also been raised with Christ in the heavenly places (Col. 2:12; 3:1; Eph. 2:4–6), the apocalyptic future collapses into the Christ-event. In this context the church becomes identified with Christ, becoming a heavenly entity and threatening to displace the apocalyptic future. Whereas Rom. 6:1–11 limits our present identification with Christ to our participation in his death, Colossians and Ephesians extend it to our participation in his resurrection as well. When participation in Christ is viewed as a completed state, Christian ethical life is distorted, because it leads to premature spiritual perfection and to a sectarian segregation from the rest of God's creation.

1 CORINTHIANS 15 AND THE RESURRECTION

Paul's argument in 1 Corinthians 15 demonstrates the importance of his apocalyptic theology. In his argument with people who have a nonapocalyptic, Hellenistic world view, Paul insists on its crucial importance for the truth of the gospel.

Context

We must first of all determine the place of 1 Corinthians 15 in the context of the whole letter, because 1 Corinthians clearly shows the precarious relation of contingency and coherent center in Paul's thought. In fact, the letter seems to consist of a series of contingent arguments. Contingency is apparent in the multiple concerns to which the letter replies and in the basic shift of the argument, once we move from chapters 1 and 2 to chapter 15. The basic core of the argument appears to center on the death of Christ in chapters 1 and 2 and on the resurrection of Christ in chapter 15. Paul seems, as it were, to divorce the death and resurrection of Christ in 1 Corinthians, because the absence of the resurrection in chapters 1 and 2 is as striking as the absence of the death of Christ in chapter 15. First Corinthians consists primarily of answers to a variety of questions and concerns that had reached Paul by letter and by personal report (1 Cor. 1:11: Chloe; 16:17: Stephanas, Fortunatus, Achaicus). Paul replies to the letter of the Corinthians in 1 Cor. 7:1—16:12 (cf. the "concerning" [*peri*] clauses), whereas he reacts in chapters 1–6 to oral reports (1:11; 5:1). This question-and-answer letter deals with a wide variety of questions: a case of incest, judicial matters, matters of worship, gnosis, marriage, church unity, spiritual gifts, and instructions about the collection. Where in all this variety is unity to be found? What is in fact the "canon in the canon" of the letter? Karl Barth has attempted to demonstrate its under-lying consistency by arguing that the contingent questions are held together by the resurrection chapter (chapter 15), which he feels constitutes the climax of the letter.[65] The argument about the resurrection of the dead, then, is not an ad hoc polemical or pastoral concern of Paul but the hidden key to the whole Epistle. Barth's thesis seems to be confirmed by the preface (1 Cor. 1:4–9), because it epitomizes the content of the letter and especially emphasizes the "waiting for the revealing of our Lord Jesus Christ" (1:7) and "his sustenance to the end" (1:8), a theme that is richly developed in chapter 15 (cf. the summary of the content of the letter in vv. 4–9: "speech" [1:5—chapters 1–4]; "gnosis" [1:5—chapters 8–10]; "spir-itual gift" [1:7—chapters 12-14]; "waiting for the revelation" [1:7—chapter 15]).[66]

The Theology of the Corinthians

The Corinthians do not live in an apocalyptic climate; they inhabit the world of Hellenistic cosmology that—though in some ways amenable to an apocalyptic mentality with its dualistic, world-despairing self-under-standing—thinks in spatial-vertical categories rather than in the temporal-historical categories of apocalyptic thought. Human destiny and hope lie in an escape from Fate or Fortune (*anankē; tychē*) and from the astrological powers that enslave people and block their entrance to the heavenly sphere. The Hellenistic age has often been called an age of anxiety (Dodds[67]) or an age of failure of nerve (Murray[68]). Notwithstanding the Pax Romana, its civil order of law, and the fair imperial administration of the provinces, factors like the cosmopolitan atmosphere, the breakdown of natural boundaries and the waning of ethnic religions, the syncretism of East and West, and the social insecurity and anomie of the lower classes all combined to create a Gnostic climate of thought that emptied life of meaning. A cosmological dualism matches an anthropology that in Platonic fashion splits body and soul, matter and spirit, and considers the material body irrelevant, if not harmful, to people's communion with the divine and to their heavenly destiny.[69] A mentality prevails in which people feel alienated from their past and anxious about their future.

Within this context, the Corinthians have received the gospel with its message of the resurrection (1 Cor. 15:1, 2; *"episteusate,"* v. 11). A breakdown of communications now ensues because of the different ideological backgrounds of the parties involved. The Corinthians deem salvation a present reality (cf. 1 Cor. 1:18: *"tois de sōzomenois ēmin"*; cf. 15:2); they know themselves to participate in Christ, who has conquered the powers that rule this world and has opened a way to the heavenly world of the Spirit. They have heard Paul's gospel of freedom from the world and its powers, which Christ has accomplished, and know themselves sacramentally united with him. They accept Paul's teaching that "all things are yours . . . the world or life or death or the present or the future . . . and you are Christ's; and Christ is God's" (1 Cor. 3:21–23; 6:11). This new knowledge (8:1) enables them to consider "all things lawful" (6:12; 10:23), that is, all things are indifferent to their new spiritual status. They believe that their measure of freedom in the gospel is dependent on their spiritual knowledge of the gospel (*gnōsis*). Moreover, their worship is one great joyful celebration of their spiritual gifts and a token of their spiritual transformation (chapter 14). Salvation means salvation from the body and from entanglement in a meaningless world. The resurrection of Christ is the apex of their religiosity. For here death has been overcome, and the Spirit has poured out on them the gift of eternal life. Resurrection power is existentially appropriated, and participation with Christ is realized through the sacraments of baptism and the Eucharist. The resurrection confirms the break between the ages, as Paul had said, and consequently the break with the material world, which after all is under the dominion of death and the hostile powers that Christ has overcome. When Paul spoke about "the god of this world" (2 Cor. 4:4), he confirmed a radical dualism between the world of the flesh and the world of the Spirit. And if "flesh and blood cannot inherit the kingdom of God, nor the perishable inherit the imperishable" (1 Cor. 15:50), then resurrection power sheds all that is material and knows the death and resurrection of Christ as the crucial moment of leaving "the earthly tent" (2 Cor. 5:1) for the "building from God, a house not made with hands, eternal in the heavens" (5:1). The resurrection of Christ means his spiritual ascent, and those in Christ are the spiritual elite; they are the "chosen ones" (1:2, 9, 26-29) who have already been united with the heavenly Lord and now wait for physical death as the moment of spiritual completion and the shedding of the body, because those who belong to Christ are already "one Spirit with him" (6:17). Within this setting of pneumatic freedom and ontological participation in Christ, the Corinthians bear witness to the gospel by demonstrating their freedom and by an ethic that proclaims in word and deed that they have become indifferent to the world and that history and human affairs, that is, bodily structures, cannot compromise and contaminate their mystic bond with Christ. In terms of their theology, then, a resurrection of the dead (i.e., a resurrection of dead bodies) is both disgusting (because the body is inimical to salvation) and unnecessary (because our spiritual union with Christ is the redemption of our true self).

Paul's Argument

Paul's apocalyptic argument collides with the Hellenistic, enthusiastic world view of the Corinthians. He argues as follows (1 Cor. 15:12-22): (1) The resurrection of Christ from the dead (ek nekrōn)—that is, from Sheol and the realm of dead bodies—necessarily implies a final resurrection of the dead (anastasis nekrōn; v. 12). (2) If there is no final resurrection of the dead, then there is no resurrection of Christ (v. 13). (3) If there is no resurrection of Christ, then there is no gospel or faith (v. 14). In verses 15, 16, and 17 the argument repeats itself: (1) If the dead are not raised, then God has not raised Christ (vv. 15, 16). (2) If Christ is not raised, then there is no gospel and no hope (vv. 17-19). Verse 20 concludes the argument of verses 12-19: "But in fact Christ has been raised from the dead, the first fruits of those who have fallen asleep."[70] The resurrection of Christ has no isolated or "completed" meaning. Although the death of Christ is a "once and for all event," the resurrection of Christ is not "completed" in its full meaning and consequence until the future resurrection of the dead.

Therefore, the resurrection of Christ cannot be asserted apart from the future apocalyptic resurrection, because it derives its meaning from its future referent (cf. Rom. 1:4). Verses 20–28 undergird this assertion more specifically; verse 20 and verses 23–28 protect the Adam typology of verses 21 and 22 against an interpretation in terms of realized eschatology. The resurrection of Christ is here interpreted as the "first fruits of those who have fallen asleep" (v. 20), that is, as the first in a series to come (cf. "the first-born among many brethren," Rom. 8:29; "the first-born from the dead," Col. 1:18). It is not an event in the midst of history but rather the event that inaugurates the end of history. And because it is a historical and "material" event for which witnesses are listed (1 Cor. 15:1–11), the nature and mode of the final resurrection in the age to come require further elaboration. Therefore, Paul discusses the question "How are the dead raised? With what kind of body do they come?" (v. 35).[71] Because the end of history is not simply history's annihilation but its transformation, there is a body that will be raised and not just a disembodied Spirit, just as there will be a radical change (v. 51: *allagēsometha*) for the living and not a negation of the body. The relation between this age and the age of glory causes difficulties for Paul as for any apocalyptic writer, because the discontinuity of "the spiritual body" with the earthly body of "flesh and blood" (v. 50) readily suggests a radical dualism between historical and posthistorical existence. However, Paul's insistence on "change" (v. 51), on the continuity of personal identity (1 Thess. 4:15), and on the somatic character of the resurrection indicates a temperate dualism and a preservation of the historical self in the midst of the end-time transformation. Paul shares a lack of clarity on this point with apocalyptic thought in general, for which the "glory" of the new age indicates the radically new character of eternal life (cf. Apocalypse of Baruch 49–51; Mark 12:25: "like angels in heaven").[72] However, Paul's occasionally severe discontinuous language about life in the age to come should not deceive us (cf. "food is meant for the stomach and the stomach for food—and God will destroy both one and the other"; 1 Cor. 6:13). Paul's ethical imperatives, for instance, presuppose the transformation, rather than the futile destiny, of the created order: "The body is not meant for immortality, but for the Lord, and the Lord for the body. And God raised the Lord and will also raise us up by his power" (1 Cor. 6:13–14). And because the risen Christ has "a body of glory" (Phil. 3:21), which is continuous with the identity of Jesus, Paul is able to witness to the transformation of reality in the age of glory, because that age will not negate the created order but rather bring it to its eschatological destiny.

Critical Evaluation

The circular nature of Paul's argument in 1 Cor. 15:12–19 is obvious and demonstrates the logical interaction between the two foci of the resurrection of Christ and the final apocalyptic resurrection. The cogency of the argument rests on a premise that is seemingly not open to discussion. However, this premise is for the Corinthians undoubtedly the questionable postulate that determines everything else. In other words, Paul's circular argument lacks a sufficient warrant, because what needs to be argued is taken for granted. Thus, Paul treats the warrant as an axiomatic premise because the very question of the Corinthians is taken for granted by Paul, that is, the necessary connection between the resurrection of Christ (which they affirm) and the futurity and materiality of a general resurrection (which they deny). "The apocalyptic connection," then, constitutes the basis of Paul's argument (15:20–28). The spiritualist interpretation of the resurrection by the Corinthians, which later became the battleground between the church and gnosticism and was so appealing to a Greek-Platonic climate of thought, is simply cast aside by Paul's apocalyptic world view. The Corinthians argue that because Christ's resurrection was a resurrection from death, it constituted his victory over death. Why, then, should the resurrection of Christ from death/from the dead* mean a resurrection (or a resuscitation) of dead bodies?† In many New Testament hymns the resurrection of Christ signifies Christ's victory over death and his status as world ruler, *kosmokrator*, that is, it means his exaltation and not specifically a "bodily" resurrection. Rather, the resurrection here celebrates simply the enthronement of Christ as "Lord," and there is no reference to Christ as the "first fruits" of the general resurrection of the dead.

Moreover, 1 Cor. 15:45 speaks about the risen Christ as "a life-giving

---

*"Christ has been raised from the dead" (*ek nekrōn egēgertai*, 1 Cor. 15:12–30). Elsewhere, simply "he has been raised" in 1 Cor. 15:4 (creed!), 14, 16, 17; or "God raised Christ" (1 Cor. 15:15). Resurrection language is often synonymous with exaltation language, and the victory over death and the powers is associated with it: Phil. 2:7: "God has highly exalted him"; 2 Tim. 1:10: "who has abolished death and has brought life and immortality to light"; 1 Tim. 3:16: "vindicated in the Spirit, seen by angels, . . . taken up in glory"; 1 Pet. 3:18: "being put to death in the flesh but made alive in the Spirit"; 1 Pet. 3:22: resurrection means "has gone into heaven and is at the right hand of God, with angels, authorities, and powers subject to him"; Heb. 2:9: "Jesus . . . crowned with glory and honor because of the suffering of death, so that . . . he might taste death for every one"; Heb. 2:14: ". . . that through death he might destroy him who has the power of death, that is, the devil."

†"Resurrection of dead [bodies]" (*anastasis nekrōn*, i.e., *sōmatōn*); cf. 1 Cor. 15:35–43; Dan. 12:2; Isa. 26:19: "their bodies shall rise"; cf. also Rom. 1:4: "*ex anastaseōs nekrōn.*"

Spirit" without mentioning his "spiritual body," and Paul refers to the "spiritual body" only in 1 Cor. 15:44 (cf. vv. 35–49; Phil. 3:21). The "image" concept (*eikōn*; 1 Cor. 15:49) does not necessarily suggest materiality, as its adoption by later Gnostics indicates. And Paul's references to the church as "Christ" (1 Cor. 12:12) and as "the body of Christ" might have suggested to the Corinthians that the body of the risen Lord was the church, that is, the body of believers rather than a heavenly spiritual body.

It is curious indeed that Paul's specific "resurrection body" argument (1 Cor. 15:35–49) is not set forth more clearly. The Corinthians could have accepted (in spiritualistic terms) the assertions of verses 35–41; the analogies of seed and grain and of the different kinds of bodies could easily be spiritualized. The stumbling block occurs when analogy shifts to ontology in verses 42–49: "It is sown a physical body, it is raised a spiritual body" (v. 44).

In other words, Paul himself is not too outspoken about a "spiritual body." He presupposes it more than he argues it (except for 1 Cor. 15:44). Thus, its rare usage by Paul leads to the possible misunderstanding that redemption is *from* the body (but cf. Rom. 8:23) and that there is no need for a heavenly body (2 Cor. 5:6–9; Phil. 1:21–23). The Corinthians may have had not only a more consistent logic than Paul but also a foothold in Christian tradition when they interpreted Christ's resurrection as his (bodiless?) exaltation to heaven.

The difficulty of belief in the resurrection of the body is vividly expressed in later Valentinian-Gnostic circles, where the belief in bodily resurrection is called "the faith of fools" (i.e., the psychics).[73] If sacramental logic dictates that cocrucifixion with Christ means death to the body of sin and death (Rom. 6:6; 7:24), then coresurrection with Christ means necessarily participation in the life of the spiritual Christ (see Chapter 10, below). Why, then, does "being in Christ" have to be contradicted by a renewal of corporeality, which in fact is a basic obstacle to union with God? Are not both cocrucifixion and coresurrection profound "images," not to be taken literally? Did not Paul himself argue in Romans 6 that our crucifixion with Christ means our death with him and our resurrection with Christ our newness of life and our future "life" with him (Rom. 6:8: *suzēsomen*)? And if the resurrection of Christ is his exaltation to God's right hand and a shedding of his material body on the cross, what is so religiously important about a resurrection of dead bodies? Such an expectation destroys the enjoyment and meaning of the full blessing of redemption. The "exaltation" theology of the Corinthians has indeed a consistent logic. Paul counters it, for example, in 1 Cor. 15:22. We expect "For as by a man came death, by a man also came *life*," but instead we read in the last clause, "By a man has come also *the resurrection of the dead*" (cf. Rom. 5:18–19, where no resurrection of the dead is mentioned).

PAUL'S DOGMATIC IMPOSITION

At first glance Paul does not seem to "understand" the Corinthian position. This is due not to poor information[74] but obviously to a clash in ideologies. Nevertheless, Paul understands very well the religious-ethical consequences of the Corinthian position. He observes that party strife, lack of moral sensitivity, contempt for one's neighbor, and religious pride are not consistent with the gospel and the love of Christ. But why can't he understand that a Hellenistic-Gentile church must base its Christian gospel and ethic on a world view that is consonant with its own culture? In other words, are Christian theology and ethics necessarily bound to a world view that is alien to its recipients, and is the gospel itself bound to the contingency and cultural relativity of a particular world view? Why, then, does Paul impose an apocalyptic world view on Gentiles and so run the risk of confusing the heart of the gospel with a system of thought that is, after all, culturally determined and cannot claim any "abiding" divine truth? How can Paul, in 1 Corinthians 15, ascribe religious and moral failure to the rejection of the apocalyptic world view? Is he so ideologically caught in his own world view that he fails to acknowledge that the gospel must tolerate a variety of world views? Is he ignorant about the Corinthian world view, or does he know it but refuse a hermeneutic of the gospel in its terms? Thus, he can even indict the Corinthian position as Epicureanism, that is, as an outright denial of eternal life, when he writes, "If the dead are not raised, 'Let us eat and drink, for tomorrow we die' " (1 Cor. 15:32). Likewise, he is puzzled by the Corinthian practice of baptism on behalf of dead relatives: "If the dead are not raised at all, why are people baptized on their behalf?" (1 Cor. 15:29).

It is curious that Paul, so conscious of his universal call to be "the apostle to the Gentiles" (Rom. 11:13), insists on a particularist Jewish apocalyptic ideology to communicate the truth of the gospel in 1 Corinthians 15. How is it possible that he who stakes his apostolic career on the claim that the Gentile does not need to become a Jew (through circumcision and Torah) before becoming a Christian nevertheless seems to insist that the Gentile must adopt a Jewish ideology or mentality in order to become a Christian? Does he not say,

> For though I am free from all men, I have made myself a slave to all, that I might win the more. . . . To those outside the law, I became as one outside the law . . . that I might win those outside the law. . . . I have become all things to all men, that I might by all means save some. I do it all for the sake of the gospel, that I may share in its blessings [1 Cor. 9:19-23].

First Corinthians 15 provides us with an impressive example that the coherent center of the gospel is, for Paul, not simply an experiential reality of the heart or a Word beyond words that permits translation into a multitude of world views. Harry Emerson Fosdick's dictum about the gospel as an "abiding experience amidst changing world views," or Bultmann's demythologizing program for the sake of the kerygmatic address of the gospel, is in this manner not true to Paul's conception of the gospel. However applicable the gospel must be to a Gentile in his contingent situation, it does not tolerate a world view that cannot express those elements inherent in the apocalyptic world view and that to Paul seem inherent in the truth of the gospel (cf., e.g., the charge of de Lagarde against Paul's introduction of rabbinic thought forms into the simple gospel of Jesus[75]). Paul's gospel does seem welded to the apocalyptic world view. And far from considering the apocalyptic world view a husk or discardable frame, Paul insists that it belongs to the inalienable coherent core of the gospel. The charge that Paul universalizes and absolutizes a cultural-temporal world view and makes it normative for the truth of the gospel must be taken seriously, because Paul connects the coherent center of the gospel with the particularity of an apocalyptic idiom. It seems that Paul sacrifices dialogical contingency to dogmatic necessity by imposing a particular world view on Hellenistic believers. And if Paul imposes a dogmatic interpretive scheme on the "core" of the gospel, he seems to require not only faith as *fiducia* but also faith as *assensus*, that is, as "assent" to a specific world view. This seems to restrict severely the interaction between the contingency and the coherent core of the gospel, that is, its character as language-event for a particular situation.

Indeed, according to Paul, the gospel is integrally connected with his apocalyptic world view: he cannot conceive of the resurrection of Christ—which the Corinthians affirm (1 Cor. 15:1, 2, 11)—apart from the apocalyptic general resurrection of the dead. Both stand or fall together. And it is not just a question of "communications"; it is not a linguistic problem that can be solved if only Paul can adjust his language and find a common ground. There are profound substantive issues involved in the language that concern the truth of the gospel. It seems that for Paul the apocalyptic world view is so interwoven with the truth of the gospel that if they are separated the gospel will be torn apart. If this is true, we have reached an important hermeneutical insight. Whenever apocalyptic categories are dismissed as husk or cultural accident or literal obsolescence, resurrection-language is transmuted into something else, for example, into the immortality of the soul, or our heavenly ascent, or into an existential possibility and especially into a denial of the created order. Thus, the rejection of apocalyptic categories as inconsistent with modernity and a scientific world view bears directly on the truth of the gospel! For Paul, the issue of "apocalyptic categories" is not a provincial idiosyncrasy but is interwoven with profound christological, anthropological, and ethical issues. Paul's problem with the Corinthians is at bottom their denial that spirituality is commensurate with materiality and historical existence. And this problem can only be solved, according to Paul, when the truth of the gospel (i.e., its coherent apocalyptic theme) is understood and appropriated.

As we will see, the interrelation of Spirit and body forms the basic theme of 1 Corinthians. The Spirit is for Paul determined by the apocalyptic future and does not signify the perfected state of present spirituality. It is the power that transforms the created order and directs it toward its consummation. When the Spirit is divorced from apocalyptic categories, it distorts the meaning of the gospel by unduly spiritualizing it. The Spirit, therefore, is connected with life in the body, with life for other bodies, and with eternal life as qualified by a body. And the totality of life in the body and for other bodies manifests itself concretely in the one "body of Christ," which constitutes the church. For that one ontological body of Christ does not mean an undifferentiated oneness of all who share the Spirit but rather the psycho-physical and cultural variety and mutual interdependence of its members, so that each member occupies a different function in the body (see Chapter 14, below). Oneness "in Christ" does not neutralize the historical specificity of human "bodies" (notwithstanding Gal. 3:28). It is the historical particularity of each member in "the body of Christ" that makes love (*agape*) and upbuilding (*oikodomē*) possible and necessary. Thus, the one body of Christ is not a pneumatic, ahistorical elite, but a communion of "diverse bodies" whose particularity must be respected (1 Cor. 12:14). Because the relation of spirituality to materiality in a historical context is the Corinthian problem, its solution is conceivable to Paul only in the apocalyptic structure of the gospel, for in this framework alone can the resurrection of Christ be correctly perceived in terms of its consequences for life in the body. This raises the hermeneutical question whether only an apocalyptic interpretation of the gospel can achieve Paul's program of correlating Spirit and body in the gospel.* If, however, "the resurrection of Christ" is the historically unique apostolic bedrock of the gospel, and if it is inseparably connected with the apocalyptic future—if, in other words, the resurrection within its apocalyptic coordinates is an event to which the Corinthians and all other Christians have access only in its apostolic and Pauline interpretation (1 Cor. 15:2)—then its translation into another world view (e.g., "Christ is alive again" or "Christ has conquered death") is insufficient. Indeed, the history of dogma shows that the loss of an apocalyptic interpretation of the resurrection of Christ (e.g., in categories of immortality or enthusiasm in the Spirit) leads to a perversion of the gospel because it ignores the temporal and cosmic coordinates of the resurrection of Christ. Paul, then, does not so much "misunderstand" the Corinthians but rather understands precisely the reason for their perversion of the gospel, that is, their rejection of its apocalyptic coordinates.

1 CORINTHIANS 15 AND THE THEME OF THE LETTER

Both 1 Corinthians as a whole and chapter 15 in particular raise fundamental questions about the nature of Paul's way of doing theology. In chapter 15 Paul seems to impose an apocalyptic world view on the nonapocalyptic world view of his audience and so to sacrifice dialogical contingency to a dogmatic conception of the coherent core of the gospel. Moreover, the letter as a whole reads like a series of contingent theological statements that do not seem to cohere into what we have claimed to be the coherent apocalyptic theme of Paul's gospel. When Karl Barth locates the coherent theme of 1 Corinthians in its climactic chapter 15, he makes an important contribution to the relation between contingency and coherent theme in the letter.[76] However, "the canon in the canon" of 1 Corinthians is not as easily established as Barth thinks.

Paul certainly does argue in such a contingent manner that the Corinthians may well have misinterpreted the coherent core of the gospel. The tradition that Paul inherited from Antioch centered on the death and resurrection of Christ (1 Cor. 15:3–5; cf. also 1:13, 18; 2:2; 6:14; 8:11). However, although 1 Cor. 15:3–5 explicitly cites the tradition of both the

---

*For example, a correlation not in terms of the apocalyptic future but in terms of the cross of Christ as the basis for ethical life (i.e., the body as locus of the cross and cross-bearing [2 Cor. 4:10–11]).

death and resurrection of Christ, Paul focuses solely on the resurrection clause in his interpretation of the gospel in chapter 15 ("he was raised on the third day," v. 4), and omits any explication of the death of Christ.

In 1 Corinthians 1 and 2, to the contrary, the gospel is interpreted solely in terms of the death (cross) of Christ, and there is no reference to the resurrection of Christ.* It seems that the diverse polemical situations of the letter compel Paul to such a diversity and contingency of argumentation that the death and resurrection of Christ are torn apart and the "whole" gospel of Paul, that is, its coherent core (cf. *to euangelion*, 15:1[77]) is thwarted. The contrast with Romans 6 is striking because here the integral unity of dying and rising with Christ is impressively explicated.

Barth's claim about 1 Corinthians 15 as the coherent core and key to the whole letter presupposes that at chapter 15 the readers still have chapters 1 and 2 clearly in mind and are able to integrate the different foci of these chapters. Paul's strategy comes as a surprise, because the death of Christ would have helped Paul to clarify the nature of the resurrection in chapter 15, as much as the resurrection of Christ would have helped him in his argument in chapters 1 and 2.

Paul's firm resolution "For I decided to know nothing among you except Jesus Christ and him crucified" (1 Cor. 2:2), which constitutes the heart of his gospel, is virtually ignored in chapter 15. Because the polemical edge of chapter 15 is directed against the enthusiastic life-style of the Corinthians, the message of cross and resurrection would have clarified the nature of the resurrection in chapter 15. For if the resurrection is primarily the victory over sin (Rom. 6:10) and a new service in the body (Rom. 6:12), the correlation of Spirit and life in the body, which the pneumatic Corinthians reject, is based on our participation in the death and resurrection of Christ (Rom. 6:1-10). In other words, if the resurrection of Christ is primarily a victory over sin and in that sense a victory over death, why doesn't 1 Corinthians 15 integrate sin and death and relate them to the cross and resurrection in such a way that the victory over death is more than a promise of a future resurrection-body, more than

---

*Compare the following discussion of themes in 1 Corinthians with the themes of Jürgen Moltmann in the *Theology of Hope* and in *The Crucified God*. Precisely how are "the resurrection of the crucified Christ" and "the cross of the risen Christ" related? How is the suffering of God in the Son and with us related to the triumph of God in the resurrection of Christ and in the final kingdom? Why are the apocalyptic coordinates of the *Theology of Hope* so subordinated to the suffering love of God in *The Crucified God*? Does Moltmann disjoin here the themes of the cross and the resurrection, a disjunction not unlike Paul's when we compare 1 Corinthians 1 and 2 to 1 Corinthians 15?

physical "survival" in the afterlife? Do we not have to say in terms of the argument of Romans 6 that victory over death is primarily a victory over sin (Rom. 6:10) because sin is "the sting of death" (1 Cor. 15:56)? And does not the cross of Christ signify precisely this victory over sin? The consequence of this victory is a new life of service to God in the body as "men who have been brought from death to life" (Rom. 6:13), a "newness of life" (Rom. 6:4) of those who after the destruction of the body of sin (Rom. 6:6) can now present their "bodies as a living sacrifice, holy and acceptable to God" (Rom. 12:1). The Corinthian divorce of Spirit and body could have been met by grounding the Christian ethic (in terms of a correlation of Spirit and body) in the death and resurrection of Christ. As it is now presented in 1 Corinthians 15, this ethic rests on the resurrection argument alone: the resurrection of Christ promises a future resurrection-body, so that the body is ethically significant—something the Corinthians deny.

Again, in 1 Corinthians 1 and 2, the resurrection of Christ could have assisted Paul in clarifying the cross as "God's power" (1 Cor. 1:24) and his own preaching as "the power of God and the demonstration of the Spirit" (2:1–5). In short, why is the resurrection as part of "the things of first importance" (*en prōtois*, 15:3) not the theme or a theme of chapters 1 and 2 as well, and why are these "things of first importance"—which include the death of Christ—interpreted in chapter 15 solely in terms of the resurrection and not in terms of Christ's death?

The interaction between coherent core and contingency is a definite problem in 1 Corinthians. Romans and 1 Corinthians seem very different in this respect. In Romans the coherent theme is quite clear, but its contingency is unclear; in 1 Corinthians the coherent theme is unclear, but its contingency is obvious. First Corinthians 15 presents a coherent apocalyptic core, but it seems as if Paul imposes a dogmatic structure on the Corinthians which disregards their contingent situation, that is, their nonapocalyptic world view. Again, a comparison of chapters 1 and 2 with chapter 15 shows a contingent argumentation throughout the letter which seems to disregard the "whole" of Paul's gospel, that is, the death (chapters 1 and 2) *and* resurrection of Christ (chapter 15).

We must remember, however, that the letter situation, with its contingent, exhortative, and polemical arguments, is quite different from Paul's first proclamation of the gospel to the Corinthians. Thus the letter situation represents a second-level dialogue that permits greater contingent emphases than were possible in Paul's first-level foundational proclamation: "I decided to know nothing among you except Jesus Christ and him crucified" (1 Cor. 2:2).

SPIRIT AND BODY

In the light of Paul's contingent argument in 1 Corinthians, we can understand the partition theories to which the letter has been frequently subjected. Walter Schmithals,[78] for instance, assigns chapter 15 to an earlier letter (letter B), and thus isolates chapter 15 from the literary context of the whole letter, in order to explain the different emphases of chapter 1 (letter D: 1:1—4:21) and chapter 15 (letter B).[79]

Although such theories are worthy to be pursued, one wonders whether they are not an attempt to bypass the remarkable interaction in Paul between the coherent theme of the gospel and his contingent argumentation, for the letter reveals that its coherent theme revolves around the correlation of Spirit and body. The Corinthians adhere to the proposition that the material (the body) is inimical to the spiritual (the Spirit). They split apart what Paul conjoins. And so Paul consistently maintains the integration of body and Spirit throughout the letter (1 Cor. 3:16–17; 6:13–20; 9:24–27). Thus, the integration of Spirit and body in an apocalyptic perspective provides the contingent interpretation of the gospel in the Corinthian situation.

I conclude, then, that chapter 15, with its apocalyptic focus on the resurrection and its emphasis on the ultimate significance of the resurrection-body, is indeed the climax of that interpretation of the gospel that the Corinthians had to hear according to Paul. The coherent center of the gospel is in 1 Corinthians unfolded as the correlation of Spirit and body, in the light of the apocalyptic resurrection-body. To Paul, the rejection of this theme by the Corinthians means that they have rejected the gospel. Therefore, Barth is indeed correct when he claims 1 Corinthians 15 as the key to Paul's letter.[80] However, its relation to chapters 1 and 2 is more tenuous than he thinks. This applies as well to Käsemann's statement about 1 Corinthians 15: "The Risen Exalted One remains the Crucified One."[81] The resurrection of the crucified Christ may well have been the subject of Paul's foundational preaching and the underlying presupposition of the letter, but the literary structure of the letter itself does not show it.

CONCLUSION: CHRONOLOGY AND THEOLOGY

It cannot be too strongly emphasized that Paul's thought is motivated by the future consummation as God's goal with history and creation. All the ingredients of Paul's thought find their proper location only within this futurist flow. Our modern distaste for Paul's apocalyptic conceptuality thus distorts our focus. What to us is husk and peripheral is primary to Paul, and what to us is kernel and core is differently focused in Paul.

Although Christocentrism seems a true description of Paul's thought, it leads to distortions if we ignore Paul's theocentric-apocalyptic posture. Wrede comments:

> The whole Pauline conception of salvation is characterized by suspense; a suspense which strains forward towards the final release, the actual death. The earthly life is not the setting in which salvation becomes complete. In this connection we should keep before our minds with especial clearness a fact which, indeed, when we are dealing with Paul, ought never to be forgotten. He believed with all his might in the speedy coming of Christ and the approaching end of the world. In consequence, the redemptive act of Christ, which lay in the past and the dawn of the future glory lay, in his view, close together. . . . It has been popularly held that Paul departed from the view of salvation of the early Church by shifting the stress from the future to the past, looking upon the blessedness of the Christian as already attained, and emphasizing faith instead of hope. It is easy to see that this is assuredly but a half truth. All references to the redemption as a completed transaction swing around at once into utterances about the future. . . . There are deep-reaching differences between the Pauline doctrine of redemption and the thoughts of modern belief.[82]

First Corinthians 15 shows clearly the necessary relation between the resurrection of Christ and the final resurrection of the dead. The chronological proximity of this relation contains a theological necessity. On the one hand, the resurrection of Christ is a sign of the impending kingdom (1 Cor. 15:24); on the other hand, the general resurrection of the dead is the completion of the resurrection of Christ. For Paul, then, the Christ-event is at once crucial and provisional. The analogy of D-Day and V-Day illustrates this. A D-Day without an impending V-Day loses its character of D-Day. Likewise, a D-Day that is celebrated as if it were V-Day loses sight of the reality of things because it ignores God's plan of cosmic redemption and is caught in an overheated spiritualistic illusion, "as if the day of the Lord *has* come" (2 Thess. 2:2). D-Day is provisional, but it is also crucial. The Corinthians, however, with their spiritual pride, celebrate D-Day as if it were V-Day. Thus they claim for the present what God has ordained for the future and disdain historical existence and its concrete demands with their individualist mysticism.[83]

The interpreters of consistent eschatology (Albert Schweitzer, Martin Werner, Fritz Buri[84]) deserve credit for pointing to this futurist-eschatological element in the New Testament as a whole. Their critics have correctly noted that if future eschatology were such a decisive matter, the delay of the Parousia would have destroyed Christian faith. Thus, Oscar

Cullmann characterized Christ as "the center" (*die Mitte der Zeit*) of Christian faith and eschatology as a variable that was and is constantly open to shifting emphases.[85] Werner, to the contrary, argues that de-eschatologizing is the key to the development of Christian dogma.[86] It is unfortunate that the problem of the future theocentric thrust of Paul became so heavily centered on the question of chronology, that is, on the delay of the Parousia. That debate concludes prematurely that, inasmuch as the Parousia has not taken place, the center of Christian faith either lies in Christology or calls for an existentialist resolution of the early Christian hope. In fact, Paul can adjust himself remarkably well to the delay of the Parousia. If there is any "development" in his thinking, it certainly concerns the issue of its arrival. Whereas he expects to be alive at the Parousia in 1 Thess. 4:15 and 1 Cor. 15:50–52, he seems to contemplate his death before its occurrence in Phil. 1:20 and possibly in 2 Cor. 5:1–11 (cf. 2 Cor. 1:9). Even so, he can write in what was one of his last letters, "Salvation is nearer to us now than when we first believed" (Rom. 13:11; cf. Phil. 4:4). In other words, he persists in imminent expectation, notwithstanding his awareness of the delay of the Parousia. His response to the excited Thessalonians shows a restraint against chronological expecta-tions and calculations: "But as to the times and the seasons, brethren, you have no need to have anything written to you. For you yourselves know well that the day of the Lord will come like a thief in the night" (1 Thess. 5:1, 2). Although the usual indictment against apocalyptic with its calculations and timetables seems a gross exaggeration,[87] Paul's deviation from this apocalyptic practice is obvious. A similar observation can be drawn from Paul's missionary method, because it reveals no contradiction between apocalyptic fervor and missionary strategy. Paul is simply not an apocalyptic fanatic who runs breathlessly through the Roman Empire because the end of the world is imminent. He spends, for instance, one and a half years at Corinth and three years at Ephesus and contemplates a mission to Spain. Thus, eschatology and missions do not contradict each other, as if the one paralyzes the strength of the other. The mission charge in Acts 1:6–8 is much more concerned with the alternative—eschatology *or* missions—than anything in Paul. Paul can contemplate a universal mission and yet live in terms of apocalyptic imminence. It seems, therefore, that the scholarly debate on the delay of the Parousia focuses exclusively on calculating chronological time, that is, on the chronological dating that separates the Christ-event and the end time, whereas for Paul the issue is primarily not one of chronological reckoning but one of theological necessity. Chronological proximity is important as the concomitant of theological necessity, because there is a necessary relation between the "already" and the "not yet" in the gospel. It is interesting that Bultmann interprets the chronological tension in existentialist terms and thus in terms of theological necessity. However, he confuses chronological reckoning with chronological expectation, and his anthropological hermeneutic loses sight of the cosmic dimensions of the Christian hope. Thus, he ignores the "not yet" of the transformation of the creation and the "not yet" of God's final verdict on our responsibility in the last judgment. According to Paul, Christians can never surrender the universal-cosmic future horizon of the Christ-event, and the imminence of God's kingdom, if they consider the resurrection of Christ to be of fundamental importance to their faith. Indeed, the resurrection prompts Christians to an apocalyptic self-understanding in the world. For in their own bodies Christians live existentially the tension of their present incompleted existence in solidarity with an unredeemed creation, and they must therefore yearn for the consummation of the resurrection, which is nothing but God's triumph over the power of death that poisons his creation. It may be argued that the phenomenon of hope in human life points to the need for a completion that will enable us to understand fully what we now only understand fragmentarily (1 Cor. 13:12; cf. Pannenberg). This completion will resolve the tension of our present life in the body, because our lives can be complete only when they embrace our contradictions as well as those of the created order. Only then will "the last enemy," death, be swallowed up (2 Cor. 5:4) by life and by the triumph of God (see Chapter 16, below). In this light the often maligned theology of 2 Peter is in some ways on the right track, because for Peter the chronological delay of the Parousia does not mean its theological demise (2 Pet. 3:8–10).

Both the great importance and the provisionality of the Christ-event must be maintained, just as D-Day cannot be without V-Day. The Christ-event itself is misappropriated if it is not seen as the proleptic anticipation of the age to come. It is a mistake to introduce here a philosophical hermeneutic, as if Paul understands the relation between the Christ-event and the kingdom of God in terms of antinomy, paradox, or in dialectical terms, that is, within the Greek cyclical understanding of time.[88] The tension between the resurrection of Christ and the general resurrection cannot be defined without its chronological and cosmic-universal dimension. Otherwise, the apocalyptic tension becomes subject to docetic distortion. For Paul, the temporal element is necessary for the sake of the cosmic hope of the creation. Just as the "not yet" of the temporal dimension safeguards the cosmic nature of the future eschatological event,

the "already" of the Christ-event announces its imminence. A philosophical interpretation of the relation between the Christ-event and the final
glory of God in terms of dialectics and paradox constitutes a denial of the
character of the Parousia as future event in Paul, because it transforms the
expectation of an ontic event into a noetic perception and interprets it as a
perennial religious tension.

The question raised by 1 Corinthians 15 is why Paul insists on an
apocalyptic world view as an inherent part of the gospel. If the basic
problem in 1 Corinthians is the nature of Christian life as life in the body
by the Spirit, a theology of the cross, as developed in chapters 1 and 2,
might have provided a sufficient solution to the Corinthian problem of a
prematurely realized eschatology in the Spirit. In fact, the Gospel of John
shows us the possibility of such a position. Here the cross itself becomes the
moment of glorification, whereas "cross-bearing" characterizes Christian
life and heavenly immortality its victory (John 15:18–25; 16:2–4, 33;
17:14–19). Why then does Paul's "eschatological reservation" need an
apocalyptic world view? Can it not be sustained by Christian life "under
the cross"? A simple affirmation of that question is inadequate. A theology
of the cross that is unrelated to the resurrection as "first fruits" of the
kingdom of God and the future resurrection of the dead is in danger of
neglecting the created order and the hope for God's final cosmic victory
over his rebellious creation, which he promised in the resurrection of
Christ. In that case, the theology of the cross is easily transformed into a
passion mysticism and the resurrection into the noetic meaning of the
victory of the cross (cf. Bultmann). The Gospel of John shows the
limitation of such a theology of the cross, because—notwithstanding
Christian life under the cross—the cross becomes the secret hour of glory,
the "gateway" to heaven, and it ceases to have cosmic-eschatological
meaning for a fallen world. Thus, in Paul the cross is embedded in the
apocalyptic framework of the resurrection of Christ, so that the proleptic
victory of the cross and resurrection moves toward the future public
victory of God in the final resurrection. Christian life in the body by the
Spirit is indeed life under the cross. Therefore, we "proclaim the death of
the Lord" in the Eucharist (1 Cor. 11:26). But life under the cross is not
celebrated as if suffering has become acceptable or "good" in the gospel.
Life under the cross awaits God's victory, and so Paul adds, we "proclaim
the Lord's death until he comes" (1 Cor. 11:26). The "eschatological
reservation" expects the future resurrection of the dead, so that the present
paradox of victory *amid* death (2 Cor. 4:11) can be sustained by the hope
in the transformation of all creation, that is, in the victory *over* death. Only

then the song of triumph will be heard: "Death is swallowed up in victory" (1 Cor. 15:54). The "redemption of the body" (Rom. 8:23) is not a "redemption from the body" but a redemption of the total "body" of creation (Rom. 8:21). And so Paul concludes, "Therefore, my beloved brethren, be steadfast, immovable, always abounding in the work of the Lord, knowing that in the Lord your labor is not in vain" (1 Cor. 15:58).

The apocalyptic world view is the fundamental carrier of Paul's thought. Without it his basic christological focus becomes distorted. Without it the design of Paul's theology shifts from Christ as "first fruits" to Christ as the total "fulness of God" (Col. 1:19), that is, Christ as that total and completed revelation of God which exhausts all God's glory and triumph. For Paul, the "material content" (*Sachgehalt*) of the gospel is inseparable from the necessary "linguistic medium" (*Sprachgestalt*) of apocalyptic thought; in fact, the coherent theme of the gospel is unthinkable apart from apocalyptic. In that sense, apocalyptic thought patterns are not to be demythologized or regarded as incidental linguistic "husk" that can be transposed into a nonapocalyptic metaphysic. The post-Pauline history of the church shows abundantly that the gospel itself was jeopardized when nonapocalyptic thought forms became its hermeneutical carrier.

It is interesting that Christian hermeneutics has regularly adopted the dualistic component of apocalyptic—in whatever spiritualistic or existentialist terms—whereas it has neglected and/or obscured its other two components, imminence and cosmic-universalism. And so it has failed to understand Paul properly, because the dimensions of imminence and cosmic expectation are central to Paul, whereas that of apocalyptic dualism is tempered by the salvation-historical understanding of Israel's place in God's saving design for his creation.

9

The Scandal of the Cross

THE CURSE OF THE LAW

The death and resurrection of Christ constitute the central confession of the Jewish-Hellenistic Christian tradition (1 Cor. 15:3-5). Because this confession is open to a variety of interpretations, the question arises whether Paul simply transmits this tradition or reinterprets it in some manner.

Paul's persecution of the church was motivated by his Pharisaic conviction that by definition a Messiah who suffered death could not be the Messiah but had to be an impostor. Galatians 3:13 expresses this central Jewish polemic: "Cursed be every one who hangs on a tree" (Deut. 21:23). Although in Jewish penal law, stoning and not crucifixion was the method of executing criminals, the dead body was later hung on a tree to manifest publicly the divine curse in accordance with Deut. 21:23. Jesus' indictment as an impostor was not simply a human judicial act; it was confirmed by God. Paul was infuriated, not so much by someone who made messianic claims but by the claim on behalf of someone who had been condemned by the law of God. After all, messianic pretenders were not unknown in Judaism (cf. Josephus[1]), and they were tolerated until time itself proved their claims to be mistaken. Akiba, the revered rabbi of Israel, professed Bar Cocheba to be the Messiah in the rebellion of A.D. 132 against Hadrian, without stirring up any charges of heresy.

Paul's conversion revolutionized his religious convictions. Psychological factors do not adequately explain his conversion—for instance, a frustration with the burden of the law, or a belated remorse evoked by the memory of the cruel death of the innocent figure of Jesus on the cross, or the exemplary behavior of the persecuted followers of Jesus. The first of these explanations underlies many interpretations of Paul's conversion. Nietzsche paved the way when he attributed Paul's conversion to his lust for power—a lust he could finally satisfy by throwing off the yoke of the law and by venting his open hostility on what he had always secretly hated.[2] Even more popular is the tendency to read Paul through Luther and to identify Luther's monastic struggle with Paul's struggle with the law. Such a view is no longer possible after Werner Georg Kümmel's monograph "Romans 7 and the Conversion of Paul."[3] Romans 7 is

182

basically not autobiographical; to the contrary, a struggle with the law in Paul's Pharisaic career is contradicted by Gal. 1:14 and Phil. 3:6, where Paul glorifies the law during his Jewish life (cf. *simchat hattorah*, "the joy of the law"). The textual pillars of a psychological interpretation of Paul's conversion—Romans 7 and Gal. 3:24—cannot sustain it. Romans 7 is basically a retrospective analysis of Jewish existence under the law (see Chapter 11). And "the law was our custodian unto Christ" (Gal. 3:24) does not refer to the law as the pedagogue who makes us aware of sin and guilt and so prepares us for the forgiveness of sins in Christ. Rather, the law is the custodian in salvation-history who keeps us imprisoned (Gal. 3:23) until the time of Christ, so that our existence before the coming of Christ is objectively a "no-exit" situation before God (see Chapter 4, above). Moreover, it must be remembered that Paul's description of life in Christ does not employ rabbinic salvation terminology, as if Paul, after his conversion, filled his former longings with the typical language of Jewish-rabbinic soteriology. Terms like "repentance," "forgiveness," "consciousness of sins," and "conversion" (*metanoia; metanoein kai epistrephein*; Acts 3:19; 26:20) are not an integral part of Paul's soteriological vocabulary. Terms like "expiation," "sacrificial blood," and "covenant" are rarely used, and when Paul uses them, he borrows them from the Jewish-Hellenistic Christian tradition. Paul never portrays Jesus Christ as a second Moses (cf. Matthew), and language of a "new law" is impossible for him (cf. *kainē entolē*, John 13:34; *nomos kainos*, Barn. 2:6; 15:7).

Whatever the psychological basis of Paul's conversion experience may have been, it is essentially unavailable to the historian (but see Chapter 11, below). Psychological reductionism cannot take the place of historical explanation. What is most striking about Paul's conversion is its suddenness and Paul's unpreparedness.[4] Both Paul and Acts agree on this point. Paul himself speaks about it in terms of a sudden "revelation about [of?] Christ" through God's good pleasure (Gal. 1:15). What needs to be explored about the conversion is not primarily the depths of Paul's psyche but the function of the experience in Paul's life, that is, the radical consequences that Paul drew from the Christophany. It is erroneous to speculate about the secondary accounts in Acts 9, 22, and 26, as if they can yield an explanation of the Christophany, because Paul persecuted the church not for psychological reasons but for theological ones. Paul considered it simply a scandalous heresy to confess a crucified Messiah, who moreover caused his followers to tamper with the Torah. Judaism—otherwise so tolerant in doctrinal matters—cannot permit a confession that undermines its life under the Torah and must therefore eradicate it.

THE END OF THE LAW

Paul shared with all Christians an apocalyptic interpretation of the resurrection, because all Christians believed that the Christ-event had inaugurated the messianic age and the kingdom of God. However, all Christians did not draw the same conclusions from the Christ-event, for why would the confession of Jesus as the Messiah necessarily upset the basic fabric of Judaism and the Torah?

> How do we know that Paul when he was still a persecutor of Christians was suffering inward distress from his experiences of the powerlessness of the law? How did the vision of Christ bring about the resolution of this tension? How exactly did it reveal a way of salvation by which the abolition of the law was implied? In themselves, the vision of Christ and the law have nothing to do with one another. What Paul received in that moment was the conviction of the Messiahship of Jesus. While other believers were content simply to adopt this conviction, he proceeds to draw from it in some way or other the conclusion that the law was henceforth invalidated. Whether he did that at the moment or only later, we do not know. What is certain is only that he does draw this conclusion, though it is not contemplated either in the thoughts of Jesus or in those of the primitive community.[5]

Schweitzer then answers the question that was raised at the beginning of this chapter: Paul not only adopts the Antioch tradition of the sacrificial death of Christ but reinterprets it radically. But why does Paul interpret the death and resurrection of Christ as the radical end of the law? Paul reverses Judaism's most consistent indictment against Jesus' messianic status: His death is not God's curse but the redemptive center of God's judgment and love for a lost world. The consistency of this insight, with its reverberations and consequences for all Christian life, constitutes the steady anchor and depth of Paul's interpretation of the gospel. In short, Paul's radicality as persecutor has an inverse relation to his radical interpretation of the gospel. He saw more clearly than any other early Christian the destructive consequences of a crucified Messiah for the fabric of Judaism. And that radicality constitutes the constant element in Paul the Jew and Paul the Christian. What changes is not the conflict between Judaism and the gospel but its evaluation: What once was destructive is now salvific (cf. Gal. 1:23). Christ is indeed the end of the law (Rom. 10:4).

But how was it possible for Paul to transform the Jewish charge "Cursed be every one who hangs on a tree" into its opposite, "Christ redeemed us from the curse of the law, having become a curse for us"

(Gal. 3:13)?[26] Why does the death of Christ not only reverse the curse of the law (Gal. 3:13) but also signify "the end of the law" (Rom. 10:4)? As Schweitzer stated, the vision of Christ by itself had nothing to do with the abolition of the law. Other Christians did not draw the same consequences from the death and resurrection of Jesus. Yet Schweitzer's observation may be misleading, because Paul was not the first Christian to connect the death of Christ with the issue of the validity of the Torah. Other Christians had preceded Paul in the two areas that are often thought to have originated with Paul, that is, the impingement of Jesus' death on the validity of the law, and the opening up of the gospel to the Gentiles. Paul's persecution of Christians was evoked by the Stephen-Barnabas group (Acts 6:13; 11:19-26). This group not only confessed a crucified Messiah as the Messiah of God but also had begun to attack the Torah by loosening its demands and by preaching the gospel to Gentiles without circumcising them (see Chapter 11, below). Paul's persecution was motivated by two interrelated theological factors: Not only was a pseudo-Messiah, cursed by God's Torah, confessed as the Messiah of God, but that confession entailed the breakdown of the holy domain of Judaism's election privilege, that is, the admission of Gentile "sinners by nature" (Gal. 2:15) into the people of God without circumcision. This double violation of the Torah was the Achilles' heel of Paul's furor against the Jewish-Hellenistic missionary party that later settled in Antioch. It is doubtful whether early Christians themselves saw the issue this sharply. Palestinian-Jewish Christianity continued to operate within the domain of the Torah, and Hellenistic-Jewish Christianity probably did not overemphasize the incongruity between Jesus' death and the Torah. It understood itself to be liberalizing the Torah without eradicating it, and it imposed at least a minimum of Torah conditions on Gentile missions (cf. Matt. 23:23; the apostolic decree [Acts 15:20; 21:25] and the so-called Noachian Commandments). Paul radicalizes the issue in terms of an either/or. If the Torah curses Jesus, whom Christians confess as Messiah, then Jesus is not only a pseudo-Messiah but also an anti-Messiah. A pseudo-Messiah is an irritant within Judaism and can be tolerated, but an anti-Messiah who attacks the Torah must be eradicated. The Torah and a crucified Messiah collide inevitably. At this point no compromise is possible, because if the one "who hangs on a tree" is truly the Messiah, the Torah comes to its end at the tree. It is superseded and abolished by God himself. In that case, the resurrection of Christ is not only God's confirmation of Jesus' messianic claim but God's confirmation of his death, because it is embraced within God's purpose. Jesus—condemned and cursed by the Torah—is indeed the

Messiah of God who supersedes the law and abolishes the "dividing wall" (Eph. 2:14) between Jews and Gentiles. The domain of the Torah with its halakic fences—the "wall"—has been set aside: God's righteousness is "apart from the law" (Rom. 3:21), and Christ is the "end of the law" (Rom. 10:4). Therefore, the death of Christ signifies the great reversal, because the judgment of the Torah on Christ becomes instead the judgment of God in Christ on the Torah. This reversal is all the more radical because Paul does not primarily attribute the death of Christ to Jewish ignorance or criminal behavior (cf., e.g., Acts 2:23; 3:15, 17). In other words, it cannot be accounted for as a human miscarriage of justice but is a part of God's plan of salvation. God does not simply reverse a human crime against the law in the resurrection but reverses the status of the Torah itself by "sending his son" to die on our behalf (cf. Rom. 8:3; Gal. 4:4; see Chapter 11, below). Marcion came close to Paul's intent when he defined the law as the inferior revelation of the Demiurge, which the new revelation of the God of Christ abolishes. Although Gal. 3:13–20 is perhaps Paul's most radical assertion about the Torah, he is not a Marcion because he interprets "Christ redeemed us from the curse of the law" (Gal. 3:13a) by the phrase "Christ has become a curse *for us*" (Gal. 3:13b). Galatians 3:13a, then, does not permit a Marcionite interpretation, as if the phrase "Christ redeemed us from the curse of the law" simply means an abolition of an outdated law that moreover never conformed to God's intention. To the contrary, Paul takes over from the Antioch church the confession of the death of Christ "on our behalf" (Gal. 3:13b; = "for our sins," 1 Cor. 15:3). The Antioch church interprets Jesus' death as a sacrificial death, that is, as the forgiveness of the sins that the judgment of the law imposes on a disobedient people. However, Paul radicalizes this confession, because the death of Christ "for us" (that is, "for our sins") does not simply mean forgiveness under the law. It abolishes the continuing validity of the law, although it confirms its verdict. The death of Christ does not mean the continuation of the law (i.e., a new possibility of obedience under the law) or a covenant renewal (cf. Rom. 3:24). Rather, it means the termination of the law (Rom. 10:4), because it initiates a new eschatological life, where God and humankind meet under new conditions. And yet the new "access" to God (Rom. 5:2) satisfies the rightful claims of the law. "The death he died he died to sin, once for all" (Rom. 6:10) means that Christ satisfied the righteous requirement of the law (Rom. 8:4) as expressive of God's holy will, in order to establish a new relationship to God "apart from the law" (Rom. 3:21).

Paul picks up the traditional confession of the death of Christ "on our behalf" and applies it to the Torah itself. Christ died not primarily to enable sins to be forgiven under the Torah but to bring both forgiveness for sins and the end of the Torah. Galatians 2:19 states it succinctly: "For I *through the law* died *to the law* that I might live to God." "I died through the law," that is, through its divine judgment over me; "I died to the law," that is, Christ died for me and I died with Christ, so that the judgment of the law and its reign no longer apply to me. Christ both satisfied the claims of the law and abolished the law, "so that I might live to God," that is, in the new domain of a law-free intimate relationship with God. And so Paul concludes, "I have been crucified with Christ" (Gal. 2:20a), a statement that connotes both Christ's sacrificial death (2:20c: "the Son of God who—gave himself for me") and the death of the law.

The issue of the Torah is complex because Paul steers a course midway between a Marcionite and a Jewish-Christian interpretation. With Marcion he would have agreed that the Torah is invalidated in Christ, that is, that Christ is the "end of the law" for the believer (Rom. 10:4). But unlike Marcion, he does not conclude that the law is an inferior dispensation that does not conform to God's will and plan of salvation. To the contrary, Christ died "for our sins," that is, for the sins incurred under the law. Christ's death is a sacrificial death that acknowledges our just condemnation by the law, and yet the dominion of the law ceases with the sacrifice of Christ. Obedience to kosher laws (cf. the Apostolic Decree) or circumcision or any other "works of the law" constitutes a denial of Christ, because the law has been judged by God in Christ "on the tree." But this judgment does not negate the divine ontological status of the law (cf. Rom. 7:12, "the law is holy and just and good"). Rather, God's judgment pertains to the poisonous interaction of the law with the human situation. The effect of that interaction excludes humankind from eternal life. The law's holy demand is acknowledged in Christ's sacrifice "for us," but henceforth its deadly interaction and effect cease. Because Christ has opened up our new access to eternal life, Christ is both the end (*la fin*) and expiration of the law, and its fulfillment (*le but*).

The Torah in Judaism has ontological status because it expresses the totality of God's revelation. The concept of Wisdom had already achieved ontological status in the later parts of the Hebrew canon, and it came to be equated with the Logos in Hellenistic Judaism (Philo; Wisdom of Solomon). The Torah now is conjoined to Wisdom (Sirach; Wisdom of Solomon) and becomes the mediator of creation. When "rabbinic" Judaism confesses that God created the world by means of the Torah and for the sake of the Torah, this confession coincides with apocalyptic thought. In apocalyptic books like Enoch, the Torah regulates the created order, rules the various angels who supervise the elements of the world, and so enacts God's cosmic reign and purpose[7] (see Chapter 11, below). Apocalyptic and rabbinic Judaism cannot be split apart in this respect.[8]

Apocalyptic thought lends a new dimension to the historical fabric of life. Human agents, historical entities, and natural phenomena are dominated and pervaded by transcendent spiritual forces. Historical events have their ontological counterparts in suprahistory, whereas spiritual forces become active agents through mythological personification (cf. demonology and angelology). Such mythological personification abounds in the New Testament. Spiritual forces "blind" (2 Cor. 4:4) and "deceive" (Rom. 7:10), just "as the serpent deceived Eve by its cunning" (2 Cor. 11:3); they "tempt" (1 Thess. 3:5) or "hinder" ("Satan hindered us," 1 Thess. 2:18). The author of Ephesians puts it very well:

> Put on the whole armor of God, that you may be able to stand against the wiles of the devil. For we are not contending against flesh and blood, but against the principalities, against the powers, against the world rulers of this present darkness, against the spiritual hosts of wickedness in the heavenly places [Eph. 6:11–12].

Satan is no longer a messenger and servant of God—as in the Old Testament—but has become a fallen angel who is allowed to reign over this world. In apocalyptic circles, history has in many ways ceased to be the realm of human freedom and has become unequivocally evil and the realm of death. In this vein Paul can speak about Satan as "the god of this world" (2 Cor. 4:4) or about "the rulers of this world" (1 Cor. 2:8), "forces in heaven and on earth and under the earth" (Phil. 2:10; trans. mine) and about "the elemental spirits of the universe" (Gal. 4:3, 9). The domination of earthly affairs by cosmic forces gives apocalyptic thought a deterministic—if not fatalistic—outlook. Qumran, for instance, posits two different Spirits that God has implanted in people and that decide their destiny. And yet, the apocalyptic outlook does not shift into a Gnostic ontological dualism. Determinism in Jewish thought does not preclude human responsibility because a person can overcome the "evil impulse" (*yetzer harah*) by obedience to the Torah. Even 4 Ezra, which despairs of the possibility of obedience because of humankind's "corrupt heart," and the Apocalypse of Baruch do not surrender obedience to the Torah as the necessary condition for salvation. The Torah is the ontological-moral counterpower that enables one to resist the evil powers, and obedience to it is the exclusive condition for participation in the kingdom of God.

Paul's conviction that Christ is the end of the law must therefore be viewed in the context of the apocalyptic status of the law. It is not merely a moral code and covenantal gift but an apocalyptic power.

APOCALYPTIC AND THE DEATH OF CHRIST

Paul's interpretation of the death of Christ is remarkably apocalyptic:

(1) The death of Christ marks the defeat of the apocalyptic powers and is thus not merely a moral act but an apocalyptic event. (2) The death of Christ therefore signifies the final judgment of the old age. Moreover, Paul not only intensifies Jewish apocalyptic but transforms it, in that the death of Christ changes both the condition for life after death and the particularist view of Jewish apocalyptic. Furthermore, (3) the death of Christ is inseparably connected to the resurrection of Christ. Because the resurrection is an apocalyptic-cosmic event that inaugurates the cosmic triumph of God, it draws the death of Christ into its apocalyptic orbit. Finally, (4) Paul interprets the saving effects of the death and resurrection of Christ not only consecutively in the apocalyptic manner but also dialectically.

The Defeat of the Apocalyptic Powers

As to the first point, the death of Christ is, according to Paul, his victory over the powers of the old age. Paul uses traditional apocalyptic terminology sparingly and interprets it anthropologically (see below),[9] so that words such as "powers," "rulers," "lordships," "thrones," "world rulers of darkness," "the spiritual forces of darkness in the heavens" (cf. Eph. 6:12; Col. 1:16) are primarily restricted to the apocalyptic sections of 1 Cor. 15:24–28 and Rom. 8:38–39 (cf. 1 Cor. 2:6–9). He does not engage in apocalyptic timetables, descriptions of the architecture of heaven, or accounts of demons and angels; nor does he take delight in the rewards of the blessed and the torture of the wicked (cf. Revelation).

The major apocalyptic forces are, for him, those ontological powers that determine the human situation within the context of God's created order and that comprise the "field" of death, sin, the law, and the flesh. The field is an alliance of powers under the sovereign rule of death. All the powers of the field have their specific reign or dominion: persons are "under the power of sin" (*hamartia*, Rom. 3:9) or "under the power of the law" (*nomos*, Rom. 6:15); sin "reigns" (Rom. 5:21) and death (*thanatos*) "reigns" (Rom. 6:9; cf. 5:17); the flesh (*sarx*) has a "mindset" of its own (Rom. 8:5–7) or "desires" (Gal. 5:17). The field operates as an interrelated whole; its forces cannot be genetically delineated, and no power can be

viewed in isolation from the others. In Romans 7, for instance, sin enters
the human scene from the outside through the law, and the alliance of sin
and the law causes people's death (v. 11). From another angle, people are
already sold under sin before the law enters the picture, because they are
carnal (*sarkinos*, Rom. 7:14; cf. 5:12). In this case, the law only confirms
what people already are (Rom. 5:20). Again, in Rom. 8:3 the law is not
the beachhead for sin as in Rom. 7:8, 11, but is infected by the flesh (*sarx*)
and thus incapable of resisting sin. How, we may ask, can a person be both
determined by sin and thus incapable of fulfilling the law, and at the same
time be innocent of sin until the law enables sin to enter from the outside?

On the one hand, death is "the wages of sin" (Rom. 6:23), so that sin is
the agent and death its consequence; but on the other hand, death can also
be the agent and sin its instrument (1 Cor. 15:56). Death is the primal
power; it is "the last enemy" (1 Cor. 15:26) within the field of the
interlocking forces. The antithesis between the two ages can be summed
up as "the reign of death" as opposed to the "reign of life" (Rom. 5:17,
21). And death remains in some way the signature of this world, even after
its allies—the law, the flesh, and sin—have been defeated in the death and
resurrection of Christ (1 Cor. 15:24–26; see Chapter 10, below). The death
of Christ now marks the defeat of the apocalyptic power alliance and
signals the imminent defeat of death, "the last enemy" (cf. Rom. 6:7–10;
7:4–6; 8:35–39; 1 Cor. 2:6–8; cf. 15:26). It is therefore an apocalyptic
event, and not just an act of sacrificial love that evokes in us a moral
sentiment. The author of Colossians interprets Paul correctly on this point:
"He disarmed the principalities and powers and made a public example of
them, triumphing over them in him" (2:15; cf. Eph. 1:20–22).

The death of Christ truly constitutes the eschatological judgment of the
powers. "The rulers of this age" have "crucified the Lord of glory" (1
Cor. 2:8); the rebellion of the world and its powers against God reaches its
zenith in Christ's death. But it is exactly in the cross of Christ that the
world itself is judged. "For since, in the wisdom of God, the world did not
know God through wisdom, it pleased God through the folly of what we
preach to save those who believe" (1 Cor. 1:21). In that sense, the wrath of
God culminates in the death of Christ: "The Jews . . . killed both the Lord
Jesus and the prophets. . . . God's wrath has come upon them until the end
(1 Thess. 2:14–16; trans. mine). And God's apocalyptic judgment in the
death of Christ will be confirmed in the last judgment, because those who
do not believe the message of the cross "perish" (1 Cor. 1:18; 2 Cor. 2:15).
Their "end is perdition" (Phil. 3:19; cf. 1:28) and "sudden destruction"
(1 Thess. 5:3).

We must be clear about Paul's relation to the prior Christian tradition in this respect, for there can be no doubt that the Antioch tradition views the death of Christ in the context of his resurrection and the future resurrection of the dead (1 Corinthians 15). The "Maranatha" at the conclusion of the Eucharist and the imminent expectation of the Parousia in credal contexts like 1 Thess. 4:14 and 1 Cor. 11:23–26 confirm this. However, although Paul and the early tradition share an apocalyptic outlook, Paul's focus on the apocalyptic dimension of the death of Christ is specifically his own. There is definitely a characteristically Pauline "theology of the cross," about which more will be said below. The inauguration of the new age with the resurrection is contingent on the radical end of the old age in the cross, and Paul's reinterpretation of the Jewish-Hellenistic tradition must be understood in this light.

Paul reinterprets the traditional Christian conception of the righteousness of God as covenant renewal, of Christ as expiation or as the Paschal Lamb (Rom. 3:24–26; 1 Cor. 5:7), of the sacrificial blood of Christ (Rom. 3:24–25; 5:9) in terms of his understanding of the death of Christ as the judgment of the powers of this age. Traditional language does not express sufficiently for Paul the "cosmic" meaning of the death of Christ, that is, its victory over death and its allies—sin, the law, and the flesh (cf. Gal. 3:13; 4:4–5; Rom. 6:1–10; 8:3; 2 Cor. 5:20). The death and resurrection of Christ mark the discontinuity between the old age and the new because history is broken apart into the era of the Old Adam and that of the eschatological Adam (Rom. 5:12–21). The death of Christ does not refer primarily to the death of an innocent suffering martyr, which evokes remorse and moral cleansing; it does not mean a new moral beginning for the "old" person, or primarily the forgiveness of his former transgressions so that he can begin again with a clean slate. To the contrary, the death of Christ addresses itself to sin as a cosmic power and slavemaster, that is, to the human condition "under the power of sin." It announces the negation of the power of sin that controls the world, and thus it has not only a moral but also an ontological meaning. "The old has passed away . . . the new has come" (2 Cor. 5:17), and a "new creation" has been established (*kainē ktisis*, 2 Cor. 5:17; Gal. 6:15).

In this context, terms like "discontinuity" and "negation" may be misleading. The death of Christ is indeed the negation of the evil powers, but even more it is their judgment. Paul's apocalyptic thought is not synonymous with the Gnostic concept of negation, for God remains sovereign over—and faithful to—his created world. His dualism is more historical than metaphysical because it is characterized by the wrath of

God and his judgment and not by the silence of God or by God's tragic involvement in a creation that should not have been. However, the wrath of God is not simply the Stoic law of retribution in a moral universe.[10] It is God's apocalyptic judgment that brings perdition and death.[11] Rudolf Bultmann puts it well:

> God's grace is not a quality, nor his timeless kindliness, and what the gospel brings is not enlightenment as to God's hitherto misunderstood nature, as if until now he had been wrongly conceived as wrathful and ought henceforth to be regarded as gracious. On the contrary! Now, as then, God's wrath pours out "against all ungodliness and wickedness of men" [Rom. 1:18]. . . . God continues to be the judge, and Christian faith in the grace of God does not consist in the conviction that God's wrath does not exist or that there is no threateningly impending judgment [2 Cor. 5:10], but in the conviction of being rescued from God's wrath [Rom. 5:9; 1 Thess. 1:10; 5:9]. That misunderstanding, however, is based upon the false notion, that God's wrath is a quality, an emotion, wrathfulness—a notion against which the ancient church, under the influence of Stoic thinking, thought it had to defend God. In reality "wrath of God" means an occurrence, i.e., the judgment of God.[12]

AFFIRMATION AND TRANSFORMATION OF JEWISH APOCALYPTIC

As to the second point (see p. 189, above), Paul's emphasis on God's wrath and judgment not only affirms but also transforms Jewish apocalyptic thinking. It affirms it because Paul, like the apocalyptist, views God's wrath and judgment not so much as his purifying chastisement of the individual or as his pedagogy[13] but as a cosmic-apocalyptic event. This is clear in Rom. 1:18–32, where God is portrayed as the apocalyptic harvester whose wrath manifests his final judgment on history. However, Paul transforms Jewish apocalyptic because he structures the relation of particularism to universalism in the age to come in a different mood and mode. Apocalyptic exclusivism, with its reward of the faithful and its celebration of the eternal doom of the godless, is in this form not present in Paul. In fact, a major difference between the Book of Revelation and Paul is the absence of the vengeance motif, of the rejoicing in the torture of God's enemies. Paul rejects this type of exclusive particularism inherent in Jewish martyrdom theology. Moreover, the death and resurrection of Christ radically change the definition of faith and its reward.

The Jewish-apocalyptic resurrection from the dead involves a change from mortal to glorious bodies as a reward of "the righteous" for their faithfulness and obedience (cf. Apocalypse of Baruch 49-51). Paul also speaks about resurrection life as a reward for obedience, but this aspect dwindles before the knowledge that only the death and resurrection of Christ saves both Jews and Gentiles from the death sentence of the wrath and judgment of God (Rom. 1:16—3:20). In other words, the death of Christ is the proleptic division between this age of judgment and death and the new age of life; it is an abyss that no one escapes and before which all humankind comes to nought. In Judaism, sin and death are powers that have lost their cutting edge for those who are faithful to the Torah. They believe that sin can be overcome in this life by human effort and that death has lost its power (see Chapter 10, below). According to Paul, death is not a temporary abode in Sheol for those who have kept the Torah, a time that will end when God rewards them in the final judgment with resurrection life. He transforms Jewish-apocalyptic thought by radicalizing not only God's wrath, but also the powers of sin and death ("the last enemy"). The death of Christ becomes the focus of God's judgment, and faith in Christ's death for us will be the norm for the future last judgment. Because all have sinned, all must die. The death of Christ signifies the apocalyptic judgment on all humankind, and his resurrection signifies the *sola gratia* of new life in Christ for all. In this sense, the division in humankind is constituted not by those faithful to the Torah and those who are wicked but by the death of Christ. For the death of Christ signifies God's universal judgment on all: "Since all have sinned and fall short of the glory of God" (Rom. 3:23). Thus, all fall under God's wrath and judgment and all are justified in Christ (Rom. 5:18).

Paul's definition of faith and obedience differs from Jewish apocalyptic because the object of faith is the death and resurrection of Christ as God's judgment and gift of new life. Faith and endurance are indeed the necessary prerequisites for participation in God's kingdom, but they are a faith and endurance that have participated in Christ's death and have therefore gone through the abyss of God's judgment.

This is not the place for a full discussion of the issue of particularism and universalism in Paul.[14] There are texts that, when pushed logically, favor universalism, whereas other texts compel a particularist interpretation. However, the following considerations seem relevant here:

1. Paul's contextual arguments cannot be pressed into a systematic-dogmatic construal.

2. Ontological statements about God's cosmic triumph over the evil powers and about the destiny of the creation in God's kingdom must be distinguished from anthropological statements.

3. The final apocalyptic triumph of God does not permit a permanent pocket of evil or resistance to God in his creation.

4. The solution to the "dark side" of the created world lies in God's imminent eschatological triumph, in which evil, tragedy, and everything in creation that opposes God will be overcome or taken up in God's glory.

5. The stance of faith is inseparable from the Christian hope in God's triumph. Therefore, the last judgment is not a survival in Paul's thought but integral to it; it measures our faithfulness to the new life that Christ has given us and thus involves judgment and exclusion from eternal life throughout.

6. The corporate nature of Paul's thought (cf. the motif of "the one and the many" in Rom. 5:12–21) does not permit an atomistic analysis of the number of the elect. And the universalistic thrust of Paul's thought cannot be logically pressed, because the context decides at every turn Paul's argumentative stance; he can stress either the universal reign of grace or the necessity of faith as the condition for participating in eternal life.

7. The destruction of the godless and the judgment of the believers is the consequence of Paul's insistence on the necessary condition of faith that marks our obedience to Christ. However, the destruction, judgment, or torment of nonbelievers does not mean that God's triumph is ultimately marred by an ultimate resistance of evil to his will. This hermeneutical consequence is not directly apparent in Paul's letters, but it is the necessary consequence of the theme of the triumph of God that dominates his thought.

The death of Christ is the apocalyptic judgment of the world: "the death he died he died to sin, once for all" (Rom. 6:10). And to be "crucified with Christ" (Rom. 6:6) means to be subjected to God's judgment. The synoptic Gospels point to this apocalyptic character of Jesus' death when they associate his death with apocalyptic phenomena like darkness (Mark 15:33) and earthquakes (Matt. 27:51) and so confirm John's statement that the cross of Jesus is "the judgment of this world" (John 12:31).

The Death and Resurrection of Christ

As to the third point (p. 189, above), the apocalyptic-cosmic interpretation of the death of Christ is the consequence of its inseparable connection with the resurrection of Christ. When that connection is misinterpreted, both cross and resurrection lose their ontological, "cosmic"-apocalyptic significance and collapse into either a theology of glory or an individualized theology of the cross. In both cases, the "apocalyptic connection" of the Christ-event with the future triumph of God is denied and displaced by a Christomonism that entails a false perspective on both the death and resurrection of Christ.

The resurrection as a historical event must be distinguished from the resurrection as a kerygmatic event. Bultmann states:

> The resurrection is not a mythological event adduced in order to prove the saving efficacy of the cross, but an article of faith just as much as the meaning of the cross itself. Indeed, faith in the resurrection is really the same thing as faith in the saving efficacy of the cross, faith in the cross as the cross of Christ. Hence, you cannot first believe in Christ and then in the strength of that faith believe in the cross. To believe in Christ means to believe in the cross as the cross of Christ. The saving efficacy of the cross is not derived from the fact that it is the cross of Christ: it is the cross of Christ because it has this saving efficacy. Without that efficacy, it is the tragic end of a great man.[15]

Bultmann correctly sees the inseparable connection between cross and resurrection in Paul; texts like 1 Cor. 15:3-5, Rom. 4:24-25, 8:34, 2 Cor. 5:15, and 1 Thess. 4:14 testify to their early Christian credal correlation. However, Bultmann fuses historical fact and interpretation in such a way that the historical character of the resurrection event ceases to be important.

> The cross is not an isolated event, as though it were the end of Jesus which needed the resurrection subsequently to reverse it. When he suffered death, Jesus was already the Son of God and his death by itself was the victory over the power of death. ... The resurrection of Jesus cannot be a miraculous proof by which the skeptic might be compelled to believe in Christ. ... You cannot prove the redemptive efficacy of the cross by invoking the resurrection.[16]

In fusing interpretation and event in such a way that the resurrection becomes the hermeneutic of the event of the cross, Bultmann imposes an individualistic-imitative dimension onto the theology of the cross. The truth of the cross is, for him, the existential decision of becoming "cross-bearers," that is,

> to take on oneself the cross, to allow it to become the determinative power of one's life, to let oneself be crucified with Christ.[17]

> To believe in the cross of Christ does not mean to concern ourselves with a mythical process wrought outside of us and our world . . . but rather to make the cross of Christ our own, to undergo crucifixion with him.[18]

In contrast to Bultmann and kerygmatic theologians like Ernst Fuchs, Gerhard Ebeling, and Willi Marxsen,[19] I believe that the death and resurrection of Christ are not one event for Paul but two distinct historical events that can neither be fused nor separated. Our debt to the Enlightenment and the historicism of Ernst Troeltsch,[20] with its criteria of probability, historical analogy, and causal dependency, cannot be superimposed on Paul. The historicity of the resurrection cannot be swept under the rug because it is contrary to modern taste. Bultmann[21] criticizes Paul for his attempt to prove the resurrection in 1 Corinthians 15, whereas Barth denies any such attempt by Paul.[22] However, there can be no doubt that Paul speaks about the death and resurrection of Christ as two distinct events. He cites the resurrection "on the third day" (1 Cor. 15:4) not only because it conforms to scriptural warrant (Hos. 6:2) but probably also as a historical reminiscence of the resurrection event.[23] Moreover, he underscores the reality of Jesus' death with the phrase "he was buried" (1 Cor. 15:4). Bultmann's interpretation would seem to favor a direct ascension by Jesus from the cross to heaven, which the text nowhere indicates.[24] Furthermore, Paul cites witnesses to the historical miracle of the objective resurrection event (1 Cor. 15:5-7), without which the gospel would have been in vain (vv. 14-19). No meditation on the cross alone would have turned its curse into its saving efficacy!

For Paul, the death and resurrection of Christ are cosmic-ontological events. The resurrection has inaugurated a new ontological reality, that is, the reality of resurrection life as "the new creation" that—however proleptic—has changed the nature of historical reality. The shortcoming of a kerygmatic interpretation of the cross, such as Bultmann's, lies in its inability to do justice to the resurrection as a historical-apocalyptic event. Indeed, when the resurrection is denied its ontological-apocalyptic character, the death of Christ is individualized into an existentialist event that no longer has cosmic significance for the created order.

Consecutive and Dialectical Interpretations

As to the fourth point (see p. 189, above), death and resurrection are first of all consecutive events in Paul.

> Christ being raised from the dead will never die again; death no longer has dominion over him [twice: *ouketi*]. The death he died he died to sin, once for all [*ephapax*], but the life he lives he lives to God [Rom. 6:9-10].

> For he was crucified [past tense] in weakness, but lives [present tense] by the power of God [2 Cor. 13:4].

But if we have died with Christ, we believe that we shall also live with him [Rom. 6:8].

Since, therefore, we are now justified by his blood, much more shall we be saved by him from the wrath of God [Rom. 5:9].

This consecutive, linear interpretation is in the manner of apocalyptic thought: after the judgment of death comes the glory of the resurrection and the new life, just as after the death of the kernel comes the grain (1 Cor. 15:36–38). The temporal sequence of death and resurrection enables Paul to accentuate the different nature of the old and the new, that is, the nature and sequence of death and life. The cross accentuates the judgment and death of the old age, whereas the resurrection and the Spirit announce the newness of the coming age.

In this context we can understand why the "rabbinic" language of sacrifice and atonement is unsatisfactory for Paul. Although it expresses judgment and forgiveness, it is incapable of stating the new ontological state of life that succeeds the judgment of God in the death of Christ. Forgiveness means acquittal of punishment but not the destruction of the power of sin or the "new creation" of the Christian's participation in the resurrection mode of life.

The sequential interpretation of death and resurrection stresses the finality of the death of Christ, that is, the "once for all" character of the destruction of the evil powers. However, the resurrection of Christ has a different type of finality because it is incomplete apart from its consummation in the new age. In other words, there is a soteriological identity of Christians with Christ in the death of Christ but not in the resurrection of Christ. Christ has died and has been raised. Believers have also died with Christ but have not yet been raised (Rom. 6:5–8). The resurrection of Christ is the first in a series to come, a series that will be completed only at the general resurrection of the dead. Therefore, Christ is the "first fruits" (*aparchē*) of the general resurrection (1 Cor. 15:20). The symmetry between Christ's death and his resurrection breaks down in its application to Christian life (see Chapters 10 and 12, below).

What strikes us in Paul is that a dialectical relation between the death and resurrection of Christ intersects the consecutive relation. And this may well be Paul's unique contribution to the theology of the cross. Life is not just life after death but also life in the midst of death, just as "power" does not only succeed "weakness" (1 Cor. 15:43) but manifests itself as weakness: "For when I am weak, then I am strong" (2 Cor. 12:10). The catalogs of "dangerous situations" (*peristaseis* = crisis situations: 1 Cor.

4:9–13; 2 Cor. 4:7–12; 6:3–10; 11:23–29; Rom. 8:35–39) claim that not only do life and power exist after or even notwithstanding human weakness but that they manifest themselves *as* weakness.[25] Christian life is truly cruciform: "For while we live we are always being given up to death for Jesus' sake, so that the life of Jesus may be manifested in our mortal flesh. So death is at work in us, but life in you" (2 Cor. 4:11–12).

The central section of Romans (chapters 5–8) is an important commentary on the interaction of the consecutive and dialectical relation of death and life, as grounded in the death and resurrection of Christ. The love of God in the death of Christ causes us to "rejoice in our hope of sharing the glory of God" (Rom. 5:2), a theme that is subsequently elaborated on in Rom. 8:18–39. But this hope in the coming glory is intersected by a "rejoicing in our sufferings" (Rom. 5:3; 8:17, 37), not only because "life" succeeds suffering but also because "life" unfolds itself as suffering: "and if [we are] children, then heirs, heirs of God and fellow heirs with Christ, provided we suffer with him in order that we may also be glorified with him" (Rom. 8:17). Furthermore, Paul frequently refrains from assigning death and resurrection to distinct spheres, as if the death of Christ refers only to judgment and his resurrection only to life. The love of God and its life-giving power occur at times in texts where the resurrection is not explicitly mentioned (Rom. 5:6–8; 8:32; Gal. 2:20; 2 Cor. 5:15; see Chapter 12, below). Similarly, the salvation occurrence in Christ is sometimes stated in "sending" formulas, where there is no explicit reference to the death and resurrection of Christ (Gal. 4:4) or where it must be inferred (Rom. 8:3; 2 Cor. 5:21).

THE THEOLOGY OF THE CROSS

Although Paul distinguishes the death and resurrection of Christ as events, he often interprets them as constituting a single meaning. The context determines in each case whether the elements of judgment or those of love and life prevail. This is especially true in Paul's theology of the cross.

Paul's theology of the cross is his unique contribution to the interpretation of the death and resurrection of Christ.[26] Contrary to widespread opinion, the theology of the cross is rare in the New Testament. It must be distinguished in some ways from a theology of the death and resurrection of Christ and from that of the suffering of Christ. The interactions among these various forms of reflection on the death of Christ do not permit us to fuse them, because they have distinct meanings.

The "cross" never appears within the traditional sequence of "he died and rose again/was raised." Although the credal statement "Christ died for you" probably lurks behind the query "Was Paul crucified for you?" (1 Cor. 1:13), it is the only time that Paul interprets the "death" formula in terms of the "cross." Contrary to our common speech about "cross and resurrection," there is no "cross-resurrection" formula in Paul; the focus on the death of Christ in the terminology of "the cross" is often so exclusive that in most contexts no explicit "life" terminology relieves its darkness and judgment. This observation is confirmed by the fact that "the cross" is never associated with the sacrificial formulas "*hyper*" and "*peri*" (= "on behalf of"). Whereas "death" and "dying" (*thanatos, apothneskein*) are regularly connected with the resurrection and frequently with the sacrificial motif of the death of Christ, the latter motif is absent in the terminology of the cross (but cf. Gal. 6:14: "But far be it from me to glory except in the cross of our Lord Jesus Christ, *by which [di' hou]* the world has been crucified to me, and I to the world").

The cross is Paul's most succinct interpretation of the death of Christ and functions as its specific apocalyptic hermeneutic. Because the terminology of "the cross" (and "to crucify") occurs infrequently in Paul, the specificity of its occurrence suggests its profound meaning, just as the specifically Pauline meaning of "grace" (*charis*) is quantitatively inversely related to its qualitative importance.

Theologies of Suffering

The terminology of the cross is never directly related to suffering or to God's suffering. A word of caution is necessary at this point. The cross of Christ does not permit a passion mysticism, a contemplation of the wounds of Christ or a spiritual absorption into the sufferings of Christ (*conformitas crucis*).[27] Paul never sanctifies or hallows death, pain, and suffering. There is no hint of a masochistic delight in suffering. The death of Christ is efficacious only because it stands within the radius of the victory of the resurrection (cf. Rom. 6:8, 10; 14:9; 2 Cor. 13:4; 1 Thess. 4:14). Indeed, the resurrection of Christ interprets the death of Christ as sacrificial, that is, as the act of God's or Christ's love (Rom. 5:6-8; 2 Cor. 5:14-15). Although the death of Christ qualifies the resurrection of Christ as that of the Crucified One,[28] the death of Christ does not in and by itself inaugurate the new age or in and by itself legitimize and sanctify suffering and death as the way in which God executes his lordship in an evil world, that is, as suffering love. There is no Christomonism of the cross, no passion mysticism or patri-passionism in Paul. The issue of God's suffering love versus his impassibility is not to be imported into Paul's thought. The later emphasis in church history on God's impassibility (*apatheia*) presupposes a Greek metaphysical scheme that has no connection with Paul's conception of God's future apocalyptic sovereignty over his creation. Paul confines the realms of suffering and death to this world and does not make them constituent aspects of God's being. The glory of God as the destiny of creation is not contaminated by—or coordinated with—notions of the virtues of suffering, pain, or death. The final state of God's glory is characterized by "imperishability" (*aphtharsia*) and "immortality" (*athanasia*, 1 Cor. 15:53; "imperishability . . . glory . . . power," 1 Cor. 15:42). The "spiritual body" (*sōma pneumatikon*) implies the future elimination of the mortal and suffering character of Christian life in this world (Rom. 8:11). And even the time of Jesus' lordship in glory is not that of a "Jésus sera en agonie jusqu'à la fin du monde. Il ne faut pas dormir pendant ce temps-là" (Pascal[29]) but a state in which "death [and suffering] has no longer dominion over him" (Rom. 6:9). Indeed, suffering is not a constituent part of the Trinitarian being of God in Paul. In fact, Paul has only an incipient doctrine of the Trinity (1 Cor. 12:4–11; 2 Cor. 13:14). Christ is never called "God"—not even in Rom. 9:5—but remains the "Son of God," "Lord," and "Christ," one who is subordinate to the Father, for whose glory he acts and dies (Phil. 2:11) and to whom he will "subject" himself at the end time (1 Cor. 15:28). We must therefore not read later Trinitarian developments into Paul. Paul's "Trinitarian" construal is apocalyptic-monarchic (1 Cor. 15:28), that is, Christ and the Spirit function as apocalyptic heavenly "assistants" of God—not unlike Irenaeus's concept of Christ and the Spirit as God's "hands." We can say that Paul is moving toward a fuller Trinitarian conception; for example, God's love for the world in the cross of Christ (Rom. 5:6, 8) moves toward the idea of a "crucified God." Yet because Paul does not have a full Trinitarian scheme, it would be inappropriate to incorporate suffering into the being of God[30] or to equate God's compassion for the world with the finality of the cross of Christ as "the crucified God." The components of the apocalyptic glory and triumph of God do not permit God's suffering to be taken up into the future glory. We conclude, then, that the idea of the risen Christ who bears in heaven the marks of the crucified one may perhaps be the necessary consequence of a hermeneutical reflection on Paul's thought, but it cannot be imported into the historical Paul himself.

Paul is in many ways different from the other so-called early theologians of the cross—Ignatius, 1 Peter, Mark, and John. Ignatius is preoccupied with becoming a disciple of Christ. Because he believes that his Christian faith will only be complete when he is allowed to be devoured by the lions as a martyr in Rome, he focuses on the imitation of the passion of Christ. Contrary to Paul, "suffering" is a central term for Ignatius's passion mysticism (cf. *pathos, paschō*). The terminology of suffering also predominates in 1 Peter, whereas "cross" terminology is absent (cf. *paschō*, "to suffer": 1 Pet. 2:19–25; 3:14, 17; 4:1, 15, 19; 5:10; *pathēmata*, "sufferings": 1 Pet. 1:11; 4:13; 5:1, 9). Although Paul uses the motif of suffering, it is limited to a few texts (Phil. 1:29; 1 Thess. 2:14; 2 Cor. 1:6; Rom. 8:17), and never refers to the death of Christ. Paul never says, "Christ suffered and was raised." However, because in 1 Peter, Jesus' innocent suffering is the great paradigm and example for suffering Christians, he—unlike Paul—does not develop a theology of the cross but focuses on the suffering death of Christ as the visible model for Christian imitation and discipleship.

Mark is often characterized as "the Pauline gospel." Yet unlike Paul and like 1 Peter, Mark is more a theologian of the sufferings of Christ than a theologian of the cross. The passion of Christ becomes in Mark the paradigm for Christian discipleship. Although the words of the angel— "You seek Jesus of Nazareth, who was crucified. He has risen, he is not here" (Mark 16:6)—have a Pauline connotation, Mark's intent is clear in a saying like "If any man would come after me, let him deny himself and take up his cross and follow me" (Mark 8:34; cf. Matt. 10:38; 16:24; cf. Luke 9:23 ["daily"]; 14:27). Likewise, the passion predictions in Mark (8:28; 9:31; 10:30) point to "following Jesus on the way [to the cross]" (Mark 10:21, 52). A theological interpretation of the terminology of the cross is virtually absent in Mark[31] because the discipleship motif of following Jesus in his suffering predominates. However, Jesus' cry of abandonment (Mark 15:34) constitutes in its context a profound reflection on the meaning of the cross. The bleakness and the lonely forsakenness of the man on the cross, the total breakdown of the Jewish religious establishment, and the final apocalyptic judgment on Judaism are as striking here as the insight of the Gentile centurion that the suffering figure on the cross is truly the King of the Jews and the Son of God. The cross has no need, as it were, of the confirmation of the resurrection. It is itself both the judgment of the world, and the victory over the world. Although Mark is here close to Paul, the passion motif as constitutive of the hidden victory of Christ moves in a different direction from Paul.

Although the cross is central for John, his interpretation is very different from that of Paul. John fuses cross and resurrection in such a way that the cross is no longer a scandal but the gateway to glory. Because it signifies Jesus' "being lifted up" (*hypsoun*) into heaven, it becomes the hour of his glory (John 12:27–33), whereas for Paul the cross is a scandal and the hour of the weakness of Christ (1 Cor. 1:25; 2 Cor. 13:4).[32]

The Death of Jesus in the Early Church

The distinctive character of Paul's theology of the cross reveals itself when we compare it with the interpretation of the death of Jesus in the early church. When Jewish Christianity emerged out of Judaism, it had to come to terms with the problem of a crucified Messiah. Its polemic with Judaism could not be fruitful unless the death of the Messiah was accounted for. The debate centered necessarily on Scripture as the common authority for both parties. Although the character of the debate changed after Hellenistic Christianity turned its back on Judaism, it continued well into the second century (cf. Justin's *Dialogue with Trypho*).

Acts portrays the various ingredients of the Christian answer to the Jewish charge "Cursed be every one who hangs on a tree" (Gal. 3:13). Although it is hazardous to trace the genetic development of the debate, Jewish Christianity originally seems to underplay the death of the Messiah, and it concentrates on Jesus' resurrection as God's reversal of an ignominious death. At this stage, the resurrection of Christ functions to confirm God's vindication of Jesus' messianic claim and marks the inauguration of the appearance of the Son of man or "the Son" (1 Thess. 1:10) from heaven to usher in the kingdom of God. The petition "Maranatha" (1 Cor. 16:22; Rev. 22:20; Didache 16) expresses the fervent eschatological longing that is aroused by the resurrection and the gift of the Spirit. The "reversal scheme" attributes the death of Jesus primarily to the ignorance or wickedness of the Jews (Acts 3:17; 2:23). Although Acts ascribes the death of Jesus to the "definite plan and foreknowledge of God" (2:23), the death itself has no redemptive significance, for the removal of its "scandal" engages the apologetic energy of Jewish Christians. The exegesis of Scripture, then, provides the warrant for God's "plan and foreknowledge" (Acts 2:23–28). We do not know whether the original line of defense was based on a global appeal to "the scriptures" (*hai graphai*) or on specific proof-texts from Scripture. The first option suggests itself in the pervasive use in Luke-Acts of the salvation-historical phrase "it was necessary" (*dei*, Luke 9:22; 13:33; 17:25; 21:9; 22:37; 24:7, 26, 44; Acts 1:16; 17:3), especially when we see it in conjunction with the global reference to the Scriptures in a text like Luke 24:44, "everything written about me in the law of Moses and the prophets and the psalms must [*dei*] be fulfilled" (cf. also Luke 24:27, "in all the scriptures").

However, the reference to "according to the scriptures" in 1 Cor. 15:3,

4 may well reflect an earlier tradition and may have specific proof-texts in mind (although the sacrificial reference to Isaiah 53 is certainly not a formulation of the Jerusalem church). Luke-Acts probably reflects a later stage in the debate with Judaism, when Christianity is in the process of appropriating the Old Testament as its own Scripture that now in its totality testifies to Christ.

The church as well as the Qumran community employs the so-called pesher-hermeneutic that interprets Scripture in terms of its eschatological fulfillment in the present. Christian interpretation searches the Scripture for prophecies of Jesus' atoning death (cf., e.g., Rom. 15:3; 1 Cor. 10:11; 15:3-5; Matthew's "fulfillment" quotations; the prominent use of Psalms 22 and 69 in Mark's passion story [Mark 14, 15]). However, it seems that in its earliest stage scriptural hermeneutic is preoccupied with a defensive apologetic of the Messiah's criminal death and attempts to account for it in terms of Jewish ignorance, wickedness, or salvation-historical necessity. On this point, Luke-Acts may well reflect elements of this early Jewish-Christian tradition, because nowhere does it ascribe atoning significance to Jesus' death; instead, it focuses both on Jesus' innocent suffering and on the resurrection that must undergird Christianity's claim to be the fulfillment of Scripture (Luke 24:25-46).

However, the Hellenistic-Jewish Christian community soon ascribes atoning significance to Jesus' death and turns from apologetics to a positive theological construal (1 Cor. 15:3-5). The concept of the atoning, sacrificial death of a human being comes to Jewish-Hellenistic Christianity by way of Diaspora theology. The death of the "suffering, righteous person" as beneficial to others derives from the Wisdom of Solomon, whereas the atoning value of death stems from 2 and 4 Maccabees. In the Old Testament, sacrifice applies never to human beings but only to animals—with the single exception of Isaiah 53. Jewish-Hellenistic Christianity combines the Old Testament-Jewish idea of sacrifice with that of the atoning death of the righteous sufferer and applies it to Christ, so that Jesus' death is now viewed as both sacrificial and expiatory.

The verb "to hand over" (*paradidōmi*) in the New Testament indicates the growth of this tradition, which—according to Norman Perrin—entails three stages: (1) the historical concept of betrayal and surrender; (2) the theological idea of "being handed over by God"; and (3) the soteriological idea of Christ's self-surrender on behalf of our sins that is associated with Isaiah 53.[33] Perrin's scheme, however, needs revision, because there is no evidence in Jewish Targums that Isaiah 53 was ever applied to the Messiah as the Suffering Servant. Therefore, it is unlikely that the Jewish-Christian community interpreted Isaiah 53 in this way. Its synoptic references (Mark 10:45 par.; 14:24 par.) are surely from the hand of Mark and cannot be ascribed either to Jesus himself or to the Palestinian Christian community. Because the sacrificial tradition comes from Hellenistic Judaism, it is only there that Isaiah 53 is associated with the death of Christ (cf. 1 Cor. 15:3).*

Paul receives the credal formulations of 1 Cor. 15:3 and Rom. 4:25 from the Jewish-Hellenistic church, just as he inherits the interpretation of Jesus' death as "sacrificial offering" (Passover sacrifice [Exod. 12:12–13; 1 Cor. 5:7]; expiation [hilastērion, Rom. 3:25]) and as "covenant sacrifice" (Exod. 24:4–8; 1 Cor. 11:23) from the tradition. However, contrary to the Jewish-Hellenistic tradition, Paul interprets the death and resurrection of Christ primarily in terms of a cosmic-apocalyptic judgment and renewal. Just as in Christ's death the powers of sin, the law, the flesh, and death are judged, so in Christ's resurrection the "new creation" emerges.

THE CONTEXT OF THE CROSS IN PAUL

The cross constitutes the epitome of Paul's apocalyptic interpretation of the death and resurrection of Christ and occurs exclusively in three contexts: (1) the cross and wisdom (1 Cor. 1:17–18, 23; 2:2, 8); (2) the cross and the law (Gal. 2:20; 3:1; 5:11; 6:14); (3) the cross and the "new creation" (Gal. 5:24; 6:14; Rom. 6:6).[34]

In the context of wisdom and the law, the apocalyptic element of negation predominates. Wisdom and the law are both structures of this age, normative powers for Greeks and Jews respectively. They are symbolic abbreviations of what "the civilized and religious world" considers its highest values. In the light of the cross, however, wisdom and the law are for Paul equally "the world." In this context, the "advantage of the Jew" (Rom. 3:1) over the Gentile is ignored. The world of the law is leveled, along with that of wisdom, because both fall impartially and equally under the judgment on the cross. The utter bleakness of the cross in its negative aspect predominates here, and the motif of vicarious suffering (hyper; peri) is completely absent,[35] just as there is no reference to God's suffering love or to participation in suffering as constitutive of Christian discipleship. The unrelieved bleakness of Mark's passion story comes to mind here, with its themes of betrayal, forsakenness, and

---

*In fact, it is doubtful whether the tradition behind the credal text that Paul quotes in Rom. 4:25 interpreted the clause in Isa. 53:12c (LXX: kai dia tas hamartias autōn paredothē) as "on behalf of" (hyper) rather than as "because of" (dia). The early precredal tradition probably read, "He was put to death because of our sins," not "for the sake of our sins" (= "on behalf of"), because the motif of expiation can be gathered only from the credal clause as a whole: "who was put to death [paredothē] for [dia] our trespasses and raised for [dia] our . . . justification" (Rom. 4:25).

judgment (Mark 15). The cross simply expresses the culmination of God's wrath and judgment. It is not the world's "finest hour" but its "last hour." The cross negates and judges the worlds of religion and culture: it contradicts wisdom (1 Cor. 1:18); it crucifies the law and the world (Gal. 2:20; 6:14); it invites public hostility (Phil. 3:18); it is foolishness (1 Cor. 1:14); a scandal to Jews and folly to Gentiles (1 Cor. 1:23; cf. Gal. 5:11), and truly a manifestation of weakness (1 Cor. 1:25; 2 Cor. 13:4).

Nevertheless, the cross has not only the dimension of "death" but also the dimension of "resurrection," however implicit references to its "life"-giving power often are. The obedience of Christ unto death, "even death on a cross" (Phil. 2:8), became the occasion for his resurrection and exaltation. The cross of Christ is indeed "weakness," but after the weakness comes "life" (2 Cor. 13:4). "Our old self was crucified with him so that the sinful body might be destroyed, and we might no longer be enslaved by sin" (Rom. 6:6). Therefore, salvation and the gift of the Spirit are grounded in the publicly proclaimed, crucified Christ (Gal. 3:1-5).

In these contexts, the cross signifies both judgment and life. It is the abyss for the world, but on the other side of the abyss of death and judgment there is "life." Therefore, the cross is the ultimate ground of the event of the grace of God; it expresses the verdict of "amazing grace" at the moment when the law has condemned me. Galatians 2:20-21 states it powerfully: "I have been crucified with Christ; it is no longer I who live, but Christ who lives in me . . . I do not nullify the grace of God; for if justification were through the law, then Christ died to no purpose." Thus the cross becomes shorthand for all the blessings of God in Christ; it tears us from the old world (Gal. 6:14), from the law (Gal. 2:19), and from our old life (Rom. 6:6; Gal. 5:24) in order to grant us life in the resurrection world that Christ has initiated. The "foolishness of the cross is God's power and wisdom" (1 Cor. 1:24), so that our new life in Christ means becoming "fools" in the eyes of the world (1 Cor. 3:18; 4:10) and a surrender of boasting and prestige (1 Cor. 1:29-31). Because "those who belong to Christ Jesus have crucified the flesh with its passions and desires" (Gal. 5:24), they continue to kill the deeds of the body (Rom. 8:13; cf. Col. 3:5). We are indeed dead to sin (Rom. 6:11) and "the body is dead" (Rom. 8:10), inasmuch as our body of sin has been crucified with Christ (Rom. 6:6).

The cross, then, is the apocalyptic turning point of history. The breaking-in of the new age means the destruction and judgment of the old age. Although the cross points heavily to the negative side of God's coming triumph, the "negation" of the cross proclaims as well the joyful reality of its "affirmation." In Gal. 6:14, for instance, the crucifixion of the old world is followed immediately by the reality of the "new creation" (Gal. 6:15). The cross radically upsets the standards of the world—its investment in glory, achievement, wisdom, and religiosity. It is indeed— in John's terms—the judgment of the world (John 12:31) and can be known as God's judgment and saving power only by a radical "perceptual shift" on the part of those who are "called" and "chosen by God" (1 Cor. 1:26–29), for the cross is and remains foolishness and a scandal (Gal. 5:11) as long as Christians live in this world. It is not a pseudo-obstacle or a pseudo-foolishness that "deep gnosis" can once and for all turn into its opposite as a form of secret wisdom.[36]

The vocabulary of "the cross" does not belong to the dictionary of polite Hellenistic-Roman society. It refers to a *mors turpissima* (Tacitus), a horrendous, ignominious happening reserved for the scum of society, that is, traitors and runaway slaves.[37] A Roman citizen could never be condemned to death on a cross. This "obscene" word now becomes the apex of Paul's interpretation of Jesus' death. And its scandal makes people stumble. Paul does not give the cross a symbolic, allegorical, or aesthetic meaning, as happens in later Christian interpretations, where the wood of the cross often becomes a blossoming tree. Crucifixion evokes the picture of an abject, nude figure on a cross, subjected to the most arbitrary sadism and cruelty of the executioners. Whipping, torture, the burning out of the eyes, and maiming often preceded the actual hanging (cf. Josephus *The Jewish War* 5.44.9). It is no surprise, then, that the "scandal" of the cross runs deep in the Greco-Roman world. What distinguishes gods from human beings in Greece and Rome is their immortal nature. Celsus mocks Christians for believing that "the person of whom I am telling you is God's Son, although he was most dishonorably arrested and punished to his utter disgrace" (Origen).[38] Likewise, Lucian mocks Christians as "poor devils, who deny the Greek gods and worship instead that crucified sophist and live according to his laws."[39] Thus, the suffering of the Son of God on the cross became the principal reason for the docetic interpretation of Christ in Christian thought. The Docetists attempted to accommodate the gospel of the cross to the theory of the gods' impossibility to suffer.

> With great emphasis and sarcastic joy the enemies of Christianity always pointed to the contemptible nature of Jesus' death. A God or Son of God dying on the cross of shame, that was sufficient to undo the new religion. Jesus was persecuted and killed, but not as a just man, a new Socrates. Rather he was found to be a criminal, put on trial and so condemned to death.[40]

In the face of this most nonreligious and horrendous feature of the gospel, it was only God's grace that enabled Christians to pierce through the utter disgrace of the cross to perceive the saving nature of the death of Christ (1 Cor. 1:18), for only God's "call" could make Christ crucified their strength and wisdom. According to Gal. 5:11, the cross remains for Christians both the stumbling block and the anchor of faith: "But if I, brethren, still preach circumcision, why am I still persecuted? In that case the stumbling block of the cross has been removed [perfect tense: *katērgē-tai*]." The cross of Christ is indeed "once for all," but the scandal of the cross is not "once for all" removed. It remains a scandal and must embody itself over and over again in the lives of Christians "under the cross," so that it continues to be the surprising object of their faith-commitment.

The theology of the cross is Paul's unique apocalyptic interpretation of the events of Jesus' death and resurrection, because it constitutes in most contexts the totality of meaning implicit in the Christ-event. The future age dawns in the cross, just as the old age comes to naught in it. Although the cross is primarily the dark side of God's victory in the resurrection, its manifold meaning addresses the reality of Christian life not only as cruciform and weak but also as victorious in its cruciform mode, that is, as strong in its utter dependence on God's "transcendent power" (2 Cor. 4:7). The cross directs the Christian to his present status and mission in the world; he is not to flee from it to a premature resurrection glory in the Spirit. Therefore, the cross is a reminder for the Christian of the "now" of life in Christ and of its hidden victory. It has this power because it points to the coming reality of God's final victory in which the glorious resurrection of all reality will not only confirm but also succeed the cruciform existence of the Christian. The *dialectic* of cross and resurrection *in* this life will be embraced by the *sequence* of resurrection-life *after* our cruciform life in the final victory of God.

The death and resurrection of Christ in their apocalyptic setting constitute the coherent core of Paul's thought. I argued earlier (Chapter 7, above) that Paul's hermeneutic is distinct in two respects: (1) He is able to focus on a consistent core within the early church's multiple traditions and thereby can grasp what to him is the core of the gospel. Therefore, he achieves a consistency of interpretation amid a contingency of gospel situations and a variety of gospel traditions. (2) He is able to infuse the tradition with a deeper meaning that it did not previously possess. Paul identifies the specific core of the gospel amid the variety of theological traditions in the early church as "Jesus Christ and him crucified" (1 Cor.

2:2) and interprets this specific core in a variety of contingent situations.

The question now arises whether this distinctive trait of Paul's herme-neutic is true for his theology of the cross as well. The death and resurrection of Christ in their soteriological significance seem to constitute the dogmatic center and the abiding, timeless truth of Paul's thought. Contextual thought seems to falter here, because the pivotal center of cross and resurrection is not open to the demands of dialogical and situational modification. Paul seems simply to impose this doctrinal center on the particular needs of his churches. However, although Paul's gospel has a coherent center, the mode of its application to the situations and needs of his audiences and the nature of its specific construal must be discerned.

The claim that the dogmatic essence of Paul's thought is constituted by his theology of the cross goes awry (1) when it ignores the fact that in Paul the death and resurrection of Christ are two distinct events with a unified meaning; (2) when it defines the death and resurrection of Christ in such a Christomonistic way that its apocalyptic coordinates are overlooked; and (3) when it does not observe the incredible versatility with which Paul applies the various components of Christ's death and resurrection to varieties of contingent occasions.

THE DOGMATIC DEBATE: ANSELM AND THE "CLASSICAL" VIEW OF THE ATONEMENT

The history of Christian thought shows the danger of separating or conflating the death and resurrection of Christ. In other words, when (1) the cross is separated from the resurrection, the unitary meaning of God's redemptive act in Christ threatens to be dissolved; and when (2) the cross is conflated with the resurrection, the specific character of God's redemp-tive act in Christ is jeopardized.

In the first case, Christ is viewed as "the Lamb of God" who satisfies on behalf of humankind the wrath of God and in this way merits God's mercy as priest, representative, and sacrifice. This Anselmian view of the atonement[41] threatens to undo the redemptive initiative of God's act in Christ by splitting apart the wrath of God and the mercy of Christ. The resurrection of Christ is here, as it were, a meritorious reward by God for the sacrifice of Christ, as if Christ's death and resurrection are separable in the sense that they can be allotted to Christ on the one hand and to God on the other hand. In this case, Paul's interpretation of "the righteousness of God" is split apart into the justice and mercy of God, as if God's mercy is conditional upon the satisfaction of his justice (Rom. 3:24-26; Gal. 3:13; 2

Cor. 5:21; cf. the Reformers and the Reformed tradition). This view surrenders implicitly the unified meaning of the death and resurrection of Christ. Contrary to Anselm's intention, it seems as if a meritorious Christology "from below" becomes the condition for an act of God "from above," that is, the raising of Christ is viewed as God's reward for the obedience and sacrifice of his Son.

In the second case, the unitary meaning of the Christ-event is maintained. God is the initiator of our redemption in Christ, whereas Christ as God's "Christus Victor" (Gustaf Aulén[42]) enters the world and defeats the evil powers that control humankind. In this portrayal—which, according to Aulén, is the patristic-classical view—the mode of God's redemption in Christ threatens to become docetic, for the cross is here viewed as the place where the principalities and powers are disarmed (Col. 2:15), so that the death of Christ becomes the necessary price or ransom that the powers demand, a price paid to the devil, according to Origen. This model conflates the death and resurrection of Christ in such a way that the death of Christ is no longer seen as Christ's profound identification with the human condition, and the resurrection is no longer seen as God's vindication of the obedience of Christ.

Whereas the Anselmian view threatens to cast sin and redemption in juristic-meritorious terms, the "classical" view threatens to view sin and redemption in terms of a dualistic power struggle in which God in Christ simply conquers enemy territory by an invasion from heaven. In this scheme, sin is less a responsible guilt that must be forgiven than a power that must be eradicated, so that Anselm's dictum is relevant here: "Nondum considerasti quanti ponderis peccatum sit" (You have not yet considered the weight of sin). The death of Christ is here so conflated with his victorious resurrection that the depth, burden, and costliness of God's love in Christ are not accentuated. This results in an interpretation of "the righteousness of God" as simply God's redemptive act and ignores its Hebrew moral meaning of God's "just order." A Christology "from above" overshadows a Christology "from below," and our new creation in Christ threatens to become discontinuous with our former moral responsibility under the power of sin. This view ignores the fact that sin needs to be not only eradicated but also forgiven.

For Paul, the events of cross and resurrection cohere in a single meaning. Paul correlates God's act of love in Christ (Rom. 3:25) and the obedience of Christ (Rom. 5:19; Phil. 2:6). Thus, the death of Christ is both God's "own" love for the world (Rom. 5:6–8) and God's judgment over human sin (1 Cor. 1:18–23); it is both Christ's obedience, self-surrender, and sacrificial love for us (Rom. 5:19; Gal. 1:4; Phil. 2:6; 2 Cor. 8:9) and God's surrender of "his own Son" (Rom. 8:32).

In other words, the dogmatic debate separates where Paul correlates. In Paul the death and resurrection of Christ express both God's love and God's judgment, that is, a love that has passed through the judgment by bearing its cost and pain. Paul never separates the victory of God in Christ over the powers that enslave the creation from the solidarity of God in Christ with the creation into which God has entered in Christ. God's judgment and love "enflesh" themselves in the human situation, so that love is not simply the result of a contest of opposing powers but an overcoming of estrangement. The wrath of God and the love of God cannot be divided between God and Christ but must be held together in the being of God, as, for example, in Luther's formulation of the "right and left hand" of God (*opus proprium et alienum*). Humankind "under the power of sin" needs both forgiveness and a renewal of its being. Thus, the righteousness of God cannot be split apart into the justice and mercy of God. In Paul, the death and resurrection of Christ emphasize God's righteousness as the power of love that bears the burden of its moral character within itself and so expresses the costliness of love in the cross of Christ. Christ is not only the victorious agent from heaven who defeats the power of sin and who renews our being but also the exemplar of humanity who in his obedience fulfills the image of God and atones for human sin. In this sense the portrait of Christ in the synoptic Gospels as the one who is both victorious over Satan and obedient unto death (Mark 10:45; 14:24) cannot be surrendered when we turn to Paul. The unitary meaning of the death and resurrection of Christ points to the fact that the suffering Son of man and the victorious Son of God cannot be polarized. For the one who "is highly exalted" by God in the resurrection is also the one who "emptied himself, taking the form of a servant . . . and became obedient unto death, even death on a cross" (Phil. 2:7, 8).

A doctrinal view of the death and resurrection of Christ cannot allow the resurrection event to be swallowed up by the death of Christ, or the death of Christ to be fused into his resurrection. The danger of a Christomonistic view is that it divorces the death and resurrection of Christ from God's redemptive purpose for his creation so that it inevitably individualizes and privatizes the Christ-event. In the one case, the resurrection becomes our present individual identification with the heavenly Christ and our premature celebration of a usurped blessed state, whereas in the other case, the death becomes our existential decision to become cross-bearers in the world or our identification with God's abiding suffering love in the cross.

According to Paul, the cosmic dimensions of the death and resurrection of Christ signify that the cross is God's judgment of the world and that the resurrection is the beginning of the ontological renewal of creation that will come to completion in God's new age. Paul's soteriological apocalyptic is determined by the theocentric focus of the death and resurrection of Christ. The cross is indeed the cross of the risen Lord, and the resurrection is the exaltation of the crucified Lord, so that the signature of Christian life in this world is marked by God's grace and love. However, the cruciform life of believers in Christ has a victorious ring because it is on the way to, and lives in the dawn of, the coming cosmic triumph of God.

COHERENCE AND CONTINGENCY

The relation of core and contingency is particularly impressive in Paul's preaching of the cross and resurrection. We have noticed the variety and versatility with which Paul emphasizes the various components of the death and resurrection of Christ. In accordance with the argumentative situation and its demands, Paul can stress the resurrection (1 Corinthians 15), the cross (1 Corinthians 1, 2), the expiatory death of Christ (Rom. 3:23–25), a "sending" formula (Gal. 4:4; Rom. 8:3), or a combination of sacrificial and participatory language (2 Cor. 5:14–15). And yet the unified meaning of cross and resurrection remains present even when the two events seem separated (1 Corinthians 1 vs. 1 Corinthians 15) or when references to the cross or the death of Christ omit any mention of his resurrection.

The unitary meaning of the cross and resurrection is especially clear in Rom. 6:1–10, where both are directly applied to our life in Christ. The exception to this unitary scheme seems to be 1 Corinthians 15 (see Chapter 8, above). Although Paul cites the creed of the death and resurrection of Christ (1 Cor. 15:3), his argument is here so concentrated on the futurity of the resurrection that its modification by the death of Christ is lacking. The urgency of the situation in Corinth may have compelled Paul to this one-sided emphasis, for it would be an error to suppose that in Paul's mind the death and resurrection of Christ could ever be separated; in that sense, 1 Corinthians 1 and 2 are the presupposition and complement to 1 Corinthians 15 (cf. Barth[43]). And yet Paul himself seems occasionally to separate the death and resurrection of Christ because it is peculiar that its usual unitary meaning is not evident in his teaching on the Spirit, which is, after all, the basic power of Christian life and also—one would suspect—of life under the cross. However, this expectation is not fulfilled. As we shall see (Chapter 13, below), the Spirit is usually so directly associated with the victory of the resurrection of Christ that it is much more the power of the future triumph of God in the present than the power of the cross for our present cruciform existence.

10

The Dilemma of Sin and Death: Equivalent or Disparate Powers?

THE RELATION OF SIN AND DEATH

At this point the question arises whether a Jewish apocalyptic world view can tolerate a radical Christian modification without being changed into something else. Does Paul shift apocalyptic into a Christocentric scheme that transforms his apocalyptic theology into a form of "realized eschatology," or into an existentialist anthropology? If the death and resurrection of Christ are cosmic-apocalyptic events (see Chapters 8 and 9, above) that signify the final defeat of the powers of sin and death and inaugurate the reign of resurrection-life in Christ, how shall Christian life *in history* be interpreted? If for those "in Christ" sin and death are no more, how is it still possible to speak about historical life and finitude as we know it? Does Paul's logic push him to a view of "eschatological life," which has the ontological status of a "new creation" and is thus identical with the end of history?

Do we have to say with Rudolf Bultmann, "History has been swallowed by eschatology"?[1] Bultmann's existential interpretation of Paul's apocalyptic circumvents "realized eschatology" by focusing on the decision of faith that grants believers new life before God in every moment of their existence. Thus, chronological history has ceased to be important because eschatological life refers to the historicity of the believer's existence in faith. If we reject Bultmann's option, "realized eschatology" seems to be the only alternative. Our new being in Christ is then given to us through sacramental participation *ex opere operato* and signifies our glorification with Christ while we simply wait for the "shedding" of our body at death. According to this dualistic scheme, which divorces the Spirit from the body, death is purely a spiritual power that has been overcome in Christ. Its manifestation in physical death and finitude has no significance, because physical death is simply the natural end of all created things. Apocalyptic theology slides here into a Gnostic dualism, and the future of history and the created order are abandoned.

Paul seems caught in an insoluble problem. How can he as a Christian-apocalyptic theologian interpret the death and resurrection of Christ as "the already" of God's new age and yet leave room for the "not yet"? How can he allow for an "interim time," in which the "already" and "not yet" are not fused, when his logic seems to compel their necessary conflation? For if sin and death *have been* overcome in Christ's death and resurrection, spiritual tension must yield to the spiritual bliss of the *beati possidentes* ("blessed possessors"), with their conviction, "we have arrived, because the powers of sin and death *have been* overcome." Paul's christological center seems to leave no other option but to drown his apocalyptic theology in a realized eschatology. Even the Pauline school, which wrote Colossians and Ephesians, adopts this view: The whole revelation of God has been consummated in Christ, "in whom are hid all the treasures of wisdom and knowledge" (Col. 2:3) and in whom God "has summed up all things, things in heaven and things on earth" (Eph. 1:10; trans. mine). If Ephesians is "the quintessence of Paulinism,"[2] apocalyptic theology certainly has no essential place in Paul, and it is no wonder that Gnostics considered Paul their natural ally!

In view of the twofold fact that Christ "died to *sin*, once for all" (Rom. 6:10) and that "*death* no longer has dominion over him" (Rom. 6:9), the relation between the apocalyptic power of sin and the apocalyptic power of death becomes an urgent problem for the interpreter of Paul. Does Paul give us any guidelines for understanding the relation of sin to death? How does he account for death's continuing reign through suffering and cosmic evil in the historical existence of believers, if "the new creation" has come about in Christ's victory over sin and death? Moreover, does Paul believe that all cosmic evil can be attributed to sin, or does he leave other possibilities open? And how is the eschatological destiny of the created order related to all this?

Ambiguity seems to abound when we consider the relation between sin and death in Paul. Sin (*hamartia*) and death (*thanatos*) are the supreme powers of the old age, which in turn determine the function of the law (*nomos*) and flesh (*sarx*) in the world. Sin and death are intimate "allies" and appear as personified powers or hypostases. As we saw earlier (Chapter 9, above), they both "reign" over the old age (Rom. 5:12–21); sin is able to "deceive" (Rom. 7:10) and death has a "sting" and a victorious reign (1 Cor. 15:55). In fact, sin is the procreator of death: "As sin came into the world through one man and death through sin, and so death spread to all men because all men sinned" (Rom. 5:12). "Sin reigned in death" (Rom. 5:21) and "the body of sin" (Rom. 6:6; trans. mine) is the equivalent of "this body of death" (Rom. 7:24). The poisonous instrument of death (its "sting") is sin (1 Cor. 15:56) and "the provisions of sin are death" (Rom. 6:23; trans. mine).[3] The alliance of sin and death is intimate indeed: "When the commandment came, sin came to life and I died" (Rom. 7:9; trans. mine).

The question then is: If sin and death are interlocking realities and if sin is the progenitor of death and in turn death's deadly weapon, how can Paul say that sin *has been* overcome in Christian life, but not death, which is the effective result of sin? And if both sin and death have been defeated in Christ, how is our historical life accounted for?

SIN: THE IMPOSSIBLE POSSIBILITY

Paul's language of sin—even apart from its relation to death—seems ambiguous. Scholars have been divided for decades on the question of the place of sin in Christian life according to Paul. Pre-Christian life is indeed "under the power of sin" (Rom. 3:9). A person has "no possibility not to sin" (Augustine) because he is under slavery to sin (Rom. 6:20). And yet, sin is not the tragic signature of an evil world and a person's blind fate but rather his own responsibility: "Sin came into the world through one man . . . because all men sinned" (Rom. 5:12). Sin commences its road to power by appearing as a free choice in the context of a command, "You shall not covet" (Rom. 7:7). A person then appears to have the ability to obey the command of the law, and even when that person trespasses, he would seem to have the opportunity for repentance and atonement as this is provided for in Judaism. However, Paul radicalizes this Jewish concept of sin.[4] Once a person has transgressed, the option to obey or disobey ceases. Sin, so to speak, grows over a person's head and traps him into bondage. In other words, sin commences as a seemingly corrigible transgression by the person but ends as a power over the person. As Søren Kierkegaard says, "sin is not a negation, but a position." A comparison of Rom. 1:18—2:29 and Rom. 5:12-21 (although so different in their contexts) confirms this description. Romans 1:18—2:29 addresses the person in terms of his responsible culpability and suggests that he could have obeyed the commandment of the Creator, whereas Rom. 5:12-19 claims that all of us are primarily victims of sin (notwithstanding Rom. 5:12d), because we are descendants of Adam, that is, we are all "in Adam."

The Christ-event has broken the power of sin. There is no ambiguity on this point in Paul. Romans 6:1-14 speaks unequivocally about an "either/or," not a "both/and": "Our old man *has been* crucified with Christ," and "the body of sin *has been* destroyed [*katargēthē*]" (v. 6; trans. mine); "He who has died is freed from sin" (v. 7; cf. 1 Pet. 4:1); "Sin *shall* have no dominion over you [*ou kyrieusei:* future tense, not an imperative], since *you are* not under law but under grace" (v. 14; trans. mine). The sequence of Romans 6 strongly confirms this "either/or": "Do you not know that if you yield yourselves to any one as obedient slaves, you are slaves of the one whom you obey, *either* of sin, which leads to death, *or* of obedience, which leads to righteousness?" (v. 16). Just as a slave has no option but to obey his master, so the human being is inevitably subject to a lordship. There is no neutral ground, for one is subject either to the "lordship" of sin or to that of God. This "either/or" is confirmed by the opposition between the flesh and the Spirit in Romans 8: "Those who are in the flesh cannot please God. But you are not in the flesh, you are in the Spirit" (Rom. 8:8-9). The domains of the flesh and the Spirit are simply antithetical: "For the desires of the flesh are against the Spirit, and the desires of the Spirit are against the flesh; for these are opposed to each other, to prevent you from doing what you would" (Gal. 5:17). Indeed, "the mind-set of the flesh is death, but the mind-set of the Spirit is life and peace" (Rom. 8:6; trans. mine).

The problem of sin in Christian life has often been misinterpreted in terms of a dialectic between justification by faith and sin. Luther expressed it as *simul iustus ac peccator* ("both justified and a sinner"). The interpretation of Romans 7 as an autobiographical confession of Paul—which has been predominant since Origen, the (later) Augustine, and the Reformation— should not confuse us. After the investigations of Werner Georg Kümmel and others,[5] this position is no longer tenable. According to Paul, the Christian does not remain a sinner. Thus we cannot read Paul through the eyes of Augustine and Luther, and the formula of the Reformation—"both justified and a sinner"—cannot be the interpretive norm for Romans 7. Indeed, the introduction of ontological and judicial categories has compli- cated the debate in the history of doctrine: Is "righteousness" a forensic judgment by God, in terms of which we are "reckoned" righteous, although we remain sinful (*iustitia aliena; gratia imputata*), or does it bestow a new quality on us (*gratia infusa*)? Hans Windisch, in his debate with Bultmann, argued persuasively that the hermeneutic of *simul iustus ac peccator* should read instead *tunc peccator—nunc iustus* ("once a sinner, now justified").[6]

Not only the content but also the context of Romans 7 prevents its interpretation as a Christian confession (see Chapter 11, below), even when the use of *ego* in Rom. 7:7-25 and the shift to the present tense in Rom. 7:14-25 are appealed to in order to legitimize a Christian confes- sional interpretation. The absence of the Spirit in Rom. 7:7-25; the clash between chapters 7 and 8 with their antithesis of "flesh" (Rom. 7:14) and "the Spirit" (Rom. 8:1–11); the use of "mind" (*nous*, Rom. 7:23, 25) and the "inner man" (*ho esō anthrōpos*, Rom. 7:22)—which are not synonymous with "the Spirit"—all these factors speak against a Christian interpretation of the passage. Furthermore, the location of Romans 7 between chapters 6 and 8—where the old and the new life are simply opposed to each other— does not permit such an interpretation. Paul does not characterize Christian life in any sense as "sold under sin" (Rom. 7:14).

The thematic preface to Rom. 7:7–25 is stated in verses 5 and 6. It clearly indicates the Pauline "either/or": *"When* we *were* living in the flesh, our sinful passions, aroused by the law, were at work in our members to bear fruit for death. But *now* we are discharged from the law, dead to that which held us captive, so that we serve not under the oldness of the letter, but in the newness of the Spirit" (trans. mine). Romans 7:7–25 describes in terms of an apology of the law (vv. 7–13) the human condition under the "oldness of the letter" (vv. 14–25a), whereas Rom. 8:1–11 explicates life in the "newness of the Spirit" (Rom. 7:6). Although the life of the Christian takes place in the context of the lingering "old age," it is itself redeemed from the infectious power of sin. Paul's view of Christian life is (in Augustinian terms) a *posse non peccare* ("the possibility not to sin") set against the *non posse non peccare* of the old age ("the impossibility not to sin") and the *non posse peccare* of the future resurrection-life ("the impossibility to sin"). Sin has become an *impossible possibility*—impossible, because of the victory of Christ over sin, which is mediated to us through the Spirit, and possible because Christian life remains threatened and liable to *Anfechtung* (attack or temptation). As Christians, we no longer live the life of "the body of sin" (*sōma tēs hamartias*) or the life of the "spiritual body" (*sōma pneumatikon*), but that of the "mortal body" (*sōma thnēton*). To be sure, "weakness" (*astheneia*) is still a fact of Christian life, for it is an inherent part of historical life in the mortal body but is not to be equated with life under the power of sin. In fact, as we shall see, Paul uses the term in different contexts with a variety of meanings (Chapter 13, below).

Paul not only speaks about social domains of power (Rom. 7:5, 6) but also addresses the depth of the individual human psyche: "Those who belong to Christ Jesus have crucified the flesh with its passions and desires" (*pathēmata kai epithumiai*, Gal. 5:24). The "desire" (*epithumiā*) in a person constitutes him as "flesh" and as "sold under the power of sin" (Rom. 7:14; trans. mine). Thus, the point of departure for the plight of the person under the law is the commandment "You shall not covet" (*ouk epithymē-seis*, Rom. 7:7). Indeed, "desire" evokes the power of sin (Rom. 7:7–8), whereas in turn the power of sin provokes "desire" (Rom. 6:12). Because sin has been overcome, the "desires of the flesh" have also been eradicated by Christians (Gal. 5:16, 24). These "passions" and "desires" manifest themselves either as sensuality or as pride,[7] that is, as sexual misbehavior (Rom. 1:26–32) or as "boasting" (Rom. 3:27, 7:5[?]).

Although Paul continually struggles with the fact of sin in his churches (1 Cor. 3:1; 5:1–5), he never yields on this point. Sin is an impossible possibility, and Christians engaged in sin jeopardize their new status as Christians: "For while there is jealousy and strife among you, are you not of the flesh [*sarkikoi*], and behaving like [unconverted] men?" (1 Cor. 3:3).

To be sure, Paul can adopt the language of the Corinthian opposition and speak (albeit only once!) about "babes" in Christ (*nēpioi*, 1 Cor. 3:1) in contrast to the "mature" (*teleioi*, 1 Cor. 2:6) and "spiritual men" (*pneumatikoi*, 1 Cor. 3:1). Although Paul insists that a person's Christian status will be decided at the last judgment (1 Cor. 4:5), and although he can be surprisingly flexible about God's final judgment of mercy (1 Cor. 3:15; 5:5), he does not tolerate an existence "according to the flesh" for so-called average Christians. The differentiation between "babes" and the "perfected" (*teleioi*)—such as that made by a Gnostic like Valentinus between pneumatics (perfected Christians) and psychics ("average" Christians)—is foreign to Paul. Christian life is never life "according to/in the flesh" but always life "according to/in the Spirit."* The distinction between the *psychikos* (the unspiritual man) and the *pneumatikos* (the spiritual man) does not constitute a spiritual hierarchy in the church but simply marks non-Christian from Christian life (1 Cor. 2:14–15). Paul's antithesis of "milk" and "solid food," "babes in Christ" and "spiritual men" does not intend to excuse sin for "second-class" Christians. The context of 1 Cor. 3:1 shows such remarks to be a sarcastic indictment of the Corinthians' perfectionist claim (*teleios*): "But I, brethren, could not address you as spiritual men, but as men of the flesh, as babes in Christ. I fed you with milk, not solid food. . . ."

The Need for Sanctification

There is definitely room for Christian growth, for an increase in faith, hope, and love (see "to excel" and "to abound" [*perisseuein*]: Rom. 15:13; 1 Cor. 14:12; 15:58; 2 Cor. 9:8; Phil. 1:9; "to strive" and "to seek" [*diō-*

---

*To be sure, life "according to/in the flesh" can simply mean historical/biological existence (cf. Rom. 1:3; 4:1; 9:3, 5, 8; 1 Cor. 10:18; 2 Cor. 10:3; Gal. 2:20; Phil. 1:22, 24; Philemon 16, etc.). The reference above is to the morally pejorative meaning of life "according to/in the flesh," as, for instance, in Rom. 7:5, 18; 8:3, 8, 9, 12; 2 Cor. 1:17; 10:2, 3; 11:18.

kein; zētein]: 1 Cor. 14:1; 14:12; "to desire earnestly" [*zēloun*]: 1 Cor. 12:31; 14:1). The Thessalonians and Philippians are exhorted to "increase and abound in love" (1 Thess. 3:12), "that your love may abound more and more" (Phil. 1:9). However, Paul does not respond to the dynamic struggle of faith in daily life with static perfectionist rigidity. If the contingent character of Paul's theology needs any demonstration, it is on the level of his paraenesis. "The fact that Paul does not build or even intend to build a developed ethical system has become a commonplace in all discussions about Pauline ethics. Hans von Soden even considered it Paul's 'holy greatness' that he limited himself to lay the foundations and was not interested in explicating in a coherent fashion the 'concrete detail' in any exhaustive or systematic manner."[8]

Although there is no "growth" or "increase" of the Spirit, the Spirit itself allows growth; faith has its own "measure" (Rom. 12:3), just as there are "varieties of gifts" (*charismata*, 1 Cor. 12:4). A Christian is not to think of himself "more highly than he ought to think, but to think with sober judgment" (*sōphronein*, Rom. 12:3). In fact, "weakness" (*astheneia*) is not inconsistent with Christian life. Some Christians are "weak in faith" (Rom. 14:1), and "the Spirit helps us in our weakness; for we do not know how to pray as we ought" (Rom. 8:26). There can be a "lack of faith" (*hystērema*, Thess. 3:10), just as there is room for "progress" (*prokopē*, Phil. 1:25) and an "increase" (*auxanesthai*) in faith (2 Cor. 10:15). Believers may at times "trespass" (*paraptōma*, Gal. 6:1), and if this happens, it necessitates a "restoring" (*katartizein*, cf. Gal. 6:1; 1 Cor. 1:10; 2 Cor. 13:11). Yet amid all these contingencies and gradations of faith, Paul views sin not as "inevitable" but as an "impossible possibility." The vocabulary of sin (*parabasis; paraptōma; hamartēma; hamartia*) is seldom applied to Christian life (Gal. 6:1; but cf. 1 Cor. 5:1–5; 2 Cor. 2:7; 12:21). Sin is not to be tolerated or lamented as a necessary part of "the human condition." It belongs to the "no longer" of Christian life: "If Christ has not been raised, your faith is futile and you are still [*eti*] in your sins" (1 Cor. 15:17; cf. Rom. 6:7, 14, 22).

The power of sin has been eradicated in Christ. Although Pauline interpreters agree on this point, the radicality of Paul's position is undermined when a modern distinction between the power of sin and the sinful act is introduced. Anders Nygren's arguments on this subject are typical.[9] He interprets the *ego* of Romans 7 as a Christian confession and tries to make this consistent with Paul's statement about "freedom from the power of sin" in Romans 6. Nygren is, therefore, compelled to say, "[The Christian] really does live 'in Christ' . . . ; but at the same time he lives 'in the flesh' (Gal. 2:20) and so is a member of Adam, of the body of the old fallen humanity. Here sin still has a hold on him."[10] Nygren resolves the contradiction in Christian life between freedom from the power of sin and life "as a sinner among sinners"[11] by making a distinction between the power of sin and the sinful act. However, Paul never says "sin is in principle destroyed but *sins* continue." Paul's Jewish mind does not separate human intention from its concrete acts. He would rather define the person in terms of an inseparable intention-action axis.

The defeat of the power of sin is not an abstract article of faith, nor is it reduced to an inner motivation, for the power of sin manifests itself in specific deeds of transgression, that is, as deeds of the body (Rom. 8:13). Because sinful acts testify to the power of sin, both are eradicated in Christ. Although Paul is not preoccupied with the despair of the existentialist about the impossible possibility of being a moral being in the midst of an absurd world, neither is he preoccupied with our pietistic ideal of "sinlessness." His remarkable extroversion is grounded in the freedom for which "Christ has set us free" (Gal. 5:1), which also means the freedom from self-concern.[12] Indeed, he can be very specific about sins, if they endanger Christian communal life, but usually he is not casuistically engaged. Paul adopts the idea of "the works of the flesh" (Gal. 5:19) and the lists of vices and virtues (cf. Rom. 1:28–31) from Jewish-Christian catechetical material, but he applies them primarily to social sins, to those sins that disrupt the Christian community.[13] Furthermore, the lists of "virtues" function as paradigms for a Christian life-style rather than as a casuistic-halakic legal code. Although Paul can use the terminology of "blameless" (*amemptos*, Phil. 2:15; 3:6; 1 Thess. 3:13; *aproskopos*, 1 Cor. 10:32; Phil. 1:10), "innocent" (*akeraios*, Phil. 2:5), "holiness" (*hagiasmos*; *hagios*, Rom. 6:19, 22; 1 Thess. 4:3–4, 7), and "pure" (*eilikrinēs*, 2 Cor. 1:12; 1 Cor. 5:8), he is not preoccupied with self-analysis.

Stendahl correctly stresses that the introspective conscience of the West has imposed a hermeneutic on Paul that divorces the original from its later translation.[14] Paul is concerned about sanctification, being "without blemish," and so on, but this is set within the domain of freedom in Christ and manifests itself in apostolic service to the world, that is, in extraverted social behavior that proclaims our freedom in Christ rather than our bondage to self-preoccupation with "peccadilloes."

Our pietistic tradition with its emphasis on sanctification and sinlessness in the context of an exclusive self-preoccupation, fear of damnation, and joyless casuistry should not be read into Paul's concern for the sanctified life. Indeed, he understands his former Pharisaic life-style ("blameless" [*amemptos*] under the law, Phil. 3:6) to be radically different from his apostolic obligation; the one who did "set himself apart" from others (*pharaz:* "Pharisee") is now "set apart" by God (*pharaz* as *aphōrismenos*) to serve "both Greeks and barbarians, both the wise and the foolish" (Rom. 1:1, 14). In that sense, "sanctification" (*hagiasmos,* Rom. 6:19, 22; 1 Thess. 4:3, 7) conveys more the meaning of "consecration to God's service" (1 Cor. 1:30) than that of our pietistic conception of "sanctification."

THE TEMPTATION OF SIN AND THE ACTUALITY OF DEATH

The Reign of Death

If sin and death are interlocking powers that cannot be separated, how can Paul maintain that the power of sin has been overcome in Christian life, but not the power of death, at least not in its full range? Paul posits the power of death as "the last enemy" (1 Cor. 15:26), which will not be defeated in its total range until the final resurrection of the dead. Only at that time, *"when [hotan]* the perishable puts on the imperishable, and the mortal puts on immortality, *then [tote]* shall come to pass the saying that is written: 'Death is swallowed up in victory.' 'O death, where is thy victory? O death, where is thy sting?' " (1 Cor. 15:54-55).

Thus, whereas sin has been overcome in the death and resurrection of Christ, death still reigns, at least in some important sense. This ambiguity seems to destroy Paul's victorious confession in Rom. 6:9: "For we know that Christ being raised from the dead will never [*ouketi*] die again; death no longer has dominion over him." The resurrection of Christ proclaims the victory of Christ over death. How, then, is death still operative as the supreme power, "the last enemy," even for "those in Christ" (1 Cor. 15:26)?

Whereas in statements about sin there is a strict conformity between the christological and anthropological dimensions ("Our old self *was* crucified with him," Rom. 6:6), we observe in statements about death a disjunction and rupture between the christological and anthropological dimensions ("But if we have died with Christ, we believe that we shall also live with him," Rom. 6:8). Although Christ has defeated both sin and death, it is curious that—whereas the defeat of sin is a reality for Christians ("How can we who died to sin still live in it?" Rom. 6:2)—the defeat of death is still to come. Indeed, how can Paul speak about the destruction of sin for those in Christ, when "the provisions of sin," that is, death (Rom. 6:23), still reign, so that Christians must still die and suffer (Rom. 8:17-25)?

The disjunction between statements about sin and death is due to their distinct spheres; sin is an anthropological reality, whereas death is as well a cosmological reality. The cosmic order is not "sinful" according to Paul. It has been subjected to "death" because of humanity's sinfulness (Rom. 8:20). The power of sin, then, is anthropological, but it has cosmic consequences (Rom. 5:12–21; 8:18–27).

Paul's Ambivalence

Paul now faces a theological problem that he does not resolve consistently and one that has plagued Christian theology ever since. Paul's inconsistency about the relation of sin to death is caused by two contradictory claims.

(a) Sin and death form an inseparable alliance, and thus they both reign or fall together. In fact, death entered the world through sin (Rom. 5:12), and the "fall" of creation stems from the sinful activity of Adam, the steward of creation (Rom. 8:20). Thus, Paul's apocalyptic thinking connects death so closely with sin that cosmic death is the inevitable result of sin. In Rom. 8:2, for example, "sin and death" are inseparably related; moreover, both alike have been defeated by Christ.

This explanation, however, does not suffice, because (b) Paul can also break the relation between sin and death. If sin has been overcome by Christ, but not the range of death—it remains "the last enemy" even after the Christ-event (1 Cor. 15:26)—then suffering and death cannot be due exclusively to sin. Death executes its reign over the created order like an infectious disease even after its ally, sin, has been defeated by Christ. The relation of suffering and finitude to sin and death remains unclear. There seems to be a residue of death in the created order that is not directly related to sin.

A similar disjunction between sin and death is found in 1 Cor. 15:42–44: "What is sown is perishable, what is raised is imperishable. *It is sown in dishonor, it is raised in glory.* It is sown in weakness, it is raised in power. It is sown a physical body, it is raised a spiritual body." Paul seems to claim here that the created order itself is an order of death by divine design.[15] The apocalyptic connection between sin and death (cf. Rom. 3:23) shifts here to a type of Hellenistic cosmology that posits a dualism between the supernatural sphere and the natural sphere.

First Corinthians 15:47–50 moves in the same direction: "The first man was from the earth, a man of dust; the second man is from heaven. As was the man of dust, so are those who are of the dust. . . . Flesh and blood cannot inherit the kingdom of God, nor does the perishable inherit the imperishable." Because of its inherently perishable character, the created order is simply discontinuous with the realm of "glory" and "the spiritual body." Texts like 2 Cor. 3:18 and 4:18 seem to confirm this, because the idea of death as the "provisions of sin" and as "the last enemy" is absent in those contexts: "The things that are seen are transient [*proskaira*], but the things that are unseen are eternal [*aiōnia*]" (2 Cor. 4:18); "We all, with unveiled face, beholding the glory of the Lord, are being changed into his likeness from one degree of glory to another; for this comes from the Lord who is the Spirit" (2 Cor. 3:18).

However, Paul stands basically in the apocalyptic tradition. It considers death a hostile power that has invaded God's creation through sin: "O Adam, what have you done? For though it was you who sinned, the fall was not yours alone, but ours also who are your descendants. For what good is it to us, if an eternal age has been promised to us, but we have done deeds that bring death?" (4 Ezra 7:118; cf. 3:7-21; 2 Apoc. Bar. 17:3; 23:4; 48:42; 54:15, 19). For the apocalyptist, death is not a natural part of the created order and has a negative ontological status. The hope of the bodily resurrection of the dead confirms this estimate of death as a physico-spiritual power that rules the old age. The new age will be characterized by the destruction of death; it will be a time when the bodies of the faithful dead will be transformed into bodies of glory (2 Apocalypse of Baruch 51).

Sin and Death in the Old Testament

We must remember in this connection that the relation of sin to physical death is not a major theological problem in the Old Testament. The resurrection of the dead occurs here only at the periphery (Isaiah 25; Daniel 12). Generally speaking, physical death is accepted as a normal state of affairs. What the Old Testament believer fears is death as a power that causes a premature end to life (Isa. 38:10) or that mutilates a full life on earth, that is, death as the spiritual enemy in sickness and oppression (Ps. 18:4; 116:3). The problem of physical death emerges only occasionally, as separation from God and as the obstacle to an abiding communion with him (Psalm 73; 139; cf. "For in death there is no remembrance of thee; in Sheol who can give thee praise?" [Ps. 6:5]). However, usually a full life, many children, and death at a ripe old age are signs of blessing (Job 5:26; Gen. 15:15; 28:8; 35:29). The focus is not on death as "the last enemy" or on eternal life as the ultimate state of bliss but on death and life as a curse or blessing of this world.

Even in Genesis 1-3, death is not "the provisions of sin" (Rom. 6:23), just as "the fall" is not connected with Adam's "original" sin.

Since man is created of perishable matter, his natural condition is mortality (Gen. 3:19). The myth of the tree of life indicates, however, that the boundary between the two domains was not an absolute one. Had man persevered in obedience to God by respecting the divine commands, God would have reserved the right to change man's condition and to grant him immortality as a favor. Man's disobedience irremediably destroyed this possibility, and thenceforth death, which until that time has been virtual, became an actuality for him.[16]

Nevertheless, according to the basic conviction of the Old Testament, death is not the punishment for sin: Adam's and Eve's punishment is a life of toil and sweat, not a loss of immortality. Genesis 3:19 assumes humankind's mortal status as a natural phenomenon: "You are dust, and to dust you shall return." Moreover, the created order is not subjected to death because of Adam's "fall"; rather, the connection between human sin and the creation causes the creation to be cursed, to be a domain of toil and sweat.

SPIRITUAL DEATH VERSUS PHYSICAL DEATH?

We cannot diffuse the problem of the relation of sin to death by positing a distinction between spiritual and physical death, as if Paul regularly separates them. When Paul speaks about the power of death, he has not only spiritual death in mind. He employs the metaphorical language of a "spiritual" death: "When the commandment came, sin revived and I died" (Rom. 7:9); "So you also must consider yourselves dead to sin and alive to God in Christ Jesus" (Rom. 6:11). A text like Rom. 6:13, "Yield yourselves to God as men who have been brought from death to life [*hōsei ek nekrōn zōntas*]," certainly refers to a "spiritual" resurrection from the dead, and thus the defeat of death is here synonymous with the defeat of the power of sin. However, "death" language—as opposed to "sin" language—has an added meaning. Because death and life refer to the physical death and resurrection of Christ and to a physical resurrection from the dead, the metaphorical meaning of death does not exhaust Paul's speech about death. Death refers basically to a physico-spiritual reality, that is, a "last enemy" (1 Cor. 15:26) that rules the present age and will be defeated only at the time of the final resurrection of the dead. As long as death is present in the world, Christian life is subject to it: Christians sigh and groan for the redemption of their bodies alongside the groaning of creation itself (Rom. 8:19-23). Paul insists on the psychosomatic unity of the person and excludes the idea of an immortal soul or a disembodied spirit in the new age. The "spiritual" body is not simply a wrapper around an immortal soul but a new somatic selfhood that conforms to the goal of all creation, that is, its material transformation into the "freedom of the glory of the children of God" (Rom. 8:21). Death, then, is neither the inevitable end of life, which one can contemplate with tranquillity (the Stoics; Epicurus), nor the peaceful resting place for individual Christians who, at the moment of death, will enter immortality and eternal life. Death remains—however qualified by Christ's resurrection—the sign that we live in solidarity with the created order in its finitude and are not yet perfected. As Christians we are constantly *subjected* to the reality of death and suffering, whereas we are only *threatened* by the possibility of sin. Although we are a "new creation" in Christ and thus separated from the old age, we are still involved in the "sufferings of the present age" (Rom. 8:18), and "our outer man is wasting away" (*diaphtheiretai*, 2 Cor. 4:16). Thus, "we groan, and long to put on our heavenly dwelling" (2 Cor. 5:2), "so that what is mortal [*to thnēton*] may be swallowed up by life" (2 Cor. 5:4). Indeed, the new age will provide an ontological transformation from the "physical body" to the "spiritual body" (1 Cor. 15:46). Paul describes it as a "radical change" for the living (*allagēsometha*, 1 Cor. 15:51) and as a "resurrection" for the dead (1 Cor. 15:52).

The difficulty Paul had with the relation of sin to death is evident in the misunderstanding of his position by his Hellenistic churches. In a nonapocalyptic climate, the inseparable connection between sin and death, which seems inherent in Paul's Christology, is here understood in purely spiritual categories. Paul's Hellenistic churches must have considered the futurist eschatological resurrection from the dead to be unconvincing (1 Cor. 15:12-58; see Chapter 8, above). Paul himself had argued the theme of "the many in the one" and "the one in the many"—our incorporation in and solidarity with Christ (*en Christō*, Rom. 5:12-21; 1 Cor. 15:21-22). To Hellenistic ears this may not have sounded much different from Paul's baptismal-sacramental theme of being "together with" Christ (*syn Christō*, Rom. 6:1-10). They understood Paul to mean that just as Christ had defeated sin, so he had defeated death. Our "spiritual" resurrection (Rom. 6:13) has already lifted us with Christ into the heavenly places (cf. Eph. 2:6), because we *"have been* raised with Christ" (Col. 3:1). For if "in Christ" we have been incorporated into his death and resurrection, then our sacramental union with Christ can only mean the defeat of death. Many early Christians drew this conclusion (cf. Col. 2:12; Eph. 2:6). It was, no doubt, the conviction of the Corinthians and of "Paul's" opponents in 2 Tim. 2:17-18: "Hymenaeus and Philetus who have swerved from the truth by holding that the resurrection is past already."

They believed that death had already been defeated, together with the power of sin. A confession like 2 Tim. 1:10 shows how easily the abolition of death through the resurrection of Christ could be fused with the conviction that death in its whole range had been overcome: "the appearing of our Savior Christ Jesus, who *has abolished* [aorist tense: *katargēsantos*] death and brought life and immortality to light through the gospel" (2 Tim. 1:10; cf. also the hymnal fragment of Eph. 5:14: "Awake, O sleeper, and arise from the dead, and Christ shall give you light"). After the defeat of sin and death in the cross and resurrection, Christians can now simply wait for physical death as the final shedding of the mortal body and as the "door" to immortality. This idea was especially suitable to the Hellenistic world where, notwithstanding Epicurean skepticism about immortality, the Platonic notion of immortality and the notion of "the body is a tomb" [*sōma sēma*] were widespread. Jewish-Hellenistic literature frequently speaks about the immortality of the soul after death (Wisdom of Solomon; 2 Maccabees; see Chapter 8, above). The Gospel of John is a canonical witness to this conviction. The future resurrection functions in this Gospel only in a peripheral way and may be editorial (e.g., John 6:39, 40). John's realized eschatology has no real place for death as "the last enemy" in the eschatological future. Thus, Jesus corrects Martha's conventional understanding of a "resurrection at the last day": "I am the resurrection and the life; he who believes in me, though he die, yet shall he live, and whoever lives and believes in me shall never die" (John 11:25–26).

Paul's inconsistency about the relation of sin and death is aggravated in a nonapocalyptic climate. Here, a Hellenistic cosmology, with its dualism between Spirit and matter and between the imperishable and the perishable, displaces the apocalyptic scheme. Physicality becomes the source of evil—as already in Philo—and the material becomes in Platonic fashion the imperfect copy of the heavenly forms (cf., e.g., "copy and shadow" vs. "the heavenly sanctuary" [*hypodeigma kai skia* vs. *ta epourania,* Heb. 8:5]; "shadow" vs. "the true form" [*skia* vs. *sōma,* Col. 2:17]). Physical death is accepted—if not welcomed—as a release from the entrapment of the body, and the (immaterial) soul realizes its true destiny at death.

The "Interim" Status of Dead Christians

Although the distinction between spiritual and physical death is basically alien to Paul's apocalyptic conviction of death as "the last enemy," which will be overcome in the final resurrection of the dead, he nevertheless distinguishes occasionally between physical death and spiritual death, while he conjoins them in other contexts. Paul's statements about the interim state of the dead favor a spiritual interpretation of the power of death. Although the dead in Christ "sleep" and will not be raised into resurrection bodies until the final resurrection of the dead (1 Cor. 15:51; cf. 1 Thess. 4:15), death as "the last enemy" seems to have lost its grip on Christians who have died. The statement that death "will" not "be able to separate us from the love of God in Christ Jesus our Lord" (Rom. 8:38–39) prepares the way for Paul's desire to "depart and be with Christ, for that is far better" (Phil. 1:23). To be sure, 2 Corinthians 5 opposes the Parousia (vv. 1, 10) to the interim state of the dead. Although this state involves an incomplete and "nude" existence, it is nevertheless a form of "being at home" with the Lord (v. 8). The final resurrection of the dead seems here only relatively different from the "interim state." For "the dead in Christ" (1 Thess. 4:16), death seems to have lost its character as "the last enemy," because their communion with Christ is not interrupted by death. The idea of death as a "spiritual enemy" that *has been* overcome by Christ is more compatible with such statements than the idea of death as "the last enemy" that rules the whole cosmos until the final resurrection of the dead.

Moreover, how can the Christian claim to be already a "new creation" in Christ (2 Cor. 5:16; Gal. 6:15) and yet yearn for a radical change from "flesh and blood" to a "spiritual body" (1 Cor. 15:50–53)? Indeed, this is an acute problem, for the term "the new creation" does not just refer to a moral change but has ontological status; it is "a new act of creation."[17] Is the future "spiritual body" then only an appropriate supernatural "form,"[18] or only a somatic "wrapper" for an already redeemed spirit? Besides, how does Paul view the relation between the Christian in history and the Christian in the final resurrection state? If a radical change and a resurrection from the dead is to occur (1 Cor. 15:50–53), will that be a *creatio ex nihilo,* a totally new creation by the God "who gives life to the dead and calls into existence the things that do not exist" (Rom. 4:17)? Does this mean a "new creation" all over again?

Do we have to say, then, that "the dead in Christ" really perish until the moment of the final resurrection? In other words, how does Paul view the continuity between Christian historical life in the Spirit and in the future "spiritual body"? Does he think in terms of a transformation of bodies or in terms of a radical discontinuity between Christian life in history and in the future resurrection state? In the latter case, the continuity between life in history and in the resurrection body would lie exclusively in God (1 Cor. 15:38 [?]) rather than in the Spirit that the Christian possesses since baptism. But, if Christians really are subject to death as "the last enemy," how can Paul speak about death as unable to separate us from the love of God in Christ (Rom. 8:38), and how can there be a communion of the dead with Christ before "the last enemy" has been overcome?

Paul seems to waver between death as the physico-spiritual "last enemy"—which still reigns although sin has been defeated in Christ—and death as a purely spiritual power that has been overcome since the resurrection of Christ.

The contingent context of the argument determines Paul's particular pitch. Sometimes death is related to sin in such a way that physical death is not directly within the horizon of the discussion. Here resurrection language is primarily applied to the ethical life in its relation to sin:

> For we know that Christ being raised from the dead will never die again; death no longer has dominion over him. The death he died he died to sin, once for all. So you also must consider yourselves dead to sin and alive to God in Christ Jesus. . . . Yield yourselves to God as men who have been brought from death to life. [Rom. 6:9–13]

At other times, death is explicitly related not to sin but to the final victory of life in the resurrection of the dead. Death is now treated as "the last enemy," that is, as a physico-spiritual reality inherent in the created order until the final triumph of God (1 Cor. 15:51–58; Rom. 8:18–30). The question thus arises whether the contingency of the argumentative contexts points to a fundamental inconsistency of Paul's thought on this issue or not.

PAUL'S BASIC INTENT

Paul's basic thrust is toward the future consummation of the defeat of death, which has already been guaranteed by the death and resurrection of Christ (Rom. 8:38). The Christ-event constitutes the Christian hope; Christ is "the first fruits of those who have fallen asleep" (1 Cor. 15:20), so that the harvest will coincide with the final defeat of death (1 Cor. 15:26) and the gift of a spiritual body.

The physico-spiritual nature of death does not allow an exact correspondence with the essentially spiritual nature of sin. As we have seen, statements about sin as a power that has been eradicated in Christ do not parallel claims about the defeat of death. The reason for this is that the physico-spiritual nature of death cannot be collapsed into its purely spiritual meaning, as is clear in a text like 1 Cor. 11:29–30, where not only spiritual death but physical death is the result of God's judgment: "For any one who eats and drinks without discerning the body eats and drinks judgment upon himself. That is why many of you are weak and ill, and some have died."

Paul probably intends to say that although sin and death reigned together and were dethroned together by Christ, the defeat of the power of sin has not undone the effect of sin in the world, that is, death. The cause of the disease—sin—has been removed by the Christ-event, so that death has presumably been robbed of its deadly "sting" (1 Cor. 15:56). Death in that case is only the aftereffect of the power of sin. According to 1 Cor. 15:54, however, the power of death is present "until" (*tote*) the final resurrection of the dead. If death is only an aftereffect of sin, it would cease to be "the last enemy" (1 Cor. 15:26) that God must still overcome in the apocalyptic consummation according to Paul (1 Cor. 15:25–28). However, if sin, which is "the sting of death" (1 Cor. 15:56) has been removed, how can death still be "the last enemy," especially in the face of Rom. 8:38–39, "I am sure that neither death, nor life . . . will be able to separate us from the love of God in Christ Jesus our Lord"? Sin is certainly the cause of the power of death in the created order (Rom. 5:12, 20; 8:20). But if that is true, how—given Paul's statement that sin has been defeated in the Christ-event—can the sting of death continue to be present in the creation until the final triumph of God (1 Cor. 15:54)?

A systematic doctrinal view of Paul's thought on sin and death is impossible. To be sure, the often contradictory character of his particular emphases is held together by the central conviction that because the Christ-event has brought the end of sin for those in Christ, the end of death as a physico-spiritual power is impending, for "death no longer has dominion over [Christ]" (Rom. 6:9).

CONTEXTUAL ARGUMENTATION

This basic conviction now is interpreted in a variety of ways according to the argumentative demands of the contextual-contingent situation:

1. Within a context of realized eschatology and spiritualism, Paul emphasizes that death is still "the last enemy" in order to prevent dualistic conclusions that reject not only a responsible life in the body but also the future redemption of the created order.

2. However, where the context demands a defense of justification by faith alone apart from the law and a rejection of Jewish antinomian charges, Paul interprets the present ethical life of Christians as a victory over death, that is, he interprets it in resurrection terms, as for example in Rom. 6:13, "men who have been brought from death to life."

3. Again, in a context of martyrdom and persecution, he points to believers' victory in Christ and to their lasting communion with Christ; death has been robbed of its power (Phil. 1:21-23; Rom. 8:38). Again, the situation is different where believers grieve over the dead before the Parousia (1 Thess. 4:13-18). Here Paul teaches the future eschatological "communion of all the saints"; *all* Christians will be perfected together without a privileged position for those who are alive at the time of the Parousia (cf. 1 Cor. 15:50). Similarly, Paul can emphasize the incomplete status of the dead in Christ over against the glory of the Parousia and the resurrection body of "all" together (2 Cor. 5:1-10).

There are at least two basic elements in Paul's thought about death:

First, the final resurrection of the dead and the Parousia are the goal of the whole created order; death is "the last enemy" for both Christians and the created order in the sense that the final cosmic redemption will coincide with the final defeat of death. As all groan *together,* so all will be redeemed *together* in a final and completed way. In this context, there is therefore no ground for Christian privileges or egoistic privatistic bliss immediately after death.

The second basic element is that the "dead in Christ" (1 Thess. 4:16), however, will not be severed from their personal communion with Christ. In that sense, death has been overcome. Yet the dead must wait—whether "asleep" (1 Thess. 4:13-18) or "at home with the Lord" (Phil. 1:23; 2 Cor. 5:8)—until the final triumph of God. Although Paul does not surrender the believer's "individual" communion with Christ immediately after death, it occupies a secondary position, because Paul's primary concern is the future apocalyptic "communal" participation of all believers with Christ (1 Thess. 4:17; Rom. 6:8). This points to the solidarity of the whole created order, for just as there is a common solidarity in death, so there will be a common solidarity in eternal life at the time of the final redemption and triumph of God.

The dialectic between theocentrism and Christocentrism is especially clear in Paul's thought about sin and death. He cannot surrender "the new creation," which Christ has initiated and which means the defeat of sin and death. But neither can he surrender the future horizon of God's cosmic triumph over death and suffering. Both the actual presence of God's future in Christ and the future thrust of our present status in Christ toward the final glory of God occupy his thought. Paul's statements about sin and death confirm the interaction between contingency and coherence in his thought. I have alluded frequently to the contingent aspect of Paul's thought in this regard, which explains the variety of seemingly disjointed statements. However, the necessary diversity of emphases and the flexible character of Paul's paraenesis does not signify a bewildering contradiction, because the coherent theme of Paul's thought is constituted by the apocalyptic interpretation of the Christ-event as the prelude to God's coming triumph.

The Power of Death and the Cruciform Life

We must be aware that Paul's treatment of sin and death gives him the opportunity to define Christian existence "under the cross." For in Christ, death is not just an enemy to be endured or the result of sin's inevitable power, but a redemptive possibility. Thus, Paul's apostolic ministry is characterized as "always carrying in the body the death of Jesus, so that the life of Jesus may also be manifested in our bodies. For while we live we are always being given up to death for Jesus' sake, so that the life of Jesus may be manifested in our mortal flesh [en tē thnētē sarki]. So death is at work in us, but life in you" (2 Cor. 4:10-12); "Our hope for you is unshaken; for we know that as you share in our sufferings [pathēmata], you will also share in our comfort" (2 Cor. 1:7). Paul defines these sufferings as "the sufferings of Christ": "For as we share abundantly in Christ's sufferings, so through Christ we share abundantly in comfort too" (2 Cor. 1:5). The impending defeat of death and the loosening of its grip upon Christian life are evident in the sure hope that the spiritual defeat of death in the resurrection of Christ spells its physical and total defeat in the coming new age. But the impending defeat of death is also evident in the paradoxical fact that henceforth death must already yield to life and therefore has a victorious redemptive meaning. To be "crucified with Christ" is to participate in the "sufferings of Christ," that is, to be engaged in the redemptive activity of apostolic life in the present time (see Chapter 13, below). In a sense, the apostle invites suffering and glories in it in order to break the claim of death in the light of its ultimate defeat. Therefore, sufferings are not just to be endured as the messianic woes of the end time (Rom. 8:18), but to be gloried in (Rom. 5:3). As I stated before (Chapter 9) the chronological sequence of life after death in the apocalyptic manner is crossed by a dialectic: "When I am weak, then I am strong" (2 Cor. 12:10). Paul is aware of comfort in the midst of suffering (2 Cor. 1:5) and of life in the midst of death (2 Cor. 4:10) . Henceforth, suffering is a suffering with Christ (Rom. 8:17), because all suffering is embraced by God's saving purpose and takes place in the light of the coming glory of God. Suffering is not only relieved because of the coming glory but also imbued with secret power. It is so imbued because it manifests itself as redemptive love in the world, because it already breaks the hold of the power of death on this world. When Paul speaks about becoming "conformed to the death of Christ" and about "sharing Christ's sufferings" (Phil. 3:10; trans. mine), he grounds his conformity to the death of Christ in the hope of the final resurrection of the dead (Phil. 3:11). Thus, the dialectic of "life amid death" never overshadows the apocalyptic sequence of "life after God's final victory over death," for the dialectic operates only within the sphere of the apocalyptic hope in the coming glory of God.

Paul intends to portray Christian life in the world not only as a rejoicing in the intimate presence of God in Christ but also as a looking forward to that future of God, for which Christ lived and died, so that life's burdensome contradictions may be "swallowed up by life" (2 Cor. 5:4). The realism of Paul's thought is striking. He does not spiritualize away the reality of death that is present in the contingencies and burdens of life, nor does he relativize the victory of God in the death and resurrection of Christ. Our "new creation" in Christ is for him the proleptic manifestation of the redemption of the whole creation, when death will be "swallowed up in victory" (1 Cor. 15:54).

THE CONTINUING DILEMMA

Although we appreciate the contextual richness of Paul's thought about sin and death, it reveals an inconsistency that cannot be ignored or harmonized. This inconsistency impinges on a problem that has haunted Christians throughout the ages: the relation of suffering and evil to sin and death. If—after the Christ-event—death is still "the last enemy," whereas sin has been defeated, then suffering and evil can no longer be due exclusively to sin. We could argue that because, according to Paul, death entered the world through sin and "the creation was subjected to futility, not of its own will but by the will of him who subjected it in hope" (Rom. 8:20)—and is thus to be located in God's will because of Adam's fall—sin has not only "deadly" anthropological consequences, but cosmic-universal ones as well. In this case, creation's "fall" stems from the sinful activity of Adam, the "steward of creation."

But this cannot be the whole story, for if the power of sin has been overcome by Christ, but not the range of death—because it *remains* "the last enemy" even after the resurrection of Christ—then Christian suffering cannot be due solely to sin but must be associated with the infectious disease of death that stamps the created order. At this point the apocalyptic explanation of the power of death fails because it associates the reign of death regularly with the fall of Adam. And Paul's apocalyptic shares in this insufficient explanation. However, the natural consequence of the inconsistent relation of sin to death in his thought suggests that the power of death exceeds that of sin. Paul probably considers death in the universe to be the lingering effect of sin. But if this is true, then death would be acceptable to the Christian because its "sting"—sin—has been undone (1 Cor. 15:56). Although death would perhaps not be acceptable in an ultimate sense, the Christian could at least face it with a sense of peace. However, in that case, death would no longer be "the last enemy." If death is, and remains, the enemy for the Christian and the created order alike, then two options remain. Either death is a power that reigns independently from the power of sin, or death is still allied with the continuing power of sin, even for Christians after the Christ-event. Because Paul rules out the latter alternative, death and suffering are in some sense independent operatives in the world. Thus, for Paul, the resurrection of Christ is the promise of the total death of death, but the victory over death in its physico-spiritual sense is thus far only a reality for Christ himself and not for those in Christ.

The apocalyptic longing for the resurrection of the dead is not an incidental theory for Paul but is existentially grounded in the necessary solidarity of the Christian with a creation that is marked by suffering and death. Paul does not say, "The death he [Christ] died he died to *death,* once for all"; he does say, "The death he [Christ] died he died to *sin,* once for all" (Rom. 6:10). In the Jewish apocalyptic manner, Paul locates "the fall" of the created order in the fall of the human being. However, his interpretation of the relation of sin and death after the occurrence of the Christ-event suggests that death and suffering cannot be totally reduced to sin. There is a crucial and mysterious "dark" residue of suffering and death in God's created order that will be resolved only by the final resurrection of the dead in the glory of God.

We must remember that our modern attitude toward death as a natural phenomenon of created life derives from our philosophical heritage and its reflection upon finitude and infinitude, temporality and eternity. We associate temporality with contingency, finitude, transience, and decay, that is, with those realities that we consider inconsistent with God's unchangeable perfection and eternal immutability. However, according to Paul the goal of Christian life is not our absorption into a timeless divine nature (2 Pet. 1:4[?]) that is in principle antithetical to a transient world of finitude and decay.[19] Paul does not equate temporality with death, because he views death as a hostile intruder into God's created order, which knew no death until Adam's sin. At this point, however, the inconsistency arises. Because death cannot be completely explained by the power of sin, the power of death and suffering remains a cosmic mystery; it continues to reign over Christians even after Christ's victory over death.

Paul's theodicy is apocalyptically grounded. Only from the perspective of our final destiny in the resurrection of the dead, when death, "the last enemy," has been defeated, only from that wholistic perspective can we grasp the meaning of the parts and fragments that make up our life in the world (1 Cor. 13:12). Only at that time will the sighing of the Christian and the creation, and also our query about so much seemingly meaningless suffering in the world, make place for the joy of the total creation in the embrace and glory of God.

11

The Enigma of the Law: Instrument of God or Servant of Sin?

The law has been previously discussed in its contextual setting in Galatians and Romans (see Chapters 4-6, above). However, it deserves a fuller treatment, for it seems to constitute an enigma in Paul's thought. The enigma is this: Paul maintains that the law is the instrument of God, but he asserts at the same time that it is the servant of sin. The law is God's holy will, obedience to which is the condition for life; but God also gave the law to increase sin in order to indict its deadly character. In the following pages I do not intend to forget the contextual character of Paul's thought. However, unless Paul's various argumentative moves are simply intuitive, opportunistic impulses, they must be shown to cohere in an intelligible pattern consistent with the organizing center of his thought.

THE DUAL FUNCTION OF THE LAW

The Boundaries of the Discussion

Because the issue of the law is exceedingly complex, the interpreter must avoid both an exercise in dialectics, which defies intelligibility, and a type of analysis that oversimplifies the dialectical elements in Paul's treatment of the law. In our discussion, we must consider four basic issues:

1. The context of the discussion. A coherent view of the law cannot be bought at the expense of Paul's contextual argument, and a systematic doctrine of the law in terms of logical propositions must be ruled out. Paul's argument in Romans, for example, differs from that in Galatians, for he deals with a different problem with a different audience in those letters (see Chapter 6, above). Even within Romans itself, the context of Romans 1-3 has a focus different from that of Rom. 10:1-10, and again Romans 7 differs from both. We cannot simply import Rom. 10:3 or Phil. 3:9 with its theme of pride and striving after "their own righteousness" into the exegesis of Romans 7.

2. The leading question within a particular context concerns the posture or perspective from which Paul argues. Is he, for example, identifying

himself with a Jewish position in Romans 2 and thus with a point of view that he in fact has overcome,[1] or is he consistently arguing from his new Christian perspective and always in the same manner?

3. Even if—as seems to be the case—Paul argues consistently from a Christian perspective, how *discontinuous* is this perspective from Judaism's own position on the law? The discontinuity seems confirmed by Paul's own stance ante- and post-Christum, as Gal. 1:14 and Phil. 3:7 with their theme of the *simchat hattora* ("joy of the law") disclose. Does this mean that there is no continuous thread or common basis of argument between Paul and Judaism? Does Paul, the Christian, impose on Judaism a point of view that amounts to a fatal misunderstanding and misrepresentation of Judaism (Schoeps[2])?

Or, if he does not misunderstand Judaism, does his new allegiance to Christ logically compel him to exclude the Jewish position? Moreover, does Paul indict the Jew for an inherently false striving in obeying the law (Bultmann[3]); does he indict the Jew for his sinful acts (Wilckens[4]); or does he simply infer from his stance in the lordship of Christ that faith logically excludes the law (Sanders[5])?

4. Because of Paul's "enigmatic" statements about the law, which seem to defy systematic clarity, the "hermeneutical circle" is especially evident in our interpretation of it. The history of interpretation plays an intriguing role. The "original" and "the translation" fuse frequently in the history of Christian thought on this topic, especially when we consider the pervasive influence of "the introspective conscience of the West"[6] and its powerful manifestation in interpreters like Augustine, Luther, and Calvin. The contemporary theological climate often prejudices the discussion. For instance, our perspective on the relation of law and gospel, or on the issue of the third use of the law, is predetermined by whether we are engaged in a meaningful dialogue with Judaism, in a polemic with Judaism and Jewish Christianity, in a Lutheran-Calvinist debate, or in a discussion about social ethics. Despite these hermeneutical pressures, the crucial exegetical issue is whether Paul argues for the abrogation of the law or for a continuing validity of the law in the gospel.

Shall we sketch the relation of law and gospel in a virtually dualistic manner (Bultmann[7]), in a dialectical manner (Käsemann[8]), or in a continuous manner (Wilckens[9])? Or shall we opt for two different "patterns of religion" that run on different tracks (Sanders[10])?

THE LAW AND PAUL'S CONVERSION

We must not forget that within this context there is an urgent need for an intelligible account of Paul's call or conversion. The modern scholarly aversion to nineteenth-century psychological portraits of Paul and to adventures in psychoanalysis like those of Richard L. Rubenstein[11] has resulted in a virtual eclipse of an account of Paul's call. Indeed, we must distinguish between text and pretext, and we cannot revert to speculations about Paul's psyche which lie behind the text. Speculations about Paul's encounter with "the evil impulse" (yetzer harah) after his youthful innocence, or about his bar mitzvah and his subsequent frustration with the law are illegitimate and have no warrant in the text.

Nevertheless, unintelligibility abounds when the function of Paul's call is under discussion, especially when it relates to his former Jewish life. The adoption of a "boom" theory seems to prevail. Paul commits himself to Christ "in a flash" and in a "totally unexpected" manner. What is at stake, however, is not the element of surprise but its effect on the previous life-story of Paul. How could the Christophany have been so traumatic and so radical in its consequences unless it lit up and answered a hidden quest in his soul?

It will be necessary to find our way between a psychological description of Paul's Jewish past, which engages in illegitimate speculation, and a purely theological exposition of Paul's Christian position, as if Paul is simply engaged in a theological-dogmatic treatise when he speaks (e.g., in Romans 7) about human existence under the law without any reference to his personal experience under the law. When scholarship concentrates solely on Paul's theological exposition of the law,[12] it overlooks the distinction between faith and its theological expression and thus overlooks the matrix of Paul's theology of the law in his own experience. When the reason for Paul's adoption of Christ is exclusively located in the facticity of the Christophany, its effect on Paul's Pharisaic conviction remains obscure.

E. P. Sanders's "patterns of religions" method provides a classical example of a purely theological approach to Paul's thought on the law.[13] He compares the religion of Judaism and the religion of Paul and shows how after Paul's acceptance of the lordship of Christ the logic of his position entailed an assessment of the law that has little or no resemblance to Judaism's self-understanding about the function of the law. This approach prevents the often pejorative accounts of Judaism as inferior, legalistic, meritorious, and so on. But the price paid for this irenic treatment is that we are prevented from asking the question that is vital to our understanding of Paul: What actually was the interface between Paul the Pharisee and Paul the Christian? Why did the Christophany evoke such a crisis in his life, one that turned his former allegiance upside down and provoked a view of the Torah that differed considerably from his

Jewish-Christian brethren? Even when Paul compares his call to that of the prophets (Jeremiah; Second Isaiah), the dissimilarity transcends the similarity. For although the prophetic call provoked a radical reinterpretation of Israel's traditions, these prophets did not overturn the tradition in the radical way Paul did. My intent is not to give a psychological explanation of the Christophany but to interpret its traumatic meaning for Paul.

The Law and Romans 7

We will focus on Romans 7 as the text that raises most of the aforementioned issues. Romans 7 shows primarily the contextual nature of Paul's argument about the law. However, it also provides a clue to the basic coherence of Paul's conviction about the law.

Romans 7 is not a description of Christian life or primarily an autobiography of Paul's Pharisaic life. Rather, a Christian looks here, in the context of an apology of the law, in hindsight at the plight of the Jews under the law and describes their objective condition of despair. The depth of Paul's description suggests that a Christian interpretation of Jewish existence under the law is the primary subject matter of Romans 7. He describes the schizophrenia of the unredeemed person, who must, to his horror, admit that he is the captive of a body of death (Rom. 7:24) and a victim of sin. My "inmost self" delights in the law of God (v. 22), for the split between "willing" and "doing" (vv. 15–20) indicates that the law is good (v. 16). However, sin is the signature of my being (v. 20); it dwells within me and "occupies" me completely. Despair is the result (v. 24), for I am in a "no exit" situation. The good law is used by sin for its demonic purpose of death, for sin—like Satan—uses the law to tempt me (v. 8), indict me (v. 9), and kill me (v. 10). The law "which promised life" (v. 10) turns out to be my death. My "lust for life" that urges me to obey the law proves to be an experience of death, for the law uncovers my lust as the enemy inside (v. 7) and condemns me for it. It is interesting that in verse 7 the commandment of the law has no specific object: "You shall not covet." Its uncanny nonspecificity uncovers me as someone who is already caught in lust, before the commandment brings it into the open (v. 8).

In what sense then is Romans 7:7–13 an apology of the law? The climactic verse 13 provides the answer: The law compels sin to show its true face, so that it can no longer hide behind the law. Rudolf Bultmann interprets the phrase "sinful beyond measure" (*kath hyperbolēn hamartōlos*, v. 13) as the demonic ingenuity of sin that characterizes the law as the instigator of sin rather than as its detector.[14] This interpretation is erroneous. The law in verse 13 detects sin and makes me aware of my desperate plight. Thus Paul ends the apology of the law (vv. 7–13) in verse 13 by returning to his opening statement (cf. the similar question and the *mē genoito* response in vv. 7 and 13). To be sure, this knowledge is not therapeutic or preventive but a knowledge-unto-death, which seals my doom.

Contextual Argumentation

Romans 7 enables us to draw some specific conclusions:

1. It is primarily a Christian confession in hindsight on life under the law, because only the new Christian perception on the law is able to uncover the depth of the alliance of sin, the law, and death.

2. The context for the discussion is the apology of the law that is necessitated by the radical statement of verse 5: "While we were living in the flesh, our sinful passions, aroused by the law, were at work in our members to bear fruit for death." In fact, Rom. 7:7–24 sums up the allusions to the law in the previous chapters (Rom. 2:12, 13; 3:20, 21, 31; 4:15; 5:13, 20; 6:14, 15) which clamor for a fuller exposition. The context shows that the focus of the discussion in Romans 7 is not boasting, pride, or the person who is caught in illusion but rather the question how the ontologically holy law could cause such ontic disaster in human life. And Paul's answer is that transgressions of the law demonstrate our bondage to sin.

3. It is, therefore, erroneous to introduce the elements of false striving and boasting (Rom. 10:3; Phil. 3:9; cf. Rom. 3:27) into this context, for Paul argues not that the intent to obey the law is wrong[15] but that Jews have sealed their doom because of their factual transgressions.[16]

4. This interpretation is verified by Paul's midrashic use of Genesis 3 in Rom. 7:7–11, which he weaves together with the commandment of Exod. 20:17 (Rom. 7:7). The deception of Rom. 7:11 is not that of the law but that of sin, which like the serpent in Genesis 3 uses the commandment to uncover my "lust" (Rom. 7:7). In other words, the law itself does not primarily deceive me into false striving, self-righteousness, and illusion but convicts and condemns me. Thus, Bultmann's interpretation of the law does not apply to Romans 7:

> The way of works of the law and the way of grace and faith are mutually exclusive opposites. But why is this the case? Because *man's effort to achieve his salvation by keeping the law* only leads him into sin, indeed *this effort itself* in the end *is already sin*. It is the insight which Paul has achieved into the

nature of sin that determines his teaching on the law. This embraces two insights. One is the insight that sin is man's *self-powered striving* to undergird his own existence in forgetfulness of his creaturely existence, to procure his salvation by his own strength, that striving which finds its extreme expression in "boasting" and "trusting in the flesh." The other is the insight that man is always already a sinner, that, fallen into the power of sin, *he is always already in a falsely oriented understanding of his existence.* The reason, then, man shall not, must not, be "right-wised" by works of the law is that he must not be allowed to imagine that he is able to procure his salvation by his own strength; for he can find salvation only when he understands himself in his dependence upon God the creator.[17] [Italics mine.]

5. The theme of *superbia* (pride and false striving) is certainly present in Rom. 10:3 and Phil. 3:9 (cf. perhaps Rom. 3:27). However, this level of argument functions only after Paul has arrested the Jew in his actual transgressions of the law (Romans 7). Thus Rom. 10:3 and Phil. 3:9 discuss the status of the Jew after the gospel has been preached to him, that is, the Jew who has refused the gospel and persists in a way that has been shown to be futile. Here Paul reaches a level of new insight: Boasting is a form of illusion, because the Jew is caught in the illusion that works of the law are pleasing to God.

Moreover, although the discussion of the law in Romans resembles that in Galatians, the context is again quite different. The main pitch of the argument in Galatians is the meaning of the new lordship of Christ for the Gentiles: The law is an outmoded and unnecessary reality for Gentiles, because it was not meant for them (Gal. 3:6–14) and because it represents their former bondage to "the elemental spirits of the universe" (Gal. 4:3). Only within this primary context does Paul argue the Jewish transgressions of the law (Gal. 3:10). In other words, the basis for Paul's indictment of the law is here the new lordship of Christ and not primarily the sorry plight of the Jew under the law, as in Romans 7.

An Autobiographical Element?

The presence of an autobiographical element in Romans 7 cannot be denied. The chapter does not permit a Christian autobiography of Paul (vv. 14–25)[18] but rather describes a Christian perspective on Jewish life (vv. 4–6). However, only an autobiographical element can explain the vivid confessional cry of verse 24a.[19] Moreover, verses 14–25 seem inexplicable if they describe something that was in every sense alien to Paul's Jewish experience and that he now rehearses from a Christian perspective.

It seems that the autobiographical element in Romans 7 consists in a perceptual shift that brings to unprecedented clarity a hidden conflict—a conflict that only the Christophany unmasked and resolved. Awareness of transgression (Romans 7), hypocrisy (Rom. 2:17-29), and boasting (Rom. 2:16; 3:26), then, are components within a field that only in Christ is perceived as the condition of being "sold under the power of sin" (Rom. 7:14).

A deletion of all autobiographical inferences from Romans 7 makes the chapter theologically unintelligible and fruitless for Paul's encounter with Judaism. If the lordship of Christ is simply a totally unexpected revelation that has no experiential antecedents in Paul's Jewish life, it becomes unintelligible how and why Christ supersedes the law. For if Paul was an utterly happy Jew before he met Christ, his Christian hindsight description of Jewish life becomes inauthentic, because there is no trace of a foothold for it in his own experience. How could Paul have affirmed the credal statement "Christ died for our sins" if the problem of sin vis-à-vis the law was in no way related to his experience? If we claim that for Paul the lordship of Christ is dogmatically incompatible with the lordship of the Torah,[20] then Paul's reflections on the Torah are a purely Christian rearguard action against Judaism and the product of logical reasoning rather than of experiential conviction. To be sure, Luther's anxiety about life under the law does not have to be introduced into the debate. Luther is obviously mistaken, when he reads Romans 7 as a confession about life in Christ. However, it seems that Rom. 7:7-25 does allude to the autobiographical experience of Paul the Jew.

We may be able to understand the dialectic of Paul's situation before and after the Christ-event if we make a distinction between a person's subjective awareness and his objective condition. In Romans 7, Paul views in retrospect the objective condition of his former Jewish life, a condition that was not a matter of conscious reflection while he was a Pharisee. For a Pharisee does not operate with a model of sinlessness in his "Torah-keeping" that leads him to despair when he fails to achieve perfection. Every Jew knows himself to be vulnerable to attacks by the "evil impulse," but he also knows that the means of atonement and forgiveness are available to him in his life under the Torah. Paul could not have written Rom. 1:18—2:29 without knowing that Jews are indeed aware of sin and boasting. When he indicts the Jew for transgressing the law or for boasting while being aware of his transgression (i.e., for the sin of hypocrisy), he must have known something of both in his own Jewish life. Romans 7 becomes inexplicable in its intensity if the *"ego"* has no relation to Paul's own life. To be sure, the extent and depth of his condition under the law were hidden to Paul the Pharisee, and thus the Jew's true condition is known only in Christian retrospection. Intimations of transgression and boasting were no doubt brought to the full light of day by Christ, who in his death and resurrection both atoned for our transgressions and defeated the power of sin and the law that led to boasting. Indeed, the poisonous character of the interrelation between the law and sin is unknown to a Pharisaic Jew. To that extent the story of the law in Romans 7 is a Christian story. The alliance between sin and the law, the uncovering of "lust" as the law of my being, the deception by sin in using the law to stimulate my desire for life (v. 10) and thereby condemning me to death are all Christian insights. But this does not exclude the presence of an autobiographical element in the story.*

The fact that faith in Christ determined Paul's view of the human plight under the law does not mean that his analysis of the human plight is purely a dogmatic consequence of his soteriology. The indictment of the law is not merely a dogmatic necessity once Paul accepted the lordship of Christ. Sanders's emphasis on the priority of the lordship of Christ is correct,[21] but it needs to be balanced by another element in Paul's thought. For the movement from Christology/soteriology to anthropology is balanced by a movement from anthropology to Christology/soteriology. The latter is at least the movement of Romans 1–5, where the human need for redemption precedes the divine initiative in Christ. This indicates that Jewish existence under the law betrays an inherent weakness, to which God's act in Christ responds. Therefore, Paul does not argue in Romans 1–5 that a Christian view simply excludes the law by necessity.[22] † Rather, he

---

*James E. Loder's observations in his inaugural address "Transformation in Christian Education" (Princeton Theological Seminary, December 12, 1979) seem to undergird my analysis. Loder outlines a grammar of transformation that contains five steps: (1) a conflict borne with persistence, (2) interlude and scanning, (3) insight felt with intuitive force, (4) release and redirection of the psychic energy bound up with the original conflict, and (5) interpretation which tests the insight for coherence with the terms of the conflict and for correspondence with the public context of the original conflict.

The application of this paradigm to Paul is insofar illuminating in that Loder claims that "one may enter the sequence consciously or intentionally at any point in the structure, but still be drawn to complete the whole." In other words, we do not have to engage in psychological reductionism in interpreting Paul's call and conversion, or to posit a consciously held conflict that Paul subsequently resolves; rather, the Christophany—as the moment of resolution and new perception—compels Paul to work through the original conflict and to bring it to conscious awareness.

†I agree with Dahl's criticism of Sanders and his defense of Bultmann on this point: *faith in Christ* made Paul reach his assessment of the human plight, whereas the human plight is the logical starting point for an analysis of Paul's *theology* (Nils Alstrup Dahl, "Review of E. P. Sanders, *Paul and Palestinian Judaism*"). However, I would emphasize the factual character of Paul's indictment of Jewish transgressions in Romans 1–5, especially Romans 2, which was meant to be intelligible to his Jewish audience.

knows that Jews can be addressed in terms of their factual transgressions. He is here not ruminating on purely theological matters but is instead trying to establish a dialogue with Jews, one that is intelligible to them on their own ground.

The Coherence of Paul's Argument

The underlying coherence of Paul's view of the law consists in his radicalization of the Jewish position on "the evil impulse" and sin. Whereas for Judaism sin can be dealt with in its sacrificial system, for Paul a sinful act leads to bondage under the power of sin, that is, into the human plight of "no exit" (cf. John 8:34). This radicalization of sin—adumbrated in Qumran[23]—is the consequence of the Christophany, where a crucified Messiah was vindicated by God as Lord and as the inaugurator of the new age. Because Christ atoned on the cross for our sins, committed under the law, he not only unmasked sins as the power of sin but also defeated that power of sin in his death and resurrection.

Henceforth, the function of God's holy law was taken up and absorbed by Christ in whom "the just requirement of the law was fulfilled" (Rom. 8:4) and its deadly function under sin was abrogated. Christ was both the fulfillment and end of the law (Rom. 10:4).

THE FUNCTION OF THE LAW IN SALVATION-HISTORY

I alluded previously to the function of Rom. 7:13 as the climax of Paul's apology of the law. However, the salvation-historical function of the law demands closer scrutiny. If the law serves and executes the power of sin, how can it have a positive function in salvation-history? Apart from Rom. 7:13, Paul addresses this issue in Rom. 5:20, Gal. 3:19–25, and Rom. 11:32. It has often been argued that Paul locates the positive character of the law in its function as pedagogue or tutor for the gospel. This interpretation is erroneous, because the law is the custodian or jailer who keeps us in bondage (Gal. 3:23, 24; see Chapter 4, above). Paul's disclaimer that the law is given in order to grant life (*zōopoiēsai*, Gal. 3:21) seems to contradict Rom. 7:10 ("The very commandment which promised life" [*hē entolē hē eis zoen*]). However, from the posture of *salvation-history* (cf. Gal. 3:19–25), the law has the divine function of acting as a necessary negative instrument in order to "augment the trespasses" (Gal. 3:19; Rom. 5:20). Indeed, it was God's plan to secure our redemption at the nadir of salvation-history, that is, at the point where the law seals our no-exit situation before God. At that point God sent Christ in "the fullness of time" (Gal. 4:4; trans. mine) and reversed the downward curve of salvation-history in order to adopt us as his sons (Gal. 4:5) and transfer us to the realm of faith (Gal. 3:25) and the Spirit (Rom. 8:1–17). Thus Paul marvels in God's mysterious plan: "O the depth of the riches and wisdom and knowledge of God! How unsearchable are his judgments and how inscrutable his ways!" (Rom. 11:33).

Paul emphasizes the discontinuous character of the Christ-event in conjunction with God's continuous salvation-historical plan. The hindsight of faith perceives that even the twofold tyranny of sin and the law must yield to God's saving purpose (Gal. 3:24; Rom. 5:20–21), so that even "the dispensation of death, carved in letters on stone" had "a splendor" of its own (2 Cor. 3:7, 10). And in the light of this perception Paul confesses, "For God has consigned all men to disobedience, that he may have mercy upon all" (Rom. 11:32; cf. Gal. 3:22). The law, then, is not downgraded on idealistic grounds, as if love displaces the law as a higher virtue. Although the law is given after the promises (Gal. 3:16, 19; Rom. 4:14) and succeeds the reality of sin (Rom. 5:13, 20), it has a positive function in salvation-history, not only because it makes sin accountable before God (Rom. 4:15; 5:13) but also because it holds the whole range of history together in the plan of God. This retrospective unity of salvation-history is documented in Scripture (Gal. 3:22) and demonstrates that our sinful past is not simply ignored or forgotten but included in the embrace of God's redemptive purpose. Søren Kierkegaard indirectly comments on this:

> Forgiveness through Christ is the gentle schoolmaster who does not have the heart to recall the forgotten, but does recall it sufficiently to say: "Remember, however, that it is forgotten. It is not forgotten, but it is forgotten in the forgiveness. Every time you remember the forgiveness, then it is forgotten, but when you forget the forgiveness, then it is not forgotten and then the forgiveness is forfeited."[24]

The Gnostic is indeed the one who celebrates the new self in self-forgetfulness, because he dissociates himself radically from the nonbeing and ignorance of his past. Paul rejects such a dualism. Although the past of sin is indeed no more in Christ, it is nevertheless embraced by God's mysterious pedagogy of salvation. The law is not a supernatural mistake or a tragic flaw, for it makes sin accountable to God: "Where there is no law there is no transgression" (Rom. 4:15; cf. 3:19; 5:13, 20). However, its purpose is not ultimate damnation but demonstrates God's will to save, "that, as sin reigned in death, grace also might reign through righteousness to eternal life" (Rom. 5:21). And so the law confirms—notwithstanding its negative function—the unity of salvation-history.

Paul now views the unity of salvation-history eschatologically and not protologically. Contrary to Eph. 1:4, where God's protological plan is located in our election "before the foundation of the world,"[25] Paul deduces God's election and predestination from his eschatological vindication (Rom. 8:28–30). God's "purpose," "foreknowledge" (Rom. 8:29), and "purpose of election" (Rom. 9:11) are not a speculation about God's eternal decree before the creation of the world but are viewed from the end of history as proleptically manifest in Christ (cf. Rom. 8:29). The function of the law within the unity of salvation-history is deduced from the eschatological "fullness of time" in Christ (Gal. 4:4, trans. mine; cf. Rom. 8:29); it is viewed retrospectively rather than prospectively.

THE WORKS OF THE LAW AND
THE WORK OF FAITH

Paul's attack on "the works of the law" is often misunderstood as romantic idealism. Leo Baeck, for instance, characterizes Paul as the prototype of romantic religion that he opposes to Judaism's classical religion:

> In the Pauline, as in any romantic religion—the component of faith and revelation, of transport and ecstasy—is taken for the fulfillment of religion, for ultimate truth and perfection. . . . His faith remains purely passive, it is not faith in the challenging, commanding law of God, but merely in the gift of divine grace. . . . One might characterize the Pauline religion in sharp juxtapositions: absolute dependence as opposed to the commandment, the task of achieving freedom. . . . It is the faith that does not go beyond itself, that is not the task of life; only a "thou hast" and not a "thou shalt."[26]

However, Paul's radical attack on the works of the law is not simply the opposition of faith and work or the celebration of motivation and intentionality over actual deeds. To the contrary, Paul's Hebrew anthropology is marked by the intentionality-action axis of human existence. He commends the Thessalonians for their "work of faith" (*ton ergon tēs pisteōs*) and "labor of love" (*kopos tēs agapēs*, 1 Thess. 1:3); he warns that "each man's work will become manifest; for the Day will disclose it, because it will be revealed with fire, and the fire will test what sort of work each one has done" (1 Cor. 3:13); and he reminds the Romans that "it is not the hearers of the law who are righteous before God, but the doers of the law who will be justified" (Rom. 2:13; cf. 2:27). Just as Paul integrates rather than contrasts the last judgment with justification by faith, so he does not oppose faith to works. He would have agreed with James's protest: "Show me your faith *apart* from your works" (James 2:18).

Paul indicts works in the context of *the law,* that is, as "doing the works of the law" (the *mizwoth*).[27] For instance, in Rom. 10:4–8 Paul argues that "Christ is the end of the law, for righteousness to everyone who believes" (v. 4; trans. mine). The warrant for this claim is the antithesis of Lev. 18:5 to Deut. 30:14: the "doing of the law" (Lev. 18:5) versus "the word is near you, on your lips and in your heart" (cf. Deut. 30:14), which Paul interprets as "the word of faith" (Rom. 10:8). The antithesis of faith and "doing" the law is so acute for him that he does not hesitate to use Deut. 30:14, LXX, in contrast to its inherent meaning. The climactic clause of Deut. 30:14, "so that you can *do* it," is simply ignored (cf. LXX: *auto poiein*). Paul posits the same opposition between "doing" (Lev. 18:5) and "faith" (Hab. 2:4) in Gal. 3:11–12, not because he rejects "doing" but because he rejects doing in the context of the law. In both places Paul audaciously quotes Scripture against itself in order to create the antithesis between "the work of the law" and "faith-righteousness," and thus he effectively deletes "doing the law" from his canon of Scripture.

A frequent misinterpretation of this point must be avoided. Paul does not oppose motivation or intent to doing; he does not blame Judaism for adhering to an alleged externality of "doing works" rather than research-ing the inner impulses of the heart, and he does not psychoanalyze the mistaken intent of the Jew (cf. Bultmann[28]). Rather, he opposes "the works of the law" primarily because the system of Judaism has come to an end in the new lordship of Christ.[29] Paul's new allegiance to Christ is the primary reason for his stance toward the law, and it is this new posture that makes him say that works of the law condemn before God. Works of the law are not inherently wrong because they are works; they are primarily wrong because in the new dispensation of Christ they are clearly shown not to have been fulfilled by the Jews.

"Doing" and "works" in the context of the law are negated in Christ, for the law is now perceived to misdirect and to be sin's deceptive instrument (Rom. 10:2: Jews have a "misdirected zeal for God" [trans. mine]). Indeed, the law deceives me, for when I hear the imperative and act on it, I discover myself either as a transgressor of the law or as deluded by the law. In other words, the law informs me about my imperative, "Do this and you shall live" (Lev. 18:15; Rom. 10:5), but not about my indicative, "I am carnal, sold under sin" (Rom. 7:14), so that even prior to my attempt at obedience I am already in a state of sin.

The law requires my obedience but does not elucidate the state of my being, that is, my status as a child of Adam (Rom. 5:12). My doing, then, is misdirected, because my deeds can only confirm who I am. Because of my basic misorientation, all my deeds secretly or openly direct me to myself. Although I am "confessionally" and publicly zealously engaged in attending to God and my neighbor, I am secretly striving for my own righteousness (Rom. 10:3). The person under the law is, from the perspective of the lordship of Christ, the *homo incurvatus in se* (Luther). All his deeds only promote the attempt to secure his existence before God.

Romans 3:27 demonstrates this powerfully (see Chapter 5, above). Because the theme of Rom. 3:21-26 deals with the power of sin and its defeat by God in Christ, we expect to hear, "Where, then, is the power of sin?" However, we hear instead Paul's question to the Jew, "Where then is boasting?" (Rom. 3:27; trans. mine). In other words, the righteousness of God in Christ excludes the works of the law (3:27b), because, since God's act of righteousness in Christ, Jewish boasting in the law shows that Jews are unaware of their true condition. They boast in the law and do not perceive that they have failed to perform "the works of the law" and are thus slaves to sin.

Believers in Christ live by faith in God's liberating act of justification. They live the life of the "undivided self" that manifests itself in the unity of intention and deed. To be "crucified with Christ" means to be dead to the law and its works (Gal. 2:16-20), but it also means to live in the "new domain of the Spirit" (Rom. 7:6; trans. mine). Faith transfers me to a domain where I am freed from self-concern and thus free for the neighbor. The freedom of faith, then, is inseparable from the work of faith. However, the work of faith is qualitatively new. Paul's frequent appeals to "doing" (*poiein; prassein; ergazomai; kopian; perisseuein*) demonstrate that he does not dismiss "doing" as an ethical deed. What is at stake is Luther's insight: "Good works do not make a good man, but a good man does good works"[30] (cf. Kierkegaard: "Purity of heart is to will one thing"[31]).

At this point we are tempted to say that Paul is interested not in the quantity of works but in their quality. This, however, suggests a false alternative, as if the Jew works for a quantity of merits, whereas Paul is concerned not with concrete acts but only with their motivation.

Nevertheless, because Christ is the fulfillment of the law (cf. Rom. 8:4) and "love is the fulfilling of the law" (Rom. 13:10; cf. Gal. 5:14), works are now defined with a new focus. "The law of Christ" (Gal. 6:2; cf. 1 Cor. 9:21) is indeed the law of love that makes the Christian's work transparent to God's redemptive purpose. Therefore, Paul never uses the plural "works" (except in the Jewish context of Rom. 2:6) or the Hellenistic phrase "good works" (*kala erga;* cf. Titus 2:14; 3:8, 14; 1 Pet. 2:12). Moreover, the adjective "good" (*agathos*) is rarely added to "work" (Rom. 2:7; 2 Cor. 9:8; Phil. 1:6; but cf. 1 Tim. 2:10; 3:1; 5:10, 25; 6:18; 2 Tim. 2:21; 3:17; Titus 1:16; 2:7, 14; 3:1, 8, 14).

Christian "work" now is patterned after the "work," "labor," and "hardship" of the apostle (*ergon; kopos; mochthos;* cf. 1 Cor. 3:8; 15:58; 2 Cor. 6:5; 10:15; 11:23, 27; 1 Thess. 1:3; 2:9; 3:5). Because it means intense labor for the gospel, the quality of work is judged by its transparency. It is work "in the Lord" or "of the Lord" (cf. "fellow workers of God" [*synergoi,* 1 Cor. 3:9; 2 Cor. 6:1]; cf. also "imitators" of Christ [1 Cor. 11:1; cf. 1 Thess. 1:6; 2:14; 1 Cor. 5:16]). Thus, "fruitful labor" (Phil. 1:22) means "that in me you may have ample cause to glory in Christ Jesus, because of my coming to you again" (Phil. 1:26). "The work of faith" (1 Thess. 1:3) is—like "the fruit of the Spirit" (Gal. 5:22)— the resonance in the world and in the local congregation (Gal. 6:4) of God's redemptive love in Christ. It is therefore essentially a singular manifestation in all its various expressions; just as "the fruit [singular!] of the Spirit" is contrasted with the "works [plural!] of the flesh," so "the work of faith" is antithetical to "the works of the law."[32]

THE LAW IN THE EARLY CHURCH OUTSIDE PAUL

Paul's profile of the law comes to the fore when we compare it with its treatment in the early church. If the gospel proclaims God's righteousness through faith in Christ, why does the righteousness of God occur "apart from law" (Rom. 3:21)? It is simply not Jewish to contrast the Messiah and the law, for according to Judaism the Messiah will teach the law to the nations gathered in Jerusalem and put it within their hearts. Although the new covenant will give Israel a new heart (Jer. 31:31–34), it will not abolish the Torah, but confirm it, for the idea of a "new covenant" is possible in Judaism but a "new Torah" is unthinkable.[33]*

Thus, it is not surprising that Jewish Christians around Paul did not draw the same conclusions about the incompatibility of the Torah and Christ. Why, in fact, should there be an intrinsic connection between the confession of Christ and the abolition of the Torah, and why did Paul not follow Jewish-Christian theology with its correlation of the Torah and Christ? Or why did he not, like Matthew, view Christ as the new

---

*Versus Schweitzer et al., who posit either a new Torah or a cessation of the Torah in the messianic age.

interpreter of the Torah? Matthew makes a distinction between center and periphery within the Torah: "Woe to you, scribes and Pharisees, hypocrites! for you tithe mint and dill and cummin, and have neglected the weightier matters of the law, justice and mercy and faith; these you ought to have done, without neglecting the others" (Matt. 23:23). Matthew attacks not so much the law itself but its hypocritical observers: "The scribes and the Pharisees sit on Moses' seat; so practice and observe whatever they tell you, but not what they do; for they preach, but do not practice" (Matt. 23:2–3). In a similar vein, he warns, "Think not that I have come to abolish the law and the prophets; I have come not to abolish them but to fulfil them. For . . . till heaven and earth pass away, not an iota, not a dot, will pass from the law until all is accomplished" (Matt. 5:17). This stance agrees with Matthew's strict attitude toward the Sabbath (Matt. 24:10). In fact, every Christian is like a converted scribe who "like a householder brings out of his treasure what is new and what is old" (Matt. 13:52). Jesus radicalizes but does not abolish the law, according to Matthew; he is like a new Moses who on a new mountain radicalizes and reissues the Torah. Thus the Risen One charges his disciples to "make disciples of all nations . . . teaching them to observe all that I have commanded you" (Matt. 28:19–20). Although Matthew's gospel is for the Gentiles, his gospel contains a radicalized version of the old Torah.

Paul a Revolutionary?

Paul's revolutionary stance toward the law has earned him the epithet of apostate. But is it really so revolutionary? Paul was, after all, neither the first apostle to the Gentiles nor the first to loosen the connection between the gospel and the Torah. Others had preceded him in both areas. The Antioch church, which originated from the group around Stephen and Barnabas (Acts 8:4–8; 11:19–26), had already conducted Gentile missions in Antioch and liberalized the observance of the Torah. It not only allowed the uncircumcised Gentiles the status of "Christian proselytes" but also permitted a distinction within the law between its lesser and weightier parts. Matthew, the Gospel that originated in Syria (i.e., in the vicinity of Antioch), may well give us a picture of Antiochan theology. It seems highly probable that the Antioch church separated the cultic from the moral law and required only the observance of the "Noachian" laws for Gentile believers (cf. the apostolic decree [Acts 15:21; 21:25]). Paul is a revolutionary in that he radicalizes the issue of law and gospel: lawless Gentiles are full members of the people of God by faith alone. Paul ruptures the connection between the Torah and Christ so decisively that

Jewish life as such is invalidated (*ioudaizein;* cf. Gal. 2:14). He interprets adherence to the law in all its forms as a "rebuilding" of "those things which I tore down" (Gal. 2:18). This radicality must have caused Paul problems in the mission field, for how can he within "Torah-keeping" properly distinguish cultural-ethnic mores from vital religious elements? How can one remain "in the state in which he was called" (1 Cor. 7:20) and yet renounce the religious consequences of that state in view of the fact that in Jewish culture social and religious principles are closely interwoven.

However, for Paul, the rupture between the Torah and Christ establishes the equality of Jew and Gentile, because in Christ the "dividing wall" of the Torah (Eph. 2:14) is broken down. The "one God" of Israel's confession in the Shema (Deut. 6:4) is indeed the God of all people: "Or is God the God of Jews only? Is he not the God of Gentiles also? Yes, of Gentiles also, since God is one; and he will justify the circumcised on the ground of their faith and the uncircumcised through their faith" (Rom. 3:29, 30).

Paul in the Post-Pauline Period

In the second-century church, Paul's letters are largely ignored and his conviction about the Torah is no longer understood and therefore neutralized.[34] Jesus becomes the giver of "the new law" (Barnabas) or the *Logos* and *Nomos* (the Apologists). According to the Apologists, the *Logos* as the divine ordering principle of the universe has revealed himself in Jesus who represents the *nova lex* (*Nomos*) of the kingdom of God. The Torah is rejected as a Jewish ethnic peculiarity and accommodated to the Stoic "law of nature" (*lex naturae; nomos physeōs*), and its validity is restricted to the moral law.

Since Christianity has now become a Gentile religion and Jewish Christianity a minority, Paul's struggle with the Torah as God's unique revelation to Israel is either forgotten or argued on a different basis (Justin Martyr). Paul's claim that the Torah is ontologically divine but ontically hostile to the gospel is no longer understood. Moreover, the battle against gnosticism enhances the downfall of Paul's view of the Torah, for the law has now to be defended against Marcion and the Gnostics, who eagerly adopted Paul's hostile utterances against it. Furthermore, the Gospel tradition and the acceptance of the fourfold Gospel by the church facilitated a view of Jesus as the new teacher of the law. Henceforth, the coexistence of law and gospel will characterize the early Catholic church.

The Book of Acts already trivializes Paul's conviction about the law.

Acts pictures Paul as a true son of Jerusalem who circumcises people (Acts 16:3), keeps temple vows (21:23), and declares himself to be a Pharisee—even as a Christian (23:1). Although the Torah is "a yoke upon the neck" (15:10) and a burdensome obstacle to salvation (13:39), a minimum of law is nevertheless required by the apostolic council in the apostolic decree (15:20; 21:25). Indeed, the split betwen the cultic and moral Torah, which later became an important means to affirm the moral law and to abrogate the cultic-ceremonial law of the Old Testament, is already under way in Acts.

Likewise, the pastoral Epistles proclaim that "the law is good, if any one uses it lawfully, understanding this, that the law is not laid down for the just but for the lawless and disobedient" (1 Tim. 1:8–9). In fact, Scripture itself is regarded as a Torah for life (2 Tim. 3:16). Furthermore, the Epistle of James integrates law and gospel and ignores Paul's antithesis of "works" and "faith." The author claims that Abraham was justified "by works and not by faith alone" (James 2:24), so that faith was completed by works (2:22). James equates the "royal law, according to the scripture" (2:8) with "the law of liberty" (2:12) and understands the gospel to be a Christian interpretation of the Torah. However, he contradicts Paul's interpretation of Gen. 15:6, because he does not interpret it as faith versus works (Rom. 4:3–8). Instead, he interprets Gen. 15:6 by means of Gen. 22:9—Abraham's sacrifice of Isaac—and the story of Rahab, in order to confirm his thesis that faith is complemented by works (James 2:20–26).

The conclusion seems warranted that wherever Paul's insight into the human condition before God in Christ is downgraded and neutralized, his conviction about the law is downgraded and neutralized as well, with the result that the gospel of God's free grace—without the law—is robbed of its depth.

THE LAW AND SCRIPTURE

Although the relation of the law to Scripture is complicated in Paul, it demonstrates a new departure for a specifically Christian hermeneutic of Scripture. Despite the fact that Scripture in all its parts is the inspired, authoritative document of God's revelation to Israel, Paul makes its authority subject to Christ as the hermeneutical key to Scripture: "To this day, whenever Moses is read a veil lies over their minds; but when a man turns to the Lord the veil is removed. Now the Lord is the Spirit, and where the Spirit of the Lord is, there is freedom" (2 Cor. 3:15–17; see Chapter 7, above). Christ is the canon within the canon, so that Paul, in certain contexts, makes distinctions within Scripture between the letter and the Spirit (2 Cor. 3:6, 7; Rom. 2:29[?]), between the law and Scripture (Gal. 3:21, 22), and between the promise and the law (Gal. 3:15–21). He can even quote Scripture against Scripture when he contrasts the works of the law to faith-righteousness (Rom. 10:5–9; Gal. 3:11–12).[35]

It is impossible to impute to Paul dogmatic consistency in his interpretation of Scripture, for the contextual situation dictates his various hermeneutical moves. Judaism and Paul share the same hermeneutical techniques, but they differ profoundly in hermeneutical principle. For the Jew, "the Torah" or Pentateuch is the central core of Scripture, surrounded by "the Prophets" and "the Writings," which interpret "the Torah" and are interpreted by it. They provide mostly haggadic commentary on the Torah, whereas halakah focuses on the interpretation and elucidation of "the Torah" and becomes embodied in the halakic midrashim and the later codified Mishnah and Talmud.

Paul, to the contrary, tends to interpret "the Torah" eschatologically through the prophets (Rom. 1:2; 3:21b; cf. 16:26), as his frequent use of Second Isaiah reveals (see Chapter 7, above). At the risk of oversimplification, we can say that Scripture is interpreted essentially as "promise" by Paul, whereas it is "Torah" for the Jew.[36] God "promised beforehand" the gospel "in the holy scriptures" (Rom. 1:2), so that "scripture . . . preached the gospel beforehand to Abraham" (Gal. 3:8). Scripture, then, can be equated with the promise (Rom. 15:4; 3:21b) or is said to contain the promise (Gal. 3:17–25). Indeed, the law (= the legal code) arrives on the scene 430 years after the promise and cannot invalidate it (v. 17). But—a Jew will protest—why does the law oppose rather than confirm and sanction the promise? Is not the Torah itself the document of the promise? At this point, Paul divorces what the Jew conjoins. And Paul does so because Christ is the key to Scripture: Christ ratifies the promise by removing the law from the scene (see Chapter 7, above).

Paul's language betrays the tension inherent in his new hermeneutical key. Sometimes he identifies "scripture" (graphē) and "the law" (nomos);* sometimes he distinguishes between them. Just as he differentiates "the promise" (epangelia) from the "law" (nomos), he can also differentiate "scripture" (graphē) from "the law" (nomos). However, he does not simply equate "the promise" and "scripture" but claims that "scripture" contains both "the law" and "the promise" (Gal. 3:8, 22).[37] This terminology

---

* "Scripture" = "the law"; "the law" (nomos): Rom. 3:19; 7:1; 1 Cor. 9:8; 14:21, etc.; "scripture" (graphē): Rom. 1:2; 4:3; 9:17; 10:11; 15:4, etc.; cf. also "as it is written" (hōs gegraptai).

causes inevitable confusion, for how can "the law" be synonymous with "scripture" as a whole and yet be opposed to "the promise"? If "the promise" is the essential character of Scripture (cf. *ta logia tou theou* in Rom. 3:2), how can "the law" be opposed to the promise and still be a part of the indivisible authority of Scripture? Paul operates with a hermeneutical *discrimen* (Kelsey[38]), although he is not always consistent. It seems clear, however, that "scripture" is the overarching term, because it manifests God's plan of salvation as both promise and law (Gal. 3:8: *graphē proidousa;* Rom. 1:2: *graphai hagiai*). For how else can Paul uphold the unity of "scripture" (="the law") and yet split "scripture" (="the law") apart into "the promise" and "the law" and even oppose Scripture to Scripture (Gal. 3:11, 12). And how else can "the law" sometimes refer to the totality of "scripture" but at other times to the legal code or commandment (*entolē*) in Scripture (cf. Rom. 7:7; 13:9; 1 Cor. 9:9)?

In the salvation-historical context of Galatians, Paul presses the distinction in Scripture between "the promise" and "the law" in order to assign the law its proper function in Scripture, that is, as the negative but necessary component of salvation-history (Gal. 3:8–22). He makes a similar move in Romans. In Rom. 3:21—4:25, "scripture" (Rom. 4:2 [*graphē*]; cf. "as it is written" [Rom. 4:17]; cf. also 4:23) is both identified with "the law" (="scripture"; Rom. 3:19, 21b, 31) and yet distinguished from it (Rom. 3:21a, 28; 4:13; i.e., law = legal code).

However, in 2 Cor. 3:6, 7 the contrast is not between "the promise" and "the law" (Gal. 3:15-18) but between "the letter" (*gramma*) and "the spirit" (*pneuma;* cf. also Rom. 2:29).[39] In this context, the antithesis between the law (= *gramma*) and the Spirit (= *pneuma*) seems so absolute that the unity of Scripture (as containing both law and promise) threatens to break apart. Here the "letter" simply kills, whereas "the Spirit" gives life (2 Cor. 3:6; cf. also Rom. 7:6: "the old dominion of the letter" versus "the new dominion of the Spirit" [trans. mine]). However, 2 Cor. 3:14-16 suggests that "the letter" (= "the old covenant": v. 14) is able to become "scripture," when in Christ the veil is taken away from the hardened minds of the Jews.

"The letter" (*gramma*) is—apart from Rom. 2:27—never equated with "scripture" (*graphē*). This seems curious, because "the law"—which is regularly equated with "scripture"—is also synonymous with "the letter." However, Paul's basic hermeneutical move is identical in both instances; just as "the law" as legal code is opposed to "the promise" in "scripture," so "the letter" is opposed to "the Spirit." "The letter," then, is an extremely pejorative term. It refers to an interpretation of Scripture that belongs to the "old age" and causes death and condemnation. We can say, then, that because "scripture" (*graphē*) refers essentially to the promise within Scripture, which the death and resurrection of Christ has uncovered as its true core, "the promise" has only a negative relation to "the law" as legal code. In this way, the Christ-event assigns to Scripture (= the law) its proper function, so that law and gospel can be distinguished within the Scripture itself.

12

The Gift and the Demand
of Salvation

The "indicative" of God's redemptive act in Christ is insolubly linked to the "therefore" of the ethical "imperative." And yet, the mode of this interaction is not a timeless dogmatic construal but is directly related to the "timely" contingency of Paul's argumentation.

When Paul debates the nature of righteousness and faith with Jewish Christians or Judaizers, he emphasizes primarily "the indicative" of the gospel (Romans 1-5; Galatians 1-4). In that context "the imperative" is more presupposed than explicitly argued. It usually follows the indicative of faith-righteousness in a subsequent stage of the argument and then in relation to the lordship of Christ, our participation in him, and the gift of the Spirit (Gal. 5:1-25; Rom. 6:1—8:39). However, in a Hellenistic setting, Paul emphasizes much more the imperative and the responsibility of life in "the body," that is, in history (1 Corinthians 1-15; 2 Corinthians 1-7; cf. also 10-13). In both cases the contextual situation evokes the particular emphasis, but these emphases do not affect Paul's basic conviction about the integral connection between the indicative and the imperative (cf. the "therefore" [*oun*] that correlates the indicative and the imperative [Gal. 5:1; Rom. 6:12; cf. also Rom. 8:12; 12:1; 13:12]).

Judaizers and Jewish Christians must hear "the indicative" of the eschatological "now" of God's intervention in Christ, which eradicates "the works of the law" and any fearful striving for acceptance in the last judgment, as if the Messiah has not already come. Thus, it comes as no surprise that the apocalyptic future plays a subordinate role in Romans 1-4 and practically no role at all in Galatians 1-6. On the other hand, Hellenistic Christians must be alerted to "the imperative" of Christian life, because their exclusive celebration of the indicative—of participation in Christ—threatens to dissolve the necessary correlation of the indicative and the imperative. In this context, Paul argues the "not yet" of Christian life (i.e., the so-called eschatological reservation) in conjunction with a specific ethic. The "therefore" is thus not invariably motivated by the indicative of the Christ-event but can also be grounded in the future indicative of the last judgment and the final triumph of God; for example, "The night is far gone, the day is at hand. Let us therefore cast off the works of darkness and put on the armor of light" (Rom. 13:12, trans. mine; cf. Gal. 6:10; 1 Cor. 4:5). However, the contingency of the gospel situation does not mean "different strokes for different folks," that is, a different gospel for different occasions. Situational demands compel hermeneutical contingency, but they do not alter the coherence of the gospel. We must therefore resist "two-crater" theories (Schweitzer[1] et al.) or misconstrued "audience" theories (Lütgert[2] et al.), because a particular "crater" does not represent "the core" of the gospel and a particular audience does not create a different core of the gospel (see Chapters 2 and 5, above). Paul's gospel hinges on the eschatological promise of the lordship of Christ, because the redemptive indicative of God's reign has been inaugurated in him and issues forth in the imperative of obedience. Paul is preoccupied with interpreting the one gospel of "Jesus Christ and him crucified" (1 Cor. 2:2) in ever contingent and graphic ways.

THE SYMBOLS OF SALVATION

A Structural Analysis

Gerd Theissen has provided a structural analysis of the transfer imagery by which Paul interprets the Christ-event.[3] Although his model resembles Schweitzer's dual-crater theory, he goes beyond him in pointing to the interactions and wide range of the various metaphors and symbols. According to Theissen, two basic symbolic structures determine Paul's soteriology: a sociomorphic interaction symbolism (derived from the area of human social life) and a physiomorphic transformation symbolism (derived from the realm of organic life). The latter symbolic system addresses not personal relations—like the former—but biological and ontological structures.

Sociomorphic interaction symbolism unfolds itself in three basic metaphors: (1) the symbolism of liberation; (2) the symbolism of justification; and (3) the symbolism of reconciliation. Organic transformation symbolism also contains three basic metaphors: (1) the symbolism of physical transformation; (2) the symbolism of death and life; and (3) the symbolism of unification.

In liberation symbolism, images of social power predominate. Salvation takes place as liberation; bondage and suppression represent the unredeemed state. The enslaving powers are Satan, death, sin, and the law. Redemption is portrayed as a change in power structures; the dominant preposition is "under [the power of]" (hypo). Paul now interprets the imagery independently, because for him one dependency ("slavery") is not simply replaced by another (cf., however, Rom. 6:15–23). Therefore, Paul opposes slavery to freedom (Rom. 8:21) or sonship (Rom. 8:15; cf. Gal. 4:3–5). The transfer from slavery to freedom is described by the christological images of exaltation and ransom-redemption. In other words, liberation takes place either by a defeat of the powers or by a liberation of slaves from a hostile power. Both "power" images are connected with humiliation in Paul. The Redeemer becomes himself a "slave" (Phil. 2:7) or is killed by powers (1 Cor. 2:8) or is subjected to the law (Gal. 4:4), so that exaltation occurs because of humiliation (Phil. 2:9). In short, redemption imagery suggests the liberating activity of the Redeemer (cf. Gal. 3:13; 4:4–5: "to redeem" [ex-agorazein]; cf. Gal. 1:4: "to deliver" [ex-hairomai]).

Justification symbolism deals with the problem of guilt. The unredeemed state is represented by people's failure to obey the law, and their redemption consists in acquittal of a merited death sentence before the divine judge (cf. Rom. 14:10; cf. Rom. 2:11; 2 Cor. 5:10). Because the Oriental image of legal relations influences the imagery, legal justice is also a manifestation of benevolence by the person in power; "the thought of a benevolent salvific-justice does not, therefore, transgress the juridical framework."[4] In other words, two conceptions of legal procedure interact. On the one hand, a neutral conception of law and its impartial validity— which is irrespective of persons—demonstrates the universal indictment of humanity (Rom. 2:11). On the other hand, the neutral idea is transcended; law and grace cohere so that God sets forth the "right" "apart from the law," that is, God's covenant faithfulness transcends the impersonal justice of the law (Rom. 3:24–25).

The negativity of the law expresses itself in three ways: It brings about knowledge of sin, it stimulates people's own righteousness, and it represents the killing power of the imperative. People are lost because they live under the curse of the law, that is, under its condemning, deceiving, and killing character. Within the symbolism of justification, "transfer" terminology is often defined by the preposition "on behalf of" (hyper); Christ's death is "for us" because he takes upon himself the curse of the law and expiates its punishment because of our transgression. Yet Christ also abolishes the law and grants freedom from it (Rom. 10:4; cf. Rom. 8:3). In this context, the phrase "on behalf of" interchanges with the clause "in order that" (hina; cf. Gal. 3:13–14; 2 Cor. 5:21; Rom. 8:3–4). However, resurrection formulas do not occur in this symbolism, because God's justification in the death of Christ is primarily a sacrificial expiation.

Reconciliation symbolism stresses the contrast between enmity and peace, hate and love (cf. Rom. 5:1–12; 8:31–39; 2 Cor. 5:14–21). The basic metaphors are "reconciliation," "peace," "love" (*katallagē; eirēnē; agapē*). Whereas the liberation—and justification—symbolism functions in vertical categories (people are under the powers; Christ is above the powers; judge and sinner are located on two different judicial levels), reconciliation symbolism operates on a horizontal plane: the language of "appeal" (2 Cor. 5:20) or separation of parties predominates, not that of oppression. Cosmic powers are hostile, not because they oppress but because they separate (Rom. 8:35–39). Redemption comes to speech as access (Rom. 5:1–2), and the death of Christ is portrayed not as a defeat of the powers or as a ransom to enemies but as a manifestation of love; it is a "death for us" (*thanatos; apothnēskein hyper*) in self-surrender (Gal. 2:20; Rom. 5:8; 8:32; 2 Cor. 5:14; cf. also Rom. 14:15; 1 Cor. 8:1, 11). The resurrection of Christ—absent in the symbolism of justification—has an important function here; new life occurs after death and cannot simply be located in the death of Christ (cf. Rom. 4:25; 5:10; 8:34; 2 Cor. 5:15; 1 Thess. 5:9).

In the organic images the change takes place not in personal relations but in biological structures. The limiting boundaries of the created order are here transcended for the sake of a greater organic unity or symbiosis. This organic language creates hermeneutical difficulties for our understanding, because the focus is on a transformation of being rather than on a change in interpersonal relationships.[5]

Physiomorphic transformation is evident in 2 Cor. 3:18—4:6, 1 Cor. 15:35–57, and Rom. 5:17–21; the key terms are "image," "form," and "glory" (*eikōn; morphē; doxa*). The analogy between the Redeemer and the redeemed, that is, between image and reflection (*Bild and Spiegelbild*), shifts into ontological assimilation: "We all ... are being changed into his image/likeness" (*eikōn,* 2 Cor. 3:18). The being of the Redeemer transforms the being of the redeemed.[6]

The symbolism of death and life involves a bio- and physiomorphic symbolism (cf. Rom. 6:5: "to be grown together with him" [*symphytoi;* trans. mine]; Phil. 3:10: "to be con-formed to his death" [*symmorphizomenos;* trans. mine]; cf. also Rom. 8:17; 2 Cor. 4:10; 13:4). The Redeemer has here an "assimilating" power; his destiny is that of the redeemed. The basic theme is victory over human finitude, that is, the longing for a "new creation." Whereas in physiomorphic-transformation symbolism, dying is not a prerequisite for transformation (1 Cor. 15:51), in death and life symbolism total identification with the death and life of the Redeemer is the condition for our participation in him.

Unification symbolism emphasizes the victory over separation and human isolation. "Union" comes to speech in images of sexual intercourse and eating; a key term is "to be joined" (*kollasthai,* 1 Cor. 6:16-17; cf. 1 Cor. 7:34; Gal. 3:28). Erotic metaphors express the human desire to overcome the limitations of the self, whereas eating suggests the union of one body with other bodies. This symbolism appears especially in the motif of the "one" (*heis*) and that of "the body" (cf. Gal. 2:20; 3:28; 1 Cor. 12:12-27; Rom. 8:9-11).

According to Theissen, a comparison of the characteristic prepositions of each symbolic unit demonstrates the logic of the whole; liberation symbolism uses the preposition "under [the power of]" (*hypo*); that of justification and reconciliation employs "on behalf of" (*hyper*) and "in order that" (*hina*); transformation symbolism has "just as" (*hōs*); death and life symbolism favors "together with" (*syn*), whereas unification symbolism uses "in [Christ]" (*en*).

This structural analysis, which seems to categorize Paul's language too neatly, should not mislead us into thinking that he carefully separates the various symbolisms, as if each has a logical consistency of its own. To the contrary, the metaphors constantly interact and interweave. The metaphors of sociomorphic symbolism refer primarily to a soteriology of redemptive action; those of organismic symbolism refer primarily to a soteriology of redemptive participation. To be sure, some "fields" cohere more than others. Liberation and transformation symbolism clearly belong together, because both emphasize the exalted position of the Redeemer and the redeemed. The redeemed "likeness" (*eikōn*) and "glory" (*doxa*) of "the new man" is that of the Son who has conquered the powers and who has redeemed the enslaved (Rom. 9:29).[7] Similarly, justification symbolism coheres with that of death and life. The justification of the godless concerns a sentence of death and life, that is, condemnation and acquittal, whereas the death-life symbolism speaks about our participation in the death of Christ. Finally, the reconciliation and unification symbolisms are consonant with each other because they are both connected with victory over separation, either as a quality of the Redeemer or as that of the redeemed.

Although Theissen's analysis is not novel,[8] it illustrates effectively not only the basic components of Paul's soteriological language and their organic interaction but also his hermeneutical versatility, which renders the heart of the gospel in such a way that it speaks to the needs and demands of the socio-cultural situations of his churches. Moreover, the analysis shows that the levels of symbolic interaction do not justify a view that there is a dichotomy between juridical and mystical language[9] or an emphasis on one as opposed to the other.[10] The continuing debate about the center of Paul's thought as either "justification by faith" or "eschatological mysticism in Christ," or as a hierarchical structure, deals with wrong alternatives, because Paul's center is located in the lordship of Christ as it anticipates the final triumph of God.

Paul interprets the coherent apocalyptic core of the gospel in a variety of metaphors that interact and interweave to form an organic whole, so that a developmental or atomistic analysis of the various metaphors bypasses his hermeneutical intent. His interpretation of the gospel cannot be hierarchically structured, as if there is one primary metaphor that dominates all the others (see Chapter 2, above). We are dealing with a paradigmatic structure and with a hermeneutical field, not with rigidly defined dogmatic units that must fit a hierarchically arranged architectonic system.

THE SYMBOL OF RIGHTEOUSNESS

The symbol of righteousness seems to be the exception. Far from being a "survival" in Paul's thought or a subsidiary polemical crater (Schweitzer), it constitutes the linguistic home of Paul's conversion experience because it was the language in which he received the Christophany and by means of which he broke with his Pharisaic life, a life that circled around the issue of righteousness under the Torah.[11]

To the Jew, the Torah is the sole means of maintaining righteousness, just as righteousness is the sole means of obtaining life. The Torah is "unto justification for life" (*eis dikaiōsin zōēs*, genitive of "finality," Rom. 5:18), according to the Jewish ground rule of salvation: "He who does these things shall live in them [*ho poiēsas . . . zēsetai*]" (Lev. 18:5; cf. Gal. 3:12; Rom. 10:5). Righteousness is derived "from the law" (*ek nomou*, Rom. 10:5; Phil. 3:9; Gal. 3:21) or "through the law" (*dia nomou*, Gal. 2:21), or "by the law" (*en nomō*, Gal. 3:11; 5:14; Phil. 3:6) and is inseparable from the observance of the *mizwoth*—"the works of the law" (Gal. 2:16; Rom. 3:20; 4:2, etc.), which are inherent in "covenant-keeping."

Paul's conversion experience evokes a new depth in his understanding of "righteousness," because here Judaism and Christ fatally collide. In other words, the conversion experience comes to expression as the antithesis between the domains of the Torah and Christ, and thus "faith-righteousness" excludes and negates "works-righteousness" (e.g., Rom. 3:27–30). But why did Paul create a radical antithesis between the Torah and Christ? Most Jewish Christians were content to maintain a correlation between the two, however loose it might have been in some cases.

As we noted earlier (Chapter 8, above) the Torah in first-century

Judaism not only is a moral code—which embraces the redemption of the Exodus and the "commanding voice" of Sinai—but has gained ontological status. It summarizes everything that makes Israel "special" as the people of the election, but it has become as well the first creation of God and the reason for—and pattern of—his creation of the world. In Diaspora Judaism (Philo; Wisdom of Solomon), for instance, the Torah is closely associated with Wisdom and the Logos as the mediators of creation, and in Jewish apocalyptic circles the Torah governs the creation, its cosmic laws, and the angels who supervise the elements of the world. The ontological status of the Torah epitomizes God's exclusive self-revelation to Israel and has universal-cosmic status. Therefore, its observance is the sole means for righteousness unto life (Lev. 18:5), and because "life" is insolubly related to the Torah, disobedience means loss of eternal life and perdition.

The consequences of Paul's encounter with Christ are thus quite unbelievable, for his confession of the crucified Jesus as the Messiah entails a radical rejection of the Torah—the Torah that according to his Pharisaic past the Messiah would confirm and teach as "righteousness." How, then, is Paul able to break the insoluble connection between righteousness and the Torah, which his Pharisaic life so ardently correlated?

The answer lies in the collision between the zeal of the Pharisee and his encounter with the risen Christ. Paul's persecution of Christ was motivated by his Jewish conviction: "Cursed be every one who hangs on a tree" (Gal. 3:13; see Chapter 9, above). But now the appearance of the risen Christ demonstrated God's confirmation of a Messiah who had been cursed and crucified by the law. This meant for Paul not only the validity of the early Christian confession "Christ died for our sins and was raised for our justification" (cf. Rom. 4:25; 1 Cor. 15:3-4) but also the end of the universal-soteriological status of the Torah. Christ had died not only to forgive the sins, which were committed under the law, but also to break the power of the law itself, because the law had cursed him, whom God had vindicated. Paul's interpretation of Christ's death and resurrection never wavers. It means above all the end of the dominion of the law and our transfer to a new lordship that saves us from the law's condemnation and grants us new life in Christ. In his conversion experience, Paul discovers the strange truth that the power of sin does not collide with the Torah but allies itself with it. Otherwise, the Torah could not have condemned the Son of God, who was sent by God to redeem us. Paul then extrapolates from the confession of the church—"Christ died for our sins"—the new insight that Christ died as well to the power of sin, which the law stimulates. For "the power of sin" operates not only behind our individual "sins" (1 Cor. 15:3) but even more behind the poisonous function of the law. How otherwise could those who, like Paul, had been most faithful to the law have persecuted and crucified the Messiah of God on the very basis of the law?

It is interesting in this context that Paul rarely blames Jesus' crucifixion on the criminal act of "lawless men" (*anomoi*, Acts 2:21), that is, persons who consciously distort the law, as if a correct Jewish understanding of the law would have prevented Jesus' death. According to Paul, spiritual powers of evil operate behind the political rulers (1 Cor. 2:8; cf. Col. 2:15; Eph. 3:10; 6:12). The law itself, now, in its ontic function, is characterized as such a spiritual power (Gal. 3:13; 4:5), one that uses people for its sinful ends. It does this because it has become the servant of the power of sin. Therefore, Paul ascribes the death of Christ not primarily to men who pervert the law but to God's saving purpose and to Christ's "self-emptying" love as the necessary means for our redemption from the powers of sin, death, and the law (Gal. 3:13; 4:4–5; Rom. 8:3; 2 Cor. 5:21; cf. also Rom. 15:3; 2 Cor. 8:9; Phil. 2:6–11). Indeed, the death of Christ eradicates not only the curse of the law but also the law itself. Therefore, it does not restore the law in Christ as our new possibility for obedience. The righteousness of God in Christ is "apart from the law" (Rom. 3:21), and "Christ is the end of the law" (Rom. 10:4; cf. also Gal. 2:21).

Despite the negation of the law in Christ, it nonetheless remains God's law, "holy and just and good" (Rom. 7:12). Paul faces the alternative of viewing the law either as an inferior, mistaken revelation of God (Marcion) or as God's agent of condemnation (see Chapters 4 and 11, above). Although Paul is at times close to a Marcionite view of the law, it is his conviction that the Christ-event both fulfills (the righteous requirement of) the law (Rom. 8:4) and ends its salvific rule. The sacrificial expiation of Christ achieves what no human being could do, because he suffers in his death "for us" the punishment for sins that the law requires (Gal. 3:13).

Righteousness and Apocalyptic

The "righteousness of God" in Paul transcends its "rabbinic" interpretation of Torah-keeping. It reaches back to its prophetic and apocalyptic formulation (cf. Second Isaiah and Qumran) and radicalizes it. It denotes the victory of God and his cosmic act of redemption. God's "righteousness" in Christ not only acquits the sinner but also abolishes the power of sin by transferring us to the dominion of the lordship of Christ. And because the law is allied with the power of sin, righteousness must necessarily be "apart from the law" (Rom. 3:21). Righteousness, then, refers to our new free access to God in faith and in the Spirit as "children of God." Because it signifies our new relationship to God, it also means life in the domain of righteousness, which extends into the eschatological future (Gal. 5:5). The righteousness of God is "power for salvation" (Rom. 1:16), the gift of salvation and "the domain of salvation" (2 Cor. 5:21; Gal. 5:5; Rom. 10:10: "righteousness" = "salvation"), which inaugurates the apocalyptic destiny of the creation.[12] To live in that domain means to live as righteous people, that is, to be "upright" (*dikaios*) and to conduct one's life in obedience to the norms of the new world (Rom. 6:16–23).

According to Ernst Käsemann, the "righteousness of God" has a consistent apocalyptic meaning. As God's eschatological salvation power, it claims the creation for God's lordship and sovereignty that the Christ-event has proleptically manifested.[13] Bultmann and others contest the apocalyptic unitary meaning of "the righteousness of God."[14] Bultmann maintains that the genitive case in the term "the righteousness of God" (*dikaiosynē [tou] theou*) is a genitive auctoris (or an objective genitive) rather than a subjective genitive (Käsemann). According to Bultmann and others, "the righteousness of God" is not an attribute of God but a gift from God, that is, a righteousness bestowed on people before God in Christ. Herman Nicolaas Ridderbos, for example, points to Rom. 2:13, 3:20, 10:3, and Phil. 3:9 and states, "Righteousness is not a divine but a human quality and the nature of that quality is specified by the righteousness of God, as righteousness which is valid before God."[15] This claim is supported by Paul's formulations: "before God" (*para tō theō*, Rom. 2:13) and "in his sight" (*enōpion autou*, Rom. 3:20). Moreover, because in Rom. 10:3 and Phil. 3:9 "the righteousness of their own" and "of myself" (*idia* and *emē dikaiosynē*) is antithetical to "the righteousness of God" (*dikaiosynē [ek] [tou] theou*), the forensic, eschatological aspect of righteousness as God's justifying gift cannot be denied. It should be noted, however, that Paul's metaphors interact with each other, so that the idea of righteousness as forensic acquittal (Rom. 2:12) flows over into a broader field of meaning, where righteousness is a life-giving power and a new domain. Thus, the apocalyptic meaning of "righteousness" as life in the new age (*dikaiosynē* = *zoē*) transcends in Paul, as well as in Qumran and in other apocalyptic literature, its rabbinic referent as forensic judgment and gift. Because righteousness in Paul has both ontological cosmic and interpersonal dimensions, it describes our new being in Christ as our obedience to his lordship. Thus, Paul's hermeneutic of the lordship of Christ is based on the apocalyptic dimension of the term "righteousness"; it is both God's gift of salvation and his power that will encompass his whole creation.[16]

The phrase "the righteousness of God" (*dikaiosynē* [*tou*] *theou*)—which Paul uses only in Rom. 1:17, 3:5, 21, 22, 25, 26, 10:3, and Phil. 3:9— transcends the category of acquittal and personal relationship because it points to that order of cosmic peace (*shalōm*) and salvation (*sōtēria*) that has been proleptically manifested in Christ and that discloses itself in our obedience to his lordship (Rom. 6:16–23).[17]

Although the righteousness of God (and his verdict of justification) constitutes Paul's original hermeneutic of the Christ-event, it is not his only hermeneutic or the master symbol. In other words, "original" means first in order of time, not necessarily in order of importance. Each symbol interprets a different aspect of the one lordship of Christ that marks God's imminent triumph over evil and death. It is a sign of Paul's creativity that many of the metaphors enter Christian language through him (e.g., "reconciliation" [*katallagē*]; "freedom" [*eleutheria*]; also, in all probability, "the body of Christ" [*sōma christou*]). He may have also introduced the language of "grace" and "grace gift" (*charis; charisma*) into Christianity,[18] or at least have given these terms his own specific stamp.

The Symbol of Grace

"Grace" (*charis*) underscores the character of the Christ-event as a radically new gift that negates the old order. It signifies the complete reversal from life under the wrath of God and the power of sin to the new life of freedom and open access to God (Rom. 5:2). The language of "grace" has a specific function in Paul; it reinforces and supplements the unilateral character of God's righteousness and justifying act in the death and resurrection of Christ (Gal. 2:21; Rom. 3:24). Therefore, it protects the covenantal language of righteousness—which is inherently bilateral— against the idea of a reciprocity between God and his people, just as it protects the obedience of faith against the idea of synergism (cf. James 2:21–26). In its pregnant sense, then, grace functions as the supplementary hermeneutic of justification and faith-righteousness: "I do not nullify *the grace* of God; for if *justification* were through the law, then Christ died to no purpose" (Gal. 2:21); "You are severed from Christ, you who would be *justified* by the law; you have fallen away from *grace*" (Gal. 5:4; cf. also Rom. 3:24: "justified by his grace"; Rom. 5:1, 2; 5:17, 21).

Because "grace" expresses the utter gratuity of God's act in Christ ("a free gift" [*dōrean*]; Rom. 3:24; cf. 5:15, 17), it is an ethically vulnerable term. Just as the charge of divine caprice and injustice (Rom. 3:5; 9:19) arises in the context of God's righteousness, so does the charge of antinomianism in the context of grace: "Are we to continue in sin that grace may abound?" (Rom. 6:1; cf. vv. 14 and 15).

Paul rebuts this charge as a fatal misunderstanding of grace. Grace is not a private line to a divine reservoir of indiscriminate graciousness that increases in proportion to the increase of evil (as Rom. 5:20 might suggest). Rather, grace is an event.[19] It marks a new epoch and a new dominion of power that is antithetical to that of the power of sin: "Where sin increased, grace abounded all the more, so that, as sin reigned in death, grace also might reign through righteousness to eternal life through Jesus Christ our Lord" (Rom. 5:20–21). Just as sin has a "kingdom," so grace has its royal domain (cf. Rom. 5:21; 6:15: "under the reign of grace" [hypo charin]; trans. mine). In the light of this apocalyptic meaning of grace, the debate about Paul's view of grace in the history of Western doctrine must be taken out of its privatistic moorings and placed in its original apocalyptic setting, where it refers both to a cosmic power and to the domain of our life in Christ. Indeed, the individualistic setting of the debate about gratia imputata versus gratia infusa (imputed vs. infused grace) bypasses Paul's basic intent.

According to Gillis Petersson Wetter,[20] "grace" is not a very significant term in the New Testament.* In view of its rather different meaning in 1 Peter and Hebrews, it is possible that the term entered Christian vocabulary through the Hellenistic kerygma, although it was Paul's specific coining of the word that made it a pivotal term in Christian doctrine.[21]

Even in Paul the term does not occur as frequently as we might think. It is absent from 1 Thessalonians and Philemon and occurs once in Philippians (1:7), eight times in 1 Corinthians, sixteen times in 2 Corinthians (but ten times in a special sense in chapters 8 and 9), five times in Galatians, and twenty-one times in Romans. If we exclude the nontheological references ("thanks" [Rom. 6:17; 7:25]; "gratitude" [1 Cor. 10:30]; "thanks offering" [2 Cor. 8:4]; "gracious work" [2 Cor. 8:6] or "favor" [2 Cor. 8:4]) and the use of the term in the salutations, the greetings (although they are coined by Paul), and the references to Paul's

---

*It never occurs on the lips of Jesus; it is absent from Mark, Matthew, and 1 and 3 John; in John it is confined to the prologue (three times: John 1:14, 16, 17), whereas Luke uses it four times, but only in the general religious sense of "favor" (cf. Old Testament usage) or "gracious" (Luke 1:30; 2:40, 52; 4:22); it occurs two times in James (4:6); once in Jude (v. 4); once in 2 Peter (3:8), and only in the greetings of the Apocalypse and 2 John. Its more frequent occurrence is limited to Hebrews (seven times), 1 Peter (nine times), apart from the literature of the Pauline school (Acts, seventeen times; 1 Timothy, four times; 2 Timothy, five times; Titus, four times; Ephesians, twelve times; Colossians, five times).

apostolic office (Rom. 1:5; 1 Cor. 15:10; Gal. 1:15) and to the collection (2 Corinthians 8, 9), we discover that the specific theological "weight" of the term occurs quite infrequently. It is absent from 1 Corinthians and occurs three times in Galatians (1:6; 2:21; 5:4) and predominantly only in 2 Corinthians (1:12; 4:15; 6:1; 8:9; 12:9) and in Romans (3:24; 4:4–16; 5:2, 17, 20, 21; 6:1, 14, 15; 11:5–6 [three times]; 12:6).

It is Paul who gives the term *charis* its pivotal significance. It is surprising—in view of the central significance of *hesed* and *zedakah* ("steadfast love" and "righteousness") in the covenantal language of Israel—that Paul does not adopt the Septuagint translation of *eleos* ("mercy") for *hesed*.[22] The Septuagint translators probably sensed the aesthetic and sensuous connotations of the Greek term *charis* (attractiveness, charm, graciousness, pleasure, generosity, benevolence) and thus avoided it. Surprisingly, Paul selects *charis* for his interpretation of the Christ-event, whereas he almost avoids *eleos* (only in salvation-historical contexts [Rom. 9:23; 11:31; 15:9]). Paul probably uses *eleos* (LXX = *hesed*) sparingly because of its reference to the divine sentiment of pity in Judaism. In Judaism, *eleos* is often cast within the scheme of God's "mercy" in contrast to his "justice" (cf. the doctrine of "the scales of justice and mercy"), just as in Philo the divine predicates *theos* and *kyrios* refer respectively to God's "loving" and "punishing" attributes. Paul avoids *eleos* because in Judaism *eleos* often complements what a person lacks in works, so that God's mercy becomes a supplementary gift and not—like *charis* in Paul—the antithesis to every meritorious work.

Because "grace" has a cosmic-apocalyptic referent, it is a new *aion*, that is, a new era and dominion, that Christ has inaugurated. Its apocalyptic coordinates ("righteousness"; "life") cast it as the event of God's power and gift that unfolds itself in the variety of "grace gifts" (*charismata*) in the church (cf. esp. Rom. 12:6; 1 Cor. 12:1–11). "Grace" has the character of an event rather than the character of a divine sentiment, because it is primarily defined by God's act in Christ (Rom. 5:21; 6:14, 15).

Because grace is a free gift (Rom. 3:24; 5:15, 17), Paul uses it in an indicative sense, never in a hortatory one. Expressions like "let grace be multiplied" (1 Pet. 1:2; 2 Pet. 1:2; Jude 4) or "let us obtain grace" (Heb. 10:20) never occur in Paul. He never urges believers "that you may grow in grace and knowledge" (2 Pet. 3:10; cf. James 4:6). Moreover, "grace" is never the object of hope (but cf. 1 Pet. 1:13; 3:7[?]; Didache 16:1) or a *donum superadditum* (an "added gift"), or that quality in God that—as "mercy"—surpasses his quality as righteous judge. Furthermore, it is never used in the plural as in Philo (*charites*).

The event of grace negates the old dominion of the powers and transfers us to the lordship of Christ. Because grace always refers to our present status before God in Christ and has—unlike righteousness (Gal. 5:5; Rom. 10:10)—no future eschatological referent, its exclusive connotation of "gift" threatens to dissolve human responsibility in history and to promote quietism and passivity. Furthermore, its exclusive connotation of present fullness tends to characterize Christian life as prematurely completed. Paul's struggle with the terms *pneumatika* (spiritual gifts) and *charismata* (grace gifts) in his Hellenistic churches demonstrates the temptation of believers to appropriate grace as a possession rather than as a gift. Although the meaning of the term "gift" can shift all too readily from "a present from the giver" to "that which has been given," both the verb *charizomai* ("to give freely," Gal. 3:18; 1 Cor. 2:12; Rom. 8:32) and Paul's reflections on "faith" (*pistis*) protect "grace" against realized eschatology, spiritual complacency, and antinomian abuse. For it is "faith" that determines whether we "continue to stand in grace" (Rom. 5:2)[23] or "fall from grace" (Gal. 5:4). According to Paul, we "stand" only because we stand "in faith" (Rom. 11:20; 2 Cor. 1:24). Grace is therefore unthinkable apart from faith, just as the nature of faith is determined by grace: "the promise was made on the ground of faith, in order that it might be a matter of sheer grace" (Rom. 4:16, NEB). Paul's reflection on "faith" is thus integrally connected with his interpretation of righteousness and grace.

The Response of Faith

The "indicative" of the righteousness of God in Christ and its hermeneutical explication as grace invites an exploration of the meaning of faith. Dieter Lührmann has pointed out that "faith" is not a universal term in religious history and specifically not a propaganda term for the Hellenistic religions (vs. Bultmann).[24] To the contrary, the term must be understood in light of its Old Testament and Jewish background. For a Greek, a phrase like "faith in *christos*" would have been unintelligible,[25] the more so because for Greeks, who follow in the footsteps of Plato, "faith" (*pistis*) is inferior to "knowledge" (*noēsis; epistēmē*)—although superior to "opinion" (*eikasia*)[26]—and refers only to knowledge of the visible world. Thus, Christian apologists like Justin Martyr debate *pistis* with Jews but not with pagan Greeks.[27]

Above all, we must reject a common misunderstanding of Paul's encounter with Judaism. Paul does not simply oppose faith to works (see Chapter 11, above). Such an argument would have been ineffective, for words like "faith," "righteousness," and "God's mercy" are living realities in Judaism. Judaism does not substitute the law for God's grace, or human achievement for the righteousness of God, or works for faith.[28] To the contrary, faith is a cardinal dogma for the Jew as the daily recital of the confession (the Shema) discloses: "Hear, O Israel: the Lord our God is one Lord" (Deut. 6:4). The object of Jewish faith is the God "who gives life to the dead and calls into existence the things that do not exist" (Rom. 4:17). This confession of faith as belief now embodies itself as faithfulness and endurance, that is, as "covenant-keeping" through obedience to the *mizwoth*—"the works of the law." Furthermore, faith is not antithetical to rewards or "merit," because it is inherent in God's righteous nature that faith will be rewarded in the age to come for its steadfast endurance. The Epistle of James is a witness to this conception of faith as endurance, trust, and its "completion through works" (James 2:14–24). Indeed, James rejects a mere monotheistic confession if it is not accompanied by obedient behavior. In a similar vein, Paul also speaks about apostolic and Christian rewards (1 Thess. 2:19; Phil. 2:16; 4:1; cf. 1 Cor. 3:14). The common portrayal of Jews anxiously striving for merits in order to obtain credit with God is simply false, for it confuses God's confirmation of faithful behavior with egocentric striving and a perverted conception of God and his righteousness.[29]

Faith in Judaism has an apocalyptic dimension that subsequently passes into early Christian reflection. It is faith in God the Creator and eschatological Redeemer (cf. above: Rom. 4:17). Faith is that reality which sustains the tension between the promise of the manifestation of God's righteousness and the empirical reality of the present world that mocks the promise. The Jew lives that tension by faithfulness to the Torah, which is the pledge of God's promise. The Torah and faith are therefore inseparably related, because the righteousness of God will be enjoyed by those who are faithful to the Torah.

Paul's antithesis of faith and works constitutes a radical polemic against Judaism. Although the object of faith for Paul is also the God of the covenant, that is, God's faithfulness to his promise of righteousness, the object of faith undergoes a radical change, for Christ has become its sole focus and content (Gal. 3:25). Faith is determined by its object and not celebrated for its own sake. Although Paul describes the attitude of the believer in Rom. 4:16–22 (see Chapter 5, above) and regularly characterizes faith as obedience and trust, and as the opposite of distrust (*apistia*, Rom. 4:20), the subjective element of faith is not subordinated to its objective content. Because "faith" often refers to "the message" of the gospel, there is no divorce between *fides quae creditur* and *fides qua creditur*

(Augustine) in Paul.[30] Faith is *both* "hearing," or "obedience" (*akoē, hypakoē*) or trust, *and* "that what is heard" (*akoē;* cf. Rom. 1:5; 10:10; Gal. 3:3). The prepositions *eis, epi,* and the genitive construction *Iēsou Christou* ("*in* Jesus Christ"), describe the nature of faith; it is implicitly or explicitly always "faith *in* Jesus Christ" (except for 1 Thess. 1:8). However, this does not mean that faith has a Christomonistic focus. "Faith in [Jesus] Christ" is an abbreviation for "faith in the God, who in Christ's death and resurrection has redeemed us from the bondage of sin, and has transferred us to the dominion of his righteousness" (cf. Rom. 3:21–26). Jesus Christ is the pledge of God's imminent cosmic triumph, and thus faith in Christ is able to bear the tension between our confession of God's righteousness and our empirical reality in the world.[31]

The God "who justifies the ungodly" (Rom. 4:5) establishes his reign not because of our faithfulness to the Torah but because of his faithfulness to his promise in Christ. In that sense, 2 Cor. 1:19–20 provides a superb insight into the nature of faith:

> For the Son of God, Jesus Christ, whom we preached among you . . . was not Yes and No [*nai kai ou*]; but in him it is always Yes [*nai*]. For all the promises of God find their Yes in him [*en autō to nai*]. That is why we utter the Amen [*to amēn*] through him, to the glory of God.

Willem Cornelis van Unnik[32] has shown Paul's Hebraic play on words in these verses. The Greek *nai* translates the Hebrew *Amen,* which derives from the verb *aman* and the noun *emet* (*aman* = "to be faithful" [*hiphil:* "to establish oneself in something/someone"; "to believe"]; *emet* = "faithfulness"; cf. Isa. 7:9: "If you will not believe [*taaminu*], surely you shall not be established" [*teamenu*]). Faith, then, is epitomized in confessing and living the "amen," that is, our "yes" (Amen) to the "yes" (*Amen* = *nai*) of God's faithfulness in Christ (cf. 2 Cor. 1:18: "God is faithful"; cf. also 1 Cor. 1:9; 10:13; 1 Thess. 5:24). And the Spirit undergirds faith because the Spirit is the "down payment" of the final realization of God's promises in the glory to come (2 Cor. 1:22).

The Symbol of Freedom

Paul unfolds the righteousness of God as God's grace. Both metaphors interpret the indicative of the Christ-event, which is the sole object of faith. And faith celebrates the faithfulness of God in Christ in the midst of its suffering in an as yet unredeemed world. Faith is inseparable from the hope of righteousness (see Chapter 8, above) and from eschatological freedom: "For through the Spirit, by faith, we wait for the hope of righteousness" (Gal. 5:5); "For the goal of freedom Christ has set us free" (Gal. 5:1; trans. mine).

"Freedom" and "righteousness" interpret the Christ-event in these texts in terms of its apocalyptic goal. Like "righteousness," freedom characterizes both the liberating present experience of our life in Christ and the nature of life in the future cosmic glory of God. That "glory" will consist in freedom from death and from all the powers that still threaten us. However, "the freedom of the glory of the children of God" (Rom. 8:21) also signifies that freedom—as the character of our completed existence in glory—is the true destiny of human existence in God's design. And this freedom cannot be celebrated without the liberation of the cosmic order, of which human existence is an integral part.

"Freedom" has a threefold connotation. It denotes the past act of liberation from slavery to the powers of sin and the law; the present status of liberated believers in Christ in their joyful freedom and access to God; and the future eschatological horizon of the Christ-event as freedom from death and freedom in glory (Rom. 8:21).

The term "freedom" lacks a prehistory in the Old Testament, where it is covered by other terms like "redemption" or paraphrased as "leading you out of the house of slavery." In Judaism it becomes a "political" term only after the Maccabean wars. It occurs rarely in rabbinic literature, but when it does it points to the personal freedom that the Torah grants to its observers and students.[33] However, for the Stoics, "freedom" is a central term. It expresses the ideal of "living in accordance with nature" (the ideal of "impassibility" and "imperturbability" [apatheia; ataraxia] that marks a person's inner freedom); it refers to the Stoic's freedom from life's contingencies and troubles, but also to his stance of "self-sufficiency" (autarkeia).

In Paul, freedom has also both a negative and a positive connotation. But—contrary to the Stoic philosophy—its positive aspect denotes an active involvement with the world in accordance with God's liberating act in Christ. The Christ-event is the liberating event that has freed us not only from the law of sin and death (Rom. 8:2) but also for love (Gal. 5:13). And just as it has liberated us in Christ from the condemnation of the law and from the power of sin, it will liberate us from the signature of death that engulfs the creation as the "last enemy" (1 Cor. 15:26).

Our present freedom is marked by our open access to God and by our new status as children and sons who cry "Abba" to God the Father. Thus, we no longer fear God as our judge but live and speak with "open confidence" (parrēsia) in the joy of the Spirit (chara, Rom. 14:17; 15:13;

Gal. 5:22). Indeed, "where the Spirit of the Lord is, there is freedom" (2 Cor. 3:17), because the Spirit anticipates in the present the horizon of God's future freedom. In opposition to the Stoic philosophy, life in freedom is paradoxically life in a new "slavery," for it means the obligation to live in love (1 Cor. 9:19-23; Gal. 5:13-15). Just as love is possible because we live in freedom from fear and self-concern, so love educates for freedom because it "builds up," that is, helps others to achieve their own freedom in Christ. To be "slaves of one another" (Gal. 5:13) does not mean to enslave others; it means to set them free. Freedom from sin, then, is freedom *for* righteousness (Rom. 6:18), until that imminent moment when freedom will be righteousness, when God's righteous order will embrace the whole created order (Rom. 8:21; Gal. 5:1, 13) and we will live the life of freedom in God's glory.

Freedom summarizes Paul's interpretation of the Christ-event in both its negative aspect and its positive aspect. Freedom's negative aspect is inherent in the defeat of the powers, that is, in our freedom from the power structures of the old age through the intervention of God's act in Christ. And freedom's "affirmation" stresses our present status in Christ that frees us to serve our neighbor in love and makes us sigh for the freedom of the creation from death in the coming glory of God.

13

The Responsibility of
Life in Christ

LIFE IN CHRIST AND THE PROBLEM OF ETHICS

Life in Christ refers to life in a new epoch and a new domain. The prepositional phrase "in Christ" (*en Christo*) should not be interpreted mystically or individualistically;[1] rather, it should be considered within the apocalyptic context of Paul's thought: "For as in Adam all die, so also in Christ shall all be made alive" (1 Cor. 15:22). The phrase has essentially a participatory-instrumental meaning and signifies the transfer to the new age that has been inaugurated with the death and resurrection of Christ.

"In Christ" is not a fixed formula in Paul but is still a flexible term. Paul did not create the term, because it occurs in pre-Pauline baptismal contexts (Rom. 3:24; 1 Cor. 1:30; 6:11; Gal. 3:26[?]; cf. also 1 Cor. 1:2). Its baptismal connotation is clear when we compare 1 Cor. 6:11 with 1 Cor. 1:30: "But you were washed, you were sanctified, you were justified in the name of the Lord Jesus Christ and in the Spirit of our God" (1 Cor. 6:11); "He is the source of your life in Christ Jesus, whom God made our wisdom, our righteousness and sanctification and redemption" (1 Cor. 1:30).*

The phrase refers not only to Christ as the Lord of the new dominion and our incorporation in him but also to Christ as the agent of God who in his death and resurrection has inaugurated the new age. "In Christ" has both a local and an instrumental meaning. Although Fritz Neugebauer[2] disputes the spatial character of the term, he implies it in his characterization of "in Christ" as "being determined by the Christ-event and a being incorporated in it" (*ein Einbezogensein*).

Although the phrase has a strong instrumental character and is frequently synonymous with "through Christ" (*dia Christou*),† it belongs to

---

*It is probable that "into the name [*eis to onoma*] of the Lord Jesus" (Acts 8:16; 19:5; cf. Matt. 28:19) is identical with "in the name of . . ." (*en tō onomati*, Acts 2:38; 10:48; 1 Cor. 6:11); the terms are synonymous with "into Christ [Jesus]" (*eis Christon* [*Iēsoun*], Rom. 6:3; Gal. 3:27) and with *Christou einai* ("to belong to Christ," 1 Cor. 1:12; Gal. 3:29); *endusasthai Christon* ("to put on Christ," Gal. 3:27; cf. Rom. 13:14) and *en Christō* ("in Christ," Gal. 3:26).

†Cf. 1 Cor. 15:21–22; *di anthrōpou* = *en tō Adam* = *en tō Christō*; and the parallel to 1 Cor. 15:21–22 (*en*) in Rom. 5:18, 19 (*dia*); cf. also Rom. 5:9, 10: "Since, therefore, we are now justified *by* [in] his blood [*en tō haimati*], much more shall we be saved *by* him [*dia autou*] from the wrath of God. For if while we were enemies we were reconciled to God *by* the death [*dia tou thanatou*] of his Son, much more, now that we are reconciled, shall we be saved *in* [by] his life [*en tē zōē*]."

272

the language of incorporation and derives basically from the concept of corporate personality, that is, the idea that the head of a tribe or family is the representative embodiment of all its members.[3] According to Hebrews, the tribe of Levi "was still in the loins of his ancestor [Abraham] when Melchizedek met him" (Heb. 7:10); and according to Paul, Adam and Christ are the representative figures of the old and new humanity (1 Cor. 15:20; Rom. 5:12–21).

Although Paul inherits the term and uses it frequently, it causes him hermeneutical difficulties, for it suggests all too readily an overheated and realized eschatology where the ontological reality of the new age has already been accomplished. Its precise connotation in the Hellenistic Christian tradition before—and around—Paul is unclear, but it seems likely that it was understood in terms of a sacramental ontology, that is, as union with the glorified Christ. The indicative character of the phrase and its reference to incorporation into a new sphere suggest this. Paul now modifies the phrase in order to deemphasize its static, sacramental, and enthusiastic association. He employs it in three basic contexts:[4] (1) in relation to concepts of salvation; (2) in relation to the communal structure of the church; (3) in relation to the apostolate and other apostolic persons.* Notwithstanding Paul's antiindividualistic hermeneutic of the phrase and his emphasis on the death of Christ as constitutive of our life in Christ (cf. Rom. 3:24; 2 Cor. 5:19, 21), "incorporation" language has a logic of its own that brings us to the conclusion that what pertains to "the one" pertains as well to "all" or "the many" "in the one" (cf. Heb. 2:11: "For he who sanctifies and those who are sanctified have all one origin" [*ex henos pantes*]). Incorporation language invites realized eschatology and is unable to express the future apocalyptic dimension of Paul's thought. First Corinthians 15, for example, demonstrates the extent to which the Corinthians had rejected Paul's apocalyptic world view as inconsistent with his "in Christ" theology (see Chapter 8, above), for how is it possible for a theology of "being in Christ" to safeguard the "not yet" of our full redemption? How can anyone after reading 1 Cor. 2:6–16, with its theme of our already perfected spiritual wisdom, expect the future apocalyptic of 1 Cor. 4:4–5, 13:8–10, or 15:12–58?

It may well have been Paul's intention to connect the language of "in Christ" with the exclusive lordship of Christ and our obedience to him

---

*(1) Cf. 1 Thess. 5:18; Gal. 2:17; 3:14, 26; Rom. 3:24; 6:11, 23; 8:2, 39; 2 Cor. 5:19, 21. (2) Cf. 1 Thess. 2:14; Gal. 1:22; 2:4, 17; 3:28; Rom. 6:11; 8:1; 12:5; 2 Cor. 5:17. (3) Cf. 1 Cor. 4:15, 17; 15:31; 16:24; Rom. 9:1; 15:17; 16:3; 7, 9, 10; 2 Cor. 2:14, 17; 12:2, 19; 13:4.

(cf. the imperative connotation of the phrase "in the Lord" [*en tō kuriō*] in Paul). However, the decoding of his message no doubt caused a "spiritualistic" misunderstanding of his gospel. Although Paul counters the Corinthian theology of "in Christ" and "in the Spirit" with the claim that life "in Christ" and "in the Spirit" is inseparable from life "in the body" and cannot be conflated with life in the kingdom of God, the ontological association of participation "in Christ" and "in the Spirit" does not easily link itself with Paul's eschatological reservation.

Life "with Christ"

The phrase "with Christ" (*syn Christō*) causes similar hermeneutical difficulties. Ernst Lohmeyer, Eduard Schweizer, and others[5] have demonstrated the apocalyptic coordinates of the term (cf., e.g., Deut. 33:2, LXX; Enoch 62:14). In 1 Thess. 4:17 the reference to the Parousia of Christ climaxes with the phrase "and so we shall always be with the Lord" (*syn kyriō esometha;* cf. also Rom. 6:8; 8:32; 2 Cor. 4:4; 5:8; 13:4[?]). Christianity before and after Paul associated the traditional apocalyptic term "with Christ" with baptism as our transfer to glory. The intense early-Christian apocalyptic expectation (1 Thess. 1:10; cf. Heb. 6:5) could easily shift into realized eschatology through sacramental realism. Thus, in Titus 3:5 and Col. 1:13 (cf. 2 Cor. 5:17) the apocalyptic-cosmic "new creation" and kingdom of God have already taken place in baptism, and the phrase "with Christ" in Eph. 2:5 refers to our resurrection with Christ as an occurrence of the past: "but God . . . made us alive together with Christ . . . and raised us up with him, and made us sit with him in the heavenly places in Christ Jesus" (Eph. 2:4–6; cf. Col. 2:12, 13, 20; 3:1).

Paul now interprets the sacramental phrase "with Christ" in terms of a disjunction between Christology and anthropology. He emphasizes not only the solidarity of believers with Christ's death but also their ethical obligation to "walk in newness of life" (Rom. 6:4) and thus reserves our resurrection to glory for the end of time, when we will be what the risen Christ is now. The original temporal dimension of the phrase "with Christ" enables him to accentuate his apocalyptic perspective, which the phrase "in Christ" was not able to express: "But if we have died with Christ, we believe that we shall also live with him" (Rom. 6:8).[6] Nevertheless, the language of "with Christ" resembles that of "in Christ," because they both share the incorporation motif. Because Paul stresses the indicative character of the Christ-event, which "once for all" (Rom. 6:10) took place in the crucified "body of Christ" on Golgotha (Rom. 7:4), the apocalyptic-future perspective of "with Christ" tends at times to fuse with the ontological reality of our sacramental identification "with Christ." Indeed, 1 Thess. 5:10, Rom. 8:17, and even 2 Cor. 4:10, 13:4, do not carry (at least not explicitly) a future eschatological connotation.[7]

Nevertheless, Paul's hermeneutical intent is clear. The phrases "in Christ" and "with Christ" express for him both the ground of our new life in and through the death and resurrection of Christ and our continued participation in his lordship until the day of our eternal communion "with Christ" in God's glory. Sacramental realism does not mean an ontological usurpation of premature blessedness. Therefore, Paul's hermeneutic often interprets sacramental realism in terms of the language of justification by faith:

> I have been crucified with Christ; it is no longer I who live, but Christ who lives in me; and the life I now live in the flesh I live by faith in the Son of God, who loved me and gave himself for me. . . . For if justification were through the law, then Christ died to no purpose. [Gal. 2:20–21]

Far from divorcing a "juridical" hermeneutic from a "participation" hermeneutic,[8] Paul integrates them to protect ontology from disintegrating into a realized eschatology and so preserves the apocalyptic perspective of the lordship of Christ.

THE INDICATIVE AND THE IMPERATIVE

There is general agreement that Paul views Christian life as a "life between the times." However, Paul's apocalyptic intent is often misinterpreted in a purely Christocentric sense, which in turn leads to a misinterpretation of his ethic. Neoorthodox interpreters tend to transform the temporal sequence of apocalyptic into a metaphysical distinction between time and eternity and so reduce Paul's apocalyptic language to a hermeneutical tool that must accentuate the ultimate character of the Christ-event (see Chapter 8, above). Existentialist interpretation, with its emphasis on the "historicity" of life (*Geschichtlichkeit*), has no use for cosmic-apocalyptic imagery and chronological history (*Historie*) and so robs Paul's future apocalyptic horizon of its imminent and cosmic character. According to this interpretation, Paul supposedly entertains a notion of God as the one who always comes to us from the future.[9] Future temporal specificity is here transformed into a philosophical attribute of God as the eternal future. As a result, Paul's ethic is forced into a Christomonistic mold and interpreted purely in terms of the problem of the dialectic between the gift of salvation in Christ ("the indicative") and its demand ("the imperative").

Rudolf Bultmann discerned correctly that Paul was neither an idealist nor a confused thinker who wavered between an absolute ideal and harsh reality. The Stoic image of the moral "progressor" (*ho prokoptōn*), steadily moving to the goal of becoming a "wise man" (*sophos*)—similar to the Kantian imperative—does not apply to Paul, nor does the Gnostic image of salvation as a sacramental infusion into the believer.[10]

Bultmann argued that "the imperative" has a dialectical relation to "the indicative" in Paul, because it actualizes what the indicative makes possible. Human volition in this scheme is neither abolished nor made autonomous. Subsequently, Günther Bornkamm refined Bultmann's observations in correcting the latter's Lutheran stance on the believer as *simul iustus ac peccator*, and he argued that the believer is able to live a new moral life in Christ while anticipating the end of history.[11]

Ernst Käsemann has inserted a new dimension into the discussion.[12] With Bultmann, he locates the heart of Paul's gospel in "the righteousness of God," but he disputes Bultmann's interpretation of it (see Chapter 12, above). "The righteousness of God" has an apocalyptic derivation and denotes both God's power and His gift. It expresses God's cosmic claim on the world, which is proleptically made manifest in the lordship of Christ and in which the believer participates through obedience. The lordship of Christ, however, does not rob believers of their volition; they are not simply pawns in a cosmic struggle, because their obedience demonstrates their allegiance to God's sovereign will for his creation. According to Käsemann, the obedience of Christians must be viewed in the context of their solidarity with the created order, which comes to expression in Paul's definition of "the body" (*sōma*).[13] In other words, Käsemann advances the discussion of the relation of the indicative and imperative in Paul, which had heretofore been dominated by Bultmann's definition of "the body" as a person's relation to himself.[14] This existentialist definition of "the body" neglects its cosmic-historical character and spiritualizes a person's relation to the world. It causes an existentialist narrowing of both the indicative and imperative, because indicative and imperative are here construed as an antinomy or paradox in which God's gift in Christ is simultaneously an appeal to our decision to become bearers of the cross in each moment of time. The problem is that a precise explication of this antinomy or dialectic remains hermeneutically vague. Bultmann defined it in terms of possibility and actualization and so not only endangered Paul's emphasis on the actuality of God's act of salvation in Christ but also overemphasized the human will. The "faddish" terminology of "paradox" and "antinomy" curiously satisfied most Neoorthodox interpreters, despite the fact that it is actually a hermeneutical obfuscation. It is to Käsemann's credit that his emphasis on obedience allows the divine gift in Paul its full actuality, because "obedience" is a much "softer" claim for human participation in salvation than the existentialist focus on "decision."

Indeed, the relation between the indicative and the imperative must not be dialectically overloaded, for it points to the fact that the Christ-event awaits a cosmic consummation that will no longer have room for the imperative when the reality of "sight" displaces that of "faith" (2 Cor. 5:7). The imperative, then, must be defined—as Schweitzer said about the Sermon on the Mount—as an interim ethic. Its character as demand does not aim at obedience in separation from the future cosmic manifestation of the divine indicative or in isolation from the cosmic-redemptive outreach of Christian responsibility in the world that will be tested at the last judgment (2 Cor. 5:10; Rom. 14:12). In other words, although the interaction between indicative and imperative is based on the Christ-event, it looks forward to the theocentric confirmation of the Christ-event and to God's coming glory in a redeemed creation. The imperative is meaningful only in a world where death is still "the last enemy" and where hostile powers still threaten Christian existence. Moreover, the world's need for redemption inspires both the sighing of Christians and the imperative of their redemptive activity in the world. It stamps Christian life as both redemptively active and yet actively waiting for the Parousia of Christ.

The scheme of the indicative and imperative must be lifted out of its Christocentric and anthropocentric moorings and placed in the theocentric-cosmic perspective of Paul's Christology.

This perspective necessitates a discussion of the relation between the Spirit and the future glory of God and that between the Spirit and the body. The first topic centers on God's ultimate "indicative" in his imminent apocalyptic self-manifestation, whereas the second topic formulates the nature of "the imperative" in Paul. (See below.)

Because the obedience of the believer is grounded in the Christ-event, it is linked as well to the last judgment and the cosmic redemption of the world in the future of God. Just as the Christ-event is both crucial and provisional (see Chapter 8, above), so the imperative, which is grounded in the indicative of the Christ-event, moves from the crucial Christ-event to the suspension of its provisional character in the coming kingdom of God.

A simple indicative-imperative scheme must be dismantled in favor of a scheme that moves from the indicative of the Christ-event to the imperative of Christian obedience in order to reach its goal in the final indicative of the glory of God. Only then will the mission and work of Christ be fully realized in the celebration of *Deus Victor*. Although the indicative of the Christ-event is not the full but the proleptic realization of the future indicative of God's final glory, the imperative does not relativize God's action in Christ. It underscores our active and necessary participation in the gospel of God's coming glory: "We have been saved in this hope" (Rom. 8:24; trans. mine).

I conclude, then, that the formulation of the indicative-imperative scheme in dialectical-anthropological terms is too static. It was perhaps unduly influenced by the anthropological focus of the debate between Augustine and Pelagius about the all-sufficiency of grace versus a form of divine-human synergism. However, for Paul the indicative-imperative scheme has an apocalyptic-cosmic thrust. The imperative does not primarily answer the question "How will *I* be saved?" but rather "How are the antidivine powers of the world to be met in my redemptive activity in Christ for the sake of the world?"

It is therefore an error to defuse the future apocalyptic indicative in favor of a view that emphasizes primarily the soteriological effects of the Christ-event. In that case, ecclesiology tends to become so fused with the Christ-event that the universal dominion of the church as the body of Christ displaces the apocalyptic future glory of God. When "the divine commonwealth"[15] of the church becomes the only object of hope, the triumph of Christ becomes illegitimately identified with the triumph of the church. It is clear that both Colossians and Ephesians move in that direction.

THE FUNCTION OF THE SPIRIT

Paul's interpretation of the Spirit clarifies for his Hellenistic churches a frequent misunderstanding. Although the Spirit is indeed the power (*dynamis*) of the messianic age in the present, its integral connection with the death and resurrection of Christ qualifies its power (1) as preliminary to the final glory of God; (2) as operative in the embattled ethical situation of believers in the world; and (3) as cruciform, because it is defined by the resurrection power of a crucified Messiah.

The Spirit and the Glory

Paul regularly characterizes the Spirit as "the first fruits" (*aparchē*) and "down payment" (*arrabōn,* Rom. 8:23; 2 Cor. 1:22; 5:5; trans. mine). In both cases the genitive case—"the first fruits [the down payment] *of* the Spirit"—is appositional and not partitive. Believers have not merely received a part of the Spirit, as if it is an evolutionary power or is to be complemented by its steady increase and by a full outpouring at the Parousia. Rather, the Spirit in its totality is a presently bestowed gift, poured out at baptism (2 Cor. 1:22) and operative in historical reality until the time of the final glory that will be characterized by "imperishability," "immortality" (1 Cor. 15:53), and the "spiritual body" (1 Cor. 15:44) or "body of glory" (Phil. 3:21). Although the gift of the Spirit conveys to us the Christ-event in its redemptive presence and power, the Spirit is—like the Christ-event—a proleptic gift and a prelude to the kingdom of God. Indeed, the Spirit conveys to us the presence of the crucified and risen Christ. It is therefore a power on earth, militantly engaged, battling "against the flesh" and moving us through enemy territory toward the future of God's final victory. Thus it operates in the body (cf. 1 Cor. 6:13–20; cf. "the Spirit dwells in you" [1 Cor. 3:16; Rom. 8:11, etc.]); and it is preliminary; God prepares us (*katergazomenos*) with the gift of the Spirit (2 Cor. 5:5) for eternal life.

The Spirit has a dynamic thrust; its future intent (*phronēma*) is eternal life and eschatological peace (Rom. 8:6). The dynamic energy and movement of the Spirit, however, makes it difficult to define its dual (spatial and temporal) operation, because it not only locates us spatially in a dominion of freedom (Rom. 8:2) but also drives us toward the as yet unfulfilled future: "The hope does not disappoint us, because God's love *has been poured* into our hearts through the Holy Spirit which *has been given* to us" (Rom. 5:5); "Where the Spirit of the Lord is, there *is* freedom. And we all, with unveiled face, beholding the glory of the Lord, *are being* changed from one degree of glory to another; for this comes from the Lord who is the Spirit. . . . But we have this treasure in earthen vessels . . ." (2 Cor. 3:17, 18; 4:7); "We ourselves, who *have* the first fruits of the Spirit, groan inwardly as we *wait* for adoption as sons, the redemption of our bodies" (Rom. 8:23).

Because the thrust of the Spirit is "life and peace" (Rom. 8:6) and thus represents the messianic joy of the new age (Rom. 14:17), it does not find stasis and fulfillment in its own reality but pushes us on. It is "the first fruits" and the "down payment," not the harvest or the full payment. We do not groan because we long for the Spirit; rather, the Spirit itself is the agent that makes us "sigh" and "groan" (Rom. 8:23) and gives us endurance to wait for the final redemption of the body (Rom. 8:23, 25). It is remarkable that in the same chapter (Romans 8) the Spirit both conveys present eschatological peace and joy (vv. 1–16) and yet makes us sigh restlessly (vv. 17–27; see Chapter 16, below).

Paul's demarcation between the Spirit and the future consummation is difficult to draw in Hellenistic culture. The dualistic anthropology of the Hellenistic world, with its split of "Spirit" versus "body," or "mind" versus "body" (*pneuma* vs. *sōma; nous* vs. *sōma*), favors a fusion of the divine and the human spirit and of the reality of the heavenly kingdom of God and the human spirit. As early as Philo the ecstatic presence of the prophetic Spirit forces the mind to leave the body (*Who Is the Heir* 265). Furthermore, "Spirit" in the Hellenistic world is conceived as a heavenly substance—however ethereal—because all power is viewed in terms of a material substratum.

Since baptism, the Spirit has become the life-giving power (*pneuma zōopoioun*, 1 Cor. 15:45) in the believer and manifests itself in miraculous "heavenly" happenings like prophetic speech, ecstasy, and the gift of healing. A Hellenistic Christian now is apt to celebrate this new divine power as an infusion with divine substance, as inward "spiritual" transformation, or as the miraculous appearance of the divine in history. The Spirit produces a deification of the believers, transfers them to the heavenly world of God's kingdom, and separates them from any entanglements with the inferior material body. They know themselves already "spiritualized" and lifted out of history. Paul argues in Corinth in a setting in which the gift of the Spirit is understood as the complete presence of the kingdom (1 Cor. 4:8) and as the power that segregates bearers of the Spirit (*hoi pneumatikoi*) from the world. Because the manifestations of the Spirit (*ta pneumatika*, 1 Cor. 12:1–11) have become an exhibition before the world of the believer's separation from the world, Paul's task is to interpret the Spirit against its identification with the kingdom. We should be aware that the Gospel of John resembles in some ways the theology of the Corinthians. Because John coalesces the resurrection of Christ with the gift of the Spirit and the Parousia, he interprets the kingdom of God as the presence of the Spirit (John 13–17). Such a hermeneutic transforms the gulf between "the fallen world" and the church into an abyss, so that the church becomes, as it were, a pneumatic elite that gathers like-minded pneumatics unto itself and surrenders its redemptive mission to the world.*

In a Jewish climate this Hellenistic misunderstanding of the Spirit can be avoided. In the Old Testament, *ruah* is not so much an inherent attribute of people (but Ps. 51:10, 11; Isa. 61:1; 63:10) but a momentary, ecstatic,

---

*The Book of Acts, to the contrary, interprets the Spirit in a more Pauline manner. Although it sacrifices the dynamic historical tension between the Spirit and the kingdom of God in order to come to terms with the delay of the Parousia, the Spirit is not fused with the kingdom of God, nor has it become a substitute for the kingdom (cf. Acts 1:1–10). Acts accentuates the present time of the church as the hour of the Spirit and as the hour of missions—without sacrificing the future kingdom of God. In this way Acts guards the distinction between the Spirit and the kingdom of God.

inspirational force that "falls upon" them and "possesses" them. Not until the messianic age will it become a permanent and thoroughly ethical gift (cf. Isa. 11:1–5; Jer. 31:31–34; Ezek. 36:26–27; 37:14; Ps. Sol. 17:42; 18:8). Thus, in the prophets the Spirit has a clear future eschatological referent.[16]

Postexilic Judaism—except for Qumran[17]—often complains about the cessation of the Spirit and prophecy: "there is no longer any prophet" (Ps. 74:9); "Israel's prophets obtain no vision from the Lord" (Lam. 2:9; cf. Zech. 13:4–5; Mal. 4:5). "The rabbis frequently repeat the statement that 'with the death of Haggai, Zachariah and Malachi, the Holy Spirit ceased in Israel' and that 'the Holy Spirit was one of the five treasures of the first temple which were lacking in the second' " (Talmud B. Sotah 48a; Cant. R. A3).[18] However, the dearth of rabbinic statements about the Spirit should not deceive us. Apart from the occasional referents in rabbinic literature to the Bat Qol ("the Heavenly Voice") as referee in halakah discussions, Qumran celebrates the presence of the eschatological Spirit in its midst and testifies to a tension between the already and not yet that is similar to that of the early Christian church.[19]

The significance of Paul's interpretation of the Spirit lies in his ability to distinguish clearly between the kingdom of God and the Spirit without either relaxing their dynamic relationship (as in Acts) or fusing them (as in John). For when in the post-Pauline period the Spirit is isolated from its intimate relation to the kingdom of God, it loses its eschatological dynamic character as "first fruits" or "down payment." It now becomes either a momentary inspirational force and the power of prophetic prediction or an entity that is controlled by the church and is guided into institutional channels (the Spirit as special ministerial gift; cf. the Pastorals). Moreover, it can also become a reward for ethical behavior, that is, a *donum superadditum*, and thus not the power and ground of the moral life but rather its reward as "an added gift" (cf. The Shepherd of Hermas).

When the Spirit is fused with the kingdom, a "Corinthian theology" ensues. The Spirit is now no longer related to its Hebrew meaning of "wind in motion" or "life-giving power" but is absorbed into Hellenistic metaphysics as the substance of the divine world "above" that manifests itself as the epiphany of the divine in miraculous happenings and transforms human beings into "divine men" (*theoi andres*) and/or "royal prophets" (cf. Philo's *Life of Moses*).

The Spirit in Paul, however, has an apocalyptic mooring, because it is determined by its relation to the future glory of God (*doxa* [*tou*] *theou*). "Glory" translates the Old Testament term *kabod*, that is, the "weight" of something or someone. It describes the honor, majesty, and sovereignty of God, or more specifically, the radiant light of God's presence in the cloud of his appearance (cf. the Priestly tradent).[20] In Judaism, *kabod* is the synonym of the *shekina*, that is, the presence of God in the temple or in the rabbinic study of the Torah. However, it refers most prominently to the quality of the messianic age, that is, to the glorious life of the kingdom of God.

Whereas in the Priestly tradent the *kabod* is the cultic presence of God in the tabernacle of the desert,[21] Second Isaiah stresses its eschatological character as the glorious manifestation of God's victory: "Every valley shall be lifted up, and every mountain and hill be made low; the uneven ground shall become level, and the rough places a plain. And the glory of the Lord shall be revealed, and all flesh shall see it together" (Isa. 40:4, 5).

Paul's interpretation of the Spirit reaffirms early Christian experience in a new vein. The early Christians experienced the gift of the Spirit as the proleptic presence and signal of the imminent coming of the kingdom, manifest in such things as glossolalia, prophecy, and healings. Paul now articulates the experience of the Spirit in terms of a theological distinction between the Spirit and the final glory so as to prevent a premature fusion between the Spirit and the kingdom of God. This achievement is often called Paul's so-called "eschatological reservation."[22]

There can be no doubt that in the Hellenistic churches "the Spirit" and "the glory" rapidly became identified. Paul adopts (and quotes?) this tradition in 2 Cor. 3:18: "We all, with unveiled face, beholding the glory of the Lord, are being changed into his likeness from one degree of glory to another; for this comes from the Lord who is the Spirit." We should note that in credal contexts "glory" is often equated with "the Spirit" and "power"; Christ is raised either "by the glory of the Father" (Rom. 6:4) or "by his Spirit" (Rom. 8:11) or "by his power" (1 Cor. 6:14; cf. the parallelism in 1 Tim. 3:16: "vindicated in the Spirit," "seen by angels," "taken up in glory"). However, just as Paul qualifies the Spirit as "the first fruits" and the "down payment" of the kingdom of God, so he insists on the distinction between "the Spirit" and "the glory." This enables him not only to connect the Spirit with historical "bodily" life and Christian moral seriousness but also to preserve its eschatological dynamic as the power of the future that drives us on to the final glory. For the believers' final glory will not occur apart from the glorification of the creation: "the creation itself will be set free from its bondage to decay and obtain the freedom of the glory of the children of God" (Rom. 8:21; trans. mine). The movement in Romans 8 is from the Spirit as a present ontological reality (vv. 1–16) to the future glory, which is the content of the hope and which will embrace the whole creation (vv. 17–30). The aorist tense in

Rom. 8:30—"Those whom he justified he also glorified" (= *edoxasen*)—does not contradict the future eschatological meaning of "glory." In the context of Rom. 8:28–30, where Paul describes the absolute certainty of God's sovereign plan of salvation, he celebrates in hymnic fashion the eschatological glorification as the anticipated reality of God's plan to save.

The relation between "the glory" and "the Spirit" demonstrates the ontological aspect of the Spirit. We must be aware that "glory" is not just a liturgical metaphor for the majesty and honor of God, as when Paul speaks about "glorifying the God and Father of our Lord Jesus Christ" (Rom. 15:6). It has, like the Old Testament *kabod*, a physical connotation and refers in the context of Hellenistic culture to the ontological character of the new age: "It is sown in dishonor, it is raised in glory" (1 Cor. 15:43). The "spiritual body" (1 Cor. 15:44) is "a body of glory" (Phil. 3:21), and the eschatological destiny of the creation is to obtain "the freedom of the glory of the children of God" (Rom. 8:21). Because the Spirit is the foretaste of "the glory," it denotes an ontological reality as well and is the domain of the "new creation" (2 Cor. 5:17; Gal. 6:15), where life "in"—"according"—"to the flesh" is displaced by life "in"—"according"—"to the Spirit" (Rom. 8:4, 8). "The glory of God," of which the Spirit is "the first fruits," has the same ontological quality as "life" (*zōe*). The Spirit is not only the active power behind our moral life but also the domain and sphere of the lordship of Christ: "If we do have life in the domain of the Spirit, let us also conduct ourselves in agreement with the Spirit" (Gal. 5:25; trans. mine).[23] The Spirit as our new domain foreshadows our final freedom and glory; and the Spirit as the power of ethics pushes us toward that glory by overcoming the powers of this world: "For the desires of the flesh are against the Spirit, and the desires of the Spirit are against the flesh; for these are opposed to each other, to prevent you from doing what you would. But if you are led by the Spirit you are not under the law" (Gal. 5:17–18).

HERMENEUTICAL DIFFICULTIES

The problem with this interpretation of the Spirit and its relation to the final state of glory is provoked precisely by the ontological character of the Spirit. For how can *the finality of that what is*, that is, "the new creation" or our new and full eschatological life within the reality of the Spirit, constitute at the same time *a preliminary or proleptic stage* that yearns for its full being in the age of glory? Paul employs ontological categories in order to describe the radical nature of the negation of the old versus our new being in Christ. But it seems that these categories have no logical relation to the apocalyptic-futurist thrust of his thought. If the domain of the Spirit has true ontological status, how can it, at the same time, be relativized by its proleptic status?

Paul's language does not always match his intent. Although he intends to interpret ontological statements with the language of faith and with the "not yet" of "sight" (2 Cor. 5:7), these various "language games" do not allow logical precision; the logic of ontology does not mix with that of personal commitment and eschatological suspension.

This observation needs a fuller discussion, because it is exactly the ontological character of the Spirit that creates hermeneutical difficulties for Paul. For how can the Spirit be both an ontological entity, that is, a spatial domain within which transformation has occurred, and a temporal category, that is, the preliminary foretaste of greater things to come? In other words, how can the Spirit be both "the first fruits," claiming our ethical obedience, and a reality that as "the new creation" actualizes our full participation in the age of glory? The penultimate mixes here curiously with the ultimate!

Because the realms of faith and the Spirit speak a different "language" of salvation, Paul's hermeneutic attempts to integrate the different associations of the two languages by interpreting "Spirit" language in terms of "faith" language. We must realize that faith language does not carry the ontological connotations of Spirit language, because it is wedded to Israel's covenantal theology and is located within the "I-Thou" relationship of the covenant. For Paul, "faith" language signifies our personal relation, trust, and commitment to a gracious God, who in his forensic judgment in Christ has acquitted sinners and has granted them new access to himself. And this new relationship must face the last judgment, when our obedience and faithfulness will be judged.

It can be argued that because "faith" is not explicated in terms of an explicit ethic in Paul,[24] the forensic and interpersonal aspects of faith do not necessitate an explicit ethical imperative. Paul never speaks about "the fruit of faith," but he does speak explicitly about "the fruit of the Spirit" (Gal. 5:22).[25] Moreover, Paul rarely mentions the futurist eschatological "not yet" in his faith language (cf. Romans 1-5; Galatians 1-4 [but Gal. 5:5]).

It is quite probable that the contextual situation decides the particular pitch of Paul's argument. When Paul is engaged in a "Jewish" argument, he can assume that (former) Jews acknowledge not only the "not yet" of the messianic age and the last judgment but also the ethical zeal of "the works of the law." He must here argue against the distortion of these themes, because apocalyptic hope or fear and moral zeal are not based on "the works of the law." In this context, Paul explicates the gospel primarily as the "already" of the Christ-event that "already" entails God's justification in Christ and eschatological "peace" (Rom. 5:2) on the basis of faith alone. Because the contextual situation requires the antithesis of "works" and "faith," Paul does not employ the language of works or "the work of faith" (cf. 1 Thess. 1:3); instead, he speaks about the moral dimension of faith as trust, endurance, and hope (Rom. 5:1–4), attitudes that embrace the behavior of the believer. In this context Paul does not argue the ethical and apocalyptic dimensions of the gospel but rather corrects their Jewish misunderstanding in the light of Christ. Paul can assume here the ethical dimension of faith as trusting obedience and its proleptic dimension as hope in the promise and faithfulness of God, because they are inherent components of the Jewish religious world.

However, in a Hellenistic setting, Paul's correlation of "faith" language and the ontological language of the Spirit and participation in Christ is not appropriated. Here a selective hearing of the gospel favors only Paul's ontological categories. Contrary to Paul's intent, "Spirit" language clearly supersedes that of "faith" (cf. 1 Corinthians) and creates misunderstanding. Because in this missionary context Paul must adopt Hellenistic language, he now explicitly emphasizes both the ethical imperative of the Spirit and its future apocalyptic perspective. It is not "the already" of the gospel that needs to be heard here, but its "not yet," because Paul's Hellenistic audience fuses the Christ-event with the apocalyptic future and regards the gift of the Spirit as a sacramental substance that since baptism has transformed, if not deified, human life.

"Spirit" (*pneuma*) and "mind" (*nous*) are as popular terms in Greek culture[26] as "faith" and "trust" (*pistis*) are in Hebrew culture. The Old Testament prophets stress faith and underplay "the Spirit" (*ruah*) because of its ecstatic, momentary (and Baalistic?) character; in fact, they use the term only to describe the life-giving and ethical endowment of the messianic age (cf. Ezek. 36:26; 37:14). But in a Hellenistic climate, the Spirit is stressed and "faith" (*pistis*) is underplayed, because it conveys to the Greek the opposite of "knowledge" (*epistēmē*) and connotes something like unsubstantiated opinion (*doxa*). The Hellenistic connotation of "Spirit" lacks the personal covenantal context of "faith." It is conceived as the power and substance that has infused believers with the transforming substance of grace. These ontological dangers of Spirit language force Paul to interpret the Spirit in terms of both ethical seriousness and the "eschatological reservation." The Spirit is not synonymous with the final "glory" of the kingdom of God but is its foretaste. Paul, therefore, not only emphasizes the moral character of the Spirit but also historicizes it, although he does not deny its "miraculous" ontological and eschatological character (cf. 2 Cor. 12:12; Rom. 15:19).

Conclusion

We conclude, then, that Paul's hermeneutic is characterized by the deliberate use of a "mixed language" that ultimately defies logical precision. "Spirit" and "faith" language interpret each other (Rom. 6:8; 8:4; Gal. 2:20; 3:25-29; 5:5, 16-18), so that the eschatological richness of the gospel may be asserted and yet not distorted and so that the gift of God's ontological Spirit and power is not claimed apart from the obedience of faith. The contextual nature of Paul's argument does not imply a language split, as if a "central crater" of ontological participation in Christ is "the real core" of Paul's gospel and justification by faith is purely secondary and a survival.[27]*

THE SPIRIT AND THE BODY

According to Hermann Lüdemann, "flesh" and "Spirit" have different meanings in different contexts in Paul, and they undergird two anthropologies and soteriologies. "The first follows closely on the Hebrew *basar* and means 'man' as a natural being." The second meaning has a specific ethical connotation: "The flesh is here the necessary cause of sin and corruption and is by nature opposed to the Spirit."[28] The latter conception—derived from Hellenistic dualism—dominates Paul's soteriology, according to Lüdemann. Salvation here signifies the destruction of the flesh by the Spirit, whereas the former Hebraic conception of the flesh is coordinated with a soteriology of justification by faith and forgiveness of sins.

Although Lüdemann's "double-crater" theory is unacceptable, Paul does occasionally identify "the spirit" and "the flesh" (2 Cor. 2:12 = 7:5) when he refers to the natural human being. But normally he opposes "flesh" and "Spirit" as antithetical spheres and powers (Rom. 8:1-11; Gal. 5:17).[29] The flexibility of Paul's use of "flesh" is illustrated in 2 Cor. 10:3, where "flesh" means both the sphere of historical existence and an antidivine sphere: "For though we walk 'in the flesh' [*en sarki*], we do not fight 'according to the flesh' [*kata sarka*]" (trans. mine).

However, Paul can also equate "life in the flesh" (Rom. 8:8, 9) with

---

*E. P. Sanders is ambivalent on this point. Although he correctly states that "righteousness by faith and participation in Christ ultimately amount to the same thing" (*Paul and Palestinian Judaism*, p. 506), he elsewhere plays down the importance of justification.

"life according to the flesh" (Rom. 8:12). In this instance, both spheres are antithetical to "life in"/"according to" the Spirit (*en pneumati; kata pneuma;* Rom. 8:4, 9). "The flesh" usually epitomizes everything that opposes the new life in Christ: "While we were living in the flesh, the passions of sins stirred up by the law were at work in our members" (Rom. 7:5; trans. mine). "The works of the law" are equated (Gal. 3:2, 3) with the flesh, and so are "passions and desires" (Gal. 5:24). Believers are no longer "in the flesh, but in the Spirit" (Rom. 8:9) and serve "in the new life of the Spirit" (Rom. 7:6).

THE MEANING OF "BODY"

We must be aware of the fact that life in the new reality of the Spirit constitutes not "otherworldly" life but rather historical life in the world: the location of the Spirit is "in the body" for "other bodies."

The debate about the meaning of "the body" (*sōma*) in Paul has been dominated until recently by Bultmann: "Man is called *sōma* in respect to his being able to make himself the object of his own action or to experience himself as the subject to whom something happens. He can be called *sōma*, that is, as having a relationship to himself."[30] Indeed, Paul can interchange *sōma* with the personal pronoun, as for instance in Rom. 6:11–12: "So you also must consider *yourselves* dead to sin and alive to God in Christ Jesus. Let not sin therefore reign in your mortal *bodies*" (cf. also 1 Cor. 6:13–14).[31] However, Bultmann's definition is too narrow, because the human being not only is a body, but also has a body, that is, the body has a material substratum that binds it to the created order. According to Käsemann,[32] we are not disembodied selves but embodied selves; the body expresses our solidarity with the stuff of creation, so that the apocalyptic "redemption of our body" (Rom. 8:23) will coincide with the redemption of the creation (Rom. 8:21).

What does it mean to have the Spirit in the body? It is crucial for Paul in two respects, because it expresses (1) the solidarity of the Christian with an unredeemed world and (2) the ethical seriousness of the Christian in the world.

Solidarity with the World

Paul adopts a term that is unique in the New Testament: "the mortal body" (*sōma thnēton*). The significance of the term lies in its distinction from "the body of sin" (*sōma tēs hamartias,* Rom. 6:6) or "the flesh" (*sarx,* Gal. 5:24; cf. also "the body of the flesh" [*sōma tēs sarkos,* Col. 2:11]) and from "the spiritual body" (*sōma pneumatikon,* 1 Cor. 15:44). "The flesh" is never associated with the Spirit (but cf. 2 Cor. 4:11), whereas the Spirit is necessarily related to the body (1 Cor. 6:19; cf. 3:16).

The "mortal body" expresses our historical existence "between the times"; we are no longer "the body of sin," and we do not have as yet "the spiritual body." The multivalent contextual meaning of the term "mortal body" yields a rich meaning: the Spirit indeed operates in the mortal body, so that we can glorify and worship God in our "bodies" (1 Cor. 6:20; Rom. 12:1), whereas at the same time the body is subject to death, decay, and weakness and can even become synonymous with "the flesh" (2 Cor. 4:11).[33] Moreover, the term answers the problem of our personal identity or "continuity" amid the discontinuity of "death" in the stages of salvation, that is, it answers the problem of the continuity and discontinuity of "bodies."

Our transfer in baptism from the realm of the "body of sin" or "flesh" to that of the Spirit implies a radical discontinuity between the "old man" (*palaios anthrōpos,* Rom. 6:6) and "the new creation" (*kainē ktisis,* Gal. 6:15; 2 Cor. 5:17; cf. Rom. 6:4). Similarly, the transfer to "the spiritual body" in the final resurrection of the dead involves again a radical discontinuity, because "flesh and blood cannot inherit the kingdom of God" (1 Cor. 15:50).

"The (mortal) body" now functions as the principle of continuity between the discontinuity of the ages, because the body remains the carrier of our personal identity, although both our crucifixion with Christ in baptism and our death before the Parousia (or our radical change; 1 Cor. 15:51) imply a radical death and a radical renewal.

"The mortal body" is an "interim" reality. We are no longer "the body of sin" and not yet "the spiritual body"; we are a body that is subject both to the rule of the Spirit and to the rule of death. Indeed, the soteriological discontinuity of the "ages" suggests an anthropological discontinuity of "bodies":

Soteriological (sphere of dominions)	*Anthropological (sphere of bodies)*
the era of "sin"	"the body of sin"
the era of "Christ" and "the Spirit"	"the mortal body" ("the Spirit in the body")
the era of "God's glory"	"the body of glory" ("the spiritual body")

Notwithstanding this structure of apparent discontinuity of bodies, the soteriological discontinuity of the ages does not destroy our personal identity, because the body remains in some sense the constant amidst the discontinuity. Therefore, we are not objects of a repeated *creatio ex nihilo* but rather objects of a transformation. And this is confirmed by Paul's language of "clothing" (*enduesthai*) and by that of God's creative will at the beginning of creation—when he "willed" a body for every seed (1 Cor. 15:38). Although the "mortal body" cannot inherit the kingdom of God (1 Cor. 15:50) because of its subjection to the death and decay of the created order, it is no longer dominated by sin (Rom. 8:10) (see Chapter 10, above) and is thus capable of being the instrument of the Spirit. As "mortal bodies," believers can neither indulge in premature perfection nor languish in despair. Rather, they are reminded of the need for the final redemption of the whole mortal "body" of creation, and thus they groan in the Spirit along with the groaning of the creation for the glory to come. The "body" metaphor has a cosmic-universal connotation; "the redemption of our bodies" (Rom. 8:23) is not an individualistic matter but involves the redemption of the total body of the created order (Rom. 8:19–21).

Ethical Seriousness

Because the Spirit is the power behind the moral life and not a reward for "the works of the law," its function is unthinkable apart from life in the body. The Spirit in the mortal body expresses the ethical task of believers, so that they must manifest the victory of the Spirit in the world (see Chapter 8, above). Believers are exhorted to "glorify God in your body" (1 Cor. 6:20), and Paul insists that "the body is not meant for immorality, but for the Lord, and the Lord for the body," because "God raised the Lord and will also raise us up by his power" (1 Cor. 6:13, 14; cf. also 1 Cor. 3:16; 6:19).

Romans 12:1 epitomizes this: "I appeal to you . . . to present your bodies as a living sacrifice, holy and acceptable to God, which is your spiritual worship." The "mortal body" suggests not only the solidarity of believers with creation—because they and the created order are still subject to "death"—but also the ethical seriousness of life in the Spirit, because believers are called to challenge the power of death in the world. They can neither flee from the world into an individualistic haven of spiritual immortality—now or after death—nor consider themselves "power brokers" in a church that has usurped the kingdom of God. Instead, they must show in the midst of—and in solidarity with—this world the new life that is God's design for the future of the created order.

In that sense, Romans 8 constitutes the crown of Paul's theological achievement, for here the sighing of the creation is taken up in that of the Christian and in that of the Spirit, as all wait for the glory to be revealed and for the final redemption of the body (Rom. 8:18–27). Because life in the Spirit is life in the body, and because "the deeds of the body" (Rom. 8:13) will be judged "before the judgment seat of Christ" (2 Cor. 5:10), Paul appeals for the blameless state of the body at the Parousia (Phil. 1:10). Therefore, he pommels his body like an athlete (1 Cor. 9:27) and presses on "toward the goal for the prize of the upward[?] call of God in Christ Jesus" (Phil. 3:14).[34] The "mortal body" epitomizes the relation of the indicative and imperative (see pp. 275ff.), for only when the new indicative of God's coming glory is actualized will the imperative and "the mortal body" disappear, because the "mortal" signature of the body will "be swallowed up by life" (2 Cor. 5:4).

And so our discussion of the Spirit in relation to the body and the final glory impinges on the ethical problem of the indicative and imperative, for the imperative is not a "timeless" application of the "once and for all" redemptive indicative of the Christ-event. Rather, as we have seen, the imperative moves between the indicative of the Christ-event and its confirmation in God's coming glory. The Christian's progress is, to be sure, a "regress" to the foot of the cross (cf. Luther), but it is also a progress in the body under the reign of the Spirit toward the end of the pilgrimage in the "promised land." Thus, the justification of the sinner and the sanctification of the Christian cohere in Paul's thought, because the christological indicative does not swallow up God's future apocalyptic indicative at the end of time. The last judgment does not pale before the forensic judgment of our justification in Christ,[35] and the indicative of Christ is not "the midpoint of time" as the Christocentric center of all history.[36] Rather, "the end of time" is the continuing drawing point to which everything in Paul points: our hope, endurance, sighing, the unredeemed creation, and even the Spirit itself. Although Paul does not say with Pascal, "Jésus sera en agonie jusqu'à la fin du monde. Il ne faut pas dormir pendant ce temps-là,"[37] this sentiment is not far from him. For until Jesus Christ returns, the gospel asks us to proclaim his death and our death in him (1 Cor. 11:26), because it is our hope that the total reign of death will be swallowed up by life (2 Cor. 5:4)! Until the final redemption of the creation and the resurrection of the dead, the resurrection of Christ is not completed; it remains "first fruits." Moreover, the Spirit in us remains the Spirit in a mortal body until the final revelation of God's glory.

THE SPIRIT AND THE CROSS

The precise relationship between the Spirit and the cross is unclear in Paul. If Paul—along with the other New Testament writers—had been more explicit on this point, the history of Christian thought would not have been marked by a continuous struggle against a theology of glory. Far too often Christians have been tempted to understand the Spirit solely as the victorious Spirit of the risen Lord that inspires believers and grants them extraordinary powers. This understanding of the Spirit not only has allowed the cross to fade into the past, as if its "once for all" character is something that is behind us, but ignores the fact that the Spirit is none other than the Spirit of the *crucified* Lord.

Therefore, the question arises if there is something inherently victorious in "the Spirit" that prevents its firm association with the cross, suffering, and weakness. It cannot be denied that the Spirit has a triumphant character in Paul. He connects it more closely with the resurrection and the future glory of God than with the cross. The Spirit mediates the power of the resurrection and manifests itself in "spiritual gifts" (1 Corinthians 12–14). Hebrews speaks in a similar vein about Christians as those "who have once been enlightened, who have tasted the heavenly gifts, and have become partakers of the Holy Spirit, and have tasted the goodness of the word of God and the powers of the age to come" (Heb. 6:4–5). The Spirit is thus associated with the eschatological realities of "life and peace" (Rom. 8:6), "joy" (Rom. 15:13), and "wisdom" (1 Cor. 2:6).

Paul interprets the Spirit to the Corinthians as a power that is both ethical and penultimate. But—in the light of 1 Cor. 2:1–5, where he associates the Spirit with the crucified Christ—it is surprising that he does not ground his argument throughout 1 Corinthians in the Spirit as the Spirit of the crucified Lord. It is also strange that he does not relate it directly to the cross as the Spirit of suffering and sacrificial love in the world.

In opposition to an individualistic exhibition of spiritual gifts, Paul "ethicizes" the Spirit in 1 Corinthians 12–14 and brings it under the control of love, which is the primary "fruit of the Spirit" (cf. Gal. 5:22) and the criterion for all spiritual gifts (1 Corinthians 13). Love and upbuilding (*agapē* and *oikodomē*) must determine the quality of the Spirit and its manifestations.

However, "Jesus Christ and him crucified" (1 Cor. 2:2) is not brought into the argument in 1 Corinthians 12–14, which is all the more curious because elsewhere Paul derives Christian love from the death of Christ as the act of God's love (2 Cor. 5:14–15; cf. Gal. 2:19; 2 Cor. 8:9). In those contexts he argues that love must embrace the brother "for whom Christ has died" (Rom. 14:15; 1 Cor. 8:11).

Why, then, does not Paul ground the ethical interpretation of the Spirit in the death and resurrection of Christ in 1 Corinthians 12–14? It would have anchored the Spirit in the cross and given it a deeper meaning. This observation applies even more to 1 Corinthians 15, for here Paul omits both the death of Christ and the Spirit from the argument about the resurrection, although he cites as his theme the creed of Jesus' death and resurrection in the opening verse (v. 3) and speaks about the resurrection of Christ as "the first fruits" (v. 20)—a term elsewhere used for the Spirit (Rom. 8:23). Paul's argument in 1 Corinthians 15 focuses on the penultimate truth of the resurrection of Christ, that is, on the "not yet" of the apocalyptic glory and the resurrection of the dead. But a dogmatic proposition about the apocalyptic relation between Christ's resurrection and the final resurrection could not have been as persuasive in correcting the Corinthians' realized eschatology as a reflection on the relation between the Spirit and the cross and the meaning this has for life in the body. In other words, if Paul's real intent is to castigate the life-style of the Corinthians, why does he argue solely on the basis of the future resurrection of the dead and so force a strictly Jewish apocalyptic world view on Hellenistic Corinthians? (See Chapter 8, above.)

Although the final victory over death—"the last enemy" (1 Cor. 15:26)—is an inherent part of the gospel, wouldn't Paul have scored a more significant point if he had connected the death and resurrection of Christ—and not only the resurrection—with the final resurrection of the dead, and if he had opposed the Corinthian understanding of the Spirit by grounding it in the cross? Is not his argument in Romans 6 much more incisive and complete, because there our participation in both the cross and the resurrection establishes not only the nature of the moral life but also our hope in the resurrection of the dead (Rom. 6:1–14)? And if—as Karl Barth claims[38]—1 Corinthians 15 is the core and climax of the whole letter, why are chapters 1 and 2 so different from chapter 15? The cross dominates the argument in chapters 1 and 2, but just as the cross is absent from chapter 15, so the resurrection is (at least explicitly) absent from chapters 1 and 2 (see Chapter 8, above).

Furthermore, why is the discussion of the Spirit—which is the focus of 1 Corinthians 12–14—discontinued in chapter 15,[39] where Paul argues the "not yet" of the resurrection of the dead? Would it not have made sense to persuade the Corinthians that the Spirit, which they misunderstand as evidence of their premature perfection, is in fact only "the first fruits" of the coming glory (cf. v. 20: Christ as "the first fruits") and is, moreover, centered in the cross? And would not this have demonstrated that the heart of the Corinthian problem is not only a nonethical conception of the Spirit, or a mistaken apocalyptic perspective, but a fatal misunderstanding of the Spirit, because the Spirit as the Spirit of Christ is grounded in the cross of Christ? For a true understanding of "Jesus Christ and him crucified" (1 Cor. 2:2)—which is explicated in the context of wisdom in chapters 1 and 2—necessarily entails a proper "ethic of the body" and a proper apocalyptic perspective, as is evident, for instance, in Rom. 8:17: We are "fellow heirs with Christ, provided we suffer with him in order that we may also be glorified with him" (Rom. 8:17).

What is baffling in 1 Corinthians is not Paul's contextual way of doing theology but the incipient character of his theological construal of the relation of the cross and the Spirit. Indeed, Romans 8 demonstrates persuasively that the Spirit must be understood in terms of the cross; the "Spirit" section in Rom. 8:4–16 is here framed by the opening statement about the cross (v. 3) and by the concluding statement about suffering with Christ (v. 17).

Moreover, the Spirit is related to the cross and the believers' weakness in 1 Cor. 2:1–5, 1 Thess. 1:6, and (possibly) Rom. 5:6. "And I was with you in weakness and in much fear and trembling; and my speech and my message were not in plausible words of wisdom, but in demonstration of the Spirit and of power, that your faith might not rest in the wisdom of men but in 'the power of God' " (= "Christ crucified," 1 Cor. 1:24; 1 Cor. 2:3–5); "And you became imitators of us and of the Lord, for you received the word in much affliction, with joy inspired by the Holy Spirit (1 Thess. 1:6).

If *ei ge* ("as surely as") rather than *eti gar* ("while") is the correct reading in Rom. 5:6,[40] the Spirit is here definitely grounded in the death of Christ: "God's love has been poured into our hearts through the Holy Spirit which has been given to us [as surely as] Christ died for the ungodly" (Rom. 5:5–6).

Although the Spirit is closely related to the term "power" (*dynamis*, Rom. 15:13; 1 Thess. 1:5), it is curious that "power" but not "the Spirit" is frequently associated with the weakness and suffering of the cross.[41] Indeed, "the power of God" (*dynamis theou*, Rom. 1:16; 1 Cor. 1:10, 24; 2:5; 2 Cor. 4:7; 6:7; 13:4; cf. "the power of Christ," 2 Cor. 12:9) has a greater dialectical relation to weakness and the cross than "the Spirit" (cf. "My grace is sufficient for you, for my power is made perfect in weakness [2 Cor. 12:9; cf. 1 Cor. 1:23–25]).

Although the Spirit causes us to sigh (Rom. 8:23) and assists us in our weakness (Rom. 8:26), it is unclear whether the Spirit (a) helps us in the midst of our weakness and suffering; (b) comforts us notwithstanding our weakness; or (c) is our weakness in the world and in that sense our secret strength. Paul does not relate the last option to "the Spirit," although he does identify "power" as weakness: "For when I am weak, then I am strong" (2 Cor. 12:10).

I therefore conclude that Paul often speaks of the Spirit in an inherently triumphant manner that prevents its integral relation with the weakness and suffering of the crucified Christ. In the context of the Pauline hermeneutic of the Spirit, it is questionable whether the risen Christ "at the right hand of God" remains the crucified one (vs. Moltmann[42]). Although there are elements in the conception of the Spirit that point in this direction, the cruciform nature of the Spirit remains inchoate in Paul. The dialectic of the cruciform and yet victorious Spirit is obtuse—if not absent—because the Spirit refers primarily to the victory of the risen Christ over sin and death, which as the power of the future moves us to the apocalyptic glory of God. The Spirit, then, is much more closely related to the coming "glory" of God and the Parousia of the victorious Lord than to his abiding cross in the world. That seems to be the dominant aspect of the Spirit, notwithstanding the fact that on one occasion Paul can speak in Johannine terms about the crucifixion of Christ as constitutive of "the Lord of glory" (1 Cor. 2:8).*

RESPONSIBLE LIFE IN THE WORLD:
PAUL'S APOSTOLIC MINISTRY

The quality of "life in Christ" and "life in the Spirit" reveals itself concretely in Paul's own apostolic behavior. For an examination of his behavior, we turn to 2 Corinthians, especially chapters 10–13.

The Corinthian Opposition

Dieter Georgi and others[43] have clarified the peculiar Hellenistic-Jewish ideology of Paul's opponents in 2 Corinthians. Although these scholars

---

*An intimate relation between the Spirit and the cross in Paul is often arbitrarily assumed by systematic theologians. G. Ebeling, for instance, rejects a chronological succession of Christology and future eschatology in claiming: "What must count as a theological groundrule is this: the Spirit must be grounded in the crucified Jesus" (Gerhard Ebeling, "Erwägungen zur Eschatologie," p. 441 [trans. mine]).

may have exaggerated the syncretism of the opponents and underplayed their Jerusalem connections,[44] the midrash on Exodus 34, which Paul seems to redact in 2 Corinthians 3, exhibits a syncretistic Hellenistic-Jewish exegesis and interprets the historical Jesus as a new Moses who grants his followers participation in his glorious life.[45]

In both 2 Corinthians and Galatians, Paul's apostolate is under attack, but the issues are different. In Galatia, Paul is charged with distorting the "Jerusalem gospel," because his law-free gospel is attributed to his deviance from the gospel of the mother church in Jerusalem. In 2 Corinthians, however, the relation of law and gospel does not lie behind the attack on Paul's apostolate. The focus here is on Paul's personal status and apostolic behavior. He is charged with lack of "personal presence," spiritual greatness, and effectiveness, thereby demonstrating that he is not qualified to be an apostle. How can a man whose life is so unspectacular and whose actions are so inconspicuous claim to be an apostle of "the gospel of the glory of Christ" (2 Cor. 4:4)? Paul is simply "weak" and unimpressive (10:10). Rather than embodying the victory of Christ over the powers of this world, he seems subject to them. Although he claims to be an accredited apostle, he cannot in any sense be called a personal disciple of Jesus. Consequently, his message about Christ is not informed by the knowledge of Jesus' own glorious ministry (5:16). Moreover, he shows his timidity not only in his speech and personal presence (10:10) but also in his apparent lack of self-worth and courage. He labors for his own keep and does not claim a salary or support from his converts, as befits an apostle (12:13). He obviously lacks the Spirit, because he does not perform "the signs and wonders and mighty works" that characterize a charismatic apostle (12:12). Furthermore, his collection drive is probably an attempt to rob the church for personal gain (12:17). In short, Paul has no charisma, and there is no evidence of Christ's word and personal presence in him (13:3).

The contours of the charges against Paul seem shaped by the picture of the apostle as a divine miracle worker, one who embodies the divine presence. The opponents probably claim to know the historical Jesus by way of their Jerusalem connections, a knowledge that centers on Jesus' miracles and signs. Indeed, Jesus still communicates his powerful presence to those who belong to him and enables them to rise above the world by demonstrating his victory in their pneumatic behavior. The resurrection of Jesus assures his continuing miraculous activity and glory in his apostles and signifies their separation from a corrupt world.

The interpretation of the Old Testament apparently undergirds this picture of Jesus. Jesus is the true successor of Moses—not as the new lawgiver (cf. Matthew) but as the initiator into divine glory (2 Corinthians 3). The opposition, then, interprets Moses as Philo does in his *Life of Moses*. Although the interpretation of 2 Corinthians 3 as a reworked midrash remains conjectural,[46] the prominent use of the name of the historical Jesus in 2 Cor. 4:5, 10, 11, 14, and 11:4—so rare elsewhere in the Pauline letters (cf. Rom. 3:26; 1 Cor. 12:3; 1 Thess. 4:14)—gives credence to the presence of a "Jesus theology" in Corinth. The reference to "another Jesus," "a different Spirit," and "a different gospel" (2 Cor. 11:4), along with that to "knowing Christ according to the flesh" (2 Cor. 5:16; trans. mine), points to a type of "Divine Man" Christology (*theios anēr*) and to a gospel that consists of an aretalogy of Jesus. Jesus' divine status is here disclosed in his prophetic, miraculous activity, which is confirmed by his resurrection. In this manner, the true disciple-apostle embodies the epiphany of Jesus on earth. The Corinthian apostles subscribe to the slogan "The Christian message succeeds because it works." Its effectiveness is demonstrable in the works of these apostles, that is, in their "signs and wonders and mighty works" (2 Cor. 12:12). They boast about their missionary success (10:15; 11:10) and carry letters of recommendation (3:1) so as to recommend themselves as evidence of the truth of the gospel.

Apart from their "boasting" and "self-recommendation," they call themselves "servants of Christ" (*diakonoi Christou;* 2 Cor. 11:23). Paul uses this terminology nowhere so frequently and emphatically as in this letter.[47] Because Paul prefers elsewhere the prophetic (Old Testament) title "slave of Christ" (*doulos Christou*) as his self-designation (Rom. 1:1; Gal. 1:10; see Chapter 7, above), he probably borrows *diakonos Christou*—at least as a title—from the Corinthian apostles and applies it to himself (2 Cor. 11:23). However, its precise meaning for the Corinthian opponents remains unclear. It may refer to their mystic knowledge of Christ (2 Cor. 11:6) and to their union with him (13:3), because these apostles demonstrate as "servants of Christ" the success of a follower of Jesus (11:12) and radiate his divine glory. We may well be in the presence of a portrait of Jesus drawn in the likeness of an Apollonius of Tyana, who—according to Philostratus—was revered as a divine epiphany.

Acts and 2 Corinthians on Apostles

Certain similarities exist between apostleship according to Acts and the "super apostles" in Corinth (2 Cor. 11:5), and it may be useful to describe them before we sketch Paul's response to his Corinthian opposition.

Gerhard Friedrich[48] has drawn a connection between the Corinthian apostles and the Stephen group in Acts, not in the least because of the latter's emphasis on Moses (Acts 7:17–43; cf. 2 Corinthians 3). Indeed, Moses' reception of "living oracles" (Acts 7:38) constitutes a remarkable Jewish-Hellenistic-Christian interpretation of the Moses story, especially because Jesus is viewed as the successor to the prophet Moses, foretold by Deut. 18:15 (Acts 7:37; cf. 3:22). Moses was "beautiful before God," "instructed in all the wisdom of the Egyptians," and "mighty in his words and deeds" (*en logois kai ergois autou*, Acts 7:20–22). Although the connection between Stephen and the Corinthian apostles is highly speculative, it suggests what can happen to the Moses story in the Diaspora (cf. Philo's *Life of Moses*).

The description of apostleship in Luke-Acts resembles in some ways that of the opposition in Corinth. There may even be some similarities in their Christologies, although this again remains quite conjectural.

1. The apostles in Acts are men of eloquence who as heroes of the past deliver intricate speeches. They are accomplished interpreters of the Old Testament and achieve impressive success, which is evident in the reaction of the people; they are "cut to the quick" (Acts 2:37) and "ready for repentance" or "ready for another hearing" (Acts 13:42). No one is a match for the apostles, because the presence of the Spirit inspires their persuasive gift of speech (cf. Acts 6:10).

2. The apostles are also miracle workers and repeat the signs, wonders, and miracles of the historical Jesus (Acts 2:22; cf. 2 Cor. 12:12). According to Luke, Jesus' messianic status consists in his anointment by the Spirit to do miracles (Luke 4:18, 23). Moreover, Luke's version of the miracle stories heightens their miraculous detail and character, whereas Matthew abbreviates this element. And Luke's interest in the Spirit is characterized by its visible, effective character (e.g., Luke 3:22; 4:18–19). In Acts, Peter's shadow heals the sick (Acts 5:15), and Paul's dirty linen (19:11–12) does the same. "God did extraordinary miracles by the hands of Paul" (19:11): he exorcises the evil spirits (19:12), who even overpower Paul's opponents (19:13–16). Simon Magus is overwhelmed by the success and power of Peter and John (8:9–13). Paul and Barnabas are worshiped as Hermes and Zeus in Lystra (14:8–18), whereas Paul's sea journey to Rome is filled with heroic feats and miraculous doings (Acts 27–28). Moreover, Jesus as the successor to the prophet Moses (7:37; 3:23) is himself a prophet, who—like a Moses, Elijah, or Elisha—works "mighty works and wonders" (2:22; cf. 3:16).

3. The Corinthian apostles were no doubt ecstatics and claimed divine inspiration. Their apostolate is grounded not only in miracles but also in impressive feats like ecstasy and visions (2 Cor. 12:1; esp. 5:12–13). They accuse Paul of being "fleshly" (2 Cor. 10:2), weak, and without courage or integrity (2 Cor. 10:12; 11:7).

Ecstatic speech seems to characterize the apostles in Acts, because allusions to it occur in references to Stephen, Peter, and Agabus. Stephen is "full of grace and power," and no one can withstand "the wisdom and the Spirit with which he spoke" (Acts 6:8, 10); and he, "full of the Holy Spirit," sees at his death in a trance the glory of God and Jesus (7:55–56; cf. also the "prophetic" ecstatic speech of Peter, Agabus, and the daughters of Philip [Acts 10:34–48; 11:15; 11:27–28; 21:9]).

4. The effectiveness of the apostles is so great that whole cities come to hear them: "The word of the Lord grew and prevailed mightily" (Acts 19:20). Idolatry and magic are rooted out in Ephesus; magic books worth 50,000 pieces of silver go up in smoke (19:19), and "all the residents of Asia heard the word of the Lord, both Jews and Greeks" (19:10).

The success story of the apostles in Acts seems in many ways similar to the success that—as we saw—the opponents claim in 2 Corinthians 11–13 (cf. 11:12; 12:12).

5. The place of the death of Jesus and its redemptive function in Luke-Acts may be a clue to the function of Jesus' death in the theology of the opposition of 2 Corinthians. However, this does not apply to the theme of apostolic suffering in Luke-Acts, because the Corinthian apostles seemed to have disdained suffering. Wherever Paul goes, he arouses persecution. Peter, Stephen, and Paul are suffering, innocent martyrs, like Moses (Acts 7:29, 35, 39) and Jesus, although—except for Stephen and James—their deaths are not explicitly mentioned. Paul's call is marked by "suffering for the sake of my name" (9:16), and so he suffers persecution from beginning to end; he is persecuted in Damascus (9:23) and Jerusalem (9:29); he is stoned in Iconium (14:5), imprisoned and flogged in Philippi (chapter 16), and so on.

Acts 20–28 can indeed be characterized as Paul's *via dolorosa*; it is filled with prophetic warnings about persecutions and forebodings of his death (Acts 20:37–38). And yet Paul is not martyred at the end of Acts. Rather, the book ends on a glorious note in accordance with its theme as an apology for the Christian movement: Paul preaches the gospel in Rome "unhindered" (*akōlutōs*, Acts 28:31). According to Luke, followers of Jesus experience persecution and martyrdom, yet their suffering and/or death is not weakness but a secret triumph. Thus in Luke, Jesus delivers a homily to the women on the road to Golgotha, prays on the cross for forgiveness for his enemies, saves a lost soul before his death, and dies as a type of Socrates—a noble, morally superior suffering figure but not a victim. This is exactly what the centurion confesses: "Certainly this man was innocent" (Luke 23:47; but cf. Mark 15:39). This scenario is underscored by Pilate's frequent declarations about Jesus' innocence. Stephen's death is likewise a secret triumph, for he sees the heavens opened with the Son of man standing at the right hand of God, ready to receive him (Acts 7:55). The accent in Jesus' death is on "criminal injustice" or on cowards like Pilate or on morally corrupt killers like the Sadducees. Although the death of Jesus illustrates the evil of this world, it is transcended by its unexplained "necessity" (*dei*) in God's plan of salvation. Thus, there is no "word of the cross" (1 Cor. 1:18) or any clear reference to God's redemptive purpose in the death of Jesus. Rather, the apostles "proclaim in Jesus the resurrection from the dead" (Acts 4:2). Luke-Acts espouses a resurrection theology and stresses the victory of God notwithstanding the cross and suffering. Christianity may have had humble beginnings (but cf. Acts 26:26!), but it is a potential religious-social force in the world (Acts 19) that has even reached Rome, the heart of the Empire (Acts 28). Luke-Acts may well have agreed with Tertullian: "the blood of the martyrs is the seed of the church."[49]

Paul's Apostolic Life-style

In spite of the different theme of Acts, with its emphasis on victorious suffering and the victorious march of the gospel, some of its elements remind us of the Corinthian situation, especially the elements of success and glory. Paul is clearly on the defensive in Corinth, for nothing succeeds like success. And yet his polemic may be even sharper than in Galatians. In Corinth there is as well a "different gospel," a pseudo-gospel with pseudo-apostles (2 Cor. 11:13; cf. Gal. 1:6–9).

Paul attacks his opponents by focusing on the cruciform nature of Christian existence, in contrast to their view of it as empirically victorious and glorious. His underlying theme comes to the fore in 2 Cor. 13:4: "Christ was crucified in weakness, but lives by the power of God. For we are weak in him, but in dealing with you we shall live with him by the power of God." What is at stake is the nature of the victory of Christ as it embodies itself in Paul's apostolic experience in the world. And how different is Romans from 2 Corinthians in its reflection on Christian life! The meditative argumentative mood of Romans comes to speech in 2 Corinthians (especially in chapters 10–13) in a highly experiential manner.

These chapters have no sustained theological reflections on the relationship of Christology to anthropology or ethics (cf. Romans 5–8). Paul speaks here "from the gut," so to speak, and his hermeneutic of the gospel is carried out with experiential intensity. The human limitations and grandeur of the apostle explode here before our eyes.

These chapters exhibit Paul's personal piety and praxis, and they reveal more about his "soul'" than any psychological speculations about his conversion. Conflict is inherent in piety when it serves the world; anger and frustration combine with pride; emotional outbursts climax in joyful peace. Paul is nowhere more angry than when his own churches pervert the gospel. In fact, his indictment of the pagan world seems mild compared to his indictment of fellow Christians who pervert the gospel.

This is curious indeed when we remember the sociological-political situation of the church in the Roman world; a sociological and religious minority attempts to establish its identity apart from Judaism, Hellenistic Roman society, and its ethnic religions and "ecumenical cults" (cf. the popular mystery of Isis "with the thousand names"). In this situation of hostility, persecution, and legal insecurity, every brother and sister counts in order to secure a certain cohesiveness in the Christian movement. Tolerance and unity in the rank and file are crucial for survival. Why, then, this dangerous intolerance of Paul to the opposition, especially when it is sociologically so destructive? The answer is that Paul cannot compromise the truth of the gospel.

Exhibition of religious pride and flaunting one's union with Christ is, according to Paul, nothing but worship of "Satan" (2 Cor. 11:14) and thus a radical perversion of the gospel. The historical Jesus and his resurrection are there grasped as miraculous transformation and religious success in the world. The gospel thus creates the "superman." Both the "not yet" of the apocalyptic hope and the relation of the resurrection to the cross are undone. The coming age of glory is inserted into this world as an enclave for the pneumatic elite, and the cross is viewed as incidental to the glory of the resurrection. It seems as if the Corinthians base their theology on the "superman Jesus" of Mark 3–9 or his miracle source and omit Mark's passion story! For Paul, the resurrection confirms the cross in that it establishes Christian life "in weakness" (2 Cor. 13:4) and in a cruciform existence until the apocalyptic resurrection of the dead (2 Cor. 4:10; 5:4–10). The disjunction between the death and resurrection of Christ and our own future resurrection means that in this world the resurrection manifests itself as the victory of the cross. Thus we "always" carry "in the body the death of Jesus" (2 Cor. 4:10) and are called to redemptive suffering for the sake of the world (2 Cor. 4:12). A cruciform life-style, then, is the inevitable consequence of the confession "I have been crucified with Christ" (Gal. 2:20), because it means a glorying "in the cross of our Lord Jesus Christ, by which the world has been crucified to me, and I to the world" (Gal. 6:15; cf. Phil. 3:9). Cruciform apostolic experience is not a form of masochism or a rejoicing in passion mysticism, because it translates itself as sobriety for the sake of the public accountability and the intelligible character of the gospel over against private ecstasy (2 Cor. 5:13). It translates itself as affliction and hardship for the sake of the gospel (2 Cor. 6:3-10; 12:7-10) or as "the daily pressure upon me of my anxiety for all the churches" (11:28) or as refusing pay (12:13; 11:9) so as not to be an obstacle to the truth of the gospel (6:3). Above all, it means the distinction between "the transcendent power of God" and "the earthen vessel" of the apostle (4:7). The apocalyptic sequence of resurrection *after* death or the notion of the victory of the Spirit is absent from 2 Corinthians 10-13 (13:4?). The dialectic of cross and resurrection seems to displace any obvious marks of the resurrection in this world by the power of the Spirit. God's power in Christ is primarily viewed in this context as "weakness" and as "the sufferings of Christ" (2 Cor. 1:3-7), which conforms to the cruciform signature of apostolic experience (cf. the *peristaseis* sections ["pericopes of crisis"] in 2 Cor. 4:8-12; 6:4-10; cf. 11:23-29).[50] And yet apostolic experience in the world is not defeatist but victorious, because it lives by the promise of the final resurrection of the body and the glory of the dawning kingdom (2 Cor. 4:10-11; 5:1-10), which is even operative in the midst of suffering (2 Cor. 4:7-12; cf. 13:4).

Second Corinthians, then, demonstrates the experiential reality of "the mortal body" of the apostle, both in its subjection to death and in its redemptive activity in the world. And so the final boast of the apostle is the confession "When I am weak, then I am strong" (2 Cor. 12:10), which comes as the counterpoint to all his previous boastings and marks them as foolish (11:16—12:6). The resurrection does not gain visibility in this world in any obvious way in this Corinthian context, because Paul as an apocalyptic Christian remains pessimistic about the present status of the world. To be sure, Paul, like Luke-Acts, believes in "the triumphant march" of the gospel in the world (2 Cor. 2:14-16), but he differs from Luke-Acts as to the mode of this victory: the world does not come out to hear him when he arrives in a city, and it is not impressed by his personality. Rather, the victory of the gospel is that of the grace of God in Christ that contradicts the world and our own strength (2 Cor. 1:12; 10:3; 12:9) and yet establishes beachheads of God's dawning new world in the midst of the old world. Thus, in the light of the hope that groans for the victory of the new age (2 Cor. 4:17; 5:1–10), victory in this life is comfort in the midst of suffering and grace and power in the midst of weakness.

The "sufferings of Christ" (*ta pathēmata tou Christou*, 1:5) are not unlike the Jewish messianic woes or "tribulations" (*thlipseis*, 1:4–7; Rom. 5:3) that precede the glory to come. However, they are not just to be tolerated or endured—like the messianic woes in Judaism—but signify instead the redemptive meaning of the cross of Christ in the world. Therefore, these tribulations can become a reason for rejoicing (Rom. 5:3) and for active redemptive work in the world (cf. Rom. 8:17). And so the death of Jesus incarnates itself in the apostle's life-giving activity (2 Cor. 4:7–12), because he knows that resurrection power translates itself in this world not only as suffering in hope but also as redemptive suffering.

14

The Church as the Dawning
of the New Age

PAUL'S ECCLESIAL THOUGHT

The relationship between eschatology and ecclesiology in Paul needs careful scrutiny, for when Colossians and Ephesians are viewed as Paul's letters and as the crown of his mature thought, his ecclesiology becomes so primary that his eschatology is subsumed under it. Charles Harold Dodd, for instance, as a prominent representative of the "realized eschatology" school, traces a development in Paul from an earlier "future" eschatology to a more mature level that climaxes, in Colossians and Ephesians, in the idea of the church as the divine commonwealth.[1] A "catholic" portrayal of Paul emerges when the doctrine of the church becomes the focal point of Paul's thought. The upbuilding of the church, its ontological preexistent status, and its catholic-universal destiny now make possible a description of the church as *Christus prolongatus*, and as the *Corpus Christi mysticum* that constitutes the final fulfillment of God's promises to Israel and the goal of salvation-history. Although the pastoral Epistles have a different scope, their interest in the polity of the church, its inner cohesion and its protection against heretical disorder, emphasizes ecclesial order and organization—concerns that are quite different from Paul's. For the "historical" Paul, the church is primarily the interim eschatological community that looks forward to the future of the coming reign of God. "The body of Christ" (= the church) is not identical with the risen body of Christ,[2] and its organic growth does not displace the Parousia of Christ. Nor is the church to be identified with the kingdom of God. Although the church has a central place in Paul's thought, that interest is determined by the two foci that define the church. Eschatology and Christology are the constituents of Paul's ecclesiology, and the nature of their interrelation determines the character and function of the church. Construals that do not maintain the proper balance in the relation between eschatology and Christology misconstrue Paul's ecclesiology.

For instance, when eschatology and Christology are conflated, the concept of the church is inflated and its identification with the kingdom of God becomes a real danger. A mystical doctrine of the church catholic displaces the idea of the church as a proleptic reality, and a spiritualization of God's promises displaces God's eschatological purpose for the created world. The church is now regarded as the company of the spiritual elite, who with their endowment of the Spirit already actualize the kingdom of God in their soul (John). Or the church receives an ontological status and is an imperishable "body" that participates in divine reality (Ephesians; 2 Clement 14; Shepherd of Hermas, Visions 2.4.1).[3] In this setting, the preexistent status of the church, its ontological character, and its status as an imperishable body become the focal concerns.

When—to the contrary—eschatology and Christology are divorced from each other, apocalyptic sectarianism displaces the Christ-centered conception of the church. It so elevates eschatology over Christology that fear for the coming judgment, religious uncertainty, and a legalistic ethic become predominant. In fact, those religious movements that are most inspired by the coming Parousia of Christ usually have developed the most rigorous forms of legalism (e.g., Montanism).

And although in the Reformation the church as the *ecclesia semper reformanda* becomes subject to God's eschatological judgment, the danger of an individualistic conception of the church has in subsequent Protestant denominations often overshadowed the notion of the church as a corporate body. In that case, the church as an aggregate of justified individuals tends to overshadow its corporate character and its eschatological horizon.

We must investigate, then, the character of Paul's interest in the church, especially his construal of the relation of eschatology and Christology.

Social Concerns

Paul has often been characterized as a loner, a man who turned his back on the Jerusalem church and did his own thing. A romantic portrait of Paul long prevailed. Paul, "the man of conflict" (Riddle[4]), was the religious genius whose "heaven conquering idealism" (Holtzmann[5]) was at odds with the pragmatic reality of his churches (Weinel[6]) or whose speculative mind adapted Jesus into an inherited apocalyptic scheme (Wrede et al.[7]).

With the rise of the history-of-religions school, Paul "the mystic" or Paul "the man of the cult" displaced Paul the thinker.[8] In our time, Paul the church theologian fits the taste of our "ecumenical" age, and ecumenical discussions have often gravitated from Romans to Ephesians, that is, from the doctrinal Paul to the ecclesiastical Paul. Paul's thought is indeed remarkably "social"; as his letters show, it is evoked not so much by the needs of individuals as by the needs of his churches. Paul is primarily an apostolic missionary, and his theological reflection focuses on the social reality of the church. It has no speculative aim and is not designed as thought for the sake of thought. Moreover, his letters are not private, but personal documents that are mostly addressed to communities. The apostle Paul is not a literary genius (Kierkegaard) or a systematic theologian. Rather, his ecclesiology correlates theological thought and sociological reality in all its diversity. The members of Paul's churches are called to be Christians within a suspicious and hostile society that subjects them to legal insecurity and arbitrary persecution. Paul lives in a time when Christians are in the process of separating themselves from Judaism and the synagogue. They draw attention to themselves as a separate cult that is no longer part of the *religio licita* of Judaism in the Roman Empire. The insecurity, gossip, and persecution, already directed at Judaism, now turn against the new *superstitio prava* (Tacitus). Christians become the target of the Romans' suspicion of "secret societies," often outlawed by the emperors as pockets of disloyalty to the imperial claims of *Roma eterna* and its ethos. And apart from external pressures, there is the internal question of Christian identity. What should Christians call themselves?[9] Can they meet the charge of apostatizing from the God of the Old Testament and Judaism? And is rejection of the law a choice for moral license and a subversion of the God of the covenant? Can Christ truly be God's Messiah if he is "the end of the law"?

How, then, shall Christians understand themselves in the context of the wider world of Hellenistic-Roman society? Will they be an introverted, sectarian, apocalyptic group, waiting for God's imminent kingdom and drawing people out of society into the haven of their churches, or will they have a mission to society in accordance with the demand of the gospel?

Paul's thought has necessarily an ecclesial focus because his apostolic mandate calls him to missionize the Gentiles. He is sent out not only to found churches but also to sustain them amidst all their burdens and conflicts. "And, apart from other things, there is the daily pressure upon me of my anxiety for all the churches" (2 Cor. 11:28). Paul's ecclesial concerns are apparent in the address of his letters, because they are all directed to a community of believers. Philemon, for example, is a personal letter, written to a house church in Philemon's house.[10] The character of the address shows that Philemon is responsible not only to Paul (Philemon 8, 19) but also to the house-church members, for example, to Apphia and Archippus (Philemon 2; cf. Col. 4:17?). Similarly, not only are the persons listed in the greetings (Philemon 23–24) Paul's personal friends, but they also function as the supporters of his request. Philemon, then, is the appeal not just of an individual but of one Christian community to another as well. The same ecclesial interest is apparent in Paul's listing of co-workers and "brothers" (Gal. 1:2), and in his insistence that his letters be read by all (1 Thess. 5:27; cf. also Col. 4:15).

Moreover, the doctrinal sections of the letters issue regularly in pragmatic exhortations. The sequence of doctrine and paraenesis is not a construct of timeless speculative thought, as if—as in a philosophical treatise—"ethics" must follow "dogmatics." Rather, it shows Paul's vital interest in building up the Christian community (cf. Rom. 12:1—15:13; Gal. 5:13—6:10; Phil. 2:12–18; 1 Thess. 4:1–12; 5:1–22). Theological thought climaxes in praxis, and praxis is communal in nature. The emphasis is on communal life-style, not on individual existence. Thus, when Paul speaks about the nature of Christian life, he does so most often in communal categories. The "works of the flesh" (Gal. 5:19) and "the fruit of the Spirit" (Gal. 5:22) are predominantly social vices and virtues that are primarily addressed to the community as a whole and must guard its inner cohesion.[11]

THE UNITY OF THE CHURCH AND THE TRUTH OF THE GOSPEL

The mission of the church cannot succeed without the unity of the church in the truth of the gospel. It is interesting that Paul does not give the mission of the church a more important role than the unity of the church. Although he is occasionally concerned with the effect of the church on outsiders (Gal. 6:10; 1 Cor. 10:32; 14:23–25), there is no conscious emphasis on public relations as, for instance, in 1 Peter (1 Pet. 1:12; 3:15–17; but cf. Rom. 12:17–21; 13:1–7; Phil. 1:12–14).

Paul's primary goal is the life-style and unity of the internal life of the church (2 Cor. 6:14–15). Indeed, the unity of the church and the truth of the gospel preoccupy Paul's apostolic thought. However, the potential conflict between these two concerns is caused not by a contradiction of idealism and realism or theory and practice but by the conviction that the unity of the church can be grounded only in the truth of the gospel. In that conviction, Paul travels to Jerusalem for the apostolic council (Gal. 2:1–10) and organizes the Gentile collection for Jerusalem (Rom. 15:26–27); but in that conviction Paul also indicts Peter and Barnabas in Antioch (Gal. 2:11–14) and pronounces a curse on Judaizers in Galatia (Gal. 1:7–9) and on "the other gospel" in Corinth (2 Cor. 11:4).

However, the doctrine of the church is never a topic in Paul's letters. He inherits the term *ekklēsia* (church) from the Antioch church and the concept of "the body of Christ" rarely occurs in his correspondence. In Romans, for example, the term *ekklēsia* is absent (except in chapter 16), and the motif of "the body of Christ" occurs only in the paraenetic section of Rom. 12:4. This is all the more surprising when we recall that the unity of the church is a main concern of Romans (see Chapter 5, above).

THE BODY OF CHRIST

Although the unity of the church is given to it once and for all by God's justifying act of grace in Christ (Rom. 5:17–21; cf. 2 Cor. 5:14), this unity is always threatened by the contingencies of life, not only by the world outside the walls of the church but also by its intrusion into the church. Disunity, quarrels, factions, pride, jealousy, and immorality—sometimes "of a kind that is not found even among pagans" (1 Cor. 5:1)—threaten to tear the church apart and divide Christ himself (1 Cor. 1:13). Paul now applies a current Hellenistic-Roman metaphor of the body and its members to the church in order to guarantee its health and cohesion. The question of the provenance of the body metaphor is still unresolved,[12] although it is probably derived not from Gnostic mythology but from Stoic philosophy.[13] This unresolved question cannot obscure the fact that Paul uses the image of the body for both theological and pragmatic reasons.

The unity of the church is grounded in the redemptive act of the one Lord of the church: "Is Christ divided? Was Paul crucified for you?" (1 Cor. 1:13); "one has died for all; therefore all have died" (2 Cor. 5:14). And thus, Paul never calls for faith in the church or exhorts Christians *to become* the church or "body of Christ." The body of Christ is a given reality in Christ. Although Paul uses the body motif rarely (1 Cor. 12:12–27; Rom. 12:4–5), it belongs to a field of interrelated metaphors and images that express the reality of communal participation in Christ through our incorporation in him. It seems as if Paul is experimenting with multiple associations in expressing our new reality in Christ.[14] In fact, the extent of the field of images shows the novelty of Paul's conception and its recent introduction into Christian vocabulary. Thus, the immense and complicated discussion about the church as the body of Christ in the history of theology should not mislead us, because in Paul we are dealing not with a fixed doctrine of the church but with a powerful image.

It is impossible to trace a developmental sequence of the various images that denote our new corporate life in Christ. However, there is a movement from metaphor to ontological reality in the body image, so that Paul can even call Christ the church (1 Cor. 12:12b). In fact, the body metaphor not only summarizes and condenses the several aspects of the participation motif but also expresses the idea of mutual interdependence in the life of the church. The following motifs seem to constitute the field of images:

1. "the one" (Christ)   "the many"; "all" (Rom. 5:12–19)
                                         (cf. also 2 Cor. 5:15)
2. "we/you in Christ"   "Christ in you/in me" (Rom. 8:1;
                                         8:10; Gal. 2:20)
   "you are in the Spirit"   "the Spirit dwells in you" (Rom.
                                         8:9, 11)
3. the motif of oneness (Gal. 3:28 [heis]; cf. Eph. 2:14–15) (of persons or their activity); cf. Rom. 15:6: "together . . . with one voice" (homothymadon; en heni stomati); Phil. 1:27: "to stand firm in one spirit [en heni pneumati] with one mind [miai psychē] striving side by side for the faith of the gospel." Cf. 1 Cor. 6:17; 12:13: "one spirit"; Phil. 2:2: "of one mind" (to hen phronountes, cf. 1 Cor. 12:9, 11: "the same Spirit" [to auto pneuma]); cf. also the mutuality—and unity—motifs, e.g., 1 Cor. 1:10: "agree" (to auto legein), "united in the same mind and the same judgment" (auto nō; autē gnōmē); esp. 1 Cor. 12:25; Rom. 12:16; 15:5, where mutuality and unity are stressed (to auto and allēloi).
4. 1 and 2 and 3 are interwoven: "you are all (1) one (3) in Christ Jesus (2) (Gal. 3:28).
5. the participation motif ("one in all" or "all in one" [1]) can be combined with the sacrificial hyper ("on behalf of") motif:
   "One (1) has died on behalf of [hyper] (5) all (1), therefore all (1) have died" (2 Cor. 5:15).
6. The motif of unity, oneness, is expanded by the introduction of the body metaphor: "one (1) body (6)" (1 Cor. 6:16; 12:13).
7. The body/member metaphor enriches the participation motif because it expresses unity in diversity ("the many" [1]; "one" [3]; "in Christ" [2]). An early(?) stage is present in Rom. 12:4–5: "For as in one (3) body (6) we have many (1) members . . . , so we, though many (1), are one (3) body (6) in Christ (2) and individually members one of another" (7).
   In 1 Cor. 12:12, the metaphor is clearly expressed:
   "For just as the body (6) is one (3) and has many (1) members (7), and all (1) the members (7) of the body (6), though many, are one body, so also is Christ" (trans. mine; cf. also v. 13: "for by one (3) Spirit we were all (1) baptized into one (3) body (6) . . . and all (1) were made to drink of one (3) Spirit."

8. The transition from metaphor to ontological reality occurs (perhaps in 1 Cor. 12:12b?) in 1 Cor. 12:27:

"Now you are the body of Christ and individually members of it."

9. An ontological assertion also occurs in 1 Cor. 6:15 without the body/member metaphor: "Do you not know that your bodies are members of Christ?" The member motif is here directly applied to Christ (bodies = members in v. 15). First Corinthians 6:15 is similar to the participation motif of Gal. 3:32; 5:24: "to *belong to Christ*" (= "*to be of Christ*"; cf. also "the heavenly robe" motif of Gal. 3:27 and Rom. 13:14: "*to put on* Christ").

10. The eucharistic motif of 1 Cor. 10:17 again employs the body metaphor: "Because there is one bread, we the many are one body, for we all partake of the one bread."*

Unity and Diversity

Sacramental participation in Christ and union with Christ do not mean an undifferentiated "oneness" of the church (cf. "one [person; *heis*] in Christ Jesus"; Gal. 3:28). The equality of all in Christ does not suspend the multiformity and variety of the members. The ontological aspect of participation in Christ only seemingly suspends and diffuses the personal identity of people. In reality, ontological participation intersects with the distinct multiformity of the individual members and their several charismatic gifts and talents, which range from prophecy and glossolalia to the virtually noncharismatic activity of being a "helper" and "administrator" (1 Cor. 12:28).

The eschatological event of Christ constitutes not an aggregate of believers but "a body" with mutually interdependent members, so that the justification of the sinner is not to be interpreted in an individualistic, existentialist fashion. The *iustificatio impii* is in fact a *iustificatio impiorum*. Therefore, people are baptized "into one body—Jews or Greeks, slaves or free—and all were made to drink of one Spirit" (1 Cor. 12:13). Rudolf Bultmann must be faulted for virtually ignoring the ecclesiological-communal element in his existentialist interpretation of Paul's thought.[15]

The incorporation motif accentuates Paul's organic and historical thinking. The motif originates in the Jewish notion of corporate personality (the ancestor as the head and representative of his progeny) and has several components in Paul: (1) the one for all; (2) the one in all; (3) the

---

*First Corinthians 10:16 ("participation in the body of Christ") refers to the eucharistic body of Christ.

once for all. The "once for all" expresses the eschatological-historical event of Jesus Christ (cf. Rom. 5:15–19; 6:10) that marks the end of the old age and the inauguration of the new age. The "one for all" describes the death of Christ as the act of God's grace for his people, who henceforth participate in him ("the one in all" and "all in one"; cf. Rom. 5:12–19, 1 Cor. 15:22). In some contexts the spatial imagery "in Christ" (1 Cor. 15:22) shifts into the temporal imagery of "with Christ" (Rom. 6:1–8). It permits Paul to emphasize the historical dimension of our life in Christ because it expresses not only the apocalyptic future of the Christ-event but also its proleptic manifestation in our present existence: "If we have died with Christ, we believe that we shall also live with him" (Rom. 6:8).

The temporal phrase "with Christ" prevents the idea of a completed salvation in the present, which is apt to be associated with the spatial term "in Christ": "If any one is in Christ, he is a new creation [*kainē ktisis*]; the old has passed away, behold, the new has come" (2 Cor. 5:17; cf. Gal. 6:15; see Chapter 13, above). To be "in Christ" is indeed a "new act of creation," but this new creation must still wait for its future completion in the liberation of the whole creation (Rom. 8:21), when "we shall always be with the Lord" (1 Thess. 4:17).

The unity of the church is as important to Paul as it is to John. But in John the theological climate is different, because the oneness of the church is here grounded in the metaphysical unity of the Father and the Son (John 17:11, 21). The Gnostic motif of the ontological unity of the Redeemer and the redeemed in the spiritual oneness of the Pleroma dominates John's ecclesiological thinking (cf. also Heb. 2:11: "For he who sanctifies and those who are sanctified have all one origin"). Although John 15 speaks about the vine and the branches—an image that resembles the Pauline metaphor of the body and its members—the ontological unity of the believers has become so predominant in John that the sociological and contingent aspects of the church hardly surface (cf., however, 1, 2, and 3 John). Whereas in John the warfare of the world of darkness against the spiritual world of the church blots out everything else, Paul deals with more contingent and empirical problems, because the enmity of the world constantly threatens the unity of the community both from without and from within. Thus, he warns repeatedly and explicitly against pride, party spirit, divisions, and pagan vices (cf., e.g., Gal. 5:14—6:10).

The Tension of Love and Freedom

The body/member metaphor deals with the relation of the individual to the community in its participation in Christ. This relation bears on a major tension in Paul's thought, the tension between the truth of the gospel and the unity of the church. How shall the unity of the church—based on love, the bond of "perfect harmony" (Col. 3:14)—be maintained, when it conflicts with the truth of the gospel?

A conflict can arise between a person's stance in the truth of the gospel and his striving for the unity of the church. An expression of that problem is the tension between freedom and love. Paul discusses this issue repeatedly in the context of the unity of the church (1 Corinthians 8–10; Galatians 5; Romans 14–15). The adequacy of his argument needs careful scrutiny, for how can the truth of the gospel—the radical freedom, for which "Christ has set us free" (Gal. 5:1) and which does not tolerate any compromise with the law (Gal. 5:4)—tolerate a compromise for the sake of "a weak conscience"? Does not love for the "weak" brother in 1 Corinthians 8–10 and Romans 14–15 mean, in principle, a surrender of radical freedom, that is, a reintroduction of those "elemental spirits of the universe" (Gal. 4:4, 9)—whether idols or the law—that the death of Christ has abolished once for all? If freedom is the opposite of slavery, as Paul argues so cogently in Galatians 5, at what point does love become a surrender of freedom to slavery? At what price, then, does Paul buy the unity of the church at the price of the truth of the gospel? Christian freedom is indeed "slavery to the other in love" (douleuete, Gal. 5:13). But when does this service of love become a being enslaved by the other? At what point does love become a surrender of my stance in the truth for the sake of the unity of the church, so that I have to renounce my freedom in Christ for the sake of love for the brother? Why shouldn't I, for instance, exercise love toward people who are in error, like Judaizers or like Peter in Antioch (Gal. 2:11–14), instead of insisting that such an attitude constitutes a "yoke of slavery" (Gal. 5:1), whereas my attitude toward scrupulous Jewish Christians demands love? In that case, love seems not to educate for freedom but to demand its surrender. We can be sure that the Corinthians argued the principle of Christian freedom in the context of "knowledge" (gnōsis, 1 Cor. 8:1) when they were confronted by what must have seemed to them Judaizing or paganizing traits in their scrupulous Corinthian brethren. In our overzealous critique of "gnosis," we often fail to ask why Paul did not discern that, just as love must inform "knowledge" (gnōsis, 1 Cor. 8:1) so "knowledge" can and must clarify love (cf. the Gospel of Philip), especially when it concerns the knowledge of the truth of the gospel. Paul does not enter into a debate about the ethical limits of compromise or about the boundaries of love. The pastoral focus on the unity of the church, as grounded in the love of Christ, draws Paul away from gnosis to love (cf. "the brother for whom Christ died" [1 Cor. 8:11; Romans 14–15]).

Thus, he operates both with an ethic of theological principle and with a situation ethic and employs them in a contingent manner, because the particular situation must decide what counts as apostasy or as merely immature faith. At this point it becomes clear anew that Paul's thought is characterized by the interaction of coherence and contingency. Paul risks the charge of inconsistency, because there is no doctrinal principle or yardstick by which we can decide in advance when and where "principle" prevails over "situation," or "the truth of the gospel" prevails over "the unity" of the church.

The situational ethic often functions as an ad hoc pastoral interpretation and modification of the ethic of principle: "We know that 'an idol has no real existence,' and that 'there is no God but one.' . . . However, not all possess this knowledge. . . . Only take care lest this liberty of yours somehow become a stumbling block to the weak" (1 Cor. 8:4–9). Paul's focus on the health and unity of the church gives his thought an ecclesial and situational bent. The unity of the church is so crucial to him that it often seems as if he compromises truth and unity, freedom and love. Because the demand of the hour is unity within diversity, he is as pastor and missionary constantly engaged in translating theological principles into ad hoc situations. As long as "the truth" of the gospel is not at stake (Gal. 2:4, 14), Paul can be exceedingly flexible for the sake of multiformity within the unity of the church. We conclude, then, that the tension between theological principle and its situational interpretation, that is, the tension between "the truth" of the gospel and the unity of the church, marks Paul's apostolic career. Furthermore, it is obvious that Paul often handles this tension in such a pragmatic way that at times "the purity" of the gospel seems to be sacrificed for the sake of the unity of the church (1 Corinthians 8–10; Romans 14–15), whereas at other times the "purity" of the church in the gospel overrides everything else (Galatians). This tension has tempted many scholars to divorce Paul's thought from his practice, as if Paul "the idealist"[16] compromises the consistency of his thought and accommodates it to the empirical reality of the human situation in his mission churches. However, this divorce of coherence and contingency, of thought and practice, neglects the peculiar nature of Paul's thought, which has not only a pastoral focus on the viability and visibility of the church in the world but also a theological focus on the truth of the gospel. The notion of an invisible church or a church of sinners is foreign to Paul. He does not, for instance, discuss the church as a *corpus mixtum* (Matthew) or address the question of doubt among Christians, or even that of "little faith" (Matthew). The basic distinction is simply faith versus apostasy (*pistis/apistia*), and his references to "babes in Christ" versus "the mature in Christ" and "spiritual men" (*nēpioi; teleioi; pneumatikoi*), or his exhortations to grow in faith and so on, all aim at the visible witness of the one body of Christ. Because the unity of the church is given to it by Christ, this unity must be visible in the bond of love that "binds everything together in perfect harmony" (Col. 3:14).

We must remember, however, that whereas the church in the first and second centuries primarily aims at unity in diversity and is not engaged in a rigid orthodoxy, it is Paul who—notwithstanding his principle of "in all things charity"—insists more than any other early Christian on "in essentials, unity." His contingent interpretation of the gospel to his various churches interacts so strongly with the coherent center of his gospel that he became not only the first theologian of the church but also the one whose "doctrinal purity" made him an uneasy brother in the early catholic church, with its principle of doctrinal variety (see Chapter 7, above).

THE EKKLĒSIA

Because the church has an eschatological horizon and is the proleptic manifestation of the kingdom of God in history, it is the beachhead of the new creation and the sign of the new age in the old world that is "passing away" (1 Cor. 7:29). Therefore, the church is not identified with the kingdom of God, nor will it enter into the kingdom as a supratemporal reality. Paul does not—like the author of Ephesians—dwell on the preexistent or posthistorical reality of the church (cf. "even as he chose us in him before the foundation of the world" [Eph. 1:4]). The vocation of the church is not self-preservation for eternal life but service to the created world in the sure hope of the world's transformation at the time of God's final triumph. The last judgment is not only a judgment on the world outside the church but also a judgment that will assess the church's faithfulness to its mission in the world (cf. Rom. 14:10; 2 Cor. 5:11; cf. also 1 Pet. 4:17).

We have seen that the unity of the church and the mutual interdependence of its members is expressed in the body (*sōma*) metaphor. The *ekklēsia* ("church") concept now discloses a different aspect of the church and is in many ways unlike the body metaphor.

1. Paul himself probably introduces the body metaphor into Christian language, whereas he inherits the *ekklēsia* concept from the Jewish-Hellenistic church.

2. Paul uses the body metaphor only in 1 Corinthians 12 and Romans 12 (but cf. its frequency in Colossians and Ephesians). It occurs in a theological context, where the unity of the church is threatened, and the "bodily" character of "life together" is ignored, and where life in eschatological glory is prematurely usurped (cf. 1 Corinthians 4; 8–15). The body metaphor is related to the somatic-ethical character of Christian life as life in the body for other bodies within "the body of Christ." "For the body does not consist of one member but of many" (1 Cor. 12:14). Paul interprets the ontological oneness of "the body of Christ" in terms of diversity and multiformity, that is, as the mutuality and indispensability of all the members of the body with their various "grace gifts" (*charismata*). The body metaphor enables Paul to emphasize special traits that the traditional *ekklēsia* concept does not sufficiently address. For although the *ekklēsia* concept contains the idea of "the one assembled people of God," it is not able to stress either the Christocentric participation motif or the specific sociological dimensions of unity in the midst of diversity.

3. Thus, the emphasis on "one" (*hen*) in the metaphor of the *sōma* is absent from *ekklēsia*. Paul never refers to "the one *ekklēsia*" (*mia ekklēsia*) or to the fact that the *ekklēsia* is one. Such a qualification would be improper for *ekklēsia* because a Hellenistic political *ekklēsia* is by definition "one" as the duly established assembly of all citizens. Moreover, just as the plural is unthinkable for *sōma*, the plural is regularly used for *ekklēsia* (Rom. 16:4: "All the churches of the Gentiles"; cf. Rom. 16:16; Gal. 1:2; 2 Cor. 8:18–19, 23–24, etc.). Again, Paul refers to the body as the body of Christ, but almost exclusively to the *ekklēsia* as "the *ekklēsia* of God" (1 Cor. 10:32; 11:16, 22; 12:28; Gal. 1:13; 1 Cor. 15:9, etc.).[17] He does so in order to distinguish a Christian assembly from a political Hellenistic-Roman assembly. The body metaphor, then, is Christocentric, whereas the *ekklēsia* concept is theocentric.

4. Whereas Ephesians and Colossians refer to Christ as "the head of the body" and/or "the head of the *ekklēsia*" (Eph. 1:22; 5:23; Col. 1:18; 2:19) and speak about "the body of the church" (Col. 1:18: "he is the head of the body of the church" [trans. mine]), Paul never refers to Christ as "the head of the body" or "the head of the church," and he avoids the phrase "the body of the church." In other words, Paul does not integrate the concepts "body" and "church" but uses them in different contexts.[18] This may indicate—along with the absence of the terminology of "the head of the body"—that Paul represents an earlier stage of reflection in which *sōma* is still a recent introduction into Christian vocabulary.

5. Moreover, Paul never calls the church a synagogue (*synagōgē*) or a

building (*oikos; oikia*), and he never states that "the church is the body of Christ," but rather that "Christians belong to the body of Christ."[19]

6. Whereas the body metaphor—because of its relation to our incorporation in Christ—has implications for a concept of the universal church, this is much more difficult to establish for *ekklēsia*. In almost all cases *ekklēsia* refers to a local congregation (Rom. 16:1; 1 Cor. 11:18, 22; 14:4, 5, 12, 23, 28) or an aggregate of congregations (Rom. 16:4, 16; Gal. 1:2, 22; 1 Cor. 4:17; 7:17; 11:16; 16:1). Denis Edward Hugh Whiteley lists seven "indecisive" passages (Rom. 16:23; 1 Cor. 6:4; 10:32; 12:28; 15:9; Gal. 1:13; Phil. 3:6) where the idea of the universal church may be present. However, it is only in Colossians (1:18, 24) and Ephesians (nine times) that *ekklēsia* is used beyond doubt in a universal sense.[20]

The Ekklēsia and Israel

What, then, is the meaning of *ekklēsia* for Paul? In the Septuagint, "synagogue" (*synagōgē*) occurs almost 200 times; it translates "congregation" (*edah*) 130 times and "assembly" ("congregation"; *kahal*) 35 times. *Kahal* is rendered both as *synagōgē* (35 times) and as *ekklēsia* (almost 70 times). However, although *ekklēsia* is never the translation of *edah*, the different translations are not to be attributed to different semantic fields. Rather, they express the different options of the different translators of the Septuagint at different times. In the Masoretic text, *kahal* occurs most frequently in Deuteronomy, Ezra-Nehemiah, and 1 and 2 Chronicles and is almost synonymous with "the people" (*ha am*) or "the children of Israel" (*bene Israel*). *Edah* is the favorite term of the priestly tradent in Exodus, Leviticus, and Numbers (cf. only 3 times in the Prophets; omitted in Deuteronomy; 24 times outside the Pentateuch).

Although the Septuagint does not press the distinction between *ekklēsia* (*kahal*) and *synagōgē* (*edah*), in the New Testament only *ekklēsia* occurs, and *synagōgē* is never used for a Christian congregation, except in James 2:2. Wolfgang Schrage surmises that *synagōgē* became unsuitable for Christian usage because of its steady association with the law in the synagogue[21] and detects an anti-Jewish polemic in the use of *ekklēsia*. This seems unlikely, because in the second century both *synagōgē* and *ekklēsia* are used for Christian congregations.[22]

In New Testament times, *synagōgē*—like *proseuchē* (cf. Philo)—was probably so closely associated with the physical building of the synagogue that it did not serve its Christian purpose. *Ekklēsia*, then, was not selected as a polemical term in order to press the Christian claim to be "the new Israel" and "the true people of God." The frequent claim by scholars that

"Paul takes over the eschatological conceptuality of salvation history: *ekklēsia, hagioi, eklektoi*"; and that "the Church is the Israel of God [Gal. 6:16], the new covenant [2 Cor. 3:6]" (Conzelmann[23]) needs critical examination, because Paul's idea of the church is more complicated than this blank assertion claims. The accent in *ekklēsia* is on the local congregation, not on its catholic universality; it accentuates primarily its present activity and not its typological-eschatological relation to the people of Israel. Although Paul can speak about Israel "according to the flesh" (= "the natural Israel"? 1 Cor. 10:18) and perhaps once about the church (or about Israel?[24]) as "the Israel of God" (Gal. 6:16), he normally does not call the church the "new" or "true" Israel. This language, along with that of Christians as a "third race" (*tertium genus*), does not enter Christian vocabulary until the second century (Justin Martyr). If Paul had really viewed the Christian *ekklēsia* as the new Israel of God that inherits the privileges of Israel, he would surely have used *ekklēsia* as the central concept in Romans, especially in chapters 9–11, where the relation of the church and Israel is at stake. The nomenclature of the church as "the new Israel" clashes with Paul's eschatological hope for Israel (Rom. 11:25). The church, in its Jewish-Gentile unity, is the proleptic dawning of the future destiny of Israel, but it is not Israel's displacement. Therefore, Paul avoids the terminology of fulfillment when he speaks of God's promises to Israel and uses the proleptic term "confirm" (*bebaioun*, Rom. 4:15; 2 Cor. 1:21). We must not overlook the fact that it is Paul who maintains Israel's priority in salvation-history and who is the only New Testament theologian who safeguards Israel's future eschatological redemption. *Ekklēsia* is absent from all of Romans (except Rom. 16:1, 4, 5, 16), even from the prescript, where Paul regularly uses *ekklēsia* (1 Corinthians 1; 2 Corinthians 1; 1 Thessalonians 1; Galatians 1; cf. Phil. 4:15; Philemon 2). Instead we read, "To all God's beloved in Rome, who are called to be saints" (*klētois hagiois*, Rom. 1:7). This omission is strange in a letter where the unity of two peoples, Jew and Gentile, in one *ekklēsia* is at stake. It is possible to speculate that Paul's dialogue with Jews in Romans compels him to forego the term *ekklēsia*, because he intends to show that the true *ekklēsia* is a future eschatological reality that will only be realized when it comprises the whole people of Israel (11:25).[25]

A future-eschatological use of *ekklēsia* is, however, usually absent in Paul, because he refers to the *ekklēsia* as a present rather than as a future reality. He is not interested in an apocalyptic description of the "heavenly" church or in the future gathering of the "true" church. Therefore, an expression of eschatological hope like "May thy church be gathered from the ends of the earth" (Didache 16), which may have been current in Jewish-Hellenistic Christianity, is unthinkable for Paul. The conditions for participation in the church have been fulfilled in Christ and are not to be striven for.[26] The holiness of the church has been given to it in Christ (1 Cor. 6:11). Therefore, Christians are *now* "holy," "called," and "chosen," and the *ekklēsia* is *now* the eschatological people of God, so that Christians are not exhorted to become an *ekklēsia*, just as they are not admonished to become a body of Christ. Paul, then, in all probability does not use *ekklēsia* as a polemical term. Neither the salvation-historical fulfillment and displacement of Israel, nor its catholic universality, is central in Paul's use of the term. Instead, he emphasizes the local congregation in its concrete gathering for worship and in its present, contingent activity.

Klaus Berger has shown that the Christian meaning of *ekklēsia* is derived from Hellenistic and Hellenistic-Jewish usage (cf. Acts 19:39) and signifies the congregation as gathered in worship and only subsequently the permanence of the group of those so constituted.[27] The *ekklēsia* is primarily the cultic assembly of those who are engaged in praise and prophetic speech and who exercise judicial functions in accordance with the political usage of the term in the Hellenistic-Roman world.*

The Church as the People of God

There is, however, an ambivalence in Paul's use of *ekklēsia*. Although it is not an anti-Jewish term and not meant as the displacement of Israel, its precise relation to Israel is unclear. The *ekklēsia* is definitely the eschatological "people of God," because it gathers the "saints" (*hagioi*), the "chosen ones" (*eklektoi*), and "the called ones" (*klētoi*) of God into one eschatological unity. And when Paul claims that Abraham's seed is not the Jews but Christ and those who belong to him, the *ekklēsia* seems to be "the true Israel," that is, its replacement (Gal. 3:29; cf. also Rom. 9:8, 23–24). However, Paul never surrenders the continuity of God's story with Israel, and thus God's promises to Israel are not fulfilled in Israel's conversion to the gospel or in Israel's absorption by the *ekklēsia*: they will be fulfilled only in Israel's eschatological salvation at the time of the triumph of God (Rom. 11:25–36).

The *ekklēsia* represents the eschatological people of God as they are gathered in worship and as they witness to the coming glory of God,

---

*It is interesting to observe how frequently Paul uses *ekklēsia* for a local congregation, coming together for or engaged in judicial and/or liturgical activity (cf., esp., 1 Cor. 6:1–8; 11:18, 20, 33; 14:4, 5, 12, 19, 23, 28).

which they already celebrate by faith in giving "glory to God." In this sense the salvation-historical aspect of *ekklēsia* is evident in Paul, because the *ekklēsia* is a living witness of the ratification of God's promises to his people Israel. However, the church "of the saints" is not a sequestered cloister, barricaded against the onslaughts of the world. It represents the blueprint of the new eschatological order that will be manifested in the kingdom of God, and therefore it demonstrates its new life and open access to God in Christ in its worship and unity: "When we cry, 'Abba! Father!' it is the Spirit himself bearing witness to our spirit that we are children of God" (Rom. 8:15–16).

We can say, then, that the theme of equality and unity is present in both the *ekklēsia* and body metaphor: "For by one Spirit we were all baptized into one body—Jews or Greeks, slaves or free—and all were made to drink of one Spirit" (1 Cor. 12:13). "When you meet together, it is not the Lord's supper that you eat. . . . What! Do you not have houses to eat and drink in? Or do you despise the church of God . . . ?" (1 Cor. 11:20).

Whereas the *ekklēsia* concept stresses both the worshiping activity of the church in its "coming together" (*synerchomai*, 1 Cor. 11:18, 20, 33) and the eschatological character of the people of God in their open access to his grace (Rom. 5:2), the metaphor of the body expresses more adequately both our participation in Christ and the mutual interdependence of all the various members of the one body of Christ. Moreover, the contingent nature of Paul's gospel comes to expression in his emphasis on the local character of the *ekklēsia* and on the diversity of the charismata in the one body of Christ.

THE CHURCH IN THE WORLD

The Church and the Transformation of Society

We have discussed Paul's concept of the church in terms of its equality, diversity, unity, and ontological foundation in Christ. A practical question now arises. How does the unity and mutuality of the church manifest itself in the sociological sphere? If Paul is interested in the historical concreteness of the church and in the empirical demonstration of its eschatological unity in Christ, how does the church manifest itself as the transformation of secular values in society and as the beachhead of the coming reign of God? At this point, Paul's theology of the unity of the church must be tested in the contingent sphere of the church's daily life. Paul's "high ecclesiology" suggests not only a messianic life-style within the church but also a revolutionary impact on the values of the world, to which the church is sent out as agent of transformation and beachhead of the dawning kingdom of God.

Our expectations are, however, not unambiguously fulfilled. Paul focuses primarily on the internal religious-social life of the church, and he seems to neglect its impact on the social institutions and moral customs of his world. For instance, it is curious that Paul, who proclaims in Gal. 3:28 the equality of Jew and Greek, slave and free, male and female, elaborates elsewhere the "Jew nor Greek" clause but disregards the implications of "male nor female" and "slave nor free" (cf. Gal. 5:6; 6:15; 1 Cor. 7:19; Rom. 3:27-30, etc.). The "male nor female" clause of Gal. 3:28 is absent from the list in 1 Cor. 12:13, obviously because of Paul's trouble with ecstatic women in the Corinthian worship services (1 Corinthians 11). He insists on the importance of the "Jew nor Greek" clause because it chiefly concerns life within the church and has no direct implications for society. Equality within the church is the supreme value, and the extension of that equality into the sphere of the secular family and the social mores of society is hardly discussed. The equality of Jew and Greek concerns the intramural life of the church, because their inequality would threaten its basic existence. For how can the unity of the church be maintained and not fall apart into sectarian chaos if Jewish Christians like Peter disrupt the common eucharistic meal and segregate themselves from table fellowship (Gal. 2:11-14)? Such segregation destroys the internal life of the church and denies its ground in the cross of Christ.

Life within the Church

Before we discuss the social impact of the church on the world, the new life-style of Christians within the church needs our attention, especially the way in which the unity motif expresses itself in the worship service of the church.

The "gathering" (*synerchomai*, 1 Cor. 11:17, 18, 20, 33, 34; 14:23, 26) of the church normally takes place in private homes (Rom. 16:5, 10, 11, 14-16, 23; cf. 1 Cor. 11:20); "house churches" are the rule, and only gradually do special church buildings come into being (cf. the Christian church in Dura-Europos of the second century A.D.). Floyd Vivian Filson[28] estimates that congregations usually had no more than fifteen to thirty members, depending on the available space. The house churches form a "pneumatic democracy." Cultic borrowing from Hellenist-Roman socioreligious clubs (cf. *thiasos* and *eranos*) and the usual Hellenistic-Roman language for worship are absent; our term "worship" does not occur in Paul (*leitourgia*, *thrēskeia* [Acts 26:5]; cf. *ethelothrēskeia* [Col. 2:23]; *theosebeia* [1 Tim. 2:10]; *therapeia* [Acts 17:25]; *hierourgia* [cf. Rom. 15:16]). Early Christian self-description provides little evidence for describing early Christianity as a "cult."[29] Furthermore, there is no hierarchical division in the worship service between cultic officials and a passive laity. Official church "offices" are developed only gradually, although the Jewish-Hellenistic political and religious *ekklēsia* certainly had official rankings (cf. the rankings in the *synagōgē* of James 2:2–4). Cultic-sacrificial language is transformed metaphorically and applied to the daily life-style of the Christians (cf. "sacrifice" [*thysia*, Rom. 12:1; Phil. 2:17]; "to function as priest" [*hierourgeō*, Rom. 15:16]; "sacrifice" [*leitourgia*, Phil 2:17]). A Pauline church conforms to the picture of a Hellenistic *ekklēsia*, an assembly where praise, acclamation, and discussion (interpretation) are carried on. The common meal forms the center of the service; meal and Eucharist are not yet separated. The meal concludes with the "Eucharist" and is indeed a "dominical meal" (*kuriakon deipnon*, 1 Cor. 11:20). Although nonbelievers and sympathizers are not excluded from the assembly (*idiōtai/apistoi*, 1 Cor. 14:23–25), they are obviously excluded from the Lord's meal (cf. 1 Cor. 16:22). In principle, the service is unlike that of a secret religious society. In the church service "each one has a hymn, a lesson, a revelation, a tongue, or an interpretation" (1 Cor. 14:26), and everything focuses on the celebration of the Lord's presence "until he comes" (1 Cor. 11:26). Inquiry into the will of God for Christian edification and conduct takes place through the prophetic interpretation of Scripture: "Let all things be done for edification" (1 Cor. 14:26). The communal nature of early Christian life is remarkable. Instead of uniformity or passive dependence on "the minister," there is mutuality in service and leadership; in place of a normative-codified catechism for the community, there is lively hermeneutical activity and spontaneous utterances by the Spirit.

One searches the will of God for particular circumstances and problems. Although Jewish catechetical forms provide guidance (cf. the doctrine of the two ways in the Didache), there is no casuistry but rather flexible interpretation that is arrived at through communal discussion and consensus. The goal of worship is stated in Rom. 12:1–2: "To present your bodies as a living sacrifice, holy and acceptable to God, which is your spiritual worship. Do not be conformed to this world but be transformed by the renewal of your mind, that you may prove what is the will of God, what is good and acceptable and perfect." The "renewal of your mind" aims at the "sacrifice of your bodies," that is, the worship of God in the "bodily" situations of everyday life.[30] The church service takes place with this goal in mind. It is a collective investigation of "that which counts" (or "that which makes a difference"; *ta diapheronta*, Phil. 1:10; cf. Rom. 2:18). The "loneliness of existential decisions" in ethical situations does not conform to early Christian life, because Christians "come together" (1 Cor. 11:20) so that they may together "investigate," "test," and "approve" (*dokimazein*) what "the will of God" is, that is, "the good, the acceptable and perfect" (Rom. 12:3). In that context the *paraklēsis* (*parakalein*) of the letters occurs, that is, the mutual "encouragement and comfort" (Rom. 15:14; 1 Thess. 4:18; 5:11; cf. also Heb. 13:22). The participation of the whole community is involved: "to live in harmony," "to be of the same mind" (*to auto phronein*), "to have mutual agreement" (*to auto legein,* Rom. 15:5; Phil. 2:2; 1 Cor. 1:10; 2 Cor. 13:11). This free atmosphere of "testing" and "approving" (cf. the several connotations of the verb *dokimazein*) presupposes unity amid diversity, and equality amid the variety of "grace gifts" in which all Christians share: "each one" (*hekastos*) has a gift (1 Cor. 14:26). Moreover, the community has the charisma of "distinguishing between spirits" (*diakrisis pneumatōn*); that is, it engages in a critical testing of prophetic utterances, and the "interpretation of tongues" (*hermēneia glōssōn*) must make glossolalia intelligible and edifying. The community itself ("the others [*hoi alloi*], 1 Cor. 14:29)—and not just the prophets in its midst—interprets the utterances of prophets, just as in 1 Thess. 5:21 the "testing" (*dokimazein*) of the prophets is the task of the church as a whole.[31]

We noticed before that Paul does not write private letters; they are all addressed to the church as a whole, and he expects them to be read by the church as a whole (1 Thess. 5:27; cf. Philemon). Although Paul as apostle and founder of his churches has a special apostolic-kerygmatic authority, he wants to be engaged in a dialogue with the whole church and to participate in the give-and-take of mutual spiritual learning and sensible edification rather than act as a spellbinder (Rom. 1:11–12; cf. 15:14; cf. esp. 1 Cor. 14:6–12, 18–19). "For if we are beside ourselves, it is for God; if we are sober [*sōphronoumen*] it is for you" (2 Cor. 5:13). "Upbuilding" (*oikodomē*) is the criterion for discussion, testing, and judging in the church, because it prevents diversity from collapsing into disunity and "parties." Paul favors interpretation, prophecy, and intelligible speech (*nous*) rather than glossolalia, because those activities build up the whole church. Disorderly conduct and chaotic prophetic outbursts prevent the "order" that is necessary for "upbuilding" (1 Cor. 14:33, 40). Love is the criterion for the grace gifts in the church because it "builds up" (1 Cor. 8:1), and thus 1 Corinthians 13 must be understood within the discussion of the *church's* spiritual gifts in chapters 12–14. The nature of one's "building" on

Christ, who is the foundation, will be evaluated at the last judgment (1 Cor. 3:10-15).[32] "Upbuilding" protects the individual importance of each member of the body and protects the dignity of his charisma as indispensable for the whole body. The criterion of mutual "upbuilding" within the pneumatic democracy of the Pauline churches is so central that we know hardly anything about its "basic polity." Who conducts the services? Who decides in ambivalent cases and crises (cf., e.g., 1 Cor. 6:1-8)? Do prophets and teachers have a greater authority than the others? Except for the fundamental authority of the apostle and his co-workers within the church, we hear only about respect for "those who labor among you and are over you in the Lord and admonish you" (1 Thess. 5:12); or about the admonition "to give recognition" to "the household of Stephanas . . . and every fellow worker and laborer" (1 Cor. 16:16, 19; cf. "the bishops and deacons" [Phil. 1:1]). Because there are no "fixed offices" or rites of ordination in the church, authority is legitimized through natural gifts, which are ranked as "spiritual gifts." The leaders of the churches are probably the heads of households, administrative officers, and people with special prophetic and exegetical gifts ("prophets" and "teachers," cf. 1 Cor. 12:28). There is no reason to suspect that women did not share "leadership" on an equal basis with men, as Paul's casual references disclose (cf. Rom. 16:1-2, 3, 6, 12, 15; 1 Cor. 1:11; 16:19; Phil. 4:2, 3; Philemon 2).

The Conservatism of the Church

There can be no doubt that in the life of the early church racial, social, and sexual distinctions were abolished. "There is neither Jew nor Greek, there is neither slave nor free, there is neither male nor female; for you are all one [heis] in Christ Jesus" (Gal. 3:28). The transformation of the values of Hellenistic-Roman society within the church is revolutionary and has revolutionary implications for Christian life in society at large. Paul transforms the marriage ethic of his day by emphasizing the mutuality of the love relationship (1 Cor. 7:3-5). The extension of the equality principle within the life of the church to the marriage relationship contains the seed for a transformation of the status of the woman in society. Robin Scroggs[33] has pointed out that women served the church as equals of men, and that there is no indication that their role was in any way subordinate. He correctly dismisses 1 Cor. 14:31b-37 as an interpolation into the Epistle.* He refers to the fact that when Paul borrows Hellenistic ethical

---

*There is widespread scholarly consensus on this issue, not only because 1 Cor. 14:31b-37 conflicts with 1 Cor. 11:2-17, but also because the pericope interrupts the sequence of thought of 1 Cor. 14:26-33, 37-40.

categories he uses lists of virtues and vices, but he ignores the *Haustafel* (household rules) that figure so prominently in the deutero-Pauline Epistles (and 1 Peter), with their emphasis on the woman's subordination to her husband and her silence in the church (1 Tim. 2:12). Even more cogently he points out that Paul does not abolish the distinction between male and female—as some Gnostics did and as the Corinthians threatened to do (1 Cor. 11:1-16?)—but he does abolish value judgments based on sexual distinctions.[34]

However, it remains an open question to what extent the equality in Christ within the church is extended to society at large. Paul is really not willing or able to challenge the social structures of his society. Although he affirms the mutuality of the marriage relationship, one wonders to what extent he would have advocated the freedom for which "Christ has set us free" (Gal. 5:1) for a woman or a slave in society. Women are considered only within the marriage relationship, and not as free persons in their own right. First Corinthians 11 leaves ample room for doubt in this respect; when a woman—even within the church—manifests her freedom in prophetic speech, she is reminded of her subordination to the male on the basis of "the orders of creation." Even apart from the extension of the ecclesial equality principle into the society at large, the revolutionary impact of the equality principle is not even wholly executed within the church, as is evident in 1 Corinthians 8-10. Indeed, the issue of the strong and the weak in Corinth is directly related to socioeconomic factors of wealth and poverty. Gerd Theissen has demonstrated that Paul basically restricts his answers to the questions of "the strong" in 1 Corinthians 8-10, that is, to the affluent members of the church, who alone were able to afford meat and could indulge in gnosis, because poor people in Roman society simply could not afford meat.[35] The question of "the strong" and "the weak" is based on distinctions of wealth and property. The weak, for instance, are at a disadvantage in trying to obey Paul's orders, because their only opportunity for eating meat is in the public cultic assemblies, that are vetoed by Paul. However, private dinner parties for the rich, which are not open to the poor, are, according to Paul, religiously indifferent. Thus, the love principle that regulates the life of the church does not question or upset basic economic issues, that is, a redistribution of wealth between rich and poor. The equality of rich and poor in the church discloses a patriarchalism of love (Troeltsch[36]), that is, a philanthropic attitude toward the poor, especially during the meals preceding the Lord's Supper. However, this equality in Christ does not lead to an economic equality.[37] In other words, Paul does not address socioeconomic distinctions but restricts himself to attitudinal behavior.

Paul's social conservatism is also evident in his attitude toward slavery. The dehumanizing institution of slavery is not addressed, but only the personal relation of the slave to his master within the confines of the church, that is, the mutual attitude of care and respect as befits "brothers" (*adelphoi*). Elaine Pagels formulates it well:

> While Paul affirms the liberation of slaves and women, he declines to challenge the social structures that perpetuate their present subordination. . . . In the case of Jew and Gentile, the "new humanity" has constituted a new, present social reality for Paul. But Paul does not challenge the institutions which regulate discrimination and subordination of slaves and women. . . . This seems a double standard: to continue observing kosher laws is to deny "the freedom for which Christ died," but to continue observing social, political and marital laws and conventions remains acceptable, even commendable. Although the "new humanity" has transformed the entire relationship between Jews and Gentiles, Paul does not allow it to challenge the whole structure of the believers' social, sexual and political relationships.[38]

I am not as convinced as Pagels that the equality between Jew and Greek is as unambiguously carried out into the sphere of society as she suggests:

> In that case . . . he claims and acts out the new liberty—the equality of Jew and Gentile "in Christ"—in the present. Thus Paul dares to violate his own childhood training and his previous religious convictions; he courageously resists social pressures to break the conventions of Orthodox Judaism.[39]

In the Galatian incident,

> Paul challenges Peter, calling him a hypocrite; to revert to kosher observance in social relationships is to give up "the freedom for which Christ died"; it is to deny the new reality Christ brings to a newly unified mankind (Gal. 2:11—5:10). In the case of Jew and Gentile then, the "new humanity" has constituted a new, present social reality for Paul.[40]

Although Paul continuously stresses the unity of Jew and Gentile as essential to the life of the church, it is by no means certain that the charge against Peter of "living like a Jew" (*ioudaizein*, Gal. 2:14) applies to all Jewish life outside the church. How is it possible for Paul to acknowledge the authenticity of Jewish Christianity in Jerusalem and to expect a favorable reception there (Rom. 15:30-32), if he did not allow Jewish Christians to maintain their "Jewishness" in the world in terms of their cultural and social customs? The main point of Paul in Gal. 2:11–21 is that

Peter's behavior splits the unity of the church apart and so compels Gentiles to adopt Jewish ways as necessary for salvation. Would he have argued the same way against those who were born and raised as Jews? Doesn't the principle of 1 Cor. 7:17, 20 ("everyone should remain in the state in which he was called") also apply to Jews? Certainly in Christ "Jewish life" has become religiously indifferent, and thus Paul directs Jewish Christians not to undo the marks of their circumcision (1 Cor. 7:18). The religious significance of Torah and circumcision is done away with in Christ. But where in Jewish life can a clear division be made between national-ethnic customs and their religious "saving" significance? Would Paul have forbidden Jews to remain in their "calling" (*klēsis*, 1 Cor. 7:17-20), so that they could no longer live as Jews in terms of circumcising their children and observing kosher laws? Galatians 2:15-18 seems to argue that all Torah observance belongs to that "which I have broken down," which I, therefore, should not "rebuild." However, it is unclear how far Paul would have gone to denationalize and secularize a Jew with respect to his cultural mores and life within the Jewish community. What does it mean to become "a Jew to the Jews in order to win the Jews" (cf. 1 Cor. 9:20) or to consent to a "gospel of the circumcised" (Gal. 2:7), if Paul disallows the Jew his national identity? The extension into the larger society of the ecclesial equality between Jew and Greek would in any case not have been as significant as the challenge of the basic structures of Roman-Hellenistic society, because the distinction between Jews and Gentiles remained from the perspective of the larger society merely a *sectarian* dispute (cf. Gallio in Acts 18:15). It did not mean a revolution against societal structures, which Paul would have caused if he had applied Christian freedom to slavery, male domination, or to the state.[41]

Apart from the possibly revolutionary extension into society of the "neither Jew nor Greek" clause, Paul's attitude toward women, slaves, wealth, poverty, and the state is characterized by a social conservatism that does not extend the "ecclesial revolution" into society at large. This must have created very awkward situations. How could a slave be a total equal and a "brother" in the worship service if he had to return to the "master-slave" institution as soon as the church service in his own household was concluded? And even although we cannot import twentieth-century issues into Pauline texts, and must consider what was empirically possible for small house churches in an overwhelmingly hostile society, it is still surprising that the early Christian ethic did not carry a protest against unjust and inhuman secular institutions. The ethic does not struggle with the issue of the empirically possible versus the religiously necessary, and it does not wrestle with strategies for political and social action. Rather, we get the impression of something like a religious accommodation to the social sphere. Paul's discussion of church and state in Rom. 13:1-7 must be viewed in strictly historical and situational terms and thus against a background of Christian house-church situation(s) that are severely pressed by hostile synagogues on the one hand and Roman hostility against "superstition" on the other (cf. Tacitus's description of Christianity as *superstitio nova ac malefica*).[42] Furthermore, it has been pointed out that an oppressive taxation system (*telos*) impoverished the Christians in Rome until Nero established his tax reforms.[43] Although this must be acknowledged, the pragmatic survival of Christians in a troublesome political situation still makes Paul's ideological defense of the state difficult to understand, especially his appeal for subjection to the state and his way of describing the state and its officials in the traditional laudatory language of Hellenistic politics. To be sure, a social revolution would have wiped out the Christians, and the eschatological expectation motivated Christians to wait for "the imminent day of salvation" (cf. Rom. 13:11), because "the form of this world is already passing away" (1 Cor. 7:31). Moreover, the revolution within the church carried within itself important seeds of revolution for the structures of society. In the midst of the society, there were now after all "pockets" of a life-style that—as in the case of marriage—could and did penetrate the mores of the larger society. How can the amazing success of Christian missions otherwise be accounted for? Thus indirectly the very existence of the church provided models for a different life-style in society.

There still remains a gnawing problem. It is often said that the church's apocalyptic expectation—the expectation of the imminent coming of the kingdom of God—allowed Christians to diffuse their revolutionary impulses and to wait patiently (and socially passively?) for God's ultimate establishment of his kingdom. Social conservatism and apocalyptic enthusiasm thus seem to coincide. However, if God's coming reign will establish an order of righteousness that encompasses the created order (Rom. 8:19-21), and if the Pauline hope is not to be identified with a Gnostic discontinuity between the material and the spiritual (so that the material will simply perish and is therefore "indifferent"), then one would expect that the church as the blueprint and beachhead of the kingdom of God would strain itself in all its activities to prepare the world for its coming destiny in the kingdom of God. The hermeneutical consequence of Paul's thought on this matter suggests an active vocation and mission to the created order and its institutions, that is, the execution of our "spiritual worship" in terms of "bodily and responsible life in the world" (Rom. 12:1–2), testifying in the world to the freedom of all God's people. If the world is to be the scene of the "worship" of the Christian, then the church exists for the world in the world. Unless this is true, the sighing of the Christian for the redemption of the world (Rom. 8:19–21) is simply reduced to a faint ecclesial whisper.

15

The Destiny of Israel

ISRAEL AND THE CHURCH

It is often assumed that Paul is responsible for transferring the term "Israel" to the Christian church, so that henceforth the "true Israel" or the "Israel of God" is identified with the Christian church and denied to Israel. This supposition is erroneous. It is not until Barnabas and Justin Martyr (A.D. 150) that "Israel" is directly applied to the Christian church.[1] However complex the developments toward this "takeover" before Justin Martyr are, Paul himself never equates the church explicitly with Israel.[2] One may even argue that Paul distinguishes at times between Israel as "God's people" (*laos* = *am*) and "the Gentiles" (*ethnos*) (cf. Rom. 9:25 [Hos. 2:25]; 9:26 [Hos. 1:10]; 10:21 [Isa. 65:2]; 11:1–12; 15:10–12; 1 Cor. 10:7; 14:21; 2 Cor. 6:15; but cf. Titus 2:14; 1 Pet. 2:9).

Paul and Other New Testament Witnesses

In fact, among all the New Testament writers Paul is most passionately concerned with Israel (cf. Rom. 9:1–5; 10:1–2). He even utters the wish to be sacrificed for the sake of Israel's salvation (Rom. 9:3), and he is quite explicit about Israel's continuing and abiding privileges: "They are Israelites, and to them belong the sonship, the glory, the covenants, the giving of the law, the worship, and the promises; to them belong the patriarchs, and of their race, according to the flesh, is the Christ" (Rom. 9:4–5). How different is Paul's attitude toward Israel from that of Matthew, Luke, John, and indeed from the rest of the New Testament! Whatever their sociological settings may have been, however much they intended to give the Christian community a new identity apart from Judaism, and however much they may have reacted to Judaism's persecution of Christians, it cannot be denied that for Matthew, Luke, and John a final judgment has fallen on Israel.

In John, for instance, the Jews are equated with a fallen world and its darkness. A satanic genealogy (John 8:44) is ascribed to them, and Jesus is portrayed as a metaphysical miracle without concrete relationship to the Jewish community, although the Old Testament bears witness to Jesus and his preexistence. The true people of God are the pneumatics, who are Jesus' "own" (*idioi*), his "disciples" (*mathētai*), or his "friends" (*philoi*); and they simply displace Israel as God's people. John posits an acute break between the Israel of the Old Testament and Judaism. Jesus is indeed the Messiah of whom Moses "in the law and also the prophets wrote" (John 1:45) and "Abraham rejoiced that he was to see my day" (8:56). Yet Jesus is a stranger within Judaism. He speaks about "your law" (10:34) as if he himself is not a Jew; and he proclaims, "All who came before me are thieves and robbers" (10:8). When the Jesus of John says, "Before Abraham was, I am" (8:58), it seems that the Old Testament has been appropriated as a Christian book: it predicts the transcendent reality that has now appeared in Christ.

Matthew is quite different from John. Matthew is the spokesman of a Jewish-Hellenistic church that is conscious of its Jewish heritage but also self-conscious about its status as the true Israel, because Jesus and his new law have fulfilled the Old Testament promises (cf. the "fulfillment" quotations). This conviction manifests itself in an acrimonious polemic against the Jews (cf., e.g., the passion narrative [Matthew 26–28] and the indictment of the Pharisees [Matthew 23]). Matthew is much more Jewish and sympathetic to the Torah than Paul, yet much more hostile in his treatment of the Jews as a people. In the crucifixion scene the "crowd (*ochlos*, Matt. 27:20, 24), which throughout Matthew has been sympathetic to Jesus, suddenly becomes the "people of Israel" (*laos*, Matt. 27:25). Thus the people of Israel as a whole are responsible for Jesus' death and seal their own judgment: "His blood be on us and our children" (Matt. 27:25). For Matthew, Jesus is the new lawgiver; for Paul, Christ himself is the new Torah (1 Cor. 9:21; Gal. 6:2).

A similar situation prevails in Luke. The Gospel story is marked by the increasing hostility between Jesus and the company of the Pharisees and Sadducees which foreshadows the hour of their final condemnation. Luke's "travel narrative" (Luke 9:51—19:27) concludes with Jesus' declaration at the end of the parable of the pounds: "I tell you, that to every one who has will more be given; but from him who has not, even what he has will be taken away. But as for these enemies of mine, who did not want me to reign over them, bring them here and slay them before me" (Luke 19:26–27). The Book of Acts reports the final doom of the Jews: the Pharisees who uphold the resurrection against the Sadducees deny their own faith in rejecting Jesus' resurrection (Acts 23:6–10). Therefore, the gospel is now forever denied to the Jews and travels to the Gentiles (28:26–28). Israel has a distinct place in salvation-history, but it is only preparatory; all the Scriptures have found their fulfillment in Christ. Judaism after Christ has betrayed its own scriptural heritage. Thus Israel's "hardening" has become final. To Luke, the gospel is not a "scandal" (cf. 1 Cor. 1:23) but the salvation-historical fulfillment of the Torah (Acts 28:20–24). To be sure, Paul uses the hardening motif as well, but its Old Testament meaning prevails; the hardening occurs for the sake of a final return (Rom. 11:25). Paul then interprets "hardening" in terms of a temporary stumbling motif (*skandalon*), for he finds the reason for Israel's hardening in its religious zeal and its striving for self-righteousness in the face of the Christ-event. The Jew fails because his zeal, although sincere, is misdirected (Rom. 10:1–2). For Luke, however, the Jew fails because he is ignorant and morally corrupt. In other words, for Paul the debate with Israel is primarily religious, that is, the Jews refuse to believe in Christ because they cannot see their perversion of God's grace; for Luke, the debate with Israel is primarily moral, that is, because the Jews are immoral, they kill the innocent Jesus. Luke sees the Jews as culpable because they crucify Jesus— whereas Pilate repeatedly declares him innocent (Luke 23:4, 14, 20, 22)— and because they instigate riots against Paul and refuse to repent. Moral guilt and ignorance are Luke's basic motifs. The Jews do not understand their own religion. How can they reject Jesus as Messiah, for his resurrection fulfills the best of the Jewish tradition? Paul the Christian is consequently nothing but a consistent Pharisee: "I am a Pharisee, a son of Pharisees; with respect to the hope and the resurrection of the dead I am on trial" (Acts 23:6). The death of Christ in its redemptive sense plays no role for Luke, whereas it is central for Paul. Thus the "scandal" of the cross, which is unveiled only in its saving character by God's word in the Spirit, is focal in Paul (1 Cor. 1:18–25; Gal. 5:11) but not in Luke. Israel "stumbles" in Paul (*proskomma*) over a truly "scandalous" cross (Rom. 9:32), whereas in Luke Israel stumbles because of its ignorance and criminality.

For John, Matthew, and Luke, the church is the successor to Israel; it is the "New Israel."* In contrast to these New Testament witnesses, Paul does not identify the church with the New Israel. Although his assessment of the function of the law is negative, he is positive toward Israel as God's people. And we should notice that Israel has not only a positive function in past salvation-history but also a positive function in future salvation-history, for there will be no final eschatological deliverance without the salvation of all Israel (Rom. 11:25–26). This stance toward Israel is unique in the New Testament and postapostolic literature.

Furthermore, unlike other New Testament authors, Paul does not vent

---

*Cf. also Eph. 2:14–22: "the dividing wall" between Israel and the Gentiles not only is broken down, but also Israel is absorbed into the church; cf. also Heb. 8:13; 12:22–24.

his Christian frustration about the failure of the Jewish mission against the Jews as a people. Apart from his outburst in 1 Thess. 2:14, Paul is not openly hostile to the people of Israel, and he remains eager for their conversion and ultimate eschatological salvation.

PAUL'S DILEMMA

If Israel has a salvation-historical advantage, an urgent dilemma arises. How can Paul maintain such a position in the face of his basic theological claim that undergirds his apostolate to the Gentiles, that is, the equality of Jew and Greek in Christ on the basis of justification by faith alone (Rom. 3:28–31)? The solution to this dilemma demands a review of Paul's relation to Israel.

Israel's Priority

Liberal scholarship has often misconstrued Paul's relation to Judaism and Jewish Christianity. It portrayed Paul as the lonely genius who, after the apostolic council in Jerusalem and his quarrel with Peter and Barnabas in Antioch (Gal. 2:11–14; cf. Acts 15:37–39), breaks entirely with Jerusalem. He is described as one who turns his back on Judaism and Jewish Christianity and is intent on making Christianity an entirely Gentile religion based on a law-free gospel. This picture of a Paul who projects his own frustration with the law into a hatred for all things Jewish (cf. Nietzsche) is fundamentally mistaken. Paul is interested in the truth of the gospel, but never at the expense of the unity of the church. That unity manifests itself concretely in the one church of Jews and Gentiles. Paul does not break away on his own after his conversion but travels to Jerusalem from time to time (Galatians 1, 2; Rom. 15:25–32)—a circumstance his opponents did not hesitate to use against him when he claimed the independence of his apostolate.

The unity motif in Paul is not just a strategic move against sectarian fragmentation. It is undergirded by a theological principle: the faithfulness of God to his promises to Israel. The concept of the unity of the church and the equality of its members does not ignore the priority of the Jerusalem church, for the Jerusalem church symbolizes the connection of the church with God's promises to Israel (see Chapter 5, above). Unless that connection and continuity are maintained, God's faithfulness to his plan of salvation is jeopardized and destroyed. The relation of the church to Judaism is theologically important, because the church cannot be the people of God without its linkage with Israel as the people of God. "For I tell you that Christ became a servant to the circumcised to show God's truthfulness, in order to confirm the promises given to the patriarchs, and in order that the Gentiles might glorify God for his mercy" (Rom. 15:8–9). In other words, the gospel to the Gentiles has no foundation and no legitimacy unless it confirms the faithfulness of God to his promises to Israel. The church of the Gentiles is an extension of the promises of God to Israel and not Israel's displacement.

We must not forget that Paul's imprisonment in Jerusalem and subsequent death in Rome are brought about by his concern for Israel, that is, by his conviction that the Gentile mission is integrally connected with Jewish Christianity in Jerusalem. The collection for the Jerusalem church had been agreed upon at the apostolic council and was diligently carried out by Paul in Galatia, Macedonia, and Achaia (1 Cor. 16:1; 2 Cor. 8:9; Rom. 15:25–26). It was certainly a response to the economic needs of the Jerusalem church,[3] but it symbolized as well the unity between Jew and Gentile in the one church at a time when the mission field was divided between Gentile and Jewish missions, headed respectively by Peter and Paul (Gal. 2:6–10). However, beyond symbolizing the unity of the church, it provided a living proof of the indebtedness of the Gentiles to the Jerusalem church, a sort of thank offering to the Jewish origin of the Christian faith.[4] Therefore, Paul considers it a sacred duty to travel to Jerusalem to deliver the collection gathered among the Gentiles, although he is eager to carry his mission to Spain. Thus, the collection demonstrates the priority of Jewish Christianity and indirectly that of Israel in the thought of Paul.

> At present, however, I am going to Jerusalem with aid for the saints. For Macedonia and Achaia have been pleased to make some contribution for the poor among the saints at Jerusalem; they were pleased to do it, and indeed they are in debt to them, for if the Gentiles have come to share in their spiritual blessings, they ought also to be of service to them in material blessings. [Rom. 15:25; cf. 2 Cor. 8:14]

These spiritual blessings are no doubt the promises of God to Israel as confirmed by Jesus the crucified Messiah. A similar motif is sounded in Ephesians: "Therefore remember that at one time you Gentiles in the flesh . . . were at that time separated from Christ, alienated from the commonwealth of Israel, and strangers to the covenants of promise, having no hope and without God in the world" (Eph. 2:11–12).

The Equality of Jew and Gentile

In the light of these factors—the unity motif, the motivation for the collection, and the priority of Jerusalem—the question arises Why is Paul strictly engaged with Gentile missions? Why, if his concern is for Israel, does he not spend his energy on Jews, both in Palestine and in the Diaspora? Why does he know himself especially called as "the apostle to the Gentiles" (*ethnōn apostolos*, Rom. 11:13; cf. Gal. 1:15–16)? Is his concern for Israel, after all, nothing but a defensive, apologetic gesture, a political strategy of appeasement that conceals his real intent of destroying Israel's spiritual treasure and of establishing a purely Gentile church that is severed from Israel?

Romans 9–11 enables us to clarify the dual question of Paul's focus on Gentile missions notwithstanding his declaration of the priority of Israel in salvation-history. Paul indeed is called to be "the apostle to the Gentiles" (Rom. 11:13; cf. Gal. 1:15). His call does not negate Israel's historical mission to the world but is rather the consequence of that mission in the new messianic era that the Christ-event has inaugurated. The Old Testament citations in Romans 9–11, especially from Second Isaiah, underscore this. Israel's strategic position in salvation-history is not confined to its past, as if Israel is now absorbed by the church. Israel remains a distinct entity in the future of God's purpose. Thus, as we saw before, Paul simply refuses to equate the Gentile church with the new/true Israel. In fact, Paul considers his apostolate to the Gentiles an indirect way to bring Israel to Christ: "Inasmuch then as I am an apostle to the Gentiles, I magnify my ministry in order to make my fellow Jews jealous, and thus save some of them" (Rom. 11:13–14). The eschatological horizon of Paul's apostolate entails the vision that "until the full number of the Gentiles come in . . . all Israel will be saved; as it is written: 'The Deliverer will come from Zion . . .' " (Rom. 11:25–26). In other words, Paul's apostolate to the Gentiles is related to the salvation of Israel and does not mean a turning away from Israel.

In this connection the "mystery" of Romans 11:25 needs to be clarified: "I want you to understand this mystery, brethren: a hardening has come upon part of Israel, until the full number of the Gentiles come in, and so all Israel will be saved." What constitutes "this mystery," that is, the secret apocalyptic revelation that was granted to Paul? Furthermore, what is the meaning of "all Israel" (*pas Israel*)? Does it mean that "all Jews will be saved" (*pantes hoi ioudaioi sōthēsontai*)?[25] Does it refer to the salvation of Israel as an ethnic totality or only to a predetermined part of Israel? How does Paul understand the relation of the ethnic Israel to the "elect Israel"? These are troublesome questions in Romans 9–11.

Sometimes Paul views Israel as "the children of the promise" (vs. "the children of the flesh"), that is, as the "spiritual Israel" (Rom. 9:8), by which he presumably means Jewish Christians (Rom. 9:24). At other

times, he speaks about Israel as "the remnant" or "the seed" (*hypoleimma;*
sperma; Rom. 9:27) or as a "remnant [*leimma*] according to the election of
grace" (Rom. 11:5; trans. mine; cf. "the elect" [*eklogē*], Rom 11:7), that is,
in terms of an offshoot from ethnic Israel. And finally, he claims that in the
eschatological consummation Israel as an ethnic totality will be saved
(Rom. 11:26).

The "mystery" is often explicated as Israel's "partial hardening" (Rom
11:25) and/or as the salvation of the Gentiles prior to the salvation of Israel.
However, the words "and so" (*kai houtōs*, Rom. 11:26) are not to be
understood temporally (=*kai tote*). The mystery pertains rather to the
manner and method of salvation-history: *kai houtōs* is to be translated as
"in this manner." The hardening motif itself cannot be the mystery,
because this has been the presupposition of the argument since Rom. 11:8.[6]
Nor is the salvation of "all Israel" the mystery because, although *kai houtōs* is related to the "until" (*achri hou*) of Rom. 11:25b, Israel's salvation is
based on the "irrevocable gifts and call of God" (Rom. 11:29; trans. mine)
and on the claim that "if the dough offered as first fruits is holy, so is the
whole lump; and if the root is holy, so are the branches" (Rom. 11:16).
Instead, the mystery is the surprising wavelike or undulating dynamic of
God's salvation-history, the "interdependence"[7] of God's dealings with
Gentiles and Jews. This process takes place thus: Gentile disobedience;
Jewish disobedience becomes a means for Gentile missions; Gentile
missions, in turn, become the cause for the jealousy and conversion of
Jews; and finally, the eschatological harvest of the Gentiles will precede
the eschatological salvation of Israel. The "mystery" of God's plan
manifests itself in the inseparable connection between Israel's unbelief and
the faith of the Gentiles. However, "all Israel" (Rom. 11:26) must not be
harmonized with a permanent "hardening" of part of Israel (Rom. 11:25):
the eschatological "until" (v. 25b) intervenes here so that "all Israel" is
identical with its "fullness" (Rom. 11:12), that is, the full number of Israel
as determined by God. "All Israel," then, will no longer be a "remnant"
Israel (Rom. 11:5).

The tension between God's universal salvation ("that he may have
mercy upon all" [Rom. 11:32]) and Israel's response in faith characterizes
Romans 11. Israel's salvation ("all Israel will be saved" [Rom. 11:26]) does
not mean Israel's conversion as the result of Christian missions. "All Israel"
is not a designation for the Jewish-Christian church, because it points
clearly to an eschatological event. And yet it is not separable from Israel's
process of coming to faith and from the jealousy that the Gentiles provoke
in the present time (Rom. 11:13, 23). Paul does not envision Israel's

eschatological salvation as its absorption into the Gentile-Christian church. Indeed, Israel's destiny is here dissimilar from that portrayed in Ephesians, where Israel is absorbed in the one church of Jews and Gentiles and henceforth ceases to exist as a separate entity. On the contrary, Israel has a special eschatological destiny for Paul, for it will enter the kingdom of God as a people at the time when the mission of the church to the Gentiles has been fulfilled (Rom. 11:25–26). Jewish Christianity does not simply displace the Jewish people and does not represent their fullness; rather, Jewish Christians are the symbol of the continuing faithfulness of God to Israel and thus of Israel's priority in salvation-history and of its future eschatological deliverance as a people.

THE PRIORITY OF ISRAEL AND THE UNIVERSALITY OF THE GOSPEL

How can Israel's priority be maintained in the light of Paul's basic universality? Paul's teaching of justification by faith is based on the universality of sin and God's free gift of grace: "Since all have sinned and fall short of the glory of God, they are justified by his grace as a gift" (Rom. 3:23). And the inevitable consequence is: "[In Christ] there is neither Jew nor Greek, there is neither slave nor free . . . for you are all one in Christ Jesus" (Gal. 3:28). How can Israel's priority be maintained in the light of this, especially if Israel's "constitution," the Torah, marks its failure as God's people and is superseded by Christ. In other words, why is Paul negative about Torah-keeping, as that which defines Israel, and yet positive about Israel as God's people? That seems an outright contradiction.

Paul answers this twin issue in one basic theological move. The priority of Israel and the universality of the gospel can be maintained simultaneously because they both have a theocentric foundation. Israel's priority cannot be the occasion for its pride in being a select people—an ethnic entity, constituted by kinship and religious privilege, aware of its superiority over the Gentiles. Paul's main charge in Romans 9 is directed against this understanding of priority. Israel's priority is real, but it is not located in Israel's achievement of "covenant-keeping." It lies exclusively in God's salvation-history and therefore in His election and promises to Israel. "If the dough offered as first fruits is holy, so is the whole lump; and if the root is holy, so are the branches" (Rom. 11:16; cf. also Rom. 9:4; 11:1). This salvation-historical priority remains valid and can never be forgotten. Therefore, the eschatological fulfillment of God's promise to Israel remains a lively hope; unless Israel will be saved, God's faithfulness to his promises is invalidated. The church cannot live without the expectation of God's salvation of all Israel. Both Israel's salvation-historical priority and her future eschatological privilege manifest Israel's special function in salvation-history. Israel remains God's special people even after Christ, and Israel is not simply absorbed in the church, as if the church henceforth can call itself the new Israel. Moreover, unless God's promises to Israel can be trusted, how can the Gentiles trust His faithfulness and promise in Christ? "For the gifts and the call of God are irrevocable" (Rom. 11:29).

Israel's priority, then, rests in God's faithfulness to his promises. However, that faithfulness entails a radical contingency. God's faithfulness cannot be captured and possessed by humankind because it originates in His radical freedom and grace. The issue here is not determinism or arbitrariness on the part of God.[8] Paul's basic charge against Israel is that although it is constituted by election and grace, it has misunderstood its role as God's people: "Being ignorant of the righteousness that comes from God, and seeking to establish their own, they did not submit to God's righteousness" (Rom. 10:3). In their rejection of Christ in the gospel, the Jews manifest that they have failed to understand the promise and the demand of the Torah. They have construed the Torah as a domain of segregation from the rest of mankind, as a tool that isolates God's grace as if it is the possession of a special people. "But of Israel he says, 'All day long I have had held out my hands to a disobedient and contrary people' " (Rom. 10:21). Israel's zeal for the law has missed the mark (Rom. 10:1-3; cf. 9:30-33; 11:6). Israel was meant to be a manifestation among the nations of a people living by promise and grace as the case of their forefather Abraham shows (Romans 4; Galatians 3).* However, it has perceived this grace as exclusively meant for the people of the Torah, and so Israel has become a dis-grace in God's face. Because Christ is God's gift of grace, it has become plain with the coming of Christ that the Torah was the promise of faith for all nations through Abraham (Gal. 3:6-14). Because Israel denies that, its own Torah condemns it. It can only condemn Israel, because it requires what Israel has empirically failed to do, that is, observe the Torah as promise in faith. Israel's life under the law has become a life of condemnation before God. But now that Christ has come, the end of the condemnation has come: "Christ is the end of the law" (Rom. 10:4). Israel's eschatological destiny and privilege is therefore tied to God's original intention with her, that is, that Israel might perceive through Christ to know what it is to live by grace alone. Israel must learn

---

*The idea of Israel as God's *manifestation* among the nations is not to be confused with that of Israel's *mission* to the Gentiles. Such a mission is not a part of the normative traditions of the Old Testament and is not argued by Paul.

to extend God's promise of grace that she has received to all the Gentiles without qualification. If Jesus died for his own sinful people, how much more for the sins of the world. Israel's continuing function for the Gentile believer is grounded in both her salvation-historical priority as the people of the promise and her eschatological destiny. The consummation cannot come unless Israel is saved. For unless Israel is saved, God's faithfulness to his promises to Israel will remain forever ambiguous.

Whether Paul provides the final solution to the problem of Israel for the church is another matter. However, his insight that Judaism and Christianity are interlocking realities should occupy Christian theology at its best. The voices in the history of doctrine that either ignore Judaism altogether or use it as a platform for destructive anti-Semitic attacks have misunderstood and betrayed Paul.

EXCURSUS: PAUL AND THE
JEWISH-CHRISTIAN DIALOGUE

Pauline and Catholic Spirituality

The topic "Paul and Israel" invites a look at Pauline spirituality because it has been so frequently misunderstood. A true understanding of Pauline spirituality may not minimize the conflict between Judaism and Christianity. Yet there may be "promise in the conflict," because Paul affords an opportunity for a genuine dialogue with Judaism. In post-Pauline Christianity the dialogue practically ceased and was displaced— even in the New Testament—by hostile polemics, notwithstanding Justin Martyr's *Dialogue with Trypho* in the second century. I hope to show how ironic it is that Paul's "apostasy" from Judaism has made him the supreme anti-Semite in the history of thought.

Let me make a few preliminary remarks. A Jewish-Christian dialogue is a serious affair. If any progress is to be made and if any mutual understanding is to take place, areas of conflict and disagreement must be faced openly. Otherwise, the dialogue degenerates into an irenic get-together, where agreement is reached on inoffensive common denominators, as, for example, a common theistic postulate. In that case, Christians will tell Jews that New Testament terminology has a Hebraic base, so that ethical concerns are also vital to Christians or that Jesus was not unlike a Jewish prophet, or a Hillel or Shammai. And Jews will tell Christians that both religions should strive for an ethical monotheism in a godless world and so on. Such an approach may have served its purpose in the initial stages of ecumenical understanding and may still be useful. However, no honest dialogue can take place when conflict on a deeper level is avoided. This is a painful exercise, especially for the Christian. Christianity and Judaism do not meet in a vacuum, as if their dialogue is similar to that between, for instance, Christianity and Buddhism or Hinduism. Christianity and Judaism share a common root and a common Scripture and yet differ profoundly in the understanding of the revelation of their common God. More significantly, the Christian cannot and should not forget that his relation to the Jew throughout Christian history has been a history of perversion, misunderstanding, hatred, and persecution. Whatever the socio-psychological roots of anti-Semitism are, it is impossible for a Christian to look at a Jewish face and not remember the betrayal of whatever a religious stance means for a human being quite apart from his confessional persuasion. On this level, humanism correctly indicts the demonic and psychopathic dimensions of religious confessionalism. Although the dimension of this age-long persecution is a silent partner in the dialogue, it should not prevent the conflict. It should encourage empathy, not a watering down of the issues. No dialogue can survive without honesty, and we owe each other the honesty of where we divide at this deeper level.

The history of Jewish-Christian relations shows that nontheological factors not only intertwine with theological factors but even predominate. The depth of pagan hostility to the Jew and his particularity is easily matched by the fratricide of the Christian church. The exploration of that animosity may be more helpful to a dialogue than a discussion of the basic theological issues that divide Jew and Christian. And yet who can deny that these nontheological factors have a theological root? Who can deny that the movement of the New Testament is repeated and climaxed in the history of the church, that is, a process that moves from dialogue and an attempt to convert Jews to acts of hostility and persecution, when frustration and missionary failure are projected on the Jews, who are now indicted as the people of deicide? This angry frustration combines with the inability of the Christian to forgive the Jew for reminding him of the fact that the Jews are the elect people of God and that Christians are grafted as "unnatural branches" into Israel's election (cf. Rom. 11:24). Moreover, the betrayal by Christians of their own crucified Messiah, Jesus Christ, in their life-style often manifests itself in a transference of guilt upon the Jews: "His blood be on us and on our children" (Matt. 27:25).

An exploration of such socio-psychological factors is possibly more important than a dialogue based on an interpretation of Scripture. The primary task of the Christian toward Judaism is to safeguard the peace of the Jew in the world. And yet theological debate may at least help to remove inherited misunderstandings, for the radically different interpretation of the common Scripture by both communities reminds us that interpretation is not an exact science. To be sure, the text of Scripture illuminates and redirects our experience, but it is equally true that our own historical-collective experience illumines the text of Scripture, although it frequently distorts it as well.

Jews and Christians often view Paul in a similar way, although their evaluation of him differs profoundly. For the Jew, Paul is the apostate; for the Christian, he is the first great apostle of the gospel of the Son of God to the Gentiles. The model of the traditional Jesus-Paul antithesis is regularly the premise of this posture. The model originated in the Enlightenment and climaxed in Adolf von Harnack's statement that in the religion of Jesus—unlike in that of Paul—there was indeed a place for the Father but not for the Son.[9] The liberal attempt to free the "original" true gospel of the historical Jesus from its perversion by the dogmatic "Christ of the church" resulted in an antithesis between Jesus and the Christ. This antithesis was soon equated with that between "the religion of Jesus" and "the theology of Paul." Thus Paul became the true "founder of Christianity," the one who had perverted the gospel of Jesus with a rabbinical overlay[10] and who had turned the prophet Jesus into the Son of God,[11] or who combined Jesus' gospel with the Hellenistic mystery religions.[12] Although orthodox Christians disagreed with this picture of the development and affirmed the continuity between Jesus and Paul, they insisted that Paul was indeed the first Christian to articulate the implications of Jesus' cross and resurrection and was therefore—although not the founder—at least the first theologian of Christianity. Along these lines Paul became the originator of catholic Christianity. He was not only the most successful apostle to the Gentiles but also the theologian of the divine Sonship of Christ and of other basic Christian doctrines. Above all, Paul became the great emancipator of Christianity, the one who liberated it from its so-called Jewish limitations. Paul the catholic theologian was the "universalist," and the key to his achievement was his antipathy to everything Jewish.[13] Paul's achievement was his opposition to Jewish Christianity, especially his rejection of the privileged status of Israel and the Torah. Even the Book of Acts posits that just as the Jews were responsible for Jesus' death, so they were primarily responsible for persecuting Paul in the mission field and for his imprisonment by Rome.

Paul, the Anti-Semite

The portrait of Paul the catholic Christian was accompanied by a portrait of Paul the anti-Semite. In fact, Paul's catholicity was bought at the expense of his anti-Judaism: the more catholic, the more anti-Jewish. Although scholars like Ferdinand Christian Baur and Hans Lietzmann,[14] with their more proliferated portrait of Paul, viewed the early catholic church as a synthesis of Jewish and Pauline Christianity (and not as the product of Pauline Christianity itself), they nevertheless cast Paul as the romantic loner, a man who after the apostolic council in A.D. 50 refused any contact with Jewish Christianity and founded Gentile Christianity in opposition to Jewish Christianity. Thus, liberal scholarship located the greatness of Paul—the emancipated liberal—in his downgrading of Judaism. Julius Wellhausen's view of the Jewish law as the dead letter and of Judaism as a narrow formalism, striving for self-righteousness and heavenly merit, conforms to a popular line of interpreting Judaism that was widespread in the so-called Weber-Bousset-Schürer line of scholarship and that perverted many generations of Christian scholarship on Judaism.[15]*

Judaism now moved into this picture of Pauline Christianity. Although it could be sympathetic to the figure of Jesus, as long as he was comprehended in terms of Old Testament prophecy and Judaism,[16] it viewed Paul as the great apostate and specifically as the originator of both catholic dogma and anti-Semitism. Even interpreters who attempt a sympathetic portrait of Paul—men like Joseph Klausner, Hans Joachim Schoeps, and Samuel Sandmel[17]—cannot escape this view. However, this popular picture of Paul as the originator of catholic dogma and the enemy of Judaism is completely erroneous. It is a perversion of historical truth and entails important theological consequences. It must be emphasized that of all the New Testament authors it is only Paul who is passionately engaged with the Jews as the people of the promise and who, notwithstanding his radically different understanding of messianism, keeps his thought anchored in the Hebrew Scriptures and in the destiny of Israel as God's people. In fact, this very "Jewish" element of Paul made it impossible for the church to accept Paul as its "catholic" theologian. The eclipse of the church's understanding of Judaism has a direct relation to the eclipse of the appreciation of Paul in the early catholic church.

Pauline spirituality is in fact unique in the New Testament. It is not to

---

*It constitutes one of the great merits of Sanders's *Paul and Palestinian Judaism* that he destroyed this anti-Jewish bias in scholarship once and for all.

be equated with the catholic spirituality of the later church or even with the spirituality of many New Testament witnesses. A meaningful confrontation with Paul is possible only in the light of this insight. Paul's rabbinic interpretation of Scripture and his debate with the Torah were simply obscure to later catholic Christianity, and his view of Christ's death in the context of the law was soon forgotten. A Jewish dialogue with Christianity on a deep level is possible with Paul because he faces Jewish issues in a Jewish framework. The rest of the New Testament—apart from the historical Jesus—allows much less fruitful confrontation because it is no longer interested in Judaism as a living alternative. Instead, Judaism has in most of the New Testament become a polemical foil and a historical enemy. The synoptic Gospels and John do not stand alone on this point. Hebrews, for instance, casts the Old Testament and Judaism as the defective earthly copy of the heavenly model of Christianity (Hebrews 8–10).

What concerns us is not so much the issue of the anti-Semitic character of the New Testament but the question of how seriously Judaism is understood here in terms of its claims and promises. And it is Paul who takes Judaism seriously. He believes that Christ is the surprising answer to Judaism's religious search, and thus he never considered himself a "founder" of a new religion. For Paul, the Hebrew Scriptures climax in Christ as their eschatological confirmation. A *new scripture* (a "New Testament") was as inconceivable to him as it was for all early Christians. The "New Testament" is instead the authoritative interpretation of the Scriptures in the light of the crucified Messiah, that is, "the gospel concerning his Son" that God "promised beforehand through his prophets in the holy scriptures" (Rom. 1:2, 3).

Paul was not the one who turned the religion of Jesus into the religion about Christ. After the crucifixion and resurrection of Christ, a religion of Jesus simply did not exist. Every early Christian affirmation confessed Jesus as the Messiah. Paul simply inherited the gospel about Jesus as the Christ from the Christians whom he persecuted in his Pharisaic career and from the Antioch church that he joined after his conversion. His persecution of Christians in his Pharisaic period is unintelligible if Paul had known only the historical Jesus. What was at stake was not simply a prophetic claim by the disciples of Jesus about a Jewish prophet but their theological claim about the divine status of the crucified Messiah. Thus, a perversion by Paul of the "simple gospel of Jesus" is a historical fantasy. Before Paul's call to the apostolate, the Stephen group that founded the Antioch church had already "liberalized" the Torah with respect to the validity of the temple and the cultic law (Acts 6:13, 14). They were the first to missionize Gentiles (Acts 8:1; 11:19–26). Whatever Paul's originality may have been, he was not an innovator with respect to Christology or Gentile missions. Although he gave Christology a new interpretation and Gentile missions a new basis, he was not the innovator of the gospel but its radical interpreter.

Paul and the Early Catholic Church

Paul was not the originator of early catholic Christianity. Early catholic Christianity is a combination of many factors, but its basic theological patterns were stamped more by Johannine and Hellenistic-Christian tradition than by the Pauline letters (cf. Ignatius; the Apologists; Clement of Alexandria; Irenaeus; Origen). The concept of the *logos* provided connections with Hellenistic-Roman, and especially Stoic, thought. And the discussions that led to the formulation of the Trinity and the two natures of Christ all centered on the *logos* concept, a concept that proved helpful in stating the coequality of the Son with the Father.

In fact, it is surprising how little influence Paul's thought exercised in the early church and the extent to which he was silenced. Papias, Hegesippus, Justin Martyr, and the other Apologists do not appeal to Paul at all. Tertullian asks whether Paul has really been lost to the heretics.[18] Even 2 Peter in his apology of Paul concedes that Paul's unintelligibility is a cause for the fall of many (2 Pet. 3:15–17). Paul was not really accepted by the church until Irenaeus, and only then as a domesticated Paul, a Paul remade into a catholic Paul. He was considered to be just one among the many apostles who in no way deviated from the "rule of faith," the common apostolic tradition. In fact, the preponderance of Pauline writings in the New Testament canon is basically a historical accident. Marcion created the first New Testament canon, which contained one Gospel, Luke, and ten Pauline Epistles. His initiative caused the church to construct a canon of its own, which was more extensive than that of Marcion. In so doing, the church faced the question of whether to include or exclude Paul. The inclusion of Paul was quite natural, however, because Paul was known and read in the churches and was revered as the great missionary to the Gentiles. The church could not leave Paul to the heretics. However, Paul was neutralized in the canon. His letters were surrounded by the Acts at the beginning and with the pseudo-Pauline pastoral Epistles (and the "Catholic Epistles") at the end. Those writings, indeed, give a catholic picture of Paul. In the Book of Acts, for example, the apostle is in firm agreement with the mother church of Jerusalem and subject to its councils.

He becomes generally either an apostle committed to catholic concerns of church organization and the advocate of a moral decent life (the Pastorals), or he becomes an apostle who has lost his anchorage in Judaism and proclaims a timeless gospel that substitutes the church for the eschatological Parousia and applies the promises to Israel to the eschatological reality of the church (Ephesians). Moreover, the "Catholic Epistles" served notice that Paul was only one apostle among many in the church.

When Paul is quoted in the apostolic fathers and in the early church, it is always in terms of his moral injunctions, not in terms of his doctrinal hermeneutic. Luke's portrait of Paul in Acts shows how his admirers understand him: He is the great missionary and witness under mother church; his speeches are in no way distinct from Peter's; he simply accuses Jews of being inconsistent with their own tradition in not accepting the resurrection of Christ; and even as a Christian he still claims to be a Pharisee (Acts 23:1). Whereas the historical Paul does not allegorize the Torah frequently (cf. Gal. 4:21; 1 Cor. 10:4) but allows the Scripture to be a historical book of promise and law, later Christianity views Christ as the Logos who himself speaks in the Old Testament (cf. Heb. 2:12; 10:5-9). Subsequently, the Scriptures are appropriated as a Christian book, denied to the Jews (Barnabas), and designated as the "Old" Testament as opposed to the "New" Testament (cf. Melito of Sardis [A.D. 180]: "the books of the Old Testament"; Tertullian [A.D. 200]: *Novum Testamentum*).

Paul the Jew and Paul the Christian

What characterizes Paul's spirituality, and in what sense was his spirituality rejected or misunderstood in the postapostolic church? Paul was and remained a Jew: "Are they Hebrews? So am I. Are they Israelites? So am I" (2 Cor. 11:21). For him, Judaism is a living, historical entity, and the gospel of Christ is directed "to the Jew first and also to the Greek" (Rom. 1:16). The advantage of the Jews is real, for the promises were entrusted to them (Rom. 3:1; 9:1-5), and the Christ-event is primarily an answer to the promises to Israel (Rom. 15:8). When Paul reminds the Gentile Christians that they are "grafted, contrary to nature, into a cultivated olive tree" (i.e., Israel; Rom. 11:24), the claim of Rom. 15:8 ("Christ became a servant to the circumcised to show God's faithfulness"; trans. mine) is reiterated. For Paul, Christianity is not a *nova religio* but the answer to Israel's longing for the messianic age. Without Israel there would be no Christianity, and Christianity exists only because God elected Israel. However offensive Paul's statements may be to Jews, they are nevertheless dealing with Israel as God's people. The religious vitalities of

Israel never become an abstraction in Paul. Paul may misunderstand the Torah, but unlike later Christians he does not treat it in terms of ethnic peculiarities and cultural customs that have no revelational status (cf. Acts) or interpret it by separating universal moral law in the Old Testament from obsolete cultic law (cf. Matthew; Ptolemy to Flora). Paul may misunderstand Israel's quest for God, but he never interprets Israel in a symbolic sense. He never equates Israel with "humankind's fallen status"[19] or uses Israel as a symbol for sin or calls the devil the father of the Pharisees (cf. John). Paul does not drive a wedge between the Hebrew Scriptures and Israel in order to deny Israel its own Scriptures or in order to deny Israel its covenant with Yahweh (Barnabas). Moreover, Paul does not foster a "theft" theory ("The Scriptures belong to us Christians and not to the Jews") or a theory of "proper genealogy" ("Israel is important because it gives Christianity its prestigious antiquity, but since Christ's coming, Israel's promises have been completely fulfilled and superseded"). In short, for Paul, the gospel means the extension of the promise beyond Israel to the Gentiles, not the displacement of Israel by the Gentile church (Barnabas). Paul's basic charge against Israel is that it misunderstands its own Scripture (2 Cor. 3:17), but he does not deny Israel its Scripture; the Scriptures are ratified by the Christ-event but not antiquated as "Old" Testament. There is only *one* Scripture for Jew and Christian, although it is only properly understood in Christ (2 Cor. 3:16). The "old covenant" in Paul (2 Cor. 3:14) is not the "Old Testament" but a Jewish misinterpretation of the Scriptures, that is, understanding them as "the letter" that kills (2 Cor. 3:6).

Paul's world of thought is exceedingly complex. However, both the Gnostic Marcion and the rabbi Leo Baeck[20] are wrong when they—each in his own way—force Paul into a Gnostic world of thought. The ethical tension between the gift of grace and the ethical command is never eclipsed for the sake of a triumphalism of grace and ethical passivity, that is, for "the romantic state of the man who possesses everything" (Baeck).[21] Moreover, the religious tension between God and Christ is maintained, so that Christ is never fused with the Almighty himself (cf. "When all things are subjected to him, then the Son himself will also be subjected to him who put all things under him, that God may be all in everything" [1 Cor. 15:28; trans. mine]). Paul's spirituality is nourished by the Hebrew Scriptures and centers on those issues that the Scriptures have raised for him in the light of the Christ-event. Only when this is fully taken into account can we ask to what extent Paul has perverted his Jewish past into a mystery religion or whether he has collapsed the demand of the Torah into a Christ mysticism. Unlike later Christians who increasingly spiritualized their messianic confession and saw the Old Testament "fulfilled" in Christ, Paul speaks about Christ as the "ratification" of the Old Testament promises. Matthew and Luke, for instance, interpret the Hebrew Scriptures basically in terms of the prophetic prediction motif that is "fulfilled" in Jesus: "These are my words which I spoke to you, while I was still with you, that *everything* written about me in the law of Moses and the prophets and the psalms must be fulfilled" (Luke 24:44). The postapostolic church operates likewise in terms of prophecy and completed fulfillment in Christ. For Paul, such an allegorization and spiritualization is impossible. He struggles with the problem that although the Messiah has come, his kingdom has not. Therefore, his thought does not come to rest until it reaches the horizon of God's final eschatological kingdom that will break into history and transform all creation in accord with the messianic promises. Paul's Christology is bifocal and not unifocal; Christ is not so much the fulfillment of God's promises as the guarantee or confirmation of these promises (Rom. 4:16; 15:8; 2 Cor. 1:21). In an environment that threatened to collapse eschatology into Christology and to celebrate life in Christ as the epiphany of the divine presence on earth, so that historical life is absorbed into Christ mysticism, Paul emphasizes the "not yet" of the Christian life and stresses the need for ethical responsibility in the light of both the Christ-event and the last judgment.

Paul's apocalyptic thought causes deep misgivings in the Jewish community. Although both later Christian thought and Judaism alike dislike Paul's apocalyptic theology, Judaism has had more to fear from apocalyptic. It instinctively feels that apocalyptic threatens its "root" experience of the past. Classical Judaism of the post-Jamnia period made apocalyptic responsible for the destruction of Jerusalem, the temple, and the land because of its messianic speculations. It therefore eliminated the apocalyptic element almost completely from its heritage in the Mishnah and Talmud. A new evaluation of apocalyptic by Jewish scholars (e.g., Jochanan Bloch[22]) now seems to be forthcoming, because a great deal of the literature of the intertestamental period and Qumran can be understood only in terms of apocalyptic, and because apocalyptic can no longer be understood as a degeneration of prophecy.[23] Paul is heavily indebted to the apocalyptic ideology of his time because he had been an apocalyptic Diaspora Pharisee before his conversion. Apocalyptic is for Paul the bearer of prophecy in new circumstances. It keeps alive the prophetic promises about a new act of God in the future that will surpass God's acts in the past and bring about a transformed creation. The apocalyptic vision of God's kingdom is part and parcel of Paul's Christology, for the coming of the Messiah is the promise of God's public presence in history. Thus Paul's

Christology cannot live without the Parousia of Christ, and he is unable to collapse eschatology into Christology or to spiritualize the messianic hope, as catholic Christianity did after him. The time between Christ and the end of history is literally an interim time. It is a time of joy in Christ, as the Messiah who has come, but also a time of patience, suffering, endurance, and waiting. The interim time is to be characterized not in a purely individualistic manner but as a historical-materialistic tension; it hopes for the participation of the as yet unredeemed creation in the blessings of the messianic age and for the final deliverance of the body (Rom. 8:23), so that the body may conform to what the Christian already has received "in the Spirit." Without the redemption of creation, which like the Christian sighs and groans for its liberation (Rom. 8:19–21), the Christian cannot be a completed being. Israel occupies a special role within this apocalyptic hope because the consummation of history will not take place without Israel's participation in it (Rom. 11:26).

The distinctiveness of Paul's spirituality lies precisely in the bifocal tension of his Christology. The Messiah has come, but without his kingdom. Paul refuses to go the route of realized eschatology, so that either Christ becomes the spiritual fulfillment of all God's promises (John) or the kingdom of God becomes identified with the institution of the church in its sacramentalism and clericalism. He also refuses to go the route of a purely futurist eschatology, where the Christian confession of the crucified and risen Christ and our participation in him degenerates into an affirmation about Jesus as a new prophet or a new lawgiver, who merely announces what eventually will come to pass and what must be done in the midst of a wholly unredeemed present. Paul's spirituality lives the tension of the seemingly contradictory claim that the Messiah has come but his kingdom in its fullness is still outstanding.

Unresolved Issues

At this point a discussion with Judaism becomes possible. What is the meaning of Christ as the Messiah *without* his fully actualized kingdom?* How realistic is Paul's "materialistic" hope? How is it possible to avoid a

---

*Cf. Martin Buber's protest against the central claim of Christianity: "Peter's confession at Caesarea Philippi, that Jesus was the Christ, he wrote, was a sincere confession but not a true one, and it has not become any less untrue for having been repeated down the centuries. Why? The Messiah cannot have come at a particular moment of history because his appearing can only mean the end of history. The world was not redeemed nineteen centuries ago because we still live in an unredeemed world." (The inaugural address of Prof. Paul W. Meyer delivered at Princeton Theological Seminary on February 28, 1979, quoting Martin Buber in Franz von Hammerstein's *Das Messiasproblem bei Martin Buber*.)

spiritualization of the kingdom, when the delay of the Parousia has become so obvious? And can one speak about Christ as "the end of the law" when this world still continues under the law and needs the law for the maintenance of its moral structure? Is the prophetic-apocalyptic hope for a future new act of God a betrayal or confirmation of the open-endedness of the past in Israel's self-understanding? In other words, how are the Exodus and Sinai related to the future of the Messiah? Has Paul not really cut the connection between the Exodus-Sinai event and the times of the Messiah in his teaching about the Torah, and so betrayed the inmost heart of Judaism?

Above all, to what extent has a "crucified Messiah" and his resurrection qualified the history of the world and inaugurated something radically new, that is, "the new creation" (Gal. 6:15; 2 Cor. 5:16)? The Jew asks, "Why hasn't the Messiah come, since the world is so evil?" And the Christian must face the question "If the Messiah has come, why is the world still so evil?" (cf. Emil Fackenheim).[24]* But perhaps the more troublesome question is "How can God love the world that is so evil and obdurate in its hardness of heart that it crucifies his precious love?"

For the time being, however, let us ponder the question how the confession of Jesus as the crucified Christ relates to the issue of the Christian's continuity and discontinuity with Israel's past. Paul is clear on this point. Discontinuity does not mean the obsolescence of Israel, and continuity does not mean a conflation of the Torah and Christ. Around questions like these, the dialogue must continue.

---

*"To the Christian the Jew is the stubborn fellow who in a redeemed world is still waiting for the Messiah. For the Jew the Christian is a heedless fellow who in an unredeemed world affirms that somehow or other redemption has taken place." (Reinhold Niebuhr quoting Martin Buber in "Martin Buber: 1878-1965," p. 146.)

PART FOUR

CONCLUSION

16

The Triumph of God

THE CONTINGENCY AND COHERENCE OF THE GOSPEL

I have argued throughout this study that the nature of Paul's theological thinking is characterized by two fundamental features: the contingent particularity of his hermeneutic and his sure grasp of the coherent center of the gospel. The latter focuses on Christ as the proleptic fulfillment of the triumph of God, that is, the redemption of the created order, whereas the former manifests itself in the occasional and opportune character of the letters.

What then is the interaction between "the text" of the gospel (i.e., its coherent center) and "the context" of Paul's hermeneutic, as this applies to the particularity and variety of historical situations? Paul's hermeneutic not only distills a specific core out of the variety of gospel traditions in the early church but also "incarnates" that core into the particularity of historical occasions and contexts. Thus the universal implications of the particularity of the gospel shine forth in a manifold hermeneutic, as demanded by the circumstances. It is Paul's interpretive achievement that he combines particularity and universality, or diversity and unity, in such a way that the gospel is neither simply imposed on historical occasions as a ready-made "orthodox system" nor simply fragmented into fortuitous and accidental intuitions of thought. Above all, Paul's grasp of the gospel is evident in the linguistic imagination and versatility of his interpretation of God's act in Christ and so invites reflection on his use of language. Unless Paul's "core" is viewed in its "contingent" eventfulness, it sinks away into the abstraction of a system. Yet, unless the "contingent" character of the gospel interacts with its coherent core, Paul's hermeneutic becomes opportunistic and incidental, if not chaotic. It is important to remember in this context that the movement between "coherence" and "contingency," between "theory" and "practice," does not fit the framework of a casuistic hermeneutic that applies a general principle to a particular case, as in halakic-rabbinical hermeneutics. In Paul, the coherent center is not a frozen text or a credal sacred formula but a symbolic structure that is transparent to the primordial experience of his call. It not only breaks open traditional speech but also creates a new world for the hearer. Therefore, Paul is neither a slave of the tradition nor a syncretist

351

(see Chapter 7, above). He recasts the tradition in the freedom of the Spirit, but in such a way that he does not simply amalgamate a variety of Hellenistic religious traditions or inherited myths. Although Paul as a man of his time and culture uses obviously Jewish and Hellenistic religious categories, he neither adheres simply to their traditional meaning nor adopts them uncritically. Instead, he struggles to transform the apocalyptic language in which he lived and thought, so that it can correspond to the new event in his life, God's action in Christ for the sake of the liberation of the creation. The risen Christ is present in the gospel, because the Christ-event becomes the language-event of the gospel. Paul does not have a mystical experience to which he subsequently gives linguistic expression. On the contrary, because the experience of Christ is a linguistic experience in the prophetic-apocalyptic manner, it is "kerygma," so that Christ's presence in the world is a language-event, based on the historical event of his death and resurrection. This constitutes the crucial aspect of Paul's hermeneutic, and it determines both his relation to the tradition and his preaching of the gospel into the particularity of human situations (see Chapter 7, above).

The Character of Paul's Thought

The problem between "coherence" and "contingency" cannot be construed as the relation between abstract principle and its concrete applicability. The coherent center of the gospel is only coherent in its particularity. The gospel of "Christ crucified" ceases to be gospel unless it lights up the particular world to which it is addressed (see Chapter 3, above). The new forms of speech that Paul shares with the early Christian movement are not emotive outbursts or incoherent stammerings (glosso-lalia). Paul is a man of experience, but he is a thinker as well (see Chapter 1, above). He reflects on the revelation of Christ within the heritage of his apocalyptic-religious world and aims at clarity of thought and expression for the sake of the intelligibility of his gospel. Otherwise he cannot be a successful missionary and pastor, whose word is "a word on target" and who injects sobriety and orderly thought into the enthusiasm of the early Christian apocalyptic communities that live in expectation of the imminent end of history (2 Cor. 5:13). The interaction between experience, tradi-tion, and thought is intense. Paul is not a philosopher who abstracts from experience and engages in a project of thought for the sake of thought. But neither is he a charismatic *theios aner* ("divine man") who represents the divine epiphany on earth and lives by inspiration and miraculous deeds, nor is he a traditionalist who in halakic-Pharisaic manner transmits the Torah decisions of the rabbis. Moreover, Paul is not a storyteller, as far as we can tell from the letters. A storyteller conveys experience in narrative form as the means by which experience becomes transparent and its multivalence is expressed. Paul does not write a "Gospel," and he does not use the parable as a means of communication. Although he uses and creates powerful metaphors and images, his extended metaphors usually fail (Rom. 11:17-24) or turn into allegorizations (Rom. 7:1-3; cf. Gal. 4:21-26). Paul is a man of the proposition, the argument, and the dialogue, not a man of the parable or story (cf. his use of the diatribe). Indeed, parable, story, and image are the tools of Jesus. They are materials that derive from human experience and evoke it most directly. The story unfolds; the concept defines. The story is multidimensional, the concept singular. The story opens up horizons for imaginative participation, whereas the concept delimits a specific boundary for thought. Robert Funk says it well when he discusses the nature of language in the context of Jesus' use of the parable:

> The parable brings into the foreground language as the medium of discovery over against sedimentation-language, in which significations are preestablished. . . . All language is indirect or allusive. Speech never comes to rest in itself, as though there were nothing left to be said. . . . Rather language remains unfinished because signifying is always surpassed by the signified. Just as unspoken language, primordial discourse, precedes articulation, so it follows articulation: articulation is bounded by the silent word, from which it proceeds and to which it returns.[1]

According to Alfred North Whitehead,[2] Jesus speaks in the lowest abstractions that language is capable of—if it is to be language at all and not the fact itself. "The parable stands thus at the frontier of language and mirrors without conceptualizing the Kingdom of God."[3] Indeed, the Paul of the letters is an apocalyptic thinker, not a storyteller. Concepts and arguments must be understood before they can be appropriated. Language here functions in a different way from its use in the story or parable. A story is to be understood in terms of its total impact. The response to a story is not "What is the relation between the steps in the argument?" or "What do you mean?" Nor does our response consist of questions of cognitive intellectual understanding. Rather, our response to a story is immediate—a response of yes or no to its total impact. Paul is a theologian, probably the most important—if not earliest—theologian of the primitive church. As the apostles did before him, he shifts the language of the gospel of Jesus to a level of conceptual thinking that is easily open to abstraction by subsequent generations of his readers. Although he writes reluctantly (cf. Ernst Fuchs) and views the gospel as oral-dialogical communication (cf. the *viva vox evangelii* of Luther), he is engaged in a peculiar interaction between direct and indirect address. Direct address aims at the decision of faith, whereas scriptural exegesis with its cognitive argumentation can only mean indirect address, because it requires intellectual understanding before it can be appropriated (see Chapter 7, above).

Many scholars[4] have blamed Paul for overlaying the simple gospel of Jesus with rationalistic imports from rabbinic Jewish thought. Paul is indeed a thinker, but he is not a rationalist. What demands explanation is the modality of his thought, because the immediacy and particularity of his experience of Christ not only coincides with the tradition of the church but also finds linguistic expression in the coherent center of his gospel. The immediacy of the experience shines through its conceptual formulation in the gospel and reemerges in the particularity of Paul's hermeneutic endeavor and its evocative power. Paul moves from experience to thought and back to experience. Because the gospel demands the response of faith, the clarity of its conceptual formulation serves its situational relevance. Let me repeat Rudolf Bultmann's formulation of the theological nature of Paul's work:

> Paul's basic position is not a structure of theoretical thought. It does not take the phenomena, which encounter man and man himself whom they encounter and build them into a system, a distantly perceived *kosmos* (system) as Greek science does. Rather, Paul's theological thinking only lifts the knowledge inherent in faith itself into the clarity of conscious knowing. . . . The act of faith is simultaneously an act of knowing, and correspondingly, theological knowing cannot be separated from faith . . . theological understanding has its origin in faith.[5]

This summary of Paul as a theological thinker would be adequate if (1) Bultmann's definition of faith had a more objective character, that is, if it would focus on God's "decision" for us in the death of Christ (Rom. 5:6–8) rather than on the existential decision of faith and God's "prevenient grace"; and if (2) it underscored "conscious knowing" in terms of the historical-sociological focus and contingent particularity that it serves in Paul and from which it aims to elicit the appropriate response of faith; and—above all—if (3) "conscious knowing" included the apocalyptic-cosmic coordinates of Paul's thought.

Whereas the Pauline gospel comes to speech via various hermeneutical moves in the particularity of the human context, its coherent center focuses on the triumph of God. This theme gives Paul's gospel its dynamic, explosive character and future horizon. His theology is not contemplative or mystic, for it does not reach its goal until it climaxes in the celebration of God's final glory, that is, in that order of *shalom* and "righteousness" that God inaugurated in Christ. "History is not swallowed up in eschatology" (Bultmann)[6] by the Christ-event, so that the future becomes God's eternal presence in the now. And the eschatological expectation of the end is not so modified by the Christ-event that it becomes, as it were, a far-off termination point—a continuous and permanent variable—so that the "V-Day" of God's kingdom is in fact divorced from the "D-Day" of the Christ-event (vs. Cullmann[7]). In this construal the Christ-event has effectively displaced the event of God's coming glory and has become the center of Christian theology. This not only leads to a perversion of Paul's thought but also distorts the relation of Paul to Scripture, because the Old Testament vigorously resists the spiritualization of God's promises to Israel. In other words, a purely Christocentric interpretation of Paul no longer views the Christ-event as both crucial and provisional.

THE TRIUMPH OF GOD AS THE CENTER OF PAUL'S THOUGHT

Nils Alstrup Dahl makes some pertinent remarks about "the neglected factor in New Testament theology":

> For more than a generation the majority of New Testament scholars have not only eliminated direct references to God from their works, but also neglected detailed and comprehensive investigation of statements about God. Whereas a number of major works and monographs deal with Christology, . . . it is hard to find any comprehensive or penetrating study of the theme "God in the New Testament." . . . In a remark about Paul, R. Bultmann has stated a fundamental principle of his own: "Every assertion about God is simultaneously an assertion about man and vice versa. For this reason and in this sense, Paul's theology is at the same time anthropology."[8] In practice, Bultmann has concentrated upon the first statement, represented New Testament theology as anthropology and paid little attention to the "vice versa." O. Cullmann has stated that "Early Christian theology is in reality almost exclusively Christology." It is not clear whether or not it has ever occurred to him that this statement might also be turned the other way around.[9]

In *Christ and Time*, Oscar Cullmann makes a similar move.[10] Although he emphasizes the tension between the "already" and "not yet" in the New Testament, that is, between the Christ-event and its expected consummation in the Parousia, he actually neglects the urgency of time in early Christian experience. His focus is on Christ as "the midpoint" (*Die Mitte*). However, "midpoint" is an ambivalent term, because the temporal meaning (Christ as turning point in time) fuses with the ontological meaning (Christ as the center of salvation-history). When Cullmann states, "Eschatology is not put aside, but it is dethroned, and this holds true both *chronologically* and *essentially*,"[11] he allows a Christocentric salvation-history to displace eschatology. It is interesting to observe how often the transformation of theology into Christology runs parallel to a deapocalyp-ticizing of Paul's eschatology. This hermeneutic has caused a severe misinterpretation of Paul. When futurist, cosmic eschatology is minimized or neutralized, the final triumph of God at the end of history becomes so identified with the triumph of God in the Christ-event that the theocentric apocalyptic focus of Paul is absorbed into the Christocentric triumph of Christ. When Col. 1:19, for example, states "in him [Christ] all the fulness of God was pleased to dwell, and through him to reconcile to himself all things, whether on earth or in heaven, making peace by the blood of his cross," the author claims that the future "reconciliation of all things" has been realized in Christ (cf. also Eph. 1:10). Whenever the final victory of the reign of God becomes secondary to the present reign of Christ, the result is an ecclesiology that is no longer geared to the cosmic future triumph of God over his creation. The church now becomes dangerously identified with the kingdom of Christ (Augustine) as the place where through the sacraments souls are won for Christ, or it defines its sphere as separate from the world (the doctrine of the two kingdoms), or it begins to compete with the world for imperial glory.

An apocalyptic theologian like Paul does not permit the dialectic between the gospel and the world to overrun its chronological futurist outlook, because the promise and faithfulness of God determine the christological focus of his gospel. God's act in Christ aims at the redemp-tion of history and creation. Only at that time will God's promise to Israel, which is ratified in Christ, be fulfilled for God's whole creation, and only then will the faithfulness of God be fulfilled in the new order of "righteousness," of which Christ is the proleptic manifestation. Faith for Paul, then, is not only trust, or commitment to Christ, but the ability to sustain the contradiction between present reality and future hope and to live out of that tension.

The Neglect of Apocalyptic

One reason for the misunderstanding of Paul in the patristic period is its neglect of his Jewish apocalyptic thought. "Normative" rabbinic Judaism rejected apocalyptic in the period after Jamnia (A.D. 90) and concentrated on the halakic interpretation of the Torah in order to secure its survival. Although gnosticism is in many ways akin to apocalyptic, it transformed apocalyptic-historic dualism in a vertical ontological sense in which the "Spirit above" clashes with the "flesh below." Second- and third-century Christianity lives primarily in a Hellenistic environment, where apocalypticism becomes an irrational danger to the basic structure of the church (Montanism) or is no longer compatible with the demands of the time except as a "doctrine of the last things," like purgatory, the postmortem state of the soul, eternal life, and so on. Christianity's intellectual energy now shifts from eschatology to protology. The doctrine of God, the Creator—more presupposed than argued in the New Testament (but cf. Acts 14:15-17; 17:22-29)—becomes an important issue in the church's contact with the pagan world. According to Tertullian, heretics must be addressed differently from pagans; pagans are in need of an adequate doctrine of God, whereas Christology is the primary issue in discussions with heretics.[12] Moreover, the Logos doctrine of the Apologists must clarify the ontological relation of God and Christ, that is, as Logos *endiathetos* and *prophorikos* (the "inherent" and "outgoing" Logos), and the doctrine of the incarnation attempts to answer the Greek philosophical problem of the time, how the ontological distance between Spirit and matter is to be overcome. Theologians now must struggle against the typical Greek tendency to portray Christ in docetic terms, which denies his "incarnation" and affirms his *apatheia* (the inability to suffer).

Along these lines, Paul's apocalyptic emphasis on Christ as inaugurating the triumph of God's reign at the end of time and on the resurrection of Christ as "the first in a series to come" is displaced by protological speculations about the relation of the "persons of the Trinity" and about the immutability, perfection, and unity of God, which must protect the Trinity against "tritheism." In this context the resurrection of Christ is overshadowed by his incarnation; the resurrection now becomes a closure event that seals the end of the itinerary of the incarnate Son of God. This shift of emphasis from resurrection to incarnation involves a shift away from the theocentric to the Christocentric dimension of the gospel. Whereas the subject of the resurrection is always *God* who raised Jesus from the dead as his proleptic agent of redemption, the incarnation focuses attention on the Son of God himself as God's full revelation of himself. This shift of focus parallels the idea already present in the New Testament of the "self-rising" of Jesus (cf. "he rose from the dead").

From the patristic period until recently, the theocentric and apocalyptic center of Paul's thought has been dissipated by at least two events in the history of interpretation: (1) the rejection of the apocalyptic world view and its subsequent interpretation as (a) removable husk, (b) foil for human self-understanding, or (c) a form of realized eschatology; (2) a concomitant Christocentrism that, especially since Nicaea and Chalcedon, intended to protect the sovereignty and unity of God but actually fostered a type of Christomonism, particularly within the construal of an immanent Trinity. Christ now becomes not only the exclusive point of God's "ultimate" self-disclosure but also the exclusive place where God touches the human situation. A full immanental Trinitarian hermeneutic seems to compel an interpretation of Paul's Christology in ontological rather than functional terms and thus fuses God and Christ to the detriment of the final glory of God, to which, according to Paul, Christ is subordinate and for which he lived and died.

The Promises of God and the Old Testament

The process from theology to Christology and from apocalyptic expectation to a form of Christomonism is evident in church history. In the course of its struggle with gnosticism, the church had learned to claim the God of the Old Testament as the God of creation, covenant, and redemption. However, this did not mean a rediscovery of the theocentric emphasis of the Bible and of the nature of God as the God of the hope and promise. Although the Old Testament retained its canonical status, it now became a Christian book where Christ as the Logos speaks in the theophanies and angelophanies of the Old Testament (cf. Heb. 1:5-13; 2:5-9). The Old Testament served the anti-Gnostic debate of the church and underscored the reality of the Creator and his law. However, in this process, the Old Testament was basically spiritualized and allegorized. Christ was not only the key to Scripture but also the complete fulfillment of all the Old Testament promises. In a genuine typological scheme, the history of salvation is interpreted in terms of new historical acts of God; allegorical interpretation moves in a different direction. The interpretative key to the Old Testament became the tropological and allegorical sense, whereas the "eschatological" sense referred to the afterlife, and even so it was never a central focus of interpretation. If the Old Testament did not become a "timeless" book, it was seen as the book of the promise, which was simply fulfilled in Christ. Old Testament interpretation had to serve a Christocentrism that spiritualized the eschatological hope of the Old Testament; the concern of the Old Testament for the redemption of the land and the people, along with its political earthiness, was reinterpreted spiritually, as if the promise of God applied to the heavenly "Jerusalem" above.

This spiritualization and allegorization of the hope of the Old Testament was aided by the effects of the canonization of the Old and the New Testament canon. The rabbinic-Hebrew canon had since the Jamnia council (A.D. 90) excluded both the Apocrypha and the apocalyptic Pseudepigrapha because of its distaste for apocalyptic.[13] The canonizers of the New Testament in turn excluded two types of documents: Gnostic Gospels and Apocalypses. The exclusion of the latter category was no doubt caused by the church's distrust and rejection of Montanism. The canonizers of both the Hebrew Scriptures and the New Testament shared a common distaste for apocalyptic documents, and our present Bible is in that sense more a reflection of the religious convictions of Judaism after A.D. 90 and second-century Christianity than of the religious hopes and aspirations of the period between the Testaments and within the New Testament itself. The Protestant canon of the Bible excludes the historical and hermeneutical bridge between the Testaments (even more so when the Apocrypha of the Alexandrian canon are excluded). The absence of the historical continuity between the Testaments has important theological consequences. The intertestamental period, with its emphasis on the eschatological hope of Israel and the gradual transformation of prophecy into apocalyptic, is undercut, and, moreover, the primary apocalyptic context of the gospel is ignored. The absence of the historical continuity between the Testaments, and its displacement by "the prophetic connection" (Koch[14]) in terms of which Jesus simply fulfills the prophetic kerygma of the Old Testament, facilitated this dehistorization of the Old Testament.* The Old Testament becomes a book of predictive prophecy or an allegorical prelude to the event of Christ, or it is considered to be "law" opposed to the gospel. The dehistoricizing of the Old Testament now meant that Christology was emphasized instead of apocalyptic. The personal name "Christ" was isolated from its titular meaning; thus, Jesus Christ was no longer seen as the Messiah of Israel who, according to the Christian community, is the answer to Israel's hope in the fullness of time. Likewise, the meaning of faith as sustaining the contradiction in the present between our hope in God's promise and our present experience gave way to the idea of faith as assent to the articles of faith (the *regula fidei*

---

*To be sure, the apocalyptic-eschatological sections of the Hebrew canon are a preparation for early Christian eschatological thinking (cf. Second Isaiah; Isaiah 25, 26; Zechariah 9-14; Joel, etc.). They are, however, attached to earlier prophetic books, and, because of their position in the canon, they do not show the *historical* continuity between the Testaments.

and the creed). Moreover, the relation between eternity and time preoccupied the Platonic thinking of the patristic period: Christ's eternal preexistence, his relation to God the Father, the nature of his incarnation, and so on. However, the stature of Christ as the inaugurator of the blessings of the kingdom was forgotten, because he was viewed as the complete fulfillment of all that Israel expected from its God. The expectation of a "new heaven and a new earth" where "all flesh will see the glory of the Lord" (Isa. 40:5) was simply spiritualized away. And the consequence of this was an atemporal view of both the Old Testament and the New Testament. The canonical creation of two separate Testaments was to have disastrous theological effects; their isolation from each other became reified into a dogmatic posture that ignored the traditio-historical nature of the biblical books and impoverished their inherent hermeneutical connection.[15] Moreover, construals of a "biblical theology" have practically vanished, whereas separate theologies of Old or New Testament continue to flourish.

APOCALYPTIC IN THE HISTORY OF THEOLOGY

We have seen that the "scandal" of the cross has a precise meaning for Paul (Chapters 9 and 15, above). It refers to the means by which Israel's hope is to be fulfilled—the death of the Messiah. It is not a radical reversal or denial of the content of Israel's hope, as if the crude materialistic hope of Israel was only an adumbration of its full "spiritual" meaning in Christ. However, the inflation of Christology and the spiritualization of the Old Testament took place in an atmosphere that either suppressed apocalyptic (Montanism) or reinterpreted it in a dualistic fashion. Until recently, the history of futurist eschatology in the church has been one long process of spiritualization and/or ecclesiologizing or institutionalizing, especially under the influence of Origen and Augustine (see Chapter 8, above). Future eschatology was largely pushed out of the mainstream of the church and into heretical aberrations. These heretical aberrations are the main cause for the distaste for apocalyptic in the history of the church, because traditionally, apocalypticism minimized the central significance of Christ for our redemption. Thus, although the spiritualistic interpretation of apocalyptic sought to highlight the certainty of our redemption in Christ, its impact on the history of Christian thought has been enormous, for it contributed to the overwhelmingly negative estimate of apocalyptic by biblical and theological scholarship since the Enlightenment, and especially since Wellhausen. Wellhausen glorified Israel's prophetic period over against the so-called degeneration of the postexilic period with its apocalyptic armchair speculations and spiritually inferior reflections.[16] Moreover, as we noted before (Chapter 8, above), Neoorthodoxy collapsed apocalyptic into Christology; "eschatological" displaced the "bad" term apocalyptic and simply became a hermeneutical term for "ultimate." This culminated not only in the demything of apocalyptic in the nineteenth century and the demythologizing of Strauss and Bultmann but also in the solution of realized eschatology since Dodd.[17] All these approaches share a common stance toward myth, one that contrasts the scientific world view with the world of myth and seeks to rob apocalyptic myth of its cosmic-universal intent. Although the dualistic dimension of apocalyptic myth in Paul could easily be appropriated in an existentialist or a metaphysical framework, the real stumbling blocks of the apocalyptic myth—the dimensions of imminence and cosmic expectation—were simply removed as obsolete myth.

To be sure, scholars like Richard Kabisch, Johannes Weiss, and Albert Schweitzer[18] opened up a new chapter in the investigation of apocalyptic and its importance for New Testament thought. However, Ernst Käsemann seems to be on target in his comments on the history of research:

> The history of theology in the last two generations shows that the rediscovery of primitive Christian apocalyptic in its significance for the whole New Testament, which was the merit especially of Kabisch, J. Weiss, and A. Schweitzer, was such a shock to its discoverers and their contemporaries as we can hardly imagine. J. Weiss promptly fell back upon the liberal picture of Jesus, A. Schweitzer bravely drew the consequences from his theses about the historical Jesus (untenable theses at that), and for the rest zealous attention was given to the fields of religious history, cultic piety, and mysticism. Barth's *Romans* brought "consistent eschatology" out of its shadowy existence and made it the dominant program of exposition of the New Testament in Germany, albeit in a variety of widely differing interpretations. The tendency, to be sure, is always the same, and can hardly be better described than by a quotation from P. Althaus, *Die letzten Dinge, Lehrbuch der Eschatologie* (Gütersloh, 1957), p. 272: "The world has in principle its end in the judgment and the kingdom in Christ. In this sense every time in history, and likewise history as a whole, is an end time, because both individually and as a whole it borders upon eternity and has an immediate relation to its judgment and its redemption. To this extent all the hours of history are the selfsame last hour." It is to the credit of M. Werner that in his controversial book, *Die Entstehung des christlichen Dogmas* (Tübingen and Bern, 1941), he called to mind again the unsolved problem of primitive Christian apocalyptic that had been more or less assiduously eliminated or relegated to the outermost periphery—though to be sure he

did not anywhere lead New Testament scholars beyond Schweitzer's theses.[19]

Recently, however, many scholars have drawn renewed attention to apocalyptic in Paul[20] and so have theologians like Moltmann and Pannenberg.[21] It is often unclear, however, what hermeneutical validity is given to apocalyptic as both a historical and a present theological option.

Sanders, for example, fuses apocalyptic into the mainstream of rabbinic Judaism;[22] Hans Joachim Schoeps follows Schweitzer's interpretation[23] and focuses on a "self-contained Christ-metaphysic";[24] and even Käsemann, who posits apocalyptic as "the mother of Christian theology,"[25] marks it as a post-Easter phenomenon and exempts Jesus from it, because he "proclaimed the immediate nearness of God."[26] Moltmann's theology of hope correctly stresses the eschatologic-cosmic outlook of the New Testament.[27] However, in "the Crucified God"[28] the focal concern shifts to the event of the cross as God's basic self-disclosure, and its precise relation to the eschatological hope remains unclear. The issue, then, is not whether attention is given to apocalyptic in Paul but how it is assessed in its significance not only for his time and thought but as a viable option for our time and thought.

THE TRIUMPH OF GOD

Paul is an apocalyptic theologian with a theocentric outlook. The Christ-event is the turning point in time that announces the end of time. Indeed, Christ has become "Lord" since his exaltation and is now God's appointed world ruler who bears the divine name (Phil. 2:10), but—as Paul adds—"to the *glory* of God the Father." All that Christ does is for the sake of the final eschatological glory of God, so that people already can "glorify the God and Father of our Lord Jesus Christ" (Rom. 15:6; cf. v. 9). Paul emphasizes that it is *God* "who calls you into his own kingdom and glory" (1 Thess. 2:12); that our salvation depends on the God who is faithful unto the end (1 Cor. 1:7–9; cf. 1 Thess. 5:24; 2 Cor. 1:18); and that "when all things are subjected to him, then the Son himself will also be subjected to him who put all things under him, that God may be everything to everyone" (1 Cor. 15:28).

"Glory" (*doxa*) means overwhelmingly the "glory of God," because Paul only rarely speaks about the "glory of the Lord" (= Christ) (*doxa tou kuriou*, 1 Cor. 2:8; 2 Cor. 3:8?) or the "glory of Christ" (2 Cor. 8:23, cf. "the glory of the gospel of Christ" [2 Cor. 4:4]). In every instance, the "glory of Christ" or "the glory of the gospel" is the anticipation of the final glory of God. Paul, to be sure, has an incipient rudimentary

Trinitarian conception of God (1 Cor. 12:1-11; 2 Cor. 13:13), but Christ remains the subordinate Son, the agent of God's redemptive purpose, so that his Christology is basically functional and not metaphysical (Cullmann).[29] The climax of the history of salvation is not the resurrection of Christ and his present glory (cf. John) but the impending glory of God, on behalf of whom Christ exercises his function as "Lord" (Phil. 2:11) and as intercessor (Rom. 8:31-34). Both the Spirit (Rom. 8:26) and Christ (8:34) are the executors of God's purpose and "intercede" for us to hasten the final state of glory. Paul's apocalyptic theocentrism, then, is not to be contrasted with his Christocentric thinking, for the final hour of the glory of Christ and his Parousia will coincide with the glory of God, that is, with the actualization of the redemption of God's created order in his kingdom.

Romans 8 and the Triumph of God

Romans 8:17-39 is Paul's most impressive confession of the triumph of God. Although we may wonder whether "the one who loved us" (v. 37) is Christ (v. 35) or God (v. 39), the flow of the text suggests that God's love is documented in the love of Christ. We are "more than victors" because no power "can separate us from the love of God in Christ Jesus our Lord" (v. 39). Romans 8:35-39 explicates and climaxes the theme of the love of God that Paul had annunciated in Rom. 5:5, 8, where that love is not only the source of the death of Christ for us, "while we were yet enemies" (5:8), but also dwells in our hearts through the Spirit (5:5). This theme does not emerge again in Romans 5-8 until Rom. 8:31-39, where the text "He who did not spare his own Son but gave him up for us all" (Rom. 8:32a) picks up and reemphasizes Paul's earlier assertion, "God shows his love for us in that while we were yet sinners Christ died for us" (Rom. 5:8). The continuation of Rom. 8:32a in verse 32b ("will he not also freely give us all things [ta panta] together with him?"; trans. mine) picks up and reinterprets the sequence of Rom. 5:8 in verse 9: "Much more shall we be saved by him from the wrath of God."

God's love in Christ opens the horizon of the future consummation: "all things" (Rom. 8:32b) refers to the final defeat of the powers (Rom. 8:38-39) and our total communion with God in the new age. Because God's love in the death of Christ is for us "all" (8:32a), not only "all the blessings" of the new age will be ours but also all God's world will participate in those blessings (8:32b; cf. vv. 18, 28).

The drama of the triumph of God is narrated in Rom. 8:17-30 in a way that demonstrates profoundly how Christ both reaffirms and modifies the apocalyptic intensity of the gospel. The apocalyptic theme of the sufferings of the present age in contrast to the coming glory encompasses the whole creation (v. 18); because of man's fall, the creation sighs and groans for its redemption, and that sighing is taken up and reinforced by the Christian church. The Spirit—in concert with the groaning of the unredeemed creation—inspires the groaning of the Christian for the redemption of the body. The triumphant victory of the Spirit—located *within* the church in Rom. 8:1–16—is no longer heard here, because the Spirit itself compels the Christian to look outside the windows of the church into the created world, a world subject to "bondage to decay" (v. 21). The Christian is reminded that he is still an integral part of the unredeemed creation and will be so until the day of God's final deliverance (vv. 21, 23). The longing for the redemption of the body (v. 23) signifies that "the mortal body" of the Christian, along with the creation itself, is subject to the power of death (v. 20). Because the church is not an elite body, separated from a doomed world, but a community placed in the midst of the cosmic community of creation, its task is not merely to win souls but to bear the burdens of a creation, to which it not only belongs but to which it also must bear witness. The sufferings of this world are not a dark foil for the glory of Christian life in separation from the world but a mark of Christian solidarity with the world. The imminent and victorious character of the Spirit in Rom. 8:1–16 seems strangely hushed and contradicted by the tone of verses 17–27. Suddenly we hear not only about suffering, groaning, and perseverance (vv. 17–25), but also about the Spirit as the transcendent agent who counters our weakness and intercedes for us in words we do not even understand because we are at a loss to pray as we ought. Our present status as adopted sons in verse 15—which stimulates our cry "Abba! Father!"—becomes in verse 23 a future hope because of the state of our unredeemed bodies. It seems that the victory and joy of the Spirit are suddenly suspended. As Christians, we do not come to perfection without the unredeemed creation, to which our "bodies" bear witness (v. 23).

The basic shift from present triumph to future hope occurs in Rom. 8:17b: "Heirs of God and fellow heirs with Christ, provided we suffer with him in order that we may also be glorified with him." God's triumph will take place, notwithstanding our weakness and the sufferings of the world (vv. 18–27). However, in the light of God's coming triumph, the world's sufferings become for us a new task. The phrase "provided we suffer with him" points to our redemptive suffering in—and for—the world. Thus, God's triumph occurs *notwithstanding* our weakness and suffering (vv. 18, 26–27) but also *in the midst of* and *because of* our weakness and suffering, for the "sufferings of Christ" have a redemptive power that furthers the coming glory of God.

Before Paul moves to his celebration of the cosmic triumph of God's love (Rom. 8:31–39), he writes a catena (vv. 29–30) that sums up the ground and eschatological goal of salvation-history. Ephesians 1:1–6 is comparable to this: "Blessed be the God and Father of our Lord Jesus Christ, who has blessed us in Christ, even as he chose us in him before the foundation of the world. . . . He destined us in love to be his sons through Jesus Christ, according to the purpose of his will, to the praise of his glorious grace which he freely bestowed on us in the Beloved." But whereas Ephesians moves from Christ as the completed eschatological climax of God's purpose to our protological predestination, Paul grounds God's eternal purpose and plan in the movement of salvation-history from Christ to God's apocalyptic triumph: "Those whom he foreknew he also predestined to be conformed to the image of his Son, in order that he might be the first-born among many brethren" (Rom. 8:29; cf. 1 Cor. 15:49). The context of the catena is decisive for its interpretation: "We know that *all things* work for *good* to those who love God" (v. 28; trans. mine). This statement sums up and deepens the theme of present suffering and future glory (vv. 17–30), because in the light of the coming triumph of God (the "good"; v. 28), the future glory will wipe out the contradictions of the present. Paul even claims more than that. The present with its suffering (Rom. 8:18–27) is encompassed by God's faithfulness and sovereign purpose. "All things work for good" because all things are moving— however hidden—to God's final triumph. Thus, for the eyes of faith "all things" are encompassed by God's eternal purpose that stretches from "foreknowledge" (v. 29) to "glorification," because "those whom he justified he also glorified" (v. 30). The God of the End, who has acted in Christ, discloses for Paul the God of the Beginning. Romans 8:28–30 celebrates God's sovereignty, which is manifest in our predestination to glory through Christ's resurrection, "the first-born among many brethren" (v. 29). Christology here serves theology: it adumbrates God's majestic reign over our world. Just because the Christian knows he is anchored in that cosmic sovereignty, he may view all suffering as a "suffering with Christ" (Rom. 8:17b), because suffering is not a tragic flaw in God's creation but in some sense serves a purpose in God's triumphal plan. The claim that all things work for good for those who love God (v. 28) must be understood in its pregnant apocalyptic sense: even all hostile powers are within God's final control, and thus they must serve his ultimate purpose. The predestination language in Rom. 8:29-30 is not philosophical speculation about "beginnings," or a theory of speculative theodicy; instead, it functions as a retrospective grounding of the apocalyptic glory of God. The End, announced in Christ, manifests the eternal faithfulness of the God of the Beginning. Because of his eschatological triumph in Christ, he is indeed the God who rules history from the beginning and demands our absolute trust.

The emphasis on "all things" (panta, Rom. 8:28), "all" (ta panta, Rom. 8:33), "all of us" (hyper hymōn pantōn, Rom. 8:32), "in all these things" (en toutois pasin, Rom. 8:37; cf. "anything else" [oute tis ktisis hetera], Rom. 8:39) draws our attention in this section. It expresses the idea that the theme of the glory of God in Rom. 8:17-30 is consonant with Paul's "universalist motif," because all things work together for good (v. 28) and because "all things" will be ours in God's final glory. Therefore, we are more than victors in the midst of "all" the world's sufferings and tribulations (vv. 18-23).

The profundity of Paul's apocalyptic theology unfolds itself here. Our life and all of creation rest securely in the hand of the God who through the tears of suffering will provide the joy of our glory and so bless the seeming futility and pain of the created order. Paul's apocalyptic intensity is not akin to a dispensational speculation or a chronical reckoning that the delay of the Parousia has put to rest once for all. A hermeneutic of realized eschatology or "salvation-history" may well be our prevalent way of overcoming the embarrassment of Paul's apocalyptic.[30] However, the apocalyptic hope for Paul is an existential reality that is part and parcel of Christian life, inasmuch as it sighs and hopes for the resolution of death, suffering, and evil in the world. The intensity of the hope is all the greater not only because the Christian already lives in the dawning of God's coming reign but also because, since the coming of Christ and his victorious resurrection, suffering becomes all the more intolerable. In Paul, God's triumph is not located in the doctrine of creation, because creation is not the place where the questions of theodicy and the origin of evil in the created order are solved. God's triumph is centered not protologically but eschatologically, because the end will manifest the glorious majesty of God in the defeat of evil and death in the kingdom of God, when "the glory of the Lord shall be revealed and all flesh shall see it together" (Isa. 40:5). Only in retrospect can the Christian confess that his election and the world's history, notwithstanding its tragedies, are located in God's plan of salvation. The Christ-event—as the manifestation of God's will to save—is not to be isolated from the beginning and end of universal history. For only at the end will the purpose of God in the beginning be realized; beginning and end manifest the encompassing nature of God's plan as this has been unfolded in Christ, that is, the salvation of the created order. Thus, the delay of the Parousia cannot merely be an intellectual stumbling block that demands rational accommodations. Neither a collapsing of the tension between present and future in realized eschatology, nor a diffusing of it by postponing the end to an indefinite future, accomplishes the hermeneutical task. Indeed, the existential reality of our "mortal bodies" reminds us daily of the beckoning of the apocalyptic hour, with its blessing of righteousness for all of creation. As "mortal bodies" we not only live in solidarity with an unredeemed creation, but we are also "Christ-bearers" in our bodies, embodying in our ethical activity and life-style the *promise* of God in Christ for the future liberation of creation "from its bondage to decay" (Rom. 8:21). And our embodiment must be cruciform, because our way *from* suffering to glory entails in Christ as well a glorying *in* suffering.

The imminent triumph of God is defined by the death and resurrection of Christ and constitutes the basic coherence of the Pauline gospel in the midst of the contingent particularity of the needs of his churches.

Indeed, the Confession of 1967 states it well:

> With an urgency born of this hope the church applies itself to present tasks and strives for a better world. It does not identify limited progress with the Kingdom of God on earth, nor does it despair in the face of disappointment and defeat. In steadfast hope the church looks beyond all partial achievement to the final triumph of God.[31]

Abbreviations

IDB	*Interpreter's Dictionary of the Bible*, edited by G. A. Buttrick.
RGG	*Religion in Geschichte und Gegenwart*, 3d ed., edited by Kurt Galling et al.
TDNT	*Theological Dictionary of the New Testament*, edited by G. Kittel and G. Friedrich.
WA	*D. Martin Luthers Werke.* Kritische Gesamtausgabe (Weimar, 1883–).
WA, DB	*D. Martin Luthers Werke.* Deutsche Bibel (Weimar, 1906–61).

Notes

CHAPTER 1—Paul: Apostle to the Gentiles

1. Ignatius, "To the Romans (4:1–3)," in *The Apostolic Fathers* 1:231.

2. Rudolf Karl Bultmann, "Ignatius und Paulus," in *Studia Paulina in honorem Johannes de Zwaan*, pp. 37–51.

3. Günter Klein, "Der Abfassungszweck des Römerbriefes," in *Rekonstruktion und Interpretation*, pp. 129–44.

4. The second edition of the RSV New Testament (1971) erroneously translates *ethnē* as "nations" rather than "Gentiles." But cf. the first edition of the RSV (1946): "among all the Gentiles."

5. But cf. Birger Gerhardsson, *Memory and Manuscript.*

6. The common term for a Christian is not yet *christianos* (Acts 11:26; 26:28; 1 Pet. 4:16; Ignatius *Eph.* 11:2, etc.).

7. Heinrich Weinel, *Biblische Theologie des Neuen Testaments;* cf. idem, *Die Wirkungen des Geistes und der Geister.* Also, Paul Wernle, *Der Christ und die Sünde bei Paulus.*

8. Friedrich Nietzsche, "The Antichrist," in *The Complete Works,* 16:178–87; cf. idem, "The First Christian," in *The Dawn of Day,* pp. 56–61.

9. Cf. its documentation in William James's classic, *The Varieties of Religious Experience.*

10. Gustav Adolf Deissmann, *Paul,* pp. 4–26.

11. Cf. Heinrich Julius Holtzmann, *Lehrbuch der neutestamentlichen Theologie,* 2:164; Weinel, *Biblische Theologie,* p. 257.

12. William Wrede, *Paul,* p. 156; Martin Brückner, *Die Entstehung der paulinischen Christologie,* pp. 29, 32; Paul Wernle, *Die Anfänge unserer Religion,* pp. 27, 35, 81.

13. Deissmann, *Paul,* pp. 4–26.

14. Wrede, *Paul,* pp. 155–82.

15. Cf. the use of this image by Dwight L. Moody, "The Return of Our Lord (1877)," in *American Evangelicals, 1800–1900,* p. 185: "I look on this world as a wrecked vessel. God has given me a lifeboat, and said to me, 'Moody, save all you can.' God will come in judgment and burn up this world, but the children of God don't belong to this world; they are in it, but not of it, like a ship in the water—Christ will save His Church, but He will save them finally by taking them out of the world."

16. Rudolf Karl Bultmann, *Theology of the New Testament,* 1:190.

17. Adolf von Schlatter, *Die Theologie des Neuen Testaments und die Dogmatik,* pp. 7–82.

CHAPTER 2—The Character of Paul's Thought

1. Søren Aabye Kierkegaard, "Of the Difference between a Genius and an Apostle," in *The Present Age*, pp. 160ff.

2. Ferdinand Christian Baur, *Paul, the Apostle*. Cf. esp. Ferdinand Christian Baur, "Die Christuspartei in der korinthischen Gemeinde."

3. Richard Reitzenstein, *Die hellenistischen Mysterienreligionen*, p. 86.

4. Wilhelm Heitmüller, *Taufe und Abendmahl*, pp. 9–10, 14ff.; Wilhelm Bousset, *Kyrios Christos*, pp. 104–54.

5. Heinrich Weinel, *Biblische Theologie;* Gustav Adolf Deissmann, *Paul.*

6. Heinrich Julius Holtzmann, *Lehrbuch der neutestamentlichen Theologie* 2:150; Otto Pfleiderer, *Paulinism*, p. 156; William Wrede, *Paul*, pp. 123ff.; cf. also Paul Wernle, *Die Anfänge unserer Religion*, pp. 209ff.

7. Albert Schweitzer, *The Mysticism of Paul*, pp. 205–26, esp. p. 225.

8. Rudolf Karl Bultmann, *Theology of the New Testament*, 1:190.

9. Ibid., p. 191.

10. Leander E. Keck, *Paul and His Letters*, p. 65; Ed Parish Sanders, *Paul and Palestinian Judaism*, pp. 123, 518; Denys Edward Hugh Whiteley, *The Theology of St. Paul*, pp. xiv, 45;

11. Heinz-Dietrich Wendland, *Die Mitte der paulinischen Botschaft;* Werner Georg Kümmel, *Die Theologie des Neuen Testaments*, p. 126; Ernst Käsemann, " 'The Righteousness of God,' " in *New Testament Questions of Today.*

12. Schweitzer, *Mysticism of Paul*; William David Davies, *Paul and Rabbinic Judaism*, pp. 177, 86–110.

13. Sanders, *Paul and Palestinian Judaism*, pp. 506–8.

14. Frederick Fyvie Bruce, *Paul, Apostle of the Heart*, p. 424.

15. Nils Alstrup Dahl, "Review of Sanders, *Paul and Palestinian Judaism,*" p. 157.

16. Deissmann, *Paul*, p. 6.

17. Ernst Käsemann, "The Spirit and the Letter," in *Perspectives on Paul*, p. 138.

18. E.g., Hans Leisegang, *Der Apostel Paulus als Denker;* Johannes Weiss, *Das Urchristentum*, pp. 329ff. Cf. also Johannes Weiss, "Beiträge zur paulinischen Rhetorik," in *Theologische Studien . . . Bernhard Weiss*, pp. 190ff.; Schweitzer, *Mysticism of Paul;* Bultmann, *Theology of the New Testament*, 1:190; Hans Joachim Schoeps, *Paul;* Ernst Käsemann, "On Paul's Anthropology," in *Perspectives on Paul*, pp. 1–31; idem, "The Spirit and the Letter"; Sanders, *Paul and Palestinian Judaism*, pp. 431ff.

19. E.g., Schweitzer, *Mysticism of Paul;* Schoeps, *Paul;* Johannes Munck, *Paul and the Salvation of Mankind;* Kümmel, *Die Theologie des Neuen Testaments*, pp. 126ff.; Joseph Augustine Fitzmyer, *Pauline Theology*, pp. 30ff.; Ernst Käsemann, "On the Subject of Primitive Christian Apocalyptic," in *New Testament Questions of Today;* Peter Stuhlmacher, *Gerechtigkeit Gottes;* Sanders, *Paul and Palestinian Judaism*, pp. 8, 515.

20. Bultmann, *Theology of the New Testament*, pp. 185–352.

21. Hans Georg Conzelmann, "On the Analysis of the Confessional Formula in I Corinthians 15:3–5."

22. Charles Harold Dodd, *New Testament Studies*, pp. 67–128; cf. also John Arthur Thomas Robinson, *The Body*; Charles Henry Buck and Greer Taylor, *Saint Paul*; James D. G. Dunn, *Unity and Diversity in the New Testament*, pp. 25ff.

23. Cf. Käsemann, "On the Subject of Primitive Christian Apocalyptic." Cf. also Peter Stuhlmacher, *Gerechtigkeit Gottes*; idem, "Erwägungen zum Problem von Gegenwart und Zukunft."

24. Käsemann, "The Spirit and the Letter," p. 164.

25. Rudolf Karl Bultmann, "New Testament and Mythology," in *Kerygma and Myth*.

CHAPTER 3—Contingency and Coherence in Paul's Letters

1. Robert Walter Funk, "The Apostolic Parousia," in *Christian History and Interpretation*, pp. 263–66.

2. Hans Dieter Betz, "The Literary Composition and Function of . . . Galatians."

3. Klaus Berger, "Apostelbrief und apostolische Rede."

4. Cited in Amos Niven Wilder, *Early Christian Rhetoric*, p. 14.

5. Anders Nygren, *Commentary on Romans*, pp. 6ff.

6. Thomas Walter Manson, "St. Paul's Letter to the Romans—and Others"; John Knox, "A Note on the Text of Romans."

7. Edgar Johnson Goodspeed, *An Introduction to the New Testament*, pp. 210ff.; John Knox, *Philemon among the Letters of Paul*.

8. Albertus Frederik Johannes Klijn, *Inleiding tot het Nieuwe Testament*, p. 121.

9. Nils Alstrup Dahl, "The Particularity of the Pauline Epistles," in *Neotestamentica et Patristica*.

10. Ibid.

11. Ferdinand Christian Baur, *Paul, the Apostle*.

12. Gustav Adolf Deissmann, *Paul*, pp. 4–26.

13. John Knox, *Chapters in a Life of Paul*, p. 92.

14. Charles Harold Dodd, *The Apostolic Preaching and Its Developments*, pp. 17ff.

15. Eva Aleith, *Paulusverständnis*, pp. 119–20.

16. Cf. Adolf von Harnack, *History of Dogma*, 1:89.

17. Baur, *Paul, the Apostle*.

18. William Wrede, *Paul*, pp. 123ff.

19. Albert Schweitzer, *The Mysticism of Paul*, pp. 205–26.

20. Heinrich Weinel, *Die Wirkungen des Geistes und der Geister*; Deissmann, *Paul*; Johannes Schneider, *Die Passionsmystik des Paulus*.

21. Charles Harold Dodd, *The Meaning of Paul for Today*; cf. also, e.g., John Arthur Thomas Robinson, *Jesus and His Coming*; Charles Henry Buck and Greer Taylor, *Saint Paul*; James D. G. Dunn, *Unity and Diversity in the New Testament*.

22. Cf. U. von Wilamowitz-Moellendorff: "He writes his letters as a substitute for his personal activity." Cited by Frederick Fyvie Bruce in *Paul, Apostle of the Heart Set Free*, p. 16.

23. Cf., e.g., Ernst Käsemann in *An die Römer:* Romans is viewed essentially as "eine Summe paulinischer Theologie" (p. 372). The letter situation is acknowledged, but it does not seem to have a bearing on the interpretation. Cf. Walter Schmithal's criticism of Käsemann in *Der Römerbrief als historisches Problem*, p. 50, n. 140.

24. Leander E. Keck, *Paul and His Letters*, p. 17.

25. Rudolf Karl Bultmann, *Theology of the New Testament*, esp. "New Testament and Mythology," p. 13.

CHAPTER 4—Contextual Interpretation I

1. For a classic example, see Karl Barth, *Resurrection of the Dead,* pp. 101ff.

2. Rudolf Karl Bultmann, *Theology of the New Testament*; Hans Georg Conzelmann, *An Outline of the Theology of the New Testament*; Oscar Cullmann, *Christology of the New Testament*.

3. Günther Bornkamm, *Paul*; Herman Nicolaas Ridderbos, *Paulus*.

4. James Barr, *The Semantics of Biblical Language*, p. 233.

5. Bornkamm, *Paul*, pp. vii–viii.

6. Ibid., p. 117.

7. Ibid., p. 118.

8. Ibid.

9. Johannes Munck, *Paul and the Salvation of Mankind*.

10. Commentaries used throughout this section include: Heinrich Schlier, *Der Brief an die Galater*; Ernest DeWitt Burton, *A Critical and Exegetical Commentary on Galatians*; Franz Mussner, *Der Galaterbrief*; John Bligh, *Galatians*; Herman Nicholaas Ridderbos, *The Epistle of Paul to the Churches of Galatia*.

11. Schlier, *Der Brief an die Galater*, p. 148; cf. also on this issue Philipp Vielhauer, *Geschichte der urchristlichen Literatur*, pp. vii, 106.

12. The status of Peter as Cephas may have gained increasing importance in the early church; Matthew certainly argues this way (Matt. 16:16) and we can infer from Gal. 2:9 that in the early church James, Cephas, and John occupied authoritative roles as eschatological "pillars."

13. It is difficult to find any natural and obvious breaks in the argument from Gal. 2:11 until Gal. 5:26. For a full discussion see Mussner, *Der Galaterbrief*. In Gal. 2:15 Paul seems to address Peter in Antioch, yet moves clearly into the Galatian situation. Galatians 3:1 would seem a clear break, yet it functions as an explication for Gal. 2:19–21. Again, Gal. 4:1 and 5:1 seem to be breaks, but 4:1 is an explicit continuation of 3:15–29 ("I mean that"), whereas 5:1 is the climax of the scriptural proof of 4:21–31 with its theme of freedom. Galatians 4:12–20, with its direct personal appeal to the Galatians, seems the most obvious interruption.

14. Paul wants *ethnē* (Gentiles) and thus cites Gen. 18:18 and not Gen. 12:3 (*pasai hai phylai*) (vs. Mussner, *Der Galaterbrief*).

15. Cf. also Gal. 4:5 ("adoption as sons"), Gal. 4:6 ("sons"), Gal. 4:7 ("heir").

16. Hans Hübner, "Das ganze und das eine Gesetz"; cf. also Hans Hübner, *Das Gesetz bei Paulus*.

17. The Septuagint radicalizes the Masoretic text: "Cursed be he who does not confirm the words of this law by doing them" (Deut. 27:26).

18. *Pro* Hans Hübner, "Gal. 3:10 und die Herkunft des Paulus"; *contra* Joachim Jeremias, "Paulus als Hillelit," in *Neotestamentica et Semitica*.

19. Cf. the issue of "the fulfillment of the law" in Gal. 5:14, which will be discussed in Chapter 6, below.

20. Cf., e.g., Schlier, *Der Brief an die Galater*, pp. 109-20; John William Drane, *Paul, Libertine or Legalist?* p. 112.

21. But cf. "becoming a curse for us" (Gal. 3:13).

22. "Faith" does not occur in Gal. 3:15-21.

23. See Luther, "Lectures on Galatians," in *Luther's Works* 26:346.

24. A "third use" of the law is hardly found in Galatians, notwithstanding Gal. 5:14, 23b.

25. Richard Reitzenstein, *Die hellenistischen Mysterien-religionen*, p. 86.

CHAPTER 5—Contextual Interpretation II

1. Philipp Melanchthon, "Römerbrief-Kommentar, 1532," in *Melanchthons Werke in Auswahl* 5.

2. Cf. Walter Schmithals (*Der Römerbrief als historisches Problem*, p. 8): "Bezeichnend ist die Tatsache dass H. J. Holtzmann nie eine Vorlesung über den Römerbrief gehalten hat, weil er ihn . . . zwar als biblisch-theologische Quelle werten, aber trotz fünfzig Jahre intensiver Forschung als *Brief*, also *historisch* nicht verstehen konnte."

3. Ferdinand Christian Baur, *Paul, the Apostle*.

4. Cf. Harry Gamble, *The Textual History of the Letter to the Romans*, for an extensive discussion.

5. George La Piana, "Foreign Groups in Rome"; Wolfgang Wiefel, "The Jewish Community in Ancient Rome," in *The Romans Debate*.

6. Cf. Prisca and Aquila (Rom. 16:3), who after their expulsion from Rome went to Corinth (Acts 18:1-2) and from there to Ephesus (1 Cor. 16:19; cf. Acts 18:26); cf. Epaenetus, "the first convert in Asia for Christ" (Rom. 16:5).

7. E.g., Günther Harder, "Der konkrete Anlass des Römerbriefes"; Herbert Preisker, "Das historische Problem des Römerbriefes"; Hans Wilhelm Schmidt, *Der Brief des Paulus an die Römer*.

8. Thomas Walter Manson, "St. Paul's Letter to the Romans—and Others."

9. John Knox, "A Note on the Text of Romans," p. 191.

10. Cf. the discussion of Werner Georg Kümmel, *Introduction to the New Testament*, pp. 312ff.

11. Cf., e.g., Günther Bornkamm, "The Letter to the Romans as Paul's Last Will and Testament."

12. Cf. also Ed Parish Sanders, *Paul and Palestinian Judaism*, p. 487.

13. William G. Doty, *Letters in Primitive Christianity*, p. 79.

14. Ibid.

15. Schmithals, *Der Römerbrief als historisches Problem*, p. 210; Junji Kinoshita, "Romans—Two Writings Combined."

16. Cf. Schmithals, *Der Römerbrief als historisches Problem*, p. 20.

17. Rudolf Karl Bultmann, *Theology of the New Testament*, 2:132.

18. Francis Wright Beare, *St. Paul and His Letters*, p. 97.

19. Charles Harold Dodd, *The Epistle of Paul to the Romans*, p. 148.

20. Ibid., p. 149.

21. William Sanday and Arthur Cayley Headlam, *A Critical and Exegetical Commentary on Romans*, p. 225.

22. In *Paul, the Apostle*, Baur opened the way for such an approach in considering Romans 9–11 as "the germ and center of the whole, from which the other parts sprang." His faulty reconstruction of the problem in Rome, as if Jewish Christians are the *main* addressees in Romans, should not have blinded his opponents to the correctness of his historical method.

23. Karl Barth, *Der Römerbrief*, pp. 327ff.

24. E.g., Charles Kingsley Barrett (*A Commentary on Romans*), Karl Ludwig Schmidt (*Die Judenfrage im Lichte der Kapitel 9–11 des Römerbriefs*), Ernst Gaugler (*Der Römerbrief*), Otto Michel (*Der Brief an die Römer*), and Ernst Käsemann (*An die Römer*).

25. Barth, *Der Römerbrief*, p. 346.

26. Hans Lietzmann, *The Beginnings of the Christian Church*, pp. 108–10.

27. Cf. already Baur, *Paul, the Apostle*.

28. Barth, *Der Römerbrief*.

29. Anders Nygren, *Commentary on Romans*.

30. Karl Barth, "Vorrede zur ersten Auflage," in *Der Römerbrief*, p. 5. Translation mine.

31. Nygren, *Commentary on Romans*, pp. 6ff.

32. Ibid., p. 7.

33. Ibid., Table of Contents.

34. Cf. Egon Brandenburger, *Adam und Christus*, pp. 264–66.

35. Niklaus Gäumann (*Taufe und Ethik*, p. 23) follows the scheme closely; both Günther Bornkamm (*Paul*, p. 108) and Willi Marxsen (*Introduction to the New Testament*, p. 98) approve of it. Similar structural procedures have been advocated by Stanislaus Lyonnet ("Note sur le plan de l'Épître aux Romains"). André Feuillet ("Le plan salvifique de Dieu d'après l'Épître aux Romains"). Jacques Jean Dupont ("Le problème de la structure littéraire de l'Épître aux Romains"), and Karl Prümm ("Zur Struktur des Römerbriefes").

36. Feuillet, "Le plan salvifique de Dieu."

37. Ulrich Luz, "Zum Aufbau von Röm. 1–8," p. 163.

38. Melanchthon, "Römerbrief-Kommentar, 1532."

39. Martin Luther, "eyn lustigen aussbruch und spaciergang," "Vorrede auf die Epistel S. Pauli an die Römer," *WA, DB* 7; but cf. also on Romans 5: "Kaum gibt es in der ganzen Schrift einen Text, der diesem Kapitel gleichkommt" (*WA* 56:49, 18).

40. Paul Wernle, *Der Christ und die Sünde bei Paulus*; Otto Pfleiderer, *Das Urchristentum*; William Wrede, *Paul*, pp. 123ff.; Albert Schweitzer, *The Mysticism of Paul*, pp. 205–26.

41. Hermann Lüdemann, *Die Anthropologie des Apostels Paulus*, pp. 165, 208.

42. Cf. Sanders's essential agreement with Schweitzer (*Paul and Palestinian Judaism*, p. 486; cf. p. 438).

43. A caesura between Rom. 4:25 and Rom. 5:1 is advocated by, e.g., Dodd (*Epistle to the Romans*), Michel (*Der Brief an die Römer*), Hans Lietzmann (*An die Römer*), Nygren (*Commentary on Romans*), Schmidt (*Der Brief des Paulus an die Römer*), Günter Klein ("Der Abfassungszweck des Römerbriefes," in *Rekonstruktion und Interpretation*), Käsemann (*An die Römer*), Lyonnet ("Note sur le plan de l'Épître aux Romains"), Dupont ("Le problème de la structure littéraire"), Nils Alstrup Dahl ("Two Notes on Romans 5"), and Gäumann (*Taufe und Ethik*); a caesura between Rom. 5:11 and Rom. 5:12 by Theodor Zahn (*Der Brief des Paulus an die Römer*), Franz J. Leenhardt (*L'Épître de Saint Paul aux Romains*), Feuillet ("Le plan salvifique de Dieu"); between Rom. 5:21 and Rom. 6:1 by Bernhard Weiss (*Kritisch-exegetisches Handbuch über den Brief des Paulus an die Römer*), Ernst Kühl (*Der Brief des Paulus an die Römer*), Sanday and Headlam (*Critical and Exegetical Commentary on Romans*), Adolf von Schlatter (*Gottes Gerechtigkeit*), Paul Althaus (*Der Brief an die Römer*), Marie-Joseph Lagrange (*Saint Paul: Épître aux Romains*), Gaugler (*Der Römerbrief*), William Manson ("Notes on the Argument of Romans [ch. 1–8]," in *New Testament Essays*), Pierre Bonnard ("Où en est l'interprétation de l'épître aux Romains"), and Herman Nicolaas Ridderbos (*Aan de Romeinen*); on this issue see esp. Michael Wolter, *Rechtfertigung und zukünftiges Heil*, pp. 205ff.

44. But cf. Luz, "Zum Aufbau von Röm 1–8"; Joachim Jeremias, "Zur Gedankenführung in den paulinischen Briefen," in *Studia Paulina in honorem Johannes de Zwaan*; Gerhard Friedrich, "Römerbrief," in *RGG* 5; Dahl, "Two Notes on Romans 5."

45. Wilhelm Lütgert, *Der Römerbrief als historisches Problem*.

46. James Hardy Ropes, "The Epistle to the Romans and Jewish Christianity," in *Studies in Early Christianity*.

47. Franz J. Leenhardt, *L'Épître de Saint Paul aux Romains*.

48. Vincent Offley Eareckson in a recent Ph.D. dissertation ("The Glory to Be Revealed Hereafter") develops this line of reasoning and suggests "a chiastic argument for the demonstration of salvation to the Jew first and also to the Gentile (Rom. 1:16)" (p. 31).

Thesis: Rom. 1:16–17

Preparation	Demonstration
Gentile under sin (Rom. 1:18–32)	Jew under salvation (Rom. 3:21– 5:11)
General transition in terms of man (Rom. 2:1–16)	General transition in terms of Adam (Rom. 5:12–21)
Jew under sin (Rom. 2:17—3:8)	Gentile under salvation (Rom. 6:1– 8:27)
Summation (Rom. 3:9)	Summation (Rom. 8:28–30)
Concluding catena (Rom. 3:10–20)	Concluding catena (Rom. 8:31–39)

49. Cf. Schweitzer's argument of a repetition of Romans 1–5 in Romans 6–8 with a more adequate terminology (*Mysticism of Paul*, pp. 225ff.).

50. There has recently been progress toward a more realistic and occasional understanding of Romans. (1) Johannes Munck (*Christus und Israel*) and Bent Wenzel Noack ("Current and Backwater in the Epistle to the Romans") pointed to Romans 9–11 as an integral part of the letter. (2) The Jew in Romans 9–11 is not the *homo religiosus* in general (Bornkamm, *Paul*, p. 95) but represents the first-century Judaism that Paul must cope with in his forthcoming visit to Jerusalem (M. Jack Suggs, "'The Word Is Near You,'" in *Christian History and Interpretation*, p. 297). (3) Ernst Fuchs (*Hermeneutik*), Marxsen (*Introduction to the New Testament*), Bornkamm ("Romans as Paul's Last Will and Testament"), Jacob Jervell ("Der Brief nach Jerusalem"), Hans Werner Bartsch ("Die historische Situation des Römerbriefes"), and Dieter Georgi (*Die Geschichte der Kollekte*) direct fresh attention to the occasional and situational elements of Romans. Romans must be understood in the framework of Paul's impending visit to Jerusalem. Thus the collection visit (Rom. 15:25–33) becomes the key to Paul's real purpose, since he wants to enlist the support of the important Roman church (Rom. 1:8–15) for his collection visit in Jerusalem. He believes that Rome's prayerful intercession will accomplish his purpose and make his fears and anxiety unnecessary (Jervell, "Der Brief nach Jerusalem"). The scope of this line of argument is summed up by Fuchs: "Jerusalem is the hidden address of the Epistle to the Romans" (*Hermeneutik*, p. 191; cf. Marxsen, *Introduction to the New Testament*, p. 88). (4) Dahl ("Two Notes on Romans 5") has made an important contribution in clarifying the structural impasse with respect to Romans 5–8. He draws attention to the fact that Rom. 5:1–11 introduces succinctly such themes as "glory," "Spirit," "hope," and "salvation," which are picked up and elaborated in Romans 8. Thus Romans 8 is a full discussion of the themes of Rom. 5:1–11; consequently, the intervening chapters are not to be placed in a rigid logical structure but must be viewed as excursus, answers to objections the prior argument has raised. A new view of the perennial debate over the "structural" relation of Romans 1–4 to Romans 5–8 is thus made possible.

51. Nygren, *Commentary on Romans*, pp. 6ff.

52. Bornkamm, "Romans as Paul's Last Will and Testament."

53. Lütgert, *Der Römerbrief als historisches Problem;* Schmithals, *Der Römerbrief als historisches Problem;* Suggs, " 'The Word Is Near You' "; Bartsch, "Die historische Situation des Römerbriefes"; Luz, "Zum Aufbau von Röm 1-8"; Marxsen, *Introduction to the New Testament;* Jervell, "Der Brief nach Jerusalem"; Fuchs, *Hermeneutik;* cf. also Dahl ("Two Notes on Romans 5"); Dupont ("Le problème de la structure litteraire"); Preisker ("Das historische Problem des Römerbriefes"); Bartsch ("Die historische Situation des Römerbriefes"); Munck (*Christus und Israel*).

54. Frederick Fyvie Bruce, *Paul, Apostle of the Heart Set Free.*

55. Leander E. Keck, *Paul and His Letters.*

56. Bruce, *Paul*, p. 326.

57. Keck, *Paul and His Letters*, pp. 15-16.

58. Ibid., p. 4.

59. Kümmel, *Introduction to the New Testament*, pp. 312ff.

60. Gamble, *The Textual History of Romans*, p. 137.

61. Ibid., p. 133.

62. After completing this chapter, I discovered the similar conviction and phraseology of Gamble (ibid., p. 137): "As important as a study of the Roman background of the letter may be, it is still necessary to keep Paul's own situation in view and to grasp the epistolary situation as a whole. With Paul on the verge of embarking for Jerusalem, we might expect to discover a remarkable *coincidence and convergence* of Paul's preoccupations and the issues confronting the Roman community." (Italics mine.)

63. John Knox, "Romans 15:14-33 and Paul's Conception of His Apostolic Mission."

64. Cf., e.g., Jacob Jervell, "Der Brief nach Jerusalem."

65. Munck (*Christus und Israel*) and Dieter Georgi (*Die Geschichte der Kollekte des Paulus für Jerusalem*) point to the eschatological significance of the collection. It is the occasion that, according to Paul, will coincide with the salvation of all of Israel, as that event which according to Rom. 11:25-27 demonstrates the ingathering of the Gentiles.

66. Cf. Gottlob Schrenk, "Der Römerbrief als Missionsdokument," in *Studien zu Paulus.*

67. Fuchs, *Hermeneutik*, p. 191; Jervell, "Der Brief nach Jerusalem."

68. Cf. Ulrich Wilckens, "Über Abfassungszweck und Aufbau des Römerbriefes," in *Rechtfertigung als Freiheit.*

69. Cf. Gamble, *Textual History of Romans.*

70. Cf. Bartsch, "Die historische Situation des Römerbriefes."

71. Von Schlatter, *Gottes Gerechtigkeit*, p. 59. Cf. the quite different rendering of the RSV: "among all the nations, including yourselves"; Wilhelm Julius Mangold, *Der Römerbrief und seine geschichtlichen Voraussetzungen*, pp. 193ff.

72. Wilckens, "Abfassungszweck und Aufbau des Römerbriefs."

73. Schmithals, *Der Römerbrief als historisches Problem.*

74. Kümmel, *Introduction to the New Testament,* p. 309. Cf. esp. the elaborate statement of the problem by P. Feine, cited in Schmithals, *Der Römerbrief als historisches Problem,* p. 9.

75. N.B.: Paul does not combat a Judaizing mission in Rome. Thus the issue of circumcision, so central in Galatians, plays only a peripheral role in Romans.

76. There are five citation formulas between Rom. 2:1 and 5:11. To the contrary, only one boldface Old Testament citation and citation formula occurs between Rom. 5:12 and 8:28 (i.e., 7:7); from Rom. 5:12 to 8:39 there are only two or three explicit quotations: Isa. 50:8 (Rom. 8:33), Ps. 44:23 (Rom. 8:36).

77. Cf. Sanday and Headlam, *Critical and Exegetical Commentary on Romans;* Dodd, *Epistle to the Romans.*

78. Cf. Günther Bornkamm, "Gesetz und Natur (Röm. 2, 14–16)," *Studien zu Antike und Urchristentum,* p. 94.

79. Cf. Morna Dorothy Hooker, "Adam in Romans 1."

80. Bornkamm, "Gesetz und Natur," p. 98.

81. Paul can indeed argue in this fashion (cf. Rom. 2:17–27), but this does not exhaust the depth of his reflection on sin.

82. Cf. Krister Stendahl, "Paul among Jews and Gentiles," in *Paul among Jews and Gentiles and Other Essays,* pp. 1–7.

83. Nygren, *Commentary on Romans,* Table of Contents.

84. Dahl, "Two Notes on Romans 5."

85. Luther, "Vorrede auf die Epistel S. Pauli an die Römer."

86. But cf. Nygren, *Commentary on Romans:* "the highpoint of the epistle" (p. 20).

87. E.g., Melanchthon, "Römerbrief-Kommentar, 1532"; Feuillet, "Le plan salvifique de Dieu"; Leenhardt, *L'Épître aux Romains.* See note 43, above.

88. Only at Rom. 6:14, 15 does *nomos* occur in chapter 6.

89. Eberhard Jüngel, "Das Gesetz zwischen Adam und Christus."

90. Cf. Schmithals, *Der Römerbrief als historisches Problem.*

91. Cf. (1) "passions and desires" (*pathēmata/epithumiai,* Gal. 5:24); (2) "impurity, passion, evil desire" (*akatharsia/pathos/epithumia kakē,* Col. 3:5); (3) "in the passion of lust [*en pathei epithumias*], like the heathen [Gentiles] who do not know God" (1 Thess. 4:5; cf., esp., the lists of Eph. 2:3; 4:19; and 5:3–12). (4) "impurity" (*akatharsia,* Rom. 6:19; 1:24; 2 Cor. 12:21; Gal. 5:19; Eph. 4:19; 5:3; 1 Thess. 2:3; 4:7); (5) "licentiousness" (*aselgeia,* Rom. 13:13; 2 Cor. 12:21; Gal. 5:19; Eph. 4:19); (6) "desire" (*epithumia,* Rom. 1:24; 6:12; 13:14; Gal. 5:16, 24; Eph. 2:3; 4:22; Col. 3:5; 1 Thess. 4:5). One of the basic differences between Romans and Ephesians—which are often said to resemble each other—is the audience. "The Jewish question" preoccupies Paul in Romans; the author of Ephesians focuses on a formerly Gentile audience and its pagan sins.

92. Leo Baeck, "The Faith of Paul," in *Judaism and Christianity;* Hans Joachim Schoeps, *Paul.*

93. Schmithals, *Der Römerbrief als historisches Problem.*

94. Nils Alstrup Dahl, "The Missionary Theology in the Epistle to the Romans," in *Studies in Paul*, pp. 77, 88.

CHAPTER 6—Contextual Theology in Romans and Galatians

1. Anders Nygren, *Commentary on Romans*, p. 9; Adolf von Schlatter, *Gottes Gerechtigkeit;* Ulrich Luz, "Zum Aufbau von Röm. 1-8"; Eduard Lohse, *Grundriss der neutestamentlichen Theologie*, p. 74; Heinz-Dietrich Wendland, *Die Mitte der paulinischen Botschaft.*

2. Heinrich Weinel, *Biblische Theologie des Neuen Testaments;* Heinrich Julius Holtzmann, *Lehrbuch der neutestamentlichen Theologie;* Hermann Lüdemann, *Die Anthropologie des Apostels Paulus und ihre Stellung innerhalb seiner Heilslehre.*

3. Hans Joachim Schoeps, *Paul*, p. 224.

4. "Lehrstandpunkt": Johannes Evangelist Belser, *Einleitung in das Neue Testament*, p. 509; "dogmatische Exposition": Friedrich Adolph Philippi, *Commentar über den Brief Pauli an die Römer*, 1: xx.

5. In this respect, Romans 4 is quite similar to Hebrews with its conflation of the Old Testament promise and the Christian hope.

6. Krister Stendahl, "Paul among Jews and Gentiles," in *Paul among Jews and Gentiles and Other Essays*, pp. 1-7.

7. Charles Harold Dodd, *Epistle of Paul to the Romans*, p. 71.

8. We concentrate on the contextual interpretation of the law in these chapters; see Chapter 11, below, for a full treatment of the law.

9. Cf. for a discussion of Gal. 6:2 Donald Stoike, " 'The Law of Christ.' "

10. In personal conversation with Professor Dowey.

CHAPTER 7—Tradition and Gospel

1. Friedrich Nietzsche, "The First Christian," in *The Dawn of Day;* idem, "The Antichrist," in *The Complete Works of Friedrich Nietzsche;* Ernest Renan, *Saint Paul;* Paul Anton de Lagarde, *Deutsche Schriften.*

2. Calvin J. Roetzel, *The Letters of Paul*, p. 90.

3. William Wrede, *Paul*, pp. 166, 179.

4. Wilhelm Heitmüller, "Zum Problem Paulus und Jesus."

5. Archibald Macbride Hunter, *Paul and His Predecessors*, pp. 9ff.

6. Alfred Seeberg, *Der Katechismus der Urchristenheit;* Martin Dibelius, *From Tradition to Gospel*, pp. 238ff.

7. Richard Reitzenstein, *Die hellenistischen Mysterienreligionen*, p. 86. Cf. James D. G. Dunn, *Unity and Diversity in the New Testament*, p. 289: "Not so far from the mark then is J. W. Drane's claim that 'Paul's statements on the law in Galatians can with a great deal of justification be called blatantly Gnostic.' "

8. Krister Stendahl, "The Apostle Paul and the Introspective Conscience of the West" p. 213.

9. Ibid., p. 215.

10. Thomas Walter Manson, "The Argument from Prophecy," p. 135.

11. Edward Earle Ellis, "Midrash Pesher in Pauline Hermeneutics," in *Prophecy and Hermeneutic in Early Christianity*, pp. 179ff.

12. Cf. Joseph Barber Lightfoot, *Notes on Epistles of St. Paul*, p. 15.

13. Gerhard Sass, "Zur Bedeutung von *doulos* bei Paulus."

14. Walther Zimmerli, *Ezechiel*, 1:1–130.

15. Julius Wellhausen, *Israelitische und jüdische Geschichte*.

16. Gerhard von Rad, *Old Testament Theology*, 2:243ff.

17. However, a "new exodus" is not present in Paul. Cf. the discussion in Ed Parish Sanders, *Paul and Palestinian Judaism*, p. 512.

18. Nils Alstrup Dahl, "Contradictions in Scripture," in *Studies in Paul*.

19. *En prōtois:* "of first importance" (RSV); "first of all" (Barrett); *"hauptsachlich"* (Conzelmann).

20. Cf. Oscar Cullmann, "The Tradition," in *The Early Church*.

21. Charles Harold Dodd, *The Apostolic Preaching and Its Developments*, pp. 17ff.

22. Paul received other traditions from Antioch: words of Jesus; sacramental, confessional, credal, and hymnic materials; many paraenetic traditions.

23. Cf. Hans Lietzmann, *Messe und Herrenmahl*, p. 255.

24. Klaus Wengst, *Christologische Formeln und Lieder des Urchristentums*, pp. 11ff.

25. Hans von Campenhausen, "Das Bekenntnis in Urchristentum."

26. Cf. also Robert McQueen Grant, *Second-Century Christianity*.

27. Cf. Wengst, *Christologische Formeln und Lieder*, pp. 11ff.

28. Cf. Heitmüller, "Zum Problem Paulus und Jesus"; Heinz-Wolfgang Kuhn, "Der Irdische Jesu bei Paulus als traditionsgeschichtliches und theologisches Problem"; Ulrich Wilckens, "Jesusüberlieferung und Christuskerygma."

29. Cf. Martin Elze, "Häresie und Einheit der Kirche im 2. Jahrhundert."

CHAPTER 8—Paul's Apocalyptic Theology

1. William Morgan, *The Religion and Theology of Paul*, p. 6.

2. Philipp Vielhauer, "Introduction [to Apocalypses and Related Subjects]," in *New Testament Apocrypha*.

3. Klaus Koch, *The Rediscovery of Apocalyptic*, pp. 18–35.

4. Vielhauer, "Introduction."

5. Koch, *Rediscovery of Apocalyptic*, pp. 28–32.

6. Julius Wellhausen, "Zur apokalyptischen Literatur," in *Skizzen und Vorarbeiten*.

7. Dietrich Rössler, *Gesetz und Geschichte;* Frank Moore Cross, *The Ancient Library of Qumran and Modern Biblical Studies*, p. 54, n. 33.

8. George Foot Moore, *Judaism in the First Centuries of the Christian Era*.

9. Wilhelm Bousset, *Die Religion des Judentums im späthellenistischen Zeitalter.*

10. Rössler, *Gesetz und Geschichte.*

11. Flavius Josephus *The Jewish War 2.* 259ff.; idem, *The Antiquities of the Jews* 18–20.

12. Louis Ginsburg, "Some Observations on the Attitude of the Synagogue towards the Apocalyptic-Eschatological Writings," p. 134.

13. Ibid.

14. Cf., e.g., William David Davies, "The Jewish Background of the Teaching of Jesus," in *Christian Origins and Judaism;* Ed Parish Sanders, *Paul and Palestinian Judaism.*

15. E.g., Ginsburg, "Some Observations on the Attitude of the Synagogue," p. 134.

16. Cf. Vielhauer, "Introduction."

17. Albert Schweitzer, *The Mysticism of Paul;* Martin Werner, *Die Entstehung des christlichen Dogmas.*

18. Wellhausen, "Zur apokalyptischen Literatur"; Bernhard Duhm, *Israels Propheten,* p. 460; cf. Koch, *Rediscovery of Apocalyptic,* pp. 36ff.

19. Rudolf Schnackenburg, *God's Rule and Kingdom,* p. 69.

20. David Friedrich Strauss, *The Life of Jesus, Critically Examined.*

21. Charles Harold Dodd, *New Testament Studies,* pp. 67–128.

22. Morgan, *Religion and Theology of Paul,* p. 5.

23. Rudolf Karl Bultmann, "New Testament and Mythology," in *Kerygma and Myth,* vol. 1, esp. pp. 12ff.

24. Rudolf Karl Bultmann, *Primitive Christianity in Its Contemporary Setting,* p. 186.

25. Ibid.

26. Ibid., p. 184.

27. Rudolf Karl Bultmann, *Theology of the New Testament,* 1:322.

28. Ibid., 2:175ff.

29. Cf. Paul Ricoeur's critique (in "Préface à Bultmann," in *Le Conflict des Interprétations*) of Bultmann's attempt to search behind the language for its real intent.

30. John Goodrich Gager, "Functional Diversity in Paul's Use of End-Time Language."

31. Karl Barth, *Der Römerbrief,* p. 298; E.T., p. 314.

32. Paul Althaus, *Die letzten Dinge,* p. 272.

33. Jürgen Moltmann, *Theology of Hope;* Wolfhart Pannenberg, *Jesus—God and Man.*

34. Ernst Käsemann, "On the Subject of Primitive Christian Apocalyptic"; idem, "The Beginnings of Christian Theology," in *New Testament Questions of Today;* Peter Stuhlmacher, *Gerechtigkeit Gottes bei Paulus;* idem, "Erwägungen zum Problem von Gegenwart und Zukunft in der paulinischen Theologie"; Ulrich Wilckens, "Die Bekehrung des Paulus als religionsgeschichtliches Prob-

lem"; Hans Joachim Schoeps, *Paul;* William David Davies, *Paul and Rabbinic Judaism;* Sanders, *Paul and Palestinian Judaism;* Paul David Hanson, *The Dawn of Apocalyptic.*

35. Käsemann, "Beginnings of Christian Theology," in *New Testament Questions of Today,* p. 102.

36. Koch, *Rediscovery of Apocalyptic,* p. 47.

37. Schweitzer, *Mysticism of Paul;* Bousset, *Die Religion des Judentums.* Bousset exempts Jesus from apocalyptic and is followed in this by many other New Testament scholars.

38. Leonhard Goppelt, "Apokalyptik und Typologie bei Paulus."

39. Willi Marxsen, *Introduction to the New Testament,* p. 273.

40. Hans Georg Conzelmann, "Zur Analyse der Bekenntnisformel I. Kor. 15,3–5"; cf. also Ernst Fuchs, "Über die Aufgabe einer christlichen Theologie."

41. Sanders, *Paul and Palestinian Judaism,* p. 543.

42. Jörg Baumgarten, *Paulus und die Apokalyptik.*

43. Only Ephesians employs this terminology: Eph. 2:7 *aiōnes* (plural) *eperchomenoi;* Eph. 1:21: *ho aiōn mellōn;* Eph. 2:2; 3:9; 6:12; cf. also Matt. 13:32 vs. Mark 3:29.

44. Only Gal. 1:4 implies with "the present evil aeon" (cf. 2 Cor. 4:4: "the god of this age," trans. mine; cf. Rom. 12:2; 1 Cor. 1:20; 2:6, 8; 3:18), the *future* of the new age to come.

45. References to "the day [of the Lord; of Christ]" occur most often in traditional contexts: 1 Thess. 3:10; 5:2, 4; Rom. 2:5, 16; 13:12; 1 Cor. 1:8; 3:13; 5:5; 2 Cor. 1:14; Phil. 1:6, 10; 2:16.

46. Rudolf Karl Bultmann, *"Elpis."*

47. Bultmann, *Primitive Christianity,* p. 186.

48. Jürgen Becker, *Das Heil Gottes,* pp. 58ff.; Heinz Wolfgang Kuhn, *Enderwartung und gegenwärtiges Heil,* pp. 44–175.

49. Cf. esp. Stuhlmacher, "Erwägungen zum Problem von Gegenwart und Zukunft."

50. Cf. Ulrich Luz, "Der alte und der neue Bund bei Paulus und im Hebräerbrief."

51. Cf. Luke 24:39; Tertullian *De resurrectione carnis;* Luther's Commentary on 1 Corinthians 15; Georg Kretschmar, "Auferstehung des Fleisches," in *Leben Angesicht des Todes.*

52. E.g., Bultmann, *Primitive Christianity,* p. 186.

53. Bultmann, "New Testament and Mythology."

54. Ernst Käsemann, "On Paul's Anthropology," in *Perspectives on Paul.*

55. Bultmann, *Theology of the New Testament,* 1:viii and chaps. 4 and 5.

56. Ibid., pp. 270ff.

57. George Bertram, "Die Himmelfahrt Jesu vom Kreuz aus und der Glaube an seine Auferstehung," in *Festgabe für Adolf Deissmann,* p. 202.

58. Walter Bauer, *Das Leben Jesu im Zeitalter der neutestamentlichen Apokryphen,* p. 253.

59. 1Qh 12:11, 12; 13:19; 14:13; 16:9, 11, 12, etc.

60. Oscar Cullmann, *Christ and Time,* p. 145.

61. Archibald Macbride Hunter, *Interpreting Paul's Gospel,* p. 127.

62. For a different interpretation, cf. Andreas Lindemann, "Zum Abfassungszweck des Zweiten Thessalonicherbriefes"; cf. also Gerhard Friedrich, "1 Thessalonicher 5,1-11," in *Auf das Wort kommt es an.*

63. Both Luke and Matthew adopt a similar "postponement" strategy; cf. Luke 18:1; 21:9; 19:11; 17:20; Matt. 25:1-13, 19; 24:48.

64. Elaine Hiesey Pagels, *The Gnostic Paul;* cf. also Malcolm Lee Peel, *The Epistle to Rheginos.*

65. Karl Barth, *The Resurrection of the Dead,* pp. 13-124.

66. Cf. Peter von der Osten-Sachen, "Gottes Treue bis zur Parusie."

67. Eric Robertson Dodds, *Pagan and Christian in an Age of Anxiety.*

68. George Murray, *Five Stages of Greek Religion.*

69. The aesthetic pleasure of the beauty of the body in classic Hellenism is turned into its opposite in Hellenistic religion.

70. Paul confuses here his own apocalyptic premise with that of the Corinthians; they did not deny the resurrection of Christ and would have agreed with Paul's claims in 1 Cor. 15:17-19.

71. Joachim Jeremias ("'Flesh and Blood Cannot Inherit the Kingdom of God,'" p. 158) argues that 1 Cor. 15:50 does not mean a spiritualization of the resurrection, that it speaks rather about the change of the living at the Parousia.

72. According to the Apocalypse of Baruch 49-51, the dead are raised in their earthly state in order to secure their identity (50:3). Only after the judgment are the righteous changed.

73. Pagels, *The Gnostic Paul,* p. 84.

74. Cf. Walter Schmithals, *Die Gnosis in Korinth.*

75. Paul Anton de Lagarde, *Deutsche Schriften.*

76. Barth, *Resurrection of the Dead,* pp. 13-124.

77. Paul refers to "the gospel" as such in 1 Cor. 15:1, yet in 1 Cor. 2:2 that gospel seems to be "Jesus Christ and him crucified" as Paul's particular gospel to the Corinthians.

78. Walter Schmithals, "Die Korintherbriefe als Briefsammlung."

79. Schmithals (ibid.) divides as follows (I=1 Corinthians; II=2 Corinthians):

Brief A: I 11:2-34

Brief B: I 6:1-11 and II 6:14—7:1 and I 6:12-20 and 9:24—10:22 and 15:1-58 and 16:13-24 (*Vorbrief*)

Brief C: I 5:1-13 and 7:1—8:13 and 9:14-22 and 10:23—11:1 and 12:1-31a and 14:1c-40 and 12:31b—13:13 and 16:1-12 (*Antwortbrief*)

Brief D: I 1:1—4:21 (cf. Dahl on the importance of 1 Cor. 1-4 in: "Paul and the Church at Corinth," in *Christian History and Interpretation,* pp. 313-35)

Brief E: II 2:14—6:2 (*Zwischenbrief*)

Brief F: I 9:1-18 and II 6:3-13 and 7:2-4

Brief G: II 10:1—13:13 (*Tränenbrief*)
Brief H: II 9:1-15 (*Kollektenbrief*)
Brief I: II 1:1—2:13 and 7:5—8:24 (*Freudenbrief*)

80. Barth, *Resurrection of the Dead*, pp. 13-124.

81. Ernst Käsemann, *Der Ruf der Freiheit*, p. 86.

82. William Wrede, *Paul*, pp. 105-6, 111.

83. Cf. the temporal clauses in 1 Corinthians 15: *epeita* (v. 23); *eita* (v. 24); *tagma* (v. 23); *achri hou* (v. 25); *tote* (vv. 28, 54, 58); *prōton epeita* (v. 46); the future tenses in vv. 49-55.

84. Schweitzer, *Mysticism of Paul;* Werner, *Die Entstehung des christlichen Dogmas;* Fritz Buri, *Die Bedeutung der neutestamentlichen Eschatologie.*

85. Cullmann, *Christ and Time*, p. 139.

86. Werner, *Die Entstehung des christlichen Dogmas.*

87. Lars Hartman, "Functions of Some So-called Apocalyptic Timetables."

88. Cf. Aristotle *Physics* 1.14: "Time indeed seems to be like a circle." Cf. also the Hellenistic concept of the "wheel of birth and rebirth" (Origen *Contra Celsum* 4.68).

CHAPTER 9—The Scandal of the Cross

1. Josephus *The Jewish War* 2.259ff.; idem., *Antiquities* 18-20.

2. Friedrich Nietzsche, "The First Christian," in *The Dawn of Day;* idem, "The Antichrist," in *The Complete Works of Friedrich Nietzsche.*

3. Werner Georg Kümmel, *Römer 7 und die Bekehrung des Paulus.*

4. Johannes Munck, *Paul and the Salvation of Mankind*, pp. 13ff.

5. Albert Schweitzer, *Paul and His Interpreters*, p. 105.

6. The Torah is here discussed in relation to the death of Christ; see Chapter 11 for a comprehensive discussion of the Torah in Paul's thought. Cf. also Chapter 6, above.

7. Meinrad Limbeck, *Die Ordnung des Heils.*

8. But cf. Wilhelm Bousset, *Die Religion des Judentums im späthellenistischen Zeitalter;* Robert Henry Charles, ed., *The Apocrypha and Pseudepigrapha of the Old Testament in English*, 2:vii-xi; George Foot Moore, *Judaism in the First Centuries of the Christian Era;* Dietrich Rössler, *Gesetz und Geschichte.*

9. Cf. Jörg Baumgarten, *Paulus und die Apokalyptik*, pp. 147-97.

10. Charles Harold Dodd, *The Epistle of Paul to the Romans*, pp. 18-30.

11. Cf. "to perish" (*apolluesthai*), Rom. 2:12; 1 Cor. 1:18; 8:11; 10:9, 10; 15:18; 2 Cor. 2:15; 4:3; "to destroy" (*apolluein*), 1 Cor. 1:19; Rom. 14:15; "destruction" (*olethros*), 1 Cor. 5:5; 1 Thess. 5:3; "judgment" (*katakrima*), Rom. 5:16, 18; 8:1; (*katakrisis*) 2 Cor. 3:9; cf. Rom. 2:1; 8:34; 14:23; 1 Cor. 11:32; (*krisis tou theou*) 1 Thess. 1:5; (*katakrinein*) Rom. 2:12, 16; 3:4, etc.

12. Rudolf Karl Bultmann, *Theology of the New Testament*, 1:288.

13. Cf., however, "But when we are judged by the Lord, we are chastened

(*paideuometha* = *paideia*) so that we may not be condemned along with the world" (1 Cor. 11:32).

14. Cf. e.g., Denys Edward Hugh Whiteley, *Theology of St. Paul*, pp. 271ff.; Robert Henry Charles, *A Critical History of the Doctrine of a Future Life in Israel, in Judaism, and in Christianity*, p. 449; Jan Nicolaas Sevenster, "Some Remarks on the *Gymnos* in 2 Cor. V.3," in *Studia Paulina;* idem, "Einige Bermerkungen über den 'Zwischenzustand' bei Paulus."

15. Rudolf Karl Bultmann, "New Testament and Mythology," in *Kerygma and Myth*, 1:41.

16. Ibid., pp. 38ff.

17. Bultmann, *Theology of the New Testament*, 1:298.

18. Bultmann, "New Testament and Mythology," p. 36.

19. Ernst Fuchs, "Die Auferstehungsgewissheit nach 1. Korinther 15," in *Zum hermeneutischen Problem in der Theologie;* Gerhard Ebeling, *The Nature of Faith;* Willi Marxsen, *The Resurrection of Jesus of Nazareth*.

20. Ernst Troeltsch, *Der Historismus und seine Probleme*.

21. Bultmann, *Theology of the New Testament*, 1:295.

22. Karl Barth, *The Resurrection of the Dead*, pp. 130–40.

23. Bruce Manning Metzger, "A Suggestion Concerning the Meaning of I Cor. XV.4b."

24. George Bertram, "Die Himmelfahrt Jesu vom Kreuz aus und der Glaube an seine Auferstehung," in *Festgabe für Adolf Deissmann*.

25. Wolfgang Schrage, "Leid, Kreuz und Eschaton."

26. Heinz-Wolfgang Kuhn, "Jesus als Gekreuzigter"; Willi Marxsen, "Erwägungen zum Problem des verkündigten Kreuzes"; Wolfgang Schrage, "Das Verständnis des Todes Jesu Christi im Neuen Testament," in *Das Kreuz Jesu Christi als Grund des Heils*.

27. Jürgen Moltmann, *The Crucified God*, pp. 45ff.

28. Ibid.

29. Blaise Pascal, "Le Mystère de Jésus," in *Pensées*.

30. Moltmann, *The Crucified God*, chap. 6.

31. A theological reference to the cross occurs only in Mark 16:6; "cross" language is limited to Mark 15, where it abounds: "to crucify" (*stauroun*), Mark 15:13, 14, 20, 24, 25, 27; "cross" (*stauros*), Mark 15:21, 30, 32.

32. Cf. Kuhn, "Jesus als Gekreuzigter"; Ulrich B. Müller, "Die Bedeutung des Kreuzestodes Jesu im Johannesevangelium."

33. Norman Perrin, "The Use of (*Para*)*didonai* in Connection with the Passion of Jesus in the New Testament," in *Der Ruf Jesu und die Antwort der Gemeinde*.

34. Kuhn, "Jesus als Gekreuzigter"; Schrage, "Das Verständnis des Todes Jesu Christi im Neuen Testament."

35. The only exception is 1 Cor. 1:13.

36. Paul comes close to this in 1 Cor. 2:6–8; but cf. 1 Cor. 2:12: "the gifts bestowed on us by God" (*ta charisthenta*).

37. Martin Hengel, *"Mors turpissima crucis,"* in *Rechtfertigung.*

38. Origen *Contra Celsum* 6.10.

39. Lucian *De morte Peregrini* 11.

40. Walter Bauer, *Das Leben Jesu im Zeitalter der neutestamentlichen Apokryphen,* pp. 477, 476.

41. Anselm *Cur Deus Homo?*

42. Gustaf Aulén, *Christus Victor,* pp. 17ff.

43. Barth, *Resurrection of the Dead,* pp. 13–124.

CHAPTER 10—The Dilemma of Sin and Death

1. Rudolf Karl Bultmann, "History and Eschatology in the New Testament."

2. Frederick Fyvie Bruce, *Paul, Apostle of the Heart Set Free,* pp. 424ff.

3. Cf. Chrys C. Caragounis, *"Opsōnion":* A Reconsideration of Its Meaning."

4. Qumran already combines transgressions with the power of sin, for the confession of God's justifying grace is here coupled with the believer's knowledge to be "flesh" (1QS 11:9–11).

5. Werner Georg Kümmel, *Römer 7 und die Bekehrung des Paulus;* Rudolf Karl Bultmann, "Romans 7 and the Anthropology of Paul," in *Existence and Faith.* Herman Nicolaas Ridderbos, *Aan de Romeinen,* pp. 147–71; Krister Stendahl, "The Apostle Paul and the Introspective Conscience of the West."

6. Hans Windisch, "Das Problem des paulinischen Imperativs."

7. Cf. Reinhold Niebuhr, *The Nature and Destiny of Man,* 1:178–240.

8. Wolfgang Schrage, *Die konkreten Einzelgebote in der paulinischen Paränese,* p. 123.

9. Anders Nygren, *Commentary on Romans.*

10. Ibid., p. 247.

11. Ibid., p. 299.

12. Cf. Bultmann on "to be anxious" (*merimnan;* 1 Cor. 7:32, 33, 34; 12:25; Phil. 2:20; 4:6) in *Theology of the New Testament,* 1:226, 241–42.

13. Eduard Schweizer, "Gottesgerechtigkeit und Lasterkataloge bei Paulus," in *Rechtfertigung.*

14. Stendahl, "The Apostle Paul and the Introspective Conscience of the West."

15. The argument here differs from that in Rom. 3:23: "all have sinned and fall short of glory of God." The two texts should not be harmonized.

16. Edmond Jacob, "Death," in *The Interpreter's Dictionary of the Bible,* 1:803. Cf. also Gen. 2:17: "but of the tree of the knowledge of good and evil you shall not eat, for in the day that you eat of it you shall die."

17. Cf. Charles Kingsley Barrett, *A Commentary on the Second Epistle to the Corinthians,* pp. 170–72; cf. Peter Stuhlmacher, "Erwägungen zum ontologischen Charakter der *kainē ktisis* bei Paulus."

18. Hans Conzelmann, *1 Corinthians: A Commentary,* pp. 281–82.

19. Cf. Wolfhart Pannenberg, "Eschatologie und Sinnerfahrung"; idem,

"Tod und Auferstehung in der Sicht christlicher Dogmatik"; idem, "Die Auferstehung Jesu und die Zukunft."

CHAPTER 11—The Enigma of the Law

1. Cf. Hans Lietzmann, *An die Römer*, p. 39.
2. Hans Joachim Schoeps, *Paul*, pp. 224ff.
3. Rudolf Karl Bultmann, *Theology of the New Testament*, 1:264.
4. Ulrich Wilckens, "Was heisst bei Paulus," in *Rechtfertigung als Freiheit*, pp. 77–109.
5. Ed Parish Sanders, *Paul and Palestinian Judaism*, pp. 474ff.
6. Krister Stendahl, "The Apostle Paul and the Introspective Conscience of the West."
7. Rudolf Karl Bultmann, "Christus des Gesetzes Ende," in *Glauben und Verstehen*, 2:32–58.
8. Ernst Käsemann, "The Spirit and the Letter, " in *Perspectives on Paul*, pp. 138–66.
9. Wilckens, "Was heisst bei Paulus."
10. Sanders, *Paul and Palestinian Judaism*, pp. 12ff.
11. Richard Lowell Rubenstein, *My Brother Paul*.
12. Cf., e.g., Sanders, *Paul and Palestinian Judaism*, pp. 474ff.
13. Ibid.
14. Bultmann, *Theology of the New Testament*, 1:267.
15. Ibid., p. 264.
16. Wilckens, "Was heisst bei Paulus."
17. Bultmann, *Theology of the New Testament*, 1:264.
18. Cf., e.g., Augustine, Luther, Calvin; Barth, Knox, Nygren, Cranfield, Murray.
19. Cf. Maurice Goguel, *The Birth of Christianity*, p. 213.
20. Sanders, *Paul and Palestinian Judaism*, pp. 484ff.
21. Ibid.
22. Ibid., p. 496.
23. See n. 4 of Chapter 10.
24. Søren Aabye Kierkegaard, *The Gospel of Suffering and the Lilies of the Field*, p. 43.
25. Otfried Hofius, "Die Unabänderlichkeit des göttlichen Heilsratschlusses."
26. Leo Baeck, "Romantic Religion," in *Judaism and Christianity*, pp. 210–11. See also John Knox (*Ethic of Jesus*, p. 90), who thinks that Paul's doctrine of justification has inescapable antinomian implications; Paul's rejection of the law is too radical. "Such an understanding of the Christian's position left Paul . . . without an adequate theoretical basis for the practical ethical demands he does not fail to make upon his congregations" (ibid., p. 99).
27. Joseph Blake Tyson, " 'Works of Law' in Galatians."
28. Bultmann, *Theology of the New Testament*, 1:264.
29. Tyson, " 'Works of Law.' "

30. Martin Luther, "Röm. 12,6ff.," *WA* 17/2:34.

31. Søren Aabye Kierkegaard, *Purity of Heart Is to Will One Thing*.

32. Cf. the manifold "spirit gifts" as the expression of the *one* Spirit (1 Cor. 12:1–12).

33. Friedrich Gustav Lang, "Gesetz und Bund bei Paulus," in *Rechtfertigung*, pp. 305–21.

34. But cf. Andreas Lindemann, *Paulus im ältesten Christentum*.

35. Käsemann, "The Spirit and the Letter," p. 166.

36. However, Paul quite often cites the legal code of the Pentateuch to demonstrate God's will and commandment (for instance, Deut. 5:17–21 in Rom. 13:9; Deut. 5:21 in Rom. 7:7) or his indictment (Deut. 21:23 and 27:26 in Gal. 3:13, 10).

37. In Gal. 3:22 "the promise" seems distinct from "scripture," since "scripture" documents only our condemnation; however, in Gal. 3:8 the promise is contained in Scripture.

38. David Hugh Kelsey, *The Uses of Scripture in Recent Theology*, pp. 160ff.

39. Cf. Ernst Käsemann, *An die Römer*, pp. 70–73.

CHAPTER 12—The Gift and the Demand of Salvation

1. Albert Schweitzer, *The Mysticism of Paul*, pp. 205–26.

2. Wilhelm Lütgert, *Gesetz und Geist*.

3. Gerd Theissen, "Soteriologische Symbolik in den paulinischen Schriften"; in what follows, I paraphrase Theissen's argument.

4. Ibid., p. 288.

5. "Participation" and "juridical" categories belong to a different language game; cf. Ed Parish Sanders, *Paul and Palestinian Judaism*, p. 520.

6. Theissen, "Soteriologische Symbolik," p. 296.

7. Ibid., p. 302.

8. Cf. Gustav Adolf Deissmann (*Paul*, p. 97): the Pauline images of justification, reconciliation, forgiveness, redemption, and adoption of sons are the "one *janua vitae*" of Paul's Christ mysticism.

9. William Wrede, *Paul*, pp. 123ff.; Schweitzer, *Mysticism of Paul*, pp. 205–26.

10. William David Davies, *Paul and Rabbinic Judaism*, pp. 177, 86–110; Denys Edward Hugh Whiteley, *The Theology of St. Paul*, p. 134; Sanders, *Paul and Palestinian Judaism*, p. 520.

11. Herman Nicolaas Ridderbos, *Paulus*, p. 184.

12. Ernst Käsemann, " 'The Righteousness of God' in Paul," in *New Testament Questions of Today*.

13. Ibid.

14. Rudolf Karl Bultmann, "*Dikaiosynē Theou*."

15. Ridderbos, *Paulus*, p. 176.

16. Käsemann, " 'The Righteousness of God.' "

17. This does not deny that the verb "to justify" (*dikaioun*) and the adjective

"just"/"righteous" (*dikaios*) may have additional connotations, but cf. Rom. 5:19, where "many will be 'made righteous' " (*dikaioi katastathēsontai*) has the connotation of both a new status and a new quality.

18. According to Ernst Käsemann ("Amt und Gemeinde im Neuen Testament," in *Exegetische Versuche und Besinnungen*, 1:111), Paul coins "*charisma*" versus the Hellenistic-Christian use of "*ta pneumatika*" (cf. 1 Cor. 12:1–12). However, this cannot be substantiated (cf. Gillis Petersson Wetter, *Charis*, who points to its imperial use in Hellenistic-Roman culture). Cf. also Darrel J. Doughty, "Priority of *Charis*."

19. Rudolf Karl Bultmann, *Theology of the New Testament*, 1:288ff.

20. Wetter, *Charis*, p. 2.

21. It is also possible that by the time of 1 Peter, Hebrews, and Acts the term had lost its Pauline connotation; cf. ibid., pp. 83ff.

22. The LXX translates *hen* as *charis* and its verb form *hanan* ("to be gracious"; "to find favor") as *eleein*.

23. Although Paul does not often correlate grace and faith explicitly, it is interesting that he never uses the aorist tense for "standing" but always the perfect tense; "standing" is not a "once for all" event (cf. *hestēkenai*, Rom. 5:2; 11:20; 1 Cor. 10:12; 15:1; 2 Cor. 1:24).

24. Dieter Lührmann, *Glaube im frühen Christentum*.

25. Ibid., p. 49.

26. Cf. also *epistēmē* versus *doxa* (opinion).

27. Lührmann, *Glaube im frühen Christentum*, pp. 49, 91.

28. The term *charis* is unknown in Jewish religious literature. However, the term *eleos* is frequent; it translates in the LXX the terms *hesed* and *rachamim*. Although *eleos* often means "act of love," it frequently refers to the mercy of God (Wis. Sol. 9:1; Sir. 5:6; 16:11; 2 Macc. 6:16; 8:5; Ps. Sol. 18:3). Faith is not opposed to law-keeping; it refers both to the monotheistic confession of Israel and to faithfulness under the Law. See Herman Leberecht Strack and Paul Billerbeck, *Kommentar zum Neuen Testament aus Talmud und Midrasch*, 3:186ff.; Wilhelm Bousset, *Die Religion des Judentums im späthellenistischen Zeitalter*, pp. 193ff.; Adolf von Schlatter, *Der Glaube im Neuen Testament*, pp. 9–42; Rudolf Karl Bultmann, "*Pisteuō*," *TDNT* 6:197ff.; and esp. Sanders, *Paul and Palestinian Judaism*, pp. 81ff., 361ff.

29. Sanders, *Paul and Palestinian Judaism*, e.g., pp. 33–59.

30. Cf. Martin Buber's objection to this type of faith, in *Two Types of Faith*.

31. Lührmann, *Glaube im frühen Christentum*.

32. Willem Cornelis van Unnik, "Reisepläne und Amen-Sagen," in *Studia Paulina*.

33. Franz Mussner, *Theologie der Freiheit nach Paulus*.

CHAPTER 13—The Responsibility of Life in Christ

1. Cf. Gustav Adolf Deissmann, *Die neutestamentliche Formel "in Christo Jesu" undersucht*.

2. Fritz Neugebauer, "Das paulinische 'in Christo,' " p. 132.

3. Cf., e.g., Joshua 7; 1 Samuel 14 (cf. Denys Edward Hugh Whiteley, *The Theology of St. Paul*, pp. 45ff.).

4. Neugebauer, "Das paulinische 'in Christo,' " p. 131.

5. Ernst Lohmeyer, "*Syn Christō*," in *Festgabe für Adolf Deissmann*; Eduard Schweizer, "Die 'Mystik' des Sterbens und Auferstehens mit Christus bei Paulus."

6. It would be interesting if Rom. 6:1–10, with its *temporal* "with Christ," could be interpreted as a correction of the *spatial* incorporation motif of "in Christ" which underlies Rom. 5:12–21. However, the argument of Rom. 6:1–10 does not warrant this (cf. also 6:11, 23: "in Christ").

7. Cf. also Rom. 8:32; 1 Cor. 15:10; Phil. 3:3, 4, 9.

8. *Contra* William Wrede (*Paul*), Albert Schweitzer (*The Mysticism of Paul*), et al.

9. Cf. Rudolf Karl Bultmann, *Primitive Christianity in Its Contemporary Setting*, p. 186.

10. Rudolf Karl Bultmann, "Das Problem der Ethik bei Paulus."

11. Günther Bornkamm, "Taufe und neues Leben bei Paulus," in *Das Ende des Gesetzes*.

12. Ernst Käsemann, " 'The Righteousness of God' in Paul," in *New Testament Questions of Today*.

13. Ernst Käsemann, "On Paul's Anthropology," in *Perspectives on Paul*.

14. Rudolf Karl Bultmann, *Theology of the New Testament*, 1:195.

15. Charles Harold Dodd, *The Meaning of Paul for Today*, pp. 139ff.

16. It is indeed interesting that the prophets speak so rarely about the Spirit as a present reality. This may be due to the Baalistic connotations of the Spirit as irrational ecstatic power, which identifies with the fertility of nature.

17. Qumran exercises the gift of the prophetic spirit in its midrashic activity. See also note 59 of Chapter 8.

18. Richard Birch Hoyle, *The Holy Spirit in St. Paul*, p. 202.

19. Peter Stuhlmacher, "Erwägungen zum Problem von Gegenwart und Zukunft in der paulinischen Theologie."

20. *Kabod* can refer both to the cloud covering God's radiance and to the radiant light of God's presence.

21. In the Priestly tradition (P), the *kabod Yahweh* is distinguished from the "cloud" which surrounds the fiery *kabod* (Exod. 24:15–18; 40:34–38; cf. also Ezek. 1:28; 43:1–5). See Gerhard von Rad, "*Doxa*," in *TDNT* 2:240ff.

22. E.g., Ernst Käsemann, "On the Subject of Primitive Christian Apocalyptic," in *New Testament Questions of Today*, p. 132.

23. Cf. Franz Mussner, *Der Galaterbrief*, p. 384.

24. Except for Gal. 5:6: "faith working through love."

25. Cf., however, "the work of faith" in 1 Thess. 1:3.

26. Clearly, in classical Greek philosophy *nous* is a far more important concept

than *pneuma*. Plato elevates *nous* over *pneuma*. However, in the Gnostic climate of the Pauline churches and in the Stoic philosophy *pneuma* becomes the essential religious term. Cf. Friedrich Büchsel, *Der Geist Gottes im Neuen Testament*; Gérard Verbeke, *L'évolution de la doctrine du pneuma*; Hermann Kleinknecht and Eduard Schweizer, *"Pneuma,"* in *TDNT* 6:334–59, 396–451; Johannes Behm, *"Nous,"* in *TDNT* 4:951ff.

27. Schweitzer, *The Mysticism of Paul*, pp. 205–26.

28. Hermann Lüdemann, *Die Anthropologie des Apostels Paulus*, cited by W. David Stacey, *The Pauline View of Man*, p. 41.

29. Cf. also the Hebrew distinction between inward ("the heart"; "the Spirit") and external ("the flesh") in Rom. 2:29. (But cf. Ernst Käsemann, *An die Romer*, pp. 69ff.)

30. Bultmann, *Theology of the New Testament*, 1:195.

31. Cf. Rom. 6:13: "your members" = "yourselves."

32. "[Pauline] anthropology is cosmology *in concreto*, even in the sphere of faith" (Käsemann, "On Paul's Anthropology," in *Perspectives on Paul*, p. 27).

33. In 2 Cor. 4:10–11, body (v. 10) = mortal flesh (v. 11) (*thnētē sarx*).

34. Cf. RSV; however, in Phil. 3:14 (*"eis to brabeion tēs anō klēseōs tou theou en Christo Iēsou"*) *anō* refers to the source of the call, not its "heavenly" goal.

35. Karl Paul Donfried, "Justification and Last Judgment in Paul."

36. Oscar Cullmann, *Christ and Time*, p. 121.

37. Blaise Pascal, "Le Mystère de Jésus," in *Pensées sur la Religion*.

38. Karl Barth, *The Resurrection of the Dead*, pp. 13–124.

39. Except for 1 Cor. 15:45, "the last Adam became a life-giving Spirit" (i.e., for our life *after* the final resurrection [?]), the Spirit has no function in 1 Corinthians 15.

40. Nestle text (25th ed., 1963) vs. United Bible Societies' text (3d ed., 1975).

41. Cf., however, 1 Thess. 1:6: in v. 5 "the Spirit" is synonymous with "power," and in v. 6 the reception of the gospel occurred "in much affliction [*thlipsis*] with joy of the Holy Spirit."

42. Jürgen Moltmann, *The Crucified God*, e.g., p. 204.

43. Dieter Georgi, *Die Gegner des Paulus im 2. Korintherbrief*; cf. also Siegfried Schulz, "Die Decke des Moses"; Gerhard Friedrich, "Die Gegner des Paulus im 2 Korintherbrief," in *Abraham unser Vater*.

44. Cf. Ernst Käsemann, "Die Legitimität des Apostels."

45. Cf. Georgi, *Die Gegner des Paulus im 2. Kor*, pp. 246–300.

46. Willem Cornelis van Unnik (*Sparsa Collecta* 1:194–210) vs. Schulz ("Die Decke des Moses").

47. "Servants" (*diakonoi*): 2 Cor. 3:6; 6:4; 11:15, 23; "service" (*diakonia*): 3:7, 8, 9; 4:1; 5:18; 6:3; 8:4; 9:1, 12, 13; 11:8; "to serve" (*diakonein*): 2 Cor. 3:3; 8:19; elsewhere it occurs rarely and in a different context: 1 Cor. 3:5; Rom. 11:13; cf. Rom. 13:4 (the state); Rom. 15:8; Gal. 2:17 (Christ as servant); Rom. 16:1; Phil. 1:1 (ministerial office).

48. Friedrich, "Die Gegner des Paulus im 2. Kor."
49. Tertullian *Apology*, chap. 50.
50. Wolfgang Schrage, "Leid, Kreuz und Eschaton."

CHAPTER 14—The Church as the Dawning of the New Age

1. Charles Harold Dodd, *The Meaning of Paul for Today*, chaps. 11 and 12.
2. John Arthur Thomas Robinson, *The Body*, p. 79.
3. "Fellow citizens with the saints and members of the household of God [i.e. angels]," Eph. 2:19; cf. already Sir. 24:2.
4. Donald Wayne Riddle, *Paul, Man of Conflict.*
5. Heinrich Julius Holtzmann, *Lehrbuch der neutestamentlichen Theologie*, 2:164.
6. Heinrich Weinel, *Biblische Theologie des Neuen Testaments*, p. 322.
7. William Wrede, *Paul*; Albert Schweitzer, *The Mysticism of Paul*; Hans Joachim Schoeps, *Paul.*
8. Richard Reitzenstein, *Die hellenistischen Mysterienreligionen*; Wilhelm Bousset, *Kyrios Christos*; Wilhelm Heitmüller, *Taufe und Abendmahl bei Paulus.*
9. *Christianos* comes into existence in Antioch, according to Acts 11:26; Paul never uses it, but cf. 1 Pet. 4:16.
10. Cf. Peter Stuhlmacher, *Der Brief an Philemon.*
11. Eduard Schweizer, "Gottesgerechtigkeit und Lasterkataloge bei Paulus," in *Rechtfertigung.*
12. Cf., e.g., Ernst Käsemann, *Leib und Leib Christi*; Ernest Best, *One Body in Christ.*
13. Cf. the parable of Menenius Agrippa in Livy 2.32, about the state as a "body."
14. Cf. Denys Edward Hugh Whiteley, *The Theology of St. Paul*, pp. 198–99: "St. Paul's *doctrine* of the church is not complicated. . . . On the contrary, he says in effect that the church is the chief sphere of the activity of God in Christ, but he expresses this simple truth through a variety of metaphors, which lend to his doctrine the appearance of complexity."
15. Rudolf Karl Bultmann, *Theology of the New Testament*, 1. Only one subsection in the essay on Paul is devoted to the church (i.e., under the topic of grace), and the accent here and elsewhere is on the genetic provenance of the terms "church" and "body"; cf. 1:92–108.
16. Heinrich Weinel, *Biblische Theologie des Neuen Testaments*; cf. also Paul Wernle, *Der Christ und die Sünde bei Paulus.*
17. Cf., however, Rom. 16:16: "the churches of *Christ*"; cf. also 1 Thess. 1:1; Gal. 1:23.
18. But in 1 Cor. 12:27, 28 the image of the body (v. 27) is picked up by that of the church (v. 28); however, according to Ferdinand Hahn ("Der Apostolat im Urchristentum"), Paul makes a fresh start in v. 28.
19. Whiteley, *Theology of St. Paul*, p. 191.
20. Ibid.

21. Wolfgang Schrage, " 'Ekklesia' and 'Synagoge' "; cf. also Whiteley, *Theology of St. Paul*, p. 186; Walter Schmithals, *Der Römerbrief als historisches Problem*, p. 68.

22. Klaus Berger, "Volksversammlung und Gemeinde Gottes."

23. Hans Georg Conzelmann, *An Outline of the Theology of the New Testament*, p. 254; cf. also Paul Minear, "Church, Idea of" in *IDB* 1:608.

24. Cf. Peter Richardson, *Israel in the Apostolic Church*, pp. 74ff.

25. Berger, "Volksversammlung und Gemeinde Gottes."

26. Ibid., p. 198.

27. Ibid.

28. Floyd Vivian Filson, "The Significance of the Early House Churches."

29. Cf. Bousset, *Kyrios Christos*.

30. Cf. Ernst Käsemann, "Worship in Everyday Life," in *New Testament Questions of Today*.

31. Cf. Klaus Wengst, "Das Zusammenkommen der Gemeinde und ihr 'Gottesdienst' nach Paulus."

32. Cf. Philipp Vielhauer, *Oikodome*.

33. Robin Scroggs, "Paul and the Eschatological Woman," pp. 291ff.; idem, "Paul and the Eschatological Woman: Revisited."

34. Ibid.

35. Gerd Theissen, "Die Starken und Schwachen in Korinth," pp. 171ff.

36. Ernst Troeltsch, *The Social Teaching of the Christian Churches*.

37. Theissen, "Die Starken und Schwachen in Korinth," pp. 171ff.

38. Elaine Hiesey Pagels, "Paul and Women," p. 545.

39. Ibid.

40. Ibid.

41. Cartlidge, cited in ibid., p. 546.

42. Tacitus *Nero* 162.

43. Johannes Friedrich, Wolfgang Pöhlmann, and Peter Stuhlmacher, "Zur historischen Situation und Intention von Röm. 13:1-7"; cf. Rom. 13:7: *phoros* and *telos*, i.e., *tributum* (income tax) and *vectigal* (tolls).

CHAPTER 15—The Destiny of Israel

1. Cf. already Barn. 4:4-8; 13:1. Cf. also Peter Richardson, *Israel in the Apostolic Church*, pp. 9ff.

2. But cf. our discussion in Chapter 14, p. 317, where we argue that "sons of Abraham" in Gal. 3:7-29 refers to Christians as "true Israel."

3. Leander E. Keck, "The Poor among the Saints in the New Testament"; idem, "The Poor among the Saints in Jewish Christianity and Qumran."

4. And not a temple tax as Karl Holl argues in "Der Kirchenbegriff des Paulus," in *Gesammelte Aufsätze* 2.

5. Cf. Walter Gutbrod, *"Israēl,"* in *TDNT* 3:390.

6. Cf. Herman Nicolaas Ridderbos, *Aan de Romeinen*, p. 261.

7. Ibid.

8. However, Paul comes close to it with his image of the pot and the clay and his interpretation of Jacob and Esau: "Jacob I loved, but Esau I hated" (Rom. 9:13).

9. Adolf von Harnack, *What Is Christianity?* p. 144.

10. Paul Anton de Lagarde, *Deutsche Schriften.*

11. William Wrede, *Paul,* p. 156; von Harnack, *What Is Christianity?* pp. 183–89.

12. Richard Reitzenstein, *Die hellenistischen Mysterienreligionen.*

13. Cf. Ferdinand Christian Baur's sketch of Paul as the apostle of "true spirit" and the antagonist of Jewish Christianity; cf. also Charles Harold Dodd's *The Meaning of Paul for Today,* where Judaism is equated with narrowness and legalism, and Paul is equated with open universalism and love.

14. Ferdinand Christian Baur, *Paul, the Apostle;* Hans Lietzmann, *The Beginnings of the Christian Church.*

15. Cf. George Foot Moore, *Judaism in the First Centuries of the Christian Era;* Ed Parish Sanders, *Paul and Palestinian Judaism.*

16. Martin Buber, *Two Types of Faith;* Géza Vermès, *Jesus the Jew.*

17. Joseph Klausner, *From Jesus to Paul;* Hans Joachim Schoeps, *Paul;* Samuel Sandmel, *The Genius of Paul.*

18. Tertullian *Against Marcion* 3.5.

19. Cf., among many commentators on Romans, Karl Barth, *Der Römerbrief,* pp. 327ff.

20. Leo Baeck, "Romantic Religion," in *Judaism and Christianity,* pp. 189ff.

21. Ibid.

22. Jochanan Bloch, *On the Apocalyptic in Judaism.*

23. Cf. Julius Wellhausen, *Israelitische und jüdische Geschichte.*

24. Cf. Emil Ludwig Fackenheim, *God's Presence in History.*

CHAPTER 16—The Triumph of God

1. Robert Walter Funk, *Language, Hermeneutic, and Word of God,* p. 230.

2. Alfred North Whitehead, *Religion in the Making,* p. 56.

3. Funk, *Language, Hermeneutic, and Word of God,* p. 235.

4. Cf. Paul Anton de Lagarde, *Deutsche Schriften;* Ernest Renan, *Saint Paul;* William Wrede, *Paul.*

5. Rudolf Karl Bultmann, *Theology of the New Testament,* 1:190.

6. Rudolf Bultmann, "History and Eschatology in the New Testament," p. 16.

7. Cf. Oscar Cullmann, *Christ and Time,* p. 139.

8. Bultmann, *Theology of the New Testament,* 1:191.

9. Nils Alstrup Dahl, "The Neglected Factor in New Testament Theology."

10. Cullmann, *Christ and Time.*

11. Ibid., p. 139.

12. Tertullian *De Praescriptione Haereticorum*.

13. The Septuagint and Vulgate, however, included the Apocrypha, whereas the Reformation excluded them.

14. Klaus Koch, *The Rediscovery of Apocalyptic*, p. 37.

15. Cf. Hartmut Gese, "Erwägungen zur Einheit der biblischen Theologie," in *Vom Sinai zum Zion*; idem, *Zur biblischen Theologie*.

16. Julius Wellhausen, *Israelitische und jüdische Geschichte*.

17. David Friedrich Strauss, *The Life of Jesus, Critically Examined*; Rudolf Karl Bultmann, "New Testament and Mythology," in *Kerygma and Myth*, 1; Charles Harold Dodd, *New Testament Studies*.

18. Richard Kabisch, *Die Eschatologie des Paulus in ihren Zusammenhängen mit dem Gesamtbegriff des Paulinismus*; Johannes Weiss, *Die Predigt Jesu vom Reiche Gottes*; Albert Schweitzer, *The Quest of the Historical Jesus*.

19. Ernst Käsemann, "On the Subject of Primitive Christian Apocalyptic," in *New Testament Questions of Today*, p. 109, n. 2 (translation taken from *Journal for Theology and the Church* 6 [1969]: 100, n. 2).

20. Ibid.; Peter Stuhlmacher, *Gerechtigkeit Gottes bei Paulus*; Hans Joachim Schoeps, *Paul*; Joseph Augustine Fitzmyer, *Pauline Theology*; Werner Georg Kümmel, *Die Theologie des Neuen Testaments nach seinen Hauptzeugen Jesus, Paulus, Johannes*; Ed Parish Sanders, *Paul and Palestinian Judaism*.

21. Jürgen Moltmann, *Theology of Hope*; Wolfhart Pannenberg, *Jesus—God and Man*; cf. the comments of Koch, *The Rediscovery of Apocalyptic*, pp. 98–111.

22. Sanders, *Paul and Palestinian Judaism*, pp. 423ff.

23. Albert Schweitzer, *The Mysticism of Paul*, pp. 205–26.

24. Schoeps, *Paul*, p. 109, acknowledges this formulation as the work of Ernst Lohmeyer in *Grundlagen paulinischer Theologie* (p. 145) and goes on to comment (n. 1): "It appeals to me more than Schweitzer's much over-emphasized and ambiguous 'mysticism' or 'objective Christ-mysticism.' "

25. Käsemann, "On the Subject of Primitive Christian Apocalyptic."

26. Ernst Käsemann, "The Beginnings of Christian Theology," in *New Testament Questions of Today*, p. 101.

27. Moltmann, *Theology of Hope*.

28. Jürgen Moltmann, *The Crucified God*.

29. Oscar Cullmann, *Christology of the New Testament*, pp. 3–4.

30. Cf. James McConkey Robinson, "The Future of New Testament Theology."

31. The United Presbyterian Church in the U.S.A., "The Confession of 1967," *Book of Confessions*, 9.55.

Bibliography
of Works Cited

Aleith, Eva. *Paulusverständnis in der alten Kirche.* Berlin: A. Töpelmann, 1937.

Althaus, Paul. *Der Brief an die Römer.* Das Neue Testament Deutsch 6. 5th ed. Göttingen: Vandenhoeck & Ruprecht, 1946.

————. Die letzten Dinge: Lehrbuch der Eschatologie. 7th ed. Gütersloh: C. Bertelsmann, 1957.

Anselm. *Cur Deus Homo?*

Aristotle. *Physics.*

Aulén, Gustaf. *Christus Victor: An Historical Study of the Three Main Types of the Idea of the Atonement.* New York: Macmillan Co., 1969.

Baeck, Leo. "The Faith of Paul." In *Judaism and Christianity.* Philadelphia: Jewish Publication Society of America, 1958. Pp. 139–68.

————. "Romantic Religion." In *Judaism and Christianity.* Philadelphia: Jewish Publication Society of America, 1958. Pp. 189–292.

Barr, James. *The Semantics of Biblical Language.* London: Oxford University, 1961.

Barrett, Charles Kingsley. *A Commentary on the Epistle to the Romans.* Harper's New Testament Commentaries. New York: Harper and Brothers, 1957.

————. *A Commentary on the Second Epistle to the Corinthians.* Harper's New Testament Commentaries. New York: Harper & Row, 1973.

Barth, Karl. *The Resurrection of the Dead.* New York: Fleming H. Revell, 1933.

————. *Der Römerbrief.* 3d ed. Munich: C. Kaiser, 1924. English translation (from the 6th German ed.): *The Epistle to the Romans.* London: Oxford University, 1933.

————. "Vorrede zur ersten Auflage." Reprinted in *Der Römerbrief.* 3d ed. Munich: C. Kaiser, 1924.

Bartsch, Hans Werner. "Die historische Situation des Römerbriefes." *Studia Evangelica* 4 (Texte und Untersuchungen 102 [1968]): 282–91.

Bauer, Walter. *Das Leben Jesu im Zeitalter der neutestamentlichen Apokryphen.* Tübingen: J. C. B. Mohr (Paul Siebeck), 1909.

Baumgarten, Jörg. *Paulus und die Apokalyptik: Die Auslegung apokalyptischer Überlieferungen in den echten Paulusbriefen.* Neukirchen-Vluyn: Neukirchener, 1975.

Baur, Ferdinand Christian. "Die Christuspartei in der korinthischen Gemeinde, der Gegensatz des petrinischen und paulinischen Christenthums in der ältesten Kirche, der Apostel Petrus in Rom." *Tübinger Zeitschrift für Theologie* 4 (1831): 61–206.

————. Paul, the Apostle of Jesus Christ; His Life and Work, His Epistles and His Doctrine: A Contribution to a Critical History of Primitive Christianity. 2d ed. 2 vols. London/Edinburgh: Williams and Norgate, 1876.

Beare, Francis Wright. *St. Paul and His Letters.* Nashville: Abingdon Press, 1962.

Becker, Jürgen. *Das Heil Gottes.* Studien zur Umwelt des Neuen Testaments 3. Göttingen: Vandenhoeck & Ruprecht, 1964.

Behm, Johannes. *"Nous."* In *Theological Dictionary of the New Testament.* Edited by G. Kittel and G. Friedrich. 9 vols. Grand Rapids: Wm. B. Eerdmans, 1964–74. Vol. 4, pp. 951–60.

Belser, Johannes Evangelist. *Einleitung in das Neue Testament.* 2d ed. Freiburg im Breisgau: Herder, 1905.

Ben-Chorim, Schalom. *Paulus: Der Völkerapostel in jüdischer Sicht.* Munich: P. List, 1970.

Berger, Klaus. "Apostelbrief und apostolische Rede: Zum Formular frühchristlicher Briefe." *Zeitschrift für die neutestamentliche Wissenschaft* 65 (1974): 190–231.

————. "Volksversammlung und Gemeinde Gottes: Zu den Anfängen der christlichen Verwendung von 'ekklesia.' " *Zeitschrift für Theologie und Kirche* 73 (1976): 167–207.

Bertram, George. "Die Himmelfahrt Jesu vom Kreuz aus und der Glaube an seine Auferstehung." In *Festgabe für Adolf Deissmann zum 60. Geburtstag, 7. November 1926.* Tübingen: J. C. B. Mohr (Paul Siebeck), 1927. Pp. 187–217.

Best, Ernest. *One Body in Christ: A Study in the Relationship of the Church to Christ in the Epistles of the Apostle Paul.* London: S.P.C.K., 1955.

Betz, Hans Dieter. "The Literary Composition and Function of Paul's Letter to the Galatians." *New Testament Studies* 21 (1975): 353–80.

Bligh, John. *Galatians: A Discussion of St. Paul's Epistle.* Householder Commentaries 1. London: St. Paul Publications, 1969.

Bloch, Jochanan. *On the Apocalyptic in Judaism.* Jewish Quarterly Review Monograph Series 2. Philadelphia: Dropsie College for Hebrew and Cognate Learning, 1952.

Bonnard, Pierre. "Où en est l'interprétation de l'épître aux Romains." *Revue de théologie et de philosophie* 1 (1951): 225–43.

Bornkamm, Günther. "Gesetz und Natur (Röm 2,14–16)." In *Studien zu Antike und Urchristentum. Gesammelte Aufsätze* 2. Beiträge zur evangelischen Theologie 28. Munich: C. Kaiser, 1959. Pp. 93–118.

————. "The Letter to the Romans as Paul's Last Will and Testament." *Australian Biblical Review* 11 (1963): 2–14.

————. *Paul.* New York: Harper & Row, 1971.

————. "Taufe und neues Leben bei Paulus (Röm. 6)." In *Das Ende des Gesetzes: Paulusstudien. Gesammelte Aufsätze* 1. Beiträge zur evangelischen Theologie 16. 2d ed. Munich: C. Kaiser, 1958. Pp. 34–50.

Bousset, Wilhelm. *Kyrios Christos: Geschichte des Christusglaubens von den Anfängen des Christentums bis Irenaeus.* 2d ed. rev. Göttingen: Vandenhoeck & Ruprecht, 1921. English translation: *Kyrios Christos.* Translated by John E. Steely. Nashville: Abingdon Press, 1970.

————. *Die Religion des Judentums im späthellenistischen Zeitalter.* 3d ed. by H. Gressmann. Tübingen: J. C. B. Mohr (Paul Siebeck), 1926.

Brandenburger, Egon. *Adam und Christus: Exegetisch-religionsgeschichtliche Untersuchung zu Röm. 5,12-21.* Wissenschaftliche Monographien zum Alten und Neuen Testament 7. Neukirchen: Kreis Moers, 1962.

Bruce, Frederick Fyvie. *Paul, Apostle of the Heart Set Free.* Exeter, Devon: Paternoster, 1977.

Brückner, Martin. *Die Entstehung der paulinischen Christologie.* Strassburg: J. H. Heitz (Heitz & Mündel), 1903.

Buber, Martin. *Two Types of Faith.* New York: Harper & Row, 1961.

Buck, Charles Henry, and Taylor, Greer. *Saint Paul: A Study of the Development of His Thought.* New York: Charles Scribner's Sons, 1969.

Büchsel, Friedrich. *Der Geist Gottes im Neuen Testament.* Gütersloh: C. Bertelsmann, 1926.

Bultmann, Rudolf Karl. "Christus des Gesetzes Ende." In *Glauben und Verstehen: Gesammelte Aufsätze* 2. 4th ed. Tübingen: J. C. B. Mohr (Paul Siebeck), 1965. Pp. 32-58.

————. "*Dikaiosynē Theou.*" *Journal of Biblical Literature* 83 (1964): 12-16.

————. "*Elpis.*" In *Theological Dictionary of the New Testament.* Edited by G. Kittel and G. Friedrich. 9 vols. Grand Rapids: Wm. B. Eerdmans, 1964-74. Vol. 2, pp. 517-23, 529-35.

————. "History and Eschatology in the New Testament." *New Testament Studies* 1 (1954-55): 5-16.

————. "Ignatius und Paulus." In *Studia Paulina in honorem Johannes de Zwaan, septuagenarii.* Haarlem: Bohn, 1953. Pp. 37-51.

————. "New Testament and Mythology." In *Kerygma and Myth* 1. Edited by H. W. Bartsch. London: S.P.C.K., 1953. Pp. 1-44.

————. "*Pisteuō.*" In *Theological Dictionary of the New Testament.* Edited by G. Kittel and G. Friedrich. 9 vols. Grand Rapids: Wm. B. Eerdmans, 1964-74. Vol. 6, pp. 197-228.

————. *Primitive Christianity: In Its Contemporary Setting.* New York: Meridian Books, 1956. Reprinted 1980 by Fortress Press, Philadelphia.

————. "Das Problem der Ethik bei Paulus." *Zeitschrift für die neutestamentliche Wissenschaft* 23 (1924): 123-40.

————. "Romans 7 and the Anthropology of Paul." In *Existence and Faith: The Shorter Writings of Rudolf Bultmann.* New York: Meridian Books, 1960. Pp. 147-57.

————. *Theology of the New Testament.* 2 vols. New York: Charles Scribner's Sons, 1951-55.

Buri, Fritz. *Die Bedeutung der neutestamentlichen Eschatologie für die neuere protestan-*

tische Theologie: Ein Versuch zur Klärung des Problems der Eschatologie und zu einem neuen Verständnis ihres eigentlichen Anliegens. Zurich: M. Niehans, 1935.

Burton, Ernest DeWitt. *A Critical and Exegetical Commentary on the Epistle to the Galatians.* International Critical Commentary. Edinburgh: T. & T. Clark, 1921.

Campenhausen, Hans von. "Das Bekenntnis in Urchristentum." *Zeitschrift für die neutestamentliche Wissenschaft* 63 (1972): 210-53.

Caragounis, Chrys C. *"Opsōnion:* A Reconsideration of Its Meaning." *Novum Testamentum* 16 (1974): 35-57.

Charles, Robert Henry, ed. *The Apocrypha and Pseudepigrapha of the Old Testament in English, with Introductions and Critical and Explanatory Notes to the Several Books.* 2 vols. Oxford: Clarendon Press, 1913.

_____. *A Critical History of the Doctrine of a Future Life in Israel, in Judaism, and in Christianity.* 2d ed. London: A. & C. Black, 1913.

Conzelmann, Hans Georg. *1 Corinthians: A Commentary on the First Epistle to the Corinthians.* Hermeneia Series. Philadelphia: Fortress Press, 1975.

_____. *An Outline of the Theology of the New Testament.* New York: Harper & Row, 1969.

_____. "Zur Analyse der Bekenntnisformel I. Kor. 15,3-5." *Evangelische Theologie* 25 (1965): 1–11. English translation: "On the Analysis of the Confessional Formula in I Corinthians 15:3-5." *Interpretation* 20 (1966): 15–25.

Cross, Frank Moore. *The Ancient Library of Qumrân and Modern Biblical Studies.* London: G. Duckworth, 1958.

Cullmann, Oscar. *Christ and Time: The Primitive Christian Conception of Time and History.* Philadelphia: Westminster Press, 1950.

_____. *Christology of the New Testament.* London: SCM Press, 1959.

_____. "The Tradition." In *The Early Church.* Edited by A. J. B. Higgins. London: SCM Press, 1956. Pp. 59-99.

Dahl, Nils Alstrup. "Contradictions in Scripture." In *Studies in Paul.* Minneapolis: Augsburg Publishing House, 1977. Pp. 159-77.

_____. "The Missionary Theology in the Epistle to the Romans." In *Studies in Paul.* Minneapolis: Augsburg Publishing House, 1977. Pp. 70-94.

_____. "The Neglected Factor in New Testament Theology." *Reflection* 73:1 (1975): 5-8.

_____. "The Particularity of the Pauline Epistles as a Problem in the Ancient Church." In *Neotestamentica et Patristica: Eine Freundesgabe, Herrn Professor Dr. Oscar Cullmann zu seinem 60. Geburtstage überreicht.* Novum Testamentum, Supplements 6. Leiden: E. J. Brill, 1962. Pp. 261-71.

_____. "Paul and the Church at Corinth According to 1 Cor. 1:10—4:21." In *Christian History and Interpretation: Studies Presented to John Knox.* Edited by W. R. Farmer, C. F. D. Moule, and R. R. Niebuhr. Cambridge: At the University, 1967. Pp. 313-35.

————. "Review of E. P. Sanders, *Paul and Palestinian Judaism.*" *Religious Studies Review* 4 (1978): 153–58.

————. "Two Notes on Romans 5." *Studia theologica* 5 (1951): 37–48.

Davies, William David. "The Jewish Background of the Teaching of Jesus: Apocalyptic and Pharisaism." In *Christian Origins and Judaism.* Philadelphia: Westminster Press, 1962. Pp. 19–30.

————. *Paul and Rabbinic Judaism: Some Rabbinic Elements in Pauline Theology.* 4th ed. Philadelphia: Fortress Press, 1980. London: S.P.C.K., 1981.

Deissmann, Gustav Adolf. *Light from the Ancient East: The New Testament Illustrated by Recently Discovered Texts of the Graeco-Roman World.* London: Hodder and Stoughton, 1910.

————. *Die neutestamentliche Formel "in Christo Jesu" untersucht.* Marburg: N. G. Elwert, 1892.

————. *Paul: A Study in Social and Religious History.* 2d ed. London: Hodder and Stoughton, 1926.

Dibelius, Martin. *From Tradition to Gospel.* New York: Charles Scribner's Sons, 1965.

Dodd, Charles Harold. *The Apostolic Preaching and Its Developments.* 2d ed. New York: Harper & Row, 1951.

————. *The Epistle of Paul to the Romans.* Moffat New Testament Commentary. New York: Harper & Row, 1932.

————. *The Meaning of Paul for Today.* New York: George H. Doran, 1920.

————. *New Testament Studies.* New York: Charles Scribner's Sons, 1954.

Dodds, Eric Robertson. *Pagan and Christian in an Age of Anxiety: Some Aspects of Religious Experience from Marcus Aurelius to Constantine.* Cambridge: At the University, 1965.

Donfried, Karl Paul. "Justification and Last Judgment in Paul." *Interpretation* 30 (1976): 140–52.

Doty, William G. *Letters in Primitive Christianity.* Guides to Biblical Scholarship: New Testament Series. Philadelphia: Fortress Press, 1973.

Doughty, Darrel J. "Priority of *Charis*: An Investigation of the Theological Language of Paul." *New Testament Studies* 19 (1973): 163–80.

Drane, John William. *Paul, Libertine or Legalist?: A Study in the Theology of the Major Pauline Epistles.* London: S.P.C.K., 1975.

————. "Tradition, Law and Ethics in Pauline Theology." *Novum Testamentum* 16 (1974): 167–78.

Duhm, Bernhard. *Israels Propheten.* 2d ed. Tübingen: J. C. B. Mohr (Paul Siebeck), 1922.

Dunn, James D. G. *Unity and Diversity in the New Testament: An Inquiry into the Character of Earliest Christianity.* Philadelphia: Westminster Press, 1977.

Dupont, Jacques Jean. "Le problème de la structure littéraire de l'Épître aux Romains." *Revue biblique* 62 (1955): 365–97.

Eareckson, Vincent Offley. "The Glory to Be Revealed Hereafter: The Interpretation of Romans 8:18–25 and Its Place in Pauline Theology." Ph.D. dissertation. Princeton Theological Seminary, 1977.

Ebeling, Gerhard. "Erwägungen zur Eschatologie," in *Wort und Glaube*, vol. 3. Tübingen: J. C. B. Mohr (Paul Siebeck), 1975.

_____. "Jesus and Faith." In *Word and Faith*. Philadelphia: Fortress Press, 1963. Pp. 201–46.

_____. *The Nature of Faith*. Philadelphia: Fortress Press, 1967.

Ellis, Edward Earle. "Midrash Pesher in Pauline Hermeneutics." In *Prophecy and Hermeneutic in Early Christianity: New Testament Essays*. Wissenschaftliche Untersuchungen zum Neuen Testament 18. Grand Rapids: Wm. B. Eerdmans, 1978. Pp. 173–81.

Elze, Martin. "Häresie und Einheit der Kirche im 2. Jahrhundert." *Zeitschrift für Theologie und Kirche* 71 (1974): 389–409.

Eusebius. *The Ecclesiastical History*.

Fackenheim, Emil Ludwig. *God's Presence in History: Jewish Affirmations and Philosophical Reflections*. New York: Harper & Row, 1972.

Feuillet, André. "Le plan salvifique de Dieu d'après l'Épître aux Romains." *Revue biblique* 57 (1950): 336–87, 489–529.

Filson, Floyd Vivian. "The Significance of the Early House Churches." *Journal of Biblical Literature* 58 (1939): 105–12.

Fitzmyer, Joseph Augustine. *Pauline Theology: A Brief Sketch*. Englewood Cliffs: Prentice-Hall, 1967.

Friedrich, Gerhard. "1. Thessalonicher 5,1–11, der apologetische Einschub eines Späteren." In *Auf das Wort kommt es an: Gesammelte Aufsätze*. Edited by Johannes H. Friedrich. Göttingen: Vandenhoeck & Ruprecht, 1978. Pp. 251–78.

_____. "Die Gegner des Paulus im 2. Korintherbrief." In *Abraham unser Vater; Juden und Christen im Gespräch über die Bibel: Festschrift für Otto Michel zum 60. Geburtstag*. Edited by O. Betz, M. Hengel, and P. Schmidt. Leiden: E. J. Brill, 1963. Pp. 181–215.

_____. "Römerbrief." *Die Religion in Geschichte und Gegenwart: Handwörterbuch für Theologie und Religionswissenschaft*. 3d ed. Edited by Kurt Galling et al. 6 vols. Tübingen: J. C. B. Mohr (Paul Siebeck), 1957–62. Vol. 5, cols. 1137–43.

Friedrich, Johannes; Pöhlmann, Wolfgang; and Stuhlmacher, Peter. "Zur historischen Situation und Intention von Röm 13, 1–7." *Zeitschrift für Theologie und Kirche* 73 (1976): 131–66.

Fuchs, Ernst. "Die Auferstehungsgewissheit nach 1. Korinther 15." *Zum hermeneutischen Problem in der Theologie: Die Existentiale Interpretation*. Tübingen: J. C. B. Mohr (Paul Siebeck), 1959. Pp. 197–210.

_____. *Hermeneutik*. Bad Cannstatt: R. Müllerschön, 1954.

_____. "Über die Aufgabe einer christlichen Theologie: Zum Aufsatz Ernst Käsemanns über 'Die Anfänge christlicher Theologie.'" *Zeitschrift für Theologie und Kirche* 58 (1961): 245–67.

Funk, Robert Walter. "The Apostolic Parousia: Form and Significance." In *Christian History and Interpretation: Studies Presented to John Knox.* Edited by W. R. Farmer, C. F. D. Moule, and R. R. Niebuhr. Cambridge: At the University, 1967. Pp. 249–68.

_____. *Language, Hermeneutic, and Word of God: The Problem of Language in the New Testament and Contemporary Theology.* New York: Harper & Row, 1966.

Gäumann, Niklaus. *Taufe und Ethik: Studien zu Römer 6.* Beiträge zur evangelischen Theologie 47. Munich: C. Kaiser, 1967.

Gager, John Goodrich. "Functional Diversity in Paul's Use of End-Time Language." *Journal of Biblical Literature* 89 (1970): 325–37.

Gamble, Harry Yandle, Jr. *The Textual History of the Letter to the Romans: A Study in Textual and Literary Criticism.* Studies and Documents 42. Grand Rapids: Wm. B. Eerdmans, 1977.

Gaugler, Ernst. *Der Römerbrief.* 2 vols. Zurich: Zwingli-verlag, 1945–52.

Georgi, Dieter. *Die Gegner des Paulus im 2. Korintherbrief.* Wissenschaftliche Monographien zum Alten und Neuen Testament 11. Neukirchen-Vluyn: Neukirchener, 1964.

_____. *Die Geschichte der Kollekte des Paulus für Jerusalem.* Theologische Forschung 38. Hamburg-Bergstet: Reich, 1965.

Gerhardsson, Birger. *Memory and Manuscript: Oral Tradition and Written Transmission in Rabbinic Judaism and Early Christianity.* Uppsala: C. W. K. Gleerup, 1961.

Gese, Hartmut. "Erwägungen zur Einheit der biblischen Theologie." In *Vom Sinai zum Zion: Alttestamentliche Beiträge zur biblischen Theologie.* Beiträge zur evangelischen Theologie 64. Munich: C. Kaiser, 1974. Pp. 11–30.

_____. *Zur biblischen Theologie: Alttestamentliche Vorträge.* Beiträge zur evangelischen Theologie 78. Munich: C. Kaiser, 1977.

Ginsburg, Louis. "Some Observations on the Attitude of the Synagogue towards the Apocalyptic-Eschatological Writings." *Journal of Biblical Literature* 41 (1922): 115–36.

Goguel, Maurice. *The Birth of Christianity.* London: Allen & Unwin, 1953.

Goodspeed, Edgar Johnson. *An Introduction to the New Testament.* Chicago: University of Chicago, 1937.

Goppelt, Leonhard. "Apokalyptik und Typologie bei Paulus." *Theologische Literaturzeitung* 89 (1964): 321–44.

Grant, Robert McQueen. *Second-Century Christianity: A Collection of Fragments.* London: S.P.C.K., 1946.

Gutbrod, Walter, "*Israēl.*" In *Theological Dictionary of the New Testament.* Edited by G. Kittel and G. Friedrich. 9 vols. Grand Rapids: Wm. B. Eerdmans, 1964–74. Vol. 3, pp. 369–91.

Hahn, Ferdinand. "Der Apostolat im Urchristentum: Seine Eigenart und seine Voraussetzungen." *Kerygma und Dogma* 20 (1974): 54–77.

Hammmerstein, Franz Freiherr von. *Das Messiasproblem bei Martin Buber.* Stuttgart: W. Kohlhammer, 1958.

Hanson, Paul David. *The Dawn of Apocalyptic.* Philadelphia: Fortress Press, 1975.

Harder, Günther. "Der konkrete Anlass des Römerbriefes." *Theologia Viatorum* 6 (1954): 13–24.

Harnack, Adolf von. *History of Dogma*. 3d ed. 7 vols. London: Williams and Norgate, 1895–1900.

———. *What Is Christianity? Sixteen Lectures Delivered in the University of Berlin During the Winter Term, 1899–1900*. 3d and rev. ed. New York: G. P. Putnam's Sons, 1904.

Hartman, Lars. "The Functions of Some So-Called Apocalyptic Timetables." *New Testament Studies* 22 (1976): 1–14.

Heitmüller, Wilhelm. *Taufe und Abendmahl bei Paulus*. Göttingen: Vandenhoeck & Ruprecht, 1903.

———. "Zum Problem Paulus und Jesus." *Zeitschrift für die neutestamentliche Wissenschaft* 13 (1912): 320–37.

Hengel, Martin. "*Mors turpissima crucis*: Die Kreuzigung in der antiken Welt und die 'Torheit' des 'Wortes vom Kreuz.' " In *Rechtfertigung: Festschrift für Ernst Käsemann*. Edited by J. Friedrich, W. Pöhlmann, and P. Stuhlmacher. Tübingen: J. C. B. Mohr (Paul Siebeck), 1976. Pp. 125–84. English translation: *Crucifixion: In the Ancient World and the Folly of the Message of the Cross*. Translated by John Bowden. Philadelphia: Fortress Press, 1977.

Hofius, Otfried. "Die Unabänderlichkeit des göttlichen Heilsratschlusses: Erwängungen zur Herkunft eines neutestamentlichen Theologumenon." *Zeitschrift für die neutestamentliche Wissenschaft* 64 (1973): 135–45.

Holl, Karl. "Der Kirchenbegriff des Paulus in seinem Verhältnis zu dem der Urgemeinde." In *Gesammelte Aufsätze zur Kirchengeschichte*. 3 vols. Tübingen: J. C. B. Mohr (Paul Siebeck), 1921–28. Vol. 2, pp. 44–67.

Holtzmann, Heinrich Julius. *Lehrbuch der neutestamentlichen Theologie*. 2d ed. 2 vols. Tübingen: J. C. B. Mohr (Paul Siebeck), 1911.

Hooker, Morna Dorothy. "Adam in Romans 1." *New Testament Studies* 6 (1960): 297–306.

Hoyle, Richard Birch. *The Holy Spirit in St. Paul*. London: Hodder and Stoughton, 1927.

Hübner, Hans. "Gal 3,10 und die Herkunft des Paulus." *Kerygma und Dogma* 19 (1973): 215–31.

———. "Das ganze und das eine Gesetz: Zum Problemkreis Paulus und die Stoa." *Kerygma und Dogma* 21 (1975): 239–56.

———. *Das Gesetz bei Paulus: Ein Beitrag zum Werden der paulinischen Theologie*. Forschungen zur Religion und Literatur des Alten und Neuen Testaments 119. Göttingen: Vandenhoeck & Ruprecht, 1978.

Hunter, Archibald Macbride. *Interpreting Paul's Gospel*. Philadelphia: Westminster Press, 1955.

———. *Paul and His Predecessors*. Rev. ed. Philadelphia: Westminster Press, 1961.

Ignatius. "[Epistle] To the Romans." In *The Apostolic Fathers*. The Loeb Classical

Library 24, 25. 2 vols. Cambridge: Harvard University, 1912. Vol. 1, pp. 224–39.

Irenaeus. *Against Heresies.*

Jacob, Edmond. "Death." In *The Interpreter's Dictionary of the Bible.* Edited by G. A. Buttrick. 4 vols. Nashville: Abingdon Press, 1962. Vol. 1, pp. 802–4.

James, William. *The Varieties of Religious Experience: A Study in Human Nature.* New York: Longmans, Green, and Co., 1902.

Jeremias, Joachim. " 'Flesh and Blood Cannot Inherit the Kingdom of God.' " *New Testament Studies* 2 (1956): 151–59.

———. "Paulus als Hillelit." *Neotestamentica et Semitica: Studies in Honour of Matthew Black.* Edited by E. E. Ellis and M. Wilcox. Edinburgh: T. & T. Clark, 1969. Pp. 88–94.

———. "Zur Gedankenführung in den paulinischen Briefen." In *Studia Paulina in honorem Johannes de Zwaan, septuagenarii.* Haarlem: Bohn, 1953. Pp. 146–54.

Jervell, Jacob. "Der Brief nach Jerusalem: Über Veranlassung und Adresse des Römerbriefes." *Studia theologica* 25 (1971): 61–73.

Josephus, Flavius. *The Antiquities of the Jews.*

———. *The Jewish War.*

Jüngel, Eberhard. "Das Gesetz zwischen Adam und Christus: Eine theologische Studie zu Röm 5, 12–21." *Zeitschrift für Theologie und Kirche* 60 (1963): 42–74.

Kabisch, Richard. *Die Eschatologie des Paulus in ihren Zusammenhängen mit dem Gesamtbegriff des Paulinismus.* Göttingen: Vandenhoeck & Ruprecht, 1893.

Käsemann, Ernst. "Amt und Gemeinde im Neuen Testament." In *Exegetische Versuche und Besinnungen.* 2 vols. Göttingen: Vandenhoeck & Ruprecht, 1960–65. Vol. 1, pp. 109–34.

———. *An die Römer.* Handbuch zum Neuen Testament 8a. Tübingen: J. C. B. Mohr (Paul Siebeck), 1973.

———. "The Beginnings of Christian Theology." In *New Testament Questions of Today.* Philadelphia: Fortress Press, 1969. Pp. 82–107.

———. "Die Legitimität des Apostels." *Zeitschrift für die neutestamentliche Wissenschaft* 41 (1942): 33ff.

———. *Leib und Leib Christi: Eine Untersuchung zur paulinischen Begrifflichkeit.* Beiträge zur historischen Theologie. Tübingen: J. C. B. Mohr (Paul Siebeck), 1933.

———. "On Paul's Anthropology." In *Perspectives on Paul.* Philadelphia: Fortress Press, 1971. Pp. 1–31.

———. "On the Subject of Primitive Christian Apocalyptic." In *New Testament Questions of Today.* Philadelphia: Fortress Press, 1969. Pp. 108–37. Also translated in *Journal for Theology and the Church* 6 (1969): 99–133.

———. " 'The Righteousness of God' in Paul." In *New Testament Questions of Today.* Philadelphia: Fortress Press, 1969. Pp. 168–82.

———. *Der Ruf der Freiheit.* 3d ed. Tübingen: J. C. B. Mohr (Paul Siebeck), 1968.

_____. "The Spirit and the Letter." In *Perspectives on Paul*. Philadelphia: Fortress Press, 1971. Pp. 138–66.

_____. "Worship in Everyday Life: A Note on Romans 12." In *New Testament Questions of Today*. Philadelphia: Fortress Press, 1969. Pp. 188–95.

Keck, Leander E. *Paul and His Letters*. Proclamation Commentaries. Philadelphia: Fortress Press, 1979.

_____. "The Poor among the Saints in Jewish Christianity and Qumran." *Zeitschrift für die neutestamentliche Wissenschaft* 57 (1966): 54–78.

_____. "The Poor among the Saints in the New Testament." *Zeitschrift für die neutestamentliche Wissenschaft* 56 (1965): 100–29.

Kelsey, David Hugh. *The Uses of Scripture in Recent Theology*. Philadelphia: Fortress Press, 1975.

Kierkegaard, Søren Aabye. *The Gospel of Suffering and The Lilies of the Field*. Minneapolis: Augsburg Publishing House, 1948.

_____. "Of the Difference between a Genius and an Apostle." In *The Present Age and Two Minor Ethico-Religious Treatises*. New York: Oxford University, 1940.

_____. *Purity of Heart Is to Will One Thing: Spiritual Preparation for the Office of Confession*. Rev. ed. New York: Harper & Row, 1948.

Kinoshita, Junji. "Romans—Two Writings Combined: A New Interpretation of the Body of Romans." *Novum Testamentum* 7 (1965): 258–77.

Klausner, Joseph. *From Jesus to Paul*. New York: Macmillan Co., 1943.

Klein, Günter. "Der Abfassungszweck des Römerbriefes." In *Rekonstruktion und Interpretation: Gesammelte Aufsätze zum Neuen Testament*. Munich: C. Kaiser, 1969. Pp. 129–44.

Kleinknecht, Hermann and Schweizer, Eduard. *"Pneuma."* In *Theological Dictionary of the New Testament*. Edited by G. Kittel and G. Friedrich. 9 vols. Grand Rapids: Wm. B. Eerdmans, 1964–74. Vol. 6, pp. 332–59, 389–455.

Klijn, Albertus Frederik Johannes. *Inleiding tot het Nieuwe Testament*. Utrecht: Aula-Boeken, 1961.

Knox, John. *Chapters in a Life of Paul*. Nashville: Abingdon-Cokesbury, 1950.

_____. *The Ethic of Jesus in the Teaching of the Church: Its Authority and Its Relevance*. Nashville: Abingdon Press, 1961.

_____. "A Note on the Text of Romans." *New Testament Studies* 2/3 (1955–56): 191–93.

_____. *Philemon among the Letters of Paul: A New View of Its Place and Importance*. Rev. ed. Nashville: Abingdon Press, 1959.

_____. "Romans 15:14–33 and Paul's Conception of His Apostolic Mission." *Journal of Biblical Literature* 83 (1964): 1–11.

Koch, Klaus. *The Rediscovery of Apocalyptic: A Polemical Work on a Neglected Area of Biblical Studies and Its Damaging Effects on Theology and Philosophy*. Studies in Biblical Theology 2/22. London: SCM Press, 1972.

Kretschmar, Georg. "Auferstehung des Fleisches." In *Leben Angesicht des Todes*

Helmut Thielicke zum 60. Geburtstag. Tübingen: J. C. B. Mohr (Paul Siebeck), pp. 101–37.

Kühl, Ernst. *Der Brief des Paulus an die Römer*. Leipzig: Quelle & Meyer, 1913.

Kümmel, Werner Georg. *Introduction to the New Testament*. Rev. ed. Nashville: Abingdon Press, 1975.

————. *Römer 7 und die Bekehrung des Paulus*. Untersuchungen zum Neuen Testament 17. Leipzig: J. C. Hinrichs, 1929.

————. *Die Theologie des Neuen Testaments nach seinen Hauptzeugen Jesus, Paulus, Johannes*. Göttingen: Vandenhoeck & Ruprecht, 1969. English translation: *The Theology of the New Testament According to Its Major Witnesses: Jesus—Paul— John*. Translated by John E. Steely. Nashville: Abingdon Press, 1973.

Kuhn, Heinz-Wolfgang. *Enderwartung und gegenwärtiges Heil: Untersuchungen zu den Gemeindeliedern von Qumran mit einem Anhang über Eschatologie und Gegenwart in der Verkündigung Jesu*. Studien zur Umwelt des Neuen Testaments 4. Göttingen: Vandenhoeck & Ruprecht, 1966.

————. "Der Irdische Jesu bei Paulus als traditionsgeschichtliches und theologisches Problem." *Zeitschrift für Theologie und Kirche* 67 (1970): 295–320.

————. "Jesus als Gekreuzigter in der frühchristlichen Verkündigung bis zur Mitte des 2. Jahrhunderts." *Zeitschrift für Theologie und Kirche* 72 (1975): 1–46.

Lagarde, Paul Anton de. *Deutsche Schriften*. 5th ed. Göttingen: Dieterich, 1920.

Lagrange, Marie-Joseph. *Saint Paul: Épître aux Romains*. 3d ed. Paris: Lecoffre, 1922.

Lang, Friedrich Gustav. "Gesetz und Bund bei Paulus." In *Rechtfertigung: Festschrift für Ernst Käsemann*. Edited by J. Friedrich, W. Pöhlmann, and P. Stuhlmacher. Tübingen: J. C. B. Mohr (Paul Siebeck), 1976. Pp. 305–21.

La Piana, George. "Foreign Groups in Rome During the First Centuries of the Empire." *Harvard Theological Review* 20 (1927): 183–403.

Leenhardt, Franz J. *L'Épître de Saint Paul aux Romains*. Commentaire du Nouveau Testament 6. Neuchâtel: Delachaux & Niestlé, 1957. English translation: *The Epistle to the Romans: A Commentary*. Translated by Harold Knight. London: Lutterworth Press, 1961.

Leisegang, Hans. *Der Apostel Paulus als Denker*. Leipzig: J. C. Hinrichs, 1923.

Lietzmann, Hans. *An die Römer*. Handbuch zum Neuen Testament 8. 4th ed. Tübingen: J. C. B. Mohr (Paul Siebeck), 1933.

————. *The Beginnings of the Christian Church*. Rev. ed. New York: Charles Scribner's Sons, 1949.

————. *Messe und Herrenmahl*. Arbeiten zur Kirchengeschichte 8. Bonn: Marcus & Weber, 1926.

Lightfoot, Joseph Barber. *Notes on Epistles of St. Paul, from Unpublished Commentaries*. New York/London: Macmillan and Co., 1895.

Limbeck, Meinrad. *Die Ordnung des Heils: Untersuchungen zum Gesetzesverständnis des Frühjudentums*. Düsseldorf: Patmos, 1971.

Lindemann, Andreas. *Paulus in ältesten Christentum*. Beitrage zur Historischen Theologie 58. Tübingen: J. C. B. Mohr (Paul Siebeck), 1979.

————. "Zum Abfassungszweck des Zweiten Thessalonicherbriefes." *Zeitschrift für die neutestamentliche Wissenschaft* 68 (1977): 35–47.

Lohmeyer, Ernst. *Grundlagen paulinischer Theologie.* Beiträge zur historischen Theologie 1. Tübingen: J. C. B. Mohr (Paul Siebeck), 1929.

————. "*Syn Christō.*" In *Festgabe für Adolf Deissmann zum 60. Geburtstag, 7. November 1926.* Tübingen: J. C. B. Mohr (Paul Siebeck), 1927. Pp. 218–57.

Lohse, Eduard. *Grundriss der neutestamentlichen Theologie.* Theologische Wissenschaft 5. Stuttgart: W. Kohlhammer, 1974.

Lucian. *De Morte Peregrini.*

Lüdemann, Hermann. *Die Anthropologie des Apostels Paulus und ihre Stellung innerhalb seiner Heilslehre.* Kiel: Universitäts-Buchhandlung (P. Toeche), 1872.

Lührmann, Dieter. *Glaube im frühen Christentum.* Gütersloh: G. Mohn, 1976.

Lütgert, Wilhelm. *Gesetz und Geist: Eine Untersuchung zur Vorgeschichte des Galaterbriefes.* Beiträge zur Förderung christlicher Theologie 22. Gütersloh: C. Bertelsmann, 1919.

————. *Der Römerbrief als historisches Problem.* Gütersloh: C. Bertelsmann, 1913.

Luther, Martin. "Epistel auf den 2. Sonntag nach Epiphanias. Röm 12, 6ff." *D. Martin Luthers Werke: Kritische Gesamtausgabe.* 83 vols. Weimar: H. Böhlaus, 1883–1960. Vol. 17/2, pp. 32–60.

————. "In epistolam S. Pauli ad Galatas Commentarius [1531]. 1535." *D. Martin Luthers Werke: Kritische Gesamtausgabe.* 83 vols. Weimar: H. Böhlaus, 1883–1960. Vol. 40/1, 2. English translation: "Lectures on Galatians, 1535." *Luther's Works.* Edited by Jaroslav Pelikan. 56 vols. St. Louis/Philadelphia: Concordia and Fortress Press, 1958ff. Vols. 26–27.

————. "Vorrede auf die Epistel S. Pauli an die Römer." In *D. Martin Luthers Werke: Kritische Gesamtausgabe: Die Deutsche Bibel.* 12 vols. Weimar: H. Böhlaus, 1906–1961. Vol. 7, pp. 1–27.

Luz, Ulrich. "Der alte und der neue Bund bei Paulus und im Hebräerbrief." *Evangelische Theologie* 27 (1967): 318–36.

————. "Zum Aufbau von Röm 1–8." *Theologische Zeitschrift* 25 (1969): 161–81.

Lyonnet, Stanislaus. "Note sur le plan de l'Épître aux Romains." *Recherches de science religieuse* 39 (1951–52): 301–16.

Mangold, Wilhelm Julius. *Der Römerbrief und seine geschichtlichen Voraussetzungen.* 2d ed. Marburg: N. G. Elwert, 1884.

Manson, Thomas Walter. "The Argument from Prophecy." *Journal of Theological Studies* 46 (1945): 129–36.

————. "St. Paul's Letter to the Romans—And Others." *Bulletin of the John Rylands University Library of Manchester* 31 (1948): 224–40.

Manson, William. "Notes on the Argument of Romans (ch. 1–8)." In *New Testament Essays: Studies in Memory of Thomas Walter Manson, 1893–1958.* Edited by A. J. B. Higgins. Manchester: Manchester University, 1959. Pp. 150–64.

Marxsen, Willi. "Erwägungen zum Problem des verkündigten Kreuzes." *New Testament Studies* 8 (1962): 204–14.

————. *Introduction to the New Testament: An Approach to Its Problems.* Oxford: Blackwell, 1968.

————. *The Resurrection of Jesus of Nazareth.* Philadelphia: Fortress Press, 1970.

Melanchthon, Philipp. "Römerbrief-Kommentar, 1532." In *Melanchthons Werke in Auswahl* 5. Edited by R. Stupperich. Gütersloh: C. Bertelsmann, 1965.

Metzger, Bruce Manning. "A Suggestion Concerning the Meaning of I Cor. XV.4b." *Journal of Theological Studies* n.s. 8 (1957): 118–23.

Meyer, Paul William. "The This-Worldliness of the New Testament." Inaugural address delivered at Princeton Theological Seminary on February 28, 1979.

Michel, Otto. *Der Brief an die Römer.* Meyers kritisch-exegetischer Kommentar über das Neue Testament 4. 12th ed. Göttingen: Vandenhoeck & Ruprecht, 1963.

Minear, Paul. "Church, Idea of." In *The Interpreter's Dictionary of the Bible.* Edited by G. A. Buttrick. 4 vols. Nashville: Abingdon Press, 1962. Vol. 1, pp. 607–17.

Moltmann, Jürgen. *The Crucified God: The Cross of Christ as the Foundation and Criticism of Christian Theology.* New York: Harper & Row, 1974.

————. *Theology of Hope: On the Ground and the Implications of a Christian Eschatology.* New York: Harper & Row, 1967.

Moody, Dwight Lyman. "The Return of Our Lord (1877)." In *The American Evangelicals, 1800–1900: An Anthology.* Edited by William G. McLoughlin. New York: Harper & Row, 1968. Pp. 180–85.

Moore, George Foot. *Judaism in the First Centuries of the Christian Era: The Age of the Tannaim.* 3 vols. Cambridge: Harvard University, 1927–30.

Morgan, William. *The Religion and Theology of Paul.* Edinburgh: T. & T. Clark, 1917.

Müller, Ulrich B. "Die Bedeutung des Kreuzestodes Jesu im Johannesevangelium: Erwägungen zur Kreuzestheologie im Neuen Testament." *Kerygma und Dogma* 21 (1975): 49–71.

Munck, Johannes. *Christus und Israel: Eine Auslegung von Röm 9–11.* Aarhus: Universitetsforlaget, 1956. English translation: *Christ and Israel: An Interpretation of Romans 9–11.* Translated by Ingeborg Nixon. Philadelphia: Fortress Press, 1967.

————. *Paul and the Salvation of Mankind.* Richmond: John Knox Press, 1959.

Murray, George. *Five Stages of Greek Religion.* 3d ed. Boston: Beacon Press, 1951.

Mussner, Franz. *Der Galaterbrief.* Herders theologischer Kommentar zum Neuen Testament 9. Freiburg i.B.: Herder, 1974.

————. *Theologie der Freiheit nach Paulus.* Freiburg i.B.: Herder, 1976.

Neugebauer, Fritz. "Das paulinische 'in Christo.' " *New Testament Studies* 4 (1958): 124–38.

Niebuhr, Reinhold. "Martin Buber: 1878–1865." *Christianity and Crisis: A Christian Journal of Opinion* 25 (1965): 146–47.

———. *The Nature and Destiny of Man: A Christian Interpretation.* 2 vols. New York: Charles Scribner's Sons, 1949.

Nietzsche, Friedrich. "The Antichrist: An Attempted Criticism of Christianity." In *The Complete Works of Friedrich Nietzsche.* Edited by O. Levy. 18 vols. New York: Macmillan Co., 1910–27. Vol. 16, pp. 125–231.

———. "The First Christian." In *The Dawn of Day.* New York: Macmillan Co., 1903. Pp. 56–61.

Noack, Bent Wenzel. "Current and Backwater in the Epistle to the Romans." *Studia theologica* 19 (1965): 155–66.

Nygren, Anders. *Commentary on Romans.* Philadelphia: Fortress Press, 1972.

Origen. *Contra Celsum.*

Osten-Sachen, Peter von der. "Gottes Treue bis zur Parusie: Formgeschichtliche Beobachtungen zu 1 Kor 1,7b–9." *Zeitschrift für die neutestamentliche Wissenschaft* 68 (1977): 176–99.

Pagels, Elaine Hiesey. *The Gnostic Paul: Gnostic Exegesis of the Pauline Letters.* Philadelphia: Fortress Press, 1975.

———. "Paul and Women: A Response to Recent Discussion." *Journal of the American Academy of Religion* 42 (1974): 538–49.

Pannenberg, Wolfhart. "Die Auferstehung Jesu und die Zukunft des Menschen." *Kerygma und Dogma* 24 (1978): 104–17.

———. "Eschatologie und Sinnerfahrung." *Kerygma und Dogma* 19 (1973): 39–52.

———. *Jesus—God and Man.* 2d ed. Philadelphia: Westminster Press, 1977.

———. "Tod and Auferstehung in der Sicht christlicher Dogmatik." *Kerygma und Dogma* 20 (1974): 167–80.

Pascal, Blaise. "Le Mystère de Jésus." *Pensées sur la Religion et sur quelques autres sujects.* 2d ed. Paris: Delmas, 1952. Pp. 334–37.

Peel, Malcolm Lee. *The Epistle to Rheginos; A Valentinian Letter on the Resurrection: Introduction, Translation, Analysis and Exposition.* The New Testament Library. Philadelphia: Westminster Press, 1969.

Perrin, Norman. "The Use of (*Para*)*didonai* in Connection with the Passion of Jesus in the New Testament." In *Der Ruf Jesu und die Antwort der Gemeinde: Exegetische Untersuchungen Joachim Jeremias zum 70. Geburtstag gewidmet von seinen Schülern.* Edited by E. Lohse, C. Burchard, B. Schaller. Göttingen: Vandenhoeck & Ruprecht, 1970. Pp. 204–12. Also in *A Modern Pilgrimage in New Testament Christology.* Philadelphia: Fortress Press, 1974. Pp. 94–103.

Pfleiderer, Otto. *Paulinism: A Contribution to the History of Primitive Christian Theology.* 2d ed. 2 vols. London: Williams and Norgate, 1891.

———. *Das Urchristentum, seine Schriften und Lehren in geschichtlichen Zusammenhang beschrieben.* 2d ed. 2 vols. Berlin: G. Reimer, 1902.

Philippi, Friedrich Adolph. *Commentar über den Brief Pauli an die Römer.* 3 vols. Erlangen: Heyder & Zimmer, 1848–52.

Preisker, Herbert. "Das historische Problem des Römerbriefes." *Wissenschaftliche Zeitschrift der Friedrich-Schiller-Universität Jena* 2 (1952–53). Geisteswissenschaftliche Reihe 1, pp. 25–30.

Prümm, Karl. "Zur Struktur des Römerbriefes: Begriffsreihen als Einheitsband." *Zeitschrift für Theologie und Kirche* 72 (1950): 333–49.

Rad, Gerhard von. "*Doxa*." In *Theological Dictionary of the New Testament*. Edited by G. Kittel and G. Friedrich. 9 vols. Grand Rapids: Wm. B. Eerdmans, 1964–74. Vol. 2, pp. 238–42.

————. *Old Testament Theology*. 2 vols. New York: Harper & Row, 1962–65.

Reitzenstein, Richard. *Die hellenistischen Mysterienreligionen nach ihren Grundgedanken und Wirkung*. 3d ed. Leipzig: B. G. Teubner, 1927. English translation: *Hellenistic Mystery Religions: Their Basic Ideas and Significance*. Translated by John E. Steely. Pittsburgh: Pickwick Press, 1978.

Renan, Ernest. *Saint Paul*. New York: G. W. Carleton, 1869.

Richardson, Peter. *Israel in the Apostolic Church*. Society for New Testament Studies Monograph Series 10. London: Cambridge University, 1969.

Ricoeur, Paul. "Préface à Bultmann." *Le Conflict des Interprétations: Essais d'herméneutique*. Paris: Éditions du Seuil, 1969. Pp. 373–92. English translation: "Preface to Bultmann" in *The Conflict of Interpretations: Essays on Hermeneutics*. Edited by Don Ihde. Evanston: Northwestern University Press, 1974. Also translated in *Essays on Biblical Interpretation*. Edited by Lewis S. Mudge. Philadelphia: Fortress Press, 1980.

Ridderbos, Herman Nicolaas. *Aan de Romeinen*. Commentaar op het Nieuwe Testament. Kampen: J. H. Kok, 1959.

————. *The Epistle of Paul to the Churches of Galatia*. New International Commentary on the New Testament. Grand Rapids: Wm. B. Eerdmans, 1953.

————. *Paulus: Ontwerp van zijn theologie*. Kampen: J. H. Kok, 1966.

Riddle, Donald Wayne. *Paul, Man of Conflict: A Modern Biographical Sketch*. Nashville: Cokesbury, 1940.

Robinson, John Arthur Thomas. *The Body: A Study in Pauline Theology*. Studies in Biblical Theology 5. London: SCM, 1952; and Philadelphia: Westminster Press, 1977.

————. *Jesus and His Coming: The Emergence of a Doctrine*. Nashville: Abingdon Press, 1958.

Robinson, James McConkey. "The Future of New Testament Theology." *Religious Studies Review* 2, no. 1 (1976): 17–23.

Rössler, Dietrich. *Gesetz und Geschichte: Untersuchungen zur Theologie der jüdischen Apokalyptik und der pharisäischen Orthodoxie*. Neukirchen: Kreis Moers, 1960.

Roetzel, Calvin J. *The Letters of Paul: Conversations in Context*. Atlanta: John Knox Press, 1975.

Ropes, James Hardy. "The Epistle to the Romans and Jewish Christianity." In *Studies in Early Christianity*. Edited by S. J. Case. New York/London: Century, 1928. Pp. 353–65.

Rubenstein, Richard Lowell. *My Brother Paul.* New York: Harper & Row, 1972.

Sanday, William, and Headlam, Arthur Cayley. *A Critical and Exegetical Commentary on the Epistle to the Romans.* International Critical Commentary. 5th ed. Edinburgh: T. & T. Clark, 1902.

Sanders, Ed Parish. *Paul and Palestinian Judaism: A Comparison of Patterns of Religion.* Philadelphia: Fortress Press, 1977.

Sandmel, Samuel. *The Genius of Paul: A Study in History.* New York: Farrar, Straus & Cudahy, 1958. Reprinted 1979 by Fortress Press, Philadelphia.

Sass, Gerhard. "Zur Bedeutung von *doulos* bei Paulus." *Zeitschrift für die neutestamentliche Wissenschaft* 40 (1941): 24–32.

Schlatter, Adolf von. *Der Glaube im Neuen Testament.* 4th ed. Stuttgart: Calwer, 1927.

————. *Gottes Gerechtigkeit: Ein Kommentar zum Römerbrief.* 2d ed. Stuttgart: Calwer, 1952.

————. *Die Theologie des Neuen Testaments und die Dogmatik.* Gütersloh: C. Bertelsmann, 1909.

Schlier, Heinrich. *Der Brief an die Galater.* Meyers kritisch-exegetischer Kommentar über das Neue Testament 7. 11th ed. Göttingen: Vandenhoeck & Ruprecht, 1951.

Schmidt, Hans Wilhelm. *Der Brief des Paulus an die Römer.* Theologischer Handkommentar zum Neuen Testament 6. Berlin: Evangelische Verlagsanstalt, 1962.

Schmidt, Karl Ludwig. *Die Judenfrage im Lichte der Kapitel 9–11 des Römerbriefes.* Theologische Studien 13. 2d ed. Zollikon: Evangelischer, 1942.

Schmithals, Walter. *Die Gnosis in Korinth.* Göttingen: Vandenhoeck & Ruprecht, 1956. English translation: *Gnosticism in Corinth: An Investigation of the Letters to the Corinthians.* Translated by John E. Steely. Nashville: Abingdon Press, 1971.

————. "Die Korintherbriefe als Briefsammlung." *Zeitschrift für die neutestamentliche Wissenschaft* 64 (1973): 263–88.

————. *Der Römerbrief als historisches Problem.* Studien zum Neuen Testament 9. Gütersloh: G. Mohn, 1975.

Schnackenburg, Rudolf. *God's Rule and Kingdom.* New York: Herder and Herder, 1963.

Schneider, Johannes. *Die Passionmystik des Paulus: Ihr Wesen, ihr Hintergrund und ihr Nachwirkungen.* Untersuchungen zum Neuen Testament 15. Leipzig: J. C. Hinrichs, 1929.

Schoeps, Hans Joachim. *Paul: The Theology of the Apostle in the Light of Jewish Religious History.* Philadelphia: Westminster Press, 1961.

Schrage, Wolfgang. " 'Ekklesia' and 'Synagoge' ": Zum Ursprung des urchristlichen Kirchenbegriffs." *Zeitschrift für Theologie und Kirche* 60 (1963): 178–202.

————. *Die konkreten Einzelgebote in der paulinischen Paränese: Ein Beitrag zur neutestamentlichen Ethik.* Gütersloh: G. Mohn, 1961.

————. "Leid, Kreuz und Eschaton: Die Peristasenkataloge als Merkmale paulinischer theologia crucis und Eschatologie." *Evangelische Theologie* 34 (1974): 141–75.

―――. "Das Verständnis des Todes Jesu Christi im Neuen Testament." In E. Bizer et al., *Das Kreuz Jesu Christi als Grund des Heils.* Schriftenreihe des Theologischen Ausschusses der Evangelischen Kirche der Union 3. Gütersloh: G. Mohn, 1967. Pp. 49–89.

Schrenk, Gottlob. "Der Römerbrief als Missionsdokument." *Studien zu Paulus.* Abhandlungen zur Theologie des Alten und Neuen Testaments 26. Zurich: Zwingli-Verlag, 1954. Pp. 81–106.

Schulz, Siegfried. "Die Decke des Moses: Untersuchungen zu einer vorpaulinischen Überlieferung in 2 Kor 3,7–18." *Zeitschrift für die neutestamentliche Wissenschaft* 49 (1958): 1–30.

Schweitzer, Albert. *The Mysticism of Paul the Apostle.* New York: H. Holt and Co., 1931.

―――. *Paul and His Interpreters: A Critical History.* New York: Macmillan Co., 1951.

―――. *The Quest of the Historical Jesus: A Critical Study of Its Progress from Reimarus to Wrede.* 3d ed. London: A. & C. Black, 1954.

Schweizer, Eduard. "Gottesgerechtigkeit und Lasterkataloge bei Paulus (inkl. Kol und Eph)." In *Rechtfertigung: Festschrift für Ernst Käsemann.* Edited by J. Friedrich, W. Pöhlmann, and P. Stuhlmacher. Tübingen: J. C. B. Mohr (Paul Siebeck), 1976. Pp. 461–78.

―――. "Die 'Mystik' des Sterbens und Auferstehens mit Christus bei Paulus." *Evangelische Theologie* 26 (1966): 239–57.

Scroggs, Robin. "Paul and the Eschatological Woman." *Journal of the American Academy of Religion* 40 (1972): 283–301.

―――. "Paul and the Eschatological Woman: Revisited." *Journal of the American Academy of Religion* 42 (1974): 432–37.

Seeberg, Alfred. *Der Katechismus der Urchristenheit.* Leipzig: A. Deichert, 1903.

Sevenster, Jan Nicolaas. "Einige Bemerkungen über den 'Zwischenzustand' bei Paulus." *New Testament Studies* 1 (1954–55): 291–96.

―――. "Some Remarks on the *gymnos* in 2 Cor. V. 3." In *Studia Paulina in honorem Johannes de Zwaan, septuagenarii.* Haarlem: Bohm, 1953. Pp. 202–14.

Stacey, W. David. *The Pauline View of Man.* London: Macmillan, 1956.

Stauffer, Ethelbert. *Jesus, Paulus und Wir: Antwort auf einen Offenen Brief von Paul Althaus, Walter Künneth und Wilfried Joest.* Hamburg: Fr. Wittig, 1961.

Stendahl, Krister. "The Apostle Paul and the Introspective Conscience of the West." *Harvard Theological Review* 56 (1963): 199–215. Reprinted in *Paul among Jews and Gentiles and Other Essays.* Philadelphia: Fortress Press, 1976. Pp. 78–96.

―――. "Paul among Jews and Gentiles." In *Paul among Jews and Gentiles and Other Essays.* Philadelphia: Fortress Press, 1976. Pp. 1–77.

Stoike, Donald. " 'The Law of Christ': A Study of Paul's Use of the Expression in Galatians 6:2." Ph.D. dissertation. School of Theology at Claremont, 1971.

Strack, Hermann Leberecht, and Billerbeck, Paul. *Kommentar zum Neuen Testament aus Talmud und Midrasch.* 6 vols. Munich: Beck, 1922–61.

Strauss, David Friedrich. *The Life of Jesus, Critically Examined.* Translated from the German edition by George Eliot. London: Chapman, 1846. Reprinted 1972 by Fortress Press. Edited and with an Introduction by Peter C. Hodgson (Lives of Jesus Series).

Stuhlmacher, Peter. *Der Brief an Philemon.* Evangelisch-katholischer Kommentar zum Neuen Testament. Neukirchen-Vluyn: Neukirchener, 1975.

————. "Erwägungen zum ontologischen Charakter der *kainē ktisis* bei Paulus." *Evangelische Theologie* 27 (1967): 1–35.

————. "Erwägungen zum Problem von Gegenwart und Zukunft in der paulinischen Theologie." *Zeitschrift für Theologie und Kirche* 64 (1967): 423–50.

————. *Gerechtigkeit Gottes bei Paulus.* Göttingen: Vandenhoeck & Ruprecht, 1966.

Suggs, M. Jack. " 'The Word Is Near You': Romans 10:6–10 Within the Purpose of the Letter." In *Christian History and Interpretation: Studies Presented to John Knox.* Edited by W. R. Farmer, C. F. D. Moule, and R. R. Niebuhr. Cambridge: At the University, 1967. Pp. 289–312.

Tacitus, Cornelius. *Nero.*

Tertullian. *Against Marcion.*

————. *De Praescriptione Haereticorum.*

————. *De Resurrectione Carnis.*

Theissen, Gerd. "Soteriologische Symbolik in den paulinischen Schriften." *Kerygma und Dogma* 20 (1974): 282–304.

————. "Die Starken und Schwachen in Korinth: Sociologische Analyse eines theologischen Streites." *Evangelische Theologie* 35 (1975): 155–72.

Troeltsch, Ernst. *Der Historismus und seine Probleme. Gesammelte Schriften.* Vol. 3. Tübingen: J. C. B. Mohr (Paul Siebeck), 1922.

————. *The Social Teaching of the Christian Churches.* 2 vols. New York: Macmillan Co., 1931.

Tyson, Joseph Blake. " 'Works of Law' in Galatians." *Journal of Biblical Literature* 92 (1973): 423–31.

The United Presbyterian Church in the U.S.A. "The Confession of 1967." *The Constitution of the U.P.C.U.S.A. Part I: The Book of Confessions.* 2d ed. Philadelphia: Office of the General Assembly of the U.P.C.U.S.A., 1970.

Unnik, Willem Cornelis van. "Reisepläne und Amen-Sagen: Zusammenhang und Gedankenfolge in 2 Cor 1,15." In *Studia Paulina in honorem Johannes de Zwaan, septuagenarii.* Haarlem: Bohn, 1953. Pp. 215–34.

————. *Sparsa Collecta: The Collected Essays of W. C. van Unnik.* Novum Testamentum, Supplements 29. Leiden: E. J. Brill, 1973.

Verbeke, Gérard. *L'évolution de la doctrine du pneuma, du stoicisme à S. Augustin: Étude philosophique.* Paris: D. de Brouwer, 1945.

Vermès, Géza. *Jesus the Jew: A Historian's Reading of the Gospels.* Cleveland and London: Collins, 1973.

Vielhauer, Philipp. *Geschichte der urchristlichen Literatur: Einleitung in das Neue Testament, die Apokryphen und die Apostolischen Väter.* Berlin/New York: Walter de Gruyter, 1975.

————. "Introduction [to Apocalypses and Related Subjects]." In E. Hennecke, *New Testament Apocrypha.* Edited by W. Schneemelcher. 2 vols. Philadelphia: Westminster Press, 1963-65. Vol. 2, pp. 581-607.

————. *Oikodomē: Das Bild vom Bau in der christlichen Literatur vom Neuen Testament bis Clemens Alexandrinus.* Karlsruhe-Durlach: Gebr. Tron, 1940.

Weinel, Heinrich. *Biblische Theologie des Neuen Testaments: Die Religion Jesu und des Urchristentums.* Tübingen: J. C. B. Mohr (Paul Siebeck), 1911.

————. *Die Wirkungen des Geistes und der Geister im nachapostolischen Zeitalter bis auf Irenäus.* Freiburg i.B.: J. C. B. Mohr (Paul Siebeck), 1899.

Weiss, Bernhard. *Kritisch-exegetisches Handbuch über den Brief des Paulus an die Römer.* Meyers kritisch-exegetischer Kommentar über das Neue Testament. 7th ed. Göttingen: Vandenhoeck & Ruprecht, 1886.

Weiss, Johannes. "Beiträge zur paulinischen Rhetorik." In *Theologische Studien . . . Bernhard Weiss zu seinem 70. Geburtstage dargebracht.* Edited by C. R. Gregory et al. Göttingen: Vandenhoeck & Ruprecht, 1897. Pp. 165-247.

————. *Die Predigt Jesu vom Reiche Gottes.* 2d ed. Göttingen: Vandenhoeck & Ruprecht, 1900. English translation: *Jesus' Proclamation of the Kingdom of God.* Translated, edited, and with an Introduction by R. H. Hiers and D. L. Holland. Lives of Jesus Series. Philadelphia: Fortress Press, 1971.

————. *Das Urchristentum.* Göttingen: Vandenhoeck & Ruprecht, 1917. English translation: *The History of Primitive Christianity.* Translated by "four friends." Edited by F. C. Grant. New York: Wilson-Erickson, 1937. Reprinted in paperback by Harper Torchbooks, 1959, 2 vols.

Wellhausen, Julius. *Israelitische und jüdische Geschichte.* 9th ed. Berlin: Walter de Gruyter, 1958.

————. "Zur apokalyptischen Literatur." *Skizzen und Vorarbeiten.* 6 vols. Berlin: Reimer, 1884-99. Vol. 4, pp. 215-49.

Wendland, Heinz-Dietrich. *Die Mitte der paulinische Botschaft: Die Rechtfertigungs-lehre des Paulus im Zusammenhange seiner Theologie.* Göttingen: Vandenhoeck & Ruprecht, 1935.

Wengst, Klaus. *Christologische Formeln und Lieder des Urchristentums.* Studien zum Neuen Testament 7. Gütersloh: G. Mohn, 1972.

————. "Das Zusammenkommen der Gemeinde und ihr 'Gottesdienst' nach Paulus." *Evangelische Theologie* 33 (1973): 547-59.

Werner, Martin. *Die Enstehung des christlichen Dogmas, problemgeschichtlich darges-tellt.* 2d ed. Bern: Haupt, 1954.

Wernle, Paul. *Die Anfänge unserer Religion.* 2d ed. Tübingen: J. C. B. Mohr (Paul Siebeck), 1904.

————. *Der Christ und die Sünde bei Paulus.* Freiburg i.b.: J. C. B. Mohr (Paul Siebeck), 1897.

Wetter, Gillis Petersson. *Charis: Ein Beitrag zur Geschichte des ältesten Christentums.* Untersuchungen zum Neuen Testament 5. Leipzig: J. C. Hinrichs, 1913.

Whitehead, Alfred North. *Religion in the Making.* New York: Meridian Books, 1960.

Whiteley, Denys Edward Hugh. *The Theology of St. Paul.* Philadelphia: Fortress Press, 1964.

Wiefel, Wolfgang. "The Jewish Community in Ancient Rome and the Origins of Roman Christianity." In *The Romans Debate.* Edited by K. P. Donfried. Minneapolis: Augsburg Publishing House, 1977. Pp. 100–119.

Wilckens, Ulrich. "Die Bekehrung des Paulus als religionsgeschichtliches Problem." *Zeitschrift für Theologie und Kirche* 56 (1959): 273–93.

_____. "Jesusüberlieferung und Christuskerygma: Zwei Wege urchristlicher Überlieferungsgeschichte." *Theologia Viatorum* 10 (1965–66): 310–39.

_____. "Über Abfassungszweck und Aufbau des Römerbriefs." In *Rechtfertigung als Freiheit: Paulusstudien.* Neukirchen-Vluyn: Neukirchener, 1974. Pp. 110–70.

_____. "Was heisst bei Paulus: 'Aus Werken des Gesetzes wird kein Mensch gerecht.' " In *Rechtfertigung als Freiheit: Paulusstudien.* Neukirchen-Vluyn: Neukirchener, 1974. Pp. 77–109.

Wilder, Amos Niven. *Early Christian Rhetoric: The Language of the Gospel.* Cambridge: Harvard University, 1971.

Windisch, Hans. "Das Problem des paulinischen Imperativs." *Zeitschrift für die neutestamentliche Wissenschaft* 23 (1924): 265–81.

Wolter, Michael. *Rechtfertigung und zukünftiges Heil: Untersuchungen zu Röm 5,1–11.* Beiheft zur Zeitschrift für die neutestamentliche Wissenschaft 43. Berlin/New York: Walter de Gruyter, 1978.

Wrede, William. *Paul.* London: Philip Green, 1907.

Zahn, Theodor. *Der Brief des Paulus an die Römer.* Kommentar zum Neuen Testament 6. 2d ed. Leipzig: A. Deichert, 1910.

Zimmerli, Walther. *Ezechiel.* Biblischer Kommentar: Altes Testament. 2 vols. Neukirchen-Vluyn: Neukirchener, 1969. English translation: *Ezekiel.* Volume 1 translated by Ronald E. Clements. Philadelphia: Fortress Press, 1979. Volume 2 forthcoming.

Indexes

Index of Passages Cited

Page numbers in italics indicate that the reference is in the notes.

421

ADDITIONAL SOURCES

Index of Names

Page numbers in italics indicate that the reference is in the notes.